# SOLVING MODERN CRIME IN FINANCIAL MARKETS

# SOLVING MODERN CRIME IN FINANCIAL MARKETS

## Analytics and Case Studies

### FIRST EDITION

*Edited by*

MARIUS-CHRISTIAN FRUNZA

AMSTERDAM • BOSTON • HEIDELBERG • LONDON
NEW YORK • OXFORD • PARIS • SAN DIEGO
SAN FRANCISCO • SINGAPORE • SYDNEY • TOKYO
Academic Press is an imprint of Elsevier

Academic Press is an imprint of Elsevier
225 Wyman Street, Waltham, MA 02451, USA
The Boulevard, Langford Lane, Kidlington, Oxford OX5 1GB, UK

**Library of Congress Cataloging-in-Publication Data**
A catalog record for this book is available from the Library of Congress

**British Library Cataloguing-in-Publication Data**
A catalogue record for this book is available from the British Library

ISBN: 978-0-12-804494-0

For information on all Academic Press publications
visit our website at http://store.elsevier.com/

Typeset by SPi Global, India
Printed in USA

Working together
to grow libraries in
developing countries

www.elsevier.com • www.bookaid.org

# Contents

# III

## INVESTIGATION CRIME ON FINANCIAL MARKETS (EMPIRICAL STUDIES WITH APPLICATIONS IN R)

### 3A. Structural Changes in Time Series

### 3B. Exploring Unstructured Data

### 3C. Understanding the Balance Sheets of Financial Firms

### 3D. Fraud on the Market Theory

### 3E. Efficient Market Hypothesis Testing

### 3F. Market Prices and Trading Activity

### 3G. Order Book Analysis

### 3H. Event Study

# IV

## CASE STUDIES (APPLICATIONS IN R)

### 4A. LIBOR Manipulation

### 4B. EURIBOR Manipulation

# Preface

The recent charges by U.S. authorities against Navinder Singh Sarao[1] for market price manipulation contributing to the *Flash Crash* episode in 2010 opened a new chapter in the ontology of crime on financial markets. Sarao's character diametrically conflicts with Jordan Belfort's iconic picture not only in terms of image, but also in term of means, tools, trading style, and technology.

Sarao's "anti-golden boy" case changed in many ways the paradigm of financial markets crime. If a sole trader buying and selling American shares from his parents' basement through a complex network of offshore entities[2] was able to trigger or amplify the 2010 *Flash Crash*, there now have a new type of financial crime that needs to be investigated and a new spectrum of potential threats mainly related to use of technology and cyber-security in relation to the market infrastructures. Whatever the outcome of Sarao's case it is clear that the huge influx of technology in the investment world has brought as many threats as it has opportunities. Hence, financial crime research will need to expand in the coming years to address this and other new types of threats.

In my previous book, *Introduction to the Theories and Varieties of Modern Crime in Financial Markets*, I presented the origins and various forms of crime used in financial markets. The next step is to develop the statistical and data-mining investigation methods that can be leveraged and expanded to analyze crime in financial markets. Forward-looking analysis of financial crimes that can gain momentum in the foreseeable future is also necessary in this context.

This book covers the new types of fraud on financial markets with a focus on cryptocurrency and the sport-betting market. Case studies are presented including the LIBOR and Forex manipulation cases. A set of statistical techniques and exploratory methods is introduced in relationship to various examples of crime. The book aims to present a balanced perspective of theoretical quantitative analysis and applied cases studies and to describe them in a language accessible to the average reader in the areas of financial crime and statistics. The investigation of a financial crime or of a potential threat needs to be accompanied by a good understanding of criminal phenomena along with elements involved in offenses. The use of quantitative analytics alone cannot solely solve a given case and should be paired with strategic knowledge of the crime.

---

[1] Flash crash trader Navinder Singh Sarao "sat on £27m fortune while his mother worked two jobs" http://www.telegraph.co.uk/news/uknews/crime/11557755/Flash-crash-trader-Navinder-Singh-Sarao-sat-on-27m-fortune-while-his-mother-worked-two-jobs.html.

[2] "Flash Crash" Trader Navinder Sarao Worked With Fund Network Now Under Investigation, http://www.wsj.com/articles/flash-crash-trader-navinder-sarao-worked-with-fund-network-now-under-investigation-1434527646.

# Prologue

Despite the recent trends in technology and risk management, quantitative techniques cannot under any circumstances be solely seen as *deux ex machina* solutions for preventing and dealing with financial crime. Of course, statistics, data-mining, and computational techniques can bring more focus or accuracy in valuing the frequency and severity of a financial offense, but a crucial role of analytical methods is to provide tools for determining the causes and cradle of crime rather than predict its outcome.

The consequences of crime on financial markets in the past two decades have extended beyond the investment world and started to have a considerable impact on the real economy. The manipulation of agricultural commodities prices or interest or Forex rates can have a serious impact on the economy and even contribute to political turmoil and social unrest in certain countries or regions of the globe. The massive role played by technology in markets infrastructures adds new threats to the investment world mainly related to cyber-security issues and ultra-low latency trades.

In this context of increasing opportunity for crime, regulators, investigators, and institutions exposed to financial markets need to have appropriate methods and systems in place to detect or to find abnormalities in markets. The philosophy of such a framework should be forward-looking since the *leitmotif* of financial crime changes quickly and a static threat assessment framework would not be able to address new types of offenses. Therefore, existing statistical and data exploration methods need to be employed in a dynamic framework with learning abilities in order to tackle crime on financial markets. As past cases have shown, the various crime typologies are generally interconnected. For example, low latency market manipulation might be linked to money laundering and therefore the analytic methods need to be integrated in a holistic way.

The main challenges of addressing the variety of threats in financial crime are related to both theory and implementation. The theoretical challenges concern the choice of appropriate methods for tackling an offense and the implementation-related challenges concern the right way to build processes and systems for surveillance and detection within an organization or a market infrastructure.

# Acknowledgments

The author would like to gratefully and sincerely thank Didier Marteau, Chevalier de l'Ordre National du Merit (Knight of the National Order of Merit), Michel Mouren, Derek Cunningham, Leslie Pitts, Evgueny Kurinin, Piotr Ryzenkov, and Erika Bigg for their support.

The author is also grateful for the academic contribution, input, and support of:

- the Laboratory of Excellence for Financial Regulation in Paris (LABEX-ReFi) represented by Prof. Didier Marteau, Dr. Christian de Boissieu, and Francois Gilles Letheule for providing access to the databases (IODS, Barclays Hedge, Bankscope, Financial Times, and Bloomberg).

- Dr. Evgueny Shurmanov from the Ural State University for his continuous support and scientific collaboration.
- Dr. Aurora Castro Teixeira from the University of Porto for her efforts of organizing the most cutting-edge conference in financial crime to the Interdisciplinary Insights on Fraud and Corruption (I2FC).
- Dr. David LEE Kuo Chuen from the Singapore Management University for the cutting-edge insight on cryptocurrency.

The authors also thank Laura Hutton for her precious insight of financial crime. The author is grateful to Scott Bentley for making this project happen and to Susan Ikeda for her continuous support.

# David Lee Kuo Chuen: Interview

London, United Kingdom, April 5, 2014

## BIOGRAPHY

**David Lee Kuo Chuen—Ferrell Asset Management Pte Ltd., Singapore Management University, Singapore**

David Lee Kuo Chuen is Professor of Quantitative Finance (Practice); Director, Sim Kee Boon Institute for Financial Economics; and Academic Director, Global Master of Finance Dual Degree at Singapore Management University. A Chartered Statistician from the Royal Statistical Association, he received his Ph.D. from The London School of Economics and Political Science, University of London. In May 1999, David Lee founded Ferrell Asset Management Pte Ltd. Prior to setting up Ferrell, Dr. Lee was the Managing Director of Fraser Asset Management, the fund management unit of the Fraser-AMMB group of companies. He also served as Director of Institutional Sales at Fraser Securities and covered the Asia-Pacific equities markets.

**Marius Cristian Frunza (MCF)**: *Why is Bitcoin different from classic currencies and from other electronic currency?*

**David Lee (DL)**: It is different because cryptocurrency is not just a currency. There is a lot technology in it. A lot of people think that it is money, and that is true, but it not just money. It is programmer's money, and therefore has great potential flexibility. You can do what the program asks you to do. With Bitcoin 2.0 or Blockchain 2.0, for example, one might implement functions that are currently out of reach. Take a look at the many opportunities in smart-accounting. One simple example is that an artist can allow everybody to own his or her song. If you use cryptocurrency as a kind of token everybody can be a cryptoequity holder of the song. If somebody plays it, you will have a crypto dividend paid in cryptocurrency. This is the beauty of a programmable currency.

**MCF**: *Can cryptocurrencies be a new investment asset class?*

**DL**: At this moment cryptocurrencies are very volatile. One cause of their volatility is that the transaction levels are low, even though $8 billion in Bitcoin is changing hands. In addition, 60-70% of Bitcoins have not transacted in the last 6 months, according to the latest report. If prices are too volatile they cannot be treated as an alternative asset. You can look to the direct exposure to technology through venture capital and in start-ups through private equity way, but investing in Bitcoin is not a new investment alternative class on its own. When prices stabilize, Bitcoin will make more sense because of its predictability. Now it's difficult to value. Bitcoin is still an experiment that can go to zero, but it has a lot of upside. We see a lot of evolution in technology and new cryptocurrencies are emerging that are capable of tasks currently out of our reach.

**MCF**: *What is the role of hardware in transacting cryptocurrencies?*

**DL**: There is one thing about cryptocurrency that makes it special. Originally cryptocurrency was intended to be distributed in the network; in other words, every node would have equal access. Cryptocurrency was to be a democratic experiment in the sense that each node participates to the mining and at the same time participates in updating the transaction digital registers. But as the experiment has progressed developers have realized is that some people have better machines and higher hash rates, and they are better prepared to solve the cryptocurrency contest. They can form pools as mining costs rise, giving them further advantages. Some people can be left out in the confirmation of the public ledger. Like every democratic system, some people will tend to have more means and be able to influence other who are followers.

**MCF**: *Can cryptocurrency be sustainable without central banks?*

**DL**: I think it will coexist with central banks. Two contrasting cases are possible. At one end of the spectrum are governments that have a lot of debts. Their currencies are not reserve currencies, and there is a danger that if they run into problems people will lose confidence in their currencies. At the other end of the spectrum you have countries with lots of reserves. These countries are forming a different monetary system, as China is with BRICS banks and bilateral swaps. The Asia infrastructure bank is trying to set up a new financial system. What happens is that some governments have so much debt that they will need set up their own cryptocurrency at the country level. Their cryptocurrency will be geographically limited whether it is backed by tangible assets or other currencies. I see there is a road for those cryptocurrencies and cryptocurrencies like Bitcoin to co-exist together. If governments regulate, they can regulate the intermediaries but they cannot regulate the cryptocurrencies protocols. A lot of regulators try to understand the technology, but it evolves from day to day. The regulatory crime busters are always behind in this race. Cryptocurrencies will continue to exist with their own values for transactions complementing central government currencies.

**MCF**: *Would it be possible for a government to adopt a cryptocurrency as an official currency or in parallel?*

**DL**: I think what will happen is that governments will begin regulating intermediaries and alternative investors such as hedge funds. Those who are currently part of the system will then become the mainstream, libertarians who do not want to deal with regulation will exist in another space. Therefore, the cryptocurrencies will have two main groups mainstream and libertarian non-mainstream. The mainstream will develop much faster due to the governmental support. But the protocols will still exist as they are, and I think this experiment will end positively. Conditions will continue to evolve, and cryptocurrencies will both adapt to changes in the environment and will drive a lot of innovation. The best brains and the best developers are in that space, so you can expect innovation on an almost daily basis. That is interesting. Any government that encourages innovation will not turn down a cryptocurrency that creates something that benefits mankind. If you do not look carefully, cryptocurrencies will disrupt a lot of industries, such as banks, payment system, spot exchange, and ownership in the form of shares. Cryptocurrencies will be part of a new digital economy. For this reason I don't think governments will ban this cryptocurrencies. It is not a wise thing to do.

**MCF**: *What is the risk of cryptocurrency transactions being related to protocol?*

**DL**: One of major dangers is that cryptocurrencies involve mining, and whoever controls more than 30% of mining will have some influence. Whoever controls more than 51% can actually have a major say in rewriting the latest block chain. This could make the digital registry untrustworthy. When there is no trust in the cryptocurrency protocol the price will drop and people will abandon it. Few will be mining, and no reliable record will exist. That is the danger of minable cryptocurrencies. But there is another consensus, ledger cryptocurrencies, which are decentralized and don't need mining. For example, you could have 30-40 parties forming different nodes and agreeing on a digital ledger. I think those areas will see a lot of development. Non-minable cryptocurrencies are an area to look into as they do not pose the same danger that exists in minable cryptocurrencies.

**MCF**: *What is the risk of theft and hacking in the cryptocurrency world?*

**DL**: You can always have protocols such as proof of state or proof-of-identity and limit the mining revenue, reducing the consumption of more electricity. Regulation wise it is unclear that if somebody steals something from your computer you have the right as a property owner to go after him. Data and cryptocurrencies are digital assets. It will be interesting to see how regulations or propriety rights will be revised to address this point. The other consideration is that a cryptocurrencies are generally unregulated. They are easy to attack, like stealing coins from the intermediaries. In this context consumer protection is a key issue. Watch for new attention focused on property rights for digital assets and consumer protection in the next one or two years.

**MCF**: *The consumption of electricity for the mining process is high and the electricity price is a key factor for mining profitability. Will we see a concentration of miners in low electricity price countries?*

**DL**: These activities are already happening. Most of the farms are located in Asia, where electricity costs are lower. That's how we had a few miners controlling close to 51% of Bitcoin mining earlier this year. This concentration in itself is a danger. If mining costs go higher individuals will give up mining on their own and will join a pool, which again poses a threat of consolidating 51% of mining in the hands of a few. We can see mining moving to farms that have low electricity charges. Rental costs are also important because you cannot mine in big cities with high rent prices.

**MCF**: *Media has noted the risk of money laundering. What are your views?*

**DL**: Money laundering through cash or other financial instruments is always with us. At the same time, technology development around cryptocurrencies will continue to be innovative. People in the business of financial crime will always have to catch up with innovation. Cryptocurrencies are probably not the best way to launder the big money because transactions can be easily tracked. Cryptocurrencies are not a avenue for laundering big money; people can move only small amounts, and it is possible that people can actually move money in bigger portions. If cryptocurrency intermediaries are being regulated, if the main stream of cryptocurrencies is being regulated, and if the Bitcoin community is working to together, it will be much easier to target those illicit activities.

**MCF**: *What are the main competitors for Bitcoin?*

**DL**: One of them is XRP by Ripple, which is used by financial institutions for transactions. In XRP's case there is a ledger book of consensus, so you don't need to have all the processes Bitcoin has. You will see a lot more such innovations coming out and you will see also new kinds of cryptocurrencies such as country-based or regional cryptocurrencies with their own particular interests. Major cryptocurrencies will co-exist.

**MCF**: *Will we witness a new generation of cryptocurrencies less intensive in terms of protocol?*

**DL**: I see proof-of-identity where identity is associated with digital imprint, encrypted in that sense. This function is particularly useful if somebody wants to obtain the identity of the person using the currency. Other desirable opportunities include signing contracts by using cryptocurrencies and cryptoequity. They do not necessary involve mining but they do require proof-of-identity, not necessary based on a token, but rather based on a ledger. They would be a variation of Bitcoin that would evolve over time and we are already seeing its first phases.

# Laura Hutton: Interview

London, United Kingdom, April 5, 2014

## BIOGRAPHY

**Laura Hutton—Director of Banking Solutions, Fraud & Financial Crime Advanced Analytics Business Unit (AABU), SAS**

Laura is a director in the banking solutions team at SAS, working across the EMEA and AP region, and is responsible for the design, build, and go-to-market processes for SAS's fraud and financial crimes solutions.

Working with companies globally, Laura provides subject matter expertise across the full client engagement process from both technical and business perspectives, ensuring that SAS solutions always drive value for their customers. Laura has a specialist interest in the areas of Rogue Trading, Application Fraud, Trade Finance Fraud, Insider Fraud, FATCA, AML, and Online Fraud.

Prior to joining SAS in 2012, Laura spent 6 years at Detica NetReveal where she was responsible for the development of NetReveal's social network analysis solutions, specializing in techniques to identify and prevent fraud within the insurance and banking industries. When she left Detica she was Head of the Global Banking & Markets practice.

Laura has a First Class degree in Mathematics from the University of Durham.

**Marius-Cristian Frunza (MCF):** *For over three decades SAS has been a leading provider of analytic solutions for financial institutions. What are the new challenges for the industry in the era of big data, high-speed Internet, and ultra-high-frequency trading?*

**Laura Hutton (LH):** Let us look at unauthorized trading (the case of SocGen or the case of UBS) in which people hide their positions and their Profit and Loss. How have organizations protected themselves over the last 10-15 years? They have developed control frameworks that identify weaknesses, then they have established controls to tackle those weaknesses. One example I often cite is canceled or amended trades. Canceled and amended trades are frequently associated with high-risk trading events. So control programs identify all cancelations and amendments on a daily basis. We routinely ask our Front Office supervisor to sign off those cancelations and amendments, to say that they are fine. Now the reality is that if you are a Front Office supervisor you may well get 300 to 500 cancelations and amendments on your desk each day. You are asked to review an Excel spreadsheets and say: "Yes. Perhaps one entry corresponds to high-risk trading." You can imagine how difficult that is for a Front Office supervisor. You are looking at hundreds of rows and it is almost impossible to see which rows are fake trades and which are just business as usual.

Cancelations and amendments are just an example. You have another control that queries whether your trader is logging in at strange times during the day or night, whether she has fluctuations in her P&L, whether she has broken credit limit breaches against a counterparty, and the like. In the end there are many siloed areas in an organization, and each is running its own reports. So as a supervisor I not only receive reports containing hundred of records, but I also get 20, 30, 40+ reports on my desk everyday from all the siloed areas of my organization.

Despite everyone's best efforts this Front Office supervisor has a process-driven approach rather than one that enables him to find true exceptions. The human eye is unable to join together these disparate pieces of information. So the siloed nature of the business is very challenging. Many controls are simplistic in their calculations because they are siloed. If I am a clever trader, I can quickly learn to get around rules because SAS uses an "if" decision branch. Recent cases of unauthorized trading are good examples. Traders know the conformation process and can estimate how long they have to cancel a trade after booking it. They would also know how much credit to put against counterparties on fake trades. Where there is a rule, people find a way around it.

Those are the key technological challenges that we are addressing. The only other challenge I would mention concerns the cultural side of things. I do not mean the psychology of a real trader. Instead, I am referring to communication breakdowns among Front, Middle, and Back Office staff. Front Office traders concentrate on making money. But Back and the Middle Office staff must challenge Front Office traders about reasons for cancelling specific trades. Busy Front Office staff often do not provide complete details when describing their trading strategies, which can be difficult to understand even under the best circumstances. Therefore, the difference between Front Office and Back Office means that Back Office does not have really all the information to ask the right questions. If I were explicitly told that a trader did X, Y, Z over the past three months, that he demonstrates this type of activity, and that he did this over here, as Middle or Back Office staff member I would have more of a foundation on which to build my questions. At the moment the typical staff member asks about individual events in isolation.

**MCF:** *Since the big scandals involving financial crime allegations, major analytic software companies started developing solutions for detecting and providing information about financial crimes. Is this a point-in-time regulation-driven effect or will it become a core strategic development axis in the foreseeable future?*

**LH:** There is definitely regulatory pressure. Since the UBS case, a lot of major banks have conducted reviews of their anti-unauthorized trading measures and now rate themselves on a red, amber, and green scale. You will also find that while the Socgen and UBS cases attracted significant media attention, all organizations now have internal warning flags. These flags respond to regulatory pressures because if the banks have events, however small, they must report them to regulators. If market abuse is a regulatory requirement like Anti-Money Laundering, unauthorized trading is not. Banks need not file a report for regulators unless they have an event. When banks have an event, they come under considerable pressure to do something.

So the regulatory side is one piece, but there is also the reputational side. I think the reputational side drives things more than anything because it includes the fear factor. After Leeson nobody thought it will happen again, then Kerviel happened and nobody thought it could happen again, and then the UBS Adoboli case happened. It was a copy of the SocGen event. At that point a lot of people looked carefully and said that the same thing could happen to them. The financial loss did not concern them as much as the potential damage to their reputations. Since the financial crisis most big organizations have increasingly emphasized the protection of their reputations. Smaller organizations are perhaps still on that money-making curve or might be more willing to take on risk. We do not work as much with hedge funds because while they have very similar needs they also have a bigger appetite for risk than large international banks.

**MCF:** *What aspects of financial crime are currently addressed by the industry and what are developments do you foresee? Is there a specific focus on financial markets (e.g., securities, commodities) and market surveillance?*

**LH**: Fraud and financial crime are huge topics. If you look at retail banks, many use technology and analytics to combat them; investment banks have less interest in these tools. Retail banks have real-time transactions systems to protect against credit and debit card fraud. We have seen a large increase in application fraud, which differs from credit risk in that somebody takes money from the organization with the intention of never repaying it. Traditionally banks have analyzed credit risk and have been very good at credit risk analytics and scoring. But they are not as good at application fraud. We have also seen an increase in internal fraud, which often includes stealing for a customer, targeting elderly clients who do not have good access to their bank accounts, or colluding with vendors. Instances of collusion, or procurement fraud, is the focus of a lot of our work in South Africa and India.

Online fraud is an interesting topic. Take the United Kingdom, where you have expectations for faster payments through an increase of Internet banking. Everybody with a smartphone conducts online banking transactions, and smart phones are clearly a weak point for protecting against fraud. Banks naturally want to deliver good experiences to all of their customers. The challenge is how to give to your good customers good experiences without leaving yourself vulnerable to attacks by bad customers. We see this conundrum in all situations, from Internet banking and online transactions to online lending applications. If you apply online, you immediately become anonymous to that organization. As a good customer this system pleases me because I can apply for my loan from anywhere, but it also enables bad customers to protect themselves behind their computers. Corporate lending, which is a big part of the retail banking business, requires a more manual application process. The techniques are simple and rules based, and often a lot of data are in unstructured formats. We use our analytic capabilities to join structured and unstructured data so we can predict which loans are likely to be targets of fraud.

**MCF**: *With the "Big Data" wave institutions are creating data warehouses for various types of information, from portfolio metrics to client data and from OTC positions to social media feeds. What are the challenges for the exploration and exploitation of information held in these repositories?*

**LH**: This is a topic that puts everything into context. These organizations are very siloed in terms of data, systems, and the groups that run those systems. Everything is separate. I have seen organizations create grand 10 year plans to build big data warehouses, and these plans are illogical because it will take them a lot of time and money to bring those data together. In fact, these organizations might need to analyze those data now instead of in 10 years, and they might already be able to analyze the data where they sit *in situ*. What these organizations need is a system that deals with volume. So, for example, in an investigation of unauthorized trading one common strategy is to join up the dots across that organization and thereby analyze a trader's actions. So you have let's say 80 different systems sitting separately: everything from Teradata Oracle and Excel spreadsheets to csv files. The ideal system should be able to sit across all of those formats and ingest from where it sits. Once it has ingested those data, it should be able to draw conclusions. For an internal threat I want to the system to able to say this is the trader and this is everything she has across my siloed systems. The equivalent in an external threat is saying "this is my customer and this is everything I understand about my customer." This is what we describe as creating the holistic picture of your customer or your employee.

We can go a step further by adding information about the relationships my customer or employee has. We want to know, for example, that our employee talks to this trader by phone, she emails that researcher, and she trades on that book against that counterparty. So we create X in the context of all the relationships she has. We do exactly the same thing when we look to external threats. Of our customer Y, we can point to her loan application, her accounts, all of her transactions, and related information such as her address, the names of people she lives with, her telephone number, the names of people who receive money from her, the ATM machines she uses, and so forth. We create the social network, and I am not talking about Facebook or Twitter here. I am talking about a true social network, a fraud network analysis. Once you have that view you can apply your risk assessment.

Let's return to the unauthorized trading example. I have trader X and I know the book she trades on, the counterparties she deals with, the trades she has made, and all the controls she has ever broken. I know the relationships between her and other traders or other people within the organization. Across this view we can apply a range of techniques to detect high-risk activities.

It starts with the most simple rule. A rule could be trader X canceled more than N trades in the last days, or it could be that we joined silos and to observe toxic combinations. X has canceled a trade that was unconfirmed by a counterparty or X has had an increased number of cancelations plus she has not taken her annual leave, plus she started suddenly logging in late after everybody else has gone home. That type of analysis looks for predetermined scenarios. SAS have a catalog of scenarios and our banks have the same. We can use everybody's knowledge, but this tactic uncovers only the events you set out to discover.

Then we use data mining and data analysis to look for events of unknown patterns. If I have a holistic image of X I can analyze her. I can understand via strategies like segmentation or clustering who X should look like, and I can identify her peer group. And therefore I can recognize her deviations from the norms of her peer group.

**MCF**: *Are classic econometric tools and analytic frameworks appropriate for the analysis and detection of financial crimes? Is there a place for a new forensic science/discipline dedicated to the behavioral and analytic study of financial crimes in order to develop a specific theoretical background?*

**LH**: The techniques we use are exactly the same as those we follow in other contexts: ingesting the data, linking them together, and applying risk assessment.

We use this process for tax and VAT carousel, insurance and claim fraud, first-party bank application, unauthorized trading, and market abuse. We use SAS's traditional analytical techniques, employing segmentation clustering, which have been around for a number of years. What is different is combining them to generate data, then analyzing the data. That is what we describe as the detection piece, and it is new in that space.

The other piece we address is access to the underlying data and speed of access. So traditionally data has been seen as an enemy of organizations that want to tackle fraud. My view is that data should be a friend because if you can to use data in the right way, most of the warnings signs you need are in the data. You have to be able to harness the data in the right way.

The fundamental principle of SAS approaches is to harness the data. On one hand it is an automated detection piece: generating the data and linking them to scoring and alerting. On the other hand it is giving people a window into those data in order to explore and analyze them in better ways. In traditional reporting tools there is a high dependency on IT. Data are stored in a nice format in a nice data warehouse, and they required IT to configure a report for you. We have taken another approach based on in-memory technology that allows you to access a million if not a billion records in seconds. As a business user you can drag and drop pieces of information instantly, giving you the power to answer questions about our business. When I started to work in this area I was often looking for swings in the P&L, shifting from very positive to very negative, steadily going up, or slowly dropping. What we didn't consider was exactly the opposite. More unusual is when the P&L is completely smooth. Should I expect my P&L to be smooth when those in my peer group are not?

**MCF**: *SAS solutions are widely reputed for their ability to deal in a robust and efficient way with statistical data analysis. The financial world and especially financial markets introduce a "real-time" dimension where speed is a factor. What are the challenges of the solutions meant to detect and prevent financial crime in light of the increasing speed of transactions and operations?*

**LH**: With all of my clients I think carefully about data analysis techniques. My first question is "do I need real time?" So if I do need real time, what do I mean by real time? What do I need real time for? I need it for credit and debit card transactions because I want to stop the money; if someone's card is in the machine, I want to terminate the transaction or the payment on the internet. So it is a real-time problem in terms of the subsecond problem. Take something like application fraud. An application for a loan will never be given a note in a sub-second. Some banks from Eastern Europe want to be aggressive in order to gain market share. They want to process applications in 30 seconds or maybe in 1 to 10 minutes, which is a near real-time problem, so it doesn't need the instant response of an online transaction but it does require quick action. Other problems do not develop as quickly, such as an unauthorized trade, internal fraud, or procurement fraud.

These last problems do not manifest as quickly so you do not need to spend money to accelerate the response. In these cases what you have is a batch problem near real time. In real time, such as credit and debit card transactions and high-frequency trading, where one-thousandth of a second makes a difference, you have grades. The faster you need to respond, the most expensive and bigger the hardware you require. So you need to work out what speed you actually need and you need to use the appropriate hardware. With fraud and financial crime we offer platforms that allow everything from batch to real time and near time. Organizations can address all types of financial crimes on one platform, and they can chose their analytical and reaction

speeds. The faster they want to analyze and react, the more complex hardware they need.

**MCF**: *In the current environment "money laundering" has become a multinational/multi-asset phenomenon. Can analytic solutions bring answers alone or is expert input required? What is the right balance and the right way to mix them?*

**LH**: I do not see a challenge of mixing them as long as they are used in the right ways. As a business user I explore some data and might well identify new behaviors that are not in the automated systems. What I learn should be fed back into my automated intelligent system. Actually, I would like to look for this toxic combination scenario or look at a new analytic method that automatically defines it. I think they sit very nicely side by side as long as the right operating model is in place.

Mathematical or quantitative people need to run these analytics. A business expert who understands fraud and financial crime needs to guide those scientists to ensure you are not just running blind analytics, but you run with domain expertise in mind.

**MCF**: *For the behavioral understanding of financial crime mechanisms, Bayesian techniques and machine learning offer many upsides. How robustly can these methods be implemented in specific solutions?*

**LH**: All fundamental tools and techniques are applicable to financial crime, but that is not to say that technology should become stationary. Visual analytics is a new way at looking at data.

In terms of techniques, I think there is an increasing importance in dealing with unstructured data. SAS has traditionally used numeric data, but we also use a lot of nonnumeric data, linked text, and unstructured text to capture risk. Let's take the example of unauthorized trading for which the unstructured data analysis is very important. A lot of the banks look at the analysis in isolation, like a separate project. I don't agree with this approach, as it is part of the larger story of identifying the bank's trader and what he is doing that poses a risk to the organization. We use text analytics to join structured and unstructured data, extract them, and link the relevant information. And we go through understanding the sentiment of unstructured information to derive the risk that trader is posing. In unauthorized trading we see a strong correlation between people who cancel or amend trades at unusual hours with those who have an increase in the sentiment of urgency or mismatching between Front Office and Back Office emails. We have to be able to make the data available. In terms of analytics we use a lot of developed analytics techniques to analyze the risk. What is new is the way we link the data together. That creates the holistic image of the trader and is fundamentally new in concept. We have a greater volume of data and evolving insights in ways to link data together.

I would add that while techniques such as neural networks, decision trees, and logistic regression or segmentation have existed for some years, we are using those techniques on a new platform that delivers high performance analysis.

SAS high-performance analytics have grown in recent years to the point where we can use vast volumes of data. Those data are needed because banks want to deliver better customer experiences they do things more quickly. As we get into the big data arena, where we go across million and millions of records, unless you have a scalable high-performance analytic platform you will not be able to deliver that experience. Some open source analytical platforms do not have the scalability and they cannot take in all the information at once. We have addressed that by taking our expertise in analytics and moving on to a high-performance environment.

There are few other points I want to address. You have to be very careful that your techniques are not black box. What I mean is that if a system pumps out a result saying this transaction is high risk and has a score of 1000, how does this help an investigator? It does not. We need to use techniques that present a case and actually guide investigators in why something is high risk. So the results need to be concise and informative. As an example, for unauthorized trading space we generate an alert that says trader X is high risk because she broke rules A, B, C, plus she is not allowed in that space, plus analytically her behavior has changed over the past three days. Through the risk assessment process we use a combination of rules bases and deep analytical-based techniques and we're still trying to integrate that in a way that business people can understand. Investigators of these alerts are not mathematicians so they cannot be given blind analytics.

It is also important that investigators should be able to manage this information on a continual basis. Let's take the example of anti-money laundering, where it is important to have full audit ability from back to front. You need to know why things are high risk while others are not. Therefore, the whole process must be an open or white box rather than a black box. You need to know the scenarios that are and thresholds that are in place. You need to be able to configure and change those variables. Every organization in every country requires different types of information and their requirements are constantly changing, particularly for crimes like AML. Only an open system enables you to change and adapt over time. Certain techniques are more appropriate in certain situations. In some parts of the business some tools work better than others. For credit cards, neural networks are effective in identifying high-risk transactions. If application fraud, neural networks work less well. You are much better using decision trees or logistic regression with predetermined scenarios for those instances.

In unauthorized trading, you don't have the advantage of known outcomes to set against the predicting model, but you have a vast quantity of data that define norms. Seeing deviation from those norms is easy. So the lesson is to understand your business problem first, then choose the best techniques to detect that fraud. Because ultimately all we want to do is find the most fraud before the money is lost. For example, first party fraud was typically discovered after the fact, after the money was gone. Why look in the collections book after the money is lost? When you use logistic regression or decision tree analysis to predict what application or what insurance claims are most likely to be fraudulent, you stop the money before it disappears.

**MCF**: *For financial crime detection many solutions are specific to each intuition. Financial crime is a transnational, cross industry phenomena with global challenge. Can we imagine an industry consortium that shares the efforts for combating financial crime via big-data mining and analysis?*

**LH**: This is interesting thinking. In fraud and financial crime we have data privacy laws that often prohibit the sharing of information; every country seeks to protect the rights of the person. In fraud and financial crime investigations there are more lenient terms about what you can share. We work with a number of insurance consortia who share their claims and policy data across organizations for the sole purpose of detecting serious organized crime. There are a number of countries globally that are doing it and many more looking into it.

Banks are generally not willing to share their infrastructure because it often means sharing their data. If banks would share data across organizations, we would be able to determine who is defrauding those organizations because we would not only have the full list within a bank but also the full list across a country or countries. I do not think we are there yet, perhaps due to sensitiveness of data and competitive advantage.

In general we have seen a variety of anti-money laundering systems, fraud systems, and sanctions systems in countries worldwide. These systems do not talk to each other. We are working with a number of global organizations to consolidate the outputs of those fraud and financial crime systems. For instance, there are AML systems that generate alerts and fraud systems that generate alerts. In Mexico you have one system and a different one in the United States doing the same things. We are taking gray data, as we describe them, and linking them together at a global level, then determining what countries are missing information by looking at things in isolation. We describe this approach as a safety net proposition. It is not ripping and replacing the existing current systems. But assuming I am in global banking and I have a lot of local subsidiaries, I want to take the output of financial crime and fraud systems and link them together to make sure that they are doing everything possible to protect the business. We call it a global financial intelligence unit.

**MCF**: *Classical solutions for fighting financial crime have been focused mainly on credit card fraud, transaction fraud, securities fraud, and the like. Where do new markets (Bitcoin) or new industries (the betting and online gambling industry) fit in?*

**LH**: Banks have a lot of credit and debit cards. Banks are seeking enterprise-wide strategies and they looking at a range of business problems, including trade finance, fraud application, and online fraud. They want to optimize their anti-money laundering systems and create financial intelligence units. But this drive is not limited to banks. We do a lot of work with insurance companies on claims fraud, policy fraud, and changes by product. At banks we typically look at unsecured loans, unsecured lending, credit cards, overdraft, and personal loans; and we concentrate on portfolio-secured lending such as mortgages and on commercial business loans such as trade finance fraud. In claims, investigators used to look at motor and home insurance, but now people look at life insurance, worker compensation, and general liability. We do a lot of work with governments around VAT and carousel frauds, tax fraud. Governments want to diversify into pension fraud and benefits fraud.

I was recently with a large Asian casino that was starting to address issues such as anti-money laundering and fraud in casinos. Even if we aren't talking to Bitcoin, I went to a lecture recently on Bitcoin where people discussed how we should be protecting ourselves and about Bitcoin's concealment mechanisms for fraudsters. I think the industry is becoming more and more aware.

Awareness is also growing about telecom fraud. With a £500 smartphone I can conduct a fraudulent transaction and disappear. There are also scenarios in which people reroute networks and are not charged for roaming. They manipulate the network traffic line. Cybersecurity is an important topic and we have started doing a lot of work in this area. When considering cases of cybercrime I look at both physical and behavioral aspects. Cybercrime could be going in the backdoor of the network, and for that you should look at the network traffic. This traffic creates another big data problem because you have to get the data, then link the data and analyzing them properly. The people side is also important because people can steal and use credit card information. So we are addressing both sides.

We encourage our customers to avoid investing in "point solutions" because they create silos that allow things to flow through the cracks. Instead, we advocate enterprise-wide approaches, which call for a foundation of platforms that can ingest data, link them together, analyze data cleverly, and issue alerts about potential high-risk cases. With a tool to investigate, manage, and explore the data, they will have the capability to look across secured and unsecured products, across online and branch channels, across business domains both retail and commercial, and across physical and behavioral investments.

Of course, investment banking will need different data about retail application fraud. You will look at different scenarios and will need to apply different analytics. What you do not want is one vendor doing one thing, another vendor doing another, and no talking between their systems. You need a foundation platform that can look through different behaviors but with an integrated case management system for even simple things, such as reuse of skills within an organization. It should use an enterprise-wide approach.

But with that said we don't ask people to rip out existing systems. For instance, we do a lot of work around anti-money laundering optimization. Rather than replacing existing systems, we apply our analytics on top of their existing AML systems to prioritize their alerts from investigations and raise the most interesting ones to the top of the pile. It is a combination between being bigger and getting a strategic vision through using the strategic platform to optimize the systems you have in place.

# PART I

# MODERN FINANCIAL CRIME

# CHAPTER 1A

# Innovation and Crime

## 1 BACKGROUND

The relationship between crime and technology is relatively recent, starting in the 1990s and the Internet era. This area includes three types of crime: First, there are the traditional crime syndicates that migrated toward the technology zone because of circumstances. Second, there are types of crimes that originated from technology and exemplified by hacking and cybercrime. The third typology of crimes involves groups of individuals within organizations that developed abnormal or fraudulent behavior during the period of massive technological influx.

A few things should be noted for the first type of crime. Traditional crime syndicates have very precise and strict rules that have been in place for decades and some for centuries. These codes by their very nature restrict criminal activity, thereby increasing the occurrence of racketeering, smuggling, heisting, trafficking, etc. Activities involving technology were disregarded due to the fact that in theory are an easier target for investigators. Throughout history,

criminal syndicates did not exert direct activities on the financial markets, but instead used individuals and groups less noticeable to law enforcement. The case of Michele Sindona who was involved with Italian American and Sicilian organized crime is a good example. At the fall of the URSS the old circle of "thieves in law" (*vhor v zakone*) also subsidized cyber scams to the young but less challenged and respected hackers across the Eastern block [1]. But the change in structure of modern society inevitably brought changes in the structure of crime. The second type crimes concerns a class of educated individuals that fell into the web of illegal acts with the hope of quick returns. Hackers are probably best known to the large public but scammers involved in online gambling, digital currency, or investors relations using social media are also included. This new class covers the old world of crime and new technology entrepreneurs.

The last type of crime concerns individuals for which technology and generally speaking innovation represent a kind of no man's land in which they think everything can be tolerated. These individuals do not have a criminal

TABLE 1   SWOT Analysis of the Role of Innovation in Criminal Acts

| Strengths | Weaknesses |
|---|---|
| Speed in operations | Traceability |
| Global coverage | Audit trail for investigators |
| Low entry and exit costs | Easy to infiltrate |
| **Opportunities** | **Threats** |
| Creating new supports for crime | Attacks from other groups |
| Creating virtual traces for audit | Competition from other technologies or products |

curriculum. High-frequency trading is a relevant example, as many people in this area thought no one was watching. Manipulation such as spoofing[1] or tax arbitrage on short-term trades are other examples of this type of crime.

Table 1 shows a brief SWOT analysis of the role of innovation in criminal acts.

## 2 TECHNOLOGY LEVERAGED BY CRIME

As noted in the previous section, one of the major mutations in criminal activities occurred with the development of new technologies and more precisely with electronic communication infrastructures. Telecommunications, Internet services, and online banking changed not only the day-to-day life of our society but also brought new challenges and opportunities to the criminal world. This reshaping of crime also affected investigation procedures, especially after 9/11. Thus, in 2001 the Bush administration passed the Patriot Act in 2001, which stipulates in Title 5 that a federal agent is able to request under subpoena any information or to wiretap without the approval of a federal court, thereby helping officials to track perpetrators faster.

Most of our technological progress has been leveraged by criminals. Before analyzing large-scale scenarios such as cyber terror it should be noted that even small deviances like diffusion of non-public information in insider trading cases is much easier today than it was in the past. Organizations do use filters and tracking devices to monitor communication but the wide panel of tools and communications services make it almost impossible to keep up with the vast electronic ocean. Financial criminals use technology and innovation at all levels, from simple communication tools and social media and to high-quality fiber optics for high-frequency trading, which has a double-edge. For example, when technology is used for an illegal purpose, officials can track the whole scheme electronically, but this means the criminals can use it too, often in an attempt to throw investigators off their trail.

## 3 CRIME-DRIVEN TECHNOLOGY

One of the most sensitive and highly controversial topics is crime-driven technology, i.e., technology propelled by criminal interests. It is easy to imagine an eBay service for purchasing illegal goods and services or security software such as Bitdefender or Kaspersky, that can also be used in harmful ways, such as to generate

---

[1] By placing large buy orders, a trader can give the market the impression that there is significant buying interest, which suggests that prices will soon rise, raising the likelihood that other market participants will buy and push the prices up. The larger orders are canceled before execution.

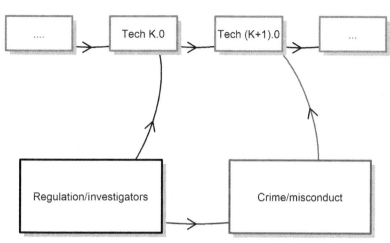

**FIGURE 1** Regulations and investigation methods do target technologies and products at in an effort to address current issues.

malware. In fact, these products do exist and are available to the public. Furthermore, some innovative products such as online gambling or betting platforms or various forms of digital currencies have been created by groups formed by criminal organizations. A good example is Liberty Gold, which used digital currency to clear illegal funds. There are similar suspicions about Bitcoin and other cryptocurrencies. The case of online betting is slightly more complex due to the fact that betting is legal in many countries, which makes its detection being a complex task. In December 2014 the Federal Bureau of Investigation busted a gambling start-up in Las Vegas with alleged ties to the organized crime and money-laundering activities, operating via Macau high-profile gamblers (junkets), online sports betting, and high-stakes poker.[2]

## 4 OUTLOOK

The first conclusion we can come to is that the current framework of regulation and surveil-

lance will very soon fail to keep up with the fast pace of innovation. Therefore, we will face a one-step behind paradigm. While as depicted in Figure 1, regulations as well as investigation methods do target technologies and products at a time in order to address current issues, there is less tendency to use a forward looking approach, often due to lack of means. By the time regulators and investigators do understand and propose ways to tackle crime in relation to technology $K.0$ a new technology $K + 1.0$ appears. New technology along with its new panel of products often go under the radar of regulations issued from the experience the previous wave a technology. This is also true for regulation of traditional financial activities.

Digital currency and cryptocurrency are good examples of this issue and will be detailed in a later section. During the Internet bubble digital currency appeared in various forms, and some digital currencies like e-Gold or Liberty Gold developed as nothing more than financial crime tools. Hence, by the time investigators manage to create a clear-cut framework to tackle those issues, another wave of technology enters the scene, making it difficult for officials to investigate and therefore prosecute these crimes. When

---

[2]FBI Takes Aim at High-Roller Junkets, http://www.wsj.com/articles/fbi-takes-aim-at-junket-ties-to-gambling-1419882338.

companies such as those involved in Bitcoin markets are finally raided by the law another cryptocurrency will be in place.

Addressing this eternal competition between crime and order, where the latter is at a disadvantage should be addressed by a change in paradigm. Regulators and investigators should envision not only surveillance tools but also innovative tools in order to keep up with the next wave of technology, thereby making it easier to assess its weaknesses and vulnerabilities. Furthermore, crime investigation should be decoupled from regulations so it does not follow only the prudential framework. Crime patterns detection are similar to *second degree* reasoning or a certain level of conceptual abstraction, hence even if the means are employed a versatile investigator should be able to determine whether there are hidden abnormal factors in a apparently normal walk of life. Today, with the help of technology, investigation should be proactive instead of passive. While these ideas are harder to implement technology progresses in all directions, which often means that solutions generated for one issue can be applied to others.

# 1B

# High-Frequency Trading

## 1 BACKGROUND

The term high-frequency trading (HFT) went viral on May 6, 2010, when it was determined to responsible for the massive market dislocation that took place during that day on the U.S. market. Fears of the European crisis caused distress in the U.S. market with increasing volatility. After this event a large-scale trade on E-Mini S&P 500 put negative pressure on the market, which was amplified by trading algorithms and HFT. Figure 1 shows the evolution of the main indexes during the "flash crash" on May 6, 2010.

The series of events started on May 6th around 2:30 p.m., when the "S&P 500 Volatility Index" went up 22.5% from the opening leave and the buy-side liquidity in the E-Mini S&P 500 futures contracts had fallen by 55%. In this environment of unusually high volatility and thinning liquidity, at 2.32 p.m. a large mutual fund trader initiated a sell for a total of 75,000 E-Mini contracts accounting for $4.1 billion.

This big sale order triggered high-frequency traders and between 2:41 p.m. and 2:44 p.m., they traded nearly 140,000 E-Mini contracts or over 33% of the total trading volume. In the next four-and-a-half minutes, prices of the E-Mini fell by more than 5% and prices of S&P 500 suffered a decline of over 6% as shown in Figure 1. As prices of the E-Mini rapidly declined, the big seller sold about 35,000 E-Mini contracts accounting for $1.9 billion of the 75,000 intended. The Chicago Mercantile Exchange paused the trade of E-Mini contracts. After the trading resumed the prices stabilized and shortly thereafter the E-Mini began to recover.

The "flash crash" caught the attention of the U.S. Securities and Exchange Commission[1] that concluded that the automated execution of a large sell order can trigger extreme price movements, especially if the automated execution

---

[1]Findings regarding the market events of May 6, 2010 http://www.sec.gov/news/studies/2010/marketevents-report.pdf.

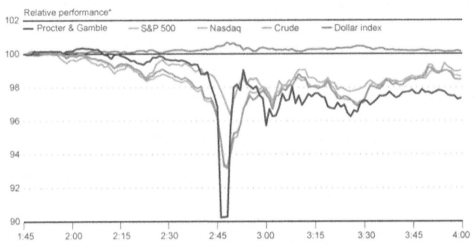

**FIGURE 1**    Evolution of the main indexes during the flash crash on May 6, 2010. *Source: Reuters.*

algorithm does not take prices into account. The interaction between automated execution programs and algorithmic trading strategies can quickly erode liquidity and result in disorderly markets.

In the aftermath market researchers showed that in 2009 HFT accounted for more than 60% of total U.S. stock volumes and generates revenues as high as $7 billion in the Unites States alone. Over the past several years revenues have shrunk dramatically, but the share of HFT in the stock trading volumes has remained significant (Figure 2).

While HFT first targeted the stock market, it expanded over time to other clusters including the derivatives and commodities markets. Figure 3 shows the evolution of daily volume and of the average difference between the timestamps of trades for the wheat futures traded on Chicago Board of Trade (CBOT).

The volumes of wheat futures started to increase massively in 2007 and concomitantly the latency proxy also diminished significantly. The new inflow of liquidity also brought higher frequency in trade execution, which is consistent with the way high-frequency traders operate.

The main question that arises in this context is whether misconduct or fraud can occur and be propagated by high-frequency traders. Market manipulation and regulation arbitrage are two possibilities that will explored.

## 2 MARKET MANIPULATION

In 2014 a highly publicized book *Flash Boys: A Wall Street Revolt* Lewis [2] blamed high-frequency traders for rigging the U.S. stock market.[2] It explains how the ability of high-frequency traders to place orders within seconds provides an advantage over slower traders, which can alter the price signal.

While the scale of "Flash Boys" manipulation is debatable, market fraud is not new. One of the first HFT firms to be tackled by the law for market manipulation was Trillium Capital, a New York-based firm.[3] Following a Financial Industry Regulatory Authority (FINRA) investigation in 2010 the firm was fined $2.3 million in sanctions.

---

[2]U.S. stock markets are rigged, says author Michael Lewis, http://www.reuters.com/article/2014/03/31/us-markets-hft-flashboys-idUSBREA2U03D20140331.
[3]Fast-trading firm hit with big fine, http://fortune.com/2010/09/13/fast-trading-firm-hit-with-big-fine/.

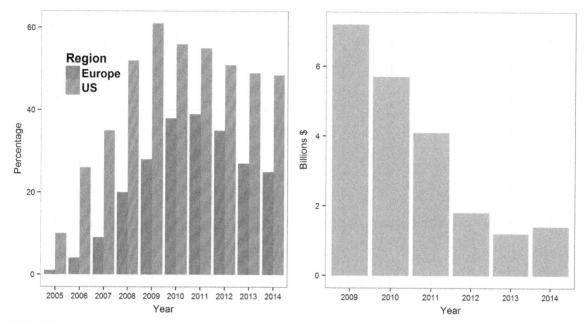

FIGURE 2 Turnover of high-frequency trading. Left: Share of the high-frequency trading in stock market volume. Right: Evolution of the revenue generated by high-frequency traders on the U.S. stock markets. *Source: TABB group.*

Over a 3-month period at the end of 2006 and the beginning of 2007 the firm placed orders to induce other traders to trade based on the mirage of demand and supply created by Trillium. Before the *fictitious* trades were entered, Trillium had limit positions that executed as a result of their traders creating buy or sell side demand, which moved the prices in certain directions. Once the real trades were executed, Trillium immediately canceled their fictitious trades and profited from their limit orders. This manipulation technique, called *smoking*, was repeated by the Trillium traders 46,000 times, generating $525,000 in profits.

In a seminal paper on HFT Biais [3] defined the main types of market abuse or manipulation involving HFT:

- **Electronic front-running** where, in exchange for kickback payments, the HFT firm is provided early notice of investors' intentions to transact by being shown initial bids and offers placed on exchanges and other trading venues by their brokers, and then race those bona fide securities investors to the other securities exchanges, transact in the desired securities at better prices, go back and transact with the unwitting initial investors to the their financial detriment.

- **Rebate arbitrage** where the HFT and brokerage firms obtain kickback payments from the securities exchanges without providing the liquidity the kickback scheme was purportedly designed to entice.

- **Slow-market (or latency) arbitrage** where the HFT firm sees changes in the price of a stock on one exchange, and picks orders sitting on slower exchanges, before those exchanges are able to react.

- **Spoofing** where the HFT firm sends out orders with corresponding cancelations, often at the opening or closing of the stock market, in order to manipulate the market price of a security and/or induce a particular

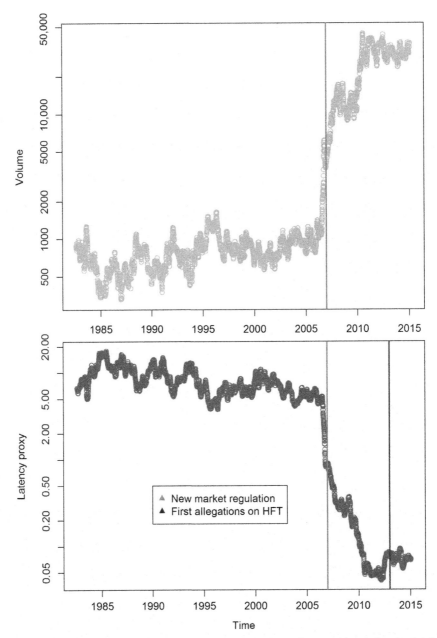

**FIGURE 3** Evolution of daily volume and of the average difference between the timestamps of trades for the wheat futures traded on CBOT. *Source: The time stamps for the trades provided by Tickdata (http://tickdata.com/) in milliseconds.*

market reaction. The high-frequency trader places a sequence of limit sell orders above the best ask, potentially for very large amounts. The hope is to torment the market and induce naïve participants to sell against the limit order to buy the high-frequency trader will have discretely placed.

- **Stuffing** where the HFT firm submits an huge number of orders to the market, which generates congestion and limits access to the market for slow traders (non-HF traders). They do not have a clear view of the current status of trading, which makes it difficult for them to execute trades. Meanwhile, fast traders who better understand what is going on and have superior access to the market engine are able to execute profitable trades at the slow traders' expense.

- **Smoking** where the HFT firm first posts alluring limit orders to attract slow traders. Then they rapidly revise these orders into less generous terms, hoping to execute profitably against the incoming flow of slow traders' market orders.

- **Layering** where the HFT defendants send out waves of false orders intended to give the impression that the market for shares of a particular security at that moment is deep in order to take advantage of the market's reaction to the layering of orders.

- **Pinging** where the HFT firm uses the tactic of entering small marketable orders—usually for 100 shares—in order to learn about large hidden orders in dark pools or exchanges. Pinging is analogous to a ship or submarine means sending out sonar signals to detect upcoming obstructions or enemy vessels. Once a firm gets a ping or a series of pings the HFT firm may engage in predatory trading activity that ensures it a nearly risk-free profit at the expense of the buy-sider that will end up receiving an unfavorable price for its large order. Scopino [4] analyzed from a legal perspective HFT and showed that some

high-speed pinging tactics arguably violate at least four provisions of the Commodity Exchange Act—the statute governing the futures and derivatives markets—and one of the regulations promulgated thereunder.

- **Abusive liquidity detection** where the HFT firm enters large orders during the pre-open or uses "pinging" to detect when a large buyer or seller get trades in ahead of them. After a profitable price movement, the trades are reversed, or in the event the price moves contrary to the position taken, the trading interest of the large buyer or seller may be viewed as a free option to trade against.

- **Contemporaneous trading** where by obtaining material, non-public information concerning the trading intentions of a client the HFT firm transacts against them.

As recent case[4] involving Athena Capital Research showed HFT firms can also be caught in the manipulation of the end-of-day prices known as *marking the close*. Athena developed strategies to dominate a trade in the last few seconds of a trading day, which made up more than 70% of the volume of these stocks in the run-up to the close on thousands of NASDAQ stocks. Athena agreed to pay a $1 million penalty to settle the case, the SEC's first on HFT manipulation. Despite all the negative media over the past year Cumming et al. [5] showed that HFT in some markets has significantly mitigated the frequency and severity of end-of-day manipulation. The effect of HFT is more pronounced than the role of trading rules, surveillance, enforcement, and legal conditions in curtailing the frequency and severity of end-of-day manipulation.

The link between exchanges with HFT firms was highlighted as a risk factor for price discovery and how some big traders might be privileged by exchanges. In 2014 BATS Global

---

[4]SEC accuses HFT firm of manipulating closing price of thousands of stocks, http://www.cnbc.com/id/102090905.

Markets, Inc., the Unite States' second biggest exchange, was the target of a class action suit related to HFT for allegedly giving preferential treatment to certain clients.[5] In the aftermath, BATS Global Markets agreed to pay a record breaking $14 million penalty to settle charges that the exchanges failed to accurately and completely disclose how order types functioned and for selectively providing such information only to certain HFT firms.

## 3 HFT AND STRUCTURED PRODUCTS: RENAISSANCE TECHNOLOGIES

With new regulations concerning proprietary trading, banks have been forced to disinvest in many of their profit-generating activities including HFT, leaving behind huge investments in systems and infrastructures. Hedge funds, which are currently the big players in algorithmic trading, have taken advantage of the opportunity to rent the banks, infrastructures and gain extra leverage.

In 2014 following a special investigation conducted by the U.S. Senate, the hedge fund Renaissance Technologies was accused of misusing complex financial structures, with the help of Barclays and Deutsche Bank, to avoid paying more than $6 billion in U.S. taxes.[6] Under U.S. legislation short-term capital gains including those from HFT were taxed at 39.6% while long-term capital gains were taxed at 20%.

Renaissance generated $34 billion in trading profits and Barclays and Deutsche Bank took in more than $1 billion in fees by creating a scheme while the gains from HFT were presented as long-term capital gains that avoided bigger taxes. Renaissance and at least 12 other hedge funds were engaged for over 6 years in HFT but they presented their gains under the form of basket options of securities, which were in accounts held for at least a year, allowing the profits to be claimed as long-term capital gains. The securities were also held in options accounts instead of traditional prime broker accounts, which were subject to an ordinary income tax rate of as high as 39% that would apply for daily trading gains.

Additionally, structured financial products helped banks bypass laws for excessive bank lending for stock speculation including the uptick rule.[7] While such structures are not illegal as noted, many represent massive schemes for tax avoidance. The real engineering behind this scheme is much more complicated, and Figure 4 gives a snapshot of the main entities involved in the process.

COLT was the name of the Barclays's project created in 2003 aimed at providing an after-tax benefit to hedge funds through the conversion of their return from the fund from short-term capital gain taxed at 39.6% to long-term capital gains taxed at 20%. Renaissance Technologies, a U.S.-based hedge fund, was the main beneficiary of the COLT project. First, the structured capital markets (as the project was labeled) involved

[5]Bats Global Markets, Inc.: HFT Litigation Securities Litigation, http://securities.stanford.edu/filings-case.html?id=105202.
[6]U.S. Senate alleges hedge fund and banks avoided $6 billion tax bill, http://www.ft.com/intl/cms/s/0/7c6ea670-1120-11e4-94f3-00144feabdc0.html#axzz3Wi7Qbn7v.

[7]The uptick rule prevents short sellers from adding to the downward momentum when the price of an asset is already experiencing sharp declines. The SEC eliminated the rule on July 6, 2007, but the rule was restated in April 2009.

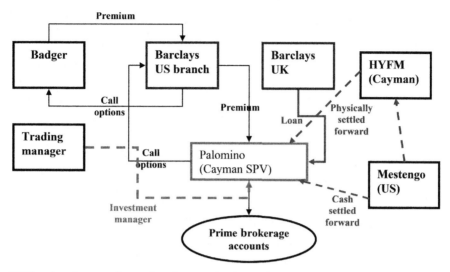

**FIGURE 4** COLT project. Structured capital markets involved several entities based both in the United States and offshore.

a few entities based both in the United States and offshore[8]:

- PalominoLtd., a Cayman Island company. Palomino's purpose was to eliminate-trade reporting obligations that would be required if Barclays participated in the transaction directly and to create a U.S. tax resident entity that in not confined by U.S. regulatory rules that applied to U.S.-formed entities.
- HYMP Ltd., also incorporated in the Cayman Islands and Mestengo Inc., used as part of a cost-efficient structure to enable Palomino to sell U.S. securities without being subject to the up-tick rules that restrict short sales of U.S. securities.

The aim of the project was not only to bypass the legal fences from the United States but also to provide leverage to Renaissance Technologies at optimal costs. Under this scheme, Palomino, a subsidiary, held at 100% by Barclays Bank PLC (UK) would borrow a few billion (let's assume 5 billion USD) from its mother company on an unsecured basis. Palomino would then establish a prime brokerage trading account with Barclays Capital Securities Lending, placing the borrowed amount into the prime brokerage accounts to be used as trading collateral. Palomino was in fact managed by Renaissance through an entity labeled in the Figure 4 as the Trading manager. The strategy was, in fact, HFT-based on long and short trades of U.S. equity stock. To enable transferring the gains from Palomino to the hedge fund Renaissance, a structured product, called *Badger*, was designed between Barclays and a subsidiary of Renaissance.

At the same time a U.S. branch of Barclays would write an American-style call option to the Badger with respect to the value of the prime brokerage accounts, for which the Bagder would pay a premium, accounting for 10% of the Palomin's loan ($500 million). Almost 5% of the call premium was the fee received by Barclays. The call option would have a term of 3 years and

[8]Subcommittee finds basket options misused to dodge billions in taxes and bypass federal leverage limits, http://www.hsgac.senate.gov/subcommittees/investigations/media/subcommittee-finds-basket-options-misused-to-dodge-billions-in-taxes-and-bypass-federal-leverage-limits.

would be cash settled. The effective strike price of the call option would be the same amount as the loans taken by Palomino. Simultaneous to its writing of the call option to Badger, Barclays would purchase an identical option from Palomino. The only difference being that the call premium paid to Palomino corresponds to the Badger's premium less the 5% of commission kept by Barclays. In the end the assets under management for Palomino were $5.48 billion: $5 billion in loans and $475 million in premiums from the options. If the Trading manager managed to increase the assets of Palomino above the $5 billion taken from Barclays, then that amount would be the payoff that would go back to Renaissance. Without the arrangement between Palomino, Metengo, and HYMF, short sales of U.S. securities by Palomino (i.e., borrowing stock from Barclays Securities and sell it on the open market) would be restricted. To manage this restriction, Palomino created identical amounts of physically long and synthetically short positions in a large number of U.S. securities so that when Palomino made sales of securities they would always be from the pool of long equity positions. As a result of a series of simultaneous transactions, each of Palomino, Mestengo, and HYMF would all have long and short positions (interests in cash or equity settled forward contracts) in the same basket of U.S. equity securities. A reduction by Palomino of its long position in certain U.S. equity securities would create a synthetic short position. The only risk beared by Barclays was the market risk generated by the fact that the Trading manager might have lost money. Therefore, Barclays put in placed fine monitoring of Palmino's book as well as of trades places with other brokers to ensure that big losing positions were cut if needed.

This complicated scheme had no other purpose than to reduce tax payments, bypass the up-tick rule, and obtain cheap loans. The Renaissance example speaks for itself not only in regard to the misconduct possible with HFT but also the complexity of the schemes used by organizations for arbitrating regulation. In addition, this example also shows the more central role played by hedge funds in the current environment of the investment industry and their close relationship with banks and investment firms.

## 4 OUTLOOK

As the events of May 6 demonstrate, especially in times of significant volatility, high trading volume is not necessarily a reliable indicator of market liquidity. *SEC report*

High-frequency traders make profit from very small differences in the prices from analyzing the micro-structure of the market and by executing a large number of trades at very high speed. The price variations relevant to HFT do not apply to traditional manipulation theories. Therefore, the real impact of HFT on financial markets is not yet clearly understand. Its supporters reaffirm that HFT brings liquidity, consistency in prices, and helps to cope with market fragmentation resulting from the co-existence between traditional exchanges and new entrants. Others claim that the low latency distorts the price discovery process and keeps out slower traders. Besides the systemic risk potentially generated by HFT, the risk of market manipulation has been noted over the past 2 years. For example, Angel et al. [6] noted that the expenditures on the speedy technologies needed for HFT is becoming a significant barrier to entry of new high-frequency traders and hence HFT is becoming more concentrated among fewer entities. This might generate in the future very big players with massive power on the markets, which may lead to further misconduct such as cartel-type behavior and manipulation attempts. Regulations can limit this by imposing floors in terms of volumes and latency.

# 1C

# Commodities Markets

## 1 BACKGROUND

The case of the rogue trader Yasuo Hamanaka, nicknamed Mister 5%, for managing 5% of global copper reserves was the first highly publicized event involving a financial crime in commodities markets. The Sumitomo event and the allegations that Hamanaka cornered the copper market came at a crucial moment for commodities markets, which started to observe a high influx of liquidity from agents other than those with transformation or merchant activities. Toward the end of the 1990s with the development of commodities futures markets many financial institutions including investment banks, assets managers, pension funds, and hedge funds started to diversify their portfolios by including commodities. Investment banks saw unique opportunities for market making of derivatives needed by purchasers of physical supply or by the commodities merchant firms such as

Louis Dreyfus, Cargill, J. Aron, etc. Hedge funds also understood that there were inefficiencies in those nascent markets that could provide strong alphas.

A comparison of U.S. equity and commodities prices (crude oil) in the United States shows that the relationship between the two markets has evolved significantly over the past two decades, as shown in Figure 1. The returns of S&P 500 futures and those of crude oil futures suffered two major turning points underlined by structural breaks tests, the first occurring in around the time of the Long Term Capital Management (LTCM) default and the other around the Lehman default (Figure 1).

The first period of modern commodities markets before the LTCM default reflected the classic features of commodities prices, which showed mean reversion [7] around a long-term tendency in price given by the offer/demand equilibrium. Futures and physical markets are highly connected, and the forward curve was generally

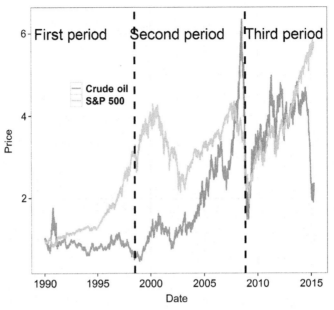

**FIGURE 1** Evolution of U.S. stock prices and oil prices since 1990. The returns of S&P 500 futures and those of crude oil futures suffered two major turning points as noted by structural breaks tests, the first occurring around the time of the LTCM default and the other around the Lehman default.

in a natural backwardation (strong convenience yield).[1]

---

[1] It should be recalled that an agent holding an investment in commodities like oil, gas, or gold has the option of flexibility with regard to consumption (no risk of commodity shortage). On the other hand, the decision to postpone consumption implies storage expenses. The net cost of these services per unit of time is termed the convenience yield $\delta$. Intuitively, the convenience yield corresponds to dividend yield for stocks, thereby the price of a forward contract is given by:

$$F_{t,T} = S_t \cdot \exp((r_{t,T} - \delta_{t,T}) \cdot (T - t)) \qquad (1)$$

where $F_{t,T}$ is the value at the moment $t$ of the futures contract for the maturity $T$, $S_t$ is the spot value at time $t$, $r_{t,T}$, and $\delta_{t,T}$ are, respectively, the values of the rate and convenience yield for the maturity $T$. Here, the quota holders will not sell their quotas to realize an arbitrage opportunity (by selling the quota and buying futures contracts). Consequently they "value" their owner-right and the convenience yield is a major element to consider when assessing commodities price.

The second period of commodities is characterized by a significant increase in liquidity but also in the volatility level. Liquidity became a fundamental driver for oil prices. In the unprecedented pace of oil and energy commodities prices during the year 2000 the mean-reversion models become irrelevant as noted by Geman [8]. Thus, in the second period there was an absence of long-term equilibrium and disconnection between the market prices from the physical demand/supply balance.

The second structural break came with the last crisis and marked the third period of the commodities markets that entered a structural contango, characterized by a negative convenience yield. In those circumstances, the roll-over costs of futures positions became significant. Granger causality tests showed a causality relationship of S&P 500 to crude oil returns. The causal transmission is valid for monthly, weekly, and daily returns and is also verified for the physical volatility levels. The oil volatility levels and the fat tails are closer to those of equity indexes than to a traditional commodity. By the third period oil as well as many commodities had less the features of alternative investments and looked more like "glorified stocks".

The changes that occurred on the commodities markets in previous decades also influenced the types of fraud. In the first period, just like in *Trading Places*,[2] frauds linked to physical trading were more common than the more recent misconduct on commodities futures markets. The controversial high-frequency trading topic is related to this area.

## 2 PHYSICAL VS. FUTURES

With all the big investment banks having extensive commodities trading operations and traditional commodities merchants such as Cargill, Louis Dreyfus, and Glencore being more involved in the derivatives market making, the natural question that arises is if the derivatives have an impact on commodities prices and if they can be used to manipulate those prices.

Gilbert [9] showed through Granger causality tests that the futures markets generally dominate the spot markets and changes in prices on the futures markets lead to price changes in spot markets more often than the reverse. This study justifies the intensification of information flow from futures to spot markets by the increase in the relative importance of electronic trading of futures contracts.

In 2014 a 2-year probe by the U.S. Senate revealed massive involvement of investment banks in physical commodities.[3] Institutions get significant exposure not only in physical trading but also in warehousing of physical commodities and transformation plants, a fact that can easily lead to price manipulation allegations. In fact, banks' ownership or investments in physical commodity businesses juxtaposed over their market-making business in the commodities derivatives gives them inside knowledge that allows them to benefit financially through market manipulation or other misconduct.

For instance, Goldman Sachs owns Metro International Trade Services, a network of metals warehouses in Detroit involved in moving aluminum from one warehouse to another, which allegedly causes long delivery times for aluminum and increased cost costumers. Table 1 shows the gross fair value of physical commodity trading inventories for the main U.S. banks involved in the commodities markets.

As a result of the Senate's report the government is considering restricting banks' physical commodity activities as they exhibited shortfalls of up to $15 billion to cover extreme loss scenarios like oil spill or potential environmental disasters specific to physical trading and storing.

**TABLE 1** Gross Fair Value of Physical Commodity Trading Inventories

| Value in billion USD | 2009 | 2010 | 2011 | 2012 | 2013 | 2014 |
|---|---|---|---|---|---|---|
| Goldman Sachs | 3.7 | 13.1 | 5.8 | 11.7 | 4.6 | 3.8 |
| JPMorgan | 10.0 | 21.0 | 26.0 | 16.2 | 10.2 | 13.9 |
| Morgan Stanley | 5.3 | 6.8 | 9.7 | 7.3 | 3.3 | – |

*Source: Financial Time & 2014 Annual reports.*

---

[2]A 1983 film starring Dan Aykroyd and Eddie Murphy, where the main characters engage in insider trading on orange juice market.

[3]Report blasts U.S. banks' physical commodities operations, http://www.ft.com/intl/cms/s/0/785e4552-700e-11e4-90af-00144feabdc0.html#axzz3X6pD5ZPM.

A traditional commodity merchant firm performs physical arbitrages due to its mining/drilling, storage, freight, and processing capacities [10]. When comparing these firms with banks involved in physical trading as explained by Pirrong [10] they show considerable diversity in their investments in physical assets, with some firms being relatively asset intensive and others being very asset light. On average, these firms are less leveraged compared to investment banks, as reflected in Table 2.

The tendency to invest in the full value chain of physical commodities from extraction to processing is also followed by banks. In addition, banks with a bigger balance sheet and larger books of derivatives can easily take the monopole niche market such as rare metals.

**TABLE 2** Assets to Equity Ratio as of 2012 for the Major Commodities Trading Firms

| Trading firm | Assets to equity ratio |
| --- | --- |
| Cargill | 2.37 |
| Archer Daniels Midland | 2.39 |
| Bunge Ltd | 2.51 |
| Wilmar | 2.76 |
| Glencore | 3.08 |
| Louis Dreyfus B.V. | 3.74 |
| Noble Group | 3.8 |
| Vitol | 4 |
| Olam | 4.02 |
| EDF Trading | 4.56 |
| Mercuria Energy Trading | 5.06 |
| BP International Ltd | 5.32 |
| Trafigura | 7.94 |
| Shell Trading International | 12.09 |
| Arcadia Energy Pte | 17.51 |
| Eni Trading Shipping | 35.09 |
| E.On Global | 111.07 |

*Source: Pirrong [10].*

Trading firms extended their activities to market making of derivatives but with smaller exposures, thereby having a lesser systemic role due to their size.

# 3 MARKET MANIPULATION IN METALS

Prices manipulation is the most ubiquitous offense in the area of commodities market, precious metals market catching the attention of investigators over the past years.

In early 2015 the U.S. Department of Justice announced an investigation of at least 10 banks, including Barclays Plc, JPMorgan Chase & Co., and Deutsche Bank AG to determine whether they manipulated prices of precious metals such as silver and gold.[4] At least two investigations had previously been conducted by various regulatory bodies concerning the rigging of gold and silver fixings and the manipulation of silver futures.

## 3.1 Gold and Silver Fixings

The legacy of gold fixing began on June 28, 2012 one day after Barclays had been fined for LIBOR manipulation. On that day one of Barclays' gold traders engaged in a fixing manipulation in order to push out of the money a digital option expiring that day in order to generate a payment of $3.5 million to a client.[5] The fix was a twice-daily (10:30 a.m. and 15:00 p.m.) auction process controlled by four banks in London, which is used by all agents involved in bullion trading. This manipulation resulted in another

---

[4]Banks Face U.S. Manipulation Probe Over Metals Pricing, http://www.bloomberg.com/news/articles/2015-02-24/banks-said-to-face-u-s-manipulation-probe-over-metals-pricing.
[5]Barclays fined $26m for trader's gold rigging, http://www.ft.com/intl/cms/s/0/08cafa70-e24f-11e3-a829-00144feabdc0.html#axzz3X6pD5ZPM.

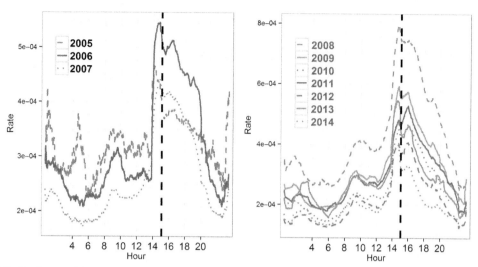

FIGURE 2   Evolution of the intra-day volatility for gold price.

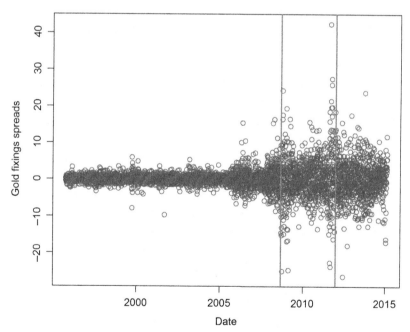

FIGURE 3   Evolution of daily difference between the p.m. and a.m. gold fixings.

fine for Barclays. Nonetheless the gold rigging was not a single event and seemingly the fixing started way before 2012. Figure 2 shows the evolution of average intra-day volatility for the price of gold computed each year, which shows since 2005 a volatility peak around 15 h p.m. corresponding to the fixing time.

The daily difference between the p.m. and a.m. gold fixings exhibited in Figure 3 shows an increased variance starting in 2005 and a pattern in the variance of the spread between 2008 and 2011.

Figure 4 shows a few concrete examples of price manipulation around the PM fixing time.

The silver fixing prices also felt the scrutiny of regulators.[6] Deutsche Bank, HSBC, and Bank of Nova Scotia have been accused of attempting to rig the fixing price of silver. The lawsuit came after a 5-year investigation of the Commodity Futures Trading Commission (CFTC), which found no evidence. Nonetheless the allegation claimed that the banks established positions in both physical silver and silver derivatives prior to the public release of silver fixing

[6]Banks accused of rigging silver price, http://www.bbc.co.uk/news/business-28509979.

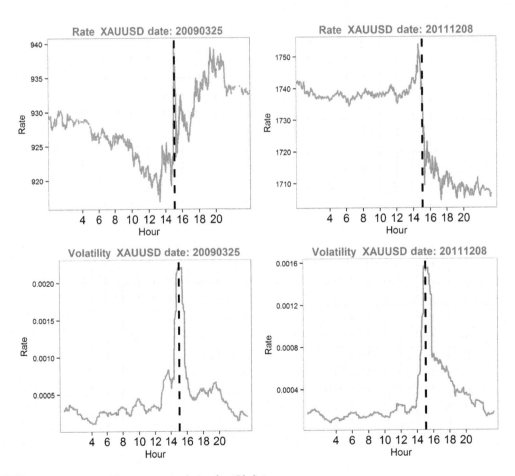

FIGURE 4   Examples of gold prices manipulation for 15 h fixing.

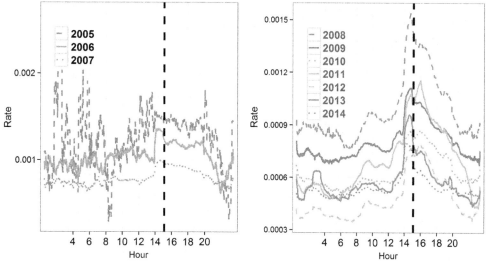

**FIGURE 5** Evolution of the intra-day volatility for the silver price rate.

results, allowing them to make illegitimate profits. The silver fixing takes place at 12 h GMT, but as Figure 5 shows the evolution of the intra-day volatility for the silver price rate shows a peak at 15 h, the gold p.m. fixing hour. Figures 6 and 7 give a few examples that occurred during the 2011 of peaks in silver prices at 15 and 12 h, respectively.

As a result of the investigations concerning price manipulation, the process of fixing for both gold and silver fixings changed on August 15, 2014.

## 3.2 Cartel on Silver Futures

Intra-day fixing manipulation is not the only fraud that occurs concerning metal prices. A class action lawsuit against JPMorgan Chase & Co. and HSBC was filed in 2010, alleging that the banks violated U.S. antitrust laws by manipulating the prices of silver futures and option contracts in tandem. Beginning in early 2008, HSBC and JPMorgan built up extremely large short positions in silver futures and options on the Commodity Exchange Inc. (COMEX), with

JPMorgan increasing its silver derivative holdings by over $6 billion or 220 million ounces.[7]

The class action suit alleges that HSBC and JPMorgan made large, coordinated trades, among other things, to artificially lower the price of silver at key times when the precious metal should have been trading at higher levels. For example, around March 14, 2008, the CME/COMEX front futures contracts traded at $20.574 per troy ounce and by October 24, 2008 they dropped to $9.25 per troy ounce. On January 8, 2010 they traded at $18.458.

The class action suit also alleged that the electronic trading helped by JPMorgan and HSBC to communicate and signal to each other their market moves (i.e., conspire and manipulate) without detection by other market participants, something that would be impossible in an open outcry pit. Note that in this particular case,

---

[7]JPMorgan Chase & Co.: iShares Silver Trust and ETF Securities Ltd. Silver Trust Securities Litigation, http://securities.stanford.edu/filings-documents/1046/SLV10_01/2010127_f01c_1007768.pdf.

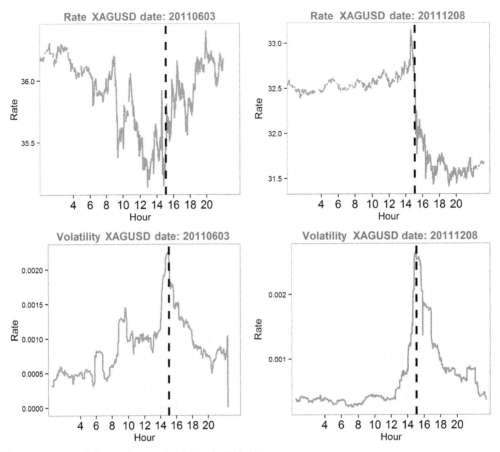

**FIGURE 6**  Examples of silver prices manipulation for 15 h fixing.

electronic trading did not bring efficiency in the market.

Figure 8 shows the evolution of gold and silver front month futures on the Chicago Mercantile Exchange (CME). Structural breaks in the relationship between silver and gold returns appear around the same dates given in the class action suit. Nonetheless the lawsuit was dismissed in March 2014 for lack of relevant evidence.

# 4 AGRICULTURAL MARKETS

The high volatility of the agricultural commodities price was noted as one of the triggers of the "Arab Spring" in Northern Africa, underlining the world risks of food. At the following G20 held in Paris in 2011 the participants agreed to introduce new rules to curb commodity price volatility[8] and to increase the transparency of information on the physical supply of agricultural commodities across the globe. Barclays, one the largest banks involved in the speculation on food including wheat, corn, and soybeans, made an estimated 500 million pounds in 2010 and 2011

[8]Sarkozy targets commodities in G20 agenda, http://www.reuters.com/article/2011/01/24/us-g20-france-idUSTRE70N5CC20110124.

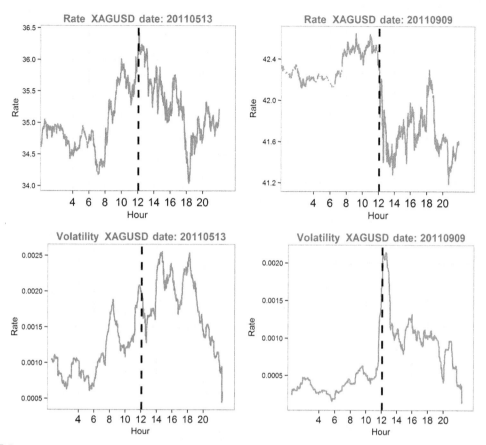

**FIGURE 7**   Examples of silver prices manipulation for 12 h fixing.

and closed its agricultural desk in 2013 because of further investigation in the post-LIBOR affair rush.[9]

Similar to energy producers and oil drillers, food companies like Nestle or Kraft have their own trading desks in charge with hedging the price risk relative to agricultural commodities.

As recent as 2015 two of these companies, Kraft and Mondelez,[10] were charged by the U.S. Commodity Futures Trading Commission for alleged wheat price manipulation on the futures markets.

Another piece in the agricultural price manipulation puzzle was given by the allegation of

[9]Barclays Stops Speculative Agricultural Commodity Trading, http://www.bloomberg.com/news/articles/2013-02-12/barclays-stops-speculative-agricultural-commodity-trading-2-.

[10]UPDATE 2-U.S. CFTC sues Kraft, Mondelez over alleged wheat price manipulation, http://www.reuters.com/article/2015/04/01/kraft-manipulation-cftc-idUSL2N0WY2IS20150401.

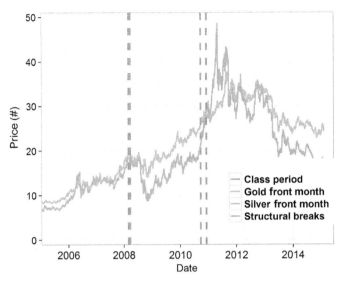

**FIGURE 8** Silver futures manipulation. Evolution of gold and silver front month futures on the CME. Structural breaks in the relationship between silver and gold returns appear around the same dates given in the class action lawsuit.

high-frequency trader influence on the commodities market.[11]

If some estimations indicate that high-frequency firms make less than 10% of overall futures softs markets, big intra-day swings in cocoa, sugar, and cotton price can be attributed to the arrival of high-frequency trading.

## 5 TAX FRAUD AND MONEY LAUNDERING

Almost all physical commodities traded through exchanges or over the counter carry various taxes, one of the most common being the Value Added Tax (VAT). VAT fraud is a common phenomenon on commodities trades including gold, diamonds, $CO_2$ emissions, gas, and electricity [11]. The shipping of physical

commodities overseas in territories with different tax and customs creates new opportunities for fraud. Physical delivery of commodities in various emerging countries also can be part of money laundering schemes due to the high value of shipments. The trade of physical commodities represents an ideal interface between *white collar* and *blue collar* crime.

## 6 OUTLOOK

Due to a foreseeable increase in demand for energy-related commodities and agricultural products prices will likely face higher volatility. In this context, the battle for profits will be less in terms of derivatives products but more in terms of storage capacities. This tendency, which has already been observed for commodities merchants, has slowly been integrated by banks in their strategies. Storage is not only a way to delay the supply but also a good tool for arbitrage and even market manipulation.

---

[11]High-speed commodities traders under scrutiny, http://www.ft.com/cms/s/0/dbfb15d6-4a83-11e0-82ab-00144feab49a.html#axzz3WZXZAAPu.

A good example is liquefied natural gas (LNG) for which storage allows not only arbitrages (winter/summer or weekend/open days) but also speculation. Therefore an agent can store the gas when the prices are low and can re-inject in the network when it becomes more expensive. LNG storage is a complex process and takes the form of seasonal or base-load storage (aquifers and depleted fields) and fast-cycle or peak-load storages (salt caverns or artificial cavities). The owner of these storage capacities and of the underlying storage process would have a significant competitive advantage. He can inject more (less) gas into their storage facilities and leaving less (more) on the market, thereby affecting the price.

Generally speaking, market manipulation is a recurrent topic in commodities markets. If the major commodities are scrutinized by regulators the more niche markets with thin liquidity will probably be future targets for market predators.

# Social Networks and Financial Crime

## 1 BACKGROUND

Social networks are massive repositories of information about people and institutions, including their opinions, views, and sentiments.[1] Basic influencer/follower relationships can be established very quickly within a social network. Influencers on social networks have been identified as users that have an impact on the activities or opinions of other users by way of followership or influence on decisions made by other users on the network. The opinions of influencers on social networks are based largely on personal views and cannot be considered absolute fact. However, their opinions have the power to affect the decisions of other users on subject such as investments. Nonetheless, the investment opinions of influential users on social networks do count, often resulting in opinion formation, which can potentially change the investment decisions of followers. Classic stock market manipulation scenarios have revealed the importance of the opinion clusters. Back in the days of cold calls, boiling rooms or aggressive mail campaigns influencers induced a certain opinion in their network of investors on the perspective of a stock or a market.

The influence of the social media upon markets is related to the concept of *sentiment* and sentiment analysis, which are detailed in a later dedicated chapter. Sentiment analysis of documents or tweets is a way of determining if the document has a positive or negative (bullish or bearish) connotation. Sentiment analysis aims to categorize a set of documents mainly through machine-learning techniques and ultimately to represent in the form of a time series the sentiment-related metric concerning a topic or a subject, like a particular stock or a market.

A few researchers have addressed the relationship between social medial and markets. Bollen et al. [12] investigated whether measurements of collective mood states derived from Twitter

---

[1]Figure 1 shows the word cloud from the tweets containing the words "financial crime."

**FIGURE 1**  "Word cloud" from the "tweets" containing "financial crime."

feeds are correlated to the value of the Dow Jones Industrial Average (DJIA) over time by analyzing the text content of daily Twitter feeds by two mood tracking tools, measuring positive vs. negative moods. Chung and Liu [13] attempted to examine Twitter's predictive potential by observing the relationship between societal Twitter trends in the technology sector and hourly stock prices of the top gainers and top losers of ten companies in the technology sector. This research is based on the hypothesis that the trending mood in Twitter about the top gainers in the technology sector will be positive, while the trending mood about top losers will be significantly more negative compared to a baseline measurement of the trending mood in the overall technology sector. Chen and Lazer [14] investigated the relationship between Twitter feed content and stock market movement and studied how well sentiment information extracted from these feeds can be used to predict future shifts in prices.

Zheludev et al. [15] presented a sentiment analysis methodology to quantify and statistically validate which assets could qualify for trading from social media analytics in an ex-ante configuration. By using sentiment analysis techniques and information theory measures the research demonstrates that social media message sentiment can contain statistically significant ex-ante information on the future prices of the S&P 500 index and a limited set of stocks, in excess of what is achievable using solely message volumes.

## 2 SOCIAL MEDIA—THE FIFTH ELEMENT

With the explosion of Internet-based social media, society has witnessed not only a new tool for information sharing and spread but also a whole new economy. Social media has opened an entirely new dimension in terms of

**FIGURE 2** New tech firms value.

consumption trends, decision making, and information flow. The relationship between the social media economy and the traditional economy has become even stronger, since the first has more power than the second. Offer and demand in the traditional economy are heavily influenced by social media through information exchange and through the trends imposed by the influencer-follower relationship. With the arrival of smart-

phones, mobile phones offering portable computers features including Internet connections, social media became a real fifth element in life. Figure 2 shows the strong growth of the main firms of the new technology wave. Both providers of smartphones and social media platforms are part of this new wave.

Since the new generation of smartphones that arrived in 2007 with the iPhone and thereafter the Android the economy of social media has impacted the classic economy on a very frequent basis. Thus, followers of social media can easily share their opinion on their experiences and preferences as well as share their choices on new trends generated by the media. This cross-breeding effect changed many traditional businesses as marketing research, advertising, and communication significantly boosted e-commerce. Social media has also affected financial services.

Social media has started to play a bigger role in relationships within the "Wall Street" world, which is influenced by the financial markets and can influence the financial markets in turn. A recent example is the foreign exchange rate rigging scandal that involved major banks such as UBS, HSBC, JPMorgan, and Citigroup and shows how social media integrates breaking news about a sector or an institution. Figure 3 shows the breakdown of the penalties for the banks in involved in the Forex rigging.

The official announcement of the penalties set by authorities was exposed by the media on November 12, 2014. A sentiment analysis applied for each of the banks involved in the Forex rigging scandal revealed a massive drift around the period of the announcement. Based on Twitter messages mentioning the names of the respective banks a sentiment rating can be constituted using

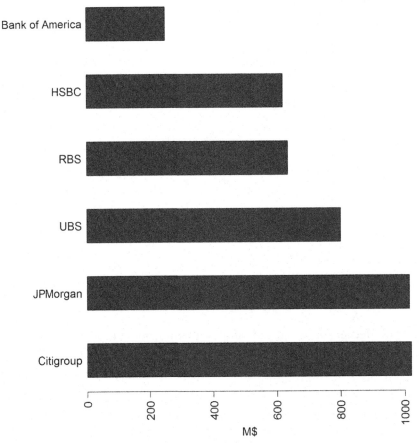

**FIGURE 3**    Breakdown of penalties for each bank involved in the Forex scandal.

an available dictionary of positive and negative content. Thus, distributions of the sentiment scores before and after the penalty announcement can indicate how social media reacted to the news. Figure 4 shows the histograms of the sentiment score for each bank before and after the announcement of the penalties for the Forex rigging

When comparing the average sentiment score for the set of tweets concerning each bank in Table 1 it appears that after the announcement there was a clear negative drift in the sentiment score. This shift can be seen most of the banks, which was confirmed by the two sample Welch tests. In order to emphasize the change in sentiment the average is computed only on the non-neutral tweets, thereby implying a sample with a non-null score.

HSBC and Citigroup showed the biggest fall in sentiment score, going from an average positive score to a negative score. For JPMorgan and Bank of America the drift is less pronounced and the mean score is negative both before and after the announcement. Interestingly, for the Royal Bank of Scotland the difference is not statistically relevant likely due to the many issues the bank was confronted with in 2014, the Forex scandal not changing the global apprehension either way, good or bad.

Figure 5 shows the evolution of stock prices for the banks affected by the penalties announced in November 2014. There is only a small negative drift and no massive bear in the prices or relevant structural breaks as the investigation started 1 year before and both banks and markets integrated the likelihood of the penalty in their financial statement figures. Nevertheless, the Forex rigging was scrutinized more by the media after the announcement in November 2014, thereby generating a massive wave of opinion on social media.

We could ask if the announcement of a massive manipulation crime affects social media in a relevant way by changing the opinion of a firm as proven by the sentiment analysis, is there another way this implication can work. Two questions arise naturally:

- Can Twitter feeds contain ex-ante information with predictive powers about the evolution of markets?
- Can a massive drift of sentiment on social media affect markets? If the answer is yes could it be possible to use social media flows by stock manipulators in order to alter or embellish the image of a company, thereby changing the market equilibrium?

For the first question there are already answers given by social media researchers, the most *viral* being the study published by Bollen et al. [12] and Zhang et al. [16] showing a positive alpha generating strategy by using tweets as leading indicators for investing in financial markets.

For the second question a hint was given in 2009 by Jonathan Fields[2] who imagined a scenario in which someone who tweets/blogs

**TABLE 1** Mean of Sentiment Score for Each Bank Before and After the Announcement of the Penalties for the Forex Rigging

| Bank | Mean score before | Mean score after | Welch test (*p*-value) |
|---|---|---|---|
| RBS | −0.28 | −0.48 | 0.17 |
| Bank of America | −0.09 | −0.15 | 0.08 |
| JPMorgan | −0.15 | −0.48 | 0.00 |
| HSBC | 0.60 | −0.31 | 0.00 |
| Citigroup | 0.37 | −0.46 | 0.00 |

[2]Is Twitter a Market Manipulator's Dream? http://www.twitip.com/is-twitter-a-market-manipulator%E2%80%99s-dream/.

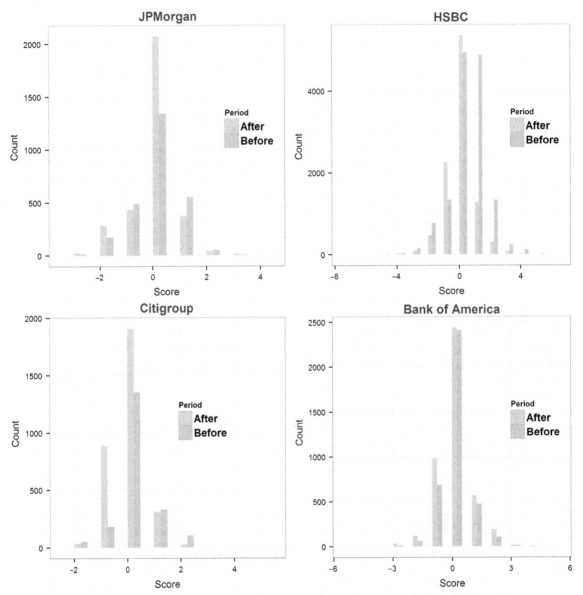

**FIGURE 4**  Forex rigging impact on banks' image through social media. Sentiment scores were measured before and after the penalty announcement date.

about the markets with a substantial following or mainstream news decides to tweet disruptive information and minutes later, after many retweets and the rumor hits mainstream blogs and media, a correction in stock price follows.

This scenario became a reality in 2013[3] when U.S. market regulators became aware of the fact. The

___

[3]For sure other episodes passed under the radar.

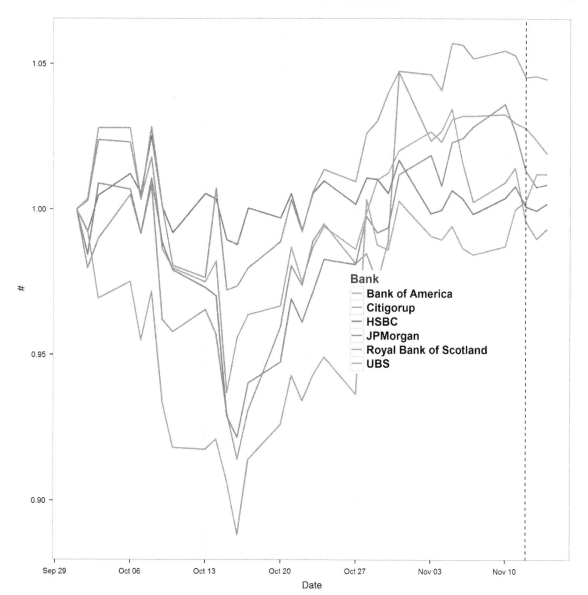

**FIGURE 5** Stock prices of banks involved FX scandal.

relationship between tweets and markets can be a very strong leverage for influencing private/public investors trading on small markets. Recently, a few of these cases recent revealed how Twitter feeds can affect markets especially when they are volatile and traded on thin liquidity.

# 3 MARKET MANIPULATION AND SOCIAL MEDIA

A case that caught the attention of regulators was related to the NASDAQ stock of the company Audience Inc., a provider of audio and voice processing components for mobile devices. On January 29, 2013 the Twitter account @mudd1waters, from an individual using the name Conrad Block, which was the actual name of the owner of Muddy Waters, mentioned in eight tweets:

> AUDIENCE noise suppression company being investigated by DOJ on rumoured fraud charges.

In fact, the assertion in the tweet was not true, but it did briefly have a dramatic impact on Audience shares, which dropped by 23% on the intra-day basis. The stock (ADNC) recovered the same day, but the amplitude of the stock plunge was an alarm signal.

However, for anyone paying attention, it is clear that there something is wrong here. For one thing, @mudd1waters tweeted only eight times, all on the same day, and all on the same subject. Later in the day, Muddy Waters Research tweeted from its actual Twitter account @muddywatersre, the following: *"There is NO report. This is a hoax. MW does not know this company."* In fact, a rogue Twitter account (@mudd1waters) was created to match the name of the equity research company Muddy Waters Research in order to spread fake news. Following the Audience Inc. case U.S. investigators such as Federal Bureau of Investigations and regulators like the Financial Industry Regulatory Authority (FINRA) started to be aware of the disruptive power of social media when used illegally.[4]

Analyzing the history of tweets concerning Audience Inc. a sentiment index is built based on dictionary of positive and negative words provided by Hu and Liu [17].[5] Figure 6 shows the evolution of the sentiment index[6] for Audience along with its stock market prices. It can be seen that a plummet occurs in the sentiment index on January 29 accompanied by a intra-day plunge in stock price. However, there was no structural change in the stock price. Interestingly, the significant changes in Twitter sentiment like that which occurred in the second half of 2012 was accompanied by a plunge in price. Prior to the hoax it became known that price and sentiment index are correlated, which probably made it a perfect target for a fraudsters trying to manipulate the stock through a rogue tweet.

## SAREPTA THERAPEUTICS

### Background

Sarepta is as a bio-pharmaceutical company focused on the discovery and development of unique RNA-based therapeutics for the treatment of rare and infectious diseases with a lead product called *Eteplirsen* for Duchenne muscular dystrophy (DMD), which was in an FDA review process.

### FDA status

There are no FDA-approved disease-modifying therapies for DMD. Throughout 2013 Sarepta communicated that they were progressing steadily on their New Drug Application, a fact that inflated its stock. However, in November 2013 the FDA stated that as a result of the test data submitted by Sarepta, they considered an approval for Eteplirsen as premature.

### Class action

One year after the @citreonresearch allegations a class action suit filed[a] accusing Sarepta of making materially false or misleading statements concerning the FDA's acceptance of Eteplirsen and also on the significance of that data set. As a result of the dissemination of the false and misleading reports, releases, and public statements, the market price of Sarepta stoke was artificially inflated throughout 2013. Figure 7 shows a strong positive momentum of both the sentiment index and stock price until October 2013 when both plunged.

---

[4]Twitter Stock Market Hoax Draws Attention of Regulators, http://www.huffingtonpost.com/2013/02/01/twitter-stock-market-hoax_n_2601753.html.
[5]Opinion Mining, Sentiment Analysis, and Opinion Spam Detection, http://www.cs.uic.edu/~liub/FBS/sentiment-analysis.html.
[6]A detailed note on the computation of the index is given in the chapter on unstructured data.

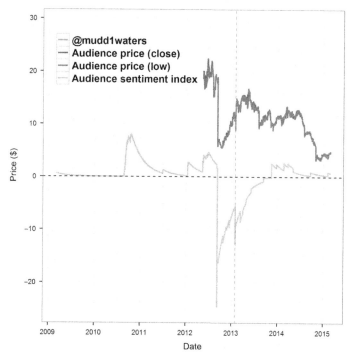

**FIGURE 6** Audience, Inc. price and sentiment index. The sentiment index plummets on January 29 accompanied by an intra-day plunge in stock price.

*Trivia*

Following the alleged hoax from @citreonresearch and the FDA news concerning Sarepta's product, in October 2013, the stock price plunged by almost $5. The aftermath indicates that the hoax might have been correct but there was not enough evidence for the positive momentum.

[a]MARK A. CORBAN vs. SAREPTA THERAPEUTICS, http://securities.stanford.edu/filings-documents/1051/SRPT00_01/2014127_f01c_14CV10201.pdf.

Another interesting case that fell apart in an unexpected way is that of the bio-tech company Sarepta Therapeutics. Only one day after the Audience hoax, a similar event occurred when a tweet from the account @citreonresearch, which mimics the name of the stock research firm Citron Research, suggested that Sarepta Therapeutics was a fraud. As a result,

Sarepta stock (SRPT) dropped over 9% in a matter of seconds. In a statement on its website, Sarepta communicated to its investors that as a growing company, it could be subject to market rumors through social media and other anonymous sources. Figure 7 shows the evolution of Sarepta's price and the sentiment index across the tweets. A drop in the sentiment index can be observed toward the end of January 2013, which does not interrupt the rally of the stock.

# 4 SOCIAL MEDIA AS A CRIME VECTOR

Many securities frauds including stock manipulation, micro-cap fraud, Ponzi schemes, and insider trading can be enhanced with the

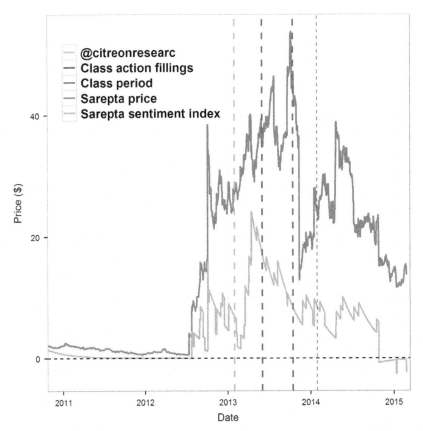

**FIGURE 7**   Sarepta therapeutics price and sentiment index. A drop in the sentiment index can be observed toward the end of January 2013, which does not interrupt the rally of the stock.

use of social media. A typical process for stock manipulation includes the following steps [18]:

1. The social-media-enhanced manipulation starts with the identification of the target: a stock that is generally volatile in a sensitive sector to news and announcement. For instance, a mining, technology, or a bio-technology company would make the perfect candidate.

2. The practical aspects consist of acquiring one or a few social media (Twitter) accounts. The creation of a new account is needed to avoid an account that is already known by the social media company. This step should make the tracking of the account difficult during the investigation process.

3. The social media fraudsters then conceive a strategy based on the rogue information they want to spread. Thus, they should take positions on target stock or on correlated assets. More sophisticated strategies include spread betting and derivatives, which are more difficult for investigators to trace.

4. The next action consists of the diffusion of hoaxes and rogue information through social media. The efficiency of this step depends on the number of accounts and on their influence within the social network.

5. If the markets react to the rogue information the fraudsters should reverse the market positions taken in step 3.

6. The last step consists of cleaning and canceling all accounts to remove any trace of the crime.

Not all stocks can be manipulated this way and the usual targets micro-cap stocks or illiquid or bogus companies. Nonetheless, recent history has shown that even major indexes can be targets for social media attacks. In 2013, an Associated Press Twitter account was hacked and a hoax tweet published claiming that President Obama had been injured in an explosion at the White House. The immediate effect of misinformation caused the S&P 500 to plunge with 0.9% in a matter of seconds, which was amplified by high-frequency trading algorithms.

Markets are vulnerable to digital market manipulation when a negative sentiment is developed on a social platform. A survey in the United Kingdom by Finextra Research showed that 62% of brokers and heads of trading desks believe social media sentiment influences share prices.[7]

## 5 HOW FAR CAN THE MISUSE OF SOCIAL MEDIA GO?

Three potential misuses of social media can occur in the future related to the way social networks design their algorithms for regulating the interactions between their users.

Some social networks like Google or Facebook determine the content that will be shown to a certain user using on proprietary algorithm. It is common knowledge that a Google

search provides different results depending on the user profile. Similarly, Facebook has algorithms that determine what users, what emotions, and what content a user can see. These kinds of algorithms can have some unexpected consequences as some users from a behavioral cluster can be shown a certain type of information that can lead them to a certain type of reaction. Why not reactions in relation to market trades?

High-frequency trading is another subject related to social media. As shown by the research review in the first section, social media content can have predictive power for financial markets. Therefore, many high-frequency trading algorithms are currently based on sentiment analysis from social media content, and the occurrence of a hoax or of a misrepresentation on social media can be amplified by high-frequency trading strategies.

Social bots, softwares that simulates human behavior in automated interactions on social network sites such as Facebook and Twitter, are from far the most dangerous in this context.

With bad bots representing almost 25% of all web traffic recent research has started to tackle this topic. Ferrara et al. [19] presented the characteristics of modern, sophisticated social bots and showed how their presence can be benign or harmful for consumers and advertisers by increasing online fraud. Social bots can be very disruptive if used during a coordinated attack on a financial target hoaxes and rogue news are tweeted and re-tweeted by the bots, thereby creating the impression of real emulation on social networks.

A clustering technique can be used to model opinion formation by assessing the affected relationships between users and also for separating real users from bots. Social bots detection is an area of research that will get a lot of attention in the future.

---

[7]Social Media and the Stock Market: A Lesson in Global Manipulation, http://www.businessesgrow.com/2014/08/14/publicly-traded-companies-wary-facebook-lesson-global-manipulation/.

# 6 OUTLOOK

Social media will continue to develop at a fast pace in the near future and will most likely affect classic information channels. Therefore, its role in feeding information to investors will become more significant. Regulators and investigators have started to become aware of the relationship between social media content and financial markets. Social networks will likely have some kind of regulatory or surveillance body in the future.

Social media can become a vector of crime on financial markets not only with stocks but also with niche commodities and Forex markets. Even the creditworthiness or the economic outlook of a country can be the object of false information on social media which could affect in market indicators (e.g., CDS, Forex rate).

Sentiment and opinion mining is a crucial area for understanding the social media phenomena and can be a useful tool for the surveillance and monitoring of social media content.

## 1 BACKGROUND

In 2014 Fortune magazine published an article by Jeffrey Robinson,[1] one of the world's biggest financial crime authors, that negatively addresses the current state of cryptocurrency (in particular Bitcoin) and gives a very somber forecast on Bitcoin's legacy. The French monthly, Marianne, was even more direct, calling Bitcoin the new scam "à-la-mode" on the Internet.[2] Despite the negative and reluctant reception from the public, cryptocurrencies are without doubt the biggest financial innovation since

---

[1] Jeffrey Robinson argues that the Bitcoin movement will end in tears for the little guy. http://fortune.com/2014/10/24/bitcoin-fraud-scam/.

[2] Marianne, Bitcoin, The giant scam on Internet, http://www.marianne.net/Bitcoin-l-arnaque-geante-sur-internet_a231609.html.

credit derivatives. Many libertarian economists see this new "virtual" currency as the Holy Grail of a new global economy trapped in a long recovery post-crisis scenario. Its supporters advocate for its advantages as sources of progress in an electronic economy and also for its role in democratizing global trade and access to currency. Whether a cryptocurrency can or cannot replace a classic one is still an open debate, it is not something likely to be seen in the next decade.

Bitcoin became popular in 2013 (Figure 5) when its exchange rate with the U.S. dollar increased from almost nothing to 1000 dollars for one Bitcoin, thereby likely creating the first virtual financial bubble.

Looking back in history it's easy to see that alternative payment methods are not new and many solutions such as PayPal, Apple Pay, and Google Wallet, which are still based on fiat currency represent viable solutions mainly for e-commerce. Beyond these digital ways of using fiat money[3] new digital currencies have risen over the past two decades, cryptocurrencies being only a sub-category of the wider class of digital currencies [20].

Attempts at creating and distributing a digital currency date back to 1990 with DigiCash Inc., founded by Chaum [21]. DigiCash introduced eCash, which was probably the first cryptocurrency. Despite its initial popularity eCash did not survive the 2000 Internet bubble.

When in 1971 the Nixon administration liberated the U.S. dollar from the Breton Woods' covenant, which implied a monetary mass backed by gold, many economists predicted the beginning of the country's economic decline. Nixon's belief that the dollar was backed by confidence, remained one of America's fundamental doctrines. However, investors wanted appetite for a currency backed by gold, and that opportunity came in early 2000 when digital gold currencies surfaced. Most of those second-generation digital currencies such as iGolder, gbullion, and e-Gold were in fact electronic money backed by ounces of gold that were stored for a fee. However, their legacy was short as the companies that ran those currencies were either shut down by the federal government for various offenses or faded away due to heavy regulatory burdens.

A digital currency that had some popularity in the pre-social media era was the Linden dollar, which was used as money in the web-based reality game Second Life. Around 2007 Second Life was seen as a promising environment for the virtual economy and the Linden dollar had some momentum but also a lot of volatility. The Linden dollar was a centralized digital currency, controlled by the owner of Second Life.

But the concept of cryptocurrency is linked to the birth of Bitcoin in 2008 and its enigmatic inventor, the famous Satoshi Nakamoto that published a working paper presenting a peer-to-peer electronic cash system. Bitcoin spread very quickly and started to be accepted as a mean of payment by major online retailers. However, its development brought questions regarding its viability in the long term, as many currencies not backed by a government did not last long. The Iraqi Swiss Dinar [22], is an example. Despite being backed in the early 1990s by the Iraqi government, the currency lost its governmental support after the first Gulf war. It continued to be used in various parts of Iraq as it was backed by neither a government nor a commodity, but it held a stable value and never collapsed over a 10-year period. The same thing happened with the Soviet ruble that continued to be used as a currency in remote places of central Asia, long after the fall of the USSR in 1991.

## 1.1 Bitcoin: Welcome to the Matrix

In contrast to its ancestors Bitcoin relies on the fact that it uses open-source software which has no owner and no legal entity behind it [20]. However, a dedicated team that does the maintenance of the software does exist. Software that

---

[3]A fiat currency is backed by a government, but is not backed by a physical commodity.

allows interface with the Bitcoin universe can be downloaded freely, and the system runs through a decentralized and fully distributed peer-to-peer network. This implies that all hardware terminals are connected to each other and each terminal can leave and rejoin the network at any time, and can later accept the information supplied by other terminals. This type of functioning revolves around the concept of *blocks*, which incorporate information about the previous validated transactions. In the physical world, this would mean the holder of a coin or a note would be able to trace all the previous owners of the money since its inception and as well as all the transactions it was a part of. The complete transaction history is stored so that anyone can verify the owner of any particular group of coins. The blocks are aggregated in historical order in a blockchain as shown in Figure 1. The number of transactions in a block is limited in size to 1,000,000 bytes to support quick propagation and to reduce anomalies. The size of each transaction is determined by the number of inputs and outputs of that transaction. The transaction information is included in the body of a block. A Bitcoin holder is connected to the system and reads the inputs from the blockchain as the history of what happened previously in terms of transactions. The blockchain is thus like a general ledger, a record of transactions available to everyone at any time.

A second particularity of this concept is that monetary transactions are possible without a third party through a cryptocurrency-specific process called mining. This feature is counterintuitive in the classic financial world, as all transactions are intermediated by at least one party and in some cases regulation pushes for intermediation. The blocks carrying transaction info are validated by the "system," and more precisely by any terminal on a randomly distributed and de-centralized basis. The blockchain cannot be overwritten once processed. In the classic banking world, at least one third party validates the transaction, but in the digital world it is the *matrix* of terminals that handles the validation. The validation is done based on a set of keys available to all terminals that should be able to read and approve the transaction. For each validated block the terminal receives an established amount of Bitcoin. This process of generating money upon validation of previous transactions is called mining. The process seems straightforward and if it would remain at this stage, the transaction validation and Bitcoin generation would be very fast. But the system introduces an additional step called "proof of work," which is a computationally intensive process and requires solving a mathematical puzzle to confirm the validation and to add a new block to the chain. The system is designed to limit the total number of Bitcoins generated (Figure 2), thereby addressing the issue of controlling monetary mass. The mining process and all of its features have already been addressed the literature Lee [20], but from the perspective of crime assessment in the crypto/digital currency world a focus on the "proof of work" is necessary.

Bitcoin uses an algorithm called *HashCash* as proof of work in the mining process. HashCash was first used as an algorithm for spam mail detection through the addition of a textual stamp

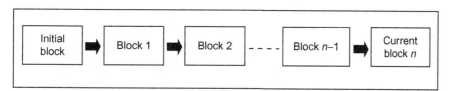

**FIGURE 1** Blocks aggregation in the blockchain. Each block includes the validation of the previous transaction contained in the previous blocks. For each new set of transactions a block is added to the blockchain that cannot be overwritten.

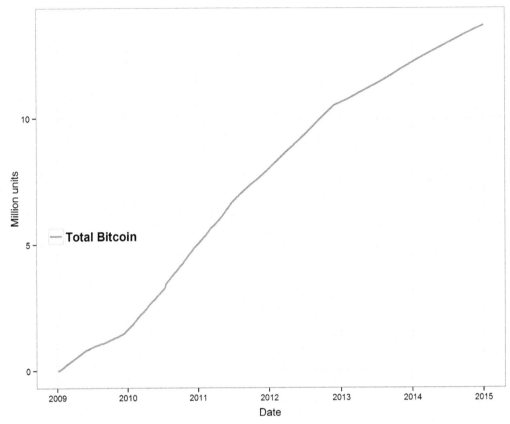

**FIGURE 2**   Evolution of total number of Bitcoins.

to the header of an email to prove the sender used a certain amount of computational memory for calculating the stamp prior to sending the email. The SHA256 (secure hash algorithm) is an algorithm used to generate values in the space of 256-bit sequences and is the cryptographic algorithm used in the proof-of-work scheme by the Bitcoin system. For instance, assuming a transaction $x$, using the value *Bitcoin transaction number 1*, its hashed assigned value through the SHA256 function is:

SHA256 ("Bitcoin transaction number 1")
= "58a9986770cb0de9fff5082dd4d72be50d
4a6650b556883832af677b0f4c3fd2"

As noted above, the HashCash proof of work consists of a puzzle. Getting the solution of this puzzle is a time and resources consuming process. For a given hash function SHA256 applied to a pending transactions $x$, let $n$ be an integer that appends $x$, $n$ is determined as the output hash which begins with a given number of zeros and is less than the target (bits header field). This puzzle has to be solved to validate the transaction. In the following example for a header starting with three zeros $n$ is 17470:

SHA256 ("Bitcoin transaction number 17470")
= "000f68b27437b33d1a76519b44a0a5
4fb12a82c80797b6b6b016556eac2942bc"

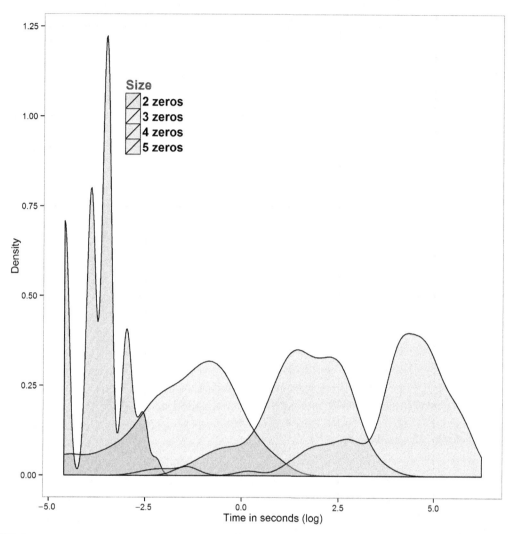

**FIGURE 3** Time for HashCash puzzle solving: Time need to solve the puzzle increases exponentially with the number of zeros.

The way the function HashCash $(x, n)$ behaves depending on $n$ is completely random and $n$ can be found only through a trail-and-error algorithm, which is obviously very intense from a computational point of view. To address this request, the value of $x$ is incremented until the conditions are met. The more number of zeros requested in the header the higher the time needed for solving the puzzle. A simple experiment ran on an Intel CPU with 2.2 GHz is exhibited in Figure 3 for solving times for size of the zero header varying from 2 to 5. With the increase in the number of Bitcoins the difficulty of the algorithm inflates (Figure 4) and more and more computation resources are needed to solve the puzzle in order to generate new Bitcoins.

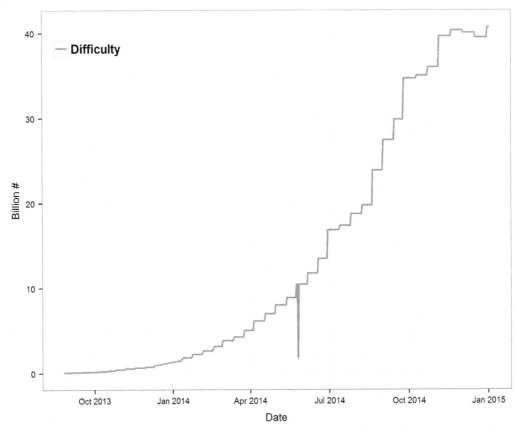

**FIGURE 4** Evolution of mining difficulty.

The difficulty of the puzzle is automatically handled by the system so that a new block can only be created every 10 minutes on average.

The bottom line is that the mining process revolves around the technology and the computing capacity for solving the increasingly complex puzzle. Bitcoin generation is in fact a competition among miners' computational power, in the same way high-frequency trading is a competition among automatic trading softwares in terms of speed. A miner with a better mining tool will have a comparative advantage, the same way a high-frequency trader with a better connection to the market. Bitcoin depends uniquely on the mining process and there is no alternative way of validating the transactions than by using "the matrix" itself. Moreover, Bitcoin depends on the increasing capacity of computation and on the miners' desire to invest in better and newer tools.

## 1.2 Is Bitcoin a New Currency, a New Commodity, or a New Right?

Before getting into the crime and fraud examples, an assessment of the nature of Bitcoin, and in general, cryptocurrencies, is needed. When looking at the historical time series of the Bitcoin/USD exchange rate it can be easily seen that it has significantly appreciated since 2013 as reflected in Figure 5. The currency shows jumps and regime changes due to a multitude of factors, such as technology advances, new arrivals in the mining arena, and changes in the confidence for

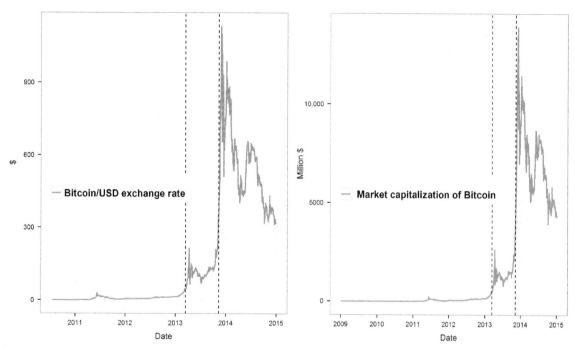

**FIGURE 5** Bitcoin market value evolution: Left: Bitcoin/USD exchange rate reached the 1000-dollar level toward the end of 2013. Right: Bitcoin market capitalization in millions of USD is mainly driven by the exchange rate.

both crypto- and real currencies. Cryptocurrencies arose as a solution at the dusk of the financial crisis to provide an alternative to the classic financial system. The increasing lack of confidence in the banking system that culminated with the Lehman default increased speculation around cryptocurrencies. Bitcoin is seen by many as a *deus-ex-machina* that came as an alternative to the current situation. Cryptomoney bypasses not only the financial system but also the governmental power related to the financial system. For these reasons Bitcoin and similar tools represent more than a simple currency.

Scholars seem to agree (Selgin [23]) that Bitcoin and in general virtual currencies are a "synthetic" commodity because they have features of both commodities and fiat money. Bitcoin offers an alternative to classic currency in the same way stamps or art objects do. Thus, Bitcoin is more like a digital commodity that has cir-

cumstantial intrinsic value related to investors' propensity toward it. The only difference from commodities is that it does not carry physical/real value (besides the value of the hardware used for mining). Bitcoin could be perceived as a virtual good or service used for transactions the same way electricity or gas is used for making houses and industries work. This argument juxtaposed with the econometric features discussed further in Table 1 makes Bitcoin more like a commodity than a currency.

Bitcoin also offers to its owner an unique opportunity to get involved in financial activities on an international level without using the classic financial system. In this new system there are or there should be no issues related to the country of domiciliation of the parties and the regulations specific to those jurisdictions. The new matrix is libertarian and equal in terms of rights to trade or transfer

**TABLE 1** Descriptive Statistics for the Daily Returns of Bitcoin/USD Exchange Rate

| Metric | Value |
| --- | --- |
| Mean | 0.0054 |
| Maximum | 0.3722395 |
| Minimum | −0.4456405 |
| Standard deviation | 0.0625 |
| Skewness | −0.262 |
| Kurtosis | 9.86 |
| Jarque-Bera test | 6562.314 ($p$-value = 0.00) |

Notes: *The series exhibit strong kurtosis and high variance. The Jarque-Bera test indicates non-Gaussian features.*

money, despite embargos or sanctions in place. At this point, the *matrix* has no *Mr. Smith* to deal with less compliant miners, which makes Bitcoin similar to a right to transfer freely value in the same way $CO_2$ or $SO_2$ allowances give the right to pollute to its owners.

Statistics of the Bitcoin/USD rate (Table 1) show that the returns exhibit strong kurtosis and high variance. The Jarque-Bera test indicates non-Gaussian features. In terms of distribution fit, the normal inverse Gaussian looks like the best candidate, as revealed in Figure 6.

When looking at the annualized volatility of the Bitcoin/USD exchange rate shown in Figure 7 it appears that cryptomoney has more fluctuation than other Forex markets. Even the U.S. dollar to Russian ruble rate since the

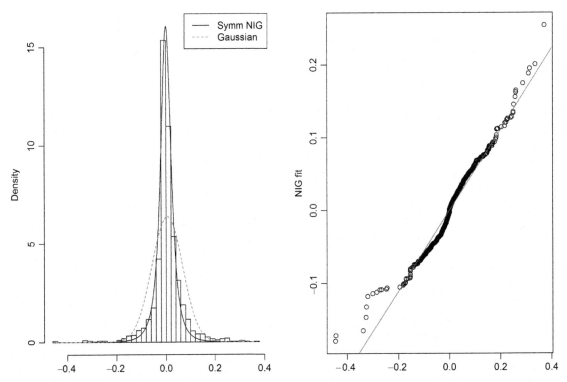

**FIGURE 6** Distribution fitting for the Bitcoins/USD daily returns. Right: Histogram of the fit for the normal inverse Gaussian compared to the Gaussian distribution. Left: QQ plot for the observed returns against the normal inverse Gaussian fit.

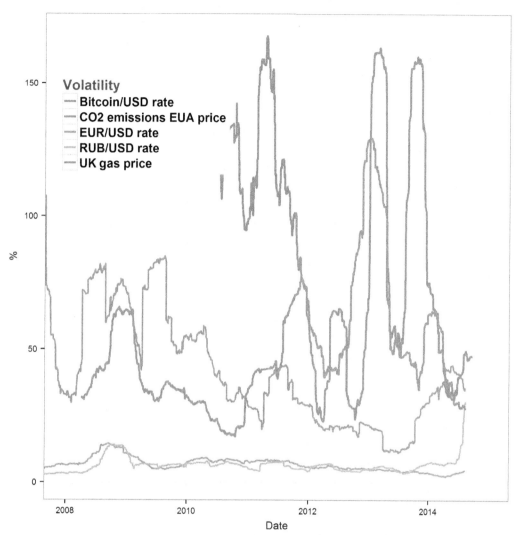

**FIGURE 7** Volatility of the Bitcoin/USD exchange rate: benchmarks with other currency.

Donbass crisis has shown lower volatility than the Bitcoin/USD. European $CO_2$ pollution rights and British gas have volatility levels comparable to the Bitcoin/USD rate, reinforcing the previously noted hypothesis about Bitcoin's nature.

Analysis of the returns with the autocorrelation function reveals strong volatility clustering effect (Figure 8), similar to what can be seen in many commodities markets from the energy complex (Table 2).

## 1.3 Bitcoin and Market Efficiency

A deposit holder in a specific currency has to keep in mind many of the aspects related to this very basic investment. First, the perspective of the currency and of the underlying economy, second the interest rate, and last but not least the creditworthiness of the bank taking the deposit if the bank is located in currency's domestic country. The strengthening of

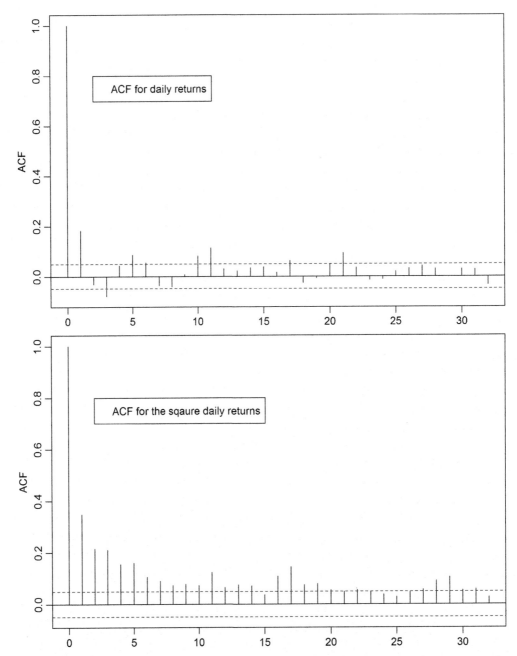

**FIGURE 8**  Autocorrelation in Bitcoin/USD rates. Top: Autocorrelation function (ACF) for the daily returns. Bottom: ACF for the squared daily returns.

**TABLE 2**  GARCH Fit Parameters

| Parameter | GARCH | | | GARCH-NIG | | | GARCH-STD | | |
|---|---|---|---|---|---|---|---|---|---|
| | Value | Std | *p*-Value | Value | Std | *p*-Value | Value | Std | *p*-Value |
| $\omega$ | 0.000 | 0.000 | 0.08 | 0.000 | 0.001 | 0.01 | 0.000 | 0.000 | 0.01 |
| $\alpha$ | 0.061 | 0.004 | 0.00 | 0.356 | 0.055 | 0.00 | 0.345 | 0.044 | 0.00 |
| $\beta$ | 0.937 | 0.003 | 0.00 | 0.642 | 0.056 | 0.00 | 0.653 | 0.051 | 0.00 |
| $\nu$ | | | | | | | 3.495 | 0.213 | 0.00 |
| $\zeta$ | | | | 0.145 | 0.035 | 0.00 | | | |
| $\xi$ | | | | 0.403 | 0.052 | 0.00 | | | |
| LL | 2647.3 | | | **2950.6** | | | 2935.3 | | |
| BIC | −3.27 | | | **−3.66** | | | −3.63 | | |

Notes: *Successful fitting of GARCH model to the daily returns of Bitcoin/USD rate underlines the existence of clustering in volatility. GARCH(1,1) model with normal inverse Gaussian innovation provides the best results.*

the American dollar during 2014 compared to the European currency is a good example of the first point. Since the Eurozone crisis the American economy has observed a faster and stronger recovery similar to the European Union and many analysts expect the U.S. dollar to be as strong as the euro. Thus, based on this appreciation we can see deposit flight toward the U.S. currency.

In the case of a cryptocurrency it would be very difficult or almost impossible to make any judgment about the economy backing the currency. In fact, the only reasoning would be linked to the degree of confidence merchants have toward that particular currency. Interest rates are another argument for holding deposits in a classic currency, but in the case of cryptocurrencies, interest rates are a complex topic. Even though some economists argue about the existence of an implied interest rate, a Bitcoin account holder does not receive interest in the same way a Yen deposit holder does.

The deposit guarantee scheme, which is proposed for almost all developed countries for deposits lower than 100 thousand dollars (euros) does not apply to cryptocurrencies, at least until banks adopt one of them.

Therefore, underlying the true nature of Bitcoin (or other virtual/cryptocurrencies) is crucial before beginning a risk assessment. Looking at its pure econometric feature it can be observed that Bitcoin is as far away from the features of a classic currency as it can be. The persistence in returns, clustering in volatility, and fat tails in Bitcoin/USD exchange rates emphasize the fact that Bitcoin should be regarded differently than other currency. Bitcoin has a lot in common with commodities, with sudden changes in the supply demand equilibrium. One of the similarities relates to energy (e.g., electricity, gas, emissions). Jumps and spikes in energy (electricity) prices are explained by the fact that small increases in demand can inflate prices rapidly, and viceversa oversupply can push prices very low if there is no need for that commodity. As shown in Figure 5 the Bitcoin/USD rate exploded in 2013, which is very uncommon for a real currency even in a growing, emerging economy. The shock observed in 2014 when Bitcoin lost almost 50% of its value to the dollar would have catastrophic consequences if this happened to a real currency. However, commodities on the energy markets this kind of variation happens frequently as regime changes in price equilibrium occur often.

As the Bitcoin becomes more popular and its flows grow in volume and frequency, the question of market efficiency is naturally raised. EUR/USD exchange is one of the most liquid markets across the globe and given its features could be a good candidate for market efficiency. In the case of Bitcoin, the language is different than that used in classic markets. A Bitcoin deposit owner is generally a Bitcoin generator if he is also involved in the mining process. The mining process adds a lot of particularities that impact market efficiency. In a classic and efficient market, all investors have homogeneous access to information and the ability to buy and sell a fraction of the available currency or stock. If a classic currency faces high and sudden depreciation the central bank can try to address the issue by buying back currency or altering interest rates. Obviously, in the case of the cryptocurrency this does not apply. The mining of currency creates an asymmetry among "investors" due to the fact that not all miners have access to the same mining tools, in terms of computation speed and so on. Thus, some have more advantages than others due to the features of their gear. Obviously, those with stronger mining tools have an advantage in price discovery. Each technological jump also creates new sources of asymmetry among miners. In theory, this heterogeneity will need to be addressed when the total Bitcoin monetary mass becomes stable, due to the fact that the mining will became more and more cost intense. If technology represents a first source of behavioral asymmetry, another source of inefficiency is the breakdown of memory and computational capacity among miners. From this point of view miner profiles vary strongly between solo miners, pool miners and farms. A solo miner might use classic technology like a central processing unit, a graphical unit, or application specific integrated circuit (ASIC) for generating Bitcoins on a standalone basis. For a solo miner the time for processing a block is given by the following equation:

$$\text{Time} = \frac{\text{Difficulty} \cdot 2^{32}}{\text{Hashrate}} \qquad (1)$$

where the hashrate depends on technology.

In theory, the average time for a solo miner using a standalone computer to solve a block is around 2000 years. Thus, the only economically feasible solutions are either a massive inflation of the mining capacity or joining mining pools. Mining farms have started to become a trend in countries where the cost of electricity and rent are cheap, since energy consumption is the main variable cost in the mining process. Table 3 shows the cost of the kWh in several countries, emphasizing the fact that Asian countries and ex-USSR

TABLE 3    Electricity Price by Country (USD/kWh)

| Country | US cents/kWh | Country | US cents/kWh |
|---|---|---|---|
| Kirgizstan | 2 | Taiwan | 12 |
| Ukraine | 3 | South Africa | 12 |
| Uzbekistan | 4.95 | Israel | 15 |
| Russia | 5 | Hong Kong | 18 |
| Thailand | 6 | France | 19.39 |
| Pakistan | 7 | United Kingdom | 20 |
| Dubai | 7.62 | Singapore | 21.53 |
| Vietnam | 8 | Japan | 22 |
| China | 8 | Sweden | 27.1 |
| Indonesia | 8.75 | Italy | 28.39 |
| Canada | 9 | Netherlands | 28.89 |
| India | 10 | Australia | 30 |
| Malaysia | 10 | Philippines | 30.46 |
| United States | 11 | Germany | 31.41 |
| | | Denmark | 40.38 |

Notes: *Countries from Southeast Asia and ex-USSR block have low prices. The only developed countries with similar levels are Canada and the United States. The European Union generally has high prices.*

republics have a net advantage in terms of electricity cost compared to developed countries.

Of course, mining farms or pools would have a net informational advantage over solo miners or smaller pools. A higher capacity for solving the cryptographic game the higher rate of block solving, thereby giving a better view of the Bitcoin inflows. If a Bitcoin pool trades Forex against a real currency, they will have more information about the volume of Bitcoins to come on the market, i.e., the impact of technology. Structurally, they are better and more informed than a solo miner. This is a crucial source of market inefficiency as a pool can generate bearish or bullish momentum on the market depending on the circumstances. The power market has similar issues in countries where there are big producers or quasi-monopolies. For example, in Germany the main power producer RWE obviously has more information about the market than a small hydro-power producer, due to its position as main supplier and trader.

Table 4 shows a series of tests for market efficiency (weak form) that discussed in detail in a separate chapter. All test statistics computed for a holding period of 10 trading days

**TABLE 4**  Tests for Assessing the Efficient Market Hypothesis (Weak Form)

| Test name | Statistic | Critical value (95%) |
| --- | --- | --- |
| Portmanteau | 10.61 | 3.8 |
| Chow and Denning | 3.53 | 1.95 |
| Wright (R1 statistics) | 9.10 | 1.99 |
| Wright (R2 statistics) | 7.79 | 2.01 |
| Wright (S1 statistics) | 13.70 | 1.93 |
| Lo and MacKinlay | 3.53 | 1.95 |
| Wald | 12.47 | 3.84 |

Notes: *The tests are performed on the time series of daily returns of Bitcoin/USD exchange rate from July 22, 2010 to December 31, 2014 assuming a holding period of 10 trading days.*

are higher than the 95% confidence level value, thereby rejecting the weak form efficiency of the Bitcoin/USD rate.

We recall that Lo and MacKinlay [24] tested the random walk process and used stock-market returns, which involves the use of specification tests based on variance estimates. In particular, this method exploits the fact that the variance of the increments in a random walk is linear in the sampling interval. This hypothesis is rejected for the timeseries of Bitcoin/USD exchange rate. Chow and Denning [25] test, a generalization of the Lo and MacKinlay test obtained from the maximum absolute value of the individual statistics confirms the results. Wright's [26] alternative non-parametric test using signs and ranks is complementary to Lo's test. Both sign (R1 and R2) and rank (S1) statistics reject the hypothesis of random walk. The Richardson and Smith [27] version of the Wald test and the Portmanteau test of Escanciano and Lobato [28] for autocorrelation also confirm these findings. Markets do not become efficient automatically from their inception. It is the actions of investors and various traders, arbitrage opportunities and putting into effect schemes to take profit from the market, which make markets efficient.

In the Bitcoin system, bringing efficiency to the market is related to mining capacity. Not all miners have the same mining capacity and the mining capacity needs to increase much faster than the Bitcoin transactions, which means a double-edge effect can occur. On the one hand, there could be a massive increase in the number of new investors that purchase and trade Bitcoin, without mining. On the other hand, the mining capacity may remain constant or progress at a much lower level. This could be the reason Bitcoin/USD became massively inefficient during 2013, when a massive inflow of demand was followed in an asymmetric manner in terms of mining ability. Figure 9 shows the random walk test applied over of a rolling window of 200 days for a holding period of 10 trading days.

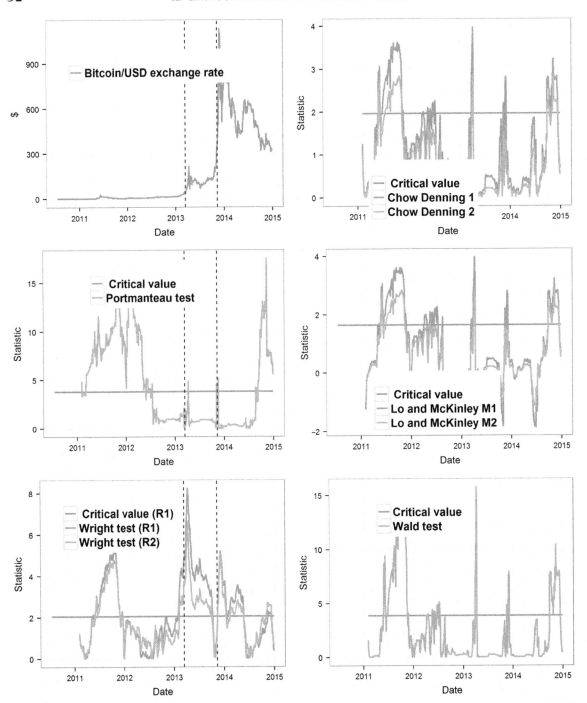

FIGURE 9  Efficiency tests applied to Bitcoin/USD daily returns for a 200-day rolling window: Portmanteau test, Wright test, Wald test, Lo and MacKinlay test, and Chow-Denning test.

The non-parametric Wright test shows the non-random walk effect that occurred in 2013.

## 1.4 Bitcoin Rush

Throughout history gold miners have been attracted to regions rich in gold and silver. From Dacia in antiquity to California and Alaska in the early years of the Industrial Revolution to Sierra Leone and Kyrgyzstan in the present, the thought of generating quick profit from mining has ignited the spirit of many. Similarly, the foreseeable gains cryptocurrency could generate has translated to not only a large number of newcomers into the cryptoworld, but also a bubble in Bitcoin's value. The current number of Bitcoin wallet users is around 2.7 million compared to only 80 thousand in early 2013.

A recent study [29] used unit root tests to investigate whether shocks in the Bitcoin/USD exchange rate have a permanent effect or a transitory effect. Smith [30] showed that the implied nominal exchange rate is highly cointegrated with the nominal exchange rate used in conventional Forex markets and that the direction of causality flows from the conventional markets to the Bitcoin market and not vice-versa, which can explain much of the volatility in Bitcoin prices.

The Granger causality test showed that there is causality between the Yuan/USD rate and the Bitcoin/USD rate. The same effect is seen for the Japanese Yen/USD. During the Bitcoin price inflation a causality relationship also existed for the Russian rubles/USD rate.

Assessment of the formation and propagation of a bubble in markets can be done in many ways. A recent approach proposed by Phillips et al. [31] includes enhanced versions of the augmented Dickey-Fuller (ADF) test: the Sup ADF test and Generalized Sup ADF test, discussed in detail in a previous chapter. The results obtained from applying this bubble-detection approach to the Bitcoin/U.S. dollar rate daily returns is shown in Table 5. The critical values for a 95% confidence level are the asymptotic values found in Phillips et al. [31].

**TABLE 5** Testing for Bubbles

| Test name | Statistic | Critical value (95%) |
| --- | --- | --- |
| Sup ADF test | 27.56 | 0.99 |
| Generalized Sup ADF test | 27.56 | 1.92 |

Notes: *Sup augmented Dickey-Fuller and generalized sup augmented Dickey-Fuller have both statistics above the 95% critical value, thereby rejecting the null hypothesis of a no bubble episode in the considered Bitcoin/USD times series.*

Figure 10 shows the evolution of statistics of two tests and gives the corresponding timing of the bubbles. The Sup augmented Dickey-Fuller test indicates two bubbles during 2013. The generalized Sup augmented Dickey-Fuller test also indicates another mini-bubble during 2012.

Bubbles are periods when markets dramatically change their features and also give a positive and yet biased signal to behavioral investors. The various cases of "fraud-on the market" described previously occurred during bubble periods when market prices were far away from norms and investors made irrational decisions. Bitcoin was no exception.

## 2 LEGAL STATUS

The conceptual debate around the nature of Bitcoin becomes much more complex when considering the legal status of the cryptocurrency. In 2014, there were very few or no official positions on the legal status of Bitcoin. But there are few exceptions. Iceland and Vietnam decided to ban Bitcoin. Iceland shutdown the flow of incoming Bitcoin, because its central bank restricts outflow of funds from the country, which was massively hit by the default of its financial sector. Vietnam also banned the trading of Bitcoin along with other electronic currencies.

Most governments have taken a "watch and see" approach to Bitcoin, i.e., making an anti-Bitcoin statement but not saying it outright. China banned banksfrom processing Bitcoin

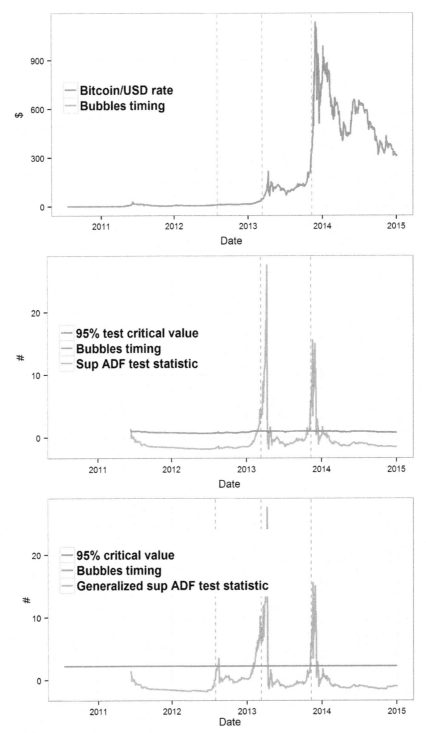

**FIGURE 10**  Bubble detection tests: Sup augmented Dickey-Fuller test indicates two bubbles during 2013. The generalized sup augmented Dickey-Fuller test also shows another mini-bubble during 2012.

transactions, shutting down the Yuan/Bitcoin exchanges operating in the mainland. Russia's main security agency made an announcement about making Bitcoin illegal, but with no issue. Some governments, like Finland, Poland, and Singapore, tried to come up with a solution to tax it.

In the United States, the Financial Crimes Enforcement Network (FinCEN) defined the circumstances under which virtual currency users could be categorized as money services businesses. These users must enforce Anti-Money Laundering and Know Your Client policies, in order to be able to identify the customers they're doing business with.

The U.S. Commodity Futures Trading Commission, which looks after financial derivatives and commodities, has not announced any clear regulation, but as many experts note, cryptocurrencies are similar in many ways to commodities and their involvement is expected to increase. The U.S. Securities and Exchange Commission published an investor alert to warn people about fraudulent investment schemes involving Bitcoin, and most likely will be involved in any serious future investigation or regulatory proposals.

# 3 DIGITAL CURRENCIES HAVE A DARK PAST

The debate around the future of cryptocurrencies and whether the classic banking system should adopt and promote this innovation is spreading rapidly among the general public. But the history of digital currency is already shaded with cases of fraud, money laundering, and ties with criminal groups. For a better understanding of crimes that reach or could potentially reach the new generation of digital currencies it is crucial to study the facts of previous cases. E-Gold and Liberty Reserve are two examples that deserve attention.

## 3.1 E-Gold

In 2008 after almost two years of court negotiations, Douglas Jackson pleaded guilty to conspiracy to operate an unlicensed money-transmitting service and conspiracy to commit money laundering. He was sentenced to 36 months of supervised released,[4] 300 h of community service, and $15 million in penalties for his companies Gold and Silver Reserve and E-Gold Limited.

The indictment was an embarrassment to the respected citizens who founded in these companies in 1996 after being convinced that gold-backed currencies, like the U.S. dollar was prior to 1971, are a much better option for investors and merchants. E-Gold backed the services accounts with gold coins stored in a bank safe deposit box in Melbourne, Florida. At that time, prior to the dotcom bubble, E-Gold was the first effective Internet-based payment system. But in the midst of roaring 1990s the effervescence of the e-commerce and online payments was raided by the new wave of cybercrime originating in many cases from the freshly dissolved Soviet block countries.

During an investigation in 2003 concerning *Shadowcrew*, a forum for cyber-scammers who trafficked in stolen credit and debit card numbers—U.S. authorities discovered that E-Gold was among their preferred money-transfer platforms, because the system allowed users to open accounts and transfer funds anonymously anywhere in the world. Indeed, E-Gold had a no Know Your Customer policy, enabling everybody and anybody to use its services. Many Internet-based payment services, including PayPal during its early years on the Web, believed they were exempt from regulation. However, E-Gold and its peers were more than online payment facilities. Users could carry a

---

[4]Bullion and Bandits: The Improbable Rise and Fall of E-Gold, http://www.wired.com/2009/06/e-gold/all/.

balance, similar to having deposits in a bank. They could also transfer money to other users. With the introduction of the U.S. Patriot Act after 9/11, international online payment and transfers became a priority, making compliance a major issue for money transmitters.

In its early days, E-Gold faced many security and performance problems due to the fact that scammers started to target E-Gold users in order to empty their accounts. Ponzi schemes were ran through or within E-Gold. When the company managed to deal with these issues, the federal indictment dismantled the operation. Before the federal motion to seize and liquidate the entire gold reserve of E-Gold under asset forfeiture law in 2008, E-Gold was processing more than $2 billion in precious metal transactions per year.

There are things to be learned from E-Gold that are relevant to the cryptocurrency community. First, an idealistic idea that gave birth to a digital currency, with a retro touch ended up in the middle of a criminal investigation. E-Gold was most likely created for a legitimate purpose to serve legitimate clients. Second, when the platform started to gain momentum, it became a target for cybercriminals involved in all types of fraud such as theft, phishing, identity theft, or Ponzi schemes. Third, larger scale criminals used E-Gold's services to pay for illegal services or items (i.e., child pornography) and to launder criminal funds. Last but not the least, E-Gold was dismantled by authorities for alleged involvement in criminal activity. In this kind of situation it is very difficult to reject the hypothesis that the operation was based on fraud, and this doubt led investigators to take radical measures. Nonetheless, randomly or not, other platforms like PayPal that faced similar issues survived the early years of web commerce and became success stories.

## 3.2 Liberty Reserve

Around the time Bitcoin started as a digital currency, the federal government busted a large-scale digital currency that appeared to be a massive platform for financial crime with alleged ties to the criminal underworld. In May 2013 U.S. authorities[5] shut down Liberty Reserve, one of the biggest companies providing digital currency and online money transfers incorporated in Costa Rica. Authorities in Spain, Costa Rica, and New York arrested five people: Arthur Budovsky (aka Eric Paltz, the principal founder of the company), Vladimir Kats (aka "Ragnar," co-founder), Ahmed Yassine Abdelghani (manager of the day-to-day operations), Allan Jimenez, Azzediine el Amine, Mark Marmilev, and Maxim Chukarev. Authorities also seized bank accounts and Internet domains associated with the company.

Interestingly, Liberty Reserve was created from the ashes of a previous failed digital currency, E-Gold, as discussed in the previous section. Liberty Reserve founders Budovsky and Kats had an unsuccessful experience running a third-party exchange service for E-Gold they started in 2006 called "Gold Age, Inc.," which functioned as an intermediation agent ("exchanger") for E-Gold, then the most popular digital currency in operation. However, in December 2006, Budovsky and Kats were convicted in New York state for operating "Gold Age, Inc." as an unlicensed money-transmitting business. The conviction was related to a bigger indictment concerning E-Gold's various offenses including money laundering.

The lessons from his first criminal conviction helped Budovsky develop a new and *improved* system of digital currency that would succeed in eluding law enforcement where E-Gold had failed, by, among other ways, locating the business outside the United States. Thus, Budovsky emigrated to Costa Rica, where in 2006 he

---

[5]Liberty Reserve, Hub For Cybercrime Money, Shut Down By U.S. Government, http://www.huffingtonpost.com/2013/05/28/liberty-reserve-cybercrime_n_3346656.html.

founded Liberty Reserve. Later on, in 2011, Budovsky formally renounced his U.S. citizenship and kept only his Costa Rican passport.

With the dismantling of E-Gold a void was left and an unfulfilled demand was there to fill. Budovsky and his new venture came there to pick up where E-Gold left off and grew exponentially. Thus, the operation became the predominant digital form of money laundering used by cyber criminals worldwide.

U.S. investigators estimated that Liberty Reserve processed more than 12 million financial transactions annually, with a combined value of more than $1.4 billion. In total from 2006 to May 2013, Liberty Reserve processed an estimated 55 million separate financial transactions and is estimated to have laundered more than $6 billion in criminal proceeds, according to the indictment. After learning the company was being investigated by U.S. officials the criminals pretend to shut down operations, but continued operating the business through a set of shell companies and shell-company accounts maintained in Cyprus, Russia, Hong Kong, China, Morocco, Spain, and Australia, among other places. The indictment shows that Liberty Reserve emerged as one of the principal means by which cyber criminals around the world distribute, store, and launder the proceeds of their illegal activities. Indeed, Liberty Reserve was a financial hub of the cybercrime world, facilitating a broad range of online criminal activity, including credit card fraud, identity theft, investment fraud, computer hacking, child pornography, and narcotics trafficking.

# LIBERTY RESERVE: THE E-HAWALA

## Background

Liberty Reserve was created around 2006 in Costa Rica by two individuals from the ex-Soviet Union block that previously operated a company linked to E-Gold. The company operated as an international platform for money transfers and payments using a digital currency system.

## Operations

Liberty Reserve provided its customers with a global money transfer system that did not required any identification, proof of address, funds origin verification, or background checks. Almost 200,000 accounts were opened with Liberty Reserve in the United States alone. In total, Liberty Reserve laundered almost $6 billion between 2006 and 2013 before being indicted.

## License-free banking

In 2009, when the Costa Rican financial regulator started to look at Liberty Reserve's activity, the company created a portal filled with rogue information that appeared to give regulators the ability to access the transactional information and monitor it for suspicious activity. In 2011, the U.S. Department of the Treasury's Financial Crimes Enforcement Network (FinCEN) issued a notice regarding the alleged criminal conduct of Liberty Reserve. Two weeks later Liberty Reserve falsely informed regulators that its business had been sold to a foreign company and would no longer be operating, while continuing to operate through shell companies controlled by Liberty Reserve directors. They also began emptying bank accounts in Costa Rica of millions of dollars and transferring the money to bank accounts in Cyprus and Russia. At the request of U.S. authorities the Costa Rican government was able to seize approximately $19.5 million in Costa Rican bank accounts.

## Organized crime ties

In 2013 Liberty Reserve directors were sentenced to 5 years in prison for conspiring to operate an unlicensed money transmitting business involved the transmission of funds derived from criminal activity.

The operating flowchart of Liberty Reserve is shown in Figure 11. In the world of financial crime, many companies start out with a legitimate business purpose and then become commingled (voluntarily or not) in committing or facilitating illegal activities. In the new wave of financial crime, Liberty Reserve being a prominent example, businesses are built for the purpose of executing criminal operations. Thus, the founders assess all risks and the ways investigators can uncover their operations. They introduce as many lines of defense as or as many obstacles as needed in order to not raise suspicions from clients, suppliers, or investigators.

Learning from the E-Gold episode, Budovsky "improved" his operation in few aspects. Liberty Reserve did not require users to verify their identity, such as by providing an official identification document or credit card. Accounts could therefore be opened easily using fictitious or anonymous identities. Liberty Reserve added many intermediaries to its clients and did not permit users to fund their accounts by transferring money directly through classic supports like credit card payments or wire transfer. Nor

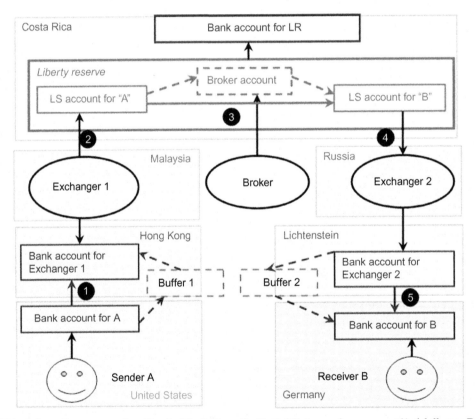

FIGURE 11  Liberty Reserve transfers: Step 1: *Client A* from the United States sends an amount X of dollars to Exchanger 1 based in Malaysia with a bank account in Hong-Kong. Step 2: Exchanger 1 credits A's account with Liberty with an equivalent amount Y of digital currency. Step 3: Client A can transfer directly or through a broker the amount Y of digital currency to B's account. Step 4: Client B transfers the amount Y to Exchanger's 2 account based in Russia. Step 5: Exchanger's 2 transfers the amount of dollars X or euros Z from its bank in Lichtenstein to B's account in Germany.

could Liberty Reserve users withdraw funds from their accounts directly, such as through an ATM. Instead, clients were required to make any deposits or withdrawals through the use of third-party called "exchangers" in order to avoid direct contact with the clients. Exchangers were third-party entities similar to traditional brokers that maintained direct financial relationships with Liberty Reserve, buying and selling digital currency in bulk in exchange for mainstream currency. The exchangers in turn bought and sold the same currency in smaller transactions with clients in exchange for mainstream currency. Liberty Reserve recommended a number of "pre-approved" exchangers. These exchangers tended to be unlicensed money-transmitting businesses operating without significant governmental oversight or regulation, concentrated in Malaysia, Russia, Nigeria, and Vietnam. The exchangers charged transaction fees for their services, typically 5% or more of the funds being exchanged. Such fees were much higher than those charged by mainstream banks or payment processors for comparable money transfers.

The use of exchangers had two consequences. On the one hand, it avoided the burden of collecting any information about its clients' banking transactions or accounts in a Know Your Client (KYC) repository, which could end up in the hands of investigators. On the other hand it introduced an additional layer in order to be able to keep clients and their operations anonymous.

As shown in Figure 11 the first step a customer A would take in order to fund a Liberty account was to transmit mainstream currency in some way from his account to an exchanger. Upon receiving the payment from client A, the exchanger credited the user's account with Liberty Reserve with a corresponding amount of digital currency. For completing a transfer to a client B, which is also a Liberty Reserve user, the amount of digital currency arrived from A to B within Liberty Reserve. Then client B was required to transfer digital currency from his Liberty account to an exchanger's account, and

in the final step the exchanger made a transfer to client B's banking account with a corresponding amount of mainstream currency.

Budovsky's concept is not new. Transferring money between two individuals from different countries goes back to even before the birth of SWIFT. In Muslim countries transfers occur through a system known as Hawala, which is graphically summarized in Figure 12. In this system a person A gives an amount X of money in a currency together with a security key to Broker 1. Broker 1 transfers the key to Broker 2 in another country. At the same time A gives the key to person B who will receive the money in the same or different currency as Broker 2 upon presenting the key. The brokers or hawaladers can also have a settlement system at higher level. Budovsky's Liberty shares most of Hawala's features, the information representing the security key being replaced with the digital currency. Further, compared to hawaladers, the exchangers have a more practical settlement system.

# 4 FINANCIAL RISK ASSESSMENT

Like any another currency used for transaction Bitcoin and in general cryptocurrencies raises many questions concerning its reliability, failure risk, and integrity. Some risks such as the production of counterfeit money or forgery are common to all currencies, but others are specific to digital or cryptocurrencies like disruption in the mining process.

As described in the second chapter, counterfeit money started almost the same time as the issuance of the first coins in Ancient China and Lydia. Plating metal coins with a gold or silver layer was one of first the forging techniques [32]. In more recent history paper money or electronic money were forged, which is likely to happen cryptocurrency. The "crypto" nature of these tools makes them in theory at least very

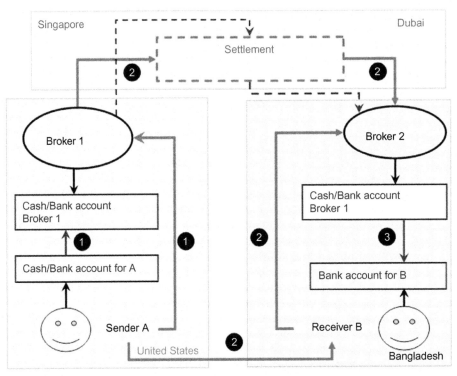

**FIGURE 12** Hawala system: Step 1: A from United States transfers money to Broker 1 and gives him information representing the security key. Step 2: Broker 1 gives information to Broker 2 in Bangladesh concerning the amount he should pay and the security key. At the same time A gives B the security key. Step 3: B based in Bangladesh presents to Broker 2 the security key and then receives the amount delivered by A. The brokers can settle the balance later through a platform that is based in Dubai.

safe from forger compared to their predecessors. For the case of Bitcoin, safety is ensured by the fact that each transaction and each unity is validated through a cryptographic algorithm publicly available and ubiquitary spread among Bitcoin miners. Thus, even if a "forged" Bitcoin is introduced into the system, a miner will realize very quickly that the transaction is not valid. It is necessary to note here that the difference between cryptocurrency and classic currency is not only semantic; in the case of cryptomoney both the currency and the transaction are verified. This eliminates in theory many risks that exist in the classic currency, like the likelihood of being paid with "things" that resemble

real money but are not. For instance, receiving change in Turkish lira coins instead of euros due to their resemblance is a common scam across Europe. Despite having a very positive outlook in terms of safety there is still risk specific to the nature of the cryptomoney and also to the infrastructure that supports it.

Figure 13 shows the different typologies of Bitcoin users and their interactions with the systems:

**1.** Users have only a Bitcoin wallet and do not mine or trade. They use a Bitcoin account like a classic web-based money account as a payment tool. They can also do

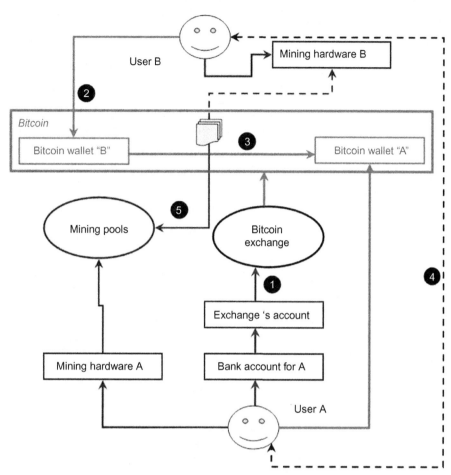

**FIGURE 13** Bitcoin user typologies and transactions. Transaction type 1: Bitcoin/classic currency trade through an organized exchange. Transaction type 2: Bitcoin account is credited by the system via successful blockchain puzzle solving. Transaction type 3: Bitcoins transferred from one user to another or constitute a payment to a provider (e.g., Amazon, e-Bay, etc.). Transaction type 4: Over-the-counter transactions paid with Bitcoins. Transaction type 5: Transaction information is sent to miner for validation.

over-the-counter transactions, with the Bitcoin transfer being compensated by another transaction involving counterparty risk.

2. Users that have a Bitcoin wallet and do mine solely for new Bitcoins, but are not involved in trading currency. They use Bitcoins for payments or over-the-counter transactions.

3. Users that have a Bitcoin wallet and do mine solely or through a mining pool and are involved in trading currency.

4. Users that have a Bitcoin wallet and are involved in trading currency but do not mine. There are basically speculators that try to make a profit from anticipating market fluctuations.

Cryptocurrencies face some of the risks common to all electronic transactions. Theft, phishing, and other electronic scams are types of fraud that can be easily leveraged in the cryptocurrency world. Given the way cryptomoney and specifically Bitcoin systems are built it should be easy to track any suspicious transactions and identify the accounts. Nonetheless, Bitcoin transactions are public but considered anonymous because nothing ties individuals or organizations to accounts that are identified in the transactions. But individuals sometimes post account numbers online in ways that can be connected to their online identities. As noted by Grinberg [22] it is possible, using statistical techniques and some identified accounts, to undo the anonymity of the system. A public ledger taking the form of a blockchain juxtaposed over "the facto" blunt transaction would make of tracking or investigating very difficult.

As other digital currencies experienced, Bitcoin and its competitors face the risk of being used by criminals as tool for money laundering. Bitcoin could and most likely already has become a main platform for illegal transactions. Perpetrators can introduce illegal funds or be paid through Bitcoin and cash out in a common currency by passing through an exchange or an over-the-counter transaction. Given the four types of users presented above the number of possible way funds can circulate from the legal to the illegal economy is almost unlimited.

The players in the arena of money laundering, terrorism financing, have a prefect home in the cryptocurrency context. The abrupt increase in international recruitment of volunteers for paramilitary and terrorist activities in the Islamic state as well as in Taliban-controlled regions in Pakistan or in the Caucasus Emirate proves the existence of a complex network of money transfers and financing that is currently under the radar. Of course, we may never know whether the young people from Europe that flew in Syria were paid through cryptocurrencies or whether

high-profile terrorists such as Doku Oumraov owned mining firms.

Like its predecessors in the digital finance world Bitcoin uses many intermediaries for its various purposes, providing services like account keeping, payment transfers, or currency exchange.

Bitcoin exchanges and brokers are risk concentrators. Some exchanges act like authentic Bitcoin clearinghouses and carry massive client positions. Like any other online platform they do have security, default, and fraud risks. Many exchanges can also have a fraudulent aim, being created uniquely for attracting funds and then vanishing.

Bitcoin's idiosyncratic risk is linked to its open-source decentralized nature and to the mining process. Bitcoin software itself can be the target of viruses or Trojan horses or other cyber-attacks. The most probable scam in the mining process would be to diminish by a small percentage the number of generated Bitcoins and to transfer this amount to the originator of the scam. Mining is still a process that is not entirely understood. The allocation algorithms vary from a mining pool to another and sometimes are unclear. Thus, a small *cut* from a mined Bitcoin would likely not be noticed by miners. Cryptoclipping[6] is a very serious threat due to previous incidents involving electronic transfers, where Trojans took a few cents from bank account without account owners realizing the loss.

The main risk of Bitcoin is linked to the likelihood that a criminal organization or group of people creates or takes over a mining pool having a significant share of the total mining capacity. In this case the security of Bitcoin based on its decentralized and distributed features would

---

[6]Clipping was probably the first fraud related to coinage in history. Clipping consists of diminishing the weight of a gold or silver coin through shaving the metal on its edges.

be seriously challenged. Thus, a group of miners could falsely validate its own transactions and be able to double spend Bitcoins and even generate counterfeit Bitcoins.

The last risk is that the Bitcoin algorithm could be hacked or distorted for illegal activities.

# 5 CLASSIC CRIMES IN THE CRYPTOCURRENCY ECONOMY

Crimes leveraged from classic online money transfer to cryptomoney include theft, cyberscam, rogue platforms, money laundering, and fraudulent investment schemes (e.g., Ponzi schemes).

## 5.1 Theft

As depicted in the movies, currency theft exists in the real world. With the diminishment of physical currency and the progress of electronic money, theft naturally moved to the cyberworld. Scammers have used methods like phishing and Trojan horses to break into banking or payment systems since the year 2000. In the early age of Internet banking major international banks were hit by hackers breaking into individual online accounts and transferring funds. The same phenomena propagated the digital currency world. The fact that many cryptocurrencies are not well understood, not regulated, and not scrutinized makes the task easier for criminals.

In March 2014 Flexcoin[7] shut down following the theft of 896 Bitcoins from its servers, amounting to $620,000. During its short-lived activity over 3 years Flexcoin, provided cloud service for sending, receiving, and storing Bitcoins, advertising itself as "the world's first Bitcoin bank."

Unlike other cryptocurrencies Bitcoins has a token equivalent, which is a physical coin loaded with the encrypted digital currency. Thus, physical theft or failure to deliver the tokens is a possible scam. For example, U.S.-based Jamie Russell[8] tried to exchange 201.7 virtual Bitcoins for 190 physical tokens from an overseas counterparty. He acknowledged a loss of almost $150,000 when the counterparty failed to deliver the tokes and cutoff communication, after the virtual Bitcoins were sent. Being based on anonymous transactions, the Bitcoin system makes it difficult for a third party to track its users operations. However, as discussed earlier the blockchain contains all transactions current and previous, which can help identify the theft. But not all Bitcoin account holders can be tracked from the virtual world in the physical world, facing the classic dilemma of the matrix dweller, which makes the work of investigators complex.

## 5.2 Money Laundering

In a testimonial published in 2013, the digital currency expert and *white hat* Fyodor Yarochkin,[9] emphasized the idea that the digital currency phenomena and its ties with organized crime is more serious than imagined. He notes that for a fee of 9% of the nominal amount criminals can materialize liquid cash through digital currency.

As noted by Bryans [33] the main features of Bitcoin proved beneficial to its survival are harmful to effective anti-money laundering regulation. The main strength of Bitcoin's anonymity is also its weakness if investigators were to try to take down the system. Without being able to tie a user to a single Bitcoin address, tracking the three phases of money-laundering (placement, layering, and integration) of criminal funds would be extremely difficult. Each mining terminal of

---

[7]Another Bitcoin Startup Tanks After $600,000 Theft, http://www.forbes.com/sites/andygreenberg/2014/03/04/another-bitcoin-startup-tanks-after-600000-theft/.

[8]Bitcoin scam costs Wisconsin man, http://time.com/4287/bitcoin-scam-costs-wisconsin-man-150000/.
[9]Liberty Reserve: Criminals face on line cash dilemma, http://www.bbc.co.uk/news/technology-22766406.

the Bitcoin network receives and processes the full ledger, and the Bitcoin network automatically scales the difficulty in completing blocks based on the total processing power of all miners, stopping the Bitcoin network from functioning requires disabling every miner on the network. Thus, investigation efforts face a target that is both difficult to identify and essentially impossible to interrupt. The black-out of the Bitcoin network is also risk in itself.

What makes Bitcoin unique for money launderers is the fact that the cryptocurrency can be used in all three phases of the laundering process.

- Bitcoin can be used as payment for illegal activities or items or in exchange for illegal funds, thereby being a possible tool for the placement stage. For instance, Bitcoins have been reportedly used on Sheep Marketplace, the underground service that replaced Silk Road, a website processing trades for drugs and other illegal goods.
- As Bitcoins can circulate anonymously from one user to another and from one country to another, it can be perfectly used in the layering step.
- As some countries start to consider Bitcoin as a legal currency, the integration phase can be conducted through the cryptocurrency, thereby representing the final step of the money-laundering process.

Bitcoin and in general cryptocurrencies are currently the perfect tool for laundering funds. The massive increase in Bitcoin transactions can bring with it many illicit users and funds.

## 5.3 Rogue Exchanges

Bitcoin systems and the software behind it are open source, free of charge, and not backed by any liability barring organization. However, in the Bitcoin universe, there are a lot of lucrative companies that provide all kind of services similar to those proposed by the pioneers of online payments and transfers. Bitcoins are generated through mining or can be purchased on exchange platforms. These exchanges, similar in aim to the Chicago Mercantile Exchange, or LIFFE, allow users to purchase or sell Bitcoins against classic currencies. For instance, a miner that generates Bitcoins might want to transform them into classic currency and needs to do it either through an exchange or an on over-the-counter basis.

Moore and Christin [34] assessed the various risks investors face from Bitcoin exchanges using data from 40 Bitcoin exchanges established over 3 years, including 18 closed exchanges. Based on a hazards model, the study shows that an exchange's transaction volume indicates whether or not it is likely to close. Less popular exchanges are more likely to be shutdown than popular ones. This conclusion proves that like any other exchange, liquidity is a crucial indicator, and thin liquidity exchanges are more likely to unviable. As shown in the following section even very popular exchanges can go bust and leave clients with massive losses. Nonetheless even in this case the exchange loses liquidity before the default occurs, a leading sign that its robustness might be affected.

A recent example of a Bitcoin exchange that closed suddenly is GBL, a Chinese Bitcoin trading platform that claimed to be based in Hong Kong and allegedly stole $4.1 million from its users' accounts.

The company[10] was launched in May 2013 with the domain *btc-glb.com* based in Beijing even though the company claimed it was based in Hong Kong. GBL users were not provided with accurate contact information on the site and the platform used a stream of information from other websites.

---

[10]Problems for Bitcoin in China as HK trader goes down, http://www.wantchinatimes.com/news-subclass-cnt.aspx?id=20131105000045&cid=1102.

Chinese authorities arrested three individuals suspected of being behind the online Bitcoin trading platform GBL in November of 2013 in several places in China. The suspects included were a 29-year-old man named Liu, who allegedly operated the service; Jin, 24, in charge of daily operations; and Huang, 33, responsible for financial management. When the platform was shut down, the site's homepage was defaced to make it look like it was targeted by hackers. However, after seeing that they could not contact anyone at GBL, users soon realized the exchange itself was a big scam and that GBL owners took off with their funds.

## 5.4 Bitcoin Exchanges Collapsing

The crash of Mtgox[11] the biggest intermediary in the Bitcoin universe, marked a turning point in public awareness of the Bitcoin (Bit con) phenomena. In February 2014 the Tokyo-based exchange closed after an alleged heist that occurred on its servers earlier in the year.

The exchange shutdown after it was discovered that an estimated 744,000 Bitcoins, representing about $350 million, had been stolen due to a hole in its security. The amount represented 6% of the 12.4 million Bitcoins in circulation worldwide at the time. The issues started for Mtgox in November 2013 when users were having problems withdrawing cash, sometimes for several weeks. Then, on February 7th of 2014 the site officially stopped all withdrawals, claiming it was temporary and due to technical issues.

A few days later Mtgox issued a statement claiming it had a problem with "transaction malleability," which implied that any user could withdraw cash and then alter the ID of the transaction to make it appear that it had never occurred, then request it again. The company indicated that it was a bug in the Bitcoin software but the Bitcoin's developer community noted that the issue had been known about for some time, and that it was less of a bug and more something developers needed to consider when creating an exchange service.

Later, in February 2014, an application for bankruptcy was submitted in Japan by Mtgox lawyers acting on behalf of the exchange, only days after MtGox went offline. They also applied to the court for protection after U.S. regulators filed a subpoena against the company. At that time, the company had outstanding debts of about 6.5 million yen ($65 million). Later in the year the Tokyo District Court from the bankruptcy trustee claimed that 202,149 Bitcoins belonging to the company were found and secure in storage.

In the aftermath of the Mtgox collapse, Kraken,[12] a company headquartered in San Francisco, was chosen by liquidators to deal with the 127,000 creditors and to distribute any remaining Bitcoins.

The Mtgox case has many things in common with other collapses in the financial world in both its origin and aftermath. Like many defaults of brokers or broker dealers (e.g., MF Global) the situation degraded very quickly. In its prime MtGox was the world's leading Bitcoin exchange, handling 70% of all transactions worldwide. In Q4 2013 the Mtgox exchange rate started to show differences compared to the average exchange rate as shown in Figure 15. The Chow test for structural breaks applied to the time series of ratios between the Mtgox rate and the average rate shows break dates in February 2013 and November 2013. In early 2013, the Bitcoin market exploded and many other exchanges started to pop up diminishing Mtgox's share in total volume as shown in Figure 14. This explains

---

[11]Mtgox Bitcoin exchange files for bankruptcy, http://www.bbc.co.uk/news/technology-25233230.

[12]Glimmer of hope for creditors in MtGox investigation, http://www.telegraph.co.uk/technology/news/11255012/Glimmer-of-hope-for-creditors-in-MtGox-investigation.html.

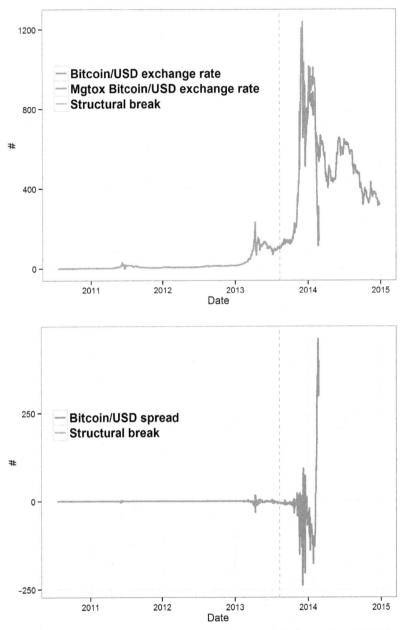

FIGURE 14  Benchmark of Bitcoin/USD rate on Mtgox vs. the average. Top: Evolution Bitcoin/USD rate on Mtgox vs. the average. Bottom: Ratio of the average Bitcoin/USD rate to Mtgox rate.

some of the market fluctuations and thus some of the rate differences.

Figure 14 depicts an episode that does not fit entirely with the official story. In Q42013 when the technical issues allegedly started, the Mtgox Bitcoin traded at a significant premium, implying that some investors were ready to pay more than average. Soon after, Mtgox Bitcoin traded at a high discount of almost $200 to the average, implying that nobody wanted to get involved with Mtgox for fear of not being able to get the money back.

The other side of the (Bit) coin that completes the puzzle is given by the findings concerning the evolution of the trading volumes in Figure 14. Indeed, Mtgox lost market share to other exchanges starting in early 2013. However, toward the fourth quarter of 2013 there was a sudden increase in liquidity at the same time the Mtgox Bitcoin traded at a premium. This information reveals a mini-bubble within Mtgox, which was confirmed also by the test used earlier. Further, on some days Mtgox appeared[13] to pass the total Bitcoin volume on all exchanges. It appears that within Mtgox one could trade a Bitcoin twice but it would only be counted only once, thereby revealing a probable issue within the Mtgox settlement (Figure 15).

This effect occurs again in February 2014 before the shutdown of the exchange. When compiling all of this information it appears the Mtgox failure involves more than an IT security issue. The fraud appeared to be coordinated over a period of a few months with a strong influx of trades and liquidity toward the end of 2013, when a buyer allegedly tried to acquire as many Bitcoins as possible on Mtgox. This micro-bull was nonetheless generated by or related to a security intruder who knew he could make a quick profit. One possible scenario could have been the ability to spend the Bitcoin from a Mtgox account twice. The fact that 6% of all existing Bitcoins disappeared indicates the intensity of the scam.

Mtgox is not the only failure due to security issues resulting from IT issues and securities fraud corroborated in a novel way. It emphasizes the fact that financial crime related to Bitcoin has a higher level of complexity than previous digital currencies.

## 5.5 Bitcoin Investment Scam

As a new tool surfing on a new bubble, Bitcoin was the perfect target for investment scams "à la Maddoff." The first case that occurred in the United States was addressed by the American SEC under the rue of securities fraud, which can provide some clues about the future regulatory framework of Bitcoin.

In 2014 an U.S. federal investigation[14] resulted in charges against Trendon Shavers, based in Texas, who ran a scam investment scheme called Bitcoin Savings and Trust. The accusations included one count of securities fraud and one of wire fraud, with each having a maximum penalty of 20 years and potential fines totaling upwards of $5 million.

Using social media, Shavers allegedly sold Bitcoin investment opportunities on various online forums promising a 7% return per week to potential investors in an environment with yearly nominal interest rates of 0.25%. He was able to raise over 700,000 Bitcoins accounting for $64 million over a period of time stretching from September 2011 to September 2012. Almost half of the Bitcoin Savings and Trust's investors lost some or all of their money. Interestingly, Shavers' attorney claimed Bitcoin was not subject to U.S. securities laws that prohibit Ponzi schemes, but the judge in that case ruled that the scam had

---

[13]The volume data used for this analysis is public unaudited data from Quandl.com.

[14]Bitcoin Ponzi scheme treated fined as securities fraud, http://www.bloomberg.com/news/2014-09-20/bitcoin-ponzi-scheme-treated-fined-as-securities-fraud.html.

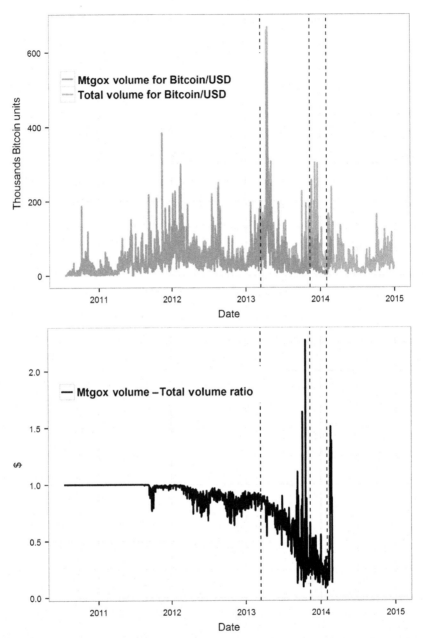

**FIGURE 15**  Benchmark of traded volumes on Mtgox vs. the total Bitcoin/USD trades. Top: Evolution of traded volumes on Mtgox vs. the total Bitcoin/USD exchanges. Bottom: Ratio of traded volumes on Mtgox to the total Bitcoin/USD exchanges.

indeed violated those laws, which are designed to protect investors from fraud.

# 6 CRYPTOMONEY SPECIFIC CRIME

Cryptomoney specific crimes are related to the process of mining and to the open-source software that governs the Bitcoin matrix. They include mining hardware scams, Bitcoin derivatives misselling, cryptoclipping, and mining pool scams.

## 6.1 Real Scams in the Virtual World: Hardware

When an acquittance with average training in technology purchased a piece of ASIC mining hardware, which never became profitable, I became suspicious. In fact, the hardware was obsolete compared to current systems' hashing rate at that time. The investment never generated profit and only a inflated electricity bill.

As a new and misunderstood technology Bitcoin attracted two categories of people. On the one hand, it was a magnet for many misinformed miners that hoped to generate easy tax-free money. On the other hand, there were scammers that took advantage of the low level of training of the first category of people and sold them goods and services that bolstered their hope for quick gains.

One example of the Bitcoin rush was Butterfly Labs, a Missouri-based company that marketed specialized hardware designed to produce Bitcoins and allegedly ran a big-scale scam with Bitcoin mining tools.[15] After investigation by Federal Trade Commission it was found that Butterfly Labs charged consumers thousands of dollars for its hardware, but then failed to provide the gear until they were practically useless,

or in many cases, did not provide the computers at all. Starting in June 2012, Butterfly Labs sold mining computers, named BitForce, advertised as cutting-edge, powerful, and efficient systems for generating Bitcoins. Consumers who bought the computers were required to pay in full, upfront. The computers ranged in price from $149 to $29,899 based on the hardware's computing power. Investigators found that in September 2013, more than 20,000 consumers had not received the computers they had purchased.

Additionally, in August of 2013 Butterfly Labs announced a new, more powerful computer to mine Bitcoins called the Monarch, which was available for $2500 to $5000. The company has delivered a few Monarch computers since August 2014. As discussed in the first section, in order to keep up with current mining technology a user needs to constantly upgrade system hardware to keep up with the mining speeds. In fact it was seen that when technology lagged it resulted in an electricity blackhole, producing less Bitcoins and eating more kWh. Butterfly Lab's delay in delivering in real-time hardware to consumers meant that Bitcoin mining computers could never generate the amount of gains they promised. By the end of 2014 the scam was shut down by U.S. investigators.

## 6.2 Bitcoin Derivatives

Bitcoins are gaining mainstream acceptance and the value is constantly fluctuating. Many brokers have seen it as an opportunity to provide their clients with a volatile asset to trade with. IG Group was the first broker to offer Bitcoin option trading. However, IG Group has since withdrawn Bitcoin as part of their pool of available assets citing it as a "management decision." Other brokers that offer Bitcoin as part of their trading options include Any Option, SetOption, and TradeRush. At TradeRush, Bitcoin is offered as a currency pair, with the Bitcoin/USD rate being the most popular pair.

---

[15]Butterfly Labs, http://www.ftc.gov/news-events/press-releases/2014/09/ftcs-request-court-halts-bogus-bitcoin-mining-operation?utm_source=govdelivery.

The Bitcoin/USD volatility can easily reach 100%, the most volatile exchange rate. While the model risk related to the binary option was discussed in a previous chapter, the case of Bitcoin/USD is even more relevant. In a strongly inefficient and incomplete market, option pricing does not fit the classic risk-neutral theory. Thus, the market maker will always have superior information especially in the case or digital options for retail customers that do not have the means or knowledge to check the real prices. With a good pool of customers, good marketing, and option prices that would imply a high markup, the digital options market is a sure profit-taking operation. The customer loses money from the moment he clicks on the bet and his losses are amplified by the volatile nature of Bitcoin.

## 6.3 Stealing GigaBits

"Time is money" says an old proverb, which can be adjusted in Bitcoin's case to "memory is cryptomoney." Butterfly Labs' case shows that the main battle for Bitcoin is in the hardware field. Thus, rogue miners can target not only users but also other computers in order to use their memory and processing power for mining. In 2013 German authorities[16] arrested two people for disseminating malwares that were mining the virtual currency by infecting its victims' computers. The accused were behind a botnet that allowed its operators to secretly use other people's computers to carry out mining. This type of *memory* fraud will follow the increasing need for mining.

## 6.4 Cryptoclipping

Cryptoclipping is a scam where a malware or Trojan horse is introduced in the Bitcoin matrix that manages to shave a small portion of the generated Bitcoin in such a way that the real

---

[16]Five held over Bitcoin scams in China and Germany, http://www.bbc.co.uk/news/technology-25217386.

miner does not realize the loss. This type of scam has long been known in banking and online payments.

## 6.5 Rogue Mining Pools

Mining pool monopole is the most serious threat in the cryptocurrency universe. The decentralized feature of the Bitcoin system is its main strength as every terminal from the matrix's node can "hash" the blockchain independently. The worstcase scenario appears when most of the mining capacity is detained by one mining pool, thereby altering the decentralized feature. If a mining pool has ownership over a high percentage of the nodes they would *de facto* centralize the mining process. Under this scenario the security of Bitcoin or another type of cryptomoney would be seriously challenged.

Let's consider a network of nodes with equal mining capacity. By assuming that a node (or a group of nodes) has mining capacity $\gamma$ higher than the other nodes, the likelihood of observing rogue validation of a blockchain can be determined. The mining can be simulated using the HashCash algorithm but with a smaller number of zeros in the header in order to make it replicable on a computer. By increasing the lengths of the input chain to be hashed the average time for solving the puzzle increases as shown in Figure 16. The increase in mining time is one of the foundations of the Bitcoin system.

A node terminal can enter a rogue activity, involving double spending-like activities or fake verifications of transactions if it manages to confirm the blockchain of a series of consecutive transactions. Thus, other terminals will need to accept the blockchain relying uniquely on that node. If that node manages to monopolize the validation process and to generate Bitcoins on rogue premises, the whole system is affected. Bitcoin and cryptocurrencies in general rely on the fact that the mining/validation is distributed and more than one node confirms transactions on a random basis. If the mining power of the network is uniformly distributed the likelihood

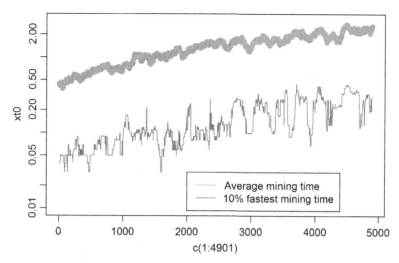

**FIGURE 16** Evolution of mining time depending on the number of transactions in the system: The average and the 10% quantile are shown.

that a node mines a series of transactions faster than its peers is very low as shown in this experiment.

Let's consider the variable $Z_{nt}$ characterizing the event where a series of $w$ transactions enter a node. $Z_{nt}$ takes the value 1 the series of transactions is validated by the same terminal. and zero otherwise. If the event occurs, assuming a series of transactions indexed $nt$, a series of mining times $\tau_{nt}$, and a series of node indexes where the mining node of the $nt$ transaction is denoted $M_{nt}$, the likelihood $Z_{nt}$ for a node $M^*$:

$$P(Z_{nt} = 1|M^*)$$
$$= \mathbf{P}(M_1 = M_2 = \ldots M_i = \ldots = M^*, \tau_i < D_{\tau_{nt}}^{-1}(\gamma)|M^*)$$
$$= \frac{\mathbf{P}(M_1 = M_2 = \ldots M_i = \ldots = M^*, \mathbf{P}(\tau_i < D_{\tau_{nt}}^{-1}(\gamma))}{P(M^*)}$$

where $i \in \{nt, nt + 1, \ldots, nt + w\}$ and $\mathbf{P}(M^*)$ is the probability that the node $M^*$ is rogue. For the event $Z_{nt}$ to occur two conditions must be met: first, all the transactions of the series need to be allocated to the same node $M^*$ and second, this node need to solve the given series of puzzles before the other nodes do. If we assume the distribution of the solving times is $D_{\tau_{nt}}$ then the

target terminal should solve faster than the time corresponding $\gamma$ quantile, $\gamma$ being the weight and the total capacity allocated to $M^*$. The simulation results are shown in Figure 17. For a terminal with a capacity higher than 30%, at least 1% of the transaction can be frauded. This ratio increase fast for a total capacity of 55% where the proportion of rogue transactions is higher than 8%.

### 6.5.1 Bitcoin's Neo

Currently, the top two mining pools account for more than 50% of the total mining capacity and the occurrence of the scenarios just discussed depends on the propensity of traders to invest in mining technology. The real threat in the short term is what can be called Bitcoin's "Neo". Under this scenario a hacker would be able to introduce a virus into the system to break the hash puzzle, or to alter the software behind the cryptocurrency. Bitcoin's "Neo" could affect not only a

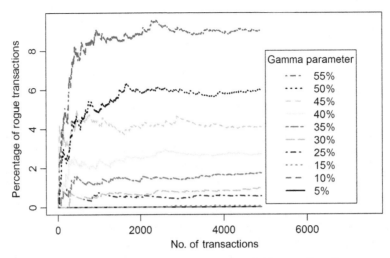

**FIGURE 17**  Rogue mining depending on the weight of mining capacity ($\gamma$) for one allegedly rogue terminal. For a terminal with a capacity higher than 30%, at least 1% of the transactions can be frauded. This ratio increases fast since for a total capacity of 55% the proportion of rogue transactions is higher than 8%.

terminal or a user but the very foundation of the Bitcoin system.

# 7 CRYPTOCURRENCY SURVEILLANCE

While transactions in the Bitcoin system are difficult to track, there are many statistics that allow surveillance at the macro level in order to assess the number of transactions and the exchange liquidity. The two simple metrics proposed below can help to monitor the turnover of the Bitcoin system and be extended to any other cryptocurrency. The first metric assesses at the time $t$ the ratio between the total number of transactions in the system and the total number of available Bitcoins. In the case of Bitcoin the denominator will be quasi-stable, because the number of new Bitcoins will diminish over time.

$$\text{Crypto-turnover}(t) = \frac{\#\text{Crypto-transactions}(t)}{\#\text{Cryptocurrency}(t)} \tag{2}$$

This ratio measured on a daily (or weekly) basis should be used as a system activity indicator. A sudden increase in this ratio may indicate that more transactions are settled through cryptomoney. If this variation is not explained by some exogenous factors like an increase in number of retailers that accept cryptocurrency. It might be warning sign for laundering patterns. The evolution of this ratio is shown in Figure 18, which shows that a first significant jump occurred in mid-2012 before the massive increase in Bitcoin price. The last change in pattern in late 2013 is most likely due to the Mtgox event.

The second metric is the ratio between the daily volume of currency exchange and the daily total number of cryptotransactions. The aim of the ratio is to monitor the relationship between the exchange activity and the cryptotransactions inside the system. This ratio should be quasi-stable because an increased (decreased) number of transactions should be accompanied by an increased (decreased) inflow or outflow of currency.

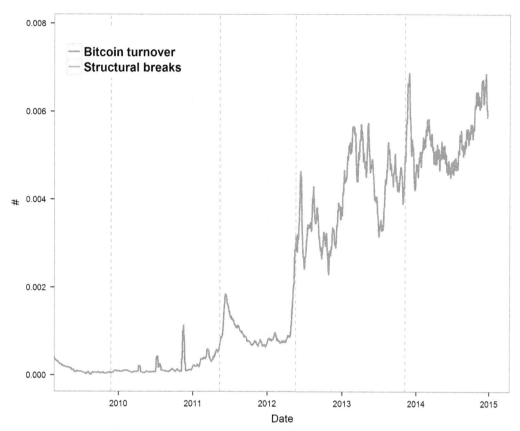

**FIGURE 18** Crypto-Turnover ratio: The ratio between the daily number of transactions and the total units of cryptocurrency. Two later structural breaks occurred in mid-2012 and late 2013.

This ratio can be computed for a certain currency $i$ at the moment $t$ or for the sum of top $N$ traded currencies:

$$\text{FX Turnover ratio}(i, t)$$

$$= \frac{\text{VolumeCurrency}_i(t)}{\#\text{Crypto-transactions}(t)} \quad (3)$$

$$\text{FX Turnover ratio}(t)$$

$$= \frac{\sum_{i=1}^{N} \text{VolumeCurrency}_i(t)}{\#\text{Crypto-transactions}(t)} \quad (4)$$

Figure 19 shows the evolution of the ratio for Chinese Yuan, U.S. dollars and Euros. The most unstable series of the ratio are those for the Bitcoin-Yuan exchanges. Most Forex trades are

in U.S. dollars. After the Chinese governmental ban of Bitcoin transactions the Forex traded volume diminished drastically. A sudden increase in this ratio on a bull in the exchange rate can signify a sudden inflow of liquidity. Conversely, a decrease in the ratio can point to an increase in the turnover of the cryptocurrency but without exchange activity, thereby requiring special attention.

Difficulty and block size evolution over time can also offer relevant information. Since the demise of Mtgox, the importance of verifying the reserves held by exchanges has become crucial and therefore the proof-of-reserve and proof-of-solvency metrics have been designed in the transaction process to prevent bankruptcy of an exchange.

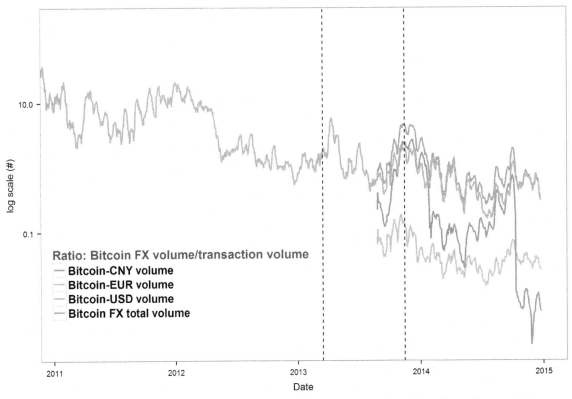

**FIGURE 19**   FX Turnover: ratio between the daily traded volume of currency and the daily volume of transaction.

## 8 OUTLOOK

Also it causes all, both small and great, both rich and poor, both free and slave, to be marked on the right hand or the forehead, so that no one can buy or sell unless he has the mark, that is, the name of the beast or the number of its name. This calls for wisdom: let the one who has understanding calculate the number of the beast, for it is the number of a man, and his number is 666. *Revelation 13:16-18*

The global economic environment has undergone significant changes in the post-crisis era. The traditionally manufacturing economy will tend, at least in the next decade, to be replaced by the services sector and physical production will move toward information technology on a much larger scale. This will bring new challenges currently faced by some dematerialized industries such as music, software, and entertainment over property rights, etc.

The financial sector will also most likely need a new approach to financing the new economy. With the emergence of peer-to-peer credit or crowd-funding new tools will be needed. As noted by Lee [20] cryptocurrencies are a serious vector for innovation in the new economy and their integration on a massive scale in the current environment is imminent. Nonetheless, it is not certain whether Bitcoin or its competitors will survive this early age of cryptomoney and end up as mainstream currency. The risks beared by cryptomoney and its users have not been studied enough and are therefore not fully understood.

The most likely scenario is that a new generation of cryptocurrency will evolve and be able to deal with the current issues to eliminate or reduce fraud such as money laundering, terrorism financing, and theft. Only when the fundamental risk is addressed will these currencies be able to gain momentum.

Regulation is another stringent point that limits the evolution of cryptomoney. No serious investor such as major banks or pension funds will step in as long as they are not sure whether there is a genuine regulatory framework in place.

Currently cryptocurrency looks in many ways like that of the $CO_2$ emission rights market before 2011, in other words a no man's land, where authorities step in only when a major crime occurs. In terms of regulation there is a need for a two-sided: on one to regulate the currency transactions, and on the other side regulation to rule the products or instruments derived from cryptocurrency. The second side is certainly more complicated as cryptomoney is an innovation tool and the number of products entering in this area could be massive.

# The Link Between the Betting Industry and Financial Crime

## 1 BACKGROUND

The allegations of Wilson Raj Perumal concerning match fixing during the last World Cup that took place in Brazil[1] showed the public the reality of betting activities within professional sports. Given its popularity, association football is one of the sports that appeared in the media over the past years as associated with illegal or criminal activity.

The use of technology in the gambling world and most specifically in the sport betting world

---

[1] The ethicscommittee of Cameron's football federation was confronted with allegations of match-fixing by "seven bad apples" in their three group games. The allegations were made in a German news magazine, *Der Spiegel*, by a convicted match fixer from Singapore. Once glorified by Pele as the African team with the highest chance to win the World Cup, Cameroon lost all its 2014 Group A games, including a 4-0 defeat by Croatia. The Indomitable Lions had Alex Song sent out for lashing out at Mario Mandzukic in that game, while teammates

Benoit Assou-Ekotto and Benjamin Moukandjo clashed later on in the game. The allegations were made by convicted football match fixer Wilson Raj Perumal, who was detained by police in Finland in April on an international arrest warrant. Prior to the game, Perumal disclosed to *Der Spiegel* the result of the Cameroon-Croatia game and that a player would be sent out, http://www.bbc.co.uk/sport/0/football/28102841.

added a new dimension to criminal involvement in sports. This phenomena has evolved to such an extent that many criminal investigation agencies now have special divisions for addressing this issue. Global organizations such as Interpol use special processes and methods to tackle match fixing [35]. Europol created a special unit called the Joint Investigation Team (JIT), codenamed Operation VETO, that ran between July 2011 and January 2013. The VETO operation was led by Europol, Germany, Finland, Hungary, Austria, and Slovenia, and was also supported by Eurojust, Interpol, and investigators from eight other European countries.

As a result, in 2013 Europol[2] and police teams from 13 European countries announced that they had uncovered an extensive global criminal network involved in widespread football match fixing. A total of 425 match officials, club officials, players, and serious criminals, from more than 15 countries, were suspected of being involved in attempts to fix more than 380 professional football matches. The activities formed part of a sophisticated organized criminal operation that generated over 8 million euros in betting profits and involved over 2 million euros in corrupt payments to those involved in the matches.

As will be discussed in the following section the term "criminal activities" has a number of connotations in relationship to professional sport, from match fixing and illegal betting to money laundering and financial crime.

Despite being a relatively recent phenomena there is relevant literature around the criminal involvement in professional sports, which also emphasizes financial crime aspects. Caruso [36] presented a simple formal model to explain that the asymmetry in the evaluation of the stake is the key factor that leads to match fixing or to tacit collusion. It was also demonstrated that when

the asymmetry in the evaluation is extremely large there is room for tacit collusion. Eventually intuition and the results of the model are applied to make a comparison between the FIFA World Cup and the UEFA Champions League tournaments. Match fixing case studies mainly focus on association football but many other sports can be targeted by criminals [37].

A European Commission study [38] showed that the European legal landscape is not uniform. While some countries focus on general offenses of corruption or fraud, others have implemented sport-specific penalties to cope with match fixing—contained either in their criminal codes (Bulgaria, Spain), sports laws (Cyprus, Poland, Greece), or special criminal laws (Italy, Malta, Portugal). In the United Kingdom, betting related match-fixing episodes are punished under the offense of cheating at gambling.

Regarding the size of the illegal sport betting market, a study from Pantheon-Sorbonne University and the International Center for Sport Security (ICSS) [39] estimated the size of the global market (legal and illegal) of sporting bets somewhere between 200 billion euros and 500 billion euros, more than 80% being illegal bets. The return rates to bettors are high in the illegal market, sometimes more than 99%.

Thus, Anderson [40] showed in a recent work that the growth of online betting gambling platforms and exchanges, and the widening of traditional sports betting markets has, in parallel, increased the vulnerability of sports to the spot fix and spread bet.

A Financial Action Task Force (FATF) study [41] addressed the issue of moneylaundering in the football sector. This study argues that money laundering through the football sector is deeper and more complex than was previously understood. The study provides strong evidence that shows that a variety of money flows and/or financial transactions may increase the risk of money laundering through football. These are related to the ownership of football clubs or players, the transfer market, betting activities,

---

[2]Results from the largest football match-fixing investigation in Europe, https://www.europol.europa.eu/content/results-largest-football-match-fixing-investigation-europe.

image rights, and sponsorship or advertising arrangements.

Another recent assessment by Fiedler [42] underlines the fact that gambling represents an ideal tool for money laundering for practical reasons. Gambling involves a huge volume of transactions and cash flows that are necessary to disguise money laundering. Over the past two decades professional sports has seen very aggressive growth in terms of revenues. This hypergrowth was heterogeneously distributed among the various sports, and was followed by many challenges in terms of regulation, governance, and financing. To illustrate this phenomena, association football is analyzed since it is the most popular sport in the world. Football Clubs do not target only to maximize their competitional results but also to have a good profitability. For instance, clubs can "own" players under very strict contractual clauses, which are very different from traditional employment contracts. Clubs can take or make loans to other clubs or national federations and use players as "collateral". "Repo"-like contracts are very common in the world of sports. Clubs can underwrite contracts with derivatives features such as paying a percentage from the resale of a player. The regulatory and supervising frameworks of professional sports are vague and not always trustworthy. These aspects combined with high financial flows makes from association football and generally from professional sports professional sports a potential target for criminal organization at all levels.

Figure 1 shows the evolution over the past several decades of the revenues of major football leagues in the main European championships. Interestingly, the revenues of the top five European leagues have experienced with few exceptions continuous double-digit growth over the past two decades.

European football has experienced strong growth in the past two decades, but more surprisingly it continued to bring in revenue even during the Eurozone crisis. On top of that, the growth rate was much higher than the growth of nominal GDP within the European Union space. Figure 2 shows a parallel between the GDP growth within the EU and association football revenue growth since 1997. With the exception of 2010, football revenues grew faster than the GDP with a peak around the year 2000. This indicates that association football might be in the light of these figures. a recession-proof sector.

The main sources of income for football clubs are match-day tickets, broadcasting events, marketing, and the footballers transfer market. Additionally, there are other products and services that do not deal directly with the sport itself but are exposed to its results including:

- Sport broadcasting rights market, which is a sophisticated market that allocates the transmissions rights for sporting events. This market has a complex structure with multiple players and intermediaries.
- Sport betting market, which represents the gambling market driven by the outcomes of sporting events. This industry gained strong momentum with the development of the Internet.

## 2 BETTING MARKET

Sport bets and financial derivatives are similar in many ways [43]. The outcome of a bet depends on the results of a particular sport event in the same way the payoff of a derivative depends on the underlying asset market prices. The total amounts staked by gamblers on a bet is equivalent to the nominal. As Levitt [43] explained, in sports betting, bookmakers announce a price, after which adjustments are small and infrequent because bookmakers do not play the traditional role of market makers matching buyers and sellers but, rather, take large positions with respect to the outcome of the game. This peculiar price-setting mechanism allows

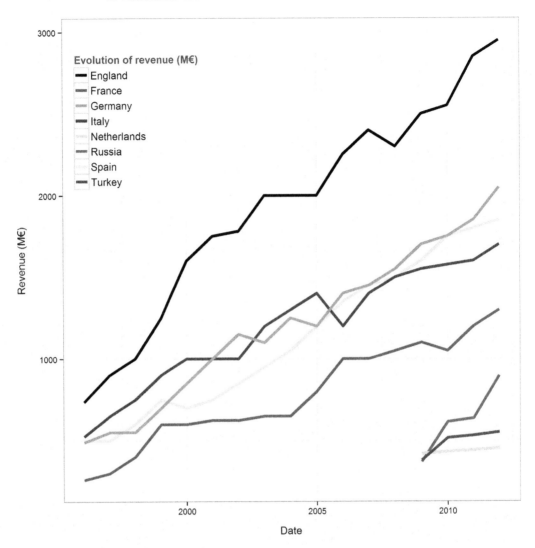

**FIGURE 1**   Top revenues in European football.

bookmakers to achieve substantially higher profits as bookmakers are more skilled at predicting the outcomes of games than bettors and systematically exploit bettor biases by choosing prices that deviate from the market-clearing price.

However, it is important to note that the majority of market makers in the financial world do take market risk and try to anticipate the momentum of the market. Thus, a trader is similar in many ways to a bookmaker. A trader takes orders from clients and also has its proprietary trading activity to generate additional profit from his understanding of the market. A bookmaker will take bets from his clients but he will offer odds based on his knowledge and anticipation of the event. We will show in

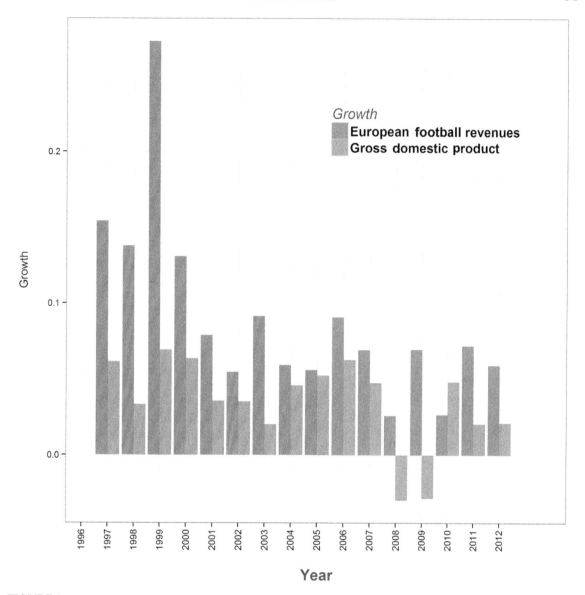

**FIGURE 2**   Growth of European Football revenues vs. EU GDP.

the following sections that the main difference between betting and financial markets is not so much linked to bookmaker vs. trader but more on investors vs. gamblers.

In the financial world many investors are institutions and asset or wealth managers. Thus, a trader taking orders from an institutional will have a well-informed counterparty. This typology of investors has access generally to extensive research and analytic resources. In the betting world, gamblers are in many cases sentiment or affection driven. Sport gamblers have more in common with casino gamblers than with financial investors. Thus, the sport betting market is inefficient due to the fact that many bets are done based on one person being a supporter of one team or one player and not on the basis of rational and objective decision-making. As a corollary it can be assumed that a trader should understand well enough the behavior of the market, while a bookmaker should understand the propensity of the public toward a team or a player. For a better understanding of the betting market the following terms need to be introduced:

- **Total turnover** or amount wagered is the total amount staked by the punters. The total turnover is similar to the premium paid for purchasing a derivative in a financial market.
- **Gross gambling revenue** represents the total amount lost by gamblers, i.e., the net cost of their gambling. Gross gambling revenue is similar to the cumulated P&L gains of a derivatives trader, which is the difference between the premium received and the costs of the hedge. Interestingly, with few exceptions bookmakers cannot always hedge and even if they can the hedges are not always efficient.

The total amount wagered through online sport betting platforms has increased at a double-digit speed in the past decade as shown in Figure 3. Thus, the gross gambling revenue was around 11 billion euros in 2012, more than double what it was in 2004. Despite the strong global recession the market of online betting has grown considerably since 2008.

Figure 4 gives a breakdown of online gambling market revenues among sport betting, casino games, poker, and bingo in 2013. The sport betting industry, which includes horse racing, represents more than 75% of the total online gambling market.

The revenues of the main online bookmakers are shown in Figure 5. William Hill, Ladbrokes, and Bet365 are the main online bookmakers in sports betting. A crucial feature of online bookmakers is that they may be are incorporated in low tax fiscal paradises (e.g., Malta, Jersey, Gibraltar, Cyprus, etc.). In addition to the low taxes, many of these locations have few regulatory systems in place for scrutinizing the activities of bookmakers. The second issue is that through online platforms gamblers domiciled in countries where gambling is banned have access to bets, thereby explaining the huge number of illegal gambling markets [39]. Therefore online betting is an efficient tool for transnational funds transfers, accounting for about 300-500 billion euro for both money-laundering and match-fixing purposes.

The betting market has a complex structure that has evolved significantly over the years and will most likely continue to evolve in the foreseeable future. The global betting market (Figure 6) can be categorized into three main zones:

- **Legal betting market**: consists of bookmakers and gamblers acting under a complaint framework. They are situated in countries where betting is legal.
- **Illegal betting market**: consists of bookmakers acting outside of the legal framework and gamblers situated in jurisdictions where betting is not legal (e.g., United States). Illegal betting is done using both online and over-the-counter systems, and it involves both cash and bank transfers.
- **Grey zone**: deals with activities that are not clearly classifiable in the legal or illegal zone. For example, a bookmaker taking illegal bets can use the legal betting market to hedge his positions. A bookmaker can take bets as black money from a customer and place it again through the legal market, creating a chain in a money-laundering scheme. A bookmaker can have clients that are part of a match-fixing syndicate and use the information from the odds of those clients to take profit in the legal market.

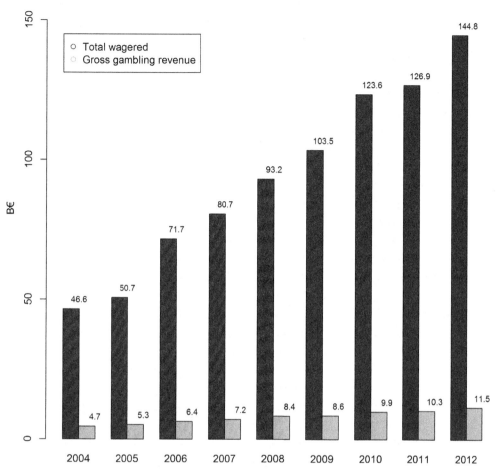

**FIGURE 3** Market for online sport betting (without horse and race bets).

There are four distinct market mechanisms for fixed-odds betting:

- The bookmaker market, which is the most popular form of sports betting (e.g., William Hill, Bet365). The odds are unilaterally determined by the bookmaker and published a few days before the event. Punters are able to make their bets at these odds while the bookmaker takes the opposite position.
- The exchange market mechanism is characterized by the fact that another punter takes the opposite side of a contract. Thus, individuals can directly trade bets with each other on a platform where bettors post the prices under which they are willing to place a bet on or against a given outcome. The latent demand for wagers is collected and presented in the order book, which publicly displays the most attractive odds with the corresponding available volumes. The bettor has the choice to either submit a limit order and wait for another participant to match her bet or to submit a market order and directly match an already offered bet. As a result,

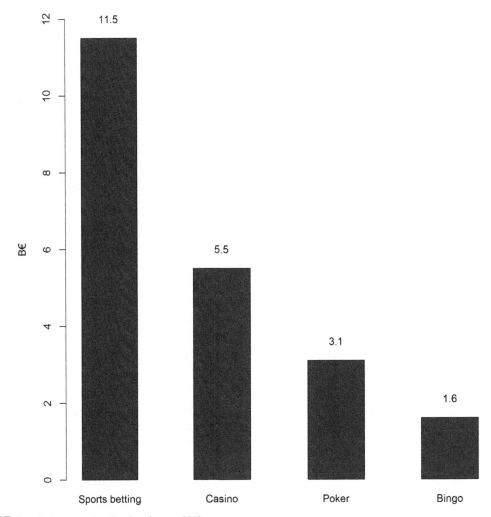

**FIGURE 4**  Market for online bookmakers in 2013.

there is a continuous double-auction process taking place on the platform. If two bettors with opposing opinions agree on a price, their demands are automatically translated into a transaction. Thus, the odds traded at a bet exchange are not determined by a specific market maker (e.g., the bookmaker) but are the result of a continuous matching of supply and demand. The provider of the platform typically charges a commission fee on the bettors' net profits. The commission fee of Betfair, for example, ranges between

2% and 5% depending on the individual's annual betting activity [44].

- Mixed markets that start as fixed odds and can be later traded during the game on an exchange basis.
- Pari-mutuel betting, which involves all gains being redistributed to the winners depending on the size of their bet.

The following sections offer more insight on modeling techniques for betting prices and the relationship between bookmaker odds and the

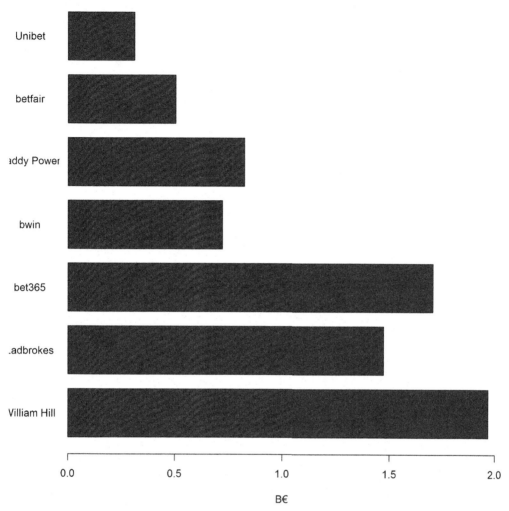

**FIGURE 5**  Market bookmakers online in 2013.

likelihood of match fixing. The main focus is on association football games but the information can be easily generalized to other sports (Figure 6).

## 3  AN INCOMPLETE AND INEFFICIENT MARKET

The highly praised theory developed by Eugene Fama in the 1960s and 1970s [45] is specific to financial markets, but some information can be leveraged easily to the betting market. This leverage makes more sense with the introduction of the exchange-based betting market (e.g., Betfair). The classic definition of efficiency cannot be applied entirely to betting as structurally the match results are not Markovian processes. Past results offer good predictive power over future results, thus technical strategies can be applied successfully in forecasting games. Bets as derivatives on the game outcome also

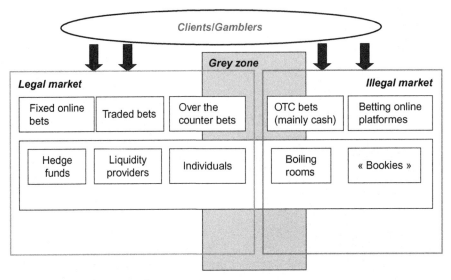

**FIGURE 6**  Structure of sports betting market.

face this constraint. Figure 7 shows the evolution of an odds[3] times series for the home games in Liverpool since 2002. The Box-Ljung test for odds values and their variations rejects the absence of autocorrelation for draw and home losses odds at 95% confidence interval. If we judge the odds as the value of a financial instrument, then the presence of inefficiency in the market should be accepted.

In theory, the outcome of total odds is constant and, so if one of the odds is not autocorrelated the other should in theory not be autocorrelated. But the outcome of odds is not constant and the sum of implied probabilities for the three odds is generally higher than 1. This type of structure of the odds market is in fact a measure of inefficiency. Both the literature and current findings underline this fact.

Many of the studies presented in this section have developed models that allow profit-taking strategies based on the historical performance of a team. Thus, the best proxy for characterizing the fixed betting market would be the weak form of the efficiency. But the bet market offers many other features such the possibility of betting on a number of goals, the spread, the number of faults, or other features of a game. The outcomes used for these bets naturally have a higher degree of randomness, and most likely the use of historical data would allow less or no profit to be taken.

One aspect of financial efficiency that can be leveraged to betting is the homogeneity of the information among punters, as well as the information available in the market and the way odds reflect this information. The following considerations around efficiency are built on the way information is captured by the punters and moreover in the way bookmakers propose their odds. The structure of bookmaker odds is a good proxy for how efficiently the information is incorporated into gambler preferences. If bookmakers see an unusual pattern in the volume or punter's strategy they adjust the odds in order to

---

[3]The Home Win, Draw, and Home Loss odds from Bet365 are considered.

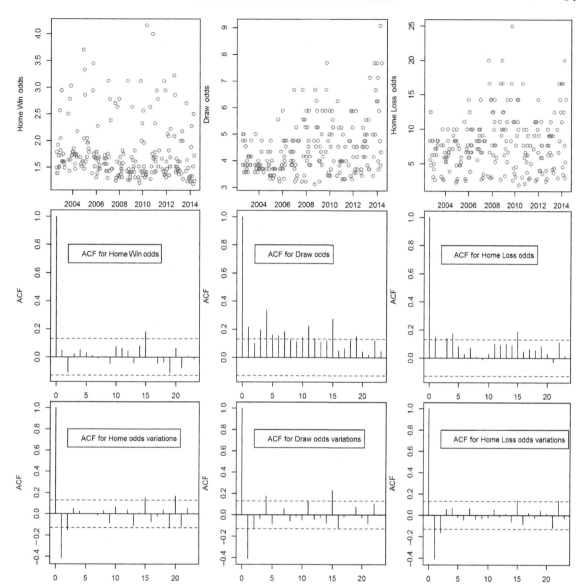

**FIGURE 7**  Liverpool's home games time series for the three fixing odds.

ensure this abnormal behavior will not result in a loss for them.

Let's assume a bookmaker offers the following fixed-odds: $o_H, o_D, o_A$. For each unity of the bet, a punter would make $o_r - 1$ with the probability of the outcome $p_r$ and lose $-1$ with the probability of the non-result $1 - p_r$, where the result $r$ states if $r \in \{H, D, A\}$. We assume here that $\sum_r p_r = 1$. The inverse of the odds $o_r$ can be interpreted as the bookmaker's probability of the desired match outcome to occur, $P(r) = \frac{1}{o_r}$. For a given match, the odds implied probabilities of all possible events sum to greater than one, $\sum_r p_r > 1$. If the sum is less than one then an opportunity for arbitrage exits. The amount above one of the sum is known as the margin or overround in legitimate gambling or as *vigorish* in illegal bookies slang. Vigorish, or simply vig, also known as *juice*, *cut*, or *take*, is the amount charged by a bookmaker, or bookie, for taking a bet from a punter. The margin is the measure associated with the efficiency of the betting market. The more efficient and liquid the market is the lower the margin is. If the market is inefficient and the bookmaker fears adverse results he charges more margin(vig). The odds can be modeled as binary options on spreads. Let $X$ be the number of goals scored by the home team and $Y$ as the number of goals scored by the away team at the game horizon $T$. The bookie is selling three types of binary options: Call, deuce, and put, defined as follows:

$$\text{Payoff} \setminus \mathbf{C}_T = \begin{cases} 1 & X - Y > 0 \\ 0 & \text{otherwise} \end{cases} \quad (1)$$

$$\text{Payoff} \setminus \mathbf{P}_T = \begin{cases} 1 & X - Y < 0 \\ 0 & \text{otherwise} \end{cases} \quad (2)$$

$$\text{Payoff} \setminus \mathbf{D}_T = \begin{cases} 1 & X - Y = 0 \\ 0 & \text{otherwise} \end{cases} \quad (3)$$

The sum of all prices of these options should be the unity corrected by the time value of the money under a risk-free rate $r$ as shown in the following equation:

$$\mathbf{P}_T + \mathbf{D}_T + \mathbf{C}_T = e^{-rT} \quad (4)$$

In reality, the total sum of these three options quoted by bookmaker is higher than 1, the difference being the gross profit of the bookmaker. The mark-up or vig includes not only the profit but also a safety cushion in case there is abnormal behavior from punters. For example, there might be private information about a game, which would be reflected as an increase of the "vig."

In our case, $X$ and $Y$ are positive discrete variables and their modeling will be addressed in a following section. In the case of financial markets, if $X$ and $Y$ are two stochastic prices[4] characterized by volatilities $\sigma_X$ and $\sigma_Y$ and correlation $\rho_{XY}$ the digital call on the spread is defined as:

$$\mathbf{C}_T = \begin{cases} 1 & X - Y > 0 \\ 0 & \text{otherwise} \end{cases} \quad (5)$$

The pricing function $\mathbf{F}$ for a digital call spread (here it is assumed the strike is null) under a risk neutral economy $\mathbf{Q}$ is given by:

$$\mathbf{C}_T = e^{-rT} E_Q[\mathbf{1}(X - Y)_+] = F(\sigma_X, \sigma_Y, \rho_{XY}) \quad (6)$$

The call put parity can be written as:

$$\mathbf{C}_T + \mathbf{P}_T = e^{-rT} \quad (7)$$

The equivalent of the overround or the profit of a digital market maker would be $\mathbf{V}_T$:

$$\mathbf{V}_T = \mathbf{C}_T + \mathbf{P}_T - e^{-rT} \quad (8)$$
$$\mathbf{V}_T = \mathbf{C}_T(\sigma_X + \sigma_X^*, \sigma_Y + \sigma_Y^*, \rho_{XY} + \rho_{XY}^*)$$
$$+ \mathbf{P}_T(\sigma_X + \sigma_X^*, \sigma_Y + \sigma_Y^*, \rho_{XY} + \rho_{XY}^*)$$
$$- e^{-rT} > 0$$

where the mark-up parameters for the volatilities are $\sigma_X^*$, $\sigma_Y^*$ and the correlation is $\rho_{XY}^*$. The mark-ups are added to the pricing, thereby generating a higher price for the digital spread calls and puts. The difference in price corresponds to the profit of the trader equivalent to the bookie's vig.

The pricing function $F$ can be determined using Mangrabe's approximation [46,47] as:

$$\mathbf{C}_T = e^{-rT} \int_{-\infty}^{+\infty} +\infty \, N\left(\frac{\rho y - x(y)}{\sqrt{1 - \rho^2}}\right) n(y) \, dy \quad (9)$$

---

[4]We would define only calls and puts on spreads.

where $N()$ is the cumulative standard density and $n()$ is normal density and:

$$\underline{x}(y) = \frac{\sigma_Y \sqrt{T} \cdot y + \mu_Y - \mu_X}{\sigma_X \sqrt{T}}$$

$$\mu_X = \log(X) + (r - 0.5 \cdot \sigma_X^2) \cdot T$$

$$\mu_Y = \log(Y) + (r - 0.5 \cdot \sigma_Y^2) \cdot T$$

The concept of risk neutrality applied to classic derivatives pricing cannot be easily leveraged to betting markets. Pricing of betting odds is more likely to give good results under the historical probability P, rather than with market implied methods. The reason is that punters do not always have a rational approach, and many bets are driven by personal affinity for a team or player. Thus, market-implied parameters might be biased by gambler behavior. This aspect could also explain why algorithms based on historical estimation provide positive returns as noted in the literature.

Shin [48] suggests that bookmakers protect themselves against the threat of insider trading by compressing the odds they offer to punters, particularly for relative outsiders. The divergence of the sum of price from unity represents the bookmaker's margin or overround, which is the equivalent of the bid-ask spread in the financial market.

As noted before, a reasonable the parallel with the derivatives would be to compare the overround with parameters mark-up in the derivatives pricing. The overround might sometimes have very interesting characteristics that could reflect asymmetry in the information spread among punters.

Bruce and Marginson [49] report that the overround is an established measure of inefficiency and can be seen as a reflection of bookmakers' collusive returns, maximizing behavior rather than simply as a response to an adverse selection problem. There is empirical support for several proposed market effects of bookmaker (market-maker) collusion.

When analyzing the evolution of "vig" over time Constantinou et al. [50] found that contrary to common views the accuracy of bookmaker odds has not improved with the bubble in betting markets. More importantly, market efficiency is questioned because of high profitability on the basis of consistent odds biases and numerous arbitrage opportunities, thereby reinforcing the assumptions made in the previous paragraph.

Figure 8 shows[5] the evolution since 2006 of the average overround proposed by the bookmakers of the main European National Football Association. It can be seen that the margin decreased continuously in the past decade due to an increase in market volume and turnover. The amount of margin charged on average varied from one country to another as seen in Table 1. Historically the lowest margin was charged for the English Premier League games as seen over the past decade. The current margin for the English League is the lowest ever and settles at around 5%. This is a natural consequence of the English Championship having the highest revenue, biggest media focus, and being the most liquid on the bet exchange. Lower league championships like Italian Serie B or English Conference show margins of 8.6% and 8.29%, respectively.

The margins depends not only on market turnover for each national league but also on idiosyncratic conditions linked to the competition itself. Thus, a measure of the margin's volatility would be relevant in this context. Table 2 reflects the benchmarks of the margins' standards deviation for the main football leagues in Europe.

The standard deviations are generally stable through time for each league. However, a few spikes can be easily spotted for the Italian Serie A in 2005 and for the Italian Serie B in 2010 and 2011. It is not a coincidence that these findings coincide with match-fixing scandals: the

---

[5]The findings are based on public historical data from http://football-data.co.uk/data.php.

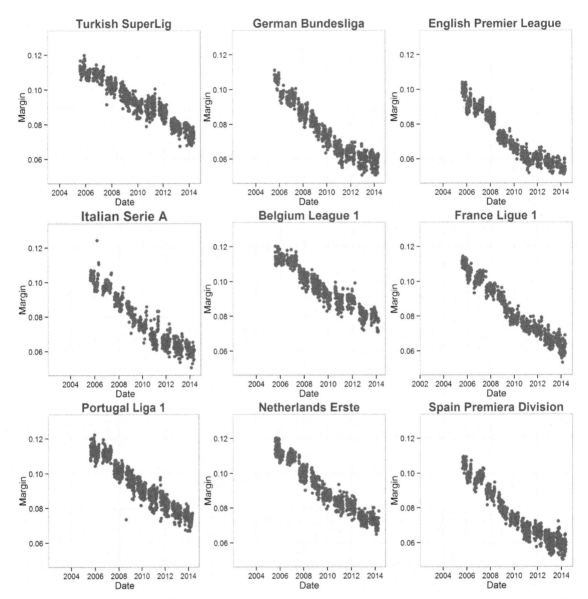

**FIGURE 8**  Evolution since 2006 of the average margin proposed by the main bookmakers for the main European National Football Association leagues.

*Calciopoli* scandal in the Italian Serie A in 2004-2005 and the *Calicoscommese* scandal in the Italian Serie B in 2010-2011. Both led to a big investigations in Italian football. The level of the margin for those years is high but not significantly higher than other leagues as seen in Table 1. The Turkish match fixing from the 2010 season does have also an increased margin volatility.

For a better understanding of margin effects a deeper assessment is given through an analysis

**TABLE 1**  Benchmarks of the Average Margin Proposed by the Main Bookmakers for European National Association Football Leagues

| Year | Holland Erediv. | Turkey | Belgium | Portugal | Spain | Germany Bundesl. | Germany Bundes. 2 | England Premier | England Conf. | Italy Serie A | Italy Serie B | France |
|---|---|---|---|---|---|---|---|---|---|---|---|---|
| 2005 | 11.15 | 11.01 | 11.29 | 11.28 | 10.19 | 10.15 | 11.2 | 9.45 | 11.47 | 10.17 | 11.15 | 10.79 |
| 2006 | 10.98 | 10.88 | 11.19 | 11.13 | 9.74 | 9.6 | 10.56 | 8.98 | 11.41 | 9.8 | 11 | 10.2 |
| 2007 | 10.17 | 10.33 | 10.32 | 10.26 | 8.94 | 8.79 | 10.03 | 8.29 | 11.02 | 8.96 | 10.72 | 9.53 |
| 2008 | 9.49 | 9.72 | 9.82 | 9.71 | 8.03 | 8.03 | 9.37 | 7.26 | 10.5 | 8.26 | 10.17 | 8.85 |
| 2009 | 8.82 | 9.2 | 9.25 | 9.19 | 7.36 | 7.45 | 8.86 | 6.67 | 9.98 | 7.63 | 9.74 | 7.93 |
| 2010 | 8.32 | 9.09 | 9.09 | 8.74 | 6.63 | 6.62 | 8.48 | 6.09 | 9.41 | 7.02 | 9.68 | 7.47 |
| 2011 | 8.22 | 8.81 | 9 | 8.49 | 6.59 | 6.52 | 8.3 | 6.08 | 9.4 | 6.65 | 9.13 | 7.24 |
| 2012 | 7.45 | 7.96 | 8.17 | 7.85 | 6.09 | 6.09 | 7.62 | 5.75 | 8.61 | 6.36 | 8.39 | 6.71 |
| 2013 | 7.3 | 7.65 | 8.02 | 7.51 | 5.94 | 5.99 | 7.38 | 5.47 | 8.69 | 6.07 | 8.29 | 6.44 |

**TABLE 2**  Benchmarks of Margin's Volatility by the Main Bookmakers for the Main European National Football Association Leagues. In Gray Color are Highlighted the Years when There were Allegation of Match Fixing. For Those Cases the Volatility is Higher Compared to Other Years

| Year | Holland Erediv. | Turkey | Belgium | Portugal | Spain | Germany Bundesl. | Germany Bundes. 2 | England Premier | England Conf. | Italy Serie A | Italy Serie B | France |
|---|---|---|---|---|---|---|---|---|---|---|---|---|
| 2005 | 0.31 | 0.3 | 0.28 | 0.33 | 0.41 | 0.51 | 0.45 | 0.57 | 0.31 | 1.28 | 0.53 | 0.4 |
| 2006 | 0.25 | 0.42 | 0.22 | 0.24 | 0.29 | 0.27 | 0.33 | 0.28 | 0.26 | 0.36 | 0.47 | 0.26 |
| 2007 | 0.35 | 0.3 | 0.28 | 0.27 | 0.3 | 0.32 | 0.35 | 0.28 | 0.49 | 0.34 | 0.45 | 0.26 |
| 2008 | 0.37 | 0.54 | 0.35 | 0.4 | 0.41 | 0.41 | 0.47 | 0.26 | 0.5 | 0.48 | 0.54 | 0.45 |
| 2009 | 0.29 | 0.28 | 0.31 | 0.29 | 0.25 | 0.3 | 0.31 | 0.29 | 0.45 | 0.72 | 0.95 | 0.25 |
| 2010 | 0.32 | 0.33 | 0.33 | 0.35 | 0.33 | 0.31 | 0.45 | 0.28 | 0.42 | 0.77 | 1.02 | 0.41 |
| 2011 | 0.31 | 0.3 | 0.3 | 0.38 | 0.26 | 0.27 | 0.36 | 0.23 | 0.55 | 0.31 | 0.38 | 0.28 |
| 2012 | 0.24 | 0.26 | 0.29 | 0.3 | 0.29 | 0.29 | 0.4 | 0.2 | 0.35 | 0.42 | 0.34 | 0.27 |
| 2013 | 0.32 | 0.3 | 0.29 | 0.35 | 0.38 | 0.32 | 0.39 | 0.28 | 0.39 | 0.27 | 0.49 | 0.35 |

of each bookmaker's margin structure. The current average margins of the bookmakers for the major football leagues are given in Table 4. The lowest margin was given by Bet365 and in particular for the English Premier League, with a margin below 3%. The leagues with the highest margin in the panel are the Turkish League, the Italian Serie B, and the English Conference. When assessing the margin on maximum odds it appears that for many leagues arbitrage opportunities do exist. For example, recall that if for a given bookmaker $j \in \overline{1, \mathbf{M}}$, one punter disposes of the odds $o_{H,j}$, $o_{D,j}$, and $o_{A,j}$, an arbitrage opportunity occurs if the following conditions are met:

$$\underbrace{\frac{1}{\max(o_{H,j})}}_{j} + \underbrace{\frac{1}{\max(o_{D,j})}}_{j} + \underbrace{\frac{1}{\max(o_{A,j})}}_{j} - 1 < 0 \quad (10)$$

In other words, if the punter can create a virtual set of odds from the maximum odds proposed by all bookmakers with an equivalent negative vig, then there is the opportunity for a risk-free profit taking strategy. Table 4 shows that the top European leagues (France, England, Spain, and Germany) offer arbitrage opportunities. On the other hand, Turkish and Belgian leagues are far from any risk-free profit as the margin for maximum odds is even higher than 1%, as they are handled cautiously by bookmaking agencies.

The average margins from the 2004 seasons given in Table 3 would have not raised any suspicions concerning a match-rigging scandal in Serie A. At a time when the overround was consistently high across all leagues, it was obviously more difficult to capture any abnormal signal through the margin level.

Figure 9 shows the evolution of the margins for Bet365 across the main leagues in Europe. A structural break can be seen in 2008 when the margin level dropped for almost all leagues. This was observed in the case of other bookmakers shown in Figure 10 for William Hill, Figure 11 for Betwin, and Figure 12 for Ladbrokes. The change occurred as a consequence of the deregulation of the gambling industry and implementation of the British Gambling Act, which allowed bookmakers to advertise through the media. This increased the competition among bookmakers for capturing the increasing volumes of the market (Table 4).

While before 2005 Bet365 had comparable margin levels for the main leagues after 2008 three levels can be distinguished: the leagues with low margin (English Premier League), few leagues with average margin (Italy, France, etc.) and those with high margins (Turkey, Belgium, Italy Serie B). The English league was the first that saw a decrease in the margin even before 2008. For the other leagues, the decrease in margin was gradual. Bet365 employed a two-regime margin strategy: one with a lower margin and another that kept the high margin.

**TABLE 3**　Benchmark of Average Margins (in percentage) from the Season 2004 Across the Major Championships and the Major Bookmakers

| Championship | Bet365 | William Hill | GamerookerB | BetWin | Ladbrokes | InterWin | Sportingbet |
|---|---|---|---|---|---|---|---|
| Netherlands | 12.39 | 12.52 | 11.52 | 11.26 | | 13.57 | 12.00 |
| Belgium | 12.43 | 12.59 | 11.50 | 11.22 | | 13.59 | 12.07 |
| Portugal | 12.42 | 12.53 | 11.46 | 11.20 | | 13.59 | 11.97 |
| Spain | 11.12 | 12.35 | 8.34 | 10.21 | | 13.62 | 9.76 |
| France | 11.76 | 12.46 | 11.26 | 10.44 | | 13.54 | 11.30 |
| Italy Serie A | 11.31 | 12.45 | 10.41 | 10.18 | 12.39 | 13.61 | 9.84 |
| Italy Serie B | 12.50 | 12.78 | 12.63 | 12.18 | 12.53 | 15.03 | 12.52 |
| Germany Bundesliga | 11.68 | 12.37 | 8.34 | 10.18 | 12.37 | 13.57 | 9.87 |
| Germany Bundesliga 2 | 12.45 | 12.36 | 10.49 | 11.16 | | 13.61 | 9.67 |
| Turkey | 11.93 | 12.52 | 11.70 | 11.29 | 11.81 | 12.48 | 9.35 |
| England | 7.86 | 12.50 | 8.06 | 10.13 | | 13.57 | 8.82 |

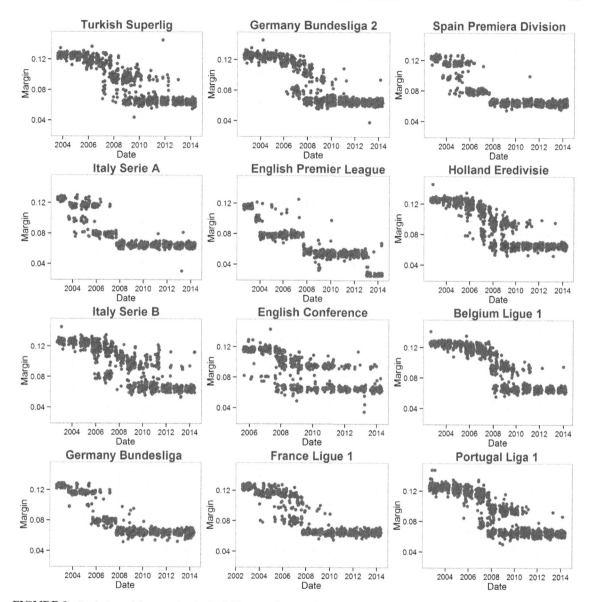

**FIGURE 9** Evolution of the margins for Bet365 across the main leagues in Europe.

Table 5 shows the margin panels for the season 2010-2011. It can be seen that in the year of *Calcioscommesse* the Italian Serie B showed higher margins than its peers. The margin for the maximum odds reaches a critical value of 2%.

The benchmark of margins' volatility represented in Table 6 shows that the Italian Serie B had the highest fluctuations in odds structure. The margins of William Hill and Bet365 were the most volatile for the second Italian echelon. The relatively high level of margins also remained for

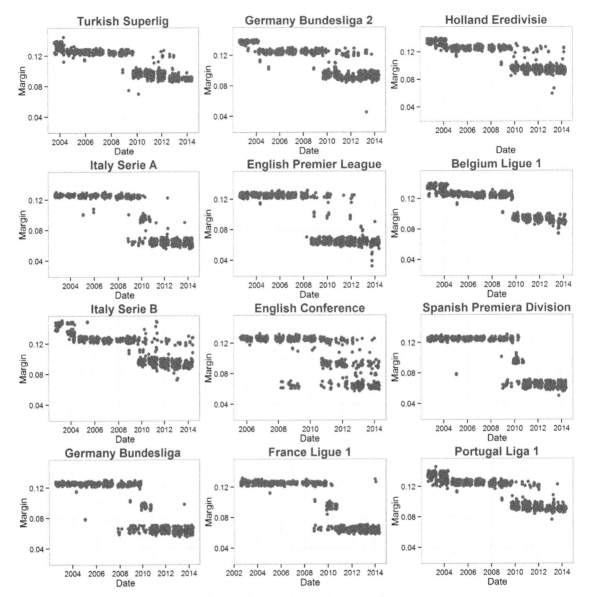

**FIGURE 10** Evolution of margins for William Hill across the main leagues in Europe.

2011-2012 when the official investigation started and the facts were made public (Table 7).

William Hill's margin is shown in Figure 10 and is globally more conservative than Bet365. In 2008 the margin contraction occurred across all studied leagues with the exception of the English Conference, where the margin range became wider.

In Figures 11 and 12 it can be seen that BetWin and Ladbrokes had unusually high margins for the English Conference even after 2008. The same effect can be seen for the Belgium and Dutch

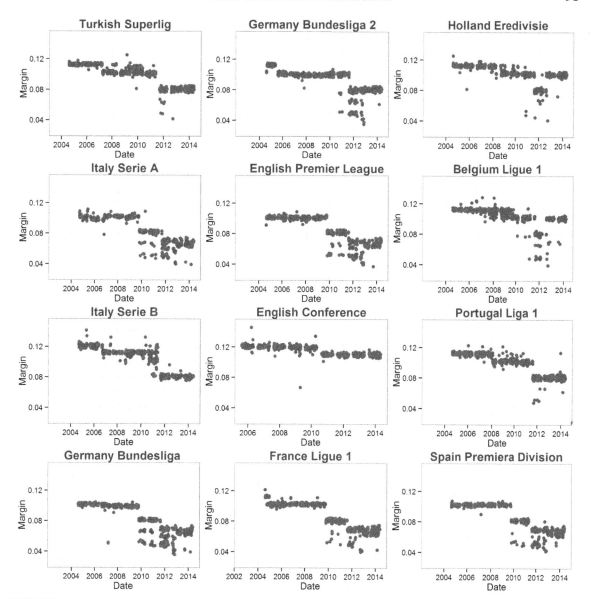

**FIGURE 11** Evolution of margins for BetWin across the main leagues in Europe.

leagues, which had minimal contractions in the average overround. The English Conference was the target of allegations of match fixing in the 2013 season, but the hypothesis that other riggings occurred silently in the past cannot be rejected.

# 4 SPORT BETTING AND FINANCIAL CRIME

The ties between sport and financial crime can be traced back to the debut of professional sports. Which match fixing in relationship

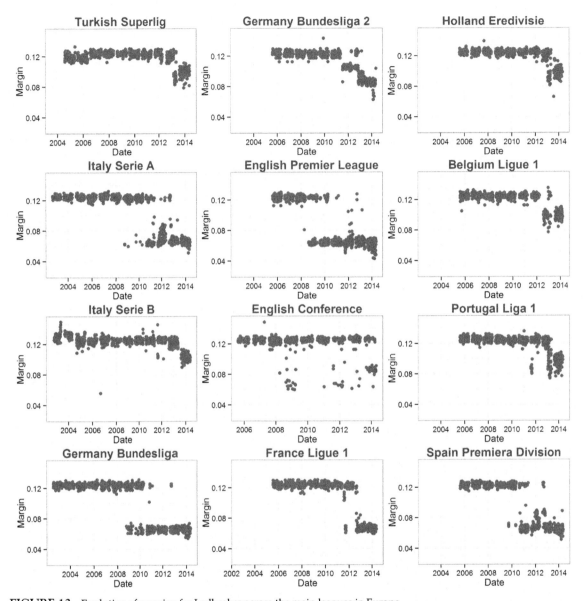

**FIGURE 12** Evolution of margins for Ladbrokes across the main leagues in Europe.

with illegal betting is the most studied and publicized form of crime, many other types of white-collar crime co-exist within the sport area. While this section is focused on the betting industry, it is worth mentioning a few other types.

The transfer market for professional athletes is a very sophisticated business with many stakeholders including clubs, players, managers, agents, brokers, scooters, etc. The amounts involved are significant as the value of an association football player can be more than

**TABLE 4**  Average Margins of the Main Bookmakers for the 2013-2014 Season

| Championship | Bet365 | William Hill | BetWin | Ladbrokes | InterWin | Average | Maximum |
|---|---|---|---|---|---|---|---|
| Netherlands | 6.53 | 9.42 | 9.95 | 9.78 | 11.35 | 7.30 | 0.61 |
| Belgium | 6.52 | 8.92 | 9.98 | 9.85 | 11.35 | 8.02 | 1.07 |
| Portugal | 6.50 | 9.03 | 8.04 | 9.67 | 11.25 | 7.51 | 0.83 |
| Spain | 6.36 | 6.28 | 6.60 | 6.49 | 8.07 | 5.94 | −0.38 |
| France | 6.47 | 6.33 | 6.59 | 6.55 | 8.07 | 6.44 | −0.03 |
| Italy Serie A | 6.45 | 6.34 | 6.58 | 6.52 | 8.05 | 6.07 | −0.10 |
| Italy Serie B | 6.72 | 9.49 | 8.06 | 10.19 | 11.07 | 8.29 | 0.74 |
| Germany Bundesliga | 6.39 | 6.36 | 6.58 | 6.56 | 8.04 | 5.99 | −0.11 |
| Germany Bundesliga 2 | 6.45 | 9.27 | 8.03 | 8.54 | 8.09 | 7.38 | 0.39 |
| Turkey | 6.42 | 9.00 | 8.07 | 10.00 | 11.31 | 7.65 | 1.07 |
| England | 2.62 | 6.27 | 6.65 | 5.93 | 8.06 | 5.47 | −0.05 |
| England Conference | 6.76 | 7.49 | 11.03 | 10.18 | 13.63 | 8.69 | 1.28 |

**TABLE 5**  Average Margins of the Main Bookmakers for the 2010-2011 Season

| Championship | B365 | William Hill | Gamebrooker | Bet Win | Ladbrokes | InterWin | Sportingbet | Average | Maximum |
|---|---|---|---|---|---|---|---|---|---|
| Netherlands | 6.85 | 9.68 | 10.03 | 10.07 | 12.49 | 13.08 | 10.12 | 8.32 | 1.39 |
| Belgium | 7.27 | 9.36 | 10.07 | 10.12 | 12.45 | 13.09 | 10.15 | 9.09 | 1.76 |
| Portugal | 6.82 | 9.59 | 10.03 | 10.01 | 12.35 | 11.19 | 10.24 | 8.74 | 1.68 |
| Spain | 6.57 | 6.68 | 7.79 | 8.00 | 7.47 | 10.17 | 10.13 | 6.63 | 0.71 |
| France | 6.51 | 6.74 | 8.78 | 7.98 | 12.35 | 10.19 | 10.12 | 7.47 | 1.31 |
| Italy Serie A | 6.69 | 6.71 | 7.87 | 8.15 | 8.40 | 10.29 | 10.15 | 7.02 | 0.96 |
| Italy Serie B | 7.81 | 10.20 | 10.19 | 10.61 | 12.51 | 11.14 | 11.13 | 9.68 | 2.23 |
| Bundesliga | 6.48 | 6.65 | 7.64 | 7.81 | 6.69 | 10.20 | 10.00 | 6.62 | 0.58 |
| Bundesliga 2 | 6.67 | 9.61 | 8.91 | 9.90 | 12.25 | 10.23 | 10.14 | 8.48 | 1.21 |
| Turkey | 6.94 | 9.49 | 10.03 | 10.05 | 12.24 | 11.36 | 10.07 | 9.09 | 1.67 |
| England | 5.45 | 6.50 | 7.68 | 8.01 | 6.50 | 10.13 | 10.12 | 6.09 | 0.63 |
| England Conference | 7.90 | 10.26 | 11.17 | 11.05 | 12.54 | 13.68 | 11.94 | 9.41 | 1.64 |

**TABLE 6** Margins Volatility of the Main Bookmakers for the 2010-2011 Season

| Championship | Bet365 | William Hill | Gamebrooker | BetWin | Ladbrokes | InterWin | Sportingbet | Average | Maximum |
|---|---|---|---|---|---|---|---|---|---|
| Netherlands | 0.90 | 0.88 | 0.31 | 0.77 | 0.31 | 0.82 | 0.26 | 0.32 | 1.00 |
| Belgium | 1.22 | 0.42 | 0.30 | 0.63 | 0.34 | 0.84 | 0.24 | 0.33 | 1.11 |
| Portugal | 0.86 | 0.86 | 0.25 | 0.53 | 0.33 | 0.48 | 0.33 | 0.35 | 1.11 |
| Spain | 0.43 | 0.93 | 0.33 | 0.64 | 2.20 | 0.39 | 0.22 | 0.33 | 0.86 |
| France | 0.37 | 0.98 | 0.46 | 0.95 | 0.31 | 0.44 | 0.25 | 0.41 | 1.61 |
| Italy Serie A | 0.86 | 0.94 | 0.62 | 0.75 | 2.75 | 0.87 | 0.24 | 0.77 | 0.93 |
| Italy Serie B | 1.78 | 1.77 | 0.70 | 0.90 | 0.98 | 0.53 | 0.33 | 1.02 | 1.41 |
| Bundesliga | 0.34 | 0.93 | 0.77 | 0.97 | 1.20 | 0.34 | 0.29 | 0.31 | 0.91 |
| Bundesliga 2 | 0.55 | 1.05 | 0.32 | 1.00 | 0.33 | 0.32 | 0.28 | 0.45 | 1.25 |
| Turkey | 0.95 | 0.54 | 0.30 | 0.46 | 0.36 | 0.29 | 0.28 | 0.33 | 1.15 |
| England | 0.29 | 0.96 | 0.29 | 0.75 | 0.82 | 0.33 | 0.25 | 0.28 | 0.70 |
| England Conference | 1.52 | 2.32 | 0.71 | 0.24 | 0.70 | 0.32 | 0.67 | 0.42 | 1.06 |

**TABLE 7** Average Margins of the Main Bookmakers for the 2011-2012 Season. The Bold Figures Highlight Italy's Serie B

| Championship | Bet365 | William Hill | GameBrooker | BetWin | Ladbrokes | InterWin | Sportingbet | Average | Maximum |
|---|---|---|---|---|---|---|---|---|---|
| Netherlands | 6.52 | 9.68 | 8.86 | 7.89 | 12.49 | 12.59 | 7.78 | 8.22 | 1.02 |
| Belgium | 6.55 | 9.26 | 9.06 | 8.02 | 12.43 | 12.52 | 7.97 | 9.00 | 1.32 |
| Portugal | 6.48 | 9.51 | 8.92 | 8.01 | 12.17 | 11.30 | 7.93 | 8.49 | 1.39 |
| Spain | 6.45 | 6.51 | 7.71 | 6.46 | 7.19 | 10.15 | 7.61 | 6.59 | 0.49 |
| France | 6.43 | 6.42 | 7.83 | 6.69 | 11.39 | 10.10 | 7.80 | 7.24 | 0.86 |
| Italy Serie A | 6.47 | 6.52 | 7.79 | 6.62 | 7.42 | 10.16 | 7.51 | 6.65 | 0.66 |
| Italy Serie B | **6.73** | **9.62** | **9.05** | **8.16** | **12.42** | **11.13** | **10.25** | **9.13** | **1.49** |
| Bundesliga | 6.39 | 6.67 | 7.60 | 6.34 | 6.52 | 10.09 | 7.69 | 6.52 | 0.46 |
| Bundesliga 2 | 6.47 | 9.47 | 8.88 | 7.67 | 10.56 | 10.15 | 7.95 | 8.30 | 0.92 |
| Turkey | 6.75 | 9.53 | 8.96 | 7.82 | 12.39 | 11.38 | 7.58 | 8.81 | 1.31 |
| England | 5.46 | 6.70 | 7.67 | 6.42 | 6.65 | 10.07 | 7.66 | 6.08 | 0.57 |
| England Conference | 6.91 | 9.52 | 10.61 | 11.02 | 12.32 | 13.69 | 10.36 | 9.40 | 1.22 |

100 million euros.[6] The payment scheme and the rights of each stakeholder are complex, huge amounts of funds being transfered through many companies or shell companies, many incorporated in tax heavens. Furthermore, many players come from emerging or underdeveloped regions where the flow of currency can involve many countries with various risk profiles. Thus, the transfer market is a perfect tool for money laundering and tax evasion.

The broadcasting rights of main sporting events such as the SuperBowl, UEFA Champions League, or the Cricket Super League is one of the main sources of revenue for professional sports, and the amount at stake is often in the range of billions. Again, the primary market for bidding for these rights and the secondary market are sophisticated and sometimes have the same features as financial markets. As immaterial products, the rights are easily sold from one company to another across many countries. In addition to money laundering and tax evasion, the risk of anti-trust exists as cartels can organize in a way that blocks access to broadcasting to other competitors.

## 4.1 Match Rigging

Arnold Rothstein and the fixing of the World Series is probably the biggest example of game fixing, which has been exploited by literature and by Hollywood productions.[7] One of the world's greatest association football players was allegedly involved in fixing the results of the 1988 Serie A at the demand of the local crime syndicate "La Cammora."[8] Over the past few

years some fixing scandals have become so obvious even to the untrained public eye that sport authorities and investigators have taken strong action against both criminals and rogue players. After recent scandals in European football leagues reputed teams like Juventus or Fenerbahce were penalized or banned from participating in higher competition. Match fixing can have the following mechanisms:

- Match rigging for obtaining a better result in order to allow one team to advance in a competition (e.g., qualification in international competition) or to avoid a demotion in an inferior league.
- Match fixing can also result from bribery of criminal syndicates to make a profit from bets on a given match.
- Transversal rigging, where two teams arrange the results of their direct game in order to make a third team profit. The profit can be in the form of a better ranking or a outcome from a bet, with the third team profiting.

The first type of rigging is one of the oldest forms in both professional and amateur sports. The line between crime and legal behavior is not clearly defined. In many competitions when a high-profile team plays a lower-profile team and the latter needs a good result whilst the better team has already secured its position it is often that the better team does not send its best players for the game. Even if the game is fair, the results will not reflect in many cases the true difference in value between the two teams. These type of behavior develops in big scale misconducts

---

[6]In 2013, Gareth Bale became the most expensive transfer in professional football for more than 91 million euros.
[7]Reference to this episode have appeared in many movies like The Godfather and the TV series Broadwalk Empire.
[8]Diego Armando Maradona was and probably still is the most popular player in Napoli and was a highly regarded figure by the local criminal clans due to his

---

flamboyant style and sanguine personality. In a trial for drug use and traffic, Maradona's bodyguard at that time, Pietro Pugliese, accused him of fixing the 1988 Serie A, by losing the title on the order of the camorristi who had bet heavily on the title shot. That year Napoli had 5 points over AC Milan, which managed to win in the last stages of the competition.

when teams or players do form cartels in order to "arrange" the results in competition. This was the case in 2005 in the Calciopoli scandal in Italy that resulted in the demotion of the then champion Juventus. For one year Juventus played in the second Italian league and in the year after many of its players were part of the Italian squad that won the World Cup in Germany. A similar case was with the Turkish Championship winner in 2011, Fenerbahce, that fixed games in order to secure the championship and to participate in the UEFA Champions League. The extensive participation of teams in the European interclub competitions and the large amounts of revenue paid by the Union of European Football Associations (UEFA) incentivized significantly the teams to compete for a better position in their national leagues.

The second type of match fixing is directly linked to the betting market. While the previous type of match fixing involves mainly high-level teams that use the fixes for a better position and a better options in the future, the betting match-fixing targets apply to all kinds of teams and leagues. Moreover, as was shown in the previous section the betting market for games involving inferior leagues or low-profile teams lacks efficiency. These types of games with low stakes and thin liquid bets are perfect targets for manipulators. Furthermore players from these teams are easier to corrupt by criminals because they respond for lower amounts of money. Thus, the rigging of low-level games can be a very lucrative business.

The third type of fixing is somewhat difficult to classify as either legal or illegal. While technically it deals with manipulation as a team or player alters the results in order to affect the ranking of another team or player, many argue that it could also be part of a team strategy to take indirectly out stronger competitors. One case proved by the literature is that of the Sumo matches as shown through a forensic statistic approach in the seminal paper of Duggan and Levitt [51].

From the perspective of football association tournaments Caruso [36] found that the role of asymmetry in the evaluation of match odds in tournaments is one of the key factors leading to concession. Thus, if during a tournament game the two opponents have different and asymmetric situations, fixing and corruption give the team with the less favorable situation an advantage. Relevant proofs can be found by comparing matches from the FIFA World Cup and the UEFA Champions League tournaments.

## SUMO: CORRUPTION, MATCH FIXING, AND ILLEGAL BETTIN

In early 2000 through the seminal book *Freakonomics*, author Levitt popularized the controversial study of sumo fixing. He showed that 70% of wrestlers with 7/7 records on the final day of the tournament (i.e., seven wins and seven losses, and one fight to go) were allegedly winning the last game. This work provides relevant statistical evidence documenting previous and unproved allegations of match rigging in sumo wrestling, a sport that dates back at least 1300 years. The study shows that non-linearity in the incentive structure of promotion leads to gains from trades between wrestlers on the margin for achieving a winning record and their opponents.

### Sumo rigging as a cartel

This cartel-type behavior where wrestlers help each other maximize their collective gain can be explained through the antitrust theory derived from Nash's equilibrium. If we assume the wrestlers' gains are similar to a derivative instrument with a non-linear payoff as reported by Levitt, and the total amount of the potential gains is pre-determined, there is indeed an incentive for splitting those gains in homogeneously rather than depending on the more random results of a tournament. From a behavior perspective the sumo rigging has many points in common with the LIBOR or gold price fixing. In all cases the main actors involved tried to fix the outcome in order to maximize the gains on a portfolio of products with nonlinear payoffs.

### Organized crime ties

Match rigging leads ineluctably to collusion into the betting world and also to a non-null intersection with the criminal world. In July 2010[a] the Japanese Sumo Association, the institution in charge with the oversight of the sport, announced the firing of a top wrestler and his manager for betting in an illegal gambling ring supervised by Japanese anti-social groups. As a result of the investigation two managers were demoted, and 18 other wrestlers were banned from competing in the following tournament. The presence of Yakuza in sumo wrestling is a silent yet strong phenomena. In the same year members of the reputed Yamaguchi-gumi clan were involved in a scandal over the sale of tickets for prized seats at the foot of the sumo ring of a high-profile tournament.

[a]Sumo's Ties to Japan Underworld Go Beyond Limits, http://www.nytimes.com/2010/07/06/world/asia/06sumo.html?pagewanted=1&hp&_r=0.

In the following sections a few major cases of match rigging are presented from a qualitative perspective. These cases will make the object of a quantitative study aimed to assess the possible link between match fixing and betting markets.

### 4.1.1 Italian Calcioscommesse

Italian football has been the target of many scandals and allegations of bribery and match throwing. But over the past 10 years two major scandals hit the Calcio, with big consequences for clubs and footballers.

In 2006, prosecutors investigated 29 games from the 2004-2005 Serie A season and one from the Serie B involving clubs such as Juventus, Fiorentina, and Lazio, which were relegated for their involvement in a match-fixing

scandal, although after appeals, only Juventus was actually demoted. Following the investigation, Juventus was stripped of two Serie A titles and demoted to Serie B, while AC Milan, Fiorentina, Lazio, Reggina, and second-division team Arezzo faced point deductions. Luciano Moggi, the alleged ringleader, attempt to arrange "friendly" match officials for some teams' games and was accused of sporting fraud and of being part of a criminal organization. No allegations of the betting market were made at that time.

At the end of 2011 another scandal surfaced culminating in the arrest of a reputed international player,[9] former Atalanta and Italy midfielder Cristiano Doni. He was banned for 3.5 years and his national squad colleague Giuseppe Signori, was banned for 5 years. Italian prosecutor Roberto Di Martino, in charge with the investigation, noted that match-fixing might have been going on for more than a decade.

By the summer of 2012 suspicions were raised for 33 matches, more than 30 arrests were reported and over 22 clubs and 61 people including 52 active players were investigated. Clubs from Serie A like Atalanta, Novara, and Sienakept were in the headlines during the investigation.

For the first time prosecutors talked about the existence of a global syndicate in charge with match fixing and betting. Stakeholders are spread across Europe to the Far East to South America and are able to arrange through a vast network the outcomes of football matches.

Despite the recent crackdowns in the Italian Calcio, FederBet [52], a specialized institution in sport rigging surveillance reported suspicions of match fixing in the 2013 season involving high-profile teams (Table 8).

[9]Ex-Italy player Cristiano Doni arrested for match fixing, http://www.bbc.co.uk/sport/0/football/16243249.

**TABLE 8** Fixed Games reported by FederBet in Italy in the 2013-2014 Season

| Date | League | Teams | Result |
|------|--------|-------|--------|
| 01.02.14 | Serie B | Padova-Carpi | 1-4 |
| 09.02.14 | Lega Pro | Paganese-Frosinone | 1-2 |
| 09.03.14 | Lega Pro | Paganese-L'Aquila | 0-1 |
| 30.03.14 | Lega Pro | Barletta-Benevento | 1-6 |
| 27.04.14 | Lega Pro | Benevento-Viareggio | 3-2 |
| 04.05.14 | Lega Pro | Prato-Benevento | 3-3 |
| 18.05.14 | Serie A | Catania-Atalanta | 2-1 |
| 25.05.14 | Serie B | Crotone-Trapani | 2-1 |
| 25.05.14 | Serie B | Cittadella-Empoli | 2-2 |

### 4.1.2 Australian Focus

The match-fixing connection seems to be dominated by Asian cartels that have a well-established worldwide network with ties to various competitions and sports. A good example is the investigation of match rigging in the Victorian league.[10] In 2013, the Australian police arrested 10 people as a result of a match-fixing investigation that was prompted by information provided by the Football Federation of Australia. Segaran Gsubramaniam, a 45-year-old from Malaysia known as "Gerry," appeared to be the brain behind a match-rigging enterprise involving several British footballers and was allegedly involved in fixing games while playing for the Melbourne-based Stars in the second-tier Victorian Premier League. The match-fixing allegations related to the Stars' last four games, in which they conceded 13 goals without scoring. They lost 16 of their 21 league matches that season, winning one and drawing four. The ring leader Gsubramaniam acted as contact between Stars players and betting syndicates and placed bets that led to winnings of more than 1.17 million pounds. This fact proves that even in second-tier leagues the betting turnover can be significant.

### 4.1.3 Turkish Football Fixed Games

Over the past decade the Turkish Football League has grown in strength both financially and performance wise. Turkish teams are in the European elite because of high revenue and stable participants in the UEFA Champions League. At the dawn of the 2013-2014 season UEFA[11] banned Fenerbahce and Istanbul rival Besiktas from all European competitions for match fixing. The Turkish teams appealed the decision but the Court of Arbitration for sport upheld the ban.

This announcement came as a result of a longer investigation inside the Turkish Championship with a focus on the 2010-2011 season, which was adjudicated by Fenerbahce. The away win of Fenerbahce against Sivasspor in the last stage of the competition with a 4-3 score was highly suspicious because allowed a title win with only 1-point difference. At that time it was Fenerbahce's second exclusion from European competition after they were withdrawn from the 2011-2012 Champions League by the domestic governing body (the Turkish Football Federation) during an investigation for match fixing. In 2012 almost 100 high-profile individuals from the Turkish football league indicted for match fixing. One of the most prominent figures was Fenerbahce Chairman Aziz Yildirim, who was convicted and sentenced to 3 years and 9 months in prison on match-fixing charges. His colleagues, Fenerbahce's board members Ilhan

---

[10]Australian match fixing: British players appear in court, http://www.bbc.co.uk/sport/0/football/24171344.

[11]Fenerbahce boss links soccer match-fixing case to Turkey corruption probe, http://uk.reuters.com/article/2014/01/20/uk-soccer-turkey-matchfixing-idUKBREA0J1GW20140120.

Eksioglu, Sekip Mosturoglu, Tamer Yelkovan, and Cemil Turan, were also found guilty of manipulating several games during the 2010-2011 Turkish Championship.

As can be seen the fixing of a tournament involves more than one team. Thus, investigators indicted several officials from Besiktas, Eskisehirspor, Sivasspor, Giresunspor, Diyarbakirspor, and Trabzonspor, the latter team losing its 2010-2011 *Spor Toto Super League* title to Fenerbahce.

In the case of the Turkish match-fixing scandal there were no alleged ties to the betting market. The fixing was aimed at securing a better place for the team to allow participation in the UEFA Champions League, a very profitable enterprise for any team.

### 4.1.4 England Conference

Match fixing in relation to the betting market is a two-dimensional phenomenon. On the one hand, the initiator of the rogue scheme has to have access to betting markets (mainly illegal ones) in order to place bets with skewed volumes. On the other hand, team officials, managers, players, or referees need to be influenced or bribed to alter the result of the game. Of course, it is more difficult to influence a first league player or referee with a high salary and substantial advertising revenues than smaller league players. Thus, structurally the most exposed competitions or sports are those that have a deep market of bets but low revenue and wages for players and officials. Thus, it is easier to bribe an England Conference player with an income of few thousand pounds per month than an NFL player earning an eight-figure income.

There were many rumors concerning fixed football games in England, but when a research report from the consortium watchdog [52] was presented in 2014 before the European Parliament, fears of massive infiltration of the English sport by Asian criminal groups started to become real. The report noted that 11 English games (Table 9) were found to involve betting fraud.

Prior to 2013, the English Football Association suspected more than a dozen active footballers were involved in match fixing in the Conference South in the 2012-2013 season. This scheme had alleged ties to match-fixing in Australian leagues as noted in an investigation led by the Daily Telegraph. In March 2013 the Association warned Conference South clubs about the likelihood of systematic fixing, after detecting abnormal betting patterns.[12]

One year later the first indictment came and Michael Boateng, a 22-year-old former defender with the Conference South club Whitehawk FC, was found guilty and sentenced to 16 months for attempted match fixing. He went to court along with Singaporean businessman Chann Sankaran and Sri Lankan citizen Krishna Ganeshan who were charged with attempting to influence the outcome of matches in League Two and the Conference South. They were both sentenced to 5 years.[13]

During the trial it was found that they had a clear strategy for lower division football clubs because the cost of bribing the players with lower wages was cheaper than approaching players from the higher leagues. For instance, Boateng was bribed by Sankaran and Ganeshan with 450 euro for helping them to alter the result of a game. The National Crime Agency tapped their hotel rooms after they tried to throw the game between AFC Wimbledon and Dagenham & Redbridge.

---

[12]Scandal of match-fixing revealed: The FA's secret list of suspects and how they are still playing in England, http://www.dailymail.co.uk/sport/football/article-2746254/SCANDAL-OF-MATCH-FIXING-REVEALED-The-FA-s-secret-list-suspects-playing-England.html.

[13]Footballer and two businessmen jailed over match-fixing plot, http://www.theguardian.com/football/2014/jun/20/footballer-businessmen-jailed-match-fixing-plot.

**TABLE 9**  Fixed Games reported by FederBet in England in the 2013-2014 Season

| Date | League | Teams | Result |
|------|--------|-------|--------|
| 02.11.13 | Conference South | Bishop Stortford-Tonbridge | 2-1 |
| 02.11.13 | Conference North | Brackley Town-Boston United | 3-2 |
| 02.11.13 | Conference North | Guiseley-Barrow | 2-1 |
| 09.11.13 | Conference North | Telford-Stalybridge | 3b-1 |
| 25.11.13 | Conference South | Havant-Chelmsford | 3-0 |
| 07.12.13 | Conference South | Bromley-Farnborough | 3-0 |
| 10.12.13 | Conference North | Oxford City-Workington afc | 1-1 |
| 13.12.13 | Conference North | Kidderminster-Alfreton | 1-3 |
| 14.12.13 | League Wales | Port Talbot-Carmanthen Town | 1-1 |
| 14.12.13 | League Wales | Bala Town-Gap | 6-0 |
| 04.01.14 | Conference North | Solihull-Stalybridge | 3-3 |
| 08.03.14 | Conference North | Forest Green-Cambridge | 3-2 |
| 20.04.14 | Premier League Woman | Notts County-Everton | 2-0 |

### 4.1.5 International Matches

Thrown games in international football are a very disputed subject, since many high-profile teams are the subjects of allegations of fixing. For instance, the victory of Argentina as host of the 1978 World Cup was allegedly the result of a series of fixing and manipulation from the pool series to the final. The aim of the fixing directed by the military dictator at that time was to ensure political momentum and popularity of the regime. Match throwing in the pool stage,[14] referees penalizing the Brazilian team, and many other examples part of the folklore of the Argentinian summer that sent Zico and Cruyff home without the Jules Rimet trophy.

Prior to the 2010 World Cup held in South Africa the *New York Times*[15] obtained a copy of an 44-page internal report about incidents from the 2010 World Cup in South Africa by football's world governing body and other related documents raising issues about betting syndicates influencing outcomes and referee honesty.

Singaporean Wilson Raj Perumal, a high-profile fixer in the betting underworld, claimed in his book that he rigged many outcomes of national football games among which was the 2010 Egypt-Australia game, won by the African team 3-0. Perumal allegedly bribed a Bulgarian referee that officiated the match to ensure that a total of three goals were scored in the

---

[14]We fixed it! Peru senator claims 1978 World Cup game against Argentina was rigged, http://www.dailymail.co.uk/sport/football/article-2098970/Argentina-cheated-World-Cup-1978-says-Peru-senator.html.

[15]Soccer match-fixing scandal deepens, http://www.theaustralian.com.au/sport/football/soccer-matchfixing-scandal-deepens/story-fn63e0vj-1226938803516.

match. According to the *New York Times* the fixes included matches as U.S.-Australia, South Africa-Guatemala, and South Africa-Denmark, the latter fixture being linked to Perumal's name.

---

## WHO'S WHO IN MATCH FIXIN

- **Arn Rothstein**, prominent criminal figure of the New-Yorkese milieu that activated during the roaring years of the Prohibition and managed to fix the World Series in 1919.
- **Otto Biederman**, reputed financier working for the organize crime in New York during the 1920s and 1930 that was able to manipulate the odds of racetracks.
- **Luciano Moggi**, president of the Italian club Juventus, which organized a fixing ring in the 2004-2005 season.
- **Dan Tan**, Singaporean citizen seen by many as the Godfather of the match-fixing Asian syndicate.
- **Wilson Raj Perumal**, Singaporean match fixer responsible for hundreds of fixed matches around the world at club and international level.

---

## 4.2 Betting and Money Laundering

Recent work by Fiedler [42] noted that gambling and mainly online gambling are effective supports for money laundering because they do not involve a physical product, thereby making it much more complicated to track the flow of money and proof real vs. virtual turnover. Gambling winnings are tax free in many jurisdictions, thereby reducing the cost to launder money.

In recent decades money laundering has evolved from a byproduct of traditional criminal activity to a full-fledged, well-established, and tailored industry. The three steps of money laundering unanimously accepted by both investigators and academics are Placement, Layering, and Integration, deployed though various tools and through customized services offered by specialized entities. As the fastest growing type of gambling, sport betting is a perfect candidate for laundering funds due to the high volumes involved.

Recent estimates [39] revealed that 140 billion euros in illicit funds are laundered through illegal betting markets annually from the total betting market, estimated to be between 200 billion and 500 billion euros, more than 80% of which is wagered on illegal markets.

Figure 13 shows the money-laundering process through the sport betting market. The initial Placement phase is realized by inducing the illicit funds in the betting systems through "rogue" punters. A rogue gambler is an individual or a group that has access to various bookmakers from both legal and illegal markets. The bets are placed with the aim of circulating it through many buffers until the bet is cleared though an legal bookmaker. Once the rogue punter places the money through a over-the-counter system, involving for instance cash, the counterparty taking the bet is in charge of the Layering phase. Thus, an "illegal" bookmaker or illegal betting platform will hedge the bet on the legal market, directly or through another connection. The layering can be a very straightforward step involving an intermediary placing a bet through a legal online platform that does not check the origin of the funds in detail. In other cases it can involve a few individuals or even legal entities that provide hedging services for bookmaking companies. The final chain in the layering consists in placing the bet on the legal market an receiving the funds cleaned which will be transferred to the legal system, thereby accomplishing the Integration step.

## 4.3 Odds Manipulation

Betting odds manipulation is an avant-garde topic indirectly discussed by researchers and about which many investigators are not yet aware. The betting market can be manipulated

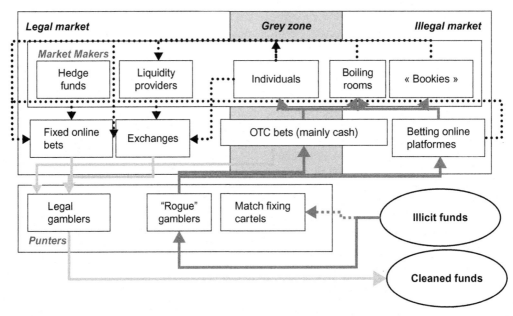

**FIGURE 13** Money laundering: Flows in the betting market for cleaning illicit funds. Dark gray arrows represent the flows related to Placement, Dashed arrows represent the flows related to Layering, and Clear gray arrows represent the flows related to Integration.

without altering the outcome of the game. Organized punters can place massive volumes on a bet or disseminate rogue information about an outcome of a match in order to provide momentum to that market. In these conditions the market will propose different odds and the manipulators will be able to liquidate their position and make a profit.

# 5 MODELING ASSOCIATION FOOTBALL OUTCOMES

For a better understanding of the betting market is it important to be able to compare the probability of the outcomes implied by the market with the probability estimates on a historical model. The models developed by Dixon and Coles [53] for fixed pre-match odds and by Dixon and Robinson [54] for dynamic live odds are among the most popular in the literature. Considering a similar framework for a set of $N$

teams let $X_{i,j}$ and $Y_{i,j}$ denote the number of goals scored in the match from team $i$ and team $j$ follow a Poisson distribution $\Lambda$ of intensities $\lambda$ and $\mu$ that are specific to that match:

$$X_{i,j} = \Lambda(\alpha_i, \beta_j, \gamma) \tag{11}$$

$$Y_{i,j} = \Lambda(\alpha_j, \beta_i) \tag{12}$$

The intensities depends on the offensive strength of the team $\alpha$ and on the defensive strength of the adversary *beta* corrected by the home factor *gamma*, corresponding to the advantage for the home team in the home matches:

$$\lambda_k = \alpha_{i(k)} \cdot \beta_{j(k)} \cdot \gamma \tag{13}$$

$$\mu_k = \alpha_{j(k)} \cdot \beta_{i(k)} \tag{14}$$

The probability that an outcome of the match between the teams $i$ and $j$ is $x - y$ given by a bivariate Poisson distribution. If a correlation factor $\rho$ is added mainly for the bias introduced by matches with a low number of goals, the probability proposed by Dixon and Coles [53] can be written as:

$$P(X_{i,j} = x, Y_{i,j} = y)$$
$$= \tau(x,y) \cdot \frac{\exp(-\lambda)\lambda^x}{x!} \cdot \frac{\exp(-\mu)\mu^y}{y!} \quad (15)$$

where the function $\tau(x,y)$ is expressed as:

$$\tau(x,y) = \begin{cases} 1 - \lambda\mu\rho & x = y = 0 \\ 1 + \lambda\rho & x = 1, y = 0 \\ 1 - \mu\rho & x = 0, y = 1 \\ 1 - \rho & x = y = 1 \\ 1 & \text{otherwise} \end{cases} \quad (16)$$

Parameters $\alpha$, $\beta$, $\gamma$, and $\rho$ can be estimated based on a historical data set of $M$ matches with score $x_k$-$y_k$ using a maximum-likelihood approach, the target function being:

$$LL(\alpha_{i(k)}, \beta_{i(k)}, \alpha_{j(k)}, \beta_{j(k)}, \gamma, \rho)$$
$$= \sum_{k=1}^{M} \log \left( \tau(x_k, y_k) \cdot \frac{\exp(-\lambda_k)\lambda_k^{x_k}}{x_k!} \cdot \frac{\exp(-\mu_k)\mu_k^{y_k}}{y_k!} \right) \quad (17)$$

The probabilities under the historical measure for a win, draw, and loss in a match between the teams $i$ and $j$ can be expressed as:

$$P(H, \lambda, \mu) = \sum_{l,m:l>m} P(X_{i,j} = l, Y_{i,j} = m | \lambda, \mu) \quad (18)$$

$$P(D, \lambda, \mu) = \sum_{l,m:l=m} P(X_{i,j} = l, Y_{i,j} = m | \lambda, \mu) \quad (19)$$

$$P(A, \lambda, \mu) = \sum_{l,m:l<m} P(X_{i,j} = l, Y_{i,j} = m | \lambda, \mu) \quad (20)$$

Nevertheless, similar to the derivatives markets the historical outcome forecast is different from bookmaker-implied outcomes. This affirmation is also supported by the research of Goddard and Asimakopoulos [55] and Kain and Logan [56], who assessed the efficiency of market bets in relationship to the historical forecast. For a given set of bookmaker odds $o_H, o_D, o_A$ the implied probabilities of the outcome are their inverses (which should be corrected by the margin effect).

We consider a set of variables $\lambda_k^p$ and $\mu_k^p$ as market premiums, which introduced in the pricing model of the outcome would provide results close to odds implied ones. These variables could be interpreted as a translation of the volatility mark-up from the derivatives world to the betting market:

$$\lambda_k^* = (\alpha_{i(k)} \cdot \beta_{j(k)} + \lambda_k^p) \cdot \gamma \quad (21)$$
$$\mu_k^* = \alpha_{j(k)} \cdot \beta_{i(k)} + \mu_k^p \quad (22)$$

The premium set $\lambda_k^p$ and $\mu_k^p$ can be calibrated by minimizing the absolute squared error (ASE) of the pricing model in regards to the market odds:

$$ASE(\lambda_k^p, \mu_k^p) = \left( \frac{1}{o_H} - P(H, \lambda^*, \mu^*) \right)^2$$
$$+ \left( \frac{1}{o_D} - P(D, \lambda^*, \mu^*) \right)^2$$
$$+ \left( \frac{1}{o_A} - P(A, \lambda^*, \mu^*) \right)^2 \quad (23)$$

# 6 DETECTION OF RIGGED MATCHES

Like many other financial markets the betting market is incomplete. Recall that a complete market is one in which there is an equilibrium price for every asset in every possible state of the world. In order for a market to be complete, it must be possible to construct any possible bets regarding any future state of the market with existing assets without friction.

In order to take into account the anticipation of the betting market regarding the outcome of the match here we introduce a market premium for both parameters $\lambda$ and $\mu$. To continue the analogy with the financial instrument let's assume that the premium is equivalent to the mark-up of the volatility that is used in pricing the vanilla option. Thus, there is a volatility premium that makes the implied volatility higher than the physical volatility. The volatility mark-up corresponds in some way to the profit of the option underwriter and also to his expectation that some massive disruption in the market might appear with huge variation, thereby involving a higher gamma risk.

Here $\lambda$ and $\mu$ would take into account the current information fixed odds might provide if punters had better recent information such as injuries, changes in management, specific patterns in direct matches with one specific team (i.e. Westham vs. Millwall). If the difference between the two premiums is significantly higher than zero the market adds a higher probability that the result will be more favorable (less adverse) to that team.

If both premiums are high but with no relevant difference, we could see a higher number of goals scored for that match. If both premiums are negative fewer goals in the match would be expected.

Anticipation might be linked to more than just knowledge. As will be shown the structure of the betting market is rather irrational and is dictated by the betting behavior of the punter. Bets should match the offer and demand of gamblers rather than the track records of the team. In football many bettors use personal affinity to a team or adversity to another in order to place a bet, rather than direct information about a team[16].

Sometimes bets are skewed if abrupt counterintuitive information appears in the market as is the case with allegations of rigged games.

---

[16]For example, a golden unspoken rule of punters on Serie B and C matches was to stay in the betting agencies and to watch the people who enter. Seeing a man would mean victory home, a woman victory away, and child a draw.

In some cases, rumors are leaked in the market, which is reflected in the bet's structure. This collusion occurs in two ways:

- Information goes to regular gamblers that use it as a hint. This information spread affects the demand to the bookmaker, which will automatically skew the odds. Let's not forget the infamous Frank Rosenthal from the iconic Oscar-winning movie "Casino" who was said "to be able to change the odds of all bookies in the country".
- Some rigging groups influence the match odds through various methods and make appropriate bets on the market. This type of behavior mainly occurs on the illegal market. The role of the transnational betting markets is fundamental. However, illegal bookmakers use legal markets in order to hedge the primary bets or to find liquidity. The primary bets on the illegal market are often big, thus the impact on the legal market is massive and again induces a regime switch in the way bets are made.

In theory, both mechanisms would have as result a strong difference in the risk premiums of the model parameters. If a fixed game occurs, and under the assumptions that there is some efficiency in the betting market, the implied parameters of the model from the bet odds could be very different. In order to see the impact it is necessary to compute the probability of the final score on the basis of the parameters calibrated under a physical measure and of those calibrated on a market implied measure. The study of the time series of the difference between $s_t = \lambda_t - \mu_t$ can provide relevant information of systemic rigging occur. Figure 14 shows the evolution of the spread estimated for various bookmaker odds for the English Premier League games.

Figure 15 shows the evolution of the spread for teams playing in the English Conference. Table 10 gives the yearly average of the spread computed for a few teams. For the 2013 season, that had strong suspicions of match fixing, teams

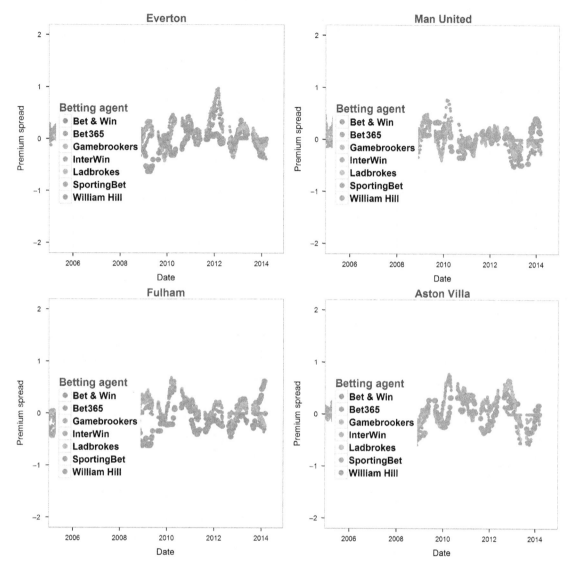

**FIGURE 14** Evolution of the spread estimated for the English Premier League games.

like Kidderminster show a sudden change in the average premium, which becomes negative. The sudden changes in the spread can be explained in the odds adjustment when the volumes are not compatible with the historical probabilities of the game.

Figures 16 and 17 show the evolution of the spread for teams playing in the Turkish League. Table 11 shows the yearly average spreads for each bookmaker. Again, a strong negative effect is seen for Fenerbahce in the 2010 season, which involved many "thrown" games.

The probability of the realized outcome can be computed with the historical parameters or with the odds-implied parameters. In an ideal

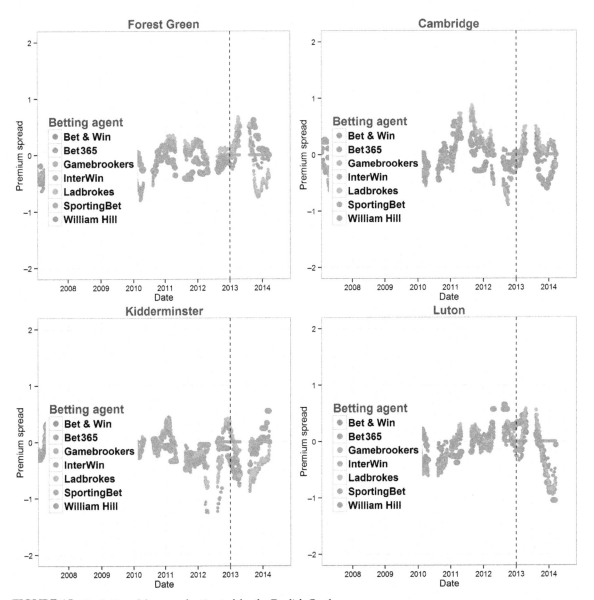

**FIGURE 15**  Evolution of the spread estimated for the English Conference.

world the difference between both would be small and centered. Figure 18 shows this difference for Fenerbahce, reflecting that after 2010 the difference was skewed toward the odds-implied probability.

The Calcioscommesse scandal initially had repercussions in the odds market as can be seen in Figure 19. For instance, Siena and Novara showed strongly negative premium spreads during the 2010-2011 season in Serie B.

**TABLE 10** Yearly Average of the Spread Estimated for the English Conference. The Bold Values Correspond to Abnormal Estimations of the Average Spread

| Team | Year | Bet365 | BetWin | GameBrokers | Interwin | Ladbrokes | Sportingbet |
|---|---|---|---|---|---|---|---|
| Forest Green | 2008 | −0.16 | −0.32 | −0.34 | −0.32 | −0.32 | −0.34 |
| | 2009 | 0.06 | −0.15 | −0.15 | −0.08 | −0.12 | −0.16 |
| | 2010 | −0.11 | 0.09 | 0.05 | 0.06 | 0.15 | 0.09 |
| | 2011 | −0.33 | 0.05 | 0.01 | 0.03 | 0.04 | 0.04 |
| | 2012 | −0.02 | 0.07 | 0.07 | 0.02 | 0.20 | 0.00 |
| | 2013 | 0.16 | **−0.35** | 0.00 | **−0.30** | **−0.26** | 0.00 |
| Aldershot | 2007 | −0.09 | −0.09 | −0.10 | −0.08 | −0.02 | −0.08 |
| | 2013 | **−0.27** | **−0.30** | 0.00 | **−0.28** | **−0.30** | 0.00 |
| Hereford | 2012 | −0.15 | −0.18 | −0.18 | −0.19 | 0.00 | 0.00 |
| | 2013 | −0.00 | 0.11 | 0.00 | 0.04 | 0.19 | 0.00 |
| Kidderminster | 2008 | −0.04 | −0.07 | −0.03 | −0.15 | 0.03 | −0.08 |
| | 2009 | 0.02 | 0.04 | 0.06 | 0.00 | 0.10 | 0.04 |
| | 2010 | −0.11 | 0.04 | −0.01 | −0.01 | 0.07 | 0.06 |
| | 2011 | −0.20 | −0.21 | −0.24 | −0.22 | −0.06 | −0.22 |
| | 2012 | −0.32 | −0.01 | −0.01 | −0.08 | −0.07 | 0.00 |
| | 2013 | 0.09 | −0.27 | 0.00 | −0.28 | −0.15 | 0.00 |
| Halifax | 2013 | −0.47 | −0.46 | 0.00 | −0.54 | −0.50 | 0.00 |
| Salisbury | 2008 | 0.09 | 0.14 | 0.08 | 0.08 | 0.16 | 0.09 |
| | 2009 | 0.10 | 0.10 | 0.12 | 0.10 | 0.20 | 0.15 |
| | 2013 | 0.00 | −0.16 | 0.00 | −0.24 | −0.16 | 0.00 |
| Cambridge | 2008 | 0.07 | 0.26 | 0.24 | 0.20 | 0.24 | 0.18 |
| | 2009 | −0.15 | −0.01 | −0.01 | −0.08 | 0.00 | 0.00 |
| | 2010 | −0.01 | 0.06 | 0.11 | −0.02 | 0.22 | 0.19 |
| | 2011 | −0.01 | 0.24 | 0.26 | 0.18 | 0.34 | 0.28 |
| | 2012 | −0.06 | −0.07 | −0.07 | −0.09 | −0.04 | 0.00 |
| | 2013 | −0.30 | −0.04 | 0.00 | −0.06 | 0.12 | 0.00 |

# 7 AMERICAN FOOTBALL

American football with its main National Football League (NFL) is one of four popular professional sports in the United States. In terms of average salaries only English Premier League NBA, Indian Premier League and Major League generate more revenue as shown in Figure 20.

Since North America (and in particular the United States) has very strict laws concerning

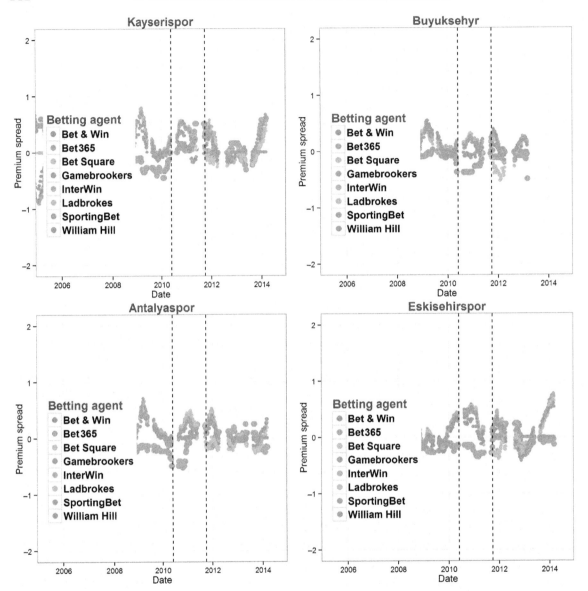

**FIGURE 16**  Evolution of the spread for teams playing in the Turkish league.

betting, match rigging appears to be less frequent than in Europe. Figure 21 shows the evolution of the overround for the NFL games including the playoff games over the past decade. The average margin is around 4%. Nonetheless, in 2014 the overround shrunk to almost 2%. In general,

the margin structure in the NFL is smaller than in the European Football Association.

One of the great football players, Charles Aaron "Bubba" Smith, who died in 2011, claimed that the 1969 Super Bowl between his Baltimore Colts and the New York Jets was

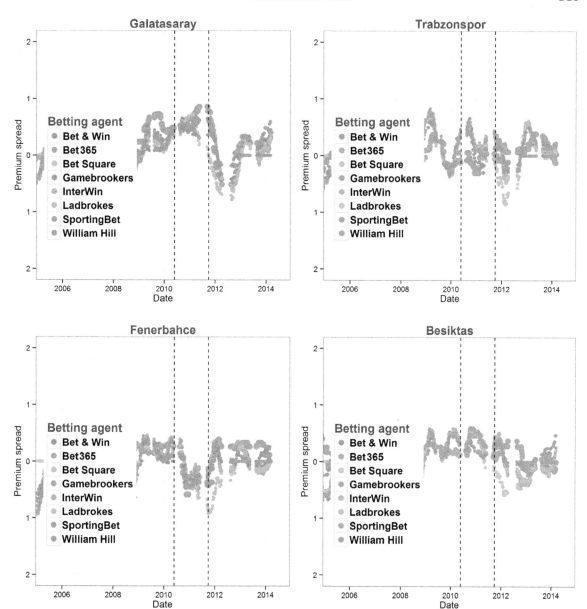

FIGURE 17    Evolution of the spread for teams playing in the Turkish league.

**TABLE 11**  Yearly Average Spread for Teams Playing in the Turkish League

| Team | Year | Bet365 | | BetWin | GameBrokers | Interwin | Ladbrokes | Sportingbet |
|---|---|---|---|---|---|---|---|---|
| | 2005 | 0.09 | 0.00 | 0.02 | 0.00 | −0.12 | 0.02 | −0.03 |
| | 2006 | 0.18 | 0.00 | −0.05 | −0.22 | −0.18 | −0.20 | −0.08 |
| | 2007 | 0.21 | −0.23 | −0.14 | −0.14 | −0.13 | −0.25 | −0.18 |
| | 2008 | 0.18 | 0.23 | 0.20 | 0.18 | 0.27 | 0.00 | 0.23 |
| Fenerbahce | 2009 | 0.40 | 0.30 | 0.34 | 0.36 | 0.39 | 0.21 | 0.28 |
| | 2010 | −0.24 | −0.02 | 0.03 | 0.05 | 0.08 | −0.05 | 0.04 |
| | 2011 | 0.10 | −0.71 | 0.11 | 0.15 | 0.12 | 0.16 | 0.17 |
| | 2012 | 0.26 | 0.12 | 0.12 | 0.12 | 0.16 | 0.12 | 0.00 |
| | 2013 | 0.24 | 0.00 | 0.00 | 0.00 | −0.04 | 0.00 | 0.00 |
| | 2005 | −0.49 | 0.00 | 0.02 | 0.01 | −0.12 | −0.08 | −0.05 |
| | 2006 | −0.28 | 0.00 | −0.20 | −0.19 | −0.28 | −0.26 | −0.18 |
| | 2007 | −0.38 | −0.26 | −0.12 | −0.09 | −0.14 | −0.08 | −0.15 |
| | 2008 | −0.12 | 0.14 | 0.16 | 0.11 | 0.05 | 0.04 | 0.14 |
| Kayserispor | 2009 | −0.32 | −0.08 | −0.12 | −0.12 | −0.13 | −0.07 | −0.14 |
| | 2010 | 0.20 | 0.38 | 0.37 | 0.42 | 0.38 | 0.31 | 0.40 |
| | 2011 | 0.00 | −0.26 | 0.00 | 0.05 | 0.18 | 0.12 | 0.05 |
| | 2012 | −0.02 | 0.05 | −0.00 | −0.00 | 0.06 | 0.00 | 0.00 |
| | 2013 | 0.26 | 0.00 | 0.33 | 0.00 | 0.22 | 0.16 | 0.00 |
| | 2005 | 0.16 | 0.00 | 0.25 | 0.06 | −0.03 | 0.13 | −0.00 |
| | 2006 | 0.12 | 0.00 | −0.20 | −0.22 | −0.30 | −0.26 | −0.24 |
| | 2007 | 0.05 | 0.14 | 0.20 | 0.16 | 0.14 | 0.04 | 0.06 |
| | 2008 | 0.06 | 0.09 | 0.06 | 0.13 | 0.12 | 0.03 | 0.14 |
| Galatasaray | 2009 | 0.55 | 0.32 | 0.42 | 0.38 | 0.43 | 0.29 | 0.38 |
| | 2010 | 0.52 | 0.61 | 0.65 | 0.60 | 0.68 | 0.68 | 0.66 |
| | 2011 | 0.13 | −0.70 | 0.38 | 0.31 | 0.42 | 0.26 | 0.29 |
| | 2012 | 0.08 | −0.06 | −0.04 | −0.04 | −0.16 | 0.00 | 0.00 |
| | 2013 | 0.27 | 0.00 | 0.22 | 0.00 | 0.09 | 0.16 | 0.00 |
| | 2005 | 0.30 | 0.00 | 0.26 | 0.12 | −0.00 | 0.20 | 0.23 |
| | 2006 | 0.38 | 0.00 | 0.20 | 0.20 | 0.05 | 0.08 | 0.17 |
| Besiktas | 2007 | 0.35 | 0.34 | 0.42 | 0.41 | 0.34 | 0.36 | 0.36 |
| | 2008 | 0.19 | 0.38 | 0.29 | 0.33 | 0.29 | 0.02 | 0.33 |
| | 2009 | 0.10 | 0.19 | 0.28 | 0.21 | 0.28 | 0.19 | 0.24 |
| | 2010 | 0.36 | 0.54 | 0.49 | 0.52 | 0.44 | 0.46 | 0.46 |
| | 2011 | 0.28 | −0.36 | 0.38 | 0.35 | 0.36 | 0.28 | 0.39 |
| | 2012 | −0.03 | −0.24 | −0.19 | −0.19 | −0.29 | −0.22 | 0.00 |
| | 2013 | 0.05 | 0.00 | 0.01 | 0.00 | −0.04 | 0.03 | 0.00 |

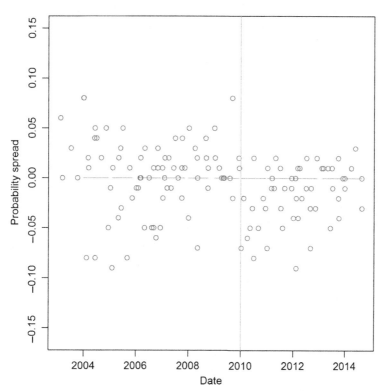

**FIGURE 18** Evolution of the difference between the historical probability and the William Hill-implied probability of the realized score for Fenerbahce.

fixed.[17] Back then the Jets beat the Colts, the favorites in Super Bowl III, in one of the biggest in America professional sports history.

A more recent allegation[18] was made in 2015 after the Seattle Seahawks victory over the Denver Broncos at the NFL's 48th Super Bowl with a final score of 43-8. Some allegations claim that the Broncos intentionally lost the championship in exchange for a large amount of money.

While the likelihood of these allegations is difficult to judge, the extrapolation of the Dixon and Coles [53] model is straightforward for American football. The probability that an outcome of a match between the teams $i$ and $j$ is $x - y$ is given by a bivariate Poisson distribution. The correlation factor $\rho$ added mainly for bias introduced by soccer matches with a low number of goals is dismissed and thus the probability can be written as:

$$P(X_{i,j} = x, Y_{i,j} = y) = \frac{\exp(-\lambda)\lambda^x}{x!} \cdot \frac{\exp(-\mu)\mu^y}{y!}$$

(24)

[17]Bubba Smith Always Alleged 1969 Super Bowl was Fixed, http://www.ibtimes.com/bubba-smith-always-alleged-69-super-bowl-was-fixed-823441.
[18]Super Bowl XLVIII Believed to have been Rigged and Currently Under Investigation by NFL, http://huzlers.com/superbowl-xlviii-believed-to-have-been-rigged-and-currently-under-investigation-by-nfl/.

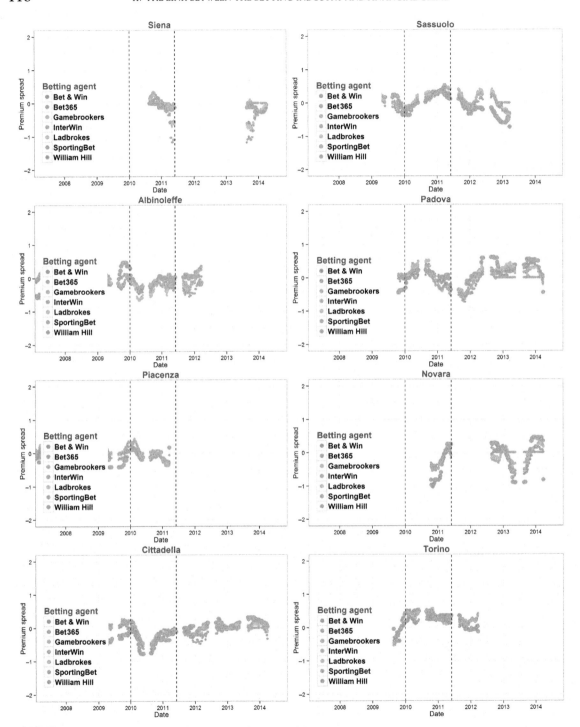

**FIGURE 19** Premium spread for various team in Serie B (Italy).

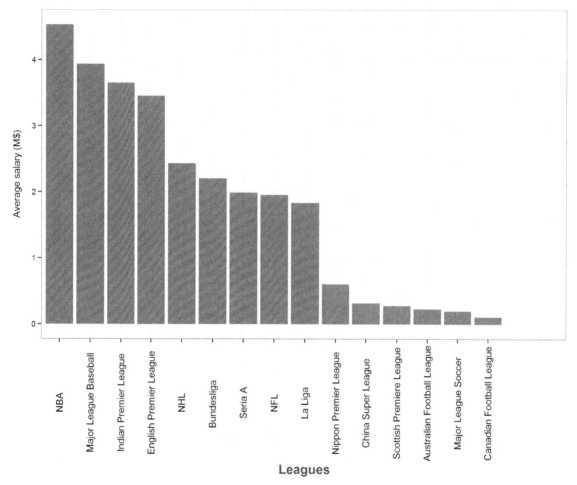

**FIGURE 20** Average salaries in professional sport leagues (2013 data).

The probabilities under the historical measure for a win and loss in an NFL match between teams $i$ and $j$ can be expressed as:

$$P(H, \lambda, \mu) = \sum_{l,m:l>m} P(X_{i,j} = l, Y_{i,j} = m|\lambda, \mu) \quad (25)$$

$$P(A, \lambda, \mu) = \sum_{l,m:l<m} P(X_{i,j} = l, Y_{i,j} = m|\lambda, \mu) \quad (26)$$

For a given set of bookmaker odds $o_H, o_D, o_A$ the implied probabilities of the outcome are their inverses (which should be corrected by the margin effect). As done before, let's consider a set of variables $\lambda_k^p$ and $\mu_k^p$ as market premiums, which introduced in the pricing model of the outcome would provide results close to the odds-implied ones.

$$\lambda_k^* = (\alpha_{i(k)} \cdot \beta_{j(k)} + \lambda_k^p) \cdot \gamma \quad (27)$$

$$\mu_k^* = \alpha_{j(k)} \cdot \beta_{i(k)} + \mu_k^p \quad (28)$$

The premium set $\lambda_k^p$ and $\mu_k^p$ can be calibrated by minimizing the absolute squared error (ASE) of the pricing model in regards to market odds:

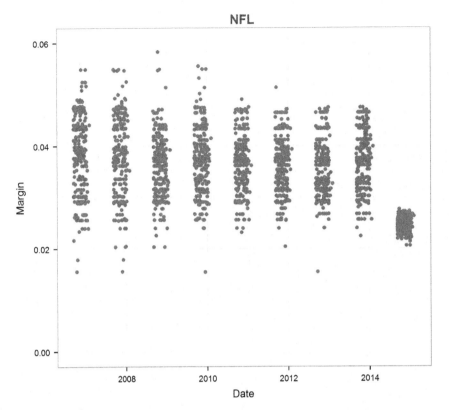

**FIGURE 21**  NFL overround.

$$ASE(\lambda_k^p, \mu_k^p) = \left( \frac{1}{o_H} - P(H, \lambda^*, \mu^*) \right)^2$$
$$+ \left( \frac{1}{o_A} - P(A, \lambda^*, \mu^*) \right)^2 \quad (29)$$

After estimating the betting odds-implied premiums, the next step in assessing whether bets capture abnormal information is to compute the spread as $s_t = \mu_t^p - \mu_t^p$. For the NFL it would be more relevant to compare regular season games to play-off games. In the structure of the NFL competition the play-off games have an increased importance. This is different from other sports like association football, where each game of the season has the same weight in deciding the competition win-

ner. Therefore, the following analysis benchmarks the spread premium computed through the described approach for regular and play-off games. Theoretically a team that had a certain pattern during the regular season should keep the same pattern in the play-offs with some noise added in due to the higher pressure of the play-offs.

Figure 22 shows the evolution of the spread premium for a teams playing at home and in regular and the play-off games. As a general observation it appears that home playing teams have a positive spread, thereby denoting a propensity of punters for the home team independently of the track record of that team. Compared to the soccer analysis the NFL teams do not show those big swings in premium from negative to positive, a sign that there is less abnormal information

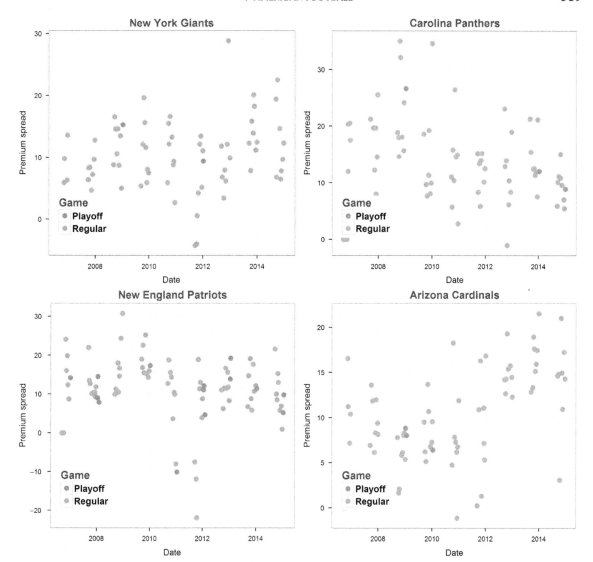

FIGURE 22 Evolution of the spread premium. The spread premium for the play-off games is very close in value to the regular season, underlining the fact that there is positive correlation between the performance of the team in the regular season and the performance during the playoff.

for the opening odds and less asymmetry in the betting patterns.

The spread premium for the play-off games is very close in value to that from the regular season, underlining the fact that there is a positive correlation between the performance of the team in the regular season and the performance during the play-offs.

The evolution of the spreads premium for Denver Broncos and Seattle Seahawks are shown in Figure 23 and Figure 24 for the home and away games respectively.

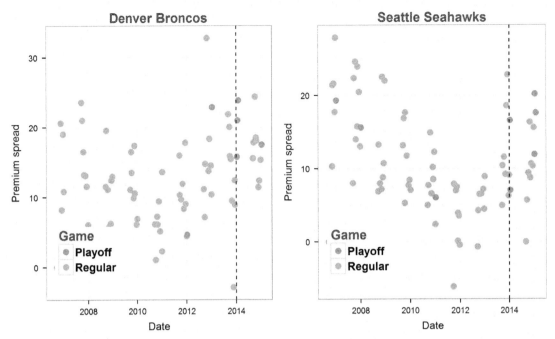

FIGURE 23   Evolution of the spread premium for Denver Broncos and Seattle Seahawks in the home games. The 2014 play-off game is indicated by a dashed line.

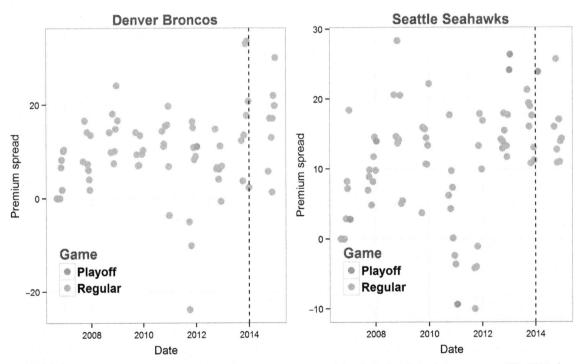

FIGURE 24   Evolution of the spread premium for Denver Broncos and Seattle Seahawks in the away games. The 2014 play-off game is indicated by a dashed line. The last game of the 2014 playoff from the right graph has a premium higher than the season average.

The spread premium for both teams during the 2014 play-off is in the range of that from the regular season. The only exception is the last game, which has a premium higher than the season. Thus, the Broncos were perceived as having a better chance to win, compared to their previous track record. Based on this finding the fairness of the game cannot be rejected, although intra-match betting data could provide additional information.

## 8 OUTLOOK

Professional sports show strong growth in revenues and also provide a favorable environment to the betting industry. Over the past 5 years both speculative allegations and courts decisions have highlighted at financial crime within the betting sector. The two main financial crimes in the betting market are match fixing and money laundering.

Match fixing is an old phenomena that was amplified by the development of the betting market. Classic match fixing to obtain a better position in a tournament is traditionally independent of betting markets. Although collusion could exit and the odds might reflect this inside information in the market. Match fixing in relation to betting aims to alter the outcome of the game though bribery in order to generate profits on the betting market. Abnormal betting patterns can be a predicting signal for this phenomena. Odds manipulation is a relatively new phenomena, similar to the manipulation of financial markets. In the dynamic market exchanges a punter or a group of punters could place bets or spread information that could alter the odds. Profit can be made through strategies at various stages of the game.

The study of the margin structures in sports can provide relevant information about the inefficiencies of the market related to the information available about a game or tournament. The models for assessing the likelihood of an outcome for a game are mainly driven by econometric estimation based on the track records of a team or player. Measuring the market premium quoted through the bookmakers odds can provide relevant information in order to assess abnormal patterns in betting.

The betting market can be used at all three stages of money laundering and leverages itself in the gray zone that exists between the legal and illegal betting markets. Thus, the gray zone allows funds to circulate from the criminal underworld to the legitimate betting market, thereby offering a straightforward channel for money laundering.

# PART II

# FORENSIC STATISTICS AS AN INVESTIGATION TOOL (THEORETICAL BACKGROUND)

# 2A

# Truth: A Game of Probabilities

The use of forensic sciences in courtrooms has become more prevalent with the increased sophistication of the investigation tools. Primary statistics are widely employed by attorneys to build their cases. A new use of statistics has emerged in litigations involving labor markets, antitrusts, and securities market cases. Nonetheless, statistical results can be easily twisted and taken out of context in order to support biased conclusions. Therefore, in courts of law the wrong judgments are made based on biased inferences.

The prosecutor's fallacy introduced by Thompson and Schumann [57] is an inconsistent statistical reasoning made in law when the context in which the accused has been brought to court is falsely assumed to be irrelevant when weighing the evidence. The prosecutor's fallacy can arise from the wrong interpretation of conditional probabilities or from data "overmining" such as when evidence is compared against a large database.

A classic example of the prosecutor's fallacy discussed in the literature Dwyer [58] is the highly publicized case of Sally Clark. Two of Sally's babies died prematurely a few weeks after birth. During a trial where she was accused of murder a medical expert witness drew on published studies to obtain a figure for the frequency of sudden infant death syndrome (SIDS) in families having some of the characteristics of the defendant's family. The probability of the event $D_1$ of death as a result of SIDS is 1 in 8500. The expert inferred a value of 1 in 73 million for the frequency of two events $D_1$ and $D_2$ of SIDS:

$$\mathbf{P}(D_1) = \frac{1}{8500} \rightarrow \mathbf{P}(D_1, D_2)$$
$$= \left(\frac{1}{8500}\right)^2 \equiv \frac{1}{73{,}000{,}000} \qquad (1)$$

In the year 2000, this led to the conviction of Sally Clark for double homicide. After the conviction, the Royal Statistical Society[1] published a note about the court's verdict:

> This approach is, in general, statistically invalid. It would only be valid if SIDS cases arose independently within families, an assumption that would need to be justified empirically. Not only was no such empirical justification provided in the case, but there are very strong a priori reasons for supposing that the

___

[1]Royal Statistical Society concerned by issues raised in Sally Clark case http://www.sallyclark.org.uk/RSS.html.

assumption will be false. [...] The well-publicized figure of 1 in 73 million thus has no statistical basis [...]
*(Source: RSS www.rss.org.uk 23rd Oct. 2001)*

In the aftermath Clark was released from jail in 2003 after winning an appeal but died four years later of alcoholism.

Fenton and Neil [59] showed that lawyers just like ordinary members of the public fall victim to arguments that have been known to mathematicians for decades to be fallacies. They also show how the prosecutor's and jury observation fallacies arise from a basic misunderstanding of conditional probability and Bayes' theorem.

If $\mathbf{P}(E)$ is the probability of having a piece of evidence $E$ in a case and $\mathbf{P}(I)$ is the probability an individual is innocent Bayes' theorem shows that the probability of having an innocent person given the occurrence of evidence is:

$$\mathbf{P}(I|E) = \frac{\mathbf{P}(I \cap E)}{\mathbf{P}(E)} = \mathbf{P}(E|I)\frac{\mathbf{P}(I)}{\mathbf{P}(E)} \qquad (2)$$

and therefore the conditional probabilities are not equal

$$P(I|E) \neq P(E|I) \qquad (3)$$

The prosecutor's fallacy usually results in assuming that the prior probability that a piece of evidence occurs conditionally to the defendant being an innocent person is equal to the probability that the defendant is innocent given the occurrence of the evidence:

$$P(I|E) = P(E|I)$$

Let's assume that on a trading floor with 200 operators there are suspicions of unauthorized

trading during a given period and the internal control decides to audit the trades of each operator. Trading book reviews establish that five traders have a high number of canceled trades during a specific period. Following the investigations one trader is fired and charged. The controllers affirm that the probability that the evidence occurs for a normal trader $\mathbf{P}(E|N)$ is very low, around 2%.

$$\mathbf{P}(E|N) = \frac{P(E \cap N)}{P(N)} = \frac{4/200}{199/200} = \frac{4}{200} \cong 2\% \qquad (4)$$

The accused trader defends himself by twisting this statistic and noting that the probability of being normal given the evidence is much higher at around 80%.

$$\mathbf{P}(N|E) = \frac{\mathbf{P}(N \cap E)}{\mathbf{P}(E)} = \frac{4/200}{5/200} = \frac{4}{5} \cong 80\% \qquad (5)$$

A court decision can be considered as a statistical hypothesis test, which rejects or fails to reject a defined null hypothesis. For example, a test could assess if the number of canceled trades is associated with a higher risk of unauthorized trading. A conclusion due to random error that the null hypothesis should be rejected, when no difference actually exists, is referred to as a "false-positive" or "Type I error." Conversely, a conclusion to fail to reject the null hypothesis, when a difference actually exists, is referred to as a "false-negative" or "Type II error." Type I and Type II errors are also known respectively as $\alpha$ and $\beta$ errors, where $\alpha$ and $\beta$ are probabilities of these errors as shown in Table 1.

TABLE 1  Type I and Type II Errors

| Statistical conclusion/reality | Null hypothesis is true: innocent | Null hypothesis is false: guilty |
|---|---|---|
| Fail to reject the null hypothesis: **Innocent** | Correct decision $\mathbf{P} = 1 - \alpha$ | False negative $\mathbf{P} = \beta$ |
| Reject null hypothesis: **Guilty** | False positive $\mathbf{P} = \alpha$ | Correct decision $\mathbf{P} = 1 - \beta$ |

Notes: *$\alpha$ is the probability of being considered guilty when in reality one is innocent. $\beta$ is the probability that one walks the court but in reality is guilty.*

Another important source of the prosecutor's fallacy is multiple testing when a big data set is assessed. Let's assume for instance that a brokerage house is searching for a suspicious trade executed on a certain stock at a certain date for a certain volume. The broker has 1 million accounts and the probability of a chance match for that pattern is 1 in 5 million. Thus, the probability of finding a match in the broker accounts is almost 18%:

$$P(I) = 1 - (1 - \frac{1}{5,000,000})^{1,000,000} = 18.1\% \quad (6)$$

Even if a suspicious trade did not occur in that account there is a non-null probability of finding a pattern identical to the first one.

Data dredging, sometimes referred to as "data fishing" or "data snooping" is a data-mining practice in which large volumes of information are analyzed with the special purpose to find a particular result or relationship. Sometimes *overmining* data leads to biased conclusions. Data dredging is sometimes described as searching more information in a data set even if actually the data set does not contain. This dredging effect can be voluntary when the analyst knows he wants to emphasize statistically something that does not exist. Therefore, one of the risks of empirical data-mining risk is that it is possible to discover meaningless or rogue knowledge. In one of the very first papers addressing the use of statistics in the courtroom Rubinfeld [60] showed how regression results could be misleading in a case. A classic example of data dredging in financial times series was provided by Leinweber [61], who showed that butter production in Bangladesh explains 75% of the variations in the S&P 500 over 10 years.

The concept of data dredging is synthesized in Bonferroni's principle, which states that if a method of finding significant items returns significantly more items than expected in the actual population, it can be assumed that most of the items found are not genuine. In the example of the broker's accounts the auditors might find

180,000 accounts when in fact none are suspicious. This means an algorithm or method for searching a particular set of data actually returns more false positives as it returns larger portions of the data than should be within that category.

Rajaraman and Ullman [62] show that for a certain amount of data, when looking for events of a certain type within that data one can expect events of this type to occur, even if the data is completely random, the number of occurrences of these events will grow as the size of the data grows. These occurrences are bogus, in the sense that they have no relevant cause other than the fact that random data will always have some number of unusual features that look significant but in reality are not.

A straightforward way to address cases where data present false positives is the Bonferroni correction [63]. It is a way to assess the conceptual soundness of cases that may fuel conspiracy theories and avoid most of the false positive responses in a search of the data.

The Bonferroni correction is a multiple-comparison correction used when several dependent or independent statistical tests are being performed simultaneously. The basic idea behind this correction is that a given $\alpha$ value may be appropriate at an individual level of a test, but it might not be appropriate for the set of all hypothesis tests. To avoid a lot of false positives, the alpha value needs to be lowered to account for the number of comparisons being performed [64].

The simplest and most conservative approach provided by the Bonferroni correction is to set the $\alpha$ value for the entire set of $n$ hypothesis tests equal to $\alpha$ by taking the confidence level value for each test equal to $\alpha/n$.

Let's assume a set of $n$ hypothesis tests denoted $\mathbf{T}_i$, where $i \in \overline{1,n}$ for hypothesis $\mathbf{H}_i$ under the assumption $\mathbf{H}_0$ that all hypotheses $\mathbf{H}_i$ are false. If the individual critical values for the test are lower or equal to $\alpha/n$:

$$\mathbf{P}(\mathbf{T}_i|\mathbf{H}_0) \leq \alpha/n \quad (7)$$

$\forall\ i\ \in\ \overline{1, n}$, then the experiment-wide critical value is:

$$P(\exists\ i\ \mathbf{T}_i | \mathbf{H}_0) \leq \alpha \qquad (8)$$

To illustrate Bonferroni's principle let's assume two data sets of the same length (i.e., 1000) normally distributed and independent with a Pearson correlation equal to zero. If two subsamples of 30 observations are chosen randomly from both sets and the correlation is computed between the subsample, the results can be surprising. When repeating the subsampling for a very large number of times the distribution of the resulting correlation is as shown in Figure 1.

The distribution of the $p$-value for the simulated samples is reflected in Figure 2, which shows uniform shape with about 5% of the sample having a relevant correlation value with a 95% confidence interval value. This finding would probably lead the data miner to the conclusion that there might be some dependency between the two sets. Therefore, the Bonferroni correction presented above implies that all the samples have a $p$-value lower than $\alpha/n$ in order to accept that the $p$-value for all tests is $\alpha$. For $\alpha$ equal to 5% and a total number of tests equal to 5000, none of the tests meet the condition, thereby implying that the experiments wide $p$-value is not inferior that 5%. Even when the miner does choose the sample selecting only those with acceptable $p$-values, the Bonferroni correction would not validate this embellished version of the experiment.

With a clear-cut framework and an appropriate understanding of the hypothesis that is tested and correct use of the statistical inferences almost anything can be proved anytime. Therefore, the use of statistics in investigations should be weighted by both ethical considerations and good sense [65, 66].

In the case of financial markets, statistics are designed to note irregularities and to emphasize differences among samples or tendencies in times series. With the emergence of big data and big data exploration the use of statistics and mining is becoming more common. Thus,

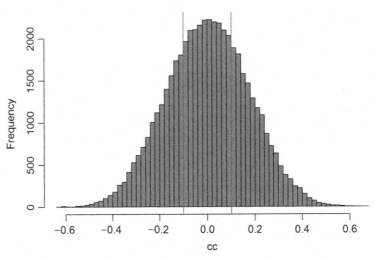

**Correlation for all samples**

FIGURE 1  Example of Bonferroni's principle: Random subsamples from two independent normally distributed data sets can be statistically correlated.

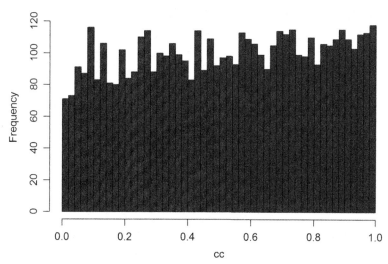

**FIGURE 2**  Example of Bonferroni's principle: Distribution of the $p$-values for the estimated correlation among the samples.

prosecutors and investigators use these tools for surveillance and also as evidence in courtrooms. The form under which statistics are used in the financial world as well as in investigatory work is continuously being reshaped due to the arrival of new markets, new products, and new types of crimes. Nonetheless, the principles of the methods remain the same and avoiding fallacies is crucial.

## 1 OUTLOOK

While prosecutors, defenders, and jury's fallacies are well described in the literature, there is a new type of fallacy in financial crime, called the fraudster's fallacy. Evidence is hard to alter in the real world but easier to change in the digital-based financial world. When a white collar crime takes place a fraudster will try to cover up the crime and change the facts in order to throw investigators off their trail or to delay prosecution. Financial offenders, whether they act in markets or elsewhere, will always try to deploy their scam in moments of volatility changing regime in the markets or political unrest in order to pass under the radar of the tests used by regulators and investigators.

# Statistical Distributions

## 1 FINANCIAL ASSET DYNAMICS

The most frequent law used in financial modeling for capturing the information contained inside the historical time series is Gaussian distribution (Geometric Brownian Motion) and its different variations regarding mean reversion and jumps:

- A Geometric Brownian Motion (GBM) is a continuous-time stochastic process in which the logarithm of the randomly varying quantity follows a Brownian motion. In this model proportional changes in the asset prices, denoted by $S$, are assumed to have constant instantaneous drift $\mu$, and volatility $\sigma$. The mathematical description of this property is given by the following stochastic differential equation:

$$\frac{\mathrm{d}S}{S} = \mu \cdot \mathrm{d}t + \sigma \cdot \mathrm{d}B \qquad (1)$$

Here $\mathrm{d}S$ represents the increment in the asset price process during a small interval of time $\mathrm{d}t$, and $\mathrm{d}B$ is the underlying uncertainly driving the model and represents an increment in a Wiener process during time $\mathrm{d}t$.

In fact, the presence of drifts in many returns times series is not economically proven. Some time series like U.S. equities series built by Schwert [68] and Siegel [69] are closer in the long run to a Gaussian model than other types are.

- In order to enrich the GBM model the mean-reversion characteristic can be introduced. The mean-reverting stochastic behavior is traditionally a characteristic of commodity spot prices and can be understood by looking at the one-factor model developed by Schwartz [7] and Campbell et al. [70] and applied to energy prices by Knittel and Roberts [71]. It is given by the following equation:

$$\frac{dS}{S} = -\alpha \cdot (\ln(S) - m) \cdot dt + \sigma \cdot dB \quad (2)$$

In this model, the spot price mean reverts to the long-term level $\overline{S}$ with $m = \ln(\overline{S})$ at a speed given by the mean reversion rate $\alpha$ and volatility $\sigma > 0$. The consequences of mean reversion can be understood by looking at the first term of Equation 2. If the spot price $S$ is above the long-term level $S$, the drift of the spot price will be negative and the price will tend to revert back toward the long-term level. Similarly, if the spot price is below the long-term level, then the drift will be positive and the price will tend to move back toward the long-term level. Defining $x = \ln S$, the conditional distribution of $x_t \mid x_{t-1}$ is given by the following expression:

$$x_t|x_{t-1} \sim N(c + \beta \cdot x_{t-1}, \sigma_\epsilon^2) \quad (3)$$

where $c = m^*(1 - e^{-\alpha})$, $\beta = e^{-\alpha}$, and $N$ denotes the Gaussian law with variance $\sigma_\epsilon{}^2$ equal to $\sigma^2(1 - e^{-2\alpha})/2\alpha$.

- To be free of the assumption that the conditional distribution of the logarithm of the security's prices is normal, the mean-reverting model can be enhanced to accommodate large movements (jumps) in spot prices. Such a popular extension of the standard mean-reverting diffusion process is the mean-reverting jump-diffusion process. A relatively simple mean-reverting jump-diffusion model for spot prices is described by the following equation:

$$\frac{dS}{S} = \alpha \cdot (\ln(S) - m)dt + \sigma \cdot dB + \kappa \cdot dQ \quad (4)$$

where the parameters are the same as in the simple mean-reverting model, $\kappa$ represents the frequency Poisson distribution of average $\lambda$, and $dQ$ is the Gaussian jump metric. Due to the introduction of jumps there are some extra parameters that come

into the model [72]. If there is abnormal information, a jump occurs and the log-price is drawn from a conditional normal distribution with mean $c + \beta \cdot x_{t-1} + \mu_\kappa$ and variance $\sigma_\varepsilon^2 + \sigma_\kappa^2$. Hence, a mean-reverting jump-diffusion process can be written as a Gaussian mixture:

$$x_t|x_{t-1} \sim (1-\lambda)\cdot N(c+\beta\cdot x_{t-1}, \sigma_\epsilon^2) + \lambda\cdot N(\mu_\kappa, \sigma_\kappa^2) \quad (5)$$

where $\mu_\kappa$ is average size of a jump and $\sigma_\kappa^2$ is the variance of the jumps.

- The existence of jumps create switches, thus we can also consider the simplest model to be as the previous one, considering a special case of the regime-switching model introduced by Hamilton [73] with a mixture of Gaussian distributions. Such modeling means that, at each time period, if there is no arrival of "abnormal" information (an event with a probability $(1-\lambda)$) the next log price is drawn by a conditional normal distribution with mean $\mu$ and variance $\sigma^2$, and if we have an arrival of "abnormal" information, a jump occurs and the log price is drawn from a conditional normal distribution with mean $\mu + \mu_\kappa$ and variance $\sigma^2 + \sigma_\kappa^2$, then the model is:

$$x_t \sim \lambda \cdot N(\mu, \sigma^2) + (1 - \lambda) \cdot N(\mu_\kappa, \sigma_\kappa^2) \quad (6)$$

where $\mu_\kappa$ is the average size of a jump and $\sigma_\kappa^2$ is the variance of the jumps.

## FOCUS: GAUSSIAN MIXTURE IN TRADING PATTERNS

Analyzing trading patterns involves many aspects, from market conditions to behavioral features. However, many unauthorized trading activities occur in plain trading such as the so-called *Delta one*, which has a constant unit delta, providing the investor with one-for-one exposure to a desired underlying asset. The mandate of the trader is to manage this position and adjust if the market has fluctuations. If a Delta one trader takes unauthorized positions not allowed by her mandate this would perturb the profile of her P&L. She will try to take more risk through those unauthorized positions in order to increase her profits.

Therefore, her P&L track should exhibit two regimes: a plain-base regime explained by her *Delta one* mandate and an abnormal regime that occurs when those fraudulent positions are traded. In the case of a scenario where the market does not have high changes in volatility such a P&L would present itself like a mixture of distributions corresponding to those two states. The Gaussian mixture fit indicates the features of each regime as well as the probability of occurrence of each state.

The hypothetical P&L of such a trader is illustrated above on the left while on the right side the fit of the Gaussian mixture is shown. The abnormal regime occurs with 45% probability (almost every other day). The normal base regime is zero centered, thus with no profit-taking inline with the Delta one mandate, while the other regime is centered around a positive value explaining the overall profit of the trader but with much higher volatility.

# 2 GENERALIZED HYPERBOLIC MODELS

A recent modeling technique discussed here permits both skewness and kurtosis in the asset returns. Indeed, these features are not accounted for in the previous model. Following the works of Eberlein and Prause [74] and Barndorff-Nielsen [75] on financial assets, we calibrate the class of generalized hyperbolic distributions to our data set. This very flexible class of distributions is able to capture heavy tails and asymmetry. It is characterized by five parameters with a parameter that permits very specific shapes. The four other parameters are linked in an easy way with the first four moments of the distribution.

This brief review of the generalized hyperbolic distribution functions focuses on the normal inverse Gaussian function. The generic form of a generalized hyperbolic model is:

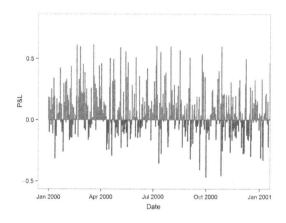

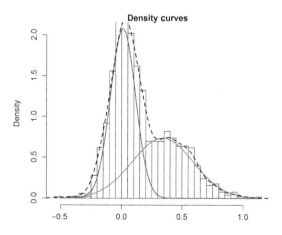

Density curves

$$f(x; \lambda; \chi; \psi; \mu; \sigma; \gamma)$$

$$= \frac{(\sqrt{\psi \chi})^{-\lambda} \psi^\lambda \left( \psi + \frac{\gamma^2}{\sigma^2} \right)^{0.5-\lambda}}{\sqrt{2\pi} \sigma K_\lambda(\sqrt{\psi \chi})}$$

$$\times \frac{K_{\lambda-0.5} \left( \sqrt{(\chi + \frac{(x-\mu)^2}{\sigma^2})(\psi + \frac{\gamma^2}{\sigma^2})} \right) e^{\frac{\gamma(x-\mu)}{\sigma^2}}}{\left( \sqrt{\left( \chi + \frac{(x-\mu)^2}{\sigma^2} \right) \left( \psi + \frac{\gamma^2}{\sigma^2} \right)} \right)^{\lambda-0.5}},$$

where $K_\lambda(x)$ is the modified Bessel function of the third kind:

$$K_\lambda(x) = \frac{1}{2} \int_0^\infty y^{\lambda-1} e^{-\frac{x}{2}(y+y^{-1})} \, dy \qquad (7)$$

With properly chosen parameters, the generalized hyperbolic reduces to the following distributions:

1. $\lambda = 1$: Hyperbolic distribution
2. $\lambda = -1/2$: NIG distribution
3. $\lambda = 1$ and $\xi \to 0$: Normal distribution
4. $\lambda = 1$ and $\xi \to 1$: Symmetric and asymmetric Laplace distribution
5. $\lambda = 1$ and $\chi \to \pm\xi$: Inverse Gaussian distribution
6. $\lambda = 1$ and $|\chi| \to 1$: Exponential distribution
7. $-\infty < \lambda < -2$: Asymmetric Student
8. $-\infty < \lambda < -2$ and $\beta = 0$: Symmetric Student
9. $\gamma = 0$ and $0 < \lambda < \infty$: Asymmetric Normal Gamma distribution

Among the generalized hyperbolic family, the normal inverse Gaussian (NIG) distribution can be obtained by setting $\lambda = -\frac{1}{2}$ in the previous equation. Thus:

$$f\left(x; -\frac{1}{2}; \chi; \psi; \mu; \sigma; \gamma\right)$$
$$= \frac{\chi^{\frac{1}{2}}\left(\psi + \frac{\gamma^2}{\sigma^2}\right)}{\pi \sigma e^{\sqrt{-\psi\chi}}}$$
$$\times \frac{K_1\left(\sqrt{\left(\chi + \frac{(x-\mu)^2}{\sigma^2}\right)\left(\psi + \frac{\gamma^2}{\sigma^2}\right)}\right) e^{\frac{\gamma(x-\mu)}{\sigma^2}}}{\left(\sqrt{\left(\chi + \frac{(x-\mu)^2}{\sigma^2}\right)\left(\psi + \frac{\gamma^2}{\sigma^2}\right)}\right)}.$$

By changing the variables of the previous equation $c = \frac{1}{\sigma^2}; \beta = \frac{\gamma}{\sigma^2}; \delta = \sqrt{\frac{\chi}{c}};$ and $\alpha = \sqrt{\frac{\psi}{\sigma^2} + \beta^2}$ we obtain a more popular representation, and the density of the NIG$(\alpha, \beta, \mu, \delta)$ distribution is equal to:

$$f_{\text{NIG}}(x; \alpha; \beta; \mu; \delta)$$
$$= \frac{\delta\alpha \cdot \exp(\delta\gamma + \beta(x-\mu))}{\pi \cdot \sqrt{\delta^2 + (x-\mu)^2}} K_1(\alpha\sqrt{\delta^2 + (x-\mu)^2}).$$

The moments (mean, variance, skewness, and kurtosis) are respectively equal to:

$$E(X) = \mu + \delta\frac{\beta}{\gamma}$$

$$V(X) = \delta\frac{\alpha^2}{\gamma^3}$$

$$S(X) = 3\frac{\beta}{\alpha \cdot \sqrt{\delta\gamma}}$$

$$E(X) = 3 + 3\left(1 + 4\left(\frac{\beta}{\alpha}\right)^2\right)\frac{1}{\delta\gamma}$$

Thus, the NIG distribution allows for behaviors characterized by heavy tails and strong asymmetries, depending on the parameters $\alpha$, $\beta$, and $\delta$.

# 3 VOLATILITY MODELS

With the development of the derivatives markets and the need for a consistent pricing model the behavior of assets volatilities started to be the object of researchers and practitioners. Typical Gaussian flat volatility failed to provide conspicuous valuations for contingencies and also underestimated risk measures such as the Value at Risk. The dynamic model with volatility clustering started to gain more momentum and to be employed by derivatives traders as well as in the assets management world. The most common models with volatility clustering are summarized below.

Let's consider that $S_t$ the asset price at time $t$ has the following dynamics under the empirical measure $P$:

$$Y_t = \ln\frac{S_t}{S_{t-1}} = r + \psi\sqrt{h_t} + \epsilon_t \qquad (8)$$

$$Y_t = \ln \frac{S_t}{S_{t-1}} = r + \psi \sqrt{h_t} + \sqrt{h_t} \cdot z_t \qquad (9)$$

where $\epsilon_t$ has zero mean and conditional variance $h_t$ under the measure **P**, $z_t$ is a i.i.d. normally distributed variable, $r$ is the one-period risk-free rate of return, and $\psi$ is the constant unit risk premium.

## 3.1 Generalized AutoRegressive Conditionally Heteroscedastic (GARCH) Model

The GARCH process introduced by Bollerslev [76] and its variations have gained increasing prominence for modeling financial assets in the last decade. The GARCH diffusion presents three particular features compared to other models. First, it assumes the present conditional variances are linearly linked to past conditional variances and to past market squared returns. Second, for an accurate calibration GARCH is greedy in terms of data. Third, the model transfers through volatility patterns the risk premium of the underlyings price. The classic GARCH framework obviously offers significant improvements in terms of econometric description compared to the classic Gaussian model. Yet Bollerslev's GARCH still remains under an assumption of normal distribution.

Further, under the framework described by Bollerslev [76], $\epsilon_t$ follows a GARCH (1,1) process:

$$\epsilon_t | \phi_{t-1} \propto N(0, h_t) \text{ or } z_t \propto N(0, 1) \qquad (10)$$

$$h_t = \alpha_0 + \alpha_1 \cdot \epsilon_{t-1}^2 + \beta_1 \cdot h_{t-1} \qquad (11)$$

where $\phi_t$ is the corresponding $\sigma$-algebra generated by the previous and present information, the unconditional variance is $h_0 = \frac{\alpha_0}{(1-\alpha_1-\beta_1)}$. The GARCH model assumes the conditional variance is a linear function of past squared disturbances and the past conditional variance, genuinely making $h_t \phi_t$ predictable.

Generalizing the above given definition a GARCH $(p,q)$ follows:

$$h_t = \alpha_0 + \alpha_1 \epsilon_{t-1}^2 + \cdots + \alpha_q \epsilon_{t-q}^2$$
$$+ \beta_1 h_{t-1} + \cdots + \beta_p h_{t-p}^2$$
$$= \alpha_0 + \sum_{i=1}^{q} \alpha_i \epsilon_{t-i}^2 + \sum_{i=1}^{p} \beta_i h_{t-i}$$

where $p \geq 0, q \geq 0, \alpha_0 > 0, \alpha_i > 0, i = 1, \ldots, q; \beta_i \geq 0, i = 1, \ldots, p$.

One of the key features of the observed behavior of financial data that GARCH models capture is volatility clustering, which may be quantified in the persistence parameter. For the model this may be calculated as:

$$\text{Persistence} = \sum_{i=1}^{q} \alpha_i + \sum_{i=1}^{p} \beta_i < 1$$

To ensure the covariance stationarity of the GARCH $(p,q)$ it is imposed that the persistence is inferior to the unity.

In order to mitigate the existence of significant kurtosis and skewness effects on asset returns, an extension of the GARCH model to non-Gaussian (generalized hyperbolic) innovations with the parametrization introduced in the previous section could be used:

$$z_t \propto GH(\lambda; \alpha; \beta; \mu; \delta) \qquad (12)$$

or

$$\epsilon_t | \phi_{t-1} \propto GH\left(\lambda; \frac{\alpha}{\sqrt{h_t}}; \frac{\beta}{\sqrt{h_t}}; \mu \sqrt{h_t}; \delta \sqrt{h_t}\right) \qquad (13)$$

$$h_t = \alpha_0 + \alpha_1 \cdot \epsilon_{t-1} + \beta_1 \cdot h_{t-1} \qquad (14)$$

GARCH diffusion presents in terms of pricing three particular features compared to other models. First, the GARCH derivatives prices depend on risk premium embedded in the underlying asset. Second, the GARCH pricing model is non-Markovian and is an interesting alternative for markets with serial dependency. Third, the GARCH model might explain some valuation bias of out-of-the-money options associated with classic models.

A few popular variations of the GARCH model include:

- **The integrated GARCH (IGARCH) [77] model** assumes the persistence is one. Omitted structural breaks should be assessed before using an IGARCH model:

$$\epsilon_t|\phi_{t-1} \propto N(0, h_t) \text{ or } z_t \propto N(0, 1) \quad (15)$$

$$h_t = \alpha_0 + (1 - \beta_1) \cdot \epsilon_{t-1}^2 + \beta_1 \cdot h_{t-1} \quad (16)$$

- **The fractionally integrated GARCH model** is an extension of the IGARCH model introduced by Baillie et al. [78] aimed at capturing the long-term persistence of volatility shocks. One way of increasing the persistence of shocks in variance is to introduce a long memory, or *fractionally integrated* model, whereas the autocorrelations of squared returns decay at a much slower rate. The basic GARCH can be rewritten with lag operators $\alpha(L) = \alpha_1 L + \cdots + \alpha_q L^q$ and $\beta(L) = \beta_1 L + \cdots + \beta_p L^p$:

$$h_t = \alpha_0 + \alpha(L)\epsilon_t^2 + \beta(L)h_t \quad (17)$$

With the notation $[1 - \alpha(L) - \beta(L)] = (1 - \Phi(L))(1 - L)$, the IGARCH $(p, q)$ the model can be redefined as:

$$(1 - \Phi(L))(1 - L)\epsilon_t^2 = \alpha_0 + [1 - \beta(L)](\epsilon_t^2 - h_t) \quad (18)$$

where the lag operator $\Phi(L)$ is built as $\Phi(L) = \Phi_1 L + \cdots + \Phi_m L^m$ and $m = \max(p, q) - 1$. Then the *fractionally integration* is obtained by replacing the operator $(1 - L)$ in the IGARCH model by the fractional operator $(1 - L)^d$:

$$(1 - \Phi(L))(1 - L)^d \epsilon_t^2 = \alpha_0 + [1 - \beta(L)](\epsilon_t^2 - h_t) \quad (19)$$

- **The Glosten-Jagannathan-Runkle (GJR)-GARCH model** introduced by Glosten et al. [79] adds asymmetry in the volatility process:

$$h_t = \alpha_0 + (\alpha_1 + c \cdot I_{t-1}) \cdot \epsilon_{t-1}^2 + \beta_1 \cdot h_{t-1} \quad (20)$$

where $I_{t-1} = \begin{cases} 0 & \epsilon_{t-1} \geq 0 \\ 1 & \epsilon_{t-1} < 0 \end{cases}$

- **The exponential GARCH (EGARCH) model** introduced by Nelson [80] aims to capture the asymmetric reaction of volatility to the positive and negative information about the market. The volatility of the EGARCH model, which is measured by the conditional variance, is an explicit multiplicative function of lagged innovations:

$$\log h_t = \alpha_t + \sum_{i=1}^{\infty} \beta_i g(z_{t-k}) \quad (21)$$

where the function $g$ is defined as $g(z_t) = \theta z_t + \gamma(|z_t| - E|z_t|)$, $g(z_t)$ having a zero mean $E[g(z_t)] = 0$. No restrictions are imposed in this version of the GARCH model. EHARCH can also assess whether the shocks in variance are persistent.

- **The asymmetric power GARCH model** introduced by Ding et al. [81] accounts for the leverage effect and also the fact that the sample autocorrelation of absolute returns is higher than that of squared returns [82]:

$$h_t^{0.5 \cdot \zeta} = \alpha_0 + \sum_{i=1}^{q} \alpha_i (|\epsilon_{t-i}^\zeta| - \gamma_i \cdot \epsilon_{t-i})^\zeta + \sum_{i=1}^{p} \beta_i h_{t-i}^{0.5 \cdot \zeta} \quad (22)$$

Note that Equation 22 with $\zeta = 2$ and $\gamma_i = 0$ matches the classic GARCH model with Gaussian innovations.

# 4 MODEL ESTIMATION

In general, distribution and volatility models are estimated using maximum likelihood. The log-likelihood function for a set or returns $r_1, r_2, \ldots, r_n$ for a parametric density function $f$ depending on parameters $\Theta$ is:

$$\ln \mathcal{LL}(\Theta ; r_1, \ldots, r_n) = \sum_{i=1}^{n} \ln f(r_i | \Theta),$$

In many cases the quasi maximum likelihood methods are employed as the estimation of a model with too many parameters (i.e., GARCH models) in one step can exhibit convergence errors.

In order to compare the adequacy of various models a few criteria are available in the literature such as the Akaike information criteria (AIC), Bayesian information criteria (BIC), the Hannan-Quinn information criteria (HQIC), and the Shibata information criteria (SIC) [83].

$$\text{AIC} = -2 \cdot \text{LL}/n + 2 \cdot k/n$$

$$\text{BIC} = -2 \cdot \text{LL}/n + k \cdot \log(n)/n$$

$$\text{HQIC} = -2 \cdot \text{LL}/n + 2k \cdot \ln(\ln(n))/n$$

$$\text{SIC} = -2 \cdot \text{LL}/n + \ln((n + 2k)/n)$$

where LL is the log likelihood, $n$ is the length of the sample, and $k$ the number of estimated parameters.

Nonetheless, it is important to emphasize that we compare non-nested models based on various distributions such as Gaussian or normal inverse Gaussian laws. Because it adopts a penalty function that in the order of $O(\log(n))$, an immediate consequence is that the BIC represents an inconsistent model selection criterion for non-nested models, thereby implying the need for an alternative criterion. Previous research [84] proposed the non-nested

information criterion (NIC) to mitigate our consistency issue. The NIC is defined as:

$$\text{NIC} = -2 \cdot \text{LL} + k \cdot \log(n) \cdot \sqrt{n} \qquad (23)$$

A straightforward test for these models is to check their estimation for the return of a stock with possible rogue accounting that pushed the price higher than the real economic value of the company. The case of ABS Industries is a good example in this sense,[1] as this company allegedly periodically communicated false information about financial situation and its business perspective. The information was also included on 10k fillings, thereby misleading investors. According to this fact the price should have suffered jumps whenever new "abnormal information was communicated" during the class period.

## ABS INDUSTRIES, INC.

### Background

ABS Industries was an Ohio corporation traded on NASDAQ under the name "ABSI." In 1996 a class action suit was filed involving a classic cooked book scheme in which the company distributed materially false financial statements reporting record and accelerating sales and earnings per share. Furthermore, the financial and other misrepresentations disseminated by ABS between 1993 and 1996 created the illusion that ABSI was enjoying growth in sales and earnings when, in reality, the growth was attributable in material part to sales improperly recorded as recording revenue.

### Cooking the books

Those acts inflated ABSI prices as high as $13.00 per share for ABSI shares. Early in 1996, when the company began to reveal its true

---

[1]HAWK vs. ABSI, http://securities.stanford.edu/filings-documents/1009/ABSI96/001.html.

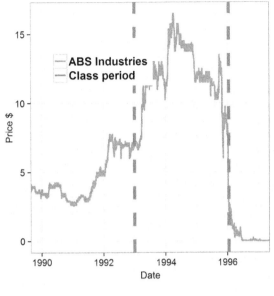

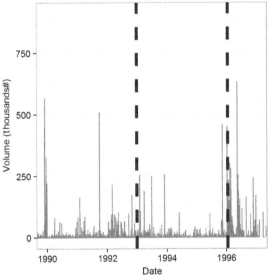

### Aftermath

After the class action suit the shares dropped even more, plummeting in the stock penny area. The company settled in 1998 for $206,000, each plaintiff receiving $5500.

Table 1 shows the result of the estimation of different distribution on the returns of ABSI during the class period. The models were implemented using the R package proposed by Breymann and Lüthi [85]. The 95% confidence interval was commuted with bootstrapping approach. The best model following the AIC criteria is the $t$-Student distribution, emphasizing that the stock prices had fat tails. The model does not impose an asymmetry as the $\beta$ parameter of the NIG distribution is not significantly different from zero.

**TABLE 1**  ABSI Daily Returns

| Parameter | Gaussian | NIG | $t$-Student |
|---|---|---|---|
| $\mu$ | 0.00 | 0 | 0 |
| | $(-0.002, 0.002)$ | $(0,0)$ | $(0,0)$ |
| $\sigma$ | 0.037 | - | 0.0391 |
| | $(0.035, 0.040)$ | - | $(0.0353, 0.0457)$ |
| $\lambda$ | - | $-0.5$ | $-1.845$ |
| | | $(-0.5, -0.5)$ | $(-2.850, -1.338)$ |
| $\nu$ | - | - | 3.692 |
| | | | $(2.67, 5.62)$ |
| $\alpha$ | - | 19.29 | - |
| | | $(13.16, 30.1)$ | |
| $\beta$ | - | 0.015 | - |
| | | $(-1.57, 1.68)$ | |
| $\delta$ | - | 0.028 | - |
| | | $(0.0215, 0.0393)$ | |
| **AIC** | 2632 | 2684 | **2691** |

Notes: *The results of the estimation of different distribution on the returns of ABSI during the class period. The models were implemented using the package proposed by Breymann and Lüthi [85]. The 95% confidence interval was commuted using a bootstrapping approach.*

financial condition and prospects, and other adverse information described herein, ABSI shares plunged from a price of $6.75 per share on January 10, 1996 to a closing price of $3.00 per share on January 13, 1996, a 55% decline resulting in damages for investors in excess of $10 million.

**TABLE 2** ABSI Volatility Models

| Parameter | GJR GARCH | | | GARCH | | | APARCH | | |
|---|---|---|---|---|---|---|---|---|---|
| | Est. | Std.err. | $p$-Value | Est. | Std.err. | $p$-Value | Est. | Std.err. | $p$-Value |
| $\alpha_0$ | 0.007 | 0 | 0 | 0.109 | 0.043 | 0.011 | 0.008 | 0.008 | 0.302 |
| $\alpha_1$ | 0.015 | 0 | 0 | 0.172 | 0.0477 | 0.000 | 0.010 | 0.010 | 0.299 |
| $\beta_1$ | 1.000 | 0 | 0 | 0.694 | 0.080 | 0.000 | 0.965 | 0.0221 | 0.000 |
| $\gamma_1$ | −0.056 | 0 | 0 | | | | −0.999 | 0.001 | 0.00 |
| $\delta$ | | | | | | | 2.021 | 0.125 | 0.000 |
| **BIC** | 2.5484 | | | 2.5440 | | | **2.5753** | | |

Notes: *Three models from the GARCH universe with Gaussian innovations estimated with the R package proposed by Ghalanos [83]. The BIC indicates that the APARCH model captures the best stock's volatility behavior, thereby incorporating the leverage effect and the persistence in absolute level of returns.*

The study of the volatility structure is presented in Table 2, which includes three models from the Generalized AutoRegressive Conditionally Heteroscedastic (GARCH) universe with Gaussian innovations estimated with the package R proposed by Ghalanos [83]. The BIC indicates that the APARCH models capture the best stock's volatility behavior, thereby incorporating the leverage effect and persistence in the absolute level of returns.

Extending further the study of the stocks that underwent a class action suit a sample of companies listed on U.S. markets is built from the Stanford Securities Class Action Clearinghouse.[2] With this database and with a daily returns data set for each stock two subsamples are considered: one prior to the class filing and one after the class filing. For each set three distributions are fitted and the best fitting model following the BIC is chosen.

Table 3 shows the break down per model for the litigated stock before and after the filing date. The total number of stocks in the post-filing sample is smaller because some companies were delisted or shut down following the investigation. It appears that the proportion of

**TABLE 3** Model Fit for Stock Price Return that was Subject to Class Action

| Model | Before fillings | % | After fillings | % |
|---|---|---|---|---|
| Gaussian | 12 | 1 | 54 | 4 |
| $t$-Student | 483 | 39 | 429 | 33 |
| Normal Inverse Gaussian | 740 | 60 | 805 | 63 |
| Total | **1235** | 100 | **1288** | 100 |

Notes: *Break down per model for the litigated stock before and after the filing date. The total number of stocks in the post-filing sample is smaller because some companies were delisted or shut down following the investigation. It appears that the proportion of stocks is closer to the Gaussian universe increase in the post-class filing samples. In both sample the NIG fits the best in most cases.*

stocks is closer to the Gaussian universe increase in the post-class filing sample. In both samples the NIG fits the best in most cases.

# 5 OUTLOOK

In the case of securities fraud the distribution cannot predict whether or not there are issues as most financial times series do not fall in the traditional model. Nonetheless, a massive change in the distribution's features or in its forecasting capacity can be a warning signal. The chapter related to distribution forecasting addresses this point.

---

[2]Stanford Securities Class Action Clearinghouse, http://securities.stanford.edu/.

# Forecasting Densities

## 1 BACKGROUND

Forecasting typically deals with the ability of a model to estimate the value of a point at a future date given the information available today. Density forecasting provides an estimate of the state of the distribution for a variable at a future moment $t + k$, given the information available at moment $t$ $(t + k > t)$.

The field of density forecasting started to receive increasing attention from researchers and bankers when financial institutions had the choice to use their own internally built models for risk management purposes. For a Value at Risk model a bank needs to prove to the regulator that the model describing the underlying distribution of a P&L profile is able to predict the behavior at a moment in the future. Thus, the Value at Risk would be a consistent estimator, which measured with the information given today, would make sense in probabilistic sense in the universe of tomorrow.

The Basel III reform imposed stressed tests to banks based on macro-economic scenarios. Therefore, density forecasting is also used to deal with the prediction of economic cycles and with the growth phases of the economy involving GDP and inflation.

There is a lot information that can be extracted from a data set based on comparing models for forecasting distributions, information that could be used for traditional risk management purposes, but also for monitoring misconduct and fraud activity.

# 2 TESTS FOR FORECASTING DENSITIES

## 2.1 Model-Free Forecasts

In the early 1990s, Diebold and Mariano [86] introduced a seminal test of the null hypothesis of no difference in the accuracy of two competing forecasts. Compared to other approaches that appeared it is based directly on predictive performance, and here we entertain a wide class of accuracy measures. More specifically the Diebold-Martino test does not make any reference to the underlying model of the forecast, but only to its outcomes.

Diebold's approach is straightforward and considers a series of forecasts $(y_t^1)$ and $(y_t^2)$ for the real-time series $y_t$ for $t \in \{1, 2, \ldots, T\}$, and the associated prediction errors $e^1$ and $e^2$ with the associated loss functions $g(y_t, y_t^1) = g(e_t^1)$ and $g(y_t, y_t^2) = g(e_t^2)$. The difference between the loss functions for the two forecasts is $d_t = g(e_t^1) - g(e_t^2)$ with an empirical expected value:

$$\bar{d} = \frac{1}{T} \sum_1^T g(e_t^1) - g(e_t^2) \qquad (1)$$

The null and alternative hypothesis of equal forecast accuracy for two forecasts is assumed to be:

- $H_0$: $\mathbf{E}(g(e_{it})) = \mathbf{E}(g(e_j t))$, or $E(d_t) = 0$
- $H_a$ $\mathbf{E}(g(e_i t)) \neq \mathbf{E}(g(e_j t))$, or $E(d_t) \neq 0$

The null hypothesis is that the two forecasts have the same accuracy. The alternative hypothesis is that the two forecasts have different levels of accuracy.

With the notations $\mu = E(d_t)$ and $f_d(0) = \frac{1}{2\pi} \sum_{k=\infty}^{\infty} E(d_t - \mu)(d(t - k) - \mu)$ the statistics for the null hypothesis $H_0$ is:

$$\sqrt{T}(\bar{d} - \mu) \rightarrow \mathbf{N}(0, 2\pi f_d(0)) \qquad (2)$$

$$\frac{\sqrt{T}(\bar{d} - \mu)}{2\pi f_d(0)} \rightarrow \mathbf{N}(0, 1) \qquad (3)$$

which can be rearranged as:

$$S_{DM} = \frac{\bar{d}}{2\pi \hat{f}_d(0)} \rightarrow N(0, 1) \qquad (4)$$

where $\hat{f}_d(0)$ is a consistent estimator for $f_d(0)$ and $S_{DM}$ denotes the Diebold-Marino statistic.

Under the null hypothesis, the test statistic Diebold-Marino is asymptotically $N(0,1)$ distributed. The null hypothesis of no difference will be rejected if the computed Diebold-Marino statistic falls outside the range of $-z_\alpha/2$ to $z_\alpha/2$, i.e., if $|S_{DM}| > z_\alpha/2$, where $z_\alpha/2$ is the upper (or positive) $z$-value from the standard normal table corresponding to half of the desired level of the test.

## 2.2 Vuong's Test for Comparing Two Distributions

Vuong [87] introduced an approach to comparing two densities for characterizing a time series. The density forecast in a time series context is based on **in-sample** fit/**out-of-sample** forecasts. This framework is implemented on the basis of a rolling window of size $m + k$, consisting of the past $m$ observations that are used to fit a density and $k$ time steps ahead observations for the forecast. Let's suppose that $X_1, \ldots, X_T$ is a random process that can be partitioned as $X_t = (Y_t, \mathbf{Z}_t)$, where $Y_t$ is the variable of interest of size $m$ and $Z_t$ is a vector of forecasts of size $k$.

The size of the total sample is $T = m + n + k$. At each moment $t$ with $t = \{m, \ldots, m + n\}$, two density forecasts based on the distribution $f$ and $g$ can be compared.[1] In Vuong's framework, the forecasts are produced based on measurable functions of the data in the rolling estimation window and the test uses the likelihood ratio

---

[1]This notation is kept for the rest of the chapter.

test for non-nested hypotheses, the differences being based on the Kullback-Leibler information criterion that measure the distance between a given distribution and the true distributions. The likelihood ratio can be written as:

$$LR_n(\hat{\theta}, \hat{\gamma}) = L(\widehat{\theta}) - L(\hat{\gamma})$$

$$= \sum_{i=1}^{n} \log(F(Y_i|Z_i, \hat{\theta})) - \log(G(Y_i|Z_i\hat{\gamma}))$$

Vuong test can be summarized as follows:

- $H_0$ The null hypothesis assuming the two distribution $f$ and $g$ are equal:

$$\mathbf{E}\left[\log \frac{f(Y_i|Z_i, \hat{\theta})}{g(Y_i|Z_i\hat{\gamma})}\right] = 0 \qquad (5)$$

- $H_{af}$ the alternative hypothesis stating that $f(\theta)$ is a better choice than $g(\gamma)$:

$$\mathbf{E}\left[\log \frac{f(Y_i|Z_i, \hat{\theta})}{g(Y_i|Z_i\hat{\gamma})}\right] > 0 \qquad (6)$$

- $H_{ag}$ the alternative hypothesis stating that $G(\gamma)$ is a better choice than $F(\theta)$:

$$\mathbf{E}\left[\log \frac{f(Y_i|Z_i, \hat{\theta})}{g(Y_i|Z_i\hat{\gamma})}\right] < 0 \qquad (7)$$

For testing the null hypothesis the following statistic is computed:

$$\frac{LR_n(\theta, \gamma)}{\sqrt{n} \cdot \widehat{\omega_n}} \to N(0, 1) \qquad (8)$$

where assuming the notation $d_i = \log(f(Y_i|Z_i\hat{\theta}))$ $- \log(g(Y_i|Z_i\hat{\gamma}))$:

$$\widehat{\omega_n} = \frac{1}{n}\sum_{t=1}^{n}[d_i]^2 - \left[\frac{1}{n}\sum_{t=1}^{n}d_i\right]^2 \qquad (9)$$

## 2.3 Weighted Logarithmic Scoring Test

Generalizing the comparison framework introduced by Vuong and assuming a loss function $S(f, y)$ depending on the density forecast $f$ and the realization $y$ of the future observations. Amisano and Giacomini [88] proposed a formal out-of-sample test for ranking competing density forecasts that are valid under very general conditions. The score proposed is:

$$S(f, y) = -\log f(y) \qquad (10)$$

The test is useful for comparing weighted averages of the logarithmic scores, thereby allowing for greater weight on particular regions of the distribution. The weighted score is:

$$S_w^f(f_t, y_t) = w(y_t) \cdot S(f_t, y_t) = w^*\left(\frac{y_t - \mu_{y_t}}{\sigma_{y_t}}\right) S(f_t, y_t) \qquad (11)$$

where $\mu_{y_t} = \frac{1}{m}\sum_{i=1}^{m} y_i$, $\sigma_{y_t} = \frac{1}{m}\sum_{i=1}^{m} y_i^2 - \left[\frac{1}{m}\sum_{i=1}^{m} y_i\right]^2$, and following weighting functions:

$$w^*(x) = \begin{cases} \phi(x) & \text{for center of} \\ & \text{distribution} \\ 1 - \phi(x)/\phi(0) & \text{for tails of distribution} \\ \Phi(x) & \text{for right tail} \\ 1 - \Phi(x) & \text{for left tail} \end{cases} \qquad (12)$$

The Giacomini-Amisano test is assumed to be the expected difference of the score for the two models $f$ and $g$, depending on parameters $\theta$ and $\gamma$, normalized by the test's standard deviation:

$$Z_n = \frac{\mathbf{E}_t(S_w^f(f_t, y_t|\theta) - S_w^g(g_t, y_t|\gamma))}{\omega_n} \qquad (13)$$

where the weighted likelihood ratio is defined for a given function $w(\bullet)$ and two alternative conditional densities forecasts $f$ and $g$, on the sample $y_i$ as follows:

$$W\Lambda_{n,i} = -w(y_i)\log(f(y_i,\hat{\theta}_m)) - \log(g(y_i,\hat{\gamma}_m)) \tag{14}$$

where $i = m+1, m+2, \ldots, m+n-k$, and $\hat{\theta}_m$ and $\hat{\gamma}_m$ are the parameters of models $f$ and $g$, estimated on the sample $y_{i*}$ with $i^* = 1, \ldots, m$. This statistic is defined as:

$$Z_n = \frac{\mathbf{E}(W\Lambda_{n,i})}{\sqrt{n}\tilde{\omega}_n} \tag{15}$$

where $\mathbf{E}(W\Lambda_{m,n,i}) = n^{-1}\sum_{i=m+1}^{m+n-k} W\Lambda_{m,i}$ and $\tilde{\omega}_n$ is a consistent estimator of the asymptotic variance $\omega_n$ computed as:

$$\tilde{\omega}_n = \frac{1}{n}\sum_{j=-k+1}^{k+1}\sum_{j=m}^{m+n-|j|} W\Lambda_{n,j}W\Lambda_{n,j+h} \tag{16}$$

where $k$ is the number of time steps ahead for which the forecast is made. The limit of this statistic for a sample sufficiently large is the normal standard distribution $N(0,1)$. A level $\alpha$ test rejects the null hypothesis of equal performance of forecasts $f$ and $g$ whenever $Z > z_\alpha/2$, where $z_\alpha/2$ is the $(1 - z_\alpha/2)$ quantile of a standard normal distribution. In case of rejection, we could choose $g$ if $W\Lambda_{m,n,i}$ is positive and $f$ if $W\Lambda_{m,n,i}$ is negative.

The Giacomini-Amisano test has many of the features of the Diebold-Marino test including the way the variance of the test is computed. As explained in a recent paper [89] the Diebold-Mariano test was intended for comparing forecasts from a model-free perspective. The Diebold-Mariano test was not intended for comparing models. Much of the large ensuing literature uses Diebold-Marino type tests for comparing models, in pseudo out-of-sample environments. While these tests are still useful tools for comparing models, they do have pitfalls and can noted counterintuitive results as pointed by Diks et al. [90] and Gneiting and Ranjan [91].

## 2.4 Threshold Weighting Test

If the Giamcomini-Amisano test is implemented with a weight function that focuses on the region of the tail or of the central part of the distributions counterintuitive results will be found. Let's consider a weighting function with the following form [72]:

- For assessing the core of the distribution
  $w(x) = \frac{1}{n}\mathbf{1}_{|x|<K*\hat{\sigma}}(x)$
- For assessing the tails of the distribution
  $w(x) = \frac{1}{n}\mathbf{1}_{|x|\geq K*\hat{\sigma}}(x)$, $\hat{\sigma}$ being the standard deviation of the sample and $K$ a constant representing the cut-off point between the core and the tail

As noted by Diks et al. [90] the above example of a weight function is often considered for evaluation of the left tail in risk management applications. The weighted logarithmic score results in predictive ability tests that are biased toward densities with more probability mass in the left tail. Hence, for the situation where $g(y) > f(y)$ for all $y$ such as $\mathbf{1}_{|y|\geq K*\hat{\sigma}}(y)$ whenever using the above weighting function for tail implies that the weighted score difference $S(g,y) - S(f,y)$ is always strictly positive. Therefore, when comparing density forecasts with different tail behavior there could be cases that a fat-tailed distribution is favored over a thin-tailed distribution, even if the true distribution that generated the data does not have heavy tails [90].

**Definition 1.** A score rule $S$ is considered *proper* if for two models $f$ and $g$ it satisfies the inequality:

$$E_f S(f,y) = \int f(y)S(f,y)\,\mathrm{d}y \leq \int f(y)S(g,y)\,\mathrm{d}y$$
$$= E_g S(g,y) \tag{17}$$

where the equality is obtained for $f = g$. In other words, the score rule will always choose the right model $g$ over the wrong model $f$ when assessing outcomes coming from model $g$.

The issue we are emphasizing here has been reported independently by Gneiting and Ranjan [91]. As they note, the weighted score introduced by Amisano and Giacomini [88] does not satisfy the properness property in the sense that there can be incorrect density forecasts that receive a higher average score than the true density.

In order to tackle this issue Gneiting and Ranjan [91] proposed a test that further develops the weighting approach of Amisano and Giacomini [88] but avoids counterintuitive inferences. Gneiting's test aims to build a proper score with respect to the above definition based on appropriately weighted versions of the continuously ranked probability score (CPRS).

For any density function $f(y)$ with a cumulative distribution function $F(z) = \int_{-\infty}^{z} f(y)\, dy$ the continuous ranked probability score is then defined as:

$$CPRS(F, y) = \int_{-\infty}^{\infty} PS(F(r), 1(y \leq r))\, dr \quad (18)$$

where

$$PS(F(r), 1(y \leq r)) = (1(y \leq r) - F(r))^2 \quad (19)$$

is the Brier probability score for the probability forecast $F_t(r) = \int_{-\infty}^{r} f(y)\, dy$ of the event $y \leq r$.

The weighted probability score described by Matheson and Winkler [92] and Gneiting and Raftery [93] is written as:

$$S^w(f, y) = -\int_{-\infty}^{\infty} PS(F(r), 1(y \leq r)w_r(r)\, dr \quad (20)$$

where the weighting function $w_r(r)$ taxes the forms presented in Equation 12. In a discrete form the above score can be approximated by assuming an equidistant discretizations of a target region with the boundaries $y_l, y_u$:

$$S_f^w(f, y) = \frac{y_u - y_l}{I - 1} \sum_{i=1}^{I} w(y_i) PS(F(y_i), I(y \leq y_i)) \quad (21)$$

where $y_i = y_l + i\frac{y_u - y_l}{I}$. The test is based on the following statistic, which is leveraged from the Amisano-Giacomini test:

$$Z_n = \frac{\mathbf{E}(S_f^w(f, y) - S_f^w(g, y))}{\widehat{\omega_n}} \quad (22)$$

where

$$\mathbf{E}_t(S_f^w(f, y)) = \frac{1}{n - k + 1} \sum_{t=m}^{m+n-k} S(f_{t+k}, y_{t+k}) \quad (23)$$

$$\mathbf{E}_t(S_f^w(g, y)) = \frac{1}{n - k + 1} \sum_{t=m}^{m+n-k} S(g_{t+k}, y_{t+k}) \quad (24)$$

and $\widehat{\omega_n}$ is an estimate of $var(\sqrt{n}(\mathbf{E}_t(S_f^w(f, y) - \mathbf{E}_t(S_g^w(g, y)))))$.

# 3 APPLICATION IN MISCONDUCT RISK MITIGATION AND FRAUD ASSESSMENT

Whenever a behavioral change occurs in the performance of an agent or in the securities returns it is usually found through the evolution of the level of a time series. However, in many cases the levels or returns of a times series do not automatically reflect the underlying changes. The place where the changes do take place is in terms of density. Two cases illustrate this situation below, first exhibiting the study of the P&L profile for a trading desk and the second the returns of a stock suspected of securities fraud.

## 3.1 P&L Profile

To illustrate density forecasting for assessing the evolution of the P&L a trading desk time series of profit and losses is simulated. The first half of the simulated series is based on a normal kernel while the second half of the series is enriched with fat tails. The aim of this simulation is to depict the case where a trading activity drifts from one type of normal strategy

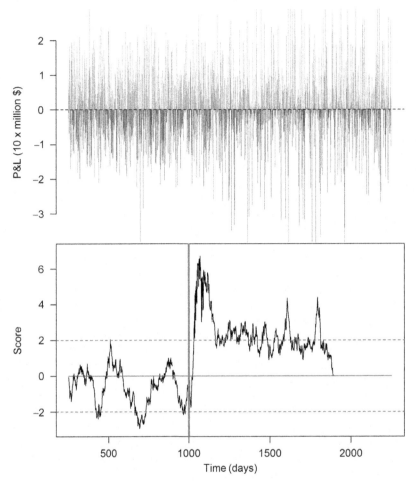

**FIGURE 1** Evolution of the P&L for a trading desk. The top graph shows the daily P&L series over a period of time. When analyzed in terms of range of outcomes, the series seems to be stationary over time. The bottom graph shows the tails weighted score benchmarking a Gaussian distribution mode against a fat-tailed model (Normal Inverse Gaussian). It can be observed that during the first 1000 trading days, the two models are no different in terms of forecasting the P&L profile. After 1000 days the Normal Inverse Gaussian model is the preferred choice for forecasting.

to an abnormal strategy that is bearing more risk. In Figure 1, the top graph shows the daily profit and loss series over a period of time. When analyzed in terms of range of outcomes, the series seems to be stationary over time. The bottom graphs show the threshold weighted test statistics benchmarking a Gaussian distribution model against a fat-tailed model (Normal Inverse Gaussian). The models are estimated over a window of 250 observations and used to forecast the 100-days ahead P&L profile. The statistics are computed over a rolling window, with the outcome as shown in the graph. It can be observed that during the first 1000 trading days, the two models are no different in terms of forecasting the P&L profile. After 1000 days the Normal Inverse Gaussian model is the preferred choice for forecasting.

In this example the density forecast emphasizes a drift in the behavior of the traders that goes points to a strategy characterized by more extreme values in the P&L profile. This drift could represent a change in underlying market volatility or a change in strategy within the limits but it can also be a signal of unauthorized or fake positions as was the case of rogue traders.

## 3.2 Securities Fraud

Another potential area of application of density forecasting is securities fraud and more specially fraud on the markets. Whenever a fraud occurs on the market either by manipulation or insider trading the price signals changes in term of levels, but also in terms of returns distribution. An alleged case of market manipulation involving the company Houston American Energy, currently in litigation in U.S. courts[2] is used as an example. Figure 2 shows the evolution of prices, volumes, and the threshold weighing test statistics before, during, and after the class period, which was between April 2010 and March 2012. The density forecast test compares a model with Gaussian log returns vs. a fat tails normal inverse Gaussian.

## HOUSTON AMERICAN ENERGY

### Background

Houston American Energy is an U.S. based company listed on the NYSE under the 'HUSA' ticker that explores and produces natural oil and gas in the United States and South America, including three exploration and production blocks leased in Columbia.

### Class action

The company disclosed materially false and misleading statements concerning the amount of recoverable oil reserves in one of the Colombian block. When financial publications began questioning HUSA's disclosures beginning in April 2010, the company denied these accusations and continued to issue false statements throughout the class period. From October 2010 Houston American was investigated for potential violations of federal securities laws concerning the company's purported reserves. Houston American received three SEC subpoenas in connection with the investigation, which were concealed until April 2012. The misleading statements inflated the price of Houston American stock from its closing price of $4 in November 2009 to a record value of $20.44 on July 6, 2011.

### Aftermath

Between September 2012 and August 2014 the case resulted in an initial dismissal from District Court to a later demand for further proceedings from the Court of Appeals.

In the case of Houston American the evolution of the test shows that at the beginning of the class period the statistics favor the fat tails model (Figure 2). As explained above, that period was characterized by an inflow of misleading statements from the firm in responses to doubts posed by a market research analysts such as Seekingalpha,[3] which as early as April 2010 indicated that HUSA might be a pump-and-dump scheme. This informational inefficiency was reflected in the stock behavior, which started to show bigger daily variations due to the fat tails effect. In the middle of the class period the behavior seemed to be stable as the statistics

---

[2]Spitzberg vs. HUSA, http://securities.stanford.edu/filings-documents/1048/HUSA00_01/20121115_r01c_12CV01332.pdf.

[3]Houston American Energy Corp. Set Up for Collapse, http://seekingalpha.com/article/197437-houston-american-energy-corp-set-up-for-collapse.

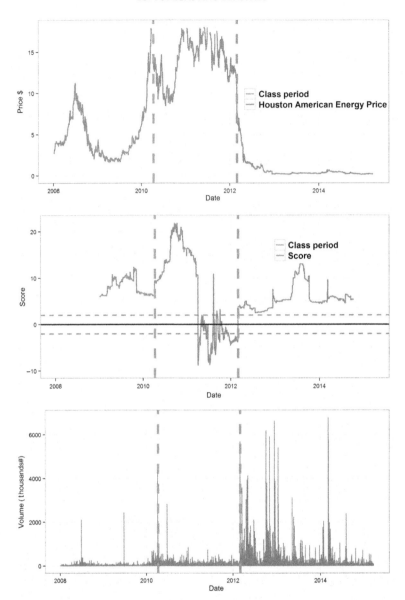

**FIGURE 2**  The upside graph shows the price of Huston American Energy stock indicating the class action. The middle graph shows the evolution of the threshold weighing test statistics during the class period, benchmarking a model with Gaussian log returns vs. a fat tails Normal Inverse Gaussian. The downside graph presents the evolution of traded volumes for the HUSA stock.

indicated that both Gaussian and NIG were similar in terms of forecast. Toward the end of the class period when the news of the situation was published the returns distributions goes again in the fat-tailed area. Independent of the outcome of the ongoing litigation this case reflects that the density forecast can peak under certain changes in behaviors of the underlying distribution for a security that is subject to any kind informational inefficiency. This topic will be detailed in the chapter dedicated to fraud on the market theory.

## 4 OUTLOOK

Density forecasting tests have many applications in risk management, mainly in the validation of risk metrics. The related literature provides a significant number of tests adapted for various situations as discussed here.

In the area of risk management assessing density forecasting accuracy is useful to ensure the consistency of risk measures such as Value at Risk. Application can also be extended to misconduct risk and fraud, ensuring the interface between risk practices and misconduct and crime monitoring. If a sudden change in the pattern of behavior of an agent or a security occurs its underlying distribution (i.e., P&L or returns) can also change. The tests for forecasting densities can monitor this change by benchmarking the predictive power of two distributions. Nonetheless, the risk manager should be aware from a qualitative perspective of the type of changes that could occur in order to choose the right distributions/models for testing.

CHAPTER

# 2D

# Genetic Algorithms

## 1 BACKGROUND

Phrases like "born criminal," or "having crime in the blood" are used in movies about violence and crime and generally aim to describe a character with inborn criminal behavior. Going beyond semantics and only focusing on white collar crime the vast number of offenses show that there are patterns or common features among individuals or organizations that commit crimes. These patterns or features evolve over time and adapt to the environment, eventually producing the next generation or typology of crime. This is true not only for crime but for almost all biological systems and is just a corollary of an older theory developed by the biologist Charles Darwin [94]. In essence, the Darwinian theory means survival of the fittest through a continuous adaptation process that implies from time to time mutation to create fitter individuals. In his theory the fittest parent also has a better chance for reproduction and hence to have offspring than less fit individuals. Evolution aims to create

better individuals that can adapt to the changing environment, with weak and unfit individuals facing extinction by natural selection. From the perspective of a genetic algorithm, solving a problem means in biological terms to find a set of individuals carrying chromosomes with the optimal features that would allow them to adapt to new conditions. Therefore, the method starts with an initial set of chromosomes, or population, which represents the initial possible solutions to the problem. As in nature, the parent chromosomes are selected based on their fitness to the environment and to produce offspring using cross-over or mutation operations. If a generation faces disease then the next generation comes from the surviving individuals. After a sufficient number of children, chromosomes are produced to form a second generation, and evolution continues on and on, producing generation after generation of those with better features. Darwin's evolution theory of natural selection states that future generations are better adapted, and in algorithm terms this means the new generation of solutions better fits to the problem.

In the field of applied mathematics genetic algorithms were introduced in the 1970s by John Holland [95]. As he explained in a seminal paper [96] genetic algorithms allow the exploration of a broader range of solutions than classic solutions do. Hence, computer programs using those algorithms *can even solve problems even their creator did not understand*. Genetic algorithms represent a class of methods using the concepts from the natural evolution process to determine a solution to a given problem.

One of the first areas of practical application, which has been popular since the late 1990s, was the prediction of financial times series. For example, Kaboudan [97] proposed a profitable trading strategy based on predictions of stock prices using a genetic algorithm introducing a metric quantifying the probability that a specific time series is predictable through such an algorithm. Another work by Mańdziuk and Jaruszewicz [98] proposed experimental evaluation of a neuro-genetic system for short-term stock index prediction using as input variables defined through technical data analysis on stocks from the German Stock Exchange, Tokyo Stock Exchange, and New York Stock Exchange together with EUR/USD and USD/JPY exchange rates. Then the genetic algorithm is applied to find an optimal set of input variables for a one-day prediction. Due to the high volatility of mutual relations between input variables, a particular set of inputs found by the genetic algorithm is valid only for a short period of time and a new set of inputs is calculated every 5 trading days. Another topic is the search for technical trading rules. Allen and Karjalainen [99] showed how genetic algorithms can be used to derive trading rules that are not ad hoc but are in a sense optimal, thereby avoiding potential bias caused by ex-post selection. Similarly, Neely et al. [100] found strong evidence of economically significant out-of-sample excess returns to genetic algorithm-based rules for time series of exchange rates for the period 1981-1999 (US dollar/Deutsche, Deutsche mark/yen). In the high-frequency trading space Dunis et al. [101] applied genetic algorithms for intra-day trading models for the USD/DEM and DEM/JPY exchange rates given by tick data.

## 2 APPLICATION IN OPTIMIZATION

Classic optimization methods like Newton-Raphson or Nelder-Mead and all the variations requiring an analytic objective function generally need many properties in terms of continuity, smoothness, and existence of an explicit Hessian with respect to the parameters to be optimized in order to produce sound results. All these methods use objective function values and the derivatives with respect to the parameters optimized to make decisions about the direction and region of search for maximum or minimum. For the rest of the chapter it is assumed the objective function to maximize is a weighted sum of a factor set $X$ with size $N_b \times n$, where $n$ is the number of parameters and $N_b$ is the number of observations in the set. Let's assume a single objective function $f : W \to R$, where the space of the solution is $W \sqsubseteq R^n$. The target of the optimization is to maximize the objective data given a set of data $X$:

$$f(w|X) = f(w_1, w_2, \ldots, w_n|X) \qquad (1)$$

The optimal solution is represented by:

$$w^* = \underset{w \in W}{\arg\max} \left( f(w|X) \right)$$
$$= \left\{ w^* \in W : f(w^*|X) \geq f(w^*|X), \forall w \text{ in } W \right\} \qquad (2)$$

A first step in the genetic algorithm is the creation of the chromosomes as a string of values through the encoding process. The encoding outcomes can be binary, real numbers, strings of characters, and even more complicated objects. In the optimization case presented in this section the chromosomes can be expressed as the set of real input variables $w$ as shown in Figure 1.

FIGURE 1  Chromosomes can be expressed as the set of real input variables $w$ for the objective function $f$.

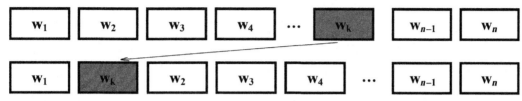

FIGURE 2  Genetic mutation. For the case of real value encoding a random gene $w_k$ is chosen and its place in the chromosome is changed.

Genetic algorithms use the following sequence of operations on the encoded set:

- Cross-over is the process in which the genes from the chromosomes of selected parents recombine and create new offsprings. There are a few types of cross-over operations including single and multiple incisions and recombination of different sequences (Figure 3). Some other operations can be logical for the case of binary data, min and max for real values, or any other functional type [102].
- Mutation implies a random change in the gene. In nature it corresponds to errors in the gene-copying process. In the case of real value encoding a random gene $w_k$ is chosen and its place in the chromosome is changed as explained in Figure 2. In addition, the mutated gene can be shocked with a small stochastic value $\delta_k$[1] to create new offsprings.
- Selection is a process based on the computation of a fitness function for each

chromosome electing the chromosomes that will generate offspring. Common examples of chromosome selection are roulette wheel,[2] and rank selection.[3]
- Elitism means that the best solution or number of high fitness solutions found in the process do not enter the selection and go further in the next generation.

Optimization through the genetic algorithm has the following steps as shown in Figure 4:

1. A population of $N_p$ initial solutions (chromosomes) is randomly generated and the fitness function is evaluated for each solution.
2. Based on the fitness value the selection assigns the elements for recombination in the next generation.
3. The selected solutions go into the recombination (cross-over) process, which generates the children population. From the two solutions chosen through the selection

---

[1]This feature is common in stochastic optimization approaches. A starting point $\mathbf{w} = (w_1, w_2, \ldots, w_n)$ is randomly generated and the objective function $f(\mathbf{w})$ is computed. A vector $\delta = (\delta_1, \ldots, \delta_n)$ is randomly generated and $f$ is computed at $(w_1 + \delta_1, \ldots, w_n + \delta_n)$ [103].

[2]Fitness level is used to associate a probability of selection with each individual solution. The population of chromosomes are like numbers on a roulette wheel and their probability of occurrence is given by their fitness.
[3]This method ranks the population according to their fitness and then every chromosome receives ranking.

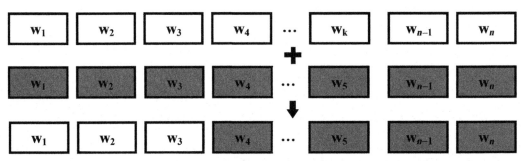

**FIGURE 3** Genetic cross-over. A single point incision creates subsequences from parent chromosomes, which are recombined in offsprings.

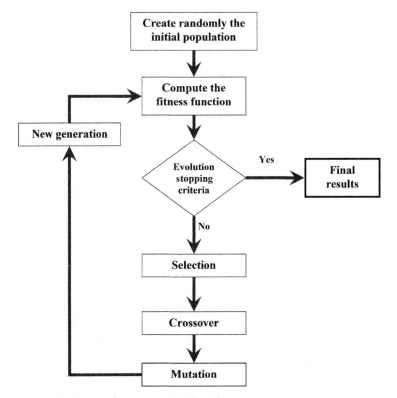

**FIGURE 4** Steps of an optimization employing a genetic algorithm.

presented above and using a cross-over operator a new offspring is created. Not all solutions need to go in the cross-over process and a cross-over rate can be imposed. Elitism can also be applied to impose the clone of the best solution.

4. The generated offspring are subjected to mutation, which occurs at a given rate.
5. Each element from the new population is assessed with the fitness function.
6. If the stopping criterion is satisfied the algorithm is stopped and the current

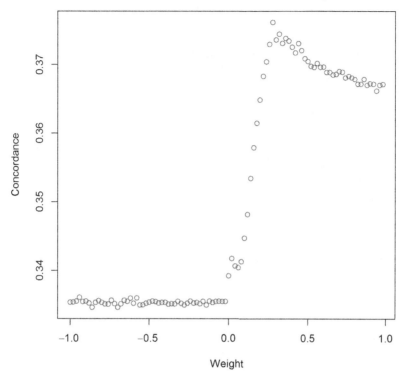

**FIGURE 5** Objective function for which the genetic algorithm is appropriate: the function has local minima, flat regions, and the first derivative is not continuous.

population is the final result; otherwise, the cycle restarts at step 2.

The traditional optimization toolboxes are very rich in terms of proposed methods, but optimization using genetic algorithms performs better when the objective function has discontinuities, or flat regions, is highly nonlinear, has stochastic features, and well-defined derivatives. Figure 5 shows an example of an objective function representing the concordance between a set of scores and a set of ordinal ratings. The input parameter is the weight of the factor in the score. It can be seen that the function has local minima, flat regions, and the first derivative is not continuous. Even a complex optimization algorithm would fail on such type of objective function and for these cases genetic algorithm are justified.

## 3 EXAMPLES

To assess the potential of misconduct risk or fraud a common way is to build a score that can reflect the riskiness of an employee, client, or counterparty. Establishing a list of factors including both qualitative and quantitative variables is not something most organizations have much experience with, and aggregating all factors into one score can be even more complex. There is already significant literature on building credit scores with genetic algorithms, especially in the area of retail banking. Desai et al. [104] investigated the predictive power of neural networks and genetic algorithms compared to traditional techniques such as linear discriminant analysis and logistic regression.

Zhang and Bhattacharyya [105] demonstrated the potential of genetic algorithms as a base classifier algorithm, which significantly outperformed the machine learning technique trained with decision trees and logistic regression. This is explained by higher diversity, both in terms of the functional form of as well as with respect to the variables defining the models. Ong et al. [106] used genetic algorithms to build credit-scoring models and compared it to other credit-scoring models including neural networks, decision trees, rough sets, and logistic regression. The study conclude that genetic algorithms can provide better performance than other models.

The problem of exploring and capturing the features of crime in a score might look similar to the development of credit scores for retail and corporate ratings, which use some genetic algorithm methods in their modeling. However, there are few issues that make the construction of a crime-rating score more complicated. First, the score can be assessed across many criteria and hence the model should be able to test the score against multiple targets. Second, the target criteria can also vary over time or have stochastic behavior. Lastly, the factors themselves might not have fixed values and should incorporate some views from experts or from external scenarios. The factor set used in this type of model incorporates cross-siloed and cross-type information. Factors can be financial ratios as well as qualitative assessments from experts or opinion metrics extracted from unstructured data (i.e., emails, or documents). All these elements make the crime rating models more complicated than the usual credit scoring models. A practical example will show some of the challenges involved in such a score. Let's assume an investment bank wants to assess the risk of crime for a set of brokerage houses, with which it has a counterparty relationship. The main frauds that are assessed through the scorecard are money laundering, market manipulation, and insider trading. The explored data results in factors that can be used in different combinations for dif-

ferent crimes. A parallel could be drawn with the gene expression in living beings. If a certain gene sequence is red in the transcription process (DNA to RNA) than a protein is synthesized, while if another region of the gene is translated then a different protein is produced. The same pool of DNA genes that are red in different sequences can generate different enzymes or different cells. In the same way, a different set of risk factors in an organization mixed in different ways can be causes of different crimes. It can be postulated that there could be a conceptual crime DNA that could exist within every organizations. The expression of those genes, depends on a lot of drivers, and can result in crimes in various types and various severities. However, this is not the main reason genetic algorithms are appropriate. When the investment bank wants to assess the crime risk for its various brokerage counterparties the following data are usually used:

- **Structured data** including all kinds of data stored in repositories mainly in numeric form.
  - *Financial data*:
    - Static: Financial ratios like leverage, liquidity, total assets, return over equity, cost efficiency, etc.
    - Dynamic: Market volatility of the main assets traded with that broker, credit default spreads, etc.
  - *Expert input* including mainly ordinal and categorical data capturing the views about a firm in a specific framework:
    - Qualitative assessment: includes grades on an ordinal scale (i.e., Good, Medium, Poor, Abnormal), management quality, reputation of the firm, clients revenue/proprietary revenue,[4] regulatory compliance, market share.

---

[4]Generally this ratio is not public but a risk manager or a relationship manager can assess it.

- Subjective features: the firm's involvement in past litigation, involvement in past investigations, senior manager with past legal issues, etc. Expert input can be converted into numeric input on a predefined base (e.g., between 0 and 100 assigning 0 for abnormal, 20 Poor, 50 Medium, and 80 for Good). Furthermore, it can be aggregated with the financial data in a set of structured data inputs.

- **Unstructured data**
  - *Text labeling*, used to identify unusual tags or names.
  - *Sentiment or opinion analysis* with e-mail or electronic exchanges between the bank and the client.
  - *Communication flows* assess the frequency and linkage complexity between the bank and its counterparties. The aim of this operation is to assess whether there are unusual patterns of communications like a trader e-mailing a risk manager or broker or with compliance, etc. This output can be transformed into a numeric value but not as a crisp variable and most likely as a range.[5]

The features of the data used in building crime scores recommends the choice of a genetic algorithm approach. Output from unstructured data can have stochastic or noisy forms, while experts' views translate into grades. The objective function would represent in this case a concordance metric between the score and a series of ordinal variables representing the riskiness of a counterparty issued from historical cases or from current assessments. This function can be changed from one generation to another, which allows integrating new data and capturing new behaviors. Crime adapts quickly to new environments. If

for instance gene's composition is decrypted at a moment $t$ and a remedy is administrated, most likely in the next generation at $t + 1$ the gene's features would be different in order to bypass the remedy.

## 3.1 Concordance Metrics

Continuing with the previous example of a brokerage house assessment a crime scoring model is based on a set of features capturing the risk of crime or misconduct. In order to find the weight of each risk driver an objective function is considered as a concordance metric between the set of scores and a set of rankings capturing the degree of crime risk of each broker. This ranking can come from historical observations of firms which were involved in fraud and misconduct cases. It can also come from expert assessments or crime agency ratings. Let's assume a data set of $n$ factors and a population of assessed brokers **B** of size $N_b$ and a matrix **X** of factor values of size $N_b \times n$ where the concordance with the ranking vector $Y$ has the following expression:

$$f(w_1, w_2, \ldots, w_n) = \langle \mathbf{X} \cdot w', \mathbf{Y} \rangle \tag{3}$$

$$= \left\langle \sum_{i=1}^{n} \mathbf{X}_{B,i} \cdot w_i, \mathbf{Y}_B \right\rangle \tag{4}$$

If the target value $Y$ includes ranks from a number of $N_e$ different experts corresponding to various crime types than the above metric should include the full expert panel. Assuming the $Y$ is a matrix of ordinal data of size $N_p \times N_e$ the full concordance is:

$$f(w_1, w_2, \ldots, w_n) = \sum_{k=1}^{N_e} \left\langle \sum_{i=1}^{n} \mathbf{X}_{B,i} \cdot w_i, \mathbf{Y}_{B,k} \right\rangle \tag{5}$$

Alternative concordance metrics are usually employed in these circumstances,

- The most common metric used is the Kendall $\tau$, which assesses the strength of association of two sets of ordinal data defined as:

---

[5]The output of unstructured data interpretation can use fuzzy inference that would result in a distribution of values conditioned by a state.

$$\tau = \frac{n_c - n_d}{0.5 \cdot N_b(N_b^2 - 1)} \quad (6)$$

where $n_c, n_d$ are the number of concordant and discordant pairs, respectively.

- The Spearman $\rho$ coefficient is defined as the Pearson correlation coefficient between the ranked variables. For the sample of size $N_b$, the $N_b$ raw scores $S_j = \sum_i^n w_i \cdot X_{j,i}, Y_j$ are converted to ranks $S_j^r, Y_j^r$, and $\rho$ is computed from:

$$\rho = 1 - \frac{6 \sum_j |S_j^r - Y_j^r|^2}{N_b(N_b^2 - 1)} \quad (7)$$

- In many cases the score should be concordant with more than one target, hence $Y$ is a matrix of size $N_b \times N_e$. As explained in the previous section the main score can be assessed against the risk of money laundering, insider trading, and market manipulation, each having a target ranking represented by a column of the matrix $Y$. The Kendall W metric allows computing the concordance against more than one ranking. Assuming that $z_{j,\bullet}(t) = \left\{ S_j^r, Y_{j,1}, Y_{j,2}, \ldots, Y_{j,N_e} \right\}$ is a discrete variable representing the score of each brokerage firm $j$ converted to ranks and the various targets ranks $Y_{j,\bullet}$, for a given number of rankings $N_e$ with the matrix $z$ of size $N_b \times N_e + 1$ the following are defined:

$$\bar{z}_{\cdot i} = \frac{1}{N_b} \sum_{j=1}^{N_b} z_{ji}$$

$$\bar{z} = \frac{1}{N_b(N_e + 1)} \sum_{j=1}^{N_b} \sum_{i=1}^{N_e+1} z_{ji}$$

$$SS_t = n \sum_{i=1}^{N_e+1} (\bar{z}_{\cdot i} - \bar{z})^2$$

$$SS_e = \frac{1}{N_b N_e} \sum_{j=1}^{N_b} \sum_{i=1}^{N_e+1} (z_{ji} - \bar{z})^2$$

Kendall's coefficient $\mathbf{W}$ is thus defined as:

$$W = \frac{12 SS_t}{(N_e+1)^2(N_b^3 - N_b)}$$

- Gini's mean difference from Borroni and Zenga [107] is a general measure of the agreement of a set of rankings. The index is used to test for the independence of two variables used to rank the units of a sample against their concordance/discordance. For a sample of ranks transformed score $S^r$ with the corresponding rankings vector $Y$, the statistic:

$$GMD(S) = \frac{\sum_{i=1}^n \sum_{j=1}^n \left| |S_i^r - Y_i| - |S_j^r - Y_j| \right|}{n(n-1)} \quad (8)$$

For a synthetic data set of 200 brokerage houses with the factors set as given in Table 1, including financial ratios, market data, qualitative input, unstructured data, and macroeconomics three model specifications are implemented.

First (Model 1) a plain model where the factors are tested against three target ranks and the concordance metric is based on the Kendall W measure. Figure 6 shows the evolution of the fitness function over 500 generations with a mutation rate of 0.1 and a cross-over rate of 0.8 [108].

The second version (Model 2) introduces an adaptive structure of the factor features. Thus, for the unstructured data if the weight of the factors in a generation is too high then the next generation of the factor level diminishes proportionally. This feature of dynamic data corresponds to a certain extent to real cases. If a broker feels there is an increased surveillance in his communication he will reduce the amount of information communicated electronically, which

**TABLE 1** Genetic Algorithm Score Weights for Various Model Specifications

| Data type | Factor | Model 1 | Model 2 | Model 3 |
|---|---|---|---|---|
| Financial ratios | Total equity | 0.36 | 0.25 | 0.21 |
| | Leverage | 0.50 | 0.30 | 0.52 |
| | Liquidity ratio | 0.40 | 0.23 | 0.24 |
| | Return over equity | 0.39 | 0.27 | 0.45 |
| | Cost to income ratio | 0.12 | 0.06 | 0.07 |
| Market data | Market volatility | 0.33 | 0.46 | 0.48 |
| | CDS spread | 0.40 | 0.33 | 0.53 |
| Qualitative inputs | Proprietary trading revenue share | 0.14 | 0.09 | 0.22 |
| | Cancelled trades | 0.52 | 0.26 | 0.30 |
| | Management legal track record | 0.51 | 0.45 | 0.62 |
| | Firm's legal track record | 0.12 | 0.05 | 0.12 |
| | Firm's investigation track record | 0.14 | 0.28 | 0.31 |
| | Reputation | 0.45 | 0.34 | 0.49 |
| | Market share | 0.57 | 0.45 | 0.45 |
| | Key persons at risk | 0.50 | 0.33 | 0.33 |
| | Local regulatory strength | 0.36 | 0.21 | 0.28 |
| Unstructured data | Sentiment in emails | 0.37 | 0.14 | 0.25 |
| | Email flows | 0.21 | 0.07 | 0.22 |
| | Unusual text | 0.23 | 0.16 | 0.29 |
| Macro | National GDP growth | 0.55 | 0.42 | 0.59 |
| | National crime index | 0.10 | 0.03 | 0.05 |

will reduce the signals in the unstructured data treatment:

$$f(w_1, w_2, \ldots, w_n)$$
$$= \left\langle \sum_{i=1}^{n} (\mathbf{X}_{B,i} - H_{B,i}(w) \cdot 1_{i \in n_{\text{unstructured}}}) \cdot w_i, \mathbf{Y} \right\rangle \tag{9}$$

where the function $H_{B,i}(w)$ is a stochastic noise function with the variance being an increasing function of $w$ for those factors concerning the unstructured data $i \in n_{\text{unstructured}}$. As expected in this specification the weight of the unstructured factors diminishes, hence some signals might go under the radar.

The third model addresses this issue by increasing the rate of mutations from 0.1 to 0.25, thereby increasing the chances of having higher figures for those weights concerning the unstructured factors. Thus, the adaptive behavior of the broker is "tricked" by the mutations rate. The new weights are higher and closer to the first specifications.

## 3.2 Multi-Objective Optimization

One of the advantages of genetic algorithms is that they can deal with multi-objective function optimization. In the previous examples if an objective function is specified for each type of crime risk or per geographical region, this can induce the existence of more than one objective functions $f_k$ in the concordance optimization. A simple way to address this issue is to consider a weighted single objective function written as:

$$f(w_1, w_2, \ldots, w_n) = \sum_k \omega_k f_k(w_1, w_2, \ldots, w_n) \tag{10}$$

A more complex approach is to optimize all objective functions concomitantly. Thus there will be a set of feasible solutions. If all objective

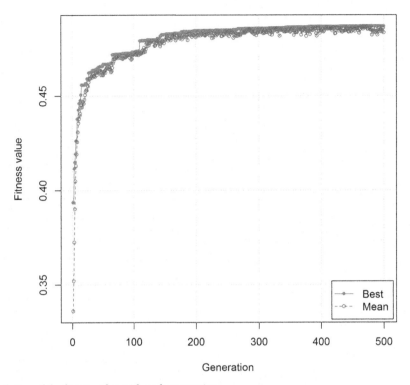

FIGURE 6 Evolution of the fitness value with each generation.

functions are for minimization, a feasible solution $\mathbf{w}^b$ is said to dominate another feasible solution $\mathbf{w}^a$:

$$\mathbf{w}^a \prec \mathbf{w}^b \ \forall i : f_i(w^a) \leq f_i(w^b) \tag{11}$$

$$\exists j : f_i(w^a) \leq f_i(w^b) \tag{12}$$

A solution is called Pareto optimal if there is no other solution or the solution space dominates it. A Pareto optimal solution cannot be improved with respect to individual function $f_i$ without worsening at least one other objective function from the set $f_{\neq i}$. The set of all feasible non-dominated solutions forms the Pareto optimal set (which generally has a high number of solutions) and the corresponding objective function

values in the objective space is called the Pareto front [109].

For the given example, Figure 7 presents the Pareto front using a method proposed by Deb et al. [110] for two objective functions corresponding to the concordance with the market manipulation ranking and money laundering ranking.

# 4 OUTLOOK

With organizations trying to get up to speed on building crime intelligence units, models that capture misconduct and fraud risk will be needed. Determining a score for assessing the risk of an employee, counterparty, or client can

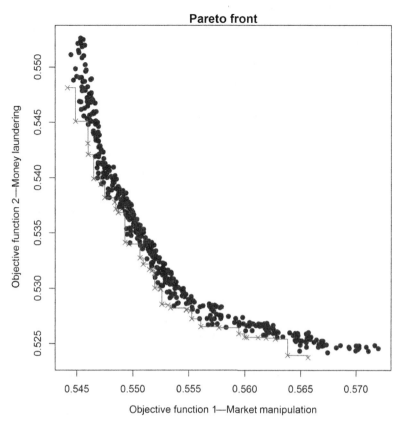

**FIGURE 7** Pareto front.

seem like a simple task but if it is used in a real environment it needs to be able to capture the particularities of criminal behavior.

As an optimization tool genetic algorithms do have many advantages for estimating the weight of such scores based on heterogeneous factors with noisy input. Given a set of risk factors in different proportions we can determine the risk of different crimes within an organization. Similar to genes in chromosomes this can result in various combinations of crime. Identifying those risks and their metamorphosis over time can justify the use of genetic algorithms not only from a purely technical perspective.

# CHAPTER

# 2E

# Statistical Hypothesis Tests

## 1 BACKGROUND

The use of quantitative techniques in the area of financial crime investigation intersects with statistical hypothesis tests. Data mining and statistics are fields that overlap, and yet also have differences. Exploratory data analysis or mining does not have any prior hypothesis to test and aims to extract the features of a data set, while statistical hypothesis testing assumes a target hypothesis to test. Nonetheless, in order to be able to generate inference based on data mining the passage through statistical hypothesis testing is difficult to avoid. Statistical hypothesis testing represents a class of methods for testing a hypothesis using the information extracted from a sample. A key concept employed in most of the tests is the significance level, which is a ruling criterion upon which a decision is made concerning the null hypothesis. Table 1 shows the various outcomes of a statistical test emphasizing the Type I and II errors.

## 2 FISHER VS. NEYMAN-PEARSON

Very early in the history of hypothesis testing two different philosophical views collided originated from two schools: Fisher on the one side and Neyman-Pearson on the other side.

The Fisher approach states only the null hypothesis $H_0$ and builds a statistic based on the data $X$. The resulting $p$-value is evidence against or in favor of a theory. In the Fisher approach, if $p$-value is very small, either something very rare has happened, or $H_0$ is false. Therefore, a $p$-value of 0.001 rejects much more strongly the null hypothesis than a $p$-value of 0.01. The Neyman-Pearson approach states two hypotheses, the null ($H_0$) and the alternative ($H_a$), and the statistics are computed for both. The fundamental difference in Fisher's school is the assessment of $\alpha$ as a probability of observing $H_0$ given the data, *a priori* chosen around 5%. If the $p$-value of the test is lower than $\alpha$ the null hypothesis is rejected with a significance level equal to $1 - \alpha$.

**TABLE 1**   Type I and Type II Errors

|       | Decision | Fail to reject $H_0$ | Reject $H_0$ |
|-------|----------|----------------------|--------------|
| Truth | TRUE | Correct decision $P = 1 - \alpha$ | Type I error $P = \alpha$ |
|       | FALSE | Type II error $P = \beta$ | Correct decision $P = 1 - \beta$ |

Notes: *Probability of making a type I error is denoted by* $\alpha$. *Probability of making a type II error is denoted* $\beta$.

The object of disagreement is the concept of significance level advocated by Neyman-Pearson. To Fisher a statistically significant result is the finding itself and not the evaluation of a coefficient, or model [111].[1] Both methods have faced criticism but in most of the economic and financial literature Neyman-Pearson's method seems to have more followers for practical reasons.

An important result is the Neyman-Pearson lemma, which is presented below. First, let's consider a random sample $X_1, X_2, \ldots, X_n$ from a probability distribution with parameter $\theta$. The likelihood ratio for comparing two simple hypotheses $H_0$ and $H_a$ is:

$$\lambda = \frac{L(\theta_1|X)}{L(\theta_0|X)} \tag{1}$$

**Neyman-Pearson Lemma.** *Assuming a positive constant k and a subset C of the sample space generating X with the following properties:*

$$\lambda(x) \geq k \text{ for } X \in C$$
$$\lambda(x) < k \text{ for } X \notin C$$
$$P(X \in C, \theta_0) = \alpha$$

*the test with critical region C will be the most powerful test for $H_0$ vs. $H_a$. $\alpha$ is the size of the test and C is the best critical region of size $\alpha$.*

A further application of this theoretical background is the field of detection aiming to choose behavioral patterns from a background with noisy information. Let's assume that for a series of hedge fund performance returns data $X$ an auditor wants to test two hypotheses: $H_1$—the hedge fund follows strictly its agreed strategy, $H_2$—the hedge funds employs a tactical strategy to increase its performance. In this condition, $H_1$ is chosen when $P(H_1|X) > P(H_2|X)$ and $H_2$ if the inequality works the other way around [113].

$$P(H_1|X) = \frac{P(X|H_1) \cdot P(H_1)}{P(X)}$$
$$P(H_2|X) = \frac{P(X|H_2) \cdot P(H_2)}{P(X)}$$

where $P(X)$ is the probability of event $X$ and $P(H_1)$ and $P(H_2)$ are the probability of the hypothesis $P(X) = P(X|H_1) \cdot P(H_2) + P(X|H_2) \cdot P(H_2)$.

$H_1$ is chosen over $H_2$ if $\frac{P(X|H_2)}{P(X|H_1)} < \frac{P(H_1)}{P(H_2)}$. The ratio $\frac{P(y|H2)}{p(y|H1)}$ is nothing more than the likelihood ratio introduced above. The Neyman-Pearson approach is obviously more efficient as it proposes a cut-off where the null is rejected. However, in the area of financial crime things are not always black or white and investigators usually deal with more than *36 shades of gray*. In this context, Fisher's method is more conceptually sound as it allows the user to compare the various *shades* as shown above.

# 3 FALLACIES OF HYPOTHESIS TEST

Despite being a useful tool, statistical hypothesis tests do have a few flaws linked to the way the list is built and also to the interpretation of

---

[1]*It is common and convenient for experimenters to take 5%. as a standard level of significance, in the sense that they are prepared to ignore all results that fail to reach this standard, and, by this means, to eliminate from further discussion the greater part of the fluctuations that chance causes have introduced into their experimental results* [112].

the results. These facts have generated a few fallacies well studied in the literature creating an argument for those statisticians that challenge the concept of statistical tests. The fallacies of hypothesis tests need to be correctly identified especially when the test results will be used in courts to prove cases of financial crime. In many cases, these tests are the main evidence, careful treatment is required.

Misinterpretation of statistical tests [111] are linked to the $p$-values and include the following:

- $p$ is the probability that the results of the test are due to chance or sampling error.
- the smaller the value $p$, the larger the effect. This fallacy is very common and is addressed by the effect size metrics.
- $p$ is the probability that the results can be replicated if the experiment was conducted a second time.
- $p$ is the probability of observing results outside the range of the observed, if the null hypothesis is true.
- $p$ is the probability of the null being true given the data $P(H_0|X) = P(H_0, X)/P(X)$, while in fact it is the probability of data given the null hypothesis $P(X|H_0)$.
- $p$ is the probability that the null is true given that we have rejected it.
- $1 - p$ is the probability that the alternative hypothesis is true given the data.
- Correlation does not imply causality. This is topic goes beyond the hypothesis testing area. However, any inference made from rejecting the null hypothesis does not imply a causality relationship for an observed concordance metric.

# 4 SCIENCE AND HYPOTHESIS TEST

In 2011 an Italian laboratory announced that theyhad found that fundamental particles (neutrinos) can travel faster than light,[2] a major breakthrough in the scientific world. The experiment, called OPERA (Oscillation Project with Emulsion-Racking Apparatus), was based 1400 m below the ground level in the Gran Sasso National Laboratory in Italy. Researchers studied a beam of particles (neutrinos) coming from the European Center of Nuclear Research (CERN), located 730 kilometers away near Geneva, Switzerland. The legitimate question was concerning the null hypothesis significance test. Furthermore, the hypothesis test could accept or reject the findings of the experiment.

Many other experiments in physics, did not use explicit and in-depth statistical significance tests, but the result were unanimously accepted. However, economic and financial literature now requires the statistical significance tests for all results communicated.

Let's assume a risk manager assesses the potential losses generated by new strategies A and B, which he wants to audit further. Let's assume the potential loss of A is $20 million with a prediction error of $10 million, while strategy B has a potential loss of $5 million with a prediction error of $1 million. The decision the risk manager should make is which strategy to audit in detail. On one hand, strategy A has a larger estimated potential loss but with a high error; on the other hand, strategy B has a lower loss but with more precision (Table 2). In many cases strategy B would be chosen for audit, given the fact that it has higher precision.

A metric similar to the $t$-statistic consisting of measuring how much larger the estimate is than the previous one would indicate that strategy B has a higher figure. However, as noted in a similar example presented by Ziliak and

---

[2]Particles break light-speed limit, http://www.nature.com/news/2011/110922/full/news.2011.554.html.

TABLE 2   Comparison Between the Estimated Loss of Strategies A and B

| Strategy | A | B |
|---|---|---|
| Estimates | 20 | 5 |
| Precision | 10 | 1 |
| Estimate/Precision | 2 | 5 |

TABLE 3   Effect Size

| Size | Distance between means (Cohen $d$) | Correlation |
|---|---|---|
| Large | 0.8 | 0.54 |
| Medium | 0.5 | 0.3 |
| Small | 0.2 | 0.1 |

McCloskey [114] the risk manager should be concerned about the size of the loss and not by the prediction quality. In this context, Fisher's views around the significance level or more correctly about the lack of a significance level are important. There is a need for a standardized metric to assess the effect observed, thereby becoming dimensionless.

## 4.1 Effect Size

Effect size is a family of metrics that measure the amplitude of a phenomena. Compared to significance tests, the metrics are independent of sample size. A statistical hypothesis test depends in most cases on the size of the sample tested. With an increase on the size of the studied sample an effect can be amplified. The problem with statistics having high significance is that $p$-values are perceived as indexes that reflect the effect size, sample size, and test type. In many cases, a statistically significant test can be the result of a large sample or a specific test used or a $p$-value. However, as is the case of the risk managers that questioned the amplitude of one strategy compared to another, there are two types of effect size to consider: for measuring association strengths and the difference between the means of the two samples. Effect size assesses whether the size is large, medium, or small based on Table 3.

Cohen's $d$, one of the most popular metrics for effect size, is defined as the difference between two means divided by a standard deviation for the pooled data, created from the two samples and following the expression:

$$d = \frac{\bar{\mu}_1 - \bar{\mu}_2}{\sigma} \tag{2}$$

where $\sigma = \sqrt{\frac{(N_1-1)\sigma_1^2+(N_2-1)\sigma_2^2}{N_1+N_2-2}}$ and the variance for a sample of data $x_i$ defined as $\sigma_1^2 = \frac{1}{n_1-1}\sum_{i=1}^{n_1}(x_{1,i} - \bar{\mu}_1)^2$. Cohen's $d$ is related to the $t$ statistics as $d \propto \frac{t}{\sqrt{N}}$. Table 3 shows the values of Cohen's $d$ for the conventional criteria that define an effect as "small," "medium," or "large." As low value of Cohen's $d$ could indicate the need for a larger size sample in a statistical test.

## 4.2 Resampling-Based Tests

Despite being challenged in some research reviews [111] as method in the field of statistical significance testing, resampling approaches do have some genuine advantages, especially if the test's statistics do not have explicit form. A simple example is assessing the frequency of suspicious transactions in a data set of trading observations. This problem becomes complex when the number of suspicious trades in the empirical set is very low or even zero and in these situations resampling-based methods could be a very good tool. Let's assume that in a data set with 1000 trades, two suspicious trades are observed, thereby implying an observed hazard rate of 0.2%. The question is how confident can we be about the estimated rate of suspicious trades. If the empirical hazard rate is 0.2%

then what is the highest number of suspicious trades that can be observed in a comparable sample?

The main point here is that the estimate of the hazard rate could be higher than 0.2% and the data sample could contain randomly only two suspicious trades; however, in other situations samples could contain more suspicious observations. For instance, assuming a data set with 1000 observations with a probability of occurrence of suspicious trades of 10% after producing many samples of this data set, we might end up with a sample containing only two rogue trades. This event is obviously rare, but shows the necessity of producing a conservative upper bound estimate of the probability of observing suspicious trades. Therefore before interpreting in any way the observed rate of suspicious frauds, one needs to estimate the theoretical probability of fraud (generating suspicious trades). In our example this can be done through bootstrapping in such way that the bootstrapped samples with less than two defaults would represent less than 5% $(1 -$ confidence interval $\alpha)$ of the total number of samples.

The test can be reduced to validating of the following null hypothesis:

- $H_0 \ \phi \leq \phi^u$
- $H_a \ \phi > \phi^u$

The problem to solve is to find the upper bound $\phi^u$ of the observed rate of suspicious rate $\phi$ so that the null hypothesis $H_0$ is not rejected with the confidence interval $\alpha$.

Given an initial data set of observations with two suspicious trades through recursive iteration the target value of the theoretic probability of fraudulent trades $(\phi)$ is increased gradually starting at 0.2%. For each iteration bootstrap samples are produced, looking for the odds of having the samples with two defaults.

For instance, from an initial sample with a theoretic probability of fraudulent trades $(\phi)$ of 0.6% (in 1000 trades there are 6 suspicious and 994 normal) a high number of samples is generated

via bootstrapping. For each sample the empirical hazard rate of suspicious trades is computed. Thus, a distribution of hazard rates is built and the distribution of these hazard rates can be visualized. For this case it appears that in more than 95% of the cases there are more than two defaults. Following this logic it can be concluded that $\phi^u = 0.6\%$ is a conservative upper bound for our initial 0.2% estimate.

To simplify the presentation without reducing the generality let's assume a data set having features from $N$ trades with $N_S$ suspicious trades. The initial sample is characterized by the indicator variable $y$, $y = (y_1, y_2, y_3, \dots, y_N)$. A bootstrap sample is created from the initial space based on the empirical distribution, putting $1/N$ weight on each observation. At this point, it should be noted that in the bootstrap process there are samples only with normal trades as well as samples with many suspicious trades. The method implemented for the computation of the $\phi$ upper bound at a given confidence level $\alpha$ has the followings steps:

1. An initial value of the upper bound of the default probability $(\phi^u)$ is set as $N_S/N$.
2. An initial sample is set with $\phi^u N$ suspicious observations $(y_{iS} = 1, iS = 1, 2, \dots, \phi^u S)$ and $N - \phi^u N$ good trades $(y_{iN} = 0, iN = \phi^u N + 1, \phi^u N + 2, \dots, N)$.
3. Independent bootstrap data sets $y_1^*, y_2^*, \dots, y_{N_{Sim}}^*$ are drawn from the initial sample. The number of resamples $N_{Sim}$ is large.
4. For each sample $y_j^*$, $j = i, 2, \dots, N_{Sim}$ the empirical hazard fraud rate is computed $\widehat{HR}_j^* = \frac{\#\{y_j^*=1\}}{N}$.
5. If the probability of observing in the distribution $HR_j^*$ values is inferior to the given default rate $N_S/N$ is lower than $1 - \alpha$[3]

---

[3] $\alpha$ is the targeted confidence level.

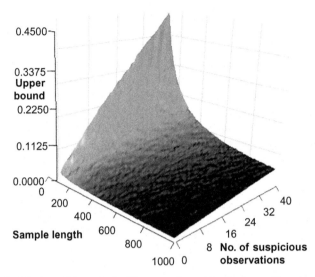

FIGURE 1    Bootstrap method for a confidence test of the upper bound for the hazard fraud rate.

$\mathbf{P}(HR^* <= \frac{N_D}{N}) < 1 - \alpha$ than $\phi^u$ $i$ the searched value. Otherwise go to the next step.

6. A new value of the upper bound of the default probability is set to $\phi^u + \epsilon$,[4] and go back to step 2. The loop is continued until the condition from step 5 is satisfied.

The results for the value of the upper bound frequency using the bootstrapping method are shown in Figure 1. The advantage of this method is that it can provide a value of the upper bound probability of fraud even if the empirical sample has no suspicious observations.

## 5 OUTLOOK

Crime investigation relies in its initial phases on the information extraction from both structured and unstructured data sets. The results of this process are in some cases presented in a plain version or as a statistical hypothesis test. Understanding the limits of the statistical test as well as the alternative interpretations (Neyman-Pearson vs. Fisher) is crucial before taking further action based on tests' outcome. The current econometric literature is very abundant in term of statistical tests, but their application requires also an appropriate knowledge of what is tested and what the test result implies.

---

[4]$\epsilon$ is the incremental step, small enough compared to the value of $\phi^u$.

# Non-Parametric Techniques

## 1 BACKGROUND

The infusion of researchers and engineers from physics and industry into the financial industry has brought with it the concept of *model*. In physics a model aims to be a mathematical representation of a phenomena with the purpose of capturing its various features. A good model should be able to explain the outcome of a phenomena. The better the representation of the model the more accurate its results in comparison to observed results.

The Black & Scholes formalism is a good depiction of the model concept as the proposed formula is able to explain the prices of vanilla derivatives. The main assumptions of the model is that the underlying returns follow a Gaussian distribution and relies on the concept of risk neutrality.

A model or parametric-based method is based on the hypothesis that the model is "the true

model" and the real-life walk follows that model. A parametric method has finite dimensionality and if we aim to improve the model, one way would be to add more dimensions, e.g., adding new parameters to the model.

The non-parametric methods do not assume either the existence of a true model or that the structure of a model is fixed. The class of techniques include statistical methods like non-parametric regression and non-parametric density kernels, but also learning techniques such as $k$-nearest neighbors, classification, and regression trees.

## 2 KERNEL DENSITY ESTIMATION

For a given data set of observations $x_1, \ldots, x_n$ a basic parametric model would aim to provide a model-based distribution that would fit the data set. A simple non-parametricrepresentation is a histogram that divides the data set space into a number of equal sub-intervals (bins) and approximates the density at the center of each interval (bin) by the proportion of points in the data set for the corresponding interval.

A parametric universe would make a hard assumption on the form of the distribution function $\mathbb{F}(x)$ [115]. In the non-parametric world the distribution function $\mathbb{F}(x)$ is estimated by:

$$\hat{\mathbb{F}}(x) = \frac{1}{n}\sum_{i=1}^{n}\mathbf{1}_{x_i \leq x} \tag{1}$$

Moving forward, the histogram kernel estimator introduces a kernel function as a mass point for each observation. Kernel estimators smooth out the contribution of each observation over a local space around that point. The density function $\hat{f}(x)$ that would correspond in the parametric world to the first derivative of $\hat{\mathbb{F}}(x)$ counts the proportion of observations in that data set that are close to the point $x$:

$$\hat{f}(x) = \frac{1}{n \cdot h}\sum_{i=1}^{n} k\left(\frac{x_i - x}{h}\right) \tag{2}$$

where $\int_{-\infty}^{\infty} k(u)\,du = 1$ and the bandwidth $h$ influences the degree of smoothing of the density function. Some popular kernel functions $k(u)$ are given in Table 1.

The extended theory of kernel estimates including the choice of bandwidth and the impact of various kernels is widely discussed in

TABLE 1   Kernel Function

| Kernel | $k(u)$ |
|---|---|
| Uniform | $\frac{1}{2}I(\mid u \mid \leq 1)$ |
| Epanechnikov | $\frac{3}{4}(1 - u^2)I(\mid u \mid \leq 1)$ |
| Gaussian | $\frac{1}{\sqrt{2\pi}}\exp(-\frac{1}{2}u^2)$ |

the literature, e.g., Pagan and Ullah [116] and Hwang et al. [117].

The kernel density can be used in almost all avenues of modeling, whereas fitting a distribution would create issues for the choice of parametric form.

Figure 1 shows the distribution of the daily volatiles for a sample of 2000 stocks. A non-parametric solution for the density would give a straightforward response if a representation for the volatility is required.

Another field where kernel density estimates are a good choice is for data sets that present abnormal shapes (two peaks histogram) or for which a model would have conceptually soundness issues. For example, the distribution of IPO discount prices of exhibited in Figure 2 for a data set of U.S. stocks would be much better represented by a model-free assumption. A parametric model would not easily fit the empirical data set and in the case where a sophisticated distribution is chosen the parameters would be less intuitive.

## 3 NON-PARAMETRIC REGRESSION

Regression analysis studies the way a system characterized by function $g(\bullet)$ responds to a set of input observations $x_1, \ldots, x_n$ generating a set of output $y_1, \ldots, y_n$. The system can be modeled as:

$$y_i = g(x_i) + \epsilon_i \tag{3}$$

where the regression function is:

$$g(X = x_i) = \mathbb{E}(Y = y_i | X = x_i) \tag{4}$$

In the parametric world there are some hard assumptions about the function $g(\bullet)$, described by a finite set of parameters, which lead to classic linear or logistic regression. Unlike the parametric approach non-parametric regression is flexible in regards to the shape of the regression curve. A straightforward method for estimating

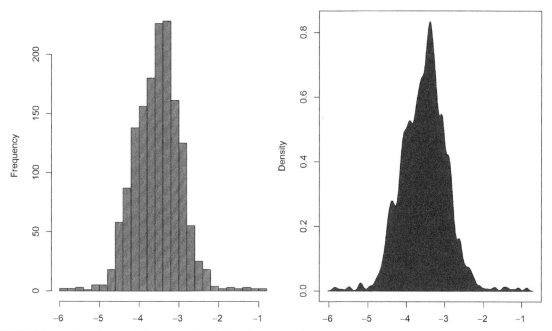

**FIGURE 1**  Stock volatility: Left: Empirical volatility histogram (log scale). Right: Kernel density estimate with Gaussian kernel function (log scale).

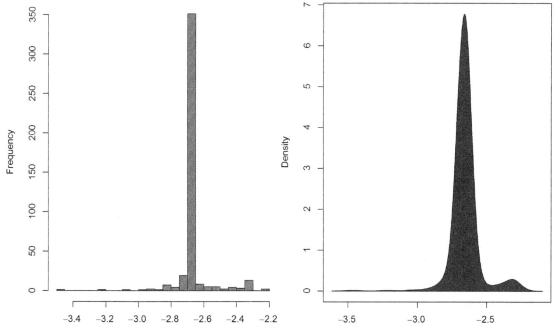

**FIGURE 2**  Price discount in IPO. Left: Histogram of the discount ratio. Right: Density estimate with an Epanechnikov kernel.

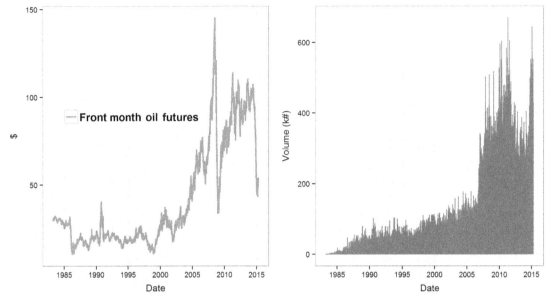

**FIGURE 3**   Oil futures: Evolution of price and volume of the front month crude oil futures.

$g(\bullet)$ in the case where the regressors are continuous was proposed first by Nadaraya and Watson [118] and Watson [119]. An immediate non-parametrical estimation of $g$ would imply computing the mean of the corresponding $Y$ for a given $x_i$. When dealing with continuous data it is more appropriate to consider a neighborhood of $x_i$:

$$\hat{g}(x) = \frac{\int yf(x,y)\,dx}{f(x)} \qquad (5)$$

For a univariate case regression $g$ can be estimated as a locally weighted average of $Y$ in the neighborhood of $x_i$, using a kernel as a weighting function in the form proposed by the Nadaraya-Watson estimator:

$$\hat{g}(x) = \frac{\sum_{i=1}^{n} k(\frac{x-x_i}{h})y_i}{\sum_{i=1}^{n} k(\frac{x-x_i}{h})} \qquad (6)$$

where $k(u)$ is the uniform kernel.

Non-parametric regression offers many choices in terms of kernel form. The method was enriched by Racine and Li [120] who proposed a generalization of the method for non-parametric regression that admits continuous and categorical data in a natural manner.

The **R** package "np" implemented by Hayfield and Racine [121] allows testing the non-parametric regression for a data set of oil futures prices and volumes (Figure 3).

Assuming a simple regression between oil prices and volumes the non-parametric and linear case can be compared as shown in Figure 4. The non-parametric allows a flexible shape that adapts to changes in the relationship between the variable. The non-parametric regression provides a $R^2$ of 0.76 compared to 0.6 for the linear case.[1]

---

[1] A special analysis of non-parametric regression for a non-stationary series is provided by Schienle [122].

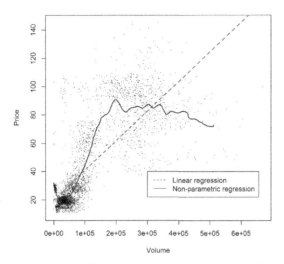

**FIGURE 4** Regression of oil prices vs. volumes. Benchmarking of non-parametric vs. linear regression. The non-parametric model allows a flexible shape that adapts to changes in the relationships between the variables.

## 4 CLASSIFICATION AND REGRESSION TREES

Decision trees, introduced by Morgan and Sonquist [123], are a class of non-parametric supervised-learning techniques used for classification and regression. Decision tree methods provide a model that predicts the value of a target variable by learning from the underlying data features and building simple decision rules.

Decision tree models are simple and efficient especially when dealing with large data set and a large number of variables. These methods partition recursively by training the data and either classifying or regressing it more efficiently than approaches that deal with the data set as a whole.

Among the many variations of decision tree techniques there is particular interest in the CART algorithm introduced by Breiman et al. [124]. CART is based on a binary decision tree that is built by dividing on a recursive basis each node into two offspring nodes. The process starts with the root containing the full data set and increases the trees by adding layers of the offsprings' nodes.

Let $Y$ by the target variable that can take ordinal categorical, nominal categorical, or continuous values. For classification purposes $Y$ is categorical with $K$ classes, its class takes values in $C = \{1, \dots, K\}$. $X_d$, $d = 1, \dots, D$ is the set of predictor variables used to train the tree in order to give the correct outputs $Y$.

In growing a CART tree (Figure 5) for each point in the sample attached to a node and a split point $x^R$ the points $x_i < x_i^R$ go to the left child (branch) and the rest go to the right child. The purpose of the CART method is to find at each bifurcation the split point $x^R$ that maximizes the splitting criteria, also called the purity criteria, where $\pi_L$ and $\pi_R$ are the probabilities of being attached to the left or right child. All possible splits consist of all possible splits corresponding to each predictor $x_i$. A tree is grown starting from the root node by repeatedly using the following steps on each node:

1. **Step 1**: Find each predictor's best split. The entries of each factor are sorted by increasing value. The sorted predictor is iterated over the full data set to find the candidate for the best split corresponding to the value that maximizes the splitting criterion.

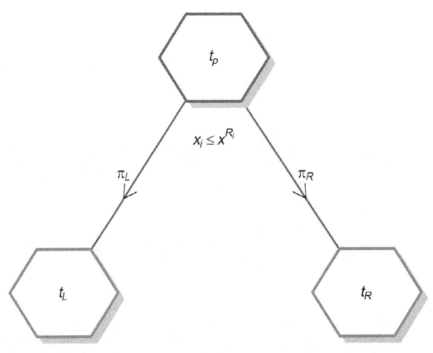

**FIGURE 5** *Tree built*: The index $t$ of nodes includes the parent node $t_p$, the child left node $t_l$, and the child right node $t_r$. For each point in the sample attached to a node and a split point $x^R$ the points $x_i < x^R$ go to the left child and the rest go to the right child. The purpose of CART is to find at each bifurcation the split point $x^R$ that maximizes the splitting criteria, also called the purity criteria, where $\pi_L$ and $\pi_R$ are the probability of being attached to the left or right child.

2. **Step 2**: Find the node's best split: For performing the split, evaluated predictors from step 1 are compared and the dichotomy that maximizes the splitting criterion is chosen.
3. **Step 3**: Build the ramification: If $x_i^R$ is the best split of the best predictor, all $x \leq x_i^R$ are sent to the left node and all $x > x_i^R$ to the right node.

## 4.1 Classification Trees

If $Y$ is a categorical variable one of the most common splitting criteria is the Gini criteria. If $x^R$ is the best split a splitting criterion $\Delta i(x^R, t)$ is calculated for every split at node $t$. Given a node $t$ the Gini impurity measure is:

$$i(s|t) = \sum_{j \neq b} p(j|t)p(b|t) = 1 - \sum_j p(j|t)^2 \quad (7)$$

where $p(b|t)$ is the conditional probability of class $b \in \{1, \ldots, K\}$ given the node $t$.

The splitting criterion to be maximized is expressed as:

$$\Delta i(x^R, t) = i(t_p) - \mathbb{E}[i(t_c)] = i(t_p) - \pi_L i(t_L) - \pi_R i(t_R) \quad (8)$$

where $\pi_L$ and $\pi_R$ are the probabilities of sending a case to the left child node $t_L$ and to the right child node $t_R$, respectively. Thus, CART chooses the best split, which is $x^R$ chosen at node $t$ which as it maximizes the splitting criterion $\Delta i(x^R, t)$:

$$\underbrace{\arg\max}_{x_i < x_i^R, i \in \{1, \ldots, D\}} [i(t_p) - \mathbb{E}[i(t_c)]]$$

$$= i(t) - \pi_L i(t_L) - \pi_R i(t_R)] \quad (9)$$

## 4.2 Regression Trees

In regression trees $Y$ is a continuous variable, with the splitting criterion $\Delta i(x^R, t) = i(t_p) - \pi_L i(t_L) - \pi_R i(t_R)$ used with the least squares deviation (LSD) as an impurity metric:

$$i(t) = 1/n \sum_{i=1}^{n} (y_i - r(\beta, x_i))^2 \qquad (10)$$

where $n$ is the sample size, $y_i$ is the training outcome, and the regression-based outcome is $r(\beta, x_i)$.

The tree-growing process stops when the offspring nodes are pure and contain only observations from the same class or under stopping criteria including the tree depth, size of a node, or the variation of the splitting criterion is smaller than a trigger. After growing the tree-pruning method can be applied for optimizing tree depth by merging offspring on the same tree branch.

## 4.3 Application to IPO litigation

A good candidate for testing the CART methodology is the modeling of the litigation process in the post-IPO process. The Stanford Securities Class action Clearinghouse[2] has a sample of IPOs that have gone through a class action suit, accounting for almost 414 cases since 1997. The aim is to assess through a decision-tree method the factors that triggered the litigation. Hence, a bigger sample is built containing both litigated and non-litigated IPOs, enriched with data from other databases concerning the IPOs provided by Kenney and Patton [125] and the IPOscoop.com.[3] The database provided by Kenney and Patton [125] gives valuable information such as the offering price, discount, and volume of shares offered. The other database IPOScoop.com, an independent online rating service for IPOs, provides details about the opening-day performance of stock. The data set of 2551 IPOs is completed with the price time series of the first 100 trading days of the stock. The factors used for classification and regression purposes are as follows:

$$Y_i = \mathbf{F}(\text{OpeningDayreturn}_i, \text{OfferingVolume}_i,$$
$$\text{Volatilty}_i, \text{Discount}_i) \qquad (11)$$

where $\text{OpeningDayreturn}_i$ is the opening return of the first day compared to the offering price, $\text{OfferingVolume}_i$ is the portion of shares offered to public from the total available shares, $\text{Volatilty}_i$ is the volatility of the returns during the first 100 days, and $\text{Discount}_i$ is the pre-IPO price discount. For the classification, $Y_i$ is a nominal value and the regression is a binary value as follows:

$$Y_i = \begin{cases} \text{Litigated} & 1 \\ \text{Not Litigated} & 0 \end{cases} \qquad (12)$$

The estimated classification tree based on the CART method provided in $R$ development by the "rpart" [126] is shown in Figure 6 before and after pruning. The misclassification error is 8.9%. The opening-day returns and the proportion of shares offered were the main driving factors for the classification trees.

The plain regression method applied in a previous chapter provided an R2 inferior to 20%. The error for the regression tree is 6.6%. The opening-day returns and the proportion of shares offered were the main driving factors, which also appear in the regression tree from Figure 7.

## 5 $k$ NEAREST NEIGHBORS

The $k$ nearest neighbor is a non-parametric classification algorithm introduced by Fix and Hodges [127] that differentiates the observations in a data set based on similarities between them. $k$ nearest neighbor is also referred to as lazy

[2]Securities Class Action Clearinghouse, http:// securities.stanford.edu/.
[3]https://www.iposcoop.com/.

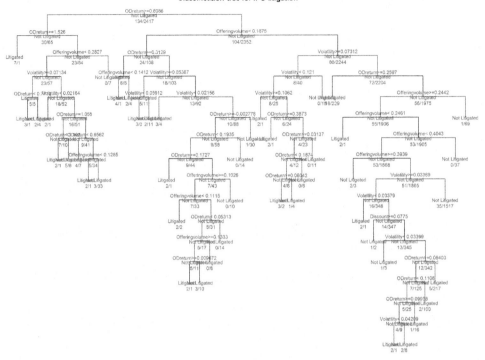

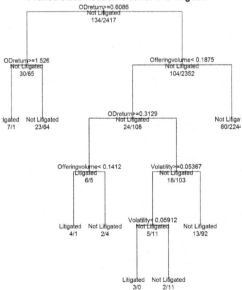

**FIGURE 6** Pre- and post-pruning classification trees for the IPO litigation, where the variable is categorical.

## Pruned classification tree for IPO litigation

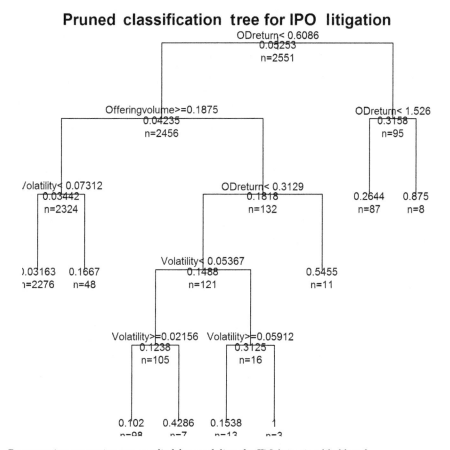

**FIGURE 7**   Post-pruning regression tree applied for modeling the IPO litigation likelihood.

learning or instance-based learning since the classification decision is made as the new observations are tested.

The method requires a training data set observation $x_1, \ldots, x_n$ where $x_i$ are labeled by the set of variables $y_1, \ldots, y_n$ where $y_i \in (1 \ldots K)$.

When classifying a new observation or set of observations $x^*$ a basic $k$ nearest neighbor has the following steps:

- **Step 1**: A positive integer $k$ is defined indicating the number of neighbors to consider for finding the similarity.
- **Step 2**: The $k$ observations in the training data set ($k$ nearest neighbor) that are the

closest to $x^*$ are chosen. Assuming the observation $x_i$ is $d$ dimensional the similarity metric between two observations $x^*$ and $x_i$ is computed usually through an Euclidean distance (the Minkowski or Mahalanobis distances are also frequent metrics):

$$\text{dist}(\mathbf{x}^*, \mathbf{x}_j)$$
$$= \sqrt{(x_{i1} - x_1^*)^2 + (x_{i2} - x_2^*)^2 + \cdots + (x_{ip} - x_p^*)^2}$$

$$(13)$$

- **Step 3**: The corresponding class $y^*$ is considered as the most frequent class among the classes of the $k$ closest neighbors.

**k-nearest neighbour**

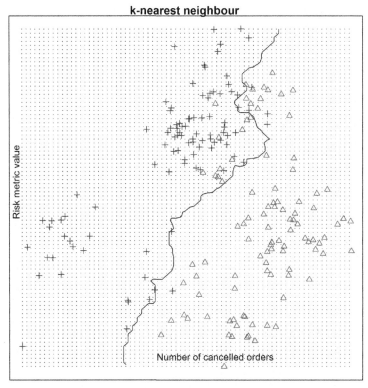

FIGURE 8  *k* nearest neighbor classification for a data set containing a daily risk measure and number of canceled trades (rescaled on a logarithm scale). The intra-day high-frequency traders (crosses) are basically characterized by a high number of canceled orders but low end-of-day risk, because most of the positions are closed. The slow traders (empty triangles) have a low number of canceled trades but a higher risk metric because they have longer term positions.

Like any other non-parametric learning technique overfitting can be a stringent issue as the algorithm may tend naturally to also learn from the noise. A way to assess the robustness of the *k* nearest neighbor algorithm is to use traditional multi-fold cross-validation. The validation would first divide the training data into *m* subsample (folds) on a random basis. For each *m*th fold the *k* nearest neighbor classifier is applied considering as training data the remaining *m* − 1 folds. The error of classification is computed and the procedure is repeated *m* times. The total error is computed as the average of all *m* accuracies.

The R implementation is frequently used for *k* nearest neighbors [128] and also for graphical

visualization through the *elemstatlearn* package proposed by Halvorsen [129].

Figure 8 employs the *k* nearest neighbor for a sample containing observations from a trading floor where there are two kinds of traders: high-frequency traders and slow traders. The first category places orders through computer-based algorithms on the market with intra-day positions, while the second category trades manually with weekly horizon positions. The data set contains a set of risk reports including daily canceled transactions and the end-of-day risk measure (value at risk). The intra-day high-frequency traders are basically characterized by a high number of canceled orders but low end-of-day risk, because most of the positions are closed. The slow traders have a low number of canceled trades but a higher risk metric because they have longer term positions.

One of the main uses of using $k$ nearest neighbor in this environment is determining when a slow frequency trader might be classified as a high-frequency trader, etc. Measuring on a dynamic basis when the features of an agent move-away from its closest peers and has more risk or canceled orders compared to similar observations is also useful. This leads us to a connected topic: outlier detection.

## 5.1 Outlier Detection

The outlier definition introduced by Hawkins [130] states that an outlier is an observation that deviates so much from other observations as to arouse suspicion that it was generated by a different mechanism. A widely used outlier detection model proposed by Breunig et al. [131] introduces the concept of a local outlier factor (LOF) for each object in the data set indicating its degree of outlier-ness on a space locate in the neighborhood of the object. Similar to $k$ nearest neighbor, the LOF of an object relies on a single parameter of $k$, which is the number of nearest neighbors used to define the local neighborhood of the object. The formalism of the method is presented briefly by introducing the following metrics.

The $k_{\text{distance}}(p)$ for an object $p$ is the distance of this object to the $k$th nearest neighbor. More concretely, it is the distance between an object $p$ and an object $o$ from the training data set $D$ where for at least $k$ objects $o' \in D$ excluding $p$ $\text{dist}(p, o') \leq \text{dist}(p, o)$ and for at most $k - 1$ objects $o' \in D$ it holds that $\text{dist}(p, o') < \text{dist}(p, o)$, thereby making $o$ the $k$th closest observations.

Given the $k_{\text{distance}}(p)$, the $k$-distance neighborhood of $p$ is defined as the set of objects $q$ whose distance from $p$ is not greater than the $k$-distance:

$$N_{k\text{-distance}(p)}(p) = \{q \in D | \text{dist}(p, q) \leq k_{\text{distance}}(p)\} \tag{14}$$

Another metric in the formalism is the local reachability density (RD) of an object $p$, which is the distance between $p$ and $o$ floored by the $k_{\text{distance}}(o)$:

$$RD_k(p, o) = \max) \{k_{\text{distance}}(o), d(p, o)\} \tag{15}$$

The local reachability density of $p$ is the inverse of the average reachability distance based on the $k$ nearest neighbors of $p$ defined as:

$$\text{lrd}_K(p) = \cfrac{1}{\left(\cfrac{\sum_{o \in N_K(p)} RD_K(p,o)}{N_K(p)}\right)} \tag{16}$$

The local outlier factor of an object $p$ is an indicator capturing the degree to which $p$ is an outlier. It is the average of the ratio of the local reachability density of $p$ and those of $p$'s $k$ nearest neighbors:

$$\text{LOF}_K(p) = \cfrac{\sum_{o \in N_K(p)} \cfrac{\text{lrd}_K(p)}{\text{lrd}_K(o)}}{|N_K(p)|} \tag{17}$$

A generalization of this method for a large data set was proposed by Knorr et al. [132].

Going back to the example of the trading floor Figure 9 shows on the left the $k$ nearest neighbors classification and on the right the detection of outliers with the LOF method for a given number of neighbors. The R development implementation is based on the work of Torgo [133].

Figure 10 shows a different application related to the detection of security risk of cyber attacks [134] on financial exchanges. The factors are the number of connections from a given server and the market volatility.

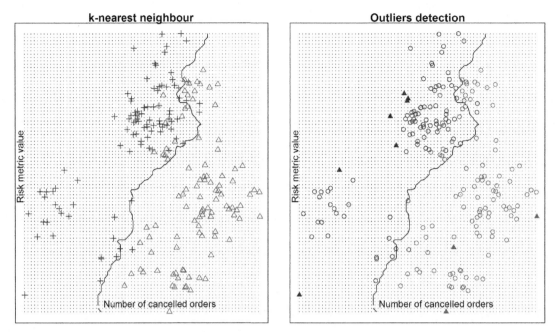

**FIGURE 9** Outlier detection for trading floor. Left: *k* nearest neighbor classification. Right: Detection of outliers with the LOF method for a given number of neighbors. The filled triangles represent the outliers from the two categories.

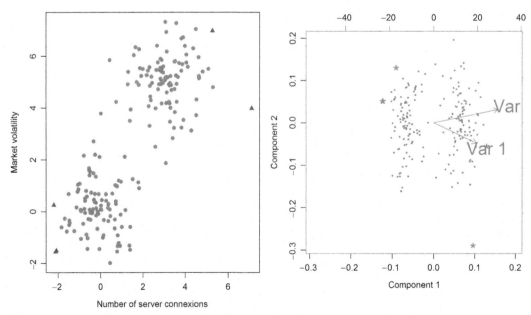

**FIGURE 10** Outlier detections for cyber attacks on market infrastructures. The factors are the number of connections from a given server and the market volatility. Left: Representation in plain factor space, where the red triangle (dark gray in print versions) are the outliers: Right: Representation in principal components space, where the stars are the outliers.

# 6 OUTLOOK

*When somebody's finger heart is better to cut the whole hand just to be sure.* View about "pruning" of the late boss of Corleonesi. *Salvatore Riina*

The non-parametric method has many advantages from a practical point of view when dealing with large data sets or when parametric models are expensive to calibrate.

The interest in non-parametric techniques for exploring financial crime goes beyond the technical aspects. Crime, be it violent or non-violent, blue or white collar, conducted on streets or in skyscrapers, follows laws that are difficult to capture by a finite set of features, thereby making it hard to fit parametric features. The basic nature of crime and especially of organized crime implies counterintuitive behaviors that are locally true but not true over a wider period of time or space.

For example, for tracking a rogue trader a scoring model would probably give less results that an outlier detection model, because a model could hardly capture all potential risks.

IPO fraud involving the listing of a bogus company would also be interesting to assess through the $k$ nearest neighbors algorithm trained on a set of existing IPOs.

The criteria and the factors that distinguish normal from abnormal are so numerous that the decision tree method would be a much more straightforward approach than a traditional parametric model.

# CHAPTER
# 2G

# Fuzzy Methods

## 1 BACKGROUND

Classification models and in general traditional statistical methods for data mining are based on binary sets. In most walks of life belonging to a class is far from being a binary choice. A simple example is the classification of the weather as good or bad based on temperature, precipitation, and sunshine. Human reasoning does not deal with a concept like the state of the weather on a binary basis. However, depending on circumstances there is a degree of truth in the statement that the weather is "bad."

The term "fuzzy logic" was introduced in 1965 by Zadeh [135] who developed the fuzzy set theory. The aim of fuzzy logic was to propose a framework closer to the way humans interact and therefore introduce a degree of truth between 0 and 1 instead of a binary state 0/1 as in classic logic. Since then, a full array of techniques and methods have been created with the aim of using fuzzy logic in various fields of data exploration.

Crime and misconduct risk assessment are mainly based on probabilistic frameworks. However, lack of historic data, complex cause-and-effect relationships, and imprecise data make it difficult to measure appropriately the impact of misconduct risk and fraud through traditional probability frameworks. Crime in the most general sense is not binary. An act cannot be classified in a straightforward way as criminal or legal.

In fact, depending on many parameters the same reality can be perceived as legitimate or criminal. The use of fuzzy logic would attach a continuous variable of the degree of criminality involved by an act. For the people involved in a crime, there are two degrees of fuzziness. First, is assessing at a moment $t$ from a set of $N$ individuals which individuals are the criminals. From a fuzzy logic perspective, every individual has a likelihood of being a criminal in relation to an act.

The second aspect is temporal in the evolution of an individual from a legitimate person toward the moment when he or she became a criminal. Legally speaking, this state is binary and courts decisions enrich the transaction matrix from one state to another. However, from a behavioral perspective the transition is continuous and smooth, and from a behavioral perspective a person does not jump from one state to another in a binary mode, which is more related to fuzzy set theory.

These tendencies have an even higher *degree of truth* when analyzing financial crime. Organizations today use extensive screenings and background checks of their employees and even on consultants to be sure that individuals with shady pasts infiltrate the organizations. Nonetheless, many big organizations find their name tied to allegations of market manipulation, money laundering, and other crimes. This means that at a certain point an individual or a group of individuals from the organization had a changed pattern of behavior that occurred over time. His status of being part of an illegal act is not 0 or 1 but most likely a continuous variable between these two borders.

The difference between traditional and fuzzy sets is established by introducing the so-called *membership function* specific to the fuzzy universe. Let's consider a finite set $X = \{x_1, x_2, \ldots, x_n\}$. A real function $\mu : X \to [0, 1]$ is called the membership function of $A$ and defines the fuzzy set $A$ of $X$. The fuzzy set $A$ of $X$ is the set of all pairs $(x, \mu(x))$. The set of elements that have a non-zero membership is called the support of the fuzzy set:

$$A \cup B = \max(\mu_A, \mu_B) \tag{1}$$
$$A \cap B = \min(\mu_A, \mu_B) \tag{2}$$

## 2 METHODS

Fuzzy techniques started being used in the financial risk management universe mainly in the area of operational risk due to the lack of historical data. Thus, the operational loss scenarios were built using the opinions from experts associating feature input into an output aimed to measure the potential loss. There is some relevant literature in the area; e.g., Stoffel et al. [136] proposed an application of the fuzzy method to analyze forensic data. Their procedure used a panel of fuzzy techniques consisting of clustering the raw data, extracting the membership functions from the data, and creating the fuzzy inference system. Shang and Hossen [137] explored avenues for using fuzzy logic models to improve risk assessment and risk decision-making. Cotofrei and Stoffel [138] proposed a fuzzy theory for enhancing the modeling phase of crime analysis processes to capture both the vague nature of forensic data and the uncertainties and conjectures characterizing the inference structures. Among the fuzzy methods used for fraud and risk assessment particular attention is given to fuzzy inference systems and fuzzy clustering.

## 2.1 Fuzzy Inference Systems

A fuzzy inference system is comprised of a method, based on fuzzy theory, which maps the input feature values to the output values. The mapping mechanism between input and output is based on a qualitative set of rules, represented by a list of if-then statements. An example related to unauthorized trading is given below for two inputs:

> If the *Market Volatility* is **High** and the *Control's quality* is **Low** *then* the frequency of *Unauthorized trading* is **High**

In this example, the input features are the market volatility and the control quality and the output is the frequency of unauthorized trades. Similar to operational risk, the misconduct risk is often assessed in an organization through scenarios built by experts in the absence of past observations related to that output. For example, if a bank did not experience any material unauthorized trading cases the only way to estimate its exposure to this risk would be to try to quantify the expert inferences, which are often vague and with a lack of accurate description of the facts and semantics.

In general, the fuzzy inference in Mamdani's version [139,140] is implemented through the following steps:

- Once the independent variables are selected a set of fuzzy rules are determined. Fuzzy rules are a collection of linguistic statements that expose the decision-making regarding outputs depending on inputs.
- The input's independent variables are fuzzified using the membership functions. Fuzzification represents the process of taking a semantic input such as high market volatility and passing it through a membership function in order to obtain fuzzy variable from 0 to 1.

- Inference rules are combined in the system by finding the consequence of the rules and deriving it on the output membership function. A fuzzy rule is based on the concept of "and" and "or". The common "fuzzy combination" operators for transcripting the rules are called T-norms:
  - **Zadeh's AND** operator
    $\mu_{A \cap B} = T(\mu_A(x), \mu_B(x))$, where $\mu_A$ is "the membership in class A" and $\mu_B$ is "the membership in class B."
    $T(\mu_A(x), \mu_B(x)) = \min(\mu_A(x), \mu_B(x))$.
  - **Zadeh's OR** $\mu_{A \cup B} = T(\mu_A(x)$, where $\mu_B(x))$ is the maximum function:
    $T(\mu_A(x), u_B(x)) = \max(\mu_A(x), \mu_B(x))$.
  
  The fuzzy "AND" is used to combine the membership functions for each rule to compute that rule's consequence.
- The output fuzzy set is generated by aggregating the results of all inference rules. The outputs of all of the fuzzy rules are combined to obtain one fuzzy output distribution, using the fuzzy "OR"

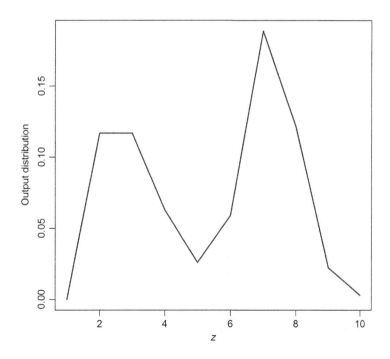

operator.[1] The following figure shows an example of the output distribution.

- The fuzzy output is defuzzified into a set of numerical values. Defuzzification is the process where a clear-cut output variable is obtained from a fuzzy system. In many cases, from a fuzzy inference a single output is desired. If a risk manager is trying to determine a trading loss from an unauthorized trading scenario the fuzzy system would have to provide a clear-cut number to indicate the size of the loss. Some defuzzification methods are proposed in the literature.
  - Center of mass method takes the output distribution and finds its weight center $z = \frac{\sum_{j=1}^{q} Z_j u_c(Z_j)}{\sum_{j=1}^{q} u_c(Z_j)}$.
  - Mean of maximum is the average of the mean of the values of $z$ at which the membership function reaches a maximum $z = \sum_{j=1}^{m} z_j^{\max}$.

A further straight-forward exploration of the fuzzy inference system is through an example aiming to classify the degree of fraud attached to a trader involved in misconduct. The example has its roots in investment banking. Fraudulent trading is mostly associated with massive losses and malversation of trader (like the forgery of back office reports). Gains are rarely associated with fraudulent behavior independent of how much the trader misbehaved. A fuzzy inference machine is built for this case with the following input variables:

- **Loss size** categorized as *low* (can be a gain), *medium, and high*. A low size loss would represent for a medium bank tens of thousands of dollars, medium is in the range of millions of dollars, and high would be hundreds of millions of dollars.

---

[1]This is not a rule as other functions can be used.

- **Degree of malversation** categorized as *low, medium, and high*. A low degree of malversation implies a minor illegal action like not communicating new positions. A medium degree example would be fabricating counterfeit proofs for order confirmations from other counterparties. An example of high is forging in the back office system and modifying the book of trades (e.g., the famous 88888 account).

The output variable is the rogue degree or (mis-behavior degree) that shows the reaction of the banks, regulators, and investigators in various cases represented by the input features. A low degree would be a management reaction either verbal or by email, a medium degree would imply the trader loses his job, and a high degree would be a legal action with detailed investigation of the organization.

A set of inference rules determined by the managing director of a trading floor are as follows:

1. *Loss Size* is **Low** or *Degree of Malversation* is **Low** then *Rogue degree* is **Low**
2. *Loss Size* is **Medium** and *Degree of Malversation* is **Any** then *Rogue degree* is **Medium**
3. *Loss Size* is **High** and *Degree of Malversation* is **High** then *Rogue degree* is **High**
4. *Loss Size* is **High** and *Degree of Malversation* is **Low** then *Rogue degree* is **Medium**
5. *Loss Size* is **Low** and *Degree of Malversation* is **High** then *Rogue degree* is **Medium**

The membership functions are Gaussian shaped and have the following expressions:

$$\mu(M, \sigma, H) = H \cdot e^{-(x-M)^2/(2 \cdot \sigma^2)} \qquad (3)$$

where $M$ is the mean, $\sigma$ is the standard deviation, and $H$ is the height.

The shape of the membership functions for the loss size and the degree of malversation are depicted in Figures 1 and 2, respectively.

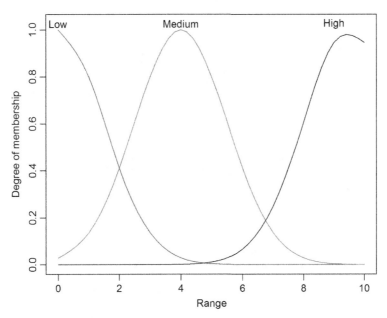

**FIGURE 1** Membership functions for the Loss Size input variable.

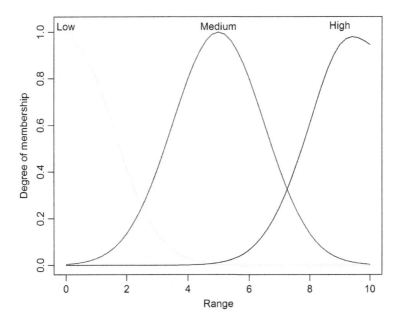

**FIGURE 2** Membership functions for the Degree of Malversation input variable.

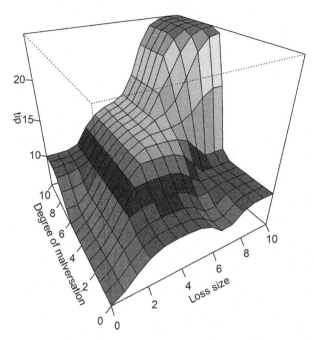

**FIGURE 3** Output surface of the fuzzy inference system. Unauthorized trading under this form is penalized only when losses are high.

Figure 3 exhibiting the output surface of the fuzzy system shows the fraud degree within the organization depending on the loss size and the degree of malversation.

It can easily be seen that unauthorized trading under this form is penalized only when losses are high. If there are not losses or even profits but the degree of malversation is high the output does not signal a fraud or abnormal behavior.

The same system can be redesigned by a risk manager keeping everything the same but changing the rules as follows:

1. *Loss Size* is **Any** or *Degree of Malversation* is **Low** then *Rogue degree* is **Low**
2. *Loss Size* is **Medium** and *Degree of Malversation* is **Medium** then *Rogue degree* is **Medium**

3. *Loss Size* is **High** or *Degree of Malversation* is **High** then *Rogue degree* is **High**

Figure 4 shows that the misbehavior of a trader is penalized whether there is loss or not on the trading desk.

When the fuzzy system is built the distribution of the output profile can be represented based on the distribution of the input variable. The only additional information is the joint distribution of the input variables. For illustration, let's assume the loss size is distributed lognormally and the degree of the malversation is normally distributed. The joint density is considered following either a Gaussian copula or a t-copula. The distribution of the rogue degree is depicted in Figure 5.

The advantage of fuzzy inference in fraud assessment is that it can deal with vagueness and

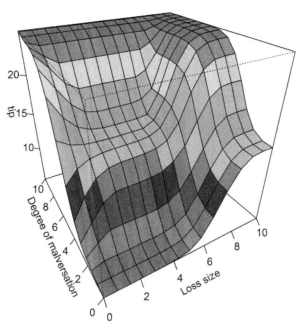

**FIGURE 4** Output surface of the fuzzy inference system. Unauthorized trading under this form is penalized whenever misbehavior occurs.

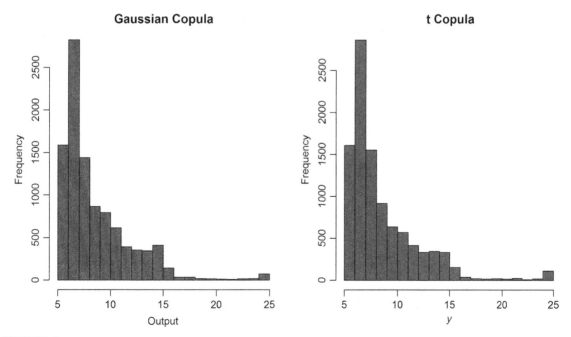

**FIGURE 5** Hist.

uncertain semantics in statements when building expert scenarios. It also allows modeling behaviors in uncertain environments where classic statistics do fail. The main disadvantage of fuzzy inference is linked to the parameters of membership functions. Small variations in the membership function can have high repercussions on the output, thereby challenging their use in highly dynamic environments.

## 2.2 Fuzzy c-Means

Fuzzy c-means is a method of clustering using fuzzy logic. While the classic $K$-means clustering attaches an observation to one cluster only, the fuzzy clustering allows one observation from the initial data set to belong to two or more clusters. This method was developed by Dunn [141] and improved by Bezdek [142] and is frequently used in pattern recognition. Fuzzy c-means assigns a membership to each observation point corresponding to each cluster center on the basis of distance between the cluster and the data point. Therefore, the closer the observations is to the cluster center the more the closer its membership is to the particular cluster center. The sum of the degrees of membership of each data point in respect to all the clusters should be equal to one. The algorithm relies on minimization of the following objective function:

$$J_m = \sum_{i=1}^{N} \sum_{j=1}^{L} \mu_{i,j}^m \|x_i - c_j\|^2, \quad 1 \le m < \infty \quad (4)$$

where $N$ is the number of data, $L$ is the number of clusters, $\mu_{i,j}$ is the degree of membership of the point $x_i$ in the cluster $j$, and $\| * \|$ is any distance metric (Euclidean) between a given point and the center of a cluster.

Fuzzy classification is based on iterative optimization of the objective function, with the updates of membership $\mu_{i,j}$ and the cluster centers $c_j$ for each iteration by:

$$\mu_{i,j} = \frac{1}{\sum_{k=1}^{L} \left( \frac{\|x_i - c_j\|}{\|x_i - c_k\|} \right)^{2/(m-1)}} \quad (5)$$

where $\|x_i - c_j\|$ is the distance from point $i$ to current cluster center $j$ and $\|x_i - c_k\|$ is the distance from point $i$ to cluster centers $k$:

$$c_j = \frac{\sum_{i=1}^{N} \mu_{ij}^m \cdot x_i}{\sum_{k=1}^{N} \mu_{ij}^m} \quad (6)$$

The clustering process stops when $\max_{i,j} |\mu_{i,j}^{n+1} - \mu_{i,j}^n| < \beta$, where $\beta$ is a termination criterion taking values between 0 and 1, and $n$ denotes the iteration number. Implementation of fuzzy c-means has the following steps:

1. First, initialize the iteration counter ($n = 1$); the cluster centers are randomly attributed.
2. The membership function family $M$ is initialized $M^n = [\mu_{i,j}]$ matrix. $\mu_{i,j}$ is computed as $\mu_{i,j} = \frac{1}{\sum_{k=1}^{c} \left( \frac{\|x_i - c_j\|}{\|x_i - c_k\|} \right)^{2/(m-1)}}$.
3. For the iteration $n$ centers vectors $C^n = [c_j]$ are computed with $M^n$ using $c_j = \frac{\sum_{i=1}^{N} \mu_{i,j}^m \cdot x_i}{\sum_{k=1}^{N} \mu_{i,j}^m}$.
4. If $\|M^{n+1} - M^n\| < \beta$ the optimization ends; otherwise, the iterations counter is $n \rightarrow n + 1$ and the $\mu_{ij}$ is updated at step 2.

Fuzzy c-means is well adapted for overlapped observations and in these cases it does perform better than the classic $K$-means algorithm. Unlike $K$-means, which performs better when the cluster's observations are perfectly separable and points belong to one cluster exclusively, for fuzzy c-means each observation is assigned a membership to each cluster, with the membership function indicating the degree of belongingness to that cluster. The main drawback of fuzzy c-means is that a lower value of termination criteria provides a better result but requires a higher number of iterations and higher computational power.

# 3 OUTLOOK

Risk regulators are very cautious about using techniques that are not well-known, especially for fraud and white collar crime assessment. Data-free models or light data estimations that rely heavily on scenarios and employ methods from the space of Bayesian calculus, neural networks, and also Fuzzy techniques are used with circumspection as their output depend highly on a few parameters aimed at capturing expert opinions on an agent's behavior. While for regulatory purposes the use of fuzzy methods can be challenged for decision making, risk management, and surveillance they do represent efficient tools. In fraud area a fuzzy expert systems can be a useful tool for a misconduct risk manager to investigate a suspicious trader to look closer at an activity that doesn't follow the known patterns. Therefore, the use of fuzzy methods is expected to grow in the area of fraud and crime analysis.

CHAPTER

# 2H

# Clustering Techniques

## 1 BACKGROUND

Machine learning as a discipline emerged at the same time as computer science and the development of powerful computing tools. Machine learning aims to design systems able to provide output and input responses without being specially instructed. In the financial industry, machine learning plays a crucial role in many fields like algorithmic trading and risk management. Among the many applications of machine learning of particular interest is classification applications. Assuming a given data set of inputs $x_1, \ldots, x_n$, a machine-learning algorithm aims to provide to each observation a class $z_1, \ldots, z_n$. The vast panel of techniques are classified as four different kinds of machine learning [143]:

- **Supervised learning:** The machine receives a empirical set of inputs $x_1, \ldots, x_n$, a sequence of desired classes $z_1, \ldots, z_n$, and the goal of the machine is to learn to put in the correct class given a new input.
- **Reinforcement learning:** The machine interacts with its environment by producing actions $a_1, a_2, \ldots$. These actions affect the state of the environment, which in turn results in the machine receiving some scalar rewards (or punishments) $r_1, r_2, \ldots$. The goal of the machine is to learn to act in a way that maximizes the future rewards it receives (or minimizes the punishments) over its lifetime.
- **Dynamic reinforcement learning:** Similar to reinforcement learning the machine interacts with its environment, which contains other machines that can interact and learn. Thus, the goal of the machine is to adapt its action based also on other machines' current and future actions. Dynamic reinforcement learning has direct application in the high-frequency trading world where the

order placed changes the short-term behavior of the other traders. The algorithm should learn to place the order strategy in order to maximize the profit. Thus, dynamic reinforcement learning can lead or be used to generate doubtful practices in order to influence the behavior of other traders by acting on the market with certain timing of orders.[1]

- **Unsupervised learning**: The machine has a set of inputs $x_1, \ldots, x_n$, that are not classified or labeled and have no interaction with the environment. Based on the pure features of the data, unsupervised learning attempts to classify and thus can be considered as mining for patterns in the data.

In the context of financial crime, whether we deal money-laundering transactions, securities fraud, or high-frequency trading, the *a priori* labeling of the data is unobserved. With the frequency of offenses being in many cases low, there is also less interaction that could lead to learning. Thus, the predilection in exploring data in financial crime is unsupervised learning.

## 2 CLUSTERING ALGORITHMS

Among the unsupervised learning techniques, clustering is a set of methods aimed at finding similar groups in the raw data, which are called clusters. Clustering groups data instances that are similar to (near) each other in one cluster and data instances that are very different from each other into different clusters. The methods of different clustering algorithms can be classified as follows [144]:

---

[1]Smoking describes an illegal practice where a high-frequency trader first posts alluring limit orders to attract slow traders. Then they rapidly revise these orders into less generous terms, hoping to execute profitably against the incoming flow of slow traders' market orders.

- **Partitioning-based**, which divides data objects into a number of partitions, where each partition represents a cluster and each cluster must contain at least one observation and each observation must belong to exactly one group. *K*-means algorithm, *K*-modes, CLustering LARge Applications (CLARA), and fuzzy c-means are examples.
- **Hierarchical-based**, which allocates the data set in a hierarchical manner depending on the medium of proximity. Proximities are obtained by the intermediate nodes. A dendrogram represents the data sets, where individual data is presented by leaf nodes. The initial cluster gradually divides into several clusters as the hierarchy continues.
- **Density-based**, which separates the data objects based on their regions of density, connectivity, and boundaries. This method is closely related to point-nearest neighbors. A cluster, defined as a connected dense component, grows in any direction that density leads to. Density-based algorithms are capable of discovering clusters of arbitrary shapes. Density-based spatial clustering of applications with noise (DBSCAN) is a popular method from this class.
- **Grid-based**, which divides the space of the data into grids, the clustering being performed at grid level and not on the data itself, thereby having a fast processing time.
- **Model-based** optimizing which is the fit between the given data and some mathematical model, assuming the data is generated by a mixture of underlying probability distributions. The expectation maximization algorithm is a model-based clustering method.

## 3 K-MEANS

*K*-means is a partitioning clustering algorithm and is also the most popular clustering algorithm. Given a data set $x_1, \ldots, x_n$ and $K$ clusters, the algorithm assigns each $x_i$ to one of the $K$ clusters of coordinates $C_1, \ldots, C_K$ by minimizing the distance of each point to the closest cluster:

$$J = \sum_{j=1}^{K} \sum_{x_i \in C_j} ||x_i - \mu_j||^2 \qquad (1)$$

where $\mu_j$ is the mean of all observations in the cluster $C_j$.

- In the **initialization step** the cluster center is set randomly $\mu_1, \ldots, \mu_K$.
- In the **assignment step** each observation $x_i$ is assigned to the cluster with the closest mean $\mu_j$.
- In the **update step** once assigned the means are updated as follows $\mu_j = \frac{1}{\left\{C_j\right\}^*} \sum_{x_i \in C_j} x_i$.
- The stopping condition is when the centers are stable.

The $K$-means algorithm is sensitive to data points that are very far away from other data points. These points are called outliers, could be data errors or some extraordinary events.

To illustrate the way clustering methods work a set of tick data of a NASDAQ stock are used, the data set[2] including the bid and ask price as well as the bid and ask size for each timestamp measured with millisecond precision. The data set includes the order books for 5 trading days in early 2013. From the row data two samples are built. The first data set includes the averaged bid-ask spread and the intra-day volatility assessed at a given time. The second sample has two features: the total volumes of bid and ask orders for each timestamp and the maximum returns realized in a forward-looking window of 1 second assuming a trader buys at a given moment and sells at the highest price in the following second.

The results of the clustering for the first sample are shown in Figure 1 and the centers of each

clusters are given in Table 1. They show that there is a cluster with low volatility and low absolute bid-ask spread, a medium volatility and medium liquidity, and a high volatility and low liquidity cluster.

The clustering of the second sample is shown in Figure 1 and the centers of each clusters are presented in Table 2.

For the second data set the results from Table 2 show that the clusters characterized by a small total size of the order volume are characterized by a lower gain and the bigger order size by a higher profit. In other words, if at a given moment the order book is has a lot of activity a simple directional position might bring in an average positive outcome over the next second. High-frequency traders use a technique called smoking and place many orders that are canceled just to attract other traders and increase their profit likelihood. This pattern can be found by clustering and can correspond to such a malicious high-frequency trading technique (Figure 2).

The optimal number of clusters is chosen such as that the within-cluster sum of squares (WCSS) is minimized:

$$\text{WCSS}(K) = \sum_{i=1}^{K} \sum_{j \in S_i} ||\mathbf{x}_j - \boldsymbol{\mu}_i||_2^2 \qquad (2)$$

Figure 3 shows the value of the WCSS decreases with the increase of clusters for both data sets. For more than five clusters the improvement in WCSS is relatively small.

# 4 EXPECTATION MAXIMIZATION ALGORITHM

The expectation maximization (EM) method is an iterative method introduced by Dempster et al. [145] used in the context of clustering for fitting mixture models. EM algorithms assumes there is a parametric model for the set of observations and the underlying models are known,

---

[2]http://www.tickdata.com.

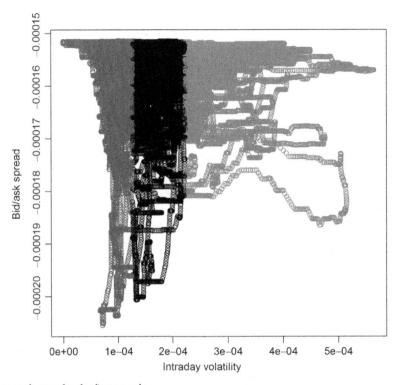

**FIGURE 1** *K*-means clusters for the first sample.

**TABLE 1** *K*-Means Clusters for the First Sample

|  | **Volatility** | **Bid ask spread** |
|---|---|---|
| Cluster 1 | 9.268411e−05 | −0.0001539647 |
| Cluster 2 | 1.604996e−04 | −0.0001552917 |
| Cluster 3 | 2.855338e−04 | −0.0001567520 |

**TABLE 2** *K*-Means Clusters for the First Sample

|  | **Volume** | **Variation** |
|---|---|---|
| Cluster 1 | 235.4379 | −0.008743369 |
| Cluster 2 | 654.8852 | 0.042125646 |
| Cluster 3 | 1177.3098 | 0.055451558 |

but the parameters of each model are not known *a priori*. Hence, going back to the initial sample of observations $(x_1, \ldots, x_n)$ and assuming that there are $K$ models for the distribution of the $x_i$ is:

$$f(x_i) = \sum_{j=1}^{K} P(C_j) f_j(x_i | C_j) \qquad (3)$$

where $P(C_j)$ is the probability of cluster $C_j$ and $f_j$ is a parametric model, usually the Gaussian distribution.

To estimate the parameters $\theta$ of the mixture models it is enough to find the maximum likelihood estimator:

$$\hat{\theta} = \arg\max_{\theta} \prod_{i=1}^{n} f(x_i | \theta) = \arg\max_{\theta} \sum_{i=1}^{n} \ln f(x_i | \theta) \qquad (4)$$

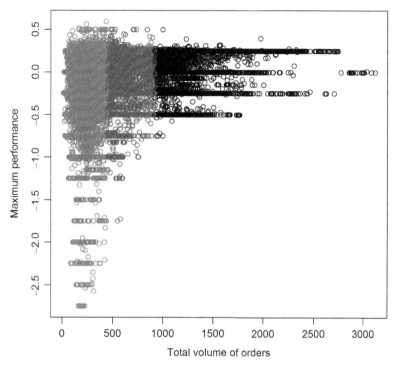

**FIGURE 2** *K*-means clusters for the second sample.

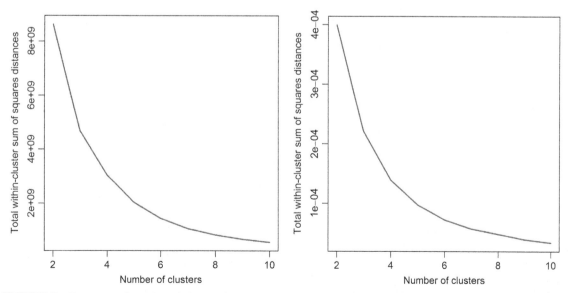

**FIGURE 3** *K*-means and number of clusters for the two samples. The value of the WCSS decreases with the increase of clusters for both data sets. For more than five clusters the improvement in WCSS is relatively small.

The problem is that $(x_1, \ldots, x_n)$ have unobserved labels or clusters. Thus, the complexity results due to the fact that both parameters and clusters $z_1, \ldots, z_n$ in $\{1, \ldots, K\}$ need to be determined. Here, the EM comes with an ingenious method of alternating between two steps:

- **Expectation:** The model parameters $\theta$ are fixed and the unobserved clusters are estimated (the probability of each element belonging to each cluster).
- **Maximization:** The clusters are fixed and the $\theta$ is obtained by maximizing the expected log likelihood of $(x_1, \ldots, x_n)$.

To be more consistent the observed data $(x_1, \ldots, x_n)$ is completed with the unobserved value of the clusters $z_1, \ldots, z_n$ such that the full data is $X_i = (x_i, z_i)$. The conditional density for the cluster $z$ given by Bayes formula is:

$$f(z|x, \theta) = \frac{f(x, z|\theta)}{f(x|\theta)} \tag{5}$$

or

$$f(x|\theta) = \frac{f(x, z|\theta)}{f(z|x, \theta)} \tag{6}$$

The log likelihood can be hence expressed as:

$$\ln f(x|\theta) = \ln f(x, z|\theta) - \ln f(z|x, \theta)$$
$$= \ln f(X|\theta) - \ln f(z|x, \theta) \tag{7}$$

For an initial value $\theta_0$ the expectation with respect to $f(z|x, \theta_0)$ is:

$$\ln f(x_1, \ldots, x_n|\theta)$$
$$= \mathbb{E}[\ln f(X_1, \ldots, X_n|\theta)|x_1, \ldots, x_n, \theta_0] \tag{8}$$
$$- \mathbb{E}[\ln f(z_1, \ldots, z_n|x_1, \ldots, x_n, \theta)|x_1, \ldots, x_n, \theta_0]. \tag{9}$$

The EM algorithm first finds the expected value of the complete-data log-likelihood $\log f(X_1, \ldots, X_n|\theta)$ with respect to the unobserved clusters $z$ given the observed data $w$ and the current parameter estimates $\theta$:

$$\mathbb{Q}(\theta|\theta_{i-1}, x_1, \ldots, x_n)$$
$$= \mathbb{E}[\ln f(X_1, \ldots, X_n|\theta)|x_1, \ldots, x_n, \theta_{i-1}] \tag{10}$$

where $\theta_{i-1}$ are the current parameter estimates we used to evaluate the expectation and $\theta$ are the new parameters that should be found to maximize the log-likelihood **Q**.

Then the EM algorithm can be completed as follows [146]:

- In the *Expectation-step* the likelihood $\mathbb{Q}(\theta|\hat{\theta}_{i-1}, x_1, \ldots, x_n)$ is computed where $x$ and $\theta_{i-1}$ are constants, $\theta$ is the variable to be found in the process, and $w$ is a random variable. This step estimates the probability of each element belonging to each cluster.
- In the *Maximization-step* the log-likelihood $\mathbb{Q}(\theta|\hat{\theta}_{i-1}, x_1, \ldots, x_n)$ is maximized and has as output:

$$\hat{\theta}_i = \arg\max_{\theta} \mathbb{Q}(\theta|\hat{\theta}_{i-1}, x)$$

The two steps are iterated until convergence is achieved. After each iteration is performed a convergence test verifies if the difference of the attributes vector of an iteration to the previous iteration is smaller than an acceptable error tolerance, given by parameter. $|\theta_i - \theta_{i-1}| < \epsilon$. When this procedure is iterated, the sequence of estimators $\hat{\theta}_0, \hat{\theta}_1, \ldots$ is obtained and it can be shown that convergence is feasible for the maximum likelihood estimator $\hat{\theta}$.

For clustering purposes-based on a Gaussian mixture in the EM algorithm each cluster $j$, of $K$ clusters is constituted a parameter vector $\theta^j$, with $\theta = \{\theta^1, \cdot\theta^K\}$ composed by the mean $\mu^j$ and by the covariance matrix $\Sigma^j$, which represent the features of the Gaussian probability distributions.

Using again the data set of the U.S. stock order book we first try to assess whether a mixture Gaussian model can be fitted to the intra-day volatility or in other words if the volatility can be clusters based on the EM algorithm.

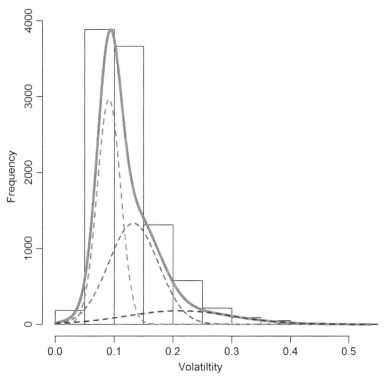

**FIGURE 4**   EM clustering of the intra-day volatility for the order-book data set, with the assumption of three clusters. The algorithm depicts the three clusters for low, medium, and high volatility regimes.

Figure 4 shows the clustering of the intra-day volatility for the order book data set, with the assumption of three clusters obtained using the R package "Rmixmod" [147]. The algorithm depicts the three clusters of volatility for low, medium, and high volatility regimes.

An example application of the EM clustering implemented with the R "**Mclust**" package [148, 149] to the order books data mining is given in Figure 5.

## 5  CLUSTERING FOR BIG DATA

The *K*-means applied to the order book of a security can require a huge data set of several gigabytes. While being generally efficient the time complexity of *K*-means is of the order $O(tkn)$, where $n$ is the number of data points, $k$ is the number of clusters, and $t$ is the number of iterations. Table 3 shows the computation time for some of the methods used on a data set with two features and a few million observations. When the data set increases and it is necessary to deal with big data, *K*-means might raise some feasibility issues as the time to results would exclude its applicability in cases where real-time response is a key factor.

Volume of data and velocity of data treatment are the main differences in clustering big data compared to conventional data clustering, as it requires substantial changes in the architecture of storage systems [144].

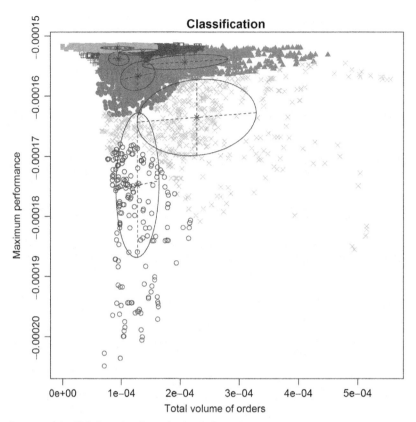

**FIGURE 5** Application of the EM clustering for order-book data mining.

A first solution came with the balanced iterative reducing and clustering using the hierarchies (BIRCH) algorithm introduced by Zhang et al. [150], which is designed for very large data sets in conditions where time and memory are limited. The BIRCH algorithm is a hierarchical-based method that has the advantage of requiring only one scan of the data set instead of needing the whole data set in advance.

BIRCH starts by scanning the database to build an in-memory tree and then applies the clustering algorithm to cluster the leafs nodes. Before discussing the steps of the algorithm a few metrics need to be introduced. For given a data set $(x_1^j, \ldots, x_n^j) \in C_j$ from the cluster $C_j$ the following metrics are defined:

- Centroid metric: $\overline{X_0} = \frac{\sum_{i=1}^{N} \overline{X_i}}{N}$.

- Radius metric: $R = \sqrt{\frac{\sum_{i=1}^{N} (\overline{X_i} - \overline{X_0})^2}{N}}$ that the measures the average distance from member points to centroid.

**TABLE 3** Computational Time for Various Clustering Method Applied to a Data Sample with 2 Million Observations

| Clustering method | Computational time |
| --- | --- |
| EM | 12.68 min |
| Hierarchical | 39.48 s |
| K-means | 10.94 s |

*Notes: The model-based methods are the most computationally intensive.*

- Diameter $D = \sqrt{\frac{\sum_{i=1}^{N}\sum_{j=1}^{N}(\overline{X_i}-\overline{X_j})^2}{N(N-1)}}$, which is the average distance between all pairs within a cluster.

Given the centroids of two clusters $C_{j_1}$ and $C_{j_2}$ the centroid Euclidean distance is defined as $D_0 = \sqrt{(X_{j_1} - X_{j_2})^2}$.

For a cluster with $N_1$ observations $(x_1, \ldots, x_{N_1})$ and another cluster with $N_2$ with $(x_{N_1+1}, \ldots, x_{N_1+N_2})$ the average inter-cluster distance $D_2$, average intra-cluster distance $D_3$, and the variance increase distance $D_4$ are:

$$D_2 = \sqrt{\frac{\sum_{i=1}^{N_1}\sum_{j=N_1+1}^{N_1+N_2}(\overline{X_i}-\overline{X_j})^2}{N_1 N_2}} \tag{11}$$

$$D_3 = \sqrt{\frac{\sum_{i=1}^{N_1+N_2}\sum_{j=1}^{N_1+N_2}(\overline{X_i}-\overline{X_j})^2}{(N_1+N_2)(N_1+N_2+1)}} \tag{12}$$

$$D_4 = \sum_{k=1}^{N_1+N_2}\left(\overline{X_k} - \frac{\sum_{i=1}^{N_1+N_2}\overline{X_i}}{N_1+N_2}\right)^2$$

$$-\sum_{j=1}^{N_1}\left(\overline{X_j} - \frac{\sum_{i=1}^{N_1}\overline{X_i}}{N_1}\right)^2$$

$$-\sum_{k=N_1+1}^{N_1+N_2}\left(\overline{X_k} - \frac{\sum_{i=N_1+1}^{N_1+N_2}\overline{X_i}}{N_2}\right)^2 \tag{13}$$

The Birch algorithm builds a dendrogram-like structure (Figure 6), called a clustering feature

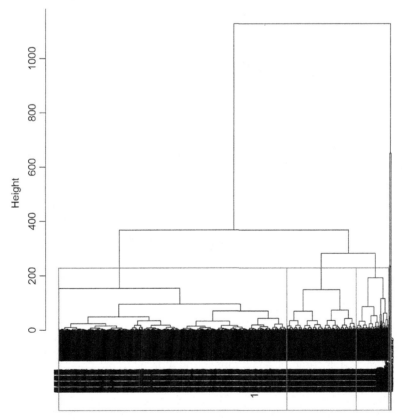

**FIGURE 6** Hierarchical clustering output.

tree (CF tree), while scanning the data set. The concepts of clustering feature and CF trees are crucial elements of BIRCH's clustering. A clustering feature has three key informations about a cluster: $(N, LS, SS)$, where $N$ is the number of objects in the cluster and $LS, SS$ are defined in the following where $N$ is the number of data points in the cluster, $LS$ is the linear sum of the $N$ data points, $LS = \sum_{i=1}^{N} \overline{X_i}$, and $SS$ is the square sum of the $N$ data points. $LS = \sum_{i=1}^{N} \overline{X_i}$. The CF structure is compact enough to calculate the intra-cluster distances.

The additive property of two CF vectors $CF_1 = (N_1, LS_1, SS_1)$ and $CF_2 = (N_2, LS_2, SS_2)$ states that the CF vector of the joint clusters $CF = (CF_1, CF_2)$ is $CF_1 + CF_2 == (N_1 + N_2, LS_1 + LS_2, SS_1 + LS_2)$ and allows to merge sub-clusters.

The BIRCH algorithm has the following steps:

- **Step 1:** The data set is scanned and an initial in-memory CF tree is built. The value of the threshold is crucial for adding points to the tree. The memory limits are addressed by increasing the threshold values, thereby building a smaller tree.
- **Step 2:** The initial tree is condensed into a smaller CF tree by removing outliers and grouping clusters.
- **Step 3:** The global clustering procedure clusters all leaf nodes on the CF values according to a hierarchical-based algorithm.
- **Step 4:** An optional cluster implies more passes over the data to refine the results.

# 6 OUTLIERS DETECTION

Outliers detection in data set is one of significant importance in data mining for financial crime as it allows detecting observations concerning transactions, accounts, or securities that have atypical patterns. From a dynamical perspective observations that are away from the clusters of their peers might raise warning signals. The notion of outliers is part of more complex clustering methods such as the BIRCH algorithm and serve only to optimize clustering process [132].

Based on clustering techniques other outlier detection methods have been developed. Pamula et al. [151] proposed a $K$-means clustering-based algorithm that starts by dividing the data set into clusters. The approach considers that the points lying near the centroid of the cluster are not candidates for outliers. A local distance-based outlier score is computed for the remaining points away from the centroids. The local distance-based outlier factor (ldof) metric [152] generalizing the local outliers factor introduced by Breunig et al. [131] for a given point $p$ is computed as:

$$\mathrm{ldof}(p) = \frac{d_p}{D_p} \qquad (14)$$

where $\mathrm{dist}(p, q) \geq 0$ $Np$ is the set of $k$-nearest, a distance measure between objects $p$ and $q$, $d_p$ is the average distance to the set $N_p$ of $k$-nearest clusters $d_p = \frac{1}{k} \sum_{q \in N_p} \mathrm{dist}(p, q)$, and $D_p$ is the average distance among objects of the set $N_p$ in $D_p = \frac{1}{k(k-1)} \sum_{q, q^* \in N_p} \mathrm{dist}(q, q^*)$. The computations needed to calculate the outlier score reduce considerably due to the pruning of points close to the cluster centroid. Based on the outlier score the points with the highest score are considered as outliers.

Dhaliwal et al. [153] proposed a similar algorithm of outliers detection used for fraud assessment of data streams. The method uses $k$-median applied to data chunks and clusters. The algorithm does not store the complete data stream but only the weighted medians found after mining a data stream cluster and passing that information along with the newly arrived data chunk to the next phase. The weighted medians found in each phase are tested for outlierness, classifying the observations as outliers or non-outliers.

Loureiro et al. [154] proposed a methodology for the application of hierarchical clustering methods to the task of outlier detection.

# 7 CLUSTERING IN FINANCIAL CRIME DETECTION

Clustering techniques are seminal tools in the area of abnormal transaction detection for tackling money laundering. Analyzing structured and unstructured data clusters might reveal similar types of accounts, transactions, individuals, or organizations. Clustering techniques are used by agencies in financial crime investigations such as the Financial Crimes Enforcement Network (FinCEN) in its Artificial Intelligence System (FAIS) for detecting atypical typologies of transaction or accounts. Clustering as part of a knowledge discovery process allows raising flags to indicate areas where further investigations may be needed.

Recently, some researchers have tested the feasibility of clustering for crime detection. Larik and Haider [155] presented a hybrid anomaly detection approach that employs clustering to establish customers' normal behavior and to determine deviation of a particular transaction from the corresponding clusters. The work suggested building an anomaly index for ranking transactions as anomalous.

Clustering can also be used in the initial phases of exploratory data mining for securities fraud detection [156].

Another area where clustering has potential application is in unstructured data mining. Bsoul et al. [157] proposed *K*-means like algorithms for clustering text files and documents used further for detecting and identifying financial crime patterns.

# 8 OUTLOOK

Clustering analysis is a fundamental tool in the exploration of data for financial crime analysis. They are already used in transaction monitoring for anti-money laundering and distributed through main solution providers such NICE Actimize and Statistical Analysis Software (SAS). Clustering techniques can easily be leveraged for monitoring the financial markets and more specifically the order books on exchanges or dark pools if available. The outliers detection method based on clustering has a foreseeable use in monitoring dynamically markets or individuals. Thus, if a feature of an individual jumps away from its group of peers (its cluster) that could be a warning sign. However, clustering algorithms face two main challenges: the ability to deal with big data and the speed of processing and capacity to provide outputs quickly. Big data clustering is used mainly in hierarchical-based methods, but the time issue remains problematic.

CHAPTER

# 21

# Support Vector Machines

## 1 BACKGROUND

In the area of financial crime, and in general in risk management, classification methods play a central role. There are at least three different streams of usefulness for those techniques. First, is the knowledge discovery, which helps to understand a portfolio or a data set, implying, for example, the identification of various clusters. Second, is the help in decision-making that requires a unique boundary between clusters in order to determine if a particular element is in one cluster or another. And lastly is the forecasting features required when a dynamic view of the behavior of a population is needed. The second feature is what organizations need in order to assess a client. Decision makers within an organization often use classification models as output in the form of a ordinal or nominal values. For instance,

credit mangers need to determine the solvency of counterparties. An anti-money laundering surveillance manager would need to know if a transaction is safe, with moderate risk or high risk. Classification models often provide a score on a continuous support, but do encounter problems when they need to transform that score into a class indicator for that observation. Thus, the classification would not only need the cluster but also a separating (hyperplane) frontier between clusters.

Figure 1 shows a two-cluster classification based on a basic *K*-means algorithm. In this example it is assumed that a series of daily observations contains data concerning proprietary trader activities. Two inputs data are shown: a P&L Index representing a score for a trader's gains and the observed number of canceled trades per day. The *K*-means classification methods emphasize the presence of two classes of

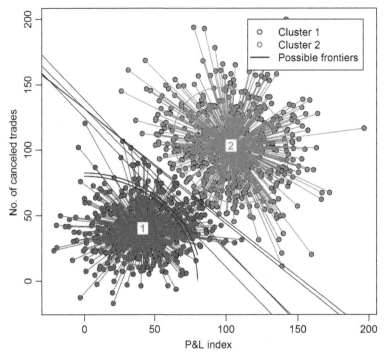

**FIGURE 1** *K*-means classification method: It emphasizes the presence of two classes of trading profiles: one with the high P&L and high number of canceled operations and another with lower P&L and the lower number of canceled operations.

trading profiles: one with high P&L and high number of canceled operations and another with a lower P&L and lower number of canceled operations. From the perspective of misconduct risk surveillance an audit of the first class would be required, as high P&L can be linked to rogue techniques implying canceled trades such as spoofing. The advantage of a clustering technique such as *K*-means is that it provides unsupervised-classification that does not need *a priori* labeling of the data to find the features of each class. As a starting point an unsupervised learning machine fits the purpose of knowledge discovery. However, from the perspective of a surveillance manager once the clusters are established it would be more difficult to implement it for supervising day-to-day operations. For example, if a new set of observations needs to

be analyzed, attaching them to a class or another can be challenging. Between the two classes, based on visual inspection many frontiers can be proposed as presented in Figure 3, thereby creating a dilemma for the risk manager: What is the frontier between the two classes?

For a given learning task, with a given finite amount of training data, the best performance will be achieved if the right balance is achieved between the accuracy attained on that particular training set and the "capacity" of the machine, which represents the ability of the machine to learn any training set without error [158].

To better depict this fact let's consider the case of a trading risk misconduct risk manager that oversees traders for misconduct risk using software based on machine-learning algorithm. The risk manager needs to assess the behavior of a new trader hired on the floor. different behavior which needs to be included in a new. If a risk managers uses a machine learning tool with too much "capacity," it would conclude that a new trader has different behavior and requires to be assigned to a new class. If the software is based on machine learning with too little capacity it would assess that the new trader as being different form the rest of the "good" traders on the floor and classify him as rogue. Both cases are extreme scenarios of machine learning. The theory of statistical learning developed by Vapnik [159] aims to deal with these issues in the machine-learning space.

## 2 ALGORITHM OVERVIEW

Among the supervised machine-learning techniques a particularly interesting method is the so-called "support vector machines" (SVM). SVM techniques emerged in the early 1990s based on cutting-edge results from the 1960s developed by the Soviet scientists Vladimir Vapnik and Alexey Chervonenkis [160]. Given a set of training observations, two categories, and set of indicators attaching a category to each observation, a SVM training algorithm proposes a model that assigns new observations into one category or the other. Thus, a SVM works as a non-probabilistic binary classifier, where the shape of the frontier type can be pre-defined.

Let's consider a set of objects $x_i \in X$ and a set of class labels $y_i \in Y$ and a machine that should learn the mapping $x_i \to y_i$ [158]. A deterministic learning machine is defined by a set of possible mappings $x_i \to f(x_i, \alpha)$, where the functions $f(x_i, \alpha)$ themselves depend on parameters $\alpha$. The expectation of the test error for a trained machine can be written in continuous form as $R(\alpha)$:

$$R(\alpha) = \int (0.5 \cdot |y - f(x, \alpha)|) \, dP(x, y) \qquad (1)$$

where $P(x, y)$ is the joint distribution function of $x$ and $y$.

The empirical risk $R_{\text{emp}}(\alpha)$ or the training error is defined as the measured mean error rate on the training set for a finite number of observations $N$ in the training set:

$$R_{\text{emp}} = \frac{1}{N} \sum_{i=1}^{N} \underbrace{(0.5 \cdot |y_i - f(x_i, \alpha)|)}_{\text{loss function}} \qquad (2)$$

The test error is the sum of the training error and of a term depending on the model complexity:

$$
\begin{aligned}
\text{Test Error} = & \, \text{Training Error} \\
& + \text{Complexity of set of Models}
\end{aligned}
\qquad (3)
$$

An important result proposed by [161] gives the following inequality:

$$R(\alpha) \le R_{\text{emp}} + \sqrt{\frac{h(\log(2N/h) + 1) - \log(\eta/4)}{N}} \qquad (4)$$

where the inequality holds with a probability of $1 - \eta h$ is a non-negative integer called the Vapnik-Chervonenkis (VC) dimension, and is a measure of capacity.

For the case of a learning machine with a high capacity set of functions, the training error is low, but the machine could also have overfitting. For the case of a simple learning machine with low complexity, the training error could be high. Therefore, from a set of several functions $f(x, \alpha)$, the function that has the lowest upper bound depicted in the previous inequality should be chosen.

### 2.1 Linear SVM

As mentioned above "Support Vector Machines" (SVM) are supervised learning models with associated learning algorithms that analyze data and recognize patterns, used for classification and regression analysis. More formally, a support vector machine constructs a hyperplane or set of hyperplanes in a high or infinite-dimensional space, which can be used for classification, regression, or other tasks. Intuitively, a good separation is achieved by the hyperplane that has the largest distance to the nearest training data point of any class (margin), since in general the larger the margin the lower the generalization error of the classifier.

For the linear version of the SVM the function can be expressed as $f(x) = w \cdot x + b$, where $x \in \Re^d$ and $w \in \Re^d$. The data points that lie closest to the separation hyperplane are called the support vectors and are the most difficult to classify (Figure 2):

$$\begin{cases} w \cdot x_i + b \geq 1 & y_i = 1 \\ w \cdot x_i + b \leq 1 & y_i = -1 \end{cases} \qquad (5)$$

which can also be expressed as:

$$y_i(w \cdot x_i + b) \geq 1 \; \forall i \qquad (6)$$

The margin is defined as $2/||w||$ and is visually represented in Figure 2. The SVM algorithm finds the hyperplane that gives the maximum margin by minimizing $||w||^2$. The SVM algorithm is trained through an optimization process by minimizing the following expression with respect to $w$ and $b$ (Figure 3):

$$L = \underbrace{\sum_{i=1}^{N}(a_i|1 - y_i \cdot (w \cdot x_i + b)|)}_{\text{Training error}} + \underbrace{0.5 * ||w||^2}_{\text{Complexity term}}$$

$$(7)$$

Interpretation of the linear SVM classification results has the advantage that it can be done by graphical visualization. The SVM separation frontier with its thresholds can be represented within a two-dimensional graph for all combinations of inputs even for multi-dimensional matrices X (Figure 5).

A learning SVM is closer to an optimization algorithm than a computing greedy search method. The SVM also has the advantage delivering a unique solution, since the optimality

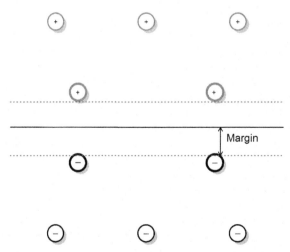

FIGURE 2   Linear version of the SVM. The data points with wider line width that lie closest to the separation hyperplane are called the support vectors and are the most difficult to classify.

## Linear separable features

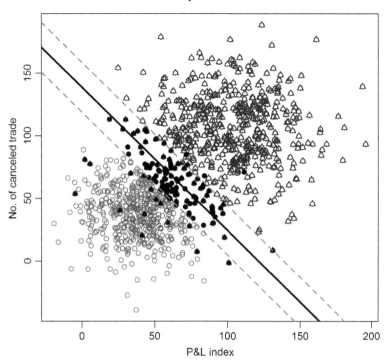

**FIGURE 3**  SVM linear algorithm searches for the hyperplane that offers the best separation between the two classes.

problem is convex. For comparison, neural networks do have multiple solutions associated with local minima and hence may not be robust over different training samples. The SVM process is a statistical optimizer that receives labeled observations as input and gives as output a function that can be used to classify future test data.

## 2.2 Linear Non-Separable SVM

Figure 4 shows a case of non-separable observations, where the observations from the training set from one class are on both sides of the foreseeable separation zone. Therefore, the data set is not perfectly separable and the challenge is to minimize the misperformance of the learning machine.

To take into account the new geometry the constraints from Equation 5 need to be relaxed and an extra cost function cost should be considered. Thus, the positive variables $\xi_i, i = 1, \ldots, l$ shown in Figure 4 should be introduced in the original constraints:

$$\begin{cases} w \cdot x_i + b \geq 1 - \xi_i & y_i = 1 \\ w \cdot x_i + b \leq -1 = \xi_i & y_i = -1, \ \xi_i \geqslant 0, \forall i \end{cases} \quad (8)$$

The objective function to be minimized for the SVM algorithm is:

$$L = \sum_{i=1}^{N} (a_i|1 - y_i \cdot (w \cdot x_i + b) - \xi_i|) + C \cdot \sum_{i=1}^{N} \xi_i + 0.5 * ||w||^2 \quad (9)$$

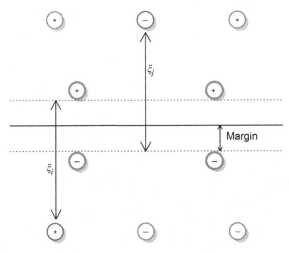

**FIGURE 4**   SVM for non-separable data. An extra cost function cost should be considered based on distances $\xi_i$.

## 2.3 Nonlinear SVM

The SVM methods can also be applied for nonlinear separation shapes.

A straightforward solution is to map the training observations into a richer feature space with nonlinear features, then construct a hyperplane in that space so all other equations presented before remain the same. Formally, the new mapping function can be rewritten with the function $\Phi(x)$:

$$f(x) = w \cdot \Phi(x) + b \qquad (10)$$

The SVM equation can be rewritten with a modification of the parameters **w**:

$$f(x) = \underbrace{\sum_{i=1}^{N} a_i \Phi(x_i)}_{w} \Phi(x) + b = \sum_{i=1}^{N} a_i \underbrace{\Phi(x_i)\Phi(x)}_{K(x_i,x)} + b$$

$$(11)$$

where the $K(x_i, x)$ is the kernel function:

$$K(x_i, x) = \Phi(x_i)\Phi(x) \qquad (12)$$

**TABLE 1**   Errors

| Kernel | Error | True positive ratio |
|--------|-------|---------------------|
| Linear | 0.01 | 0.857 |
| RBF | 0.009 | 0.859 |
| Laplace | 0.42 | 0.62 |
| Bessel | 0.019 | 0.826 |

A few kernels used in the SVM algorithm are given as follows:

$$\begin{cases} \text{Polynomial} & K(x,y) = (x \cdot y + 1)^p \\ \text{Gaussian radial} & K(x,y) = e^{-||x-y||^2/(2 \cdot \sigma^2)} \\ \quad \text{basis} \\ \text{Hyperbolic tangent} & K(x,y) = \tanh(\kappa x \cdot y - \delta) \\ \text{Laplace} & K(x,y) = e^{-||x-y||/\sigma} \\ \text{Bessel} & K(x,y) = \frac{B_{v+1}^n(\sigma||x-y||)}{||x-y||^{-n(v+1)}} \end{cases}$$

$$(13)$$

Table 1 shows the errors and true positive performance ratios of various kernels applied to the initial example.

Figure 5 shows a few examples of SVM algorithms with nonlinear kernels.

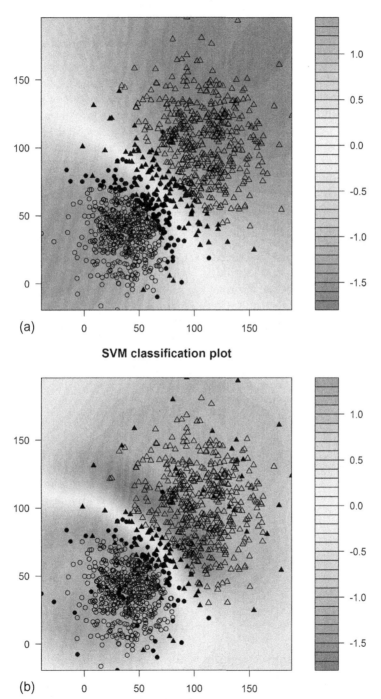

**FIGURE 5** SVM classifications for various kernels. (a) Laplacian kernel; (b) Radial basis Gaussian kernel.

## 2.4 Multi-Class SVM

The SVM algorithm was developed originally to separate binary classes through maximized margin criterion. However, in real life classification problems often require more than two classes. Therefore, the multi-class SVM deals with the situations of a mapping $x_i \rightarrow y_i$, where $y_i \in \{1, 2, \ldots, l\}$ and $l$ is the number of classes.

A few approaches have been developed for the multi-class SVM, leveraging the binary case. A first approach [162] builds $l$ different binary SVM classifiers and each machine is trained using the data from the $m$th class as positive observations and the remaining $l - 1$ classes as negative examples. This multi-class SVM (one vs. rest) is determined by searching for the $l$ binary classifiers that optimize the total search problem. A second approach introduced by Knerr et al. [163] for multi-class classification is the pairwise decomposition that evaluates all possible pairwise classifiers and thus builds $l(l - 1)/2$ individual SVM binary classifiers.

A global multi-class SVM built was proposed by Weston and Watkins [164] and consists of minimizing the following function:

$$\min_{w_m \ b \in \Re^l \ \xi \in \Re^{lxN}} L = 0.5 \sum_{m=1}^{l} w_m^T \cdot w_m$$

$$+ C \sum_{i=1}^{N} \sum_{t \neq y_i} \xi_{i,t} \quad (14)$$

with the following constraints:

$$w_{y_i}^T \Phi(x_i) + b_{y_i} \geq w_t^T \Phi(x_i) + b_t + 2 - \xi_{i,t} \ \xi_{i,t} \geq 0$$
$$i \in 1, 2 \ldots N \ t \in \{1, \ldots, l\} \setminus y_i \quad (15)$$

Despite being a global algorithm it requires high computational time to converge.

# 3 PERFORMANCE ASSESSMENT OF THE SVM

## 3.1 Cross-Validation

A natural choice for testing the performance of cross-validation is a standard technique for adjusting parameters of predictive models [165]. In a typical cross-validation, the available data consists of a set $S = \{X, Y\}$ of observation $X$ and labels $Y$, sliced into $K$ subsets $S_1, S_2, \ldots, S_K$. Each observation with its label from $S = \{X, Y\}$ is randomly assigned to one of the subsets such that there are almost an equal number of observations. In the cross-validation process an individual SVM is built by applying the algorithm to $S_1$ for all $i = (1, \ldots, K)$. $S_i$ represents the union of all observations with the exception of those in the $i$ fold. This trained machine on each fold is then tested by using the observations in $S_i$. The average of the $K$ outcomes of the model represent the cross-validation performance.

## 3.2 Bootstrapping

Assessing the range of the SVM parameters **w** and **b** is a useful result mostly when there is a need to measure the confidence interval for the algorithm's parameters. The SVM can be applied to many cases with various types of data set and the results can be highly dependent on the features of the underlying data: scarcity, homogeneity of the classes, etc. Following Efron [166] let's assume an initial training data set with $N$ observations with the features $x_1, x_2, \ldots, x_N$ and labels $y_1, y_2, \ldots, y_N$. Bootstrap samples are created from the initial space based on the empirical distribution, putting $1/N$ weight on each observation. The method implemented for the SVM parameterization has the following steps:

1. Independent bootstrap indexes $i_1, i_2, i_3, \ldots, i_N$ with values between 1 and $N$.
2. The bootstrap data sets $x_{i_1}^*, x_{i_2}^*, \ldots, x_{i_{N_{Sim}}}^*$ with labels $y_{i_1}^*, y_{i_2}^*, \ldots, y_{i_{N_{Sim}}}^*$ are drawn from the initial sample. The number of resamples $N_{Sim}$ is aimed to be large.
3. For each sample $y_j^*, j = i, 2, \ldots, N_{Sim}$ a SVM trained with the parameters $\hat{w}_j^*, \hat{b}_j^*$ is computed.
4. The bootstrap cumulative vector of distributions of each SVM parameter from the set $\hat{\theta}^* = (\hat{w}^*, \hat{b}^*)$ is constructed.

$$B_\theta(s) = \frac{\#\{\hat{\theta}_j^* < s\}}{N_{Sim}}, \quad -\infty < s < \infty \quad (16)$$

5. The quantity $z_0 = \Phi^{-1}(B_\theta(\hat{\theta}))$ is empirically computed. $\Phi$ is the cumulative density of the Gaussian distribution.
6. The bootstrap interval of the SVM parameters is set $\theta$ is defined to be:

$$\theta \in [B_\theta^{-1}(\Phi(2z_0 + z^{(\alpha)})), B_\theta^{-1}(\Phi(2z_0 + z^{(1-\alpha)}))] \quad (17)$$

where $z^{(\alpha)}$ is the $100 \cdot \alpha$ percentile for a standard normal distribution.

Figure 6 shows the distribution of the parameters (slope and offset) for a linear SVM from the previous example. The distributions of the error and of the classification performance are also plotted. The confidence interval indicates that the estimated parameters are stable.

## 3.3 SVM Optimism

When measuring the performance of SVM classification a question naturally arises: How well will the machine perform on a set different than the training set? In general, the original data is split into a training and a test sample. The SVM algorithm is trained on the training sample set and tested later on the test sample. In many cases of data mining for financial crime the available data set is limited and splitting the set in training and testing samples would reduce considerably the amount of information available to build the SVM. One drawback of traditional sample training and out-of-sample performance testing is that by splitting the data, the size of the data set used to train the SVM is smaller than the full available data. One strategy to deal with this drawback is to assess the performance of the SVM though a bootstrap type method proposed by Medema et al. [167] in the area of credit risk, derived from Efron and Tibshirani [168]. The main idea behind it is to compare the performance measure of a SVM algorithm on different bootstrap samples and to determine the difference in performance through a metric called optimism, which is deducted as follows:

- A number of $N$ bootstrap samples are generated from the initial data set.
- $N$ SVMs are trained on each of the bootstrap samples.
- The trained machines are applied to the original sample to computed $N$ SVM measures of classification performance.
- The initial trained sample is applied to the bootstrap samples used as testing samples to give $N$ measures.
- The SVM optimism is calculated for each bootstrap sample by taking the difference between the measure based on the SVM based on the original sample and the measure based on the SVM built on the bootstrap sample. This results in $N$ values of optimism.
- The overall optimism is the average of the $N$ values of optimism.

To determine the discrimination or calibration of the final model, the overall optimism is subtracted from the measure calculated on the final model, which is fitted based on the original sample (Figure 7).

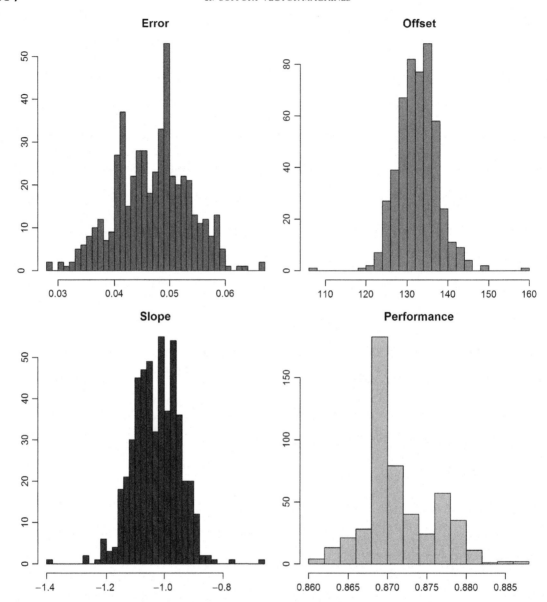

**FIGURE 6**    Bootstrapping techniques applied to a SVM algorithm.

## 4 APPLICATIONS OF THE SVM

Applications of the SVM algorithm have gained momentum in credit risk modeling, natural language processing, and fraud detection.

Pang et al. [169] used the SVM algorithm to address the problem of classifying documents by overall sentiment, determining whether a review is positive or negative in sentiment classification as traditional topic-based categorizations.

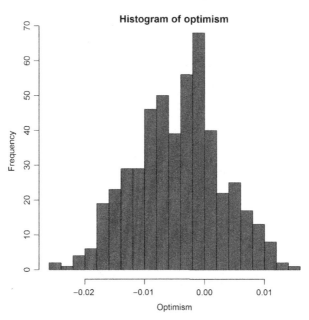

FIGURE 7  Optimism measured for a SVM.

Auria and Moro [170] provide through a SVM technique higher accuracy of company classification as solvent and insolvent. Their out-of-sample accuracy tests confirmed that the SVM outperformed other techniques like discriminatory analysis and Logit models. Huang et al. [171] studied corporate credit rating analysis with machine learning techniques including the SVM with a prediction accuracy around 80% for the U.S. and Taiwan markets.

There has also been a recent but steady trend of applying the SVM in the area of financial fraud. For example, Huang [172] proposed a fraud-detection model based on SVM techniques for detecting companies with potential fraud problems showing the ability to detect financial statement fraud 1 year before the beginning of fraud event. DeBarr and Wechsler [173] used data-mining techniques including SVM algorithms to predict fraud in insurance auto claims. Sharma and Panigrahi [174] presented various applications of data-mining techniques for the

detection of financial-accounting fraud and proposed a framework for data-mining techniques based on accounting fraud detection, emphasizing the use of SVM algorithms in this area.

## 5 OUTLOOK

The SVM algorithm will continue to expand in applications in the financial crime area. The main advantage of the SVM is its extended area of use to various fields and the capacity to incorporate various types of information. In the area of misconduct and crime on financial markets the detection involves both numerical data as well as text. To classify the transactions or behavior both types of data need to be integrated in order to capture not only the risk return features but also opinion/sentiment keyword content in text. The Forex manipulation is a good example in this sense, since the surveillance of the trader included data from the chat rooms used for organizing the manipulation.

# Determining the Accuracy of a Fraud-Detection Model

## 1 BACKGROUND

Since the seminal paper by Gini [175] there has been research on the Gini coefficient as a measure of income inequality, but the applications for credit risk modeling are relatively scarce. Some recent literature has proposed few methods for measuring the variance of the Gini coefficient estimator. For example, Lerman and Yitzhaki [176] and Ogwang [177] showed that the Gini coefficient could be derived as the regression coefficient of a linear regression, thereby providing automatically a variance estimator. Resampling methods were developed by Yitzhaki [178] who proposed a jackknife approach for Gini coefficient's variance. Yitzhaki [178], Karagiannis

and Kovacevic [179], Giles [180], and Tasche [181] developed methods designed for the Gini coefficient's application to classification model validation, based on the Mann-Whitney test.

In the context of the Gini's coefficient for assessing the discriminatory power of binary classification models (e.g., fraudulent vs normal deals) a special focus is needed on the scarce data samples and on the reliability of the Gini coefficient for such samples. The concept of model "luckiness" is introduced here, which represents the capacity of a model to correctly rank fraudulent observations, without having a score distribution that clearly separates normal from fraudulent observations. For instance, a data set of observations of rogue trading with a low number of unauthorized trades (i.e., less than 5) with a "lucky" model might assign to those unauthorized trades lower scores than to normal trades but without providing significant distance between both populations. For these cases the Gini coefficient would have a high value and therefore would validate the use of a wrong model.

## 2 THE GINI COEFFICIENT PHILOSOPHY: FROM MEASURING INCOME REPARTITION INJUSTICE TO RATING MODEL VALIDATION

Over the past 90 years, the Gini index has become one of the principal inequality measures in the field of economics [175]. With the increased focus on risk management, Gini's coefficient was leveraged for the validation of classification models and is today the most common method used to assess the effectiveness of a risk-scoring methodology.

A popular definition for Gini's coefficient among economists is the average absolute difference of incomes of two randomly selected individuals that hence reflects the income inequality in the population. Let $F(y) = P(Y \leq y)$ be the cumulative distribution function of a continuous random variable $Y$, referred by economists as the income variable. If $X$ and $Y$ are two independent random variables describing the income of two distinct random individuals, following the same distribution $\mathbf{F}$, the Gini coefficient is given by the equation:

$$G = \frac{1}{2\mu} E |X - Y|$$
$$= \frac{1}{2\mu} \int_0^\infty \int_0^\infty |x - y| \, dF(x) \, dF(y) \qquad (1)$$

where obviously $\mu = E(Y) = \int_0^\infty y \, dF(y)$.

By writing $|x - y| = 2 \cdot \max(x, y) - (x + y)$ and integrating the Gini coefficient can be written in a form often used in scoring validation:

$$G = \frac{1}{\mu} \int_0^\infty (2F(y) - 1) y \, dF(y) \qquad (2)$$

Following Frunza [182] and Tasche [181] a formalism for measuring the discriminative power of a fraud detection model is developed. Thus, let's consider a fraud likelihood scoring index $Y$ and a sample space $Z$, taking values $z \in \{F, N\}$. The $F$ state is given to a fraudulent event and $N$ to a normal event. Let's consider a probability measure $P$ over the space $Z$ and a collection of events from a set of observations collected in a $\sigma$ – algebra $F$.

Let's assume the total empirical probability of fraud (hazard rate of fraud) $\pi$ and the two conditional distribution functions are $F_F(y)$ and $F_N(y)$. The distribution function $F(y) = P[Y \leq y]$ of the marginal (or unconditional) distribution of the score $Y$ can be represented as:

$$F(y) = \pi F_F(y) + (1 - \pi) F_N(y) \qquad (3)$$

Many statistical tools are available for measuring the discriminatory power in one of these ways. A selection of popular tools in the industry are considered. These metrics are given under the assumption that the cumulative distribution is a continuously smooth function.

The cumulative accuracy profile (or CAP) is a useful graphical tool for investigating the discriminatory power of rating systems. The expression of the CAP can be written as:

$$\text{CAP}(u) = F_F(F^{-1}(u)) \qquad (4)$$

The accuracy ratio is the area between the diagonal line and the CAP curve and can be considered a measure of discriminatory power:

$$AR = \frac{2 \int_0^1 CAP(u)\, du - 1}{1 - \pi} \qquad (5)$$

The receiver operating characteristic (or ROC) is another graphical tool for investigating discriminatory power. The expression of the ROC curve is:

$$ROC = F_F(F_D^{-1}(u)) \qquad (6)$$

graphically resulting in a plot of $F_N(s)$ and $F_F(s)$. The further measure of discriminatory power is the area under the curve (AUC) defined as the area between the ROC curve and the axis of abscissa. This area can be calculated as the integral of the ROC curve from 0 to 1:

$$AUC = \int_0^1 F_F(F_N^{-1}(t))\, dt = \int_{-\infty}^{+\infty} F_N(y)(f_F(y))\, dy \qquad (7)$$

Alternatively, the AUC can be described as a probability, namely that the score of a normal event selected at random is higher than the score of an independently selected fraudulent event. Hence,

$$AUC = P[S_F < S_N] \qquad (8)$$

where $S_N$ and $S_F$ are independent and distributed according to $F_N$ and $F_F$, respectively. This can also be developed from Equations 7 and 5 that AUC $= \frac{AR+1}{2}$.

With the formalism defined here the Gini coefficient can be analytically as:

$$G = 2 \int_0^1 F_F(u)\, dF(u) - 1 \qquad (9)$$

**Proposition 1.** *Gini's coefficient defined under the formalism of a fraud-scoring framework given in Equation 9 is equivalent to the expression derived for the revenue inequality in Equation 2, under the* assumption that the credit score variable stands in place of the revenue variable.

*Proof.* From Equation 3 it can be derived:

$$f(y) = \pi f_F(y) + (1 - \pi) f_N(y) \qquad (10)$$

where $f, f_F$, and $f_N$ are the density attached to $F$, $F_F$, and $F_N$, respectively. More, it can be determined that $f_F = P(z = F|Y = y)f(y)/\pi$, where $\pi = \int P[z = F|Y = y]f(y)\, dy$. Thus, it can be developed under the following form:

$$f_F = \frac{P(z = F|Y = y)f(y)}{\int P[z = F|Y = y]f(y)\, dy} \qquad (11)$$

By integrating this equation the share of the total number of rogue events received by this part of the portfolio is given by the following expression:

$$F_F(s) = \frac{\int_{-\infty}^s yf(y)\, dy}{\int_{-\infty}^\infty yf(y)\, dy} = \frac{1}{\mu} \int_{-\infty}^s yf(y)\, dy \qquad (12)$$

where $\mu = \int_{-\infty}^\infty yf(y)\, dy$

Thus, the Gini coefficient can be written as:

$$G = 2 \int_0^1 F_F(u)\, dF(u) - 1 \qquad (13)$$

$$= \frac{2 \int_0^1 (\int_{-\infty}^u yf(y)\, dy) dF(u)}{\mu} - 1$$

$$= \frac{2 \int_0^1 (\int_{-\infty}^u y\, dF(\mathbf{y})) dF(u)}{\int_{-\infty}^\infty yf(y)\, dy} - \frac{\int_{-\infty}^\infty yf(y)\, d\mathbf{y}}{\int_{-\infty}^\infty yf(y)\, dy}$$

$$= \frac{2 \int_0^1 (\int_0^{F(y)} d\mathbf{F}) y\, dF(y)}{\mu} - \frac{\int_0^1 y\, dF(y)}{\mu}$$

$$= \frac{\int_0^1 2F(y) y\, dF(y) - \int_0^1 y\, dF(y)}{\mu}$$

$$= \frac{1}{\mu} \int_0^1 (2F(y) - 1) y\, dF(y)$$

$\square$

The Gini coefficient relates to these measures in the following way:

$$G = \text{AR} \cdot (1 - \pi) \qquad (14)$$
$$G = (2 \cdot \text{AUC} - 1)(1 - \pi)$$

The discriminatory power metrics for fraud-scoring modes are applied in a discrete space so the previous expressions for AUC, AR, and Gini coefficient should be revisited in a discrete way. First, the density function is written in the following form:

$$F(y) = \frac{1}{N} \sum_{i \in U} \delta y_i \leq y \qquad (15)$$

where $\delta y_i \leq y$ takes the value 1 if $y_i \leq y$ and the value 0 otherwise.

If $Y_F$ and $Y_N$ denote the score distributions for rogue and normal events in the data set a simple calculation shows that the area AUC below the ROC curve is:

$$\text{AUC} = \sum_{i=1}^{k} \frac{1}{2} \cdot (P(Y_F \leq y_i)$$
$$+ P(Y_F \leq y_{i-1}))P(Y_N = y_i) \qquad (16)$$
$$= \sum_{i=1}^{k} (P(Y_F \leq y_i)$$
$$+ \frac{1}{2} P(Y_D = y_{i-1}))P(Y_N = y_i)$$
$$= \sum_{i=1}^{k} (P(Y_F \leq y_i)P(Y_N = y_i))$$
$$+ \frac{1}{2} \sum_{i=1}^{k} (P(Y_F = y_{i-1})P(Y_N = y_i))$$
$$= P(Y_F < Y_N) + \frac{1}{2} P(Y_F = Y_N)$$

With a similar approach the AR is written in the following form:

$$\text{AR} = P[Y_F < Y_N] - P[Y_F > Y_N] \qquad (17)$$

The equivalent of Equation 14 in the simple continuous case on a population indexed after the score $y_i$, $i = \overline{1, n}$ is:

$$G = \frac{\sum_{i=1}^{n}(2i - 1)y_i}{n \sum_{i=1}^{n} y_i} - \frac{n + 1}{n} \qquad (18)$$

Although the Gini coefficient is probably the most commonly used tool for discriminatory power, it is usually reported without any acknowledgment of the fact that it is simply a sample statistic. As such, it has a sampling variance, and ideally a standard error should be reported. Moreover, for certain types of scarce data environments, this statistic is applied very often to small samples (less than 30 observations) or a very low number of fraud events (less than 5), thereby raising a lot of uncertainty around the relevance of a Gini coefficient measured in such conditions. Thus, in the following sections we focus on various approaches for Gini coefficient's variance computation.

On the one hand, the Gini coefficient reflects the model's capacity to discriminate *bad* from *good* events (observations), but on the other hand it assesses the quality of the model itself. However, under the discrete form the only input from the model is the order of the observations depending on the fraud model score. The separation power of the model, like the distance between the score distribution of *bad* and the score distribution of *good* events, is not directly taken into account. Thus, an inappropriate model with a "lucky" discriminant score and with a low number of observed fraud events can provide a good Gini coefficient.

# 3 RESAMPLING APPROACH

## 3.1 Bootstrap Approach

Efron [166] described an improved bootstrap method for confidence intervals applied to both parametric and non-parametric cases. Let's assume an initial sample $y$ of $N$ scores $y = (y_1, y_2, y_3, \ldots, y_N)$. Bootstrap samples are created from the initial space based on the empirical distribution, putting $1/N$ weight on each observation. At this point it should be noted that in the bootstrap process there are samples with no fraud observations as well as samples with only fraud observations. Obviously for those cases the Gini coefficient has no meaning and for very rare fraud events samples this method will provide unreliable results. A filter for those samples could be implemented to provide more rigorous results. The method implemented for the Gini coefficient has the followings steps:

1. Independent bootstrap data sets $y_1^*, y_2^*, \ldots, y_{N_{\text{Sim}}}^*$ are drawn from the initial sample. The number of resamples $N_{\text{Sim}}$ is large. The number of simulations and of the size of the initial sample will be discussed in a following section.

2. For each sample $y_j^*$, $j = i, 2, \ldots, N_{\text{Sim}}$ the Gini coefficient $\hat{G}_j^*$ is computed.

3. The bootstrap cumulative distribution of the Gini's coefficient values $\hat{G}^*$ is constructed.

$$B(s) = \frac{\#\{\hat{G}_j^* < s\}}{N_{\text{Sim}}}, \quad -\infty < s < \infty \quad (19)$$

4. The quantity $z_0 = \Phi^{-1}(B(\hat{G}))$ is empirically computed. $\Phi$ is the cumulative density of the Gaussian distribution.

5. The bootstrap interval of the Gini coefficient is defined to be:

$$G \in [B^{-1}(\Phi(2z_0 + z^{(\alpha)})), B^{-1}(\Phi(2z_0 + z^{(1-\alpha)}))] \quad (20)$$

where $z^{(\alpha)}$ is the $100 \cdot \alpha$ percentile for a standard normal distribution. If $B(\hat{G}) = 0.5$, half of the values of Gini's coefficient of bootstrap samples are less than the actual estimate of $\hat{G}$, then $z_0 = 0$.

For cases where the number of rogue events is small the distribution of the Gini's coefficients computed from the various bootstrapped samples might be asymmetric. Thus, the previous $\alpha$ confidence interval should take into account this fact through an acceleration constant "a" that depends on the skewness as follows:

$$G \in [B^{-1}(\Phi(z[\alpha])), B^{-1}(\Phi(z[1 - \alpha]))] \quad (21)$$

$$\text{where } z[\alpha] = z_0 + \frac{z_0 + z^{(\alpha)}}{1 - a(z_0 + z^{(\alpha)})}$$

where the acceleration constant $a = \frac{\text{SKEW}(l_G)}{6}$, $l_G = \frac{\partial b_G}{\partial G}$, and $b_G$ is the density function. The bootstrap approach gives the possibility to visualize the Gini curves corresponding to the confidence intervals as shown in Figure 1.

## 3.2 Jackknife Approach

The jackknife approach for measuring Gini coefficient's variance was proposed by the seminal work of Yitzhaki [178]. The method is straightforward. From the initial sample of length $N$, $N$ subsamples are jackknifed by eliminating one element and for each such subsample a Gini coefficient is computed. Obviously the method will give reliable results even for low fraud rate samples as only one value goes on the shelf per sample. The steps involved in the jackknife approach are:

1. Compute the Gini coefficient $G_0$ for the plain sample.

2. Generate $N$ samples with a jackknife method and compute $N$ Gini's coefficient $\hat{G}_j^*$, $j = i, 2, \ldots, N$.

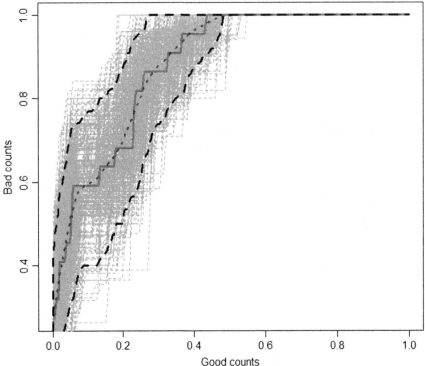

**Gini plot with confidence intervals**

FIGURE 1   Gini curve and 95% confidence interval computed via the bootstrap approach.

**3.** Compute for each generated sample the variable.

$$PG_j = N \cdot G_0 - (N - 1)\hat{G}_j^*$$

**4.** Compute the standard error for the Gini coefficient estimator:

$$\hat{\sigma}_G = \sqrt{\mathrm{Variance}(PG_j)/N}$$

**5.** Thus, the confidence interval is
$G \in [G_0 + \hat{\sigma}_G \Phi^{-1}(\alpha), G_0 + \hat{\sigma}_G \Phi^{-1}(1 - \alpha)]$.

It should be noted that large samples are needed to obtain consistent results.

# 4 ORDINARY LEAST-SQUARED APPROACH

Under the discrete form presented in Equation 18 and following Ogwang [177] and Giles [180] let's define the $\hat{\beta}$ as the linear regression estimator of $\beta$ from the following model:

$$y_i = \alpha + \beta i + \epsilon_i \tag{22}$$

where $\epsilon_i$ are zero-mean independent and homoscedasticity innovations. With this formalism the Gini coefficient can be written as:

$$G = \frac{(N^2 - 1)}{6N} \frac{\hat{\beta}}{\bar{y}} \tag{23}$$

where $N$ is the number of observations and $\bar{y}$ is the sample arithmetic mean.

Obviously we could find the variance of Gini's coefficient from the $\hat{\beta}$'s variance, but the results would be too wide given the form of Equation 22.

If $\bar{\theta}$ is considered as:

$$\bar{\theta} = \frac{\sum_{i=1}^{N} iy_i}{\sum_{i=1}^{N} y_i} \tag{24}$$

The Gini coefficient can be written in the following from equivalent to Equation 22:

$$\hat{G} = \frac{2\bar{\theta}}{N} - 1 - \frac{1}{N} \tag{25}$$

Following Giles [180], $\bar{\theta}$ can be used as the least-squared estimator in the model:

$$i = \theta + v_i \tag{26}$$

where the $v_i$s are heteroscedastic errors with variance of the form $(\sigma^2/y_i)$. Given Equation 25 the standard-error estimator for Gini's coefficient can be written as:

$$\hat{\sigma}_G = \frac{2}{N}\hat{\sigma}_{\bar{\theta}} \tag{27}$$

$\hat{\sigma}_{\bar{\theta}}$ is provided by the least-squares estimation of Equation 26 or equivalently in a regular regression:

$$i\sqrt{y_i} = \theta\sqrt{y_i} + u_i \tag{28}$$

where $u_i = \sqrt{y_i}v_i$.

In the context of a regular regression $(\theta - \bar{\theta})/\hat{\sigma}_{\bar{\theta}} \to N(0, 1)$ and thus the confidence interval for the Gini coefficient is:

$$\mathbf{P}\left(\hat{G} - \hat{\sigma}_G \Phi^{-1}\left(\frac{1+\alpha}{2}\right) \leq G \leq \hat{G}\right.$$
$$\left. +\hat{\sigma}_G \Phi^{-1}\left(\frac{1+\alpha}{2}\right)\right) = \alpha \tag{29}$$

# 5 MANN-WHITNEY APPROACH

There is also an important consequence from the representation of AUC as a probability as can be shown in Equation 16. The value of the AUC and implicitly that of Gini's coefficient can be derived through the non-parametric Mann-Whitney $U$ test.

When drawing a fraud observation with a score $y_F$ from $Y_F$ and a normal observation with score $y_N$ from $Y_N$ and setting the variable $u_{D,ND}$:

$$u_{F,N} = \begin{cases} 1 & \text{if } y_F < y_N \\ \frac{1}{2} & \text{if } y_F = y_N \\ 0 & \text{if } y_F > y_N \end{cases} \tag{30}$$

The Mann-Whitney $\hat{U}$ statistics are defined as the sum of $u_{F,N}$ over all the pairs of fraud and normal observations:

$$\hat{U} = \frac{1}{N_F \cdot N_N} \sum_{(F,N)} u_{F,N} \tag{31}$$

**Proposition 2.** *The Mann-Whitney $\hat{U}$ statistics are linked to the Gini coefficient in the following way:*

$$G = (2 * \hat{U} - 1)\frac{N_N}{N_F + N_N}$$

*Proof.*

$$\hat{U} = \frac{1}{N_F \cdot N_N} \sum_{(F,N)} u_{F,N} \tag{32}$$

$$= \frac{1}{N_F \cdot N_N} \sum_{(F,N)} \left((1_{y_F < y_N}) + \frac{1}{2}1_{y_F = y_N}\right)$$

$$= \frac{\sum_{(F,N)} 1_{y_F < y_N}}{N_D \cdot N_N} + \frac{\frac{1}{2}\sum_{(F,N)} 1_{y_F = y_N}}{N_F \cdot N_N}$$

$$= P(Y_F < Y_N) + \frac{1}{2}P(Y_F = Y_N)$$

Thus, using Equation 16 it can be shown that $\hat{U}$ = AUC. For the purpose of the discrete case, the observed default probability $\pi$ is $\frac{N_F}{N_F+N_N}$

and taking into account the relationship between AUC and Gini's coefficient from Equation 14 the demonstration is complete. $\qquad\square$

The last proposition provides two interesting results. On the one hand, the Gini coefficient can be estimated with Mann-Whitney statistics and on the other hand the variance of the $\hat{U}$ estimators can be used for computing the variance of the Gini score. For the variance $\sigma_{\hat{U}}^2$ of $\hat{U}$ the unbiased estimator $\hat{\sigma}_{\hat{U}}^2$ is found:

$$\hat{\sigma}_{\hat{U}}^2 = \frac{1}{4(N_F - 1)(N_N - 1)}\Big[1 + (N_F - 1)\hat{P}_{F,F,N} \tag{33}$$

$$+ (N_N - 1)\hat{P}_{N,N,F}$$

$$- 4(N_N + N_F - 1)\Big(\hat{U} - \frac{1}{2}\Big)^2\Big]$$

where $\hat{P}_{F,F,N}$ and $\hat{P}_{N,N,F}$ are estimators for the expressions $P_{F,F,N}$ and $P_{N,N,F}$ defined as:

$$\mathbf{P}_{F,F,N} = \mathbf{P}(Y_{F,1}, Y_{F,2} < Y_N) + \mathbf{P}(Y_N < Y_{F,1}, Y_{F,2}) \tag{34}$$

$$- \mathbf{P}(Y_{F,1} < Y_N < Y_{F,2})$$

$$- \mathbf{P}(Y_{F,2} < Y_N < Y_{F,1})$$

$$\mathbf{P}_{N,N,F} = \mathbf{P}(Y_{N,1}, Y_{N,2} < Y_F) + \mathbf{P}(Y_F < Y_{N,1}, Y_{N,2})$$

$$- \mathbf{P}(Y_{N,1} < Y_F < Y_{N,2})$$

$$- \mathbf{P}(Y_{N,2} < Y_F < Y_{N,1})$$

where the quantities $Y_{F,1}, Y_{F,2}$ are independent observations randomly sampled from $Y_F$ and $Y_{N,1}, Y_{N,2}$ are independent observations randomly sampled from $Y_N$. For $N_F, N_N \to \infty$ it is clear that $(\text{AUC} - \hat{U})/\hat{\sigma}_{\hat{U}} \to N(0, 1)$. Thus, the confidence interval of the AUC at level $\alpha$ can be computed using the following relation:

$$\mathbf{P}\Big(\hat{U} - \hat{\sigma}_{\hat{U}}\Phi^{-1}\Big(\frac{1 + \alpha}{2}\Big) \le \text{AUC}$$

$$\le \hat{U} + \hat{\sigma}_{\hat{U}}\Phi^{-1}\Big(\frac{1 + \alpha}{2}\Big)\Big) = \alpha \tag{35}$$

Equivalently the confidence interval of the Gini coefficient at level $\alpha$ is:

$$\mathbf{P}\Big(\hat{G} - \hat{\sigma}_G\Phi^{-1}\Big(\frac{1 + \alpha}{2}\Big) \le G$$

$$\le \hat{G} + \hat{\sigma}_G\Phi^{-1}\Big(\frac{1 + \alpha}{2}\Big)\Big) = \alpha \tag{36}$$

where $\hat{G} = (2 * \hat{U} - 1)\frac{N_N}{N_F + N_N}$ and $\hat{\sigma}_G = 2 \cdot \hat{\sigma}_{\hat{U}}\frac{N_N}{N_F + N_N}$.

## 6 F-GINI APPROACH

The main drawback of ordinary linear regression (OLS) and resampling approaches is the lack of focus on the way the scores are distributed. Thus, a poor model could provide a "lucky" classification for a small number of defaults and thereby generate a good Gini coefficient. The validation of a fraud-scoring model should provide some measure of the distance between the score distribution of *fraud* events and *normal* events (Figure 2). The Mann-Whitney statistics provide to a certain extent this measure but only in certain conditions of low rate of fraud events and high variance of the score $Y$, in which the Gini coefficient might be not robust. Thus, it would be useful to have a measure for both the discriminative power of a model and its capacity to separate the normal observation population from the rogue observations.

A stress-based extension of the jackknife approach is proposed. The method is identical to the jackknife with the only difference being that instead of taking out one observation, its score is replaced with a random score, simulated from a target distribution. The target distribution is Gaussian and has variance equal to the empirical variance of the sample. The Gaussian distribution is chosen as a tool for stressing the rating score of the fraud-rating model. The choice is due to its facility of implementation and to the fact that is a natural candidate for the distribution of rating errors. However, the *t*-distribution or

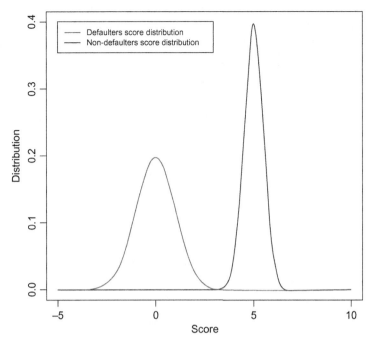

**FIGURE 2** Model discrimination.

generalized hyperbolic densities could also be good candidates. If the scoring model is good the Gini score will not be influenced by the noise in the scoring given that the two distributions of fraudulent and normal observations are very distant. If the model is poor the Gini coefficient will be significantly affected and the confidence interval will be wider. The approach has the following steps:

1. Compute the Gini coefficient $G_0$ for the plain sample.
2. Similar to jackknife create a sample by replacing the initial score $Y_i$ for one observation "$i$" with a score $Y_i^* = Y_i + \epsilon_i \widehat{\sigma_Y}$, where $\epsilon_i$ is a random number standard normally distributed and $\widehat{\sigma_Y}$ is the empirical standard deviation of the score. Here, the score $Y$ is considered to be $Y_i = -\Phi^{-1}(\mathrm{PF}_i)$, where $\mathrm{PF}_i$ is the probability that the $i_{th}$ observation provided by the scoring model is fraudulent.

3. Compute for each generated sample the Gini coefficient $\widehat{G}_j$ and the variable
   $$\mathrm{PG}_j = N \cdot G_0 - (N-1)\widehat{G}_j^*.$$
4. Repeat steps 2 and 3 for each observation in the sample: $i=1,2,\ldots,N$.
5. Repeat steps 2, 3, and 4 for a large number of times $N_{\mathrm{Sim}}$.
6. Compute the standard error for the Gini coefficient estimator:
   $$\hat{\sigma}_G = \sqrt{\mathrm{Variance}(\mathrm{PG}_j)/N}$$

7. Thus, the confidence interval is
   $G \in [G_0 + \hat{\sigma}_G \Phi^{-1}(\alpha), G_0 + \hat{\sigma}_G \Phi^{-1}(1-\alpha)].$

## 7 NUMERIC APPLICATION

The approaches described in the previous sections were tested for seven data sets with different features to assess the limits and strengths of

**TABLE 1**  Gini's Coefficient Standard Error for Target Data Set

| Method | Gini's coefficient (%) | Standard error (%) | 95% interval (%) |
|---|---|---|---|
| Bootstrap | 75.33 | 3.45 | [70.38, 81.65] |
| Jackknife | 75.33 | 4.04 | [69.77, 85.45] |
| OLS | 75.33 | 0.5 | [74.31, 76.35] |
| Mann-Whitney | 75.33 | 2.45 | [69.34, 89.15] |
| F-Gini | 75.33 | 20.03 | [39.8, 100.00] |

**TABLE 2**  Gini's Coefficient Computation Methods for Standard Error for Example 1 (Insider trading).

| Method | Gini's coefficient (%) | Standard error (%) | 95% interval (%) |
|---|---|---|---|
| Bootstrap | 67.57 | 6.12 | [52.33,78.71] |
| Jackknife | 67.57 | 6.02 | [58.41,78.14] |
| OLS | 67.57 | 1.92 | [62.14, 70.19] |
| Mann-Whitney | 67.57 | 6.14 | [59.17, 79.38] |
| F-Gini | 67.85 | 9.47 | [53.38, 84.52] |

each. A target sample was produced by sampling events from a pool of public known fraud events.

**Target Sample**: The target sample has 3720 observations in which 95 correspond to financial crime events. The fraud occurrence probability ($PF_N$) is 5.76% for the normal events and 45.19% for the fraud events ($PF_F$). The Gini coefficient and its standard error computed with various methods are given in Table 1. With a global Gini coefficient of 75.33% the scoring seems appropriate. Bootstrap, jackknife, OLS, and Mann-Whitney provide relatively low standard errors. F-Gini result is more conservative despite the fact that the average probability for defaulters and non-defaulters is significant. The low number of fraud events in the data set plays a crucial role in the accuracy of the Gini coefficient and is penalized here by the F-Gini method.

First, the linear method provides a low standard error generally constant over the past two decades with values below 1%. Jackknife, bootstrapping, and Mann-Whitney provide comparable results following the same tendency, with values below 5%. The F-Gini method is the most conservative and seems to capture the best cycle effect, oscillating around 10%.

In addition to the target data set six different subsets of observations corresponding to various types of fraud or crime typologies are studied, which will show the performance of the various methods used for computing Gini coefficient's standard error.

**Example 1** (Insider trading). The first sample is based on observations from brokerage trading accounts that might have been involved insider trading. There are two type of accounts: normal and suspicious accounts. The sample has 240 observations ($N$) and includes 20 suspicious accounts ($N_F$). The computed value of Gini's coefficient is 67.57%. The ex-ante default probabilities of observing insider trading phenomena for the suspicious and non-suspicious are $PF_F = 20.11\%$ and $PF_N = 6.52\%$. It appears that the distance between the suspicious and normal accounts is significant.

The Gini coefficients provided by the various methods are coherent, and the lowest standard error (Table 2) is given by the OLS model. The OLS method measures the accuracy of the Gini coefficient as an estimator in an estimation process and does not dissect further the underling model that generated that Gini coefficient. In all the results OLS logically provides the lowest standards error. The F-Gini standard error is the most conservative as it accounts for both Gini coefficient's precision and scoring's reliability.

**Example 2** (Pump-and-dump cases). The second example deals with a data set of microcap stock prices. Some of the stocks might have been the target of market manipulation. The data set has a higher number of observations compared to the previous example ($N = 3415$) and includes a small number of abnormal elements (stocks subject to manipulation) ($N_F = 12$) showing a

Gini coefficient of 81.71%. The ex-ante hazard rates for abnormal and normal subsets are $PF_F = 22.46\%$ and $PF_N = 3.17\%$. It appears that the distance between the manipulated and normal stock samples is significant.

The main issue in this portfolio is the scarcity of observations concerning the manipulated stocks. Both resampling procedures and $U$-tests provide more conservative figures of the standard errors (Table 3). The F-Gini standard error is twice the value of the jackknife method underlining the impact of the rating model stressing upon Gini's coefficient.

**Example 3** (Money laundering). This example contains results of a scorecard rating account with the goal of detecting the layering in a money-laundering scheme. The third sample is smaller than the previous sample but much bigger than the first one ($N = 1100$) and includes a very small number of suspicious observations ($N_F = 2$) with a Gini coefficient of 91.9%. The ex-ante hazard rate for accounts are $PF_F = 16.2\%$ and $PF_{NF} = 1.5\%$. It appears that the distance between the suspicious and normal populations is significant.

Given the fact that the data set disposes of only two observations related to the fraud the diversity of the bootstraps is low (Table 4). The model provides a perfect order and thus both the OLS and $U$-test provide a narrow interval. The jackknife method provides a more significant standard error and the F-Gini shows a 20%

**TABLE 4** Gini's Coefficient Standard Error for Example 3 (Money laundering).

| Method | Gini's coefficient (%) | Standard error (%) | 95% interval (%) |
|---|---|---|---|
| Bootstrap | 91.9 | 5.6 | [80.85, 97.08] |
| Jackknife | 91.9 | 9.7 | [73.3, 100.00] |
| OLS | 91.8 | 0.25 | [91.20, 92.25] |
| Mann-Whitney | 91.8 | 8.13 | [80.16, 99.86] |
| F-Gini | 91.9 | 19.9 | [58.36, 100.00] |

standard error underscoring the fact that a model with only two abnormal observations might have some serious reliability issues. It is obvious that for a low number of fraud observations and small samples the classic methods provide biased results. It should be recalled that Gini's coefficient was initially used for the validation of fraud models disposing of large samples with an appropriate number of fraud observations. The use of Gini's coefficient for a low default portfolio should take into account these observations and be focused on the reliability of the figure, thereby emphasizing the F-Gini approach to the confidence interval.

**Example 4** (Unauthorized trading). This example considers the assessment of traders behavior and aims to assess the likelihood of unauthorized trading. The fourth example is subsampled in order to test the various methods for a poor quality model. The number of observations is 200 and includes a significant number of rogue traders $N_F = 30$ with a very low Gini coefficient of 15.60%. The ex-ante rouge rate for rogue and normal trader populations are $PF_F = 21.74\%$ and $PF_N = 19.99\%$. It appears that the distance between the fraudulent and normal observation populations is small, emphasizing a model with low discriminatory capacity.

In this case the OLS standard error is the most aggressive (Table 5). The jackknife, Mann-Whitney, and F-Gini approaches capture the best unreliability of the model, showing confidence intervals close to zero.

**TABLE 3** Gini's Coefficient Standard Error for Example 2 (Pump-and-dump cases).

| Method | Gini's coefficient (%) | Standard error (%) | 95% interval (%) |
|---|---|---|---|
| Bootstrap | 81.71 | 6.75 | [68.94, 92.01] |
| Jackknife | 81.70 | 7.01 | [67.26, 95.71] |
| OLS | 81.71 | 0.31 | [82.33, 85.28] |
| Mann-Whitney | 81.96 | 7.51 | [68.52, 93.19] |
| F-Gini | 81.53 | 19.31 | [63.42, 100.00] |

**TABLE 5**  Gini's Coefficient Standard Error for Example 4 (Unauthorized trading).

| Method | Gini's coefficient (%) | Standard error (%) | 95% interval (%) |
|---|---|---|---|
| Bootstrap | 15.60 | 7.90 | [1.78, 28.21] |
| Jackknife | 15.60 | 8.05 | [2.34, 28.85] |
| OLS | 15.10 | 3.08 | [9.02, 21.17] |
| Mann-Whitney | 15.57 | 8.04 | [2.45, 28.90] |
| F-Gini | 15.54 | 9.11 | [0.61, 30.59] |

**TABLE 6**  Gini's Coefficient Standard Error for Example 5 (Hedge fund rating).

| Method | Gini's coefficient (%) | Standard error (%) | 95% interval (%) |
|---|---|---|---|
| Bootstrap | 85.50 | 2.40 | [82.00, 89.50] |
| Jackknife | 85.50 | 2.53 | [81.33, 89.66] |
| OLS | 85.00 | 0.61 | [83.79, 86.21] |
| Mann-Whitney | 85.92 | 0.00 | [85.92, 85.92] |
| F-Gini | 85.03 | 13.37 | [63.49, 100.00] |

**Example 5** (Hedge fund rating). A data set of hedge fund returns is considered with the aim of rating those hedge funds that communicate misleading returns. The fifth example is also built in order to test the various methods for a poor quality model, from the perspective of random scoring. A portfolio with a total of 200 hedged funds and 30 suspicious hedge funds is considered in such a way that any defaulter has a higher default probability than any non-defaulter. Thus, the expected Gini coefficient is high with a value of 85.50%. The ex-ante default probability for defaulters and non-defaulters are $PF_F = 20.98\%$ and $PF_N = 18.13\%$. It appears that the distance between the defaulted and non-defaulted populations is small, but if only the Gini coefficient was taken into account, the model would be judged as performing.

If we expect a small OLS standard error, given the fact that the model separates correctly, the $U$-test provides a null error (Table 6). This finding is explained in Equation 33, as the Mann-Whitney standard error depends directly on the number of wrongly ordered rogue hedge funds. As this "lucky" model arranges the observation in perfect order, the standard error is logically zero. The resampling methods also show a small standard error. Only the F-Gini captures the "luckiness" of the model with a higher standard error.

**Example 6** (Misselling structured products). A portfolio of structured products is considered. Depending on their complexity and the profile of

**TABLE 7**  Gini's Coefficient Standard Error for Example 6 (Misselling structured products).

| Method | Gini's coefficient (%) | Standard error (%) | 95% interval (%) |
|---|---|---|---|
| Bootstrap | 97.00 | 0.42 | [95.30, 98.29] |
| Jackknife | 97.00 | 1.10 | [94.80, 99.2] |
| OLS | 96.50 | 0.10 | [96.30, 96.71] |
| Mann-Whitney | 97.5 | 0.20 | [96.89, 97.9] |
| F-Gini | 96.5 | 35.25 | [35.05, 100.00] |

the clients that invest in those products, a scorecard assessing the probability of misselling is modeled. This example is similar to the previous example, but with a smaller number of abnormal observations. The total number of observations is significant ($N = 200$) and includes a small number of misselling cases. ($N_F = 5$) with a Gini coefficient of 97.00%. The ex-ante hazard rates for the subset containing normal cases and misselling cases are $PF_F = 21.95\%$ and $PF_N = 18.00\%$. Hence, this sample has two issues: a low number of misselling (fraud) cases and a "lucky" model.

In line with the results of the fifth data set using the resampling, the OLS and $U$-test approaches are very low and would probably give a very accurate image of the Gini coefficient (Table 7). The F-Gini standard error only increases violently near 35% indicating some structural problems in the model.

**TABLE 8** Gini's Coefficient Standard Error for Example 7 (Rogue brokers).

| Method | Gini's coefficient (%) | Standard error (%) | 95% interval (%) |
|---|---|---|---|
| Bootstrap | 80.13 | 6.47 | [63.52, 89.65] |
| Jackknife | 80.13 | 8.33 | [65.71, 92.90] |
| OLS | 79.81 | 2.91 | [70.09, 81.62] |
| Mann-Whitney | 83.92 | NA | [NA, NA] |
| F-Gini | 80.13 | 27.45 | [33.22, 100.00] |

**TABLE 9** Gini's and the Size of the Test Sample

| Criteria | Small portfolios ($N < 30$) | Large portfolios ($N \geq 30$) |
|---|---|---|
| Low number of fraud cases ($N_F < 6$) | The Gini estimation is not appropriate. | The model might be not robust (Mann-Whitney, F-Gini). |
| Non-Low High number of fraud cases ($N_F \geq 6$) | The Gini coefficient estimation is not appropriate. | All the methods for standard error are reliable. |

**Example 7** (Rogue brokers). This example is similar to the broker's scorecard model for determining those brokers involved in illegal operations (e.g., market manipulation, hard selling). The last example is artificially created and highlights three different issues: low number of fraud-related observations, scarce sample, and a "lucky model." The number of observations is limited to $N = 29$ and includes a small number of rogue brokers ($N_F = 5$) and a Gini coefficient of 80.13%. The ex-ante hazard rates for normal and rogue brokers subsets are $PF_F = 20.18\%$ and $PF_N = 17.51\%$.

Given the low number of observations related to rogue brokers and the limited number of observations the $U$-test and bootstrap methods fail to provide reliable results (Table 8). The F-Gini provides with a very high standard error exacerbating the various issues of the data set.

# 8 FOCUS ON THE SIZE OF PORTFOLIO

As discussed in the previous sections the size of the observation sample and the number of fraud cases in the sample are a key factor for computing an accurate Gini coefficient.

If the Gini coefficient is found as a result of a simple regression as presented in Equation 22 it appears obvious that we would need a significant number of observations to obtain a significant statistic result. Let's consider that 30 observations starts to constitute a sample that can provide relevant statistics (Table 9). A good model will provide an appropriate Gini coefficient and low variance (OLS) even if there is a low number of observations.

If the Gini coefficient is found as the result of a bootstrap procedure it appears obvious that the quality of the results depends on the degree of diversity of the generated sample. For example, in very rare fraud cases a large share of bootstraps will contain the same fraud cases. This along with a high Gini coefficient will provide an underestimated variance. Following the works of Frunza [182] let's consider that from six abnormal fraud events in a sample an appropriate diversity in generated samples can be observed. It should be noted here that the pure bootstrap method might not be able to provide reliable standard deviations given the fact that some samples will have no fraud cases.

For scarce fraud observations and small portfolios the Mann-Whitney approach cannot provide results as the U-test assumes it has a high number of observations for both normal and abnormal subsets.

Observations from the target data set can be used to assess the dependency between the standard error on one side and the observed fraud rate and sample size sampled the observations on the other side. The target portfolio is subsampled, controlling the length of the sample and the hazard rate. The linear, bootstrapping, and Mann-Whitney methods are used for benchmark, and a standard error surface is computed depending on the hazard rate and sample size. The results are shown in Figures 3–6.

Figure 3 shows the increase of the standard error with the diminishing sample size for the linear approach.

Figure 4 shows that the bootstrap method provides more conservative results compared to the OLS method. In addition, the error of the Gini coefficient increases with the decrease of the hazard fraud rate.

Figures 4 and 6 show the Gini's error measure through the Mann-Whitney approach for the different cases.

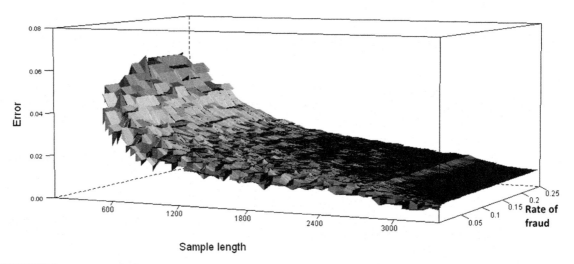

FIGURE 3    Linear standard error.

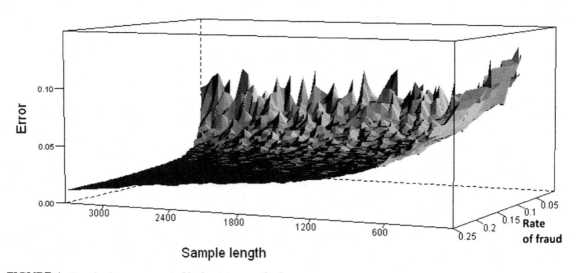

FIGURE 4    Standard error computed by bootstrap method.

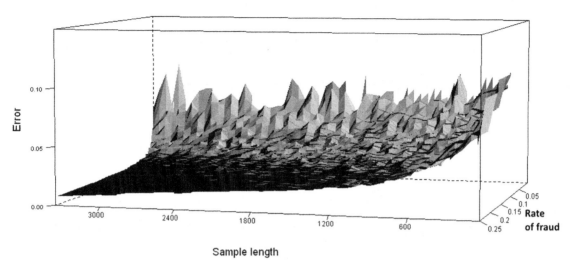

**FIGURE 5**   Mann-Whitney standard error computed for subsample of microcap manipulation cases.

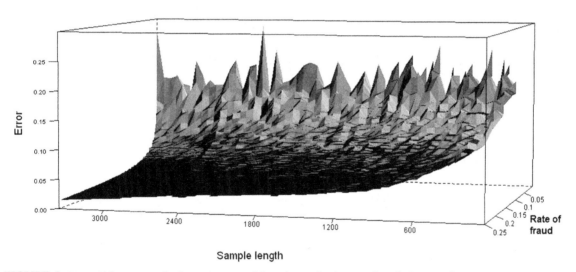

**FIGURE 6**   Mann-Whitney standard error computed for subsample of money-laundering sample.

Rare events and low-length data sets have as expected higher standard error, the Gini coefficient thereby being less reliable. Both ordinary least squares and Mann-Whitney have the same behavior, with the $U$-test being obviously more conservative.

# 9 OUTLOOK

Assessing the performance of fraud ranking/detection models is crucial for being able to rely on near-real time application. The measures derived from the Lorenz curve will continue to be highly employed in all areas of risk modeling and with growing momentum in financial crime units. Their scope varies from simple scorecard methods to complex machine-learning approaches. The Gini coefficient is one of the most popular measures for assessing the discriminatory power of a model and its relevance is crucial for assessing the quality of the underlying model.

A standard error is needed if confidence intervals or tests are to be constructed for the Gini coefficient, and various authors have proposed methods using the resampling, ordinary least squares, or $U$-test techniques. A new method, F-Gini, is proposed for measuring the reliability of the Gini coefficient. Compared to the other methods this approach also considers the model's robustness. In fact, F-Gini assesses not only the quality of the estimation, but also the quality of the underlying fraud detection model. The various methods are tested on a few data set with fraudulent and normal events (observations). It appears that the resampling methods and the $U$-test provide more conservative results. F-Gini assumes a normal target distribution for the noise introduced in the model's score and overcomes the issues of other methods, by stressing the resilience of the models' ranking ability. Thus, F-Gini is more conservative for data sets with rare fraud observations with inappropriate but "lucky" underlying scoring models.

# Benford's Law

## 1 BACKGROUND

The first mention about the way digits are distributed in data set is attributed to Simon Newcomb, an American astronomer and mathematician who published a work [183] explaining the features of the digit density. He explained that "the ten digits do not occur with equal frequency" a common known fact for the users of logarithmic tables[1] and that the first significant digit is oftener 1 than any other digit, and the frequency diminishes up to 9. Newcomb's work

was developed further in the beginning the XXth century by the French mathematician Poincaré [184], before being popularized by the seminal paper of Benford [185]. Assuming that a data set is characterized by a variable $X$ that depends on the units and has a probability distribution $P(X)$ over such variables. This probability should be invariant under a change of scale, so:

$$P(kx) = f(k)P(x) \tag{1}$$

where both densities $P(x)$ and $P(kx)$ are normalized, $\int P(x) = \int P(kx) = 1$, implying that $f(k) = 1/k$. Differentiating the above equation on the variable $k$ and fixing $k = 1$: $xP'(x) = -P(x)$.

The solution of this first-order differential equation is $P(x) = 1/x$. Under this framework the probability that the first digit takes the value $d_1$ $\mathbf{P}(D_1(X) = d_1)$ can be computed as:

---

[1] Before the invention of computers the logarithms were computed with the help of the "logarithmic tables," which were very thick books containing the results of calculations depending on various arguments for making their use more user friendly.

$$\mathbf{P}(D_1(X) = d_1) = \frac{\int_{d_1}^{d_1+1} P(x)\,\mathrm{d}x}{\int_1^{10} P(x)\,\mathrm{d}x} = \log_{10}(1 + 1/d_1) \tag{2}$$

Therefore, Benford's law is nothing more than a probability distribution expressing the likelihood of occurrence of the first digit in a set of numbers:

$$\mathbf{P}(D_1(X) = d_1) = \log_{10}(d_1 + 1) - \log_{10}(d_1)$$
$$= \log_{10}(1 + 1/d_1) \tag{3}$$

where $D_1$ is the first digit of a random variable $X$ and $d_1$ is a digit with values between 1 and 9. Figure 1 shows the distribution of the first digit Benford's law compared to the first digit of a random variable generated from a $t$-Student law.

The distribution can be extend for the second digit of a random variable number including the joint distribution for the first two digits and the

conditional distribution as follows:

$$\mathbf{P}(D_2(X) = d_2) = \sum_{d_1=1}^{9} \log_{10}(1 + (1/d_1 d_2)) \tag{4}$$

$$\mathbf{P}(D_1(X) = d_1, D_2(X) = d_2) = \log_{10}(1 + (1/d_1 d_2)) \tag{5}$$

$$\mathbf{P}(D_2(X) = d_2 | D_1(X) = d_1)$$
$$= \log_{10}(1 + (1/d_1 d_2)) / \log_{10}(1 + 1/d_1) \tag{6}$$

An elegant generalization for the distribution of the first $k$-digits in a number was given by Joenssen [186] and Hill [187]. Hence, for a random continuous variable $X$, the first $k$ digits $D_k(X)$ follow Benford's law as expressed below.

$$\mathbf{P}(D_k(X) = d_{1,k}) = \log(1 + 1/d_k) \tag{7}$$

where $D_k(X) = |x|10^{-\log(|x|)+k+1}$ and $d_{1,k} \in \{10^{k-1}, 10^{k-1} + 1, \ldots, 10^k - 1\}$.

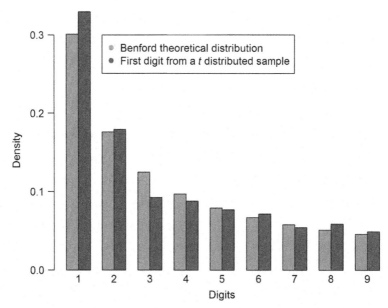

FIGURE 1   Benford's law distribution. The first digit Benford's law compares the first digit of a random variable generated from a $t$-Student law.

In theory many of the numeric series with a random feature follow Benford's law as shown by the experiment in Figure 1 and when the law is not respected there should be suspicions about the nature of the data. However, there are exceptions to this rule, especially for data that is clustered, has autocorrelation, or is generated given some constraining rules. Benford's law is used in many walks of life to identify fictitious or artificially modified numeric data samples. For instance, in experimental science when researchers alter the data manually, that set will violate Benford's law, thereby making it a good tool for investigation in many fields.

The use of Benford's law was significantly boosted by the seminal work of Nigrini [188], which showed the potential application of this tool in forensic accounting and generally in investigation for all areas involving data set. Besides the obvious fields of accounting and tax evasion investigation assessment of macroeconomic data many other areas leverage the properties of Benford's law.

For example, Graham et al. [189] applied Benford's law to assess the data concerning the catches of Atlantic lobster. On a completely different topic the results of the Iranian presidential election from 2009 were tested for fraud using the same law [190].

## 2 APPLICATION TO FRAUD ON SECURITIES MARKETS

Probably the better known research investigating thorough Benford's test crimes on financial markets is a paper published by Abrantes-Metz et al. [191] , which alerted officials about the LIBOR manipulation. Evidence of the LIBOR rate manipulation or collusion were provided via a methodology exploring the second digit distribution variant of the submission panel. The research found that over an extended period of time there were significant departures between the Benford and empirical second-digit distributions.

Karavardar [192] analyzed the Istanbul stock exchange outcomes and showed that indexes are conformable to Benford's distribution for the first digit, the second digit, and the first two digits tests in both local currency and U.S. dollars for monthly profit and losses.

Shengmin and Wenchao [193] examined the first digit distribution of two main indices in the Chinese stock market, the Shanghai Stock Exchange Composite Component index, and concluded that their behavior is compatible with Benford's. Concerning the Chinese stock market [194] found evidence using Benford's law for the influence of Chinese culture and superstition on year-round number preferences of traders, applicable only to the Hong Kong market. Furthermore, this argument explained the increased avoidance of the number 4 during the auspicious Chinese New Year, Dragon Boat, and Mid-Autumn festivals in the Hong Kong stock market.

Bharati et al. [195] studied the behavior of crude oil within various target zones and showed how prices strongly clustered around the dollar digit value of 9. Corazza et al. [196] investigated the empirical probability distribution of the first significant digit of S&P 500's stock quotations, considering the day-by-day probability distributions and concluding that the majority of such distributions follow Benford's law and that the non-Benford days are generally associated with market volatility or crash events. Another area in the financial industry exposed to the risk of fictitious figures is the hedge funds sector. Misrepresentation or manipulation of performance as well as Ponzi schemes can be investigated with Benford's law. The Maddoff scam, which was the biggest loss in the history of hedge funds and of the financial institutions, provided to its investors unrealistic returns, which were far from following Benford's law, underlining thereby the fact that they might have been the result of manual handling.

# 3 TESTING BENFORD LAW

The various tests presented in this section are implemented in the *BenfordTests* package on **R** development platform [197].

## 3.1 Pearson's $\chi^2$ Fit Test

The $\chi^2$ statistic [198] is a non-parametric statistical technique used to determine if a distribution of observed frequencies differs from the theoretical expected frequencies:

- The null hypothesis $H_0$: The data follows the specified distribution.
- The alternative hypothesis $H_a$: The data does not follow the Benford distribution.

For a simple first digit Benford's law the $\chi^2$ statistic can be plainly represented as:

$$\chi^2 = \cdot \sum_{d=1}^{9} \frac{(O_d - E_d)^2}{E_d} \qquad (8)$$

where $O_d$ is the number of observations having $d$ as the first digit and $E_d$ is the number of expected observations with the first digit $d$ given Benford's law.

Generalizing to the first $k$ digit the test can be written as:

$$\chi^2 = n \cdot \sum_{d=10^{k-1}}^{10^k-1} \frac{(\phi_d^o - \phi_d^e)^2}{\phi_d^e} \qquad (9)$$

where $n$ is the number of observations, $\phi_d^o$ is the empirical proportion of occurrence for the digit $d$, and $\phi_d^e$ denotes the expected proportion of digit $d$ given Benford's distribution.

For a given significance level $\alpha$ and a number of degrees of freedom $v = 10^k - 2$ if $\chi^2 > \chi^2_{\alpha,v}$ the null hypothesis $H_0$ is rejected, i.e., the sample does not conform to Benford's law.

## 3.2 Euclidean Distance Test

A basic test is to measure the Euclidean distance between the theoretical proportions and the observed proportion of the digits [199] with the following statistic:

$$d = \sqrt{\sum_{i=10^{k-1}}^{10^k-1} (\phi_d^o - \phi_d^e)^2} \qquad (10)$$

where $\phi_d^o$ denotes the observed frequency of digits $d$ and $\phi_d^e$ denotes the expected frequency of digits $i$.

## 3.3 Joenssen's JP-Square Test

Joenssen's JP-square test introduced by Joenssen and Muellerleile [197] performs a goodness-of-fit test based on the correlation between the first digit's distribution and Benford's distribution to assert if the data conforms to Benford's law:

$$J_P^2 = \text{sgn}(\text{cor}(\phi^o, \phi^e)) \cdot \text{cor}(\phi^o, \phi^e) \qquad (11)$$

where $\phi^o$ denotes the empirical set of proportions and $\phi^e$ denotes the expected frequency of digits $10^{k-1}, 10^{k-1}+1, \ldots, 10^k - 1$. This test assess a correlation, hence a low statistic shows discordance between the observation and Benford's law.

## 3.4 Kolmogorov-Smirnov

The traditional distribution fit test of Kolmogorov-Smirnov can also be applied in the case of Benford's law conformity assessment:

$$D_n = \sup_{d=10^{k-1},\ldots,10^k-1} \left| \sum_{j=1}^{d} (\phi_j^o - \phi_j^e) \right| \cdot vn \qquad (12)$$

where $p_i^o$ denotes the observed frequency of digits $d$ and $f_d^e$ denotes the expected frequency of digits $i$. The $D_n$ statistics follow the Kolmogorov distribution [200].

## 3.5 Chebyshev Distance Test

Another test employs the Chebyshev distance between the theoretical and observed proportions of the digits in the sample with the following statistic [201]:

$$m = \max_{d=10^{k-1},...,10^k-1} |\phi_d^o - \phi_d i^e| \qquad (13)$$

## 3.6 Mean Deviation Test

A test measuring the deviation of the mean digit of theoretical and observed distribution has the following statistic:

$$a^* = \frac{|\mu_k^o - \mu_k^e|}{(9 \cdot 10^{k-1}) - \mu_k^e} \qquad (14)$$

where $\mu_k^o$ is the observed mean of the chosen $k$ number of digits and $\mu_k^e$ is the expected/true mean value for Benford's predictions. $a^*$ conforms asymptotically to a normal distribution with strictly positive numbers under the null-hypothesis [202].

## 3.7 Freedman-Watson Test

The Freedman-Watson test, a version of the Cramer-von Mises test [203] assesses the difference between the empirical and theoretical distribution as:

$$U^2 = \frac{n}{9 \cdot 10^{k-1}} \left[ \sum_{i=10^{k-1}}^{10^k-2} (\phi_i^0 - \phi_i^e)^2 \right.$$

$$\left. - \frac{1}{1 \cdot 10^{k-1}} \left( \sum_{i=10^{k-1}}^{10^k-2} (\phi_i^0 - \phi_i^e) \right)^2 \right] \qquad (15)$$

where $U^2$ is the Watson $U^2$ statistics [204], $\phi_i^o$ denotes the observed frequency of digits $i$, and $\phi_i^e$ denotes the expected frequency of digits with $i$, $n$ being the number of observations [186].

# 4 APPLICATION TO THE LIBOR MANIPULATION

In June 2012 British regulators issued a penalty to Barclays Capital, the main bank of Exchequer, for allegations of interest rate benchmark manipulation, which resulted in the dismissal of its CEO Bob Diamond. This was the first bank in a long list involved in LIBOR and EURIBOR rigging, which revealed a cartel-type activity in which the banks were submitting rigged rates. The rigging had two purposes: alter the mark-to market of the trillion dollar market of derivatives depending on the exposure to various products and manipulate the level of rates to give the impression that their financing cost is lower than in reality. If the second effect can be emphasized by macro-analysis, the amplitude of the first side is more difficult to assess though a parametric model. A seminal paper by Abrantes-Metz et al. [191] signaled the LIBOR manipulation using a second digit test on the rates submitted by the banks from the panel. The issue with applying the Benford test to the submitted rate is that the time series of figures are stationary and are clustered around a level for a certain time. For instance, between 2005 and 2006 when the rates were high and the market had low volatility the submissions were clustered around the same centroid value, with the first two digits being stable. Over a very long period of time with many economic cycles the LIBOR rate could be compatible with Benford's law but in the short term this can be challenged. Obviously the study of second or third digits can bring additional information, but still would be affected by the stationarity. There are two ways to address this issue:

- First, is to study the conditional distribution of the second digit given the first digit, using Equation 4:

$$\mathbf{P}(D_2(X) = d_2 | D_1(X) = d_1)$$
$$= \log_{10}(1 + (1/d_1 d_2)) / \log_{10}(1 + 1/d_1)$$

$$\mathbf{P}(D_2(X) = d_2)$$
$$= \log_{10}(1 + (1/d_1 d_2)) / \log_{10}(1 + 1/d_1)$$
$$\cdot \mathbf{P}^*(D_1(X) = d_1)$$

where $\mathbf{P}^*(D_1(X) = d_1)$ is the empirical probability of the digit $d_1$.

- A second way to tackle this issue is to assess the relative spread between the banks' financing rates:

$$\text{Spread}_{i,j}^{t,h} = \text{LIBOR}_i^{t,h} - \text{LIBOR}_j^{t,h} \qquad (16)$$

where $\text{LIBOR}_i^{t,h}$ is the rate submission of the bank $i$ at time $t$ for horizon $h$. The spread measure of a moment $t$ for the LIBOR rate at horizon $h$ is expressed in basis point 0.01% and is often used by banks as it is also related to the difference between their respective CDS spreads. The series of the spreads expressed in basis points should have a random feature and therefore the first digit Benford's law can be applied.

Figures 2 and 3 show the distributions of the second digits for various banks before and after November 2007. Figure 2 indicates that the most frequent digits are 2, 3, and 4, which is coherent with the conditional distributions given the fact that the rates level before 2008 was in that region across the yield curve. After 2008 the rates started to fall and the distribution exhibited in Figure 3 shows that the theoretical distribution is closer to the uniform law.

Table 1 shows the $\chi^2$ and Kolmogorov-Smirnov (KS) statistics for the conditional second digit distribution of the LIBOR for all the banks in the panel. The values of the statistics are lower after November 2007 compared to those before 2007. This confirms the hypothesis that before the financial crisis the LIBOR manipulation involved small changes in the figures of the LIBOR in order to maximize the profit of the banks on their underwritten products exposed to LIBOR values.

Figure 4 shows a comparison of the theoretical Benford and observed distributions for the first digits of the spread during a period of 1 week across all horizons. The digit 1 is more frequent and the shape is similar to Benford's law, yet the tests ($\chi^2$ and Kolmogorov-Smirnov) reject the compatibility at a 95% confidence interval. Indeed, it should be recalled that the LIBOR submissions are not exactly market observed values and are in fact communicated by banks as an indicator of their financing cost. Therefore, the human impact exists in those numbers reflecting a rounding effect or other expert-based opinions, which would explain why the observed spread digits do not follow Benford's law.

However, a way to assess the impact of the human impact on the LIBOR submission is to study the evolution of the various conformity tests statistics present in the previous chapter over time. Figure 5 shows the evolution of the $\chi^2$, Kolmogorov-Smirnov, JP, and Euclidean tests between 2005 and 2009 across a set of first digits for spreads including all LIBOR horizons. The tests present a peak of non-compatibility in the period before the crisis June 2006 to June 2007. During this period suspicions of manipulation are high as revealed by the investigations. In this period the fraudsters did not aim to significantly change the level of LIBOR but to twist in small amounts the values to alter the valuation of some derivatives indexed on LIBOR. Thus, the change in LIBOR submission concerned mainly the second and third digits, which is reflected in the first and second digits of the spread. In 2008 the test showed much lower values, hence the submission were more compatible with Benford's law and less suspicious. In fact, in 2008 the manipulation that twisted the last digits became more massive and banks submitted systematically much lower rates (around 1%) in order to induce the idea that market had no liquidity issues (as shown in a following chapter). Under this assumption the rates were probably submitted randomly but on a lower level without a specific intention to alter the mark-to market of

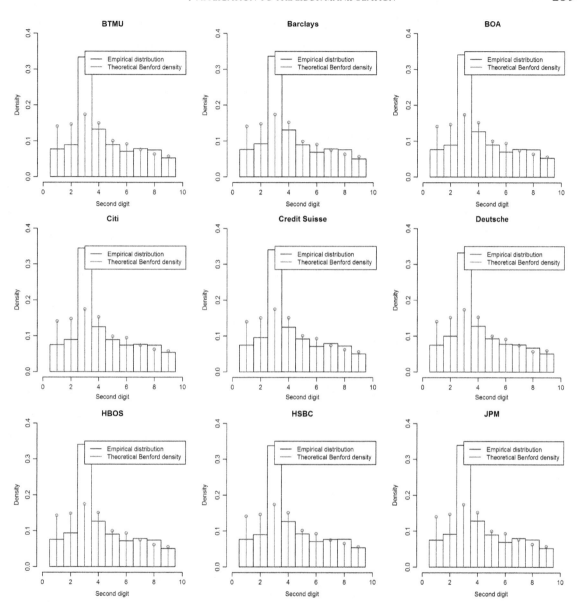

FIGURE 2 Conditional distribution of the second digit for LIBOR submission of various banks before November 2007.

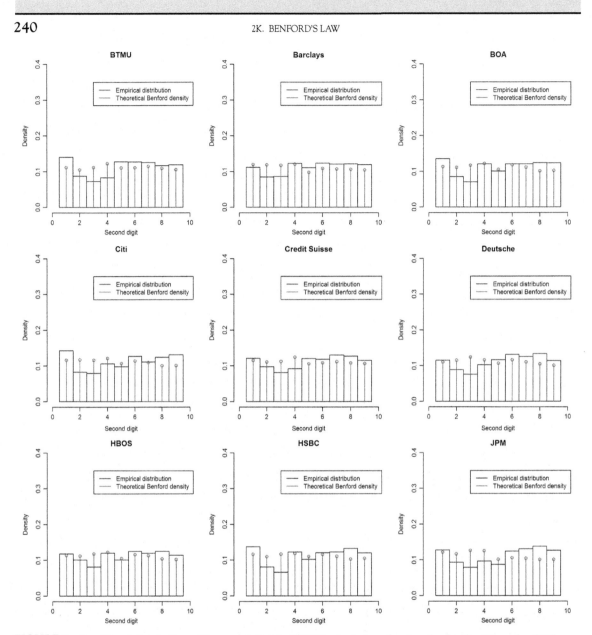

FIGURE 3   Conditional distribution of the second digit for LIBOR submission of various banks after November 2007.

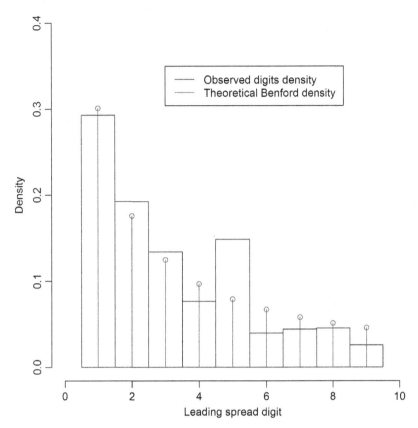

**FIGURE 4** Comparison of the theoretical Benford and observed distributions for the first digits of the spread across all LIBOR maturities.

## FIXING A STEEPENER

### Definition

Steepeners usually take the form of an interest rate swap, where one party pays the other a fixed rate and receives a floating rate equal to the difference between the long- and short-term rates. Steepeners use high leverage, where the difference between the two rates is multiplied by up to 50 times to produce a higher return:

$$\text{Payoff} = \text{Fixed rate} - \max(f + (\kappa_1 \cdot \text{CMS}_{10y})$$
$$- (\kappa_2 \cdot \text{LIBOR}_{6m}), 0, 0)$$

where $\text{CMS}_{10y}$ is the value of credit maturity swap of 10 years maturity and $\kappa_1$ and $\kappa_2$ are multipliers that determine the leverage.

### Rigging a steepener

It is enough that at each date of swap payment the bank manipulates the LIBOR 6m compared to the equivalent $\kappa_1 \cdot CMS_{10y}/\kappa_2$. This action could diminish the payment toward the counterparty or maximized the payment to be received from that counterparty.

### Trivia

Many city councils, regions, and municipalities used credit-embedding steepeners for making the cost of the loan cheaper. However, after 2007 they realized that steepeners were in fact *deepeners* that pushed them into deep distress.

**TABLE 1** $\chi^2$ and KS Statistics for the Conditional Second Digit Distribution of the LIBOR for All the Banks in the Panel

| Bank | Before Nov. 2007 | | After Nov. 2007 | |
|------|------------------|--|-----------------|--|
|      | $\chi^2$ statistics | KS statistics | $\chi^2$ statistics | KS statistics |
| BTMU | 903.5 | 12.2 | 101.5 | 4.3 |
| Barclays | 919 | 12 | 61.5 | 4.6 |
| BOA | 969.4 | 12.3 | 88.9 | 3.6 |
| Citi | 986.3 | 12.5 | 100.3 | 4.4 |
| Credit Suisse | 944.1 | 12.1 | 63.2 | 4.5 |
| Deutsche | 870.1 | 11.8 | 92.7 | 5.3 |
| HBOS | 951.9 | 12.3 | 43.4 | 3.1 |
| HSBC | 932.6 | 12.2 | 109.3 | 4 |
| JPM | 953.5 | 12.1 | 131.6 | 7 |
| Lloyds | 965.7 | 12.2 | 111 | 3.9 |
| Norinchuckin | 902.4 | 12.2 | 71.4 | 3.3 |
| Rabobank | 944.9 | 12.3 | 77.7 | 3.7 |
| RBS | 922.2 | 11.6 | 56.3 | 3.6 |
| UBS | 896.6 | 11.8 | 75.9 | 3.4 |
| WestLB | 938.6 | 12.2 | 67.5 | 3 |
| RBC | 1235.5 | 12.5 | 83.9 | 3.8 |

*The values of the statistics are lower after November 2007 compared to those before 2007.*

a product. Therefore, this randomness makes the series of spreads closer to a Benford behavior.

The last piece of analysis consists of comparing the evolution of tests for various LIBOR maturities (between overnight and 1 year). As shown in Figure 6 some maturities between 2 months and 6 months are more distant from the Benford-like behavior as revealed by the $\chi^2$ test and the Joenssen's JP-square, which assumes that they were probably the target of manipulation. The $\chi^2$ test statistic explodes during the 2006 to 2007 period, while the correlation index of the JP text plunges at the same time. Indeed, this maturity, especially the 6-month LIBOR, was used as a benchmark in almost all derivative contracts.

Another issues that can explain this behavior is the fact that at that time interest rate structured products were very popular on the market. One of the strategies was aimed at benefitting from differences between two maturities on the yield curve. This product was massively marketed by investment banks and was called a curve steepener. It was indexed between the value of a long-term rate observed on the swap market and the 6-month LIBOR. Before maturity of a product a small change in the LIBOR can let the steepener out of the money and give the client a zero payoff after he paid a premium for the product at initiation. It was, in fact, an easy way to make money without being investigated since no one though an interest rate spread could be fixed.

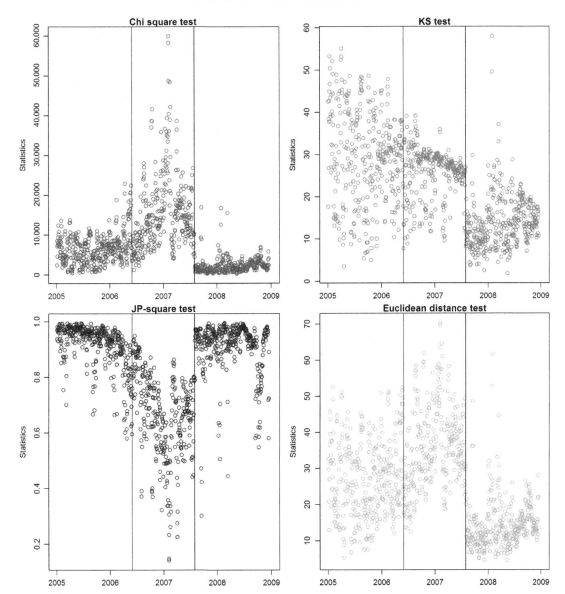

**FIGURE 5** Evolution of the $\chi^2$, Kolmogorov-Smirnov, JP, and Euclidean tests between 2005 and 2009 across a set of first digits for spreads including all LIBOR horizons.

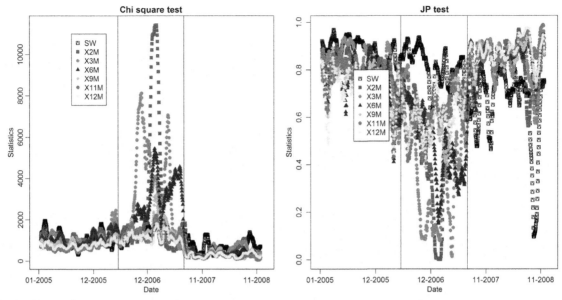

**FIGURE 6** $\chi^2$ test and the Joenssen's JP-square for various maturities (1 week, 2, 3, 6, 9, 11, and 12 months). The 2, 3, and 6 months maturities have the highest peaks in the $\chi^2$ statistics and lowest in the JP-square test.

## 5 OUTLOOK

The literature around Benford's law including both theoretical and fraud detection application is experiencing a fast growth in terms of numbers and topics.[2] Since Ningrini's seminal work [188] concerning the use of Benford's law as a forensic accounting tool the field of application has extended consistently in the investigation of securities markets. The manipulation of market benchmarks (e.g., LIBOR, EURIBOR Forex, and metals) and of hedge fund performance presented an opportunity to test the applicability of Benford's law for fraud detection. Manipulations impact the second or the third digit of the interest rate benchmarks and the various test showed that they do not comply with Benford's law. A future area of exploration can be the market for commodities, which are either traded on thin

**TABLE 2** $\chi^2$ and Kolmogorov-Smirnov Tests Applied to Salmon Price Variations

| Test | Digits | Statistics | *p*-value |
|------|--------|-----------|-----------|
| $\chi^2$ | 1 | 9.0989 | 0.33 |
| K-S | 1 | 0.7795 | 0.25 |
| $\chi^2$ | 2 | 406.38 | **0.00** |
| K-S | 2 | 1.17 | 0.089 |

liquidity or established as the oil International Swaps and Derivatives Association (ISDA) index or the prices of niche soft commodities.

Figure 7 shows Benford's law for the first and second digit distribution of the monthly variations of the Nordic salmon price between 1895 and 2015. As shown in Table 2 the $\chi^2$ and Kolmogorov tests are appropriate for the first digit but only the last one confirms the distribution for the second digit of the monthly variations. This niche market with non-continuous quotations can be a target of price manipulation or misreporting of the benchmark figures.

---

[2]Benford Online Bibliography, http://www. benfordonline.net/list/chronological.

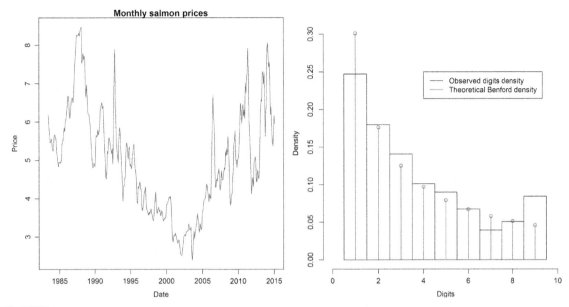

FIGURE 7   Salmon prices over the past 20 years and first digit distribution of price variations.

# PART III

# INVESTIGATION CRIME ON FINANCIAL MARKETS (EMPIRICAL STUDIES WITH APPLICATIONS IN R)

# CHAPTER
# 3A

# Structural Changes in Time Series

## 1 BACKGROUND

Institutions put in place many monitoring and reporting parameters for various activities. These reports consolidate variables relative to agents' behavior, performance of a department, and risks taken, over a certain period of time. These times series can often contain sudden changes in behavior, due to a modification in controls and internal policy, regulatory effects, or sudden shocks in markets, or a recession in the real economy.

A simple illustration is given in Figure 1, which shows the number of canceled operations on a trading desk in a certain period of time. A new control is imposed at certain moment that requires the authorization from the risk controller for overpassing the risk limits. As a result, the number of canceled trades diminishes significantly. Later in the history the desk proposed a new product to clients which was hedged with plain vanilla instruments. The canceling of the

hedges is not required to be approved and thus after the promotion of the new product the tendency of the number of cancelations went up. This increase could be a natural effect of the hedging strategy or the result of another position presented to risk department as part of a hedges.

This change in the average number of cancelations can be detected by a simple $t$-test of the two populations before and after the change in policy or before and after the launch of the new product. The relevant part of a control function is to determine with precision the date of the change. With a time series of a number of cancelations a structural break test for many breaks at unknown date would correctly note the changes of the appropriate date.

## 2 OVERVIEW OF STRUCTURAL BREAK TESTS

Of course, this is a very simple introductory example, as structural break tests provide a rich

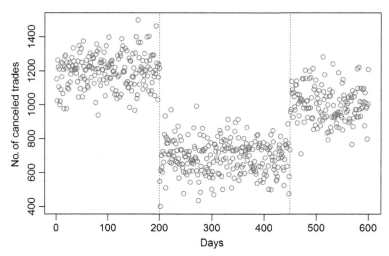

**FIGURE 1** Evolution of number of canceled operations on a trading floor. The dashed line indicates the structural breaks that represent the impact of changes in the desk's activity.

panel of options for assessing various situations like changes in mean, in variance, or in dependency between time series. Since the seminal paper of Chow [205] the econometric literature has had a growing focus on structural changes in time series. To assess if a series has a structural break in its relationship with another explanatory variable at a given *a priori* known moment $T_a$ the simplest way is to perform regression on the full sample and then to regress on the subsets before and after the given break date. The results can be compared with a $F$-test to assess whether a single regression is more efficient than two separate regressions involving splitting the data into two sub-subsets. In the second case, where there is a full structural break, we have two separate models, expressed as:

$$\mathbf{y}_t = \begin{cases} \beta_1^I x_t + \epsilon_t & t \le T_a \\ \beta_2^I x_t + \epsilon_t & t > T_a \end{cases} \quad (1)$$

where $y_t$ is the dependent variable, $x_t$ is the explanatory factors, $\epsilon_t$ are the residuals, and $\beta_1^I$ and $\beta_2^I$ are the regression parameters previous to the moment $T_a$ and after the moment $T_a$,

respectively. A partial structural break is written as:

$$\mathbf{y}_t = \begin{cases} \beta_0^I z_t + \beta_1^I x_t + \epsilon_t & t \le T_a \\ \beta_0^I z_t + \beta_2^I x_t + \epsilon_t & t > T_a \end{cases} \quad (2)$$

where $z_t$ are the set of explanatory factors that do not switch after moment $T_a$ and $\beta_0^I$ are their respective parameters.

For the case of the full break let's denote by SSE, the sum of the squared errors, for the plain regression across the entire sample of size $N$ and $SSE_1$ and $SSE_2$ the sum of squared errors for the regression performed on the subset of data before and after the moment $T_a$. The quantity $\mathbf{F}$ is defined as:

$$\mathbf{F} = \frac{SSE - (SSE_1 + SSE_2)/m}{(SSE_1 + SSE_2)/(N - 2m)} \to \mathbf{F}(m, N - 2m) \quad (3)$$

which follows an $\mathbf{F}$ distribution, where $m$ represents the number of factor in the vector $\beta$.

The null hypothesis of the parameter stability is rejected based on the $F$-test built above:

- $H_0: \beta_1^I = \beta_2^I$
- $H_a: \beta_1^I \ne \beta_2^I$

The case when the moment of the structural break is known is rare in practice and especially in the case of financial crime, when the moment a times series is disturbed is not known precisely. However, in recent financial history times series have shown a few famous structural breaks, one of them being in the months preceding the Lehman default. Therefore, most time series related to the financial sector change around September 2008. Figure 2 shows the evolution of the S&P 500 index and the variance structural breaks. It appears that in June 2008 the market suffer a massive dislocation. A similar event is indicated by the test in July 1998 year that shows the defaults of Long-Term Capital Management and of the Russian debt.

When analyzing a stock price the test for this known date should be taken into account to avoid the wrong conclusions. A good example of the Lehman effect on markets is the case of Integrity Bancshares, Inc., a company operating in the consumer financial services sector and listed on NASDAQ. On September 12, 2008, a complaint was filed in the Superior Court of Fulton County, Georgia, starting that certain SEC filings by Integrity contained materially false and misleading statements regarding Integrity's financial and operating results. The plaintiffs

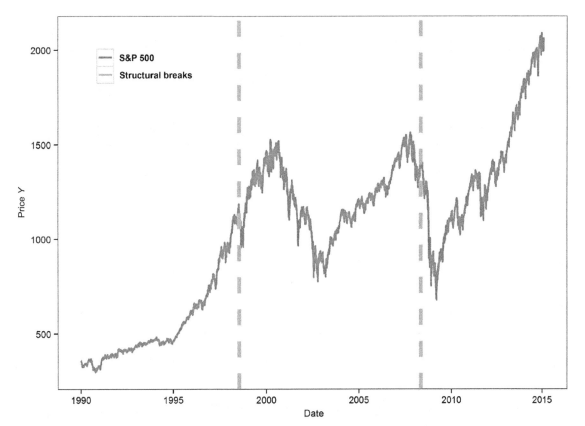

FIGURE 2 Evolution of the S&P 500 index structural breaks in June 2008 when the market suffered a massive dislocation and in July 1998 when the Long Term Capital Management and the Russian defaulted.

wanted to recover damages from the defendant under allegations of violation of the anti-fraud provisions. Indeed, Integrity's stock (ITYC) price suffered a severe deprecation in the second quarter of 2008. The stock's return showed a structural break in the linear relationship with the daily returns of Integrity prices $\mathbf{r}_t^{\text{ITYC}}$ and the return NASDAQ index $r_t^{\text{NASDAQ}}$:

$$\mathbf{r}_t^{\text{ITYC}} = \begin{cases} \alpha_1 + \beta_1 r_t^{\text{NASDAQ}} + \epsilon_t & t \leq T_{\text{Lehman}} \\ \alpha_2 + \beta_2 r_t^{\text{NASDAQ}} + \epsilon_t & t > T_{\text{Lehman}} \end{cases}$$

(4)

This shock, which occurred somewhere in the summer of 2008 (Figure 3), occurred only few days before the Lehman default, without realizing that it was a systemic shock and not idiosyncratic. One month later in October 2008 the plaintiffs withdrew their complaint after realizing that the financial sector had bigger problem than Integrity's allegedly misleading statements.

It is more complicated if the date of structural break is unknown and if there are several break dates in the series. A major contribution

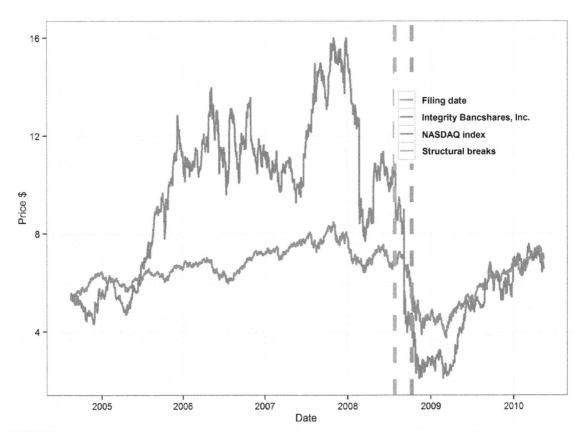

FIGURE 3   Integrity's stock price. A structural break occurs in July 2008 followed in September by the class action suit.

came from Bai and Perron [206] who proposed an algorithm based on dynamic programming that allows efficiently modeling many structural changes and construction of confidence interval [207] for particular break dates. An overview of the method is warranted. When considering multiple linear regression with $y_t$ the dependent variables and $z_t$ and $x_t$ are the explanatory variable with $k$ breaks, which can be written as:

$$
\mathbf{y}_t = \begin{cases}
\beta_0^I z_t + \beta_1^I x_t + \epsilon_t & 0 \leq t < T_1 \\
\beta_0^I z_t + \beta_2^I x_t + \epsilon_t & T_1 \leq t < T_2 \\
\cdots \\
\beta_0^I z_t + \beta_{k+1}^I x_t + \epsilon_t & T_k \leq t < T
\end{cases} \quad (5)
$$

where $T_1, T_2, \ldots, T_k$ denote the break points. With this notation both the number of breaks $k$ and the indices $T_i, i \in \overline{1,k}$ are not known. The sum of the squared residuals for this multiple regression is:

$$
S_T(T_1, T_2, \ldots, T_k) = \sum_{i=1}^{k+1} \sum_{t \in [T_{i-1}, T_i]} (y_t - \beta_0^I z_t + \beta_i^I x_t)^2
$$

$$(6)$$

Based on a least-squared method the set of breaks dates should satisfy:

$$
(T_1^*, T_2^*, \ldots, T_k^*) = \underbrace{\arg\min}_{T_1, T_2, \ldots, T_k} S_T(T_1, T_2, \ldots, T_k)
$$

$$(7)$$

This optimization is addressed though a dynamic programming algorithm from a recursive form of the objective function from a method proposed by Brown et al. [208].

Brown et al. [208] developed a test based on cumulated residuals recursive least-squares estimates of $\beta$ based on estimating. This test for structural stability of the regression coefficients is computed from the standardized recursive residuals, which take the following form:

$$
\tilde{\epsilon}_t = \frac{y_t - \hat{\beta}_{t-1}^I x_t}{\sqrt{1 + x_t^I (X_{t-1}^I X_{t-1})^{-1} x_t}} \quad (8)
$$

where $\hat{\beta}_t^I$ is the linear regressor estimator based on all observations up from 0 to moment $t$ and $X_t$ is the regressor matrix based on $\tilde{\epsilon}_t$, which is a centered process with a variance $\tilde{\sigma} = \frac{1}{n-k} \sum_{t=j+1}^{n} (\tilde{\epsilon}_t - \bar{\epsilon})^2$ under the null hypothesis:

$$
W_t = \sum_{i=j+1}^{T} \frac{\tilde{\epsilon}_i}{\overline{\sigma}_\epsilon} \quad (9)
$$

Under the null hypothesis the limiting process for the empirical fluctuation process $W_t$ is the standard Brownian motion (Weiner process) $W_t$. More precisely, the following functional central limit theorem holds:

$$
W_t \to W \text{ when } t \to \infty \quad (10)
$$

Under the alternative hypothesis for a structural change at $T_a$, the recursive residuals will have a mean zero until the moment $T_a$.

Going back to the first example with the canceled trades let's assume the trading desk enters a "painting the screen" illegal operation, which is a price manipulation strategy of influencing the price by placing trades in agreement with other trades. Thus, the number of canceled operations remains the same on average but has bigger variations depending on the needed position for manipulating the price. Figure 4 shows the evolution of the number of canceled trades, and the structural breaks at the variance level indicating the dates when the variance increases and then decreases. The empirical fluctuation process is depicted in the second graph indicating the moment when the *cumulated residual sum* became significantly different from zero. These moments correspond to the dates of the breaks determined by a Bui and Perron test and are a useful visualization tool proposed by Zeileis et al. [209] in the R-based **strucchange** package.

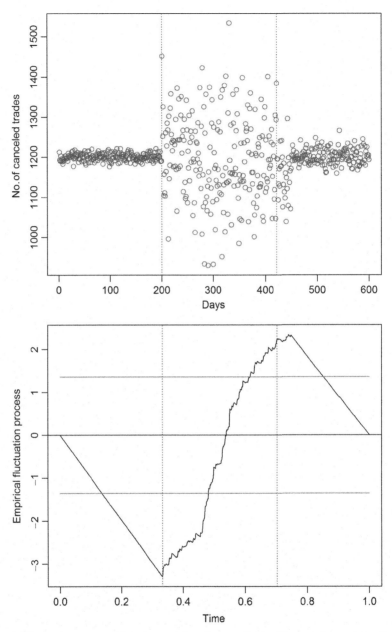

**FIGURE 4** Empirical fluctuation process. The moment when the *cumulated residual sum* became significantly different from zero corresponds to the dates of the breaks determined by a Bui and Perron test.

# 3 APPLICATION TO SECURITIES CLASS ACTIONS

## 3.1 Initial Public Offering

As shown in a previous chapter IPOs are often part of securities litigations involving allegations of fraud due to the complexity of the process and the way the information is or is not spread among investors. Can occur after a certain period from the date of the IPO, especially when the stock does not reach its target value or follows a different pattern. In this case, a structural break test could determine what time the stock started **stalling**.

A good example is the NASDAQ listed Extensity, Inc., which in January 26, 2000, commenced an IPO for its shares of common stock at an offering price of $20 per share. At that time Extensity filed a registration statement, which incorporated a prospectus, with the SEC. Toward the end of 2001 a class action suit was filed in regard to the IPO. The complaint alleged that the IPO prospectus was materially false and misleading because it failed to disclose, among other things, that the underwriters had solicited and received excessive and undisclosed commissions from certain investors in exchange for which the underwriters allocated to those investors material portions of the restricted number of Extensity shares issued in connection with the IPO. Furthermore, it was alleged that the underwriters had entered into agreements with customers whereby the underwriters agreed to allocate Extensity shares to those customers in the Extensity's IPO in exchange for which the customers agreed to purchase additional Extensity shares in the after-market at predetermined prices.

Employing a framework similar to that from Equation 4 but with unknown breaking dates the test reveals that 1 year after the IPO (Figure 5) a structural break occurred in the stock price behavior, which could be linked to the sale of the extra shares allocated to preferential investors.

## 3.2 Misleading Statements

If a firm submits a misleading statement to investors in order to boost the stock price or to avoid a turndown when the market finally incorporates the true state of affairs the market price will change suddenly in behavior. Therefore, structural breaks can provide useful information about the role of abnormal information spread to investors.

Accredited Home Lenders was among the first companies that experienced the subprime crisis in early 2007. In April 2007 a class action suit was filed against the company that allegedly issued materially false and misleading statements regarding its business and financial results. As a result of these false statements, the Accredited stock traded at artificially inflated prices, reaching a high of $58.45 per share on May 11, 2006.

The class action suit alleged[1] that Accredited concealed from the investing public several relevant fact:

- The forward financial projections and reported results were based on defective assumptions and/or manipulated facts due to the lack of requisite internal controls.
- The financial statements were materially misstated due to its failure to properly account for its allowance for loan repurchase losses.
- The underwriting guidelines were tighten given the deterioration and the increased volatility in the sub-prime market, which would have a direct material negative impact on its loan productions going forward.
- There were no reasonable basis to make projections about its 2007 results.

---

[1] Accredited Home Lenders Holding Company Securities Litigation, http://securities.stanford.edu/filings-case.html?id=103727.

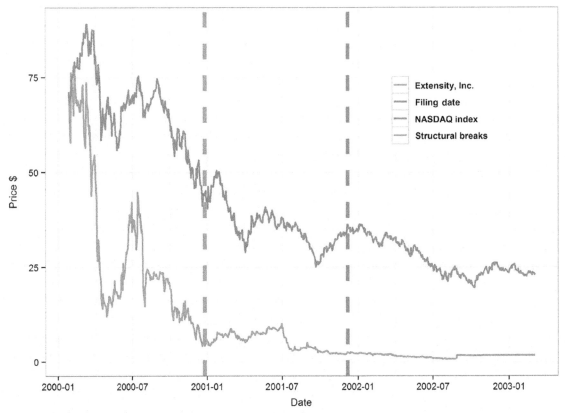

**FIGURE 5**  One year after Extensity's IPO a structural break occurred in the stock price behavior, which could be linked to the sale of the extra shares allocated to preferential investors.

After news of the class action suit seeped into the market, Accredited's shares went in bearish territory due to massive selling pressure, which resulted in losing more than 65% from their year high to $3.97 per share. In addition, in March 2007, Accredited issued a press release announcing that it had paid approximately $190 million in margin calls on its facilities since January 2007.

Figure 6 shows that a structural break occur in the second semester of 2006 as the Accredited stock price seems to go change its relationship with the NASDAQ index. This corresponds to the period when management allegedly produced bogus forecasts for the following year.

In July 2009 after the "subprimes" turmoil, the two parties have reached a $22 million cash settlement for the class action suit brought against bankrupt subprime lender Accredited Home Lenders Holding Co. and its directors and officers. Despite this settlement if allegations cannot be rejected this would imply that the first signs of distress in the American subprime market occurred in 2006, which pushed Accredited's directors and officers to allegedly cook books and manipulate.

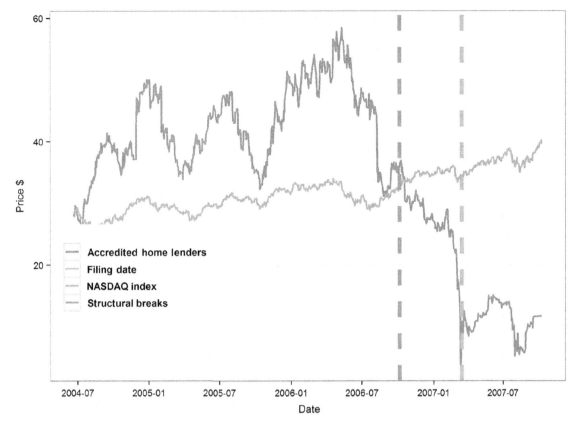

**FIGURE 6** Accredited home lenders.

## 3.3 Pump and Dump

The *pump-and-dump* crimes on listed stocks described previously are an interesting study case for which structural breaks tests can provide relevant information. A stock raided by a deliberate manipulation act changes the patterns during the time of the crime. This can be seen through the structural breaks in price levels, returns, or even in volatility as illustrated by the following:

$$r_t^S = \begin{cases} \alpha_0 + \beta_0 r_t^F + \epsilon_{1,t} & \text{var}(\epsilon_{1,t}) = \sigma_1^2; \quad t \le T_{PD} \\ \alpha_0 + \beta_0 r_t^F + \epsilon_{2,t} & \text{var}(\epsilon_{2,t}) = \sigma_2^2; \quad t > T_{PD} \end{cases}$$

(11)

where $r_t^S$ is the return of the manipulated stock, $r_t^F$ the returns of a benchmark index, $\sigma_1$ and

$\sigma_2$ are the standard deviations of the regression residuals before and after the break date, $T_{PD}$, allegedly around the moment of the pump-and-dump scheme.

A recent example of pump and dump is linked to Liberty Silver,[2] a company engaged in the exploration and development of mineral properties in North America. Liberty Silver describes itself as an "advanced exploration play in Nevada with potential opportunity to quickly become a low cost, open pit operation" and also

---

[2]Class Action Complaint against Liberty Silver Corporation, http://securities.stanford.edu/filings-documents/1051/LBSV00_01/2013911_f01c_13CV80923.pdf.

as an option on an undeveloped silver prospect near Lovelock, Nevada.

Figure 7 shows the price and volume of Liberty's stock,associated with the dates for structural breaks that occurred after the class action suit filing date. Currently the company is under investigation by the SEC. The action filing alleges various attempts at creating presents various actions that allegedly had the role to create artificial momentum of Liberty stock. These actions occurred in temporal window near the structural breaks as follows:

- In March 25, 2010, shares of Liberty Silver began trading heavy volume on Pink Sheets (OTCBB) (structural break in **August 2010**).
- On November 11, 2011, Liberty Silver announced a $3.25 million nonbrokered finance deal from a Panamanian company called "Look Back Investments" (structural break in **November 2011**).
- In a further effort to leverage more shares, legitimize Liberty Silver, and drive the stock price higher, Genovese attempted a merger with a company with more liquidity. On July 16, 2012, Liberty Silver announced that it would make a tender offer for Sennen Resources, a reputable Toronto Stock Exchange listed company with nearly $14 million in cash (structural break in **March 2012**).

## LIBERTY SILVER
### Robert Genovese

The central figure in the ongoing class action suit is Robert Genovese, a Canadian businessman. He was a penny stock promoter using television shows, newsletters, news releases, and emails to get the public to invest in his recommended stocks. Many of his investments were managed through a firm called BG Capital.

### Architecture of the pump

To inflate the price of Liberty Silver Genovese employed the use of "Midas Letter," stock research newsletter used to pump up Liberty Silver's stock value, which doubled the value of the stock in 2 months. Genovese entered into a close relationship with the New York brokerage house John Thomas Financial and with its owner, Anastasios Belesis. Genovese allegedly used Belesis and John Thomas Financial as a "boiler room" to buy and sell large quantities of stock in Liberty Silver and to artificially inflate the price of the stock.

### Alleged collateral damages

Genovese allegedly had a repeated pattern of pump-and-dump manipulations in numerous other schemes, including companies like Clearly Canadian Brands, Neptune Society, and Envoy Communications.

### Trivia

In 2004, a lawsuit was filed against Genovese for allegations of insider trading on a different stock. He ignored the court's rulings but later agreed to a settlement of $3.25 million.

Another relevant example of pump-and-dump type is the case of Galena Biopharma.[3] Galena was a biotechnology company based in Portland, Oregon, focused on the development and commercialization of targeted innovative oncology treatments that address the major unmet medical needs of advanced cancer care.

Early in 2014 a class action suit was filed against Galena Biopharma with allegations of stock pumping using specialized firms of investors relations. In July 2013, Galena entered into a contract with The DreamTeam Group, for

---

[3]Deering vs. Galena Biopharma, http://securities.stanford.edu/filings-documents/1051/GBI00_01/2014103_f01x_14CV00367.pdf.

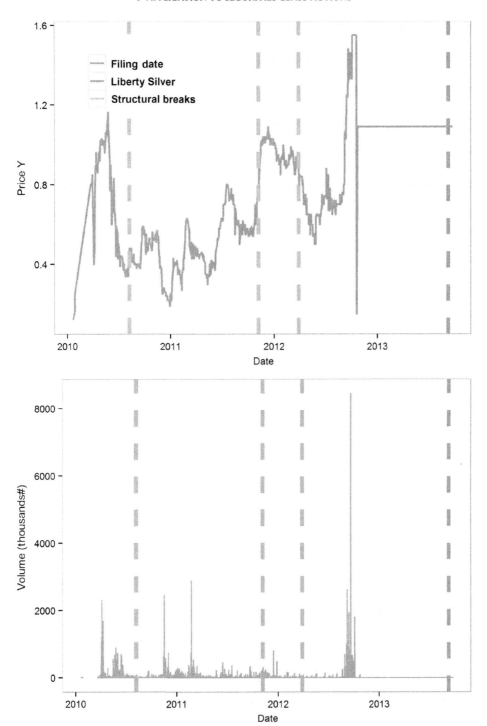

**FIGURE 7**   Prices and volumes of Liberty Silver listed on Pink Sheets.

$50,000 for 240 days of advertising, branding, marketing, investor relations, and social media services. The class action suit alleges that DreamTeam wrote fraudulent articles about Galena who maintained editorial control and final approval over all articles.

The first article placed by DreamTeam after the July 2013 contract appeared in August 2013, on the online investment advice website Seeking Alpha. Six month later in March 2014, a financial analyst published his investigation of the relationship between Galena and DreamTeam on Seeking Alpha. Two days later Galena announced that it was under investigation by the SEC, concerning certain matters relating to the company and an outside investor-relations firm.

As shown in Figure 8 Galena's stock price changed in pattern in 2013 when the relationship with the DreamTeam firm was engineered. Following those announcements the price peaked early in 2014 after plunging back around March 2014. The break test shows that both returns and volumes traded went on a different path around the time Galena allegedly smoothed its way to investors.

# 4 OUTLOOK

Structural break tests provide a retrospective look at the behavior of a times series in relationship with its own feature or with its movement with other factors. Given the large amount of information available within organizations from both internal and external sources, which is structured as times series, these types of analysis can be useful in understanding the various changes that might have occurred in the past.

Performance of rogue funds, returns of manipulated stock, or surveillance metrics of unauthorized traders can show structural

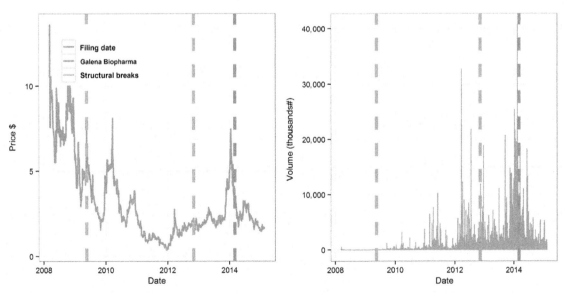

FIGURE 8 Galena stock price and volumes. Galena's stock price changed in 2013 when the relationship with the DreamTeam firm was engineered.

changes around the times the stock in question migrates toward illegal activity. Hence, structural change tests can be useful to assess if behavior went below the radar or once the investigation is in progress to assess how long the abnormal activity was occurring.

Structural break tests are backward-looking methods, but the literature proposes improved versions for cases when breaks occur toward the end of the observation data set, thereby making them useful as an active near-real time surveillance approach.

## 1 BACKGROUND

Until recently the use of analytic methods within the financial world concerned exclusively numerical structured data. The entire science of applied financial mathematics gravitates toward the numeric universe, which accounts for nearly 20% of the total available information, thereby leaving the rest of the 80% of the information less covered.

The challenge of unstructured data analysis is linked to the fact that document, audio, and video tracks have a high number of features and involve *a priori* background knowledge of the topic addressed in the language of the supports. Numeric structured data can more easily be explored and analyzed without specific information about the set. Even a small set of documents (e.g., e-mails or tweets) contains a large number of patterns, hence the need for interactive information exploration. The use of unstructured data in criminal investigations started with the use of tapped conversations between alleged members of organized crime. For example, it helped the FBI track down leaders of Italian-American crime rings in 1980s.

Post-9/11, several federal agencies and governments across the world invested in research to proactively monitor terrorist activities and foil their attempts at committing unlawful acts detrimental to civil society. Text analytics play a key role in such research areas where the objective is to intercept, translate, and analyze all communication channels the extremist organizations may be using. While it may be easy to track e-mail communication, it is not easy to tap phone conversations and convert them to text. There are several voice-to-text conversion software tools available in the market today but the accuracy and precision by which they perform need improvement. Fraud analysis is playing a larger role today as banks try to find irregular patterns and seek signals to alert them of financial fraud. Certain types of fraud within organizations may be difficult to detect unless appropriate monitoring systems are in place to keep a tab on employees and communication channels such as e-mail.

The discipline that deals with the human language, as it appears in written document, e-mails, web pages, tweets, social media, and scientific articles, in thousands of languages and varieties is called natural language processing. NLP emerged in the 1950s as a multi-field discipline that aims to analyze and understand the languages humans use naturally.

## 2 PRINCIPLES OF TEXT EXPLORATION

Text mining can be defined as a process aimed at extracting useful information from a collection of unstructured data sources through the identification and exploration of interesting patterns [210]. The purpose of text mining approaches is to extract the various features and to summarize them in a numeric set.

With the increasingly available computing power, the methods for unstructured data exploration are based more and more on statistical and machine-learning algorithms. Among the areas of unstructured data exploration that have gained momentum in crime investigations is information extraction and sentiment analysis.

The aim of information extraction is to extract the information contained in documents as well as the relationship between the extracted information within the documents. From a predefined set of semantic data, documents can be represented as sets of entities and frames. A frame according to Fillmore [211] is a cognitive structure representing a conceptual structure

based on various entities. Thus, information extraction can be seen as a limited form of complete text comprehension [210]. For a more genuine description let's assume the following text order confirmation within a trading floor: *Jaffar sells 100 GSTI to Gabriel at 100$.*

$$
\underbrace{[\dots]\underset{\text{Seller}}{Jaffar} \text{ sells } \underset{\text{Volume}}{100} \underset{\text{Tick}}{\text{"GSTI"}} \underset{\text{underlying}}{\text{shares}} \text{ to } \underset{\text{Buyer}}{Gabriel} \text{ at } \underset{\text{Price}}{100\$}[\dots]}_{\text{Trade}}
$$

$$(1)$$

A successful information-extraction process should be able to assess where the sentence starts and ends, the entities and their features (e.g., *shares* is a noun representing a financial entity) as well as the structure including a *buyer*, a *seller*, a traded *entity*, and a *price*.

Another area of text mining is text classification on the basis of a predetermined set of categories. Classification can be done through rules-based approach and with (supervised) machine-learning techniques that determine the classifier's framework based on the learning process from a labeled data set. Sentiment and opinion analysis is a specific type of classification that aims to assess the opinions, sentiments, evaluations, preferences, choices, review, views, emotions, etc., expressed in a set of documents. The following sections contain a review of methods used for sentiment analysis and information extraction, specifically part-of-speech tagging.

## 3 PART-OF-SPEECH TAGGING

Part-of-speech tagging (POS tagging) is a method that has as input a source of text written or expressed in a language that assigns parts of speech to each word, such as a noun, verb, adjective, adverb, etc. POS tagging is generally the first part of analyzing text based on human language. Table 1 shows the tags for various

**TABLE 1** Tags Listed from Penn Treebank [212]

| Tag | Description |
|-----|-------------|
| CC | Coordinating conjunction |
| CD | Cardinal number |
| JJ | Adjective |
| NN | Noun, singular or mass |
| RB | Adverb |
| VB | Verb, base form |
| VBD | Verb, past tense |

The Company has a fast growing perspective

DT　　NN　　VB　DT　JJ,VB　**NN,VB,JJ**　NN

grammar parts, as used in the Penn Treebank [212] tag set, which is the current standard.[1]

Before the tagging process begins, the first step is the text preprocessing is needed to obtain a set of words (tokens) to process. Two steps are generally implemented: sentence detection and tokenization. Sentence-boundary detection requires marking the start and end of sentences, which is a simple task that can be complicated in documents containing abbreviations and titles. Tokenization is a process of converting sentences into chain words or tokens (words, punctuation) within a sentence. A straightforward example for POS tagging is represented by the following tweets which should be tagged as follows:

The Company has a fast growing perspective

DT　　NN　　VB　DT　JJ　NN　　NN

However, few words can be assigned various POS tags. The role of an appropriate POS tagging process is to assign the right tags given the context:

---

[1] Automatic Mapping Among Lexico-Grammatical Annotation Models, http://www.comp.leeds.ac.uk/ccalas/tagsets/upenn.html.

Given a set of $n$ words $w_1, w_2, \ldots, w_n$ the POS tagging should find the corresponding set of possible tags $t_1, t_2, \ldots, t_n$. There are a few approaches to doing this: rules-based and machine-learning methods. Machine-learning techniques are either generative or discriminative. Generative methods are based on models of probability distributions. Discriminative methods are estimated posterior probabilities based on observations. Logistic regression and conditional random fields (CRFs) are examples of discriminative methods, while Naive-Bayes classifiers and hidden Markov models (HMMs) are examples of generative methods [213].

In a simple rules-based POS tagging example we assign, for instance, a word the most frequent tag from a training corpus data set. If a given token $w$ has a possible set of $m$ tokens then the probability of assigning a token $t_i$ to the word is:

$$P(t_i|w) = \frac{\#(w, t_i)}{\#(w, t_1) + \#(w, t_2) + \#(w, t_3) + \cdots + \#(w, t_m)} \quad (2)$$

where $\#(w, ti)$ is the number of times token $w$ corresponds to tag $t_i$ in the training corpus.

This simple frequency-based rule can be enriched with a rules-based tagger [214, 215] that takes into account the context of word order to assign a tag. Rules have the following form: *If a token $w$ is tagged $t_j$ and it is in context C, then the should be changed to $t_k$.*

The rules-based tagger has many advantages such as a vast reduction in required stored information, ease in comprehension of a set of meaningful rules, ease of finding, and implementation simplicity.

## 3.1 Tagging with Hidden Markov Model

A Hidden Markov Model (HMM) is a system where a variable can switch (with varying probabilities) between several states, generating one of several possible output symbols with each switch (also with varying probabilities). In this process a sequence of symbols is produced by starting in an initial state, transitioning to a new state, emitting a symbol selected by the state, and repeating this transition/emission cycle until a designated final state is reached. The sets of possible states and unique symbols may be large, but finite and known. We can observe the outputs, but the system's internals features (i.e., state-switch probabilities and output probabilities) are "hidden." A HMM [216] consists of the following elements:

- $Q = \{q_1, q_2, q_3, \ldots, q_f\}$ is a set of states: where $q_1$ is the start state and $q_f$ is the final state.
- $\pi$ is an initial probability distribution over states and $\pi_i$ is the probability at start for state $i$.
- $A = Q \times Q \rightarrow [0,1]$ is a transition probability matrix of $F \times F$ probabilities of transitioning between any pair of $F$ states prior probability (tag sequence).
- $O = \{O_1, O_2, O_3, \ldots, O_N\}$ is a sequence of $N$ observations (tokens/words) from a vocabulary $V$.
- $B = Q \times O \rightarrow [0,1]$ denotes the emission probabilities, a sequence of observation likelihoods (probability of observation generated at state) or the likelihood of a word sequence given a tag sequence.

A first-order Markov model $\lambda$ is represented by the set (p, A, B) satisfying the conditions $\sum_{q \in Q} \pi_q = 1$, $\sum_{q^* \in Q} A_{q,q^*} = 1$, and $\sum_{o \in O} B_{q,o} = 1$. In this context the main goal of the HMM is to compute the most likely state trajectory $S = \{s_1, s_2, \ldots, s_T\}$ in $Q$ given the model and the sequence $T = \{t_1, t_2, \ldots, t_T\}$ in $O$, $\underbrace{\arg\max}_{q \in Q} P(T, S|\lambda)$ [210].

Enumerating all possible state sequences $S$ for a given word sequence $T$ and choosing the one maximizing $P(T, S|\lambda)$ by computing all $F^T$ possibilities is infeasible in practice. The Viterbi

algorithm proposes a dynamic programming approach to computing the best sequence of states for each subsequence from 1 to $T$ that ends in state $qf$. If the initial word sequence is $T_n = (t_1, t_2, \ldots, t_n)$ among all sequences ending with $qf$, let $\delta(qf)$ denote the probability $P(T_n, s_n = qf|\lambda)$ of generating this initial segment following those optimal states. $\delta$ can be recursively obtained as follows:

$$\delta_1(qf) = \pi(qf) \cdot B(qf, t_1) \tag{3}$$

$$\delta_{n+1} = \max_{q' \in Q} \delta_n(q') \cdot A(q', qf) \cdot A(q, t_{n+1}), \tag{4}$$

where $q' = \underbrace{\arg\max}_{q' \in Q} \delta_n(q') \cdot A(q', qf) \cdot A(q, t_{n+1})$

$$\tag{5}$$

Then, the best state sequence among is given by choosing the highest probability endpoint and then backtracking from there to find the highest probability state path. The complexity of Viterbi's algorithm is $F^2 T$.

### 3.1.1 Conditional Random Fields

Conditional random fields (CRFs) are a family of discriminative models first proposed by Lafferty et al. [217], Culotta et al. [218], and Sutton and McCallum [219]. The most common CRFs resemble to HMMs in that the next state depends on the current state and at the same time generalizes the logistic regression to sequential data. A CRF is based on feature functions having as inputs:

- a sentence $T = (t_1, t_2, \ldots, t_n)$
- the position $i$ of a word in the sentence
- the label $s_i$ of the current word
- the label $s_{i-1}$ of the previous word

A simple example of a feature function is labeling a word following an adjective as a noun:

$$f(T, i, s_i, s_{i-1}) = \begin{cases} 1 & \text{if } s_i = \text{ADJECTIVE and} \\ & s_i = \text{NOUN} \\ 0 & \text{otherwise} \end{cases}$$

$$\tag{6}$$

A CRF algorithm assigns each feature function $f_j$ a weight $\lambda_j$. Given a sentence $T$, the score labeling $s$ of $T$ is found by adding up the weighted features over all words in $T$:

$$\text{score}(s|T) = \sum_{j=1}^{m} \sum_{i=1}^{n} \lambda_j f_j(T, i, s_i, s_{i-1}) \qquad (7)$$

where score $(s|T)$ is a sum over each feature function $j$, and over each position $i$ of the sentence. These scores can be put into probabilities $p(s|T)$ as follows:

$$p(s|T) = \frac{e^{\sum_{j=1}^{m} \sum_{i=1}^{n} \lambda_j f_j(T,i,s_i,s_{i-1})}}{\sum_{s^*} e^{\sum_{j=1}^{m} \sum_{i=1}^{n} \lambda_j f_j(T,i,s_i^*,s_{i-1}^*)}} \qquad (8)$$

The above equation looks like a sequential version of a logistic regression. CRF is trained by maximizing the log likelihood of a given training set $(s, T)$.

## 3.2 Semantic Role Labeling

While POS tagging adds a grammar label to each word of sentence, the next step is to add semantics to tags in order to put them in a relationship with the sentences. In the previous example of a trade confirmation a semantic role labeling would identify the various roles of the transaction (buyer, seller, volume, price).

$$\underset{\text{Seller}}{\text{Jaffar}} \text{ sells } \underset{\text{Volume}}{100} \underset{\text{Tick}}{\text{"GSTI"}} \underset{\text{underlying}}{\text{shares}}$$

$$\text{to } \underset{\text{Buyer}}{\text{Gabriel}} \text{ at } \underset{\text{Price}}{100\$} \qquad (9)$$

Semantic role labeling was developed by the works of Gildea and Jurafsky [220], who presented a system for identifying the semantic relationships, or semantic roles, filed by constituents of a sentence within a semantic frame. The primary task of semantic role labeling is to indicate exactly what semantic relations hold among a predicate and its associated participants and properties, with the relations drawn from a pre-specified list of possible semantic roles for that predicate [221].

# 4 SENTIMENT ANALYSIS

Another topic relative to unstructured data concerns sentiment and opinion analysis, which is a subfield of language processing concerned with extracting emotions from text.

## 4.1 Unsupervised Learning

Sentiment and opinion analysis through unsupervised learning is straightforward and does not require *a priori* labeling of the analyzed data. A consistent unsupervised-learning algorithm was proposed by Turney [222] for classifying reviews as recommended or not recommended. This opinion classification method relies on estimation of the average semantic orientation of the analyzed phrases based on the attributes contained in the phrase. Therefore, text preprocessing needs to be applied to the assessed phrase in order to identify the "epithets" containing adjectives or adverbs. The part-of-speech tagging algorithm presented in the previous section is used.

A phrase is assumed to have a positive semantic orientation if it has good associations (e.g., "exceptional") and a negative semantic orientation if it has bad associations (e.g., "shady"). The Turney [222] approach computes the semantic orientation of a phrase using the mutual information between the given phrase and a set of positive words (e.g., good, excellent) minus the mutual information between the given phrase and set of negative words (i.e., bad, poor). The unsupervised machine for sentiment classification can be completed as follows:

- The first step computes the mutual information of a phrase based on the semantics of two consecutive words (i.e., a noun followed by an adjective or vice versa,

**TABLE 2** Tagging

| First word | Second word | Third word |
|---|---|---|
| JJ | NN or NNS | Anything |
| RB, RBR, or RBS | JJ | Not NN nor NNS |
| JJ | JJ | Not NN nor NNS |
| NN or NNS | JJ | Not NN nor NNS |
| RB, RBR, or RBS | VB, VBD, VBN, or VBG | |

i.e., "high profits"). Hence, in this step, which is based on POS tagging, two consecutive words with tags corresponding to the patterns in the following table are extracted from the phrase. Table 2 shows a few rules for selecting the words relevant to Turney [222] analyzing the sentiment in a sentence.

- In the second step pointwise mutual information (PMI) [223] between two words, $w_1$ and $w_2$, is computed as follows:

$$\text{PMI}(w_1, w_2) = \log_2 \left( \frac{P(w_1 \cap w_2)}{P(w_1) \cdot P(w_2)} \right) \quad (10)$$

where $p(w_1 \& w_2)$ is the probability that word1 and word2 co-occur in the same phrase and $p(w_1)$, $p(w_2)$ are the probability of occurrence of the respective words. Hence, the ratio between $p(w_1 \& w_2)$ and $p(w_1)p(w_2)$ is a measure of the degree of statistical dependence between the words. The log of this ratio is the amount of information captured though the presence of one of the words when we observe the other.

- The third step is to compute semantic orientation (SO) of a phrase X, which is calculated as follows:

$$\text{SO}(X) = \text{PMI}(X, \text{"buy"}) - \text{PMI}(X, \text{"sell"}) \quad (11)$$

The words "buy" and "sell" were chosen to exemplify the sentiment related to the views of a set or analyst phrases concerning a stock. Buy would be a bullish sentiment denoting a positive opinion and sell would be a bearish sentiment with a negative forecast. The last step is to calculate an index of semantic orientation of the phrases based on a dictionary of positive and negative words, $w_p$ and $w_n$, with sizes of $N_p$ and $N_n$, respectively:

$$\text{ISO}(X) = \sum_{i=1}^{N_p} \sum_{j=1}^{N_n} \text{PMI}(X, wp_i) - \text{PMI}(X, wn_j) \quad (12)$$

Once the index computed it is possible to classify the phrases as positive if the index is positive and negative if the index is negative.

## 4.2 Supervised Learning

Supervised-learning techniques in the area of sentiment analysis require a labeled training data set of documents and include simple methods like Naive-Bayes and more complex, random forest, or support vector machine methods.

### 4.2.1 Naive-Bayes-Based Classifiers

One of the simplest methods and yet showing reasonable performance at classifying opinions in text is the Bayes rules-based approach. In plain words Bayesian or Naive-Bayesian classifier are supervised-learning methods trained on a set of labeled documents or phrases.

Given a document $d$ to be classified in terms of opinion based on a finite set of features (words) in $n_d$ dimensions $(w_1, w_2, \ldots, w_{n_d})$ the probability of belonging to a class $C$ given those features is $P(c|w_1, w_2, \ldots, w_{n_d})$. The appropriate class $c$ is given by solving the following problem:

$c_{\text{maximum a posteriori}}$

$$= \arg\max_{c \in C}(P(c|d))$$

$$= \arg\max_{c \in C}(P(c|w_1, w_2, \ldots, w_{n_d}))$$

$$= \arg\max_{c \in C}(P(c) \prod_{i \in \overline{1,n_d}} P(w_i|c))$$

Figure 1 shows the relationship between the class and the various words in the document. The words as attributes of the class are assumed to be independent. In the log space the above equation becomes:

$$c_{\text{map}} = \arg\max_{c \in C}(\log)P((c)) + \sum_{i \in \overline{1,n_d}} \log(P(w_i|c)) \tag{13}$$

A classification function $F_c$ has the following form:

$$F_c = \log(P(c = \text{"Positive"}))$$

$$+ \sum_{i \in \overline{1,n_d}} \log(P(w_i|c = \text{"Positive"})) \tag{14}$$

$$- \log(P(c = \text{"Negative"}))$$

$$+ \sum_{i \in \overline{1,n_d}} \log(P(w_i|c = \text{"Negative"})) \tag{15}$$

and under this formalism a document $d$ is classified as the class $c = $ positive for $F_c > 0$ and negative if $F_c$ is negative.

If the classifier encounters a word that has not been seen in the training set, the probability of both the classes (positive and negative) would become zero and the classification function would provide an error. This issue can be addressed by Laplacian smoothing:

$$P(w_i|c) = \frac{\#(w_i) + k}{(k+1) \sum_c \#(w_i)} \tag{16}$$

where $k$ is a constant usually considered as 1 and $\sum_c \#(w_i)$ is the sum of all words in class $c$.

Sentiment analysis does have acceptable performance as shown in the literature. Lewis [224] and Domingos and Pazzani [225] show that Naive-Bayes is optimal for certain problem classes with highly dependent features (Figure 2).

Naive-Bayes is the simplest form of Bayesian network in which all attributes are independent given the value of the class variable. One approach to enriching Naive-Bayes is to extend its structure to represent explicitly the dependencies among attributes. An augmented Naive-Bayes (ANB) is an extended Naive-Bayes

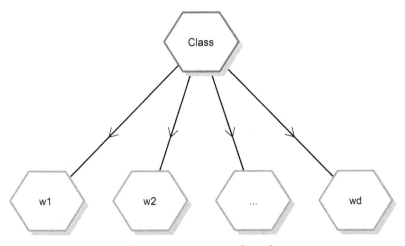

FIGURE 1   Naive-Bayes classifiers: the attributes $w_1, \ldots, w_{n_d}$ are independent.

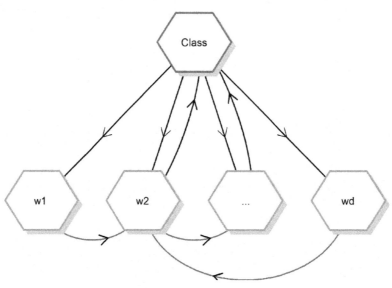

**FIGURE 2** Augmented Naive-Bayes classifiers: the attributes $w_1, \ldots, w_{n_d}$ are interconnected.

in which the class node directly points to all attribute nodes, and there exist links among attribute nodes [226]. From the view of probability, an ANB algorithm represents a joint probability distribution:

$$P(c|w_1, w_2, \ldots, w_{n_d}) = \frac{P(c, w_1, w_2, \ldots, w_{n_d})}{P(d)}$$
$$= \frac{P(c) \prod_{i=1}^{n_d} P(w_i|pa(w_i), c)}{P(d)}$$
$$(17)$$

where $pa(x_i)$ denotes an assignment to values of the parents of $w_i$.

### 4.2.2 Support Vector Machine

A support vector machine was applied to text categorization by Joachims [227] and benchmarked to other machine-learning methods by Pang et al. [169]. Let's assume a basic case with a categorization set $C$ having only the classes $C = (-1, +1)$ corresponding to negative and positive sentiment documents.

Let's assume the following sentiment prediction linear form for any data point $x_i$:

$$f(x_i) = d \cdot x_i + b \quad f(x_i) \in C \qquad (18)$$

where $f(x_i)$ assigns a value of $-1$ indicating one class and a value of $+1$ to the other class.

Consider two training samples, $Tr_+$ and $Tr_-$, corresponding to *a priori* labeled documents as positive and negative. The support vector machine finds a hyperplane that separates the two sets with maximum margin (or the largest possible distance from both sets). This search corresponds to a constrained optimization problem by letting $C \in (1, -1)$ be the correct class of document $x_i$, and the solution can be written as $d$ and $b$ by maximizing the following expression:

$$F(x) = 0.5 * |d|^2 - \alpha \sum_{j \in (+, -)} \max(0, 1 - c_j(d \cdot x_j + b))$$
$$(19)$$

where $c_+ = 1$ and $c_- = -1$.

Pang et al. [169] show that the support vector machine algorithms outperforms Naive-Bayes classifiers.

# 5 APPLICATIONS IN FINANCIAL CRIME

Information extraction is a crucial task for making unstructured data appropriate for financial-crime detection. When caught in the web of illegal acts criminals usually use codified language. This applies not only to spoken language but also to written language. Hence, criminals often use nicknames, abbreviations, or codified language. Coded language or street slang is a practice that is as old as the crime world itself. For instance, Bernardo Provenzano, the former head of the Italian Mafia, used to send his handwritten messages on small handwritten pieces of paper pieces in Sicilian dialect mainly containing quotes from the New Testament, which were supposed to mean something to the receiver, who upon delivery of the message, was supposed to burn it to destroy the proof.

In another real-life situation concerning cases of insider trading,[2] the scammers used codified language to designates stocks, order type (buy or sell), and volumes they wanted to trade. A stock was designated by a dish name, the volumes to trade as the number of dishes, and the direction based on adjectives such as tasty or adverbs like much. An excerpt of their conversation is as follows:

> Let's have as much Chinese as we can. Today will be the last day we can do this... all looks good on the Chinese.

Expanding this example it can be seen that unstructured data mining can be relevant for scanning and monitoring this kind of behavior. This procedure would include the following steps:

- First, through language tagging trained on specific trading floor language sets the real semantic role labels can be identified:

$$
\underbrace{\text{Let's}}\quad \underbrace{\text{buy}}_{\text{operations}}\quad \text{to}\quad \underbrace{200}_{\text{volume}}\quad \underbrace{\text{ramens}}_{\text{underlying}} .
$$
$$
\text{I think they will be}\quad \underbrace{\text{tasty}}_{\text{market view}} \qquad (20)
$$
$$
\text{over}\ \underbrace{\text{the next week}}_{\text{investment horizons}} .
$$

Strategy recommendation frame

Using the right semantic role labeling algorithm to estimate trading floor language it can be seen that *ramen* is similar to a stock ticker and *tasty* is similar to a market view, interpreted in the context of trading frame.

- The second step is to decode the message with the appropriate semantic role tags from the current language to the trading language.

> Let's buy to 200 "TICKER" I think they will be bullish over the next week.

This translation does not look like a culinary choice but more like an investment recommendation.

- The third step is sentiment analysis of the various phrases or document/e-mails/SMS exchanged over time. The sentiment can be positive or negative in relation to a target. A sentiment index can be built over the period of time investigated.
- The fourth step is to assess the predictive power of the sentiment index from the monitored scan of any of the stocks the individual in question has access to.
- The fifth step occurs if a pattern measured in the previous step is relevant. Then it will extend the investigation to other commentary elements like accounts with brokerage firms, etc.

Another area of application is the assessment of the social networks and Internet content

---

[2]Dentist and son jailed for three years for insider trading, http://www.telegraph.co.uk/news/uknews/crime/6780821/Dentist-and-son-jailed-for-three-years-for-insider-trading.html.

for manipulating the price of stocks. A good example is the case of Galena Biopharma,[3] a bio-technology company that hired a promotion company called The DreamTeam Group to provide with of advertising, branding, marketing, investor relations, and social media services in July 2013. The promotion company diffused information controlled by Galena's executives mostly with the aim to inflate the stock.

A good way to illustrate this concept is to assess the sentiment orientation of the Twitter messages related to Galena Biopharma. The tweets did not occur on a daily basis and were clustered around days when there was a focus from analysts. Therefore, the classic sentiment index is not applicable as the raw daily sentiment orientation is discontinuous for the days with no related tweets. To address this issue we assume the sentiment from a given day attenuates exponentially over the period with no new updates. When a new tweet appears it is cumulated over the existing signal. The procedure for building a sentiment index has the following steps:

1. For the initial day $t = t_0$ the sentiment index is $SI(t) = \sum_{Tw(t)} w_i \cdot SO_i(Tw(t))$, representing the sum of all sentiment orientation metrics for each tweet from that day $Tw(t)$ weighted by $w_i$, depending on the influence of the person who tweeted.

2. For the next day $t = t_0 + 1$:

   - If there is no tweet $Tw(t) = \emptyset$, then $SI(t) = e^{\alpha} \cdot SI(t-1)$, where $\alpha < 0$ represents the decay speed of the sentiment.
   - If there are tweets $Tw(t) \neq \emptyset$ in that day, then $SI(t) = e^{\alpha} \cdot SI(t-1) + \sum_{Tw(t)} w_i \cdot SO_i(Tw(t))$.

3. Repeat the previous steps until the end of the considered time period.

Figure 3 shows the price of Galena's stock along with the sentiment index built using the previous algorithm ($w_i = 1$ and $\alpha = -0.01$). Visually it appears that the Twitter activity started to increase in the second semester of 2013 after the DreamTeam was signed in and the sentiment index started to get bullish along with the Galena prices. In early March the arrangement was revealed and the sentiment index dropped rapidly in negative territory and the stock plummeted consecutively.

A third area of application was explored by the work of Haggerty et al. [228], who proposed a framework for the forensic investigation of e-mail data. In particular, this technique focuses on the triage and analysis of unstructured data to identify key individuals and relationships within an e-mail network (e.g., the Enron e-mail corpus). It illustrates the advantage of triaging data to identify actors and potential sources of further evidence and the application of social network analysis techniques for visualization of unstructured data, which can bring further evidence to an investigation.

# 6 OUTLOOK

The exploration of unstructured data can only create positive momentum due to its ubiquitous application. The financial industry has more awareness of the unstructured data mainly due to its crucial role in dealing with misconduct risk and financial crime. Currently unstructured data is used in money laundering and terrorist financing investigations, but its many areas of application are have not yet been fully explored.

The first level of concern for institutions is their internal communication and external communication between the agents of an organization and agents in other organizations. As was

---

[3]Deering vs. Galena Biopharma, http://securities.stanford.edu/filings-documents/1051/GBI00_01/2014103_f01x_14CV00367.pdf.

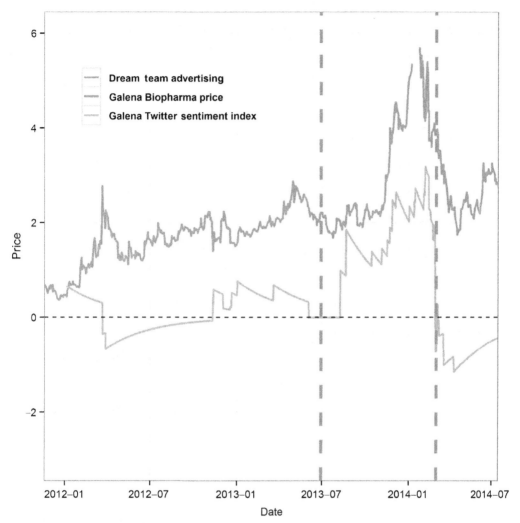

**FIGURE 3**  Galena Biopharma: Market price and Twitter sentiment index.

seen in recent cases such as Enron and the Forex manipulation case, investigators do use messages, e-mail, and documents.

The second level is the public information existing on the Internet through blogs, websites, and social media, which can have a strong influence on the information available on financial supports.

The third level is the initiative like that taken in the United States by the Obama Administration with the development of the National Security Agency.

To accomplish these types of unstructured data exploration it is necessary to have the right means in terms of hardware that provide powerful computing capacities and methods. Unstructured data is probably one of the areas that will see the fastest development in the next few year with much of it in relationship to crime analysis.

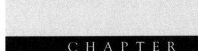

# Understanding the Balance Sheets of Financial Firms

## 1 BACKGROUND

The literature related to corporate financial statements assessment for the detection of fraud and misleading information is relatively rich. However, research on analyzing the financial statements of financial institutions is relatively scarce and crime-related research in this area is even scarcer.

There is some research focused on the fraudulous financial statement in financial institutions but it is focused mainly on traditional banks. Green and Reinstein [229] studied the effects of regulation and increased public scrutiny on financial statement fraud, focusing on publicly owned banks and savings and loan institutions as a backdrop. This work noted how the characteristics of bank fraud have changed over the past two decades through changes in regulations of banks and savings and loans. In regards to investment banking and trading activities there is less focus on the dynamics of financial statements and on the type of fraud that could exist. Investment banks have a different business model than traditional commercial and retail banks. The main activity of the latter is to provide credit inflows to the economy and to finance their balance sheets through collecting deposits from customers. Traditional banks tend to have longer-term horizons for both assets and liabilities. Investment firms including broker-dealers and proprietary trading companies do not generally collect deposits from clients and finance themselves on the short-term credit markets. Their assets concentrate on big derivatives portfolios. With the financial crisis many investment banks were forced by regulation to apply for bank licenses in order to fall under the banking prudential framework to allow them to collect deposits from customer and to diversify their financing profiles.

Within investment firms one of the main issues raised during the crisis that led to the default of many institutions was the role played by the trading activities for account or proprietary trading. Until recently, proprietary trading, which is nothing more than speculative activities using the firm's capital, was a main source of revenue for investment banks but also for traditional banks with investment or trading arms. For the latter category, the situation was considered as critical as clients' deposits are exposed to the risk of bets on derivatives markets. A high-level analysis of statements of the financial

institutions over the past decade in relationship to the weight of their proprietary trading activity and level of their ROE brings more clarity on this aspect

Thus, a support vector machine algorithm with a linear kernel is used to classify a data set of observations labeled as commercial and investment banks. The algorithm confirms the existence of two different classes that do not depend on the activity of the institutions, since the populations are not fully separable. Figure 1 shows that on the one hand there are institutions with low proprietary trading and low profitability, and on the other hand there are institutions with high profitability and high proprietary trading. In the middle there is a thick gray zone of firms that are in the *"middle,"* i.e., banks that have both investment and commercial

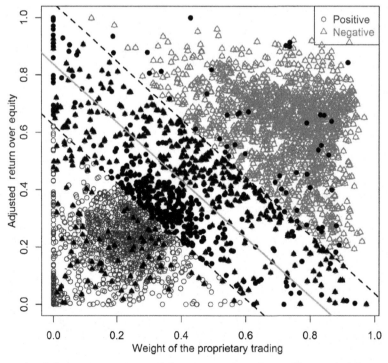

**FIGURE 1**　On the one hand, there are institutions with low proprietary trading and low profitability and on the other hand, there are institutions with high profitability and high proprietary trading. Other firms exist in the thick gray zone.

activities and enhance profit through trading on the markets. The evidence of this analysis is not conclusive as many biases could be introduced in this approach due to size and activity profile. Further analysis is required to understand the structure of the derivatives portfolios of investment banks and the relationship to generated profits.

## 2 (UN)FAIR VALUE

The origin of many issues in the investment world revolves around the concept of fair value, which drives the valuation of assets and liabilities related to trading activities. International accounting standards, both those produced by the International Accounting Standards Board (IASB; International Financial Reporting Standards, IFRS) and by the Financial Accounting Standards Board (FASB) (U.S. GAAP) require that a bank's trading book is valued at "fair value" (fair value), commonly associated with market prices. There are two sides in the debate regarding the value of an asset or liability compared to its trading price [230].

First, is it legitimate to value an instrument based on a market price from a low volume of transactions? Is there a minimum transaction flow that ensures the legitimacy of this price? Several economists have addressed these issues and so a price is inherently associated with transaction volume and not a stock. Pro-cyclical consequences are known to use market price associated with low trading volumes, illustrated by the acceleration of the crisis following the financial credit crunch of 2007. In the spring of 2007, the valuation of structured credit products, lower rates, and equity markets combined within a broader context of low liquidity resulted in a negative view of the accounting valuation of trading bank portfolios. This change immediately led to a deterioration of bank results and a simultaneous decrease in their equity. Banks were then brought into reduce portfolio risk by selling assets, increasing the downward pressure on prices, and inducing further reductions of the results and equity. On the other hand, is it legitimate to value trading portfolios even in the absence of an active market whereby no trading price is available? In this case, the accounting standard setters propose to substitute the mark-to-market model with the mark-to-model that is based on internal assumptions from the bank.

The accounting standards also define the three valuation levels applicable to trading portfolios [230, 231]. Depending on the approach to obtaining the fair value instruments they are classified as Levels 1, 2, and 3.

- **Level 1**[1] For the instruments whose value can easily be obtained using market parameters applicable to similar instruments, where trading positions that can be unwound in an active market are valued at market prices. It is, for example, the case for an initial 10-year maturity swap, valued 3 months later, but not listed on the market (a 9.75-year maturity swap is not liquid), and whose valuation can be obtained using the rate curve for the quoted market rates and a simple interpolation model.

---

[1] "Level 1 inputs are quoted prices in active markets for identical assets or liabilities the entity can access at the measurement date. A quoted market price in an active market provides the most reliable evidence of fair value and is used without adjustment to measure fair value whenever available, with few exceptions. If an entity holds a position in a single asset or liability and the asset or liability is traded in an active market, the fair value of the asset or liability is measured within Level 1 as the product of the quoted price for the individual asset or liability and the quantity held by the entity, even if the market's normal daily trading volume is not sufficient to absorb the quantity held and placing orders to sell the position in a single transaction might affect the quoted price." IFRS 13 standards.

- **Level 2**[2] The valuing of the positions on assets belonging to Level 2 is primarily based on the use of observable parameters, but is also suitable for other instruments. It is, for example, used for the case of options, as the valuation depends on an unobservable variable, the implied volatility, but can also be estimated using the implied volatility of an option listed on a comparable underlying. This is particularly true for credit default swaps, where the valuation over time can be established from the credit spreads of comparable issuers and, in general, any structured credit products and securitization results whose value depends on three parameters: the probability of default, by the securities issuer, the correlation between the events of default and the recovery rate in the event of default. These parameters can be estimated with difficulty from securities of comparable market prices. Therefore, we can consider that the valuations of Level 2 portfolios come with significant risk and the recording of valuation changes in the accounting result raises a real regulatory question.

- **Level 3**[3] Accounting standard setters accept the valuation of unlisted trading portfolios on liquid markets or whose valuation parameters cannot be estimated on the market by a "pricing model" based on unobservable parameters. Structured credit products like those that flooded the market during the subprime crisis or toxic loans for municipalities or even investment products like targeted accrual redemption notes (TARN), discussed in a previous chapter, are classified as Level 3. In this regard, the portfolio valued by the "pricing model" may be the source of negative externalities.

It is clear that the weight of the valuation at market price is marginal in all banks. At Goldman Sachs, on the only derivatives portfolio valued at "fair value," the weight of "mark-to-model" of 99.98%, the "mark-to market" accounting for only 0.02% on a portfolio of approximately 860 billion (Table 1).

It is observed that a 10% change in the value of an Level 3 portfolio, estimated on the basis of unobservable inputs, is $1.5 billion, an amount close to the bank's income over the same period ($2 billion). Our assumption that the portfolio valued at the pricing model, using estimates that are difficult to control, can serve as a variable adjustment for the result and therefore be as the source of the collective losses offset in time seems

---

[2]"Level 2 inputs are inputs other than quoted market prices included within level 1 that are observable for the asset or liability, either directly or indirectly. Level 2 inputs include quoted prices for similar assets or liabilities in active markets; quoted prices for identical or similar assets or liabilities in markets that are not active; inputs other than quoted prices that are observable for the asset or liability, for example: interest rates, and yield curves observable at commonly quoted intervals, implied volatilities and credit spreads; inputs that are derived principally from or corroborated by observable market data by correlation or other means (market corroborated inputs)." IFRS 13 standards.

[3]"Level 3 inputs are unobservable inputs for the asset or liability (IFRS 13:86). Unobservable inputs are used to measure fair value to the extent that relevant observable inputs are not available, thereby allowing for situations in which there is little, if any, market activity for the asset or liability at the measurement date. An entity develops unobservable inputs using the best information available in the circumstances, which might include the entity's own data, taking into account all information about market participant assumptions that is reasonably available." IFRS 13 standards.

TABLE 1    Break Down of Goldman-Sachs's Derivatives Assets by Level Type

| In millions $ | Derivatives assets at fair value as of March 2012 | | | | |
| --- | --- | --- | --- | --- | --- |
| | Level 1 | Level 2 | Level 3 | Cross-level netting | Total |
| Interest rates | 149 | 574,153 | 260 | – | 574,562 |
| Credit | – | 103,453 | 11,612 | – | 115,065 |
| Currencies | – | 73,684 | 1379 | – | 74,763 |
| Commodities | – | 35,198 | 860 | – | 36,058 |
| Equities | 31 | 58,180 | 1412 | – | 59,623 |
| Gross fair value of derivative assets | 180 | 844,368 | 15,523 | – | 860,071 |

empirically validated. Kolev [232] studied the correlation of the price of bank shares with the valuation at "fair value" levels 1, 2, and 3, to validate two hypotheses:

- Investors have some confidence in the evaluations of "fair value," which should lead to a positive correlation between the share price and the value of various financial assets at "fair value."
- Investors have greater confidence in the evaluations of the market price than those of the pricing model, and greater confidence in Level 2 evaluations than in Level 3 evaluations.

It is observed that the share price is positively correlated to the different portfolios valued at "fair value," but that the strongest correlation is with the portfolio valued at market price, which then decreases for Level 3 valued portfolio. Therefore, investors only grant limited credit to Level 3 valuations.

## 3 TRADING BOOKS AND PROFITABILITY

Using data from the financial reports of major American and European banks, recorded during the period 2007-2013, the historical evolution of some useful regulatory ratios to measure the strength or fragility of valuation estimates produced by banks on their trading portfolio is depicted. Using the ratio of the portfolio valued at the "pricing model," based on observable or unobservable parameters, the overall portfolio of the bank estimated is at "fair value" or the ratio "(L2 + L3)/(L1 + L2 + L3)." This indicator is somehow an estimate of the strength of the valuation at "fair value" produced by banks.

Resuming a dataset concerning a sample of Wall Street banks Figure 2 shows the part of the mark-to model in the total assets valued at fair value. The portfolio of assets consists of traded instruments (stocks, bonds, etc.) and derivatives (swaps, futures, options, structured credit products, etc.). Its value is more than $1000 billion for the majority of the banks in the considered sample. The weight of the mark-to-model is clearly dominant in the portfolio valuation structure at "fair value," and the sample mean on U.S. banks is about 85%. Only 15% of the assets are valued at the average market price, showing that the debate on the mark-to-market model is not the one on which prudential and accounting regulators should focus on. For some banks, the ratio is even close to 100%, the trading result in these cases being massively influenced by valuation changes in estimates produced by a model. Two issues, however, must correct this argument, which might lead regulators to consider

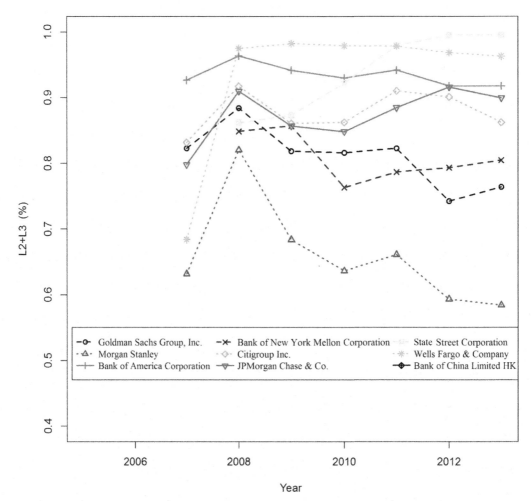

**FIGURE 2**   U.S. banks: weight of the mark-to-model l is clearly dominant in the portfolio valuation structure at "fair value," the sample mean on U.S. banks is about 85%.

that the mark-to-model creates an incentive within U.S. investment banks to develop trading activity in derivatives and structured credit products not directly quoted on the market, with the sole objective to benefit from the risk assumptions.

On the one hand, the positions valued as assets are at least partially offset by the positions recorded as liabilities, which limits the potential gains and, of course, the risk that covers only the "net" position. On the other hand, the

trading result consists of a "realized" and an "unrealized" part. The accounting representation of a position will necessarily be confronted at maturity, and its economic reality and unrealized gains will turn into actual losses if they were overvalued.

The situation for European banks is significantly different. Even if the mark-to-model remains the dominant mode of registration of positions, its relative weight is significantly lower, as Figure 3 shows. The average relative

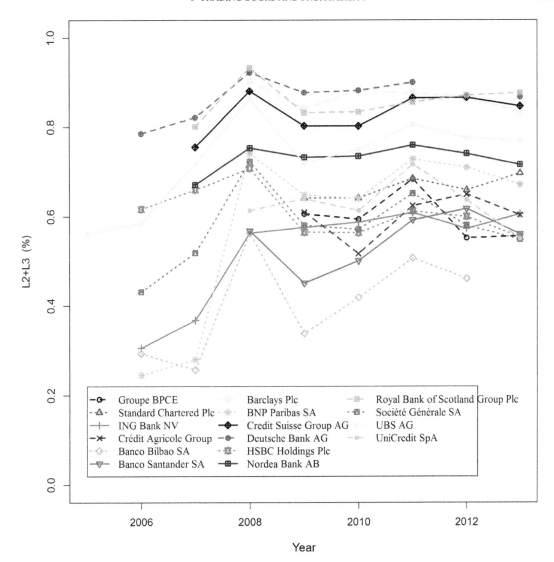

**FIGURE 3** Mark-to-model weight in the total assets of European banks valued at fair value. British and Swiss Banks, along with Deutsche Bank, have the highest ratios, superior to 80% since 2007, with French banks being slightly behind with ratios closer to 60%.

weight calculated on our sample of European banks is 70%, with quite different situations within Europe for individual banks.

Although the relative weight of the mark-to-model in European banks is lower than that observed in U.S. banks, the overall conclusion drawn from our diagnosis remains that most

banks' trading portfolios are valued using the "pricing model," which includes an unreliable dimension, impacting not only the profit but also the market risk estimation and the downstream calculation of regulatory capital. Therefore this generates an uncertainty in measuring the strength of bank.

We can clearly see in both Figures 2 and 3 that the impact of the carve out in October 2008, when banks were permitted under pressure from regulators, to temporarily transfer some of their registered portfolios at market prices (Level 1) to Levels 2 and 3. The liquidity crisis after the bankruptcy of Lehman Brothers led to a collapse in market prices and was also rendered insignificant due to the low volume of associated transactions. Their application to the valuation of Level 1 portfolios would have had a very adverse effect on the accounting profit of banks and their need for regulatory capital.

## 3.1 Banks' Revenue and Size of the Mark-to-Model Portfolio

An econometric test could confirm the hypothesis that the size of the portfolio valued on the pricing model is a determining element in the banks' results. The general model considers a linear dependence between net banking income ($R_{inv}$) (the difference between revenue and operating expenses on the perimeter of the investment bank) and the valuation of balance-sheet items and off-balance items accounted for at "fair value" and broken down by level:

$$R_{inv} = \alpha + \beta_1 \cdot L_1 + \beta_2 \cdot L_2 + \beta_3 \cdot L_3 + \epsilon \quad (1)$$

where $L_1$, $L_2$, and $L_3$ are the amounts of assets of Levels 1, 2, and 3 is the constant and $\beta_1$, $\beta_2$, and $\beta_3$ are the sensitivities for each level. Remember that the assets at "fair value" are either balance-sheet assets (i.e., debt securities, equities, structured loans, etc.), or derivatives, which, however, account for most of valuations at "fair value." Our hypothesis is confirmed if the student $t_i$ coefficient on the variable $\beta_i$ is such that $t_3 > t_2 > t_1$.

A normalization of data is conducted to make the information for different-sized institutions comparable by dividing the net banking income $R_{inv}$ and the $L_1$, $L_2$, and $L_3$ values of each institution by the average level of their portfolio valued at "fair value" over the course of the observation

period. The results of the test for the period 2007-2011 relating to Equation 1 are summarized in Table 2.

Multi-varied regression shows that Levels 2 and 3 have a significant impact on the income of the investment bank, with Level 3, as expected, being the most discriminating. The three variables alone explain about 30% of the banks' revenue variance.

Table 3 describes the results of Equation 1 where we regress the net revenue to the gross amount of assets and liabilities measured at "fair value." Therefore, when taking the effects of compensation into account and making the hypothesis that the gross sum is a good indicator to estimate the relative weight of each of the valuation methods, it is observed that the aggregate

**TABLE 2**　Regression Results Between the Income of the Sample of Banks and Assets per Level ($R^2 = 27.56\%$)

| Parameter | Estimation | Standard deviation | $t$-Value | $p$-Value |
|---|---|---|---|---|
| $\alpha$ | 0.002635 | 0.002831 | 0.931 | 0.3538 |
| $\beta_1$ | 0.008885 | 0.005572 | 1.595 | 0.1134 |
| $\beta_2$ | 0.005310 | 0.002427 | 2.188 | **0.0306** |
| $\beta_3$ | 0.098800 | 0.022040 | 4.483 | **1.67e−05** |

Note: Bold values in the third column indicated $p$-values inferior to <5%.

**TABLE 3**　Regression Results Between the Incomes of Investment Banks and the Assets and Liabilities by Level ($R^2 = 26.01\%$)

| Parameter | Estimation | Standard deviation | $t$-Value | $p$-Value |
|---|---|---|---|---|
| $\alpha$ | 0.00297 | 0.00285 | 1.042 | 0.2995 |
| $\beta_1$ | 0.00905 | 0.00564 | 1.605 | 0.1110 |
| $\beta_2$ | 0.00479 | 0.00256 | 1.869 | 0.0641 |
| $\beta_3$ | 0.07202 | 0.01740 | 4.137 | **6.49e−05** |

Note: Bold values in the third column indicated $p$-values inferior to <5%.

of assets and liabilities at Level 3 becomes the only significant factor in the model.

By reducing the scope for a sub-sample including only the largest sample investment banks it can be seen that the effect is vastly amplified. The results given in Table 4 show that $R^2$ increases significantly, from about 30% to 54%, while the portfolio valued using "mark to model" $L_3$ becomes the variable whose explanatory power is clearly the most significant (Table 4).

Figure 4 describes the relationship between standardized banking net revenue (net revenue/average valuations at "fair value") and the standardized Level 3 portfolio (L3/average valuations at "fair value"). It confirms the existence of a growing and statistically significant relationship between the two variables.

The statistical study does not question the assumption that the portfolio of assets and liabilities valued as Level 3 "mark-to-model" is a key element of the statistically significant result of net banking income. The relationship between the banks' result and the portfolios valued at "fair value" is clearly more significant in the Level 3 portfolio than in sub-portfolio Level 2 and especially for portfolio Level 1, and our results do not allow the questioning of the assimilation of this method of accounting valuation as "mark-to-myth." The scientific fragility of

**TABLE 4** Regression Results Between the Income of Investment Banks and Assets per Level ($R^2 = 53.79\%$)

| Parameter | Estimation | Standard deviation | t-Value | p-Value |
|---|---|---|---|---|
| $\alpha$ | 0.002748 | 0.003515 | 0.782 | 0.43 |
| $\beta_1$ | 0.010610 | 0.019538 | 0.543 | 0.58 |
| $\beta_2$ | −0.001020 | 0.003209 | −0.318 | 0.75 |
| $\beta_3$ | 0.207135 | 0.036305 | 5.705 | 0.00 |

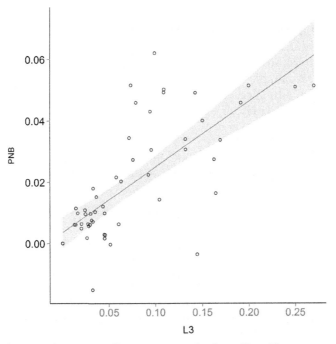

**FIGURE 4** Relationship between the revenue of large investment banks and Level 3.

evaluations exposes this portfolio to major revisions, where the consequences can be systemic, as illustrated by the over-valuation of the portfolios of structured credit products during the 2007-2008 crisis.

## 3.2 Trading ROE and Mark-to-Model

The main risk indicator for trading activates is the value at risk (VaR) that corresponds to the maximum potential loss on the trading portfolio within 99% confidence interval and in the case of an adverse market scenario, over 10 working days. The new regulations applicable to market risk are replacing the VaR with the expected shortfall representing the expected losses that are bigger than the VaR, the confidence level being reduced to 97.5% (two standard deviations in the normal law instead of 2.33). However, the 2007-2013 data, which is used in this section is part of the current regulatory environment. The report "VaR/portfolio valuation at fair value" gives information about the importance of the diversification effect of the positions recorded as assets and liabilities. A very low ratio may lead the regulator to question the estimate of the compensation of implicit risk in the covariance matrix. If the model-based valuation represents a significant fraction of the estimated fair value portfolio, the calculation of regulatory capital based on the VaR can be hazardous and might request an appropriate review.

Banks' trading results are measured by the difference between the valuation of the trading portfolio at the end of the accounting period and recovery early in the period, plus or minus the gain or loss realized during the period. This result is a gross result, estimated before any allocation of costs. This is the result produced by the banks in their accounting reference documents and, of course, is an assessment increased by the outcome of analytical accounting. The figures obtained for the corresponding Return over Equity (ROE) are therefore obviously not directly

comparable to the ROE usually published, but provide information on the "raw" return of regulatory capital market activity. The data available is used to calculate the rate of ROE-trading activity, defined and measured by the ratio between the trading income and associated regulatory funds. This ROE therefore measures the profitability of an investment in regulatory capital dedicated to market activity funds. Our data sample covered the period 2006-2012 and only capital used to hedge market risk was taken into account in accordance with the prudential rules Basel II, focusing in particular on the risk of the trading portfolio. Regulatory capital is calculated using the VaR, defined by the maximum market loss associated with a 99% confidence interval, assuming a non-adjustment of the portfolio over the next 10 working days. Mathematically, the VaR is the 99% quantile of the distribution of gains and losses of the trading portfolio estimated in 10 working days.

Many methods for calculating VaR can be applied (parametric VaR, historical VaR, Monte Carlo, etc.), the development perspective of which is not the subject of this text. In practice, banks usually estimate the VaR over the period of a day, called "one-day VaR," then multiply the estimate obtained by the root of 10, according to a procedure acceptable under the general assumption that the performance of the portfolio is distributed according to a normal distribution. The VaR data published by banks is used in accounting reference documents, which are certainly end-of-period data, but are very close to the average daily VaR for the corresponding periods (annual or quarterly). Regulatory capital is equal to the 10-day VaR, multiplied by a scaling factor whose level is at least equal to 3, depending on the intrinsic quality of the model (algorithms and parameters). Model quality is assessed by the regulatory authorities with past performance being measured by the number of exceptions, theoretically equal to 1% of the observations. The scaling factor is calculated as follows:

Scaling factor $= 3 + CF$ (model)

$$+ CF \text{ (past performance)} \quad (2)$$

where CF is the complementary factor applied to the model, depends not only on its intrinsic quality but also on the quality of the bank's risk control system. Not having the precise information on the scaling factor of the banks in our sample, a coefficient of 4.5 is used for those banks for which data is not available. This factor seems to be the most frequently used by the supervisory authorities. Consequently, the ROE is calculated using the following formula:

$$ROE = \frac{\text{Trading P\&L}}{\text{VaR}_{1 \text{ day}} \cdot \sqrt{10} \cdot \text{scaling factor}} \quad (3)$$

Figures 5 and 6 outline the historical evolution of ROE (ratio of "gross profit/regulatory capital") for U.S. and European banks since 2006.

Estimated levels show the very high profitability of trading, certainly measured before any cost allocation. The measured ROE for trading activities is the ratio between the gross income and regulatory capital allocated to cover market risk. Regardless of the absolute level of ROE, it can be observed that the profitability of trading operations has remained stable since 2008, and strengthening prudential and regulatory measures are not being translated, contrary to what one might think, in a decrease of the result reported to regulatory capital.

The case of European banks is not overtly different, since the absolute levels of ROE has also been very high and stable since 2008, despite the strengthening of prudential standards. Figures 6 describes the ROE of major European banks. These results suggest that market activities produce excessive returns per unit of risk or regulatory capital, compared to other banking or non-banking activities. Therefore, three assumptions can be made:

- The trading result is overstated, perhaps because of the importance of the mark-to-model in the valuation of portfolios valued at "fair value."
- The level of capital allocated to market-risk hedging is undervalued, perhaps due to the diversification effect associated with the VaR, which is an aggregate indicator of market risk of which the estimate depends primarily on the covariance matrix between the yields of the various risk factors, that are difficult to estimate due to the nonstationary nature of the series.[4]
- The logic of the calculation of regulatory capital explains the figures obtained. Under the assumption that the daily return of the portfolio follows a normal process, the expected annual yield increases with time, as volatility increases with the square root of time.

During 1 year it is normal for the yield to be much higher than the amount of capital calculated from the earnings' volatility over a period of only 10 working days. There is a "methodological space" sufficient to produce perfectly scientifically legitimate VaR, but at very different and difficult to control levels. The question for the regulator is whether the method of calculation of regulatory capital is based on scientifically

---

[4]In its 2013 annual report Goldman-Sachs stated: "When calculating VaR, we use historical simulations with full valuation of approximately 70,000 market factors. VaR is calculated at a position level based on simultaneously shocking the relevant market risk factors for that position. We sample from 5 years of historical data to generate the scenarios for our VaR calculation. The historical data is weighted so that the relative importance of the data reduces over time. This gives greater importance to more recent observations and reflects current asset volatilities, which improves the accuracy of our estimates of potential loss. As a result, even if our inventory positions were unchanged, our VaR would increase with increasing market volatility, and vice versa."

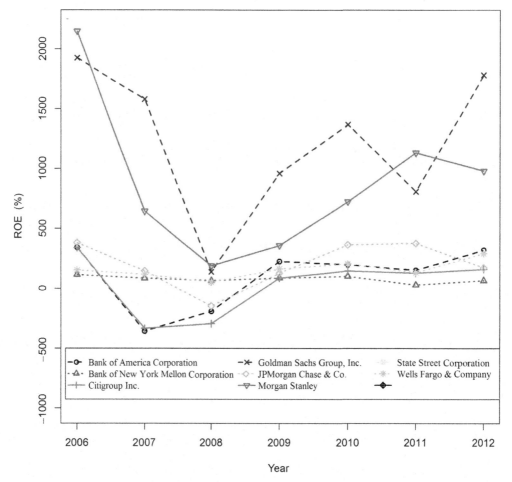

**FIGURE 5**  Ratio between gross income and regulatory capital allocated to cover market risk for American banks.

sound estimates of VaR or based on the input parameters (volatilities and correlations) whose levels are hardly controllable, especially given that the entry valuations, accounting for more than 70%, are established on the basis of a "pricing model." From this point of view, as indicated previously, the first regulatory adjustment was made following the implementation of Basel 2.5 at the end of 2011 in some jurisdictions, including Europe (but not in the United States).

This agreement is reflected in particular by raising the level of funds related to the trading portfolio, which comprises three main components:

- A requirement established according to the current VaR calculated with a confidence interval of 99% over a 10-day period, including a retrospective observation period of at least 1 year.
- A requirement based on a measure of "stressed" VaR whose calculation is similar to the current VaR, but undertaken over a period of 12 months of strong turbulence.

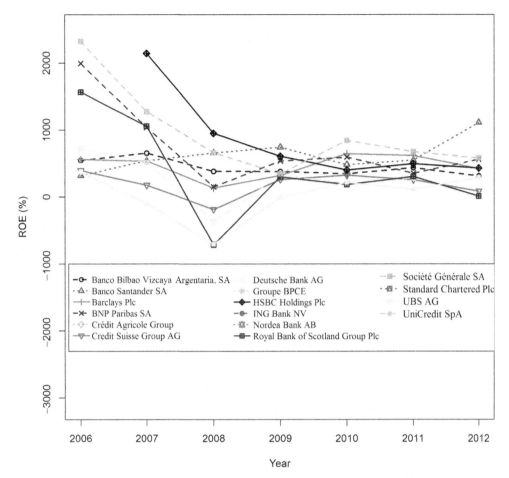

**FIGURE 6**  Ratio between gross income and regulatory capital allocated to cover market risk for European banks.

- A requirement for additional capital, based on the exposure value of credit risk and to cover losses on credit products if a rating changes or defaults (IRC incremental risk charge), calculated over a period of 12 months with a 99.9% confidence interval.

Through a cross-sectional regression conducted between the ROE of banks in year $t$ on the variation between year $(t-1)$ and $t$ of the relative weights of mark-to-market, the mark-to-model Level 2, and mark-to-model Level 3, expressed as follows:

$$\text{ROE}_t = \alpha^i + \beta^i \cdot \Delta L^i_{t-1,t} + \epsilon \quad i = (1,2,3) \quad (4)$$

where $\text{ROE}_t$ is the return over equity in year $t$ and $\Delta L^i_{t-1,t}$ is the relative variation of the weight at level $i$ between years $t$ and $t - 1$. The results of the three regression are described in Table 5.

The relative weight of assets valued at mark-to-market does not, in any way, influence the banks' trading result. The relative weight of assets valued at mark-to-model (Level 2) only marginally affects the banks' trading results, but the results are nonetheless significant. The relative weight of assets valued at mark-to-model (Level 3) is the variable that has the $R^2$ with a value of 0.20, which is not very high, but is still close to the $R^2$ levels observed on stocks betas,

**TABLE 5**  Regression Results

| Parameter | Estimate | Std. error | $t$-Value | $p$-Value |
|-----------|----------|-----------|-----------|-----------|
| $\alpha_1$ | 357% | 0.7501 | 4.763 | 0.00 |
| $\beta_1$ | 19.46 | 9.8588 | 1.974 | 0.04 |
| $R^2$ | 0.1 | | | |
| $\alpha_2$ | 372% | 0.763 | 4.875 | 0.00 |
| $\beta_2$ | 19.245 | 9.616 | 2.001 | 0.06 |
| $R^2$ | 0.11 | | | |
| $\alpha_3$ | 565% | 1.324 | 4.271 | 0.00 |
| $\beta_3$ | 282.488 | 132.305 | 2.135 | 0.04 |
| $R^2$ | 0.2 | | | |

Notes :*The relative weight of assets valued at mark-to-market does not, in any way, influence the banks' trading results. The relative weight of assets valued at mark-to-model L2 only marginally affects the banks' trading results, but the results are nonetheless significant. The relative weight of assets valued at mark-to-model L3 is the variable that has the highest $R^2$.*

which is widely used in portfolio management. The regression coefficient is also highly significant and a positive sign, as to be expected. One can thus consider that the banks' incentive to develop positions valued at "pricing model" is an assumption which is not challenged by our results.

## 3.3 Mark-to-Model vs. Mark-to-Misrepresentation

An example relevant for the potential role of mark-to-model valuations in the development of illegal fraudulent behaviors is a case involving the Bank of Montreal. The Canadian bank needed to restate its financial statements by $190 million in 2007 as a result of valuation fraud related to Level 3 assets. The valuations involved natural gas options that were traded by one of the bank's senior commodity traders, who was responsible for assigning fair values to the books on daily basis. If the derivatives involved were actively traded on a recognized market, the mark-to-market basis was used in valuing the derivatives (Level 1 instruments).

However, when no such market existed, the mark-to-model approach was used (Level 2 or 3 instruments). When the mark-to-model method was used, Bank of Montreal's internal controls required that an independent price verification be obtained. If the independent price was lower than the value calculated by the trader, a valuation reserve for the difference was established. The selection of the outside party to provide the independent valuation was done by personnel from a separate department outside that of the trader, in order to comply with segregation of duties. The trading unit had successfully resisted efforts from another unit of the bank to use a multi-contributor independent valuation service. As a result, the same outside company, Optionable, had been used exclusively as the broker for the trades and to verify the trader's valuations since 2003. Therefore, a relationship developed between the Bank of Montreal trade and three individuals at Optionable.

In effect, earning so much of its revenue from a single source impaired Optionable's independence, which created the incentive to cooperate with the trader at Bank of Montreal. This relationship led to an unlawful practice in which the three individuals at Optionable simply returned values to Bank of Montreal's back office mirroring those provided by the trader. The *mark-to-myself* trader would e-mail twice a month his list of inflated values to his contacts at Optionable, easily circumventing the internal control the Bank of Montreal thought was in place. Later that same day, Optionable would e-mail its list of supposedly independent values to Bank of Montreal's back office. These e-mails contained values exactly matching those of the trader, thus covering up the inflated values. Over the six quarters from 2005 through 2007, the Bank of Montreal's trader overvalued his book by a total of $600 million, trader's fraud accounting for about $350 million.

The fraud scheme began in the summer of 2006 when, after a lengthy battle between the two groups at the Bank of Montreal, the bank finally contracted a multi-contributor valuation service called Totem. Totem's valuations were below those provided by Optionable. After repeated efforts by the fraudulent trader to manipulate these values, by early 2007 the scheme came to an end. In addition to the impact on Bank of Montreal, the shareholders of Optionable also felt the effects of the fraud once it came to light.[5]

## OPTIONABLE: A COMPANY PROVIDIN MARK-T-MISREP-RESENTATION

The fraudulent trader sent his inflated values to Optionable, which later would send its list of supposedly independent values to the Bank of Montreal's back office with the values received from the trader. Optionable earned 24% of its 2006 revenues from the trades carried out by the Bank of Montreal trader.

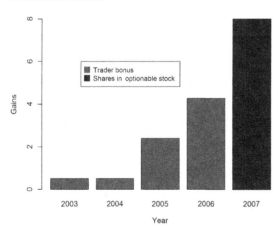

The Bank of Montreal trader's bonus reached over $4 million as a result of the fraud. Two bank

executives that owned Optionable stock made $8 million when they sold shares in Optionable stock in 2007, before the stock crashed by 82% after Bank of Montreal suspended the contract.

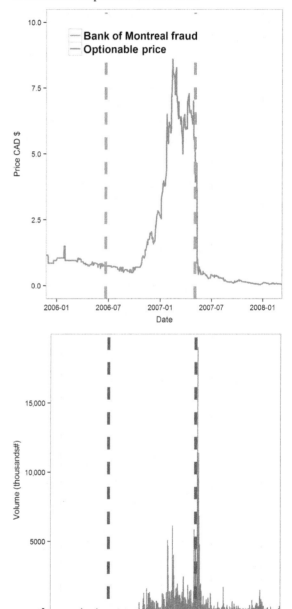

[5]http://www.fraudconference.com/uploadedFiles/ Fraud_Conference/Content/CourseMaterials/ presentations/23rd/cpp/5I7IGerryZack.pdf.

# 4 COUNTERPARTY RISK MEASURE AND BALANCE SHEET

The dialectic of mark-to-model versus the mark-to-market is not the only issue concerning the valuation of the derivatives portfolios. The Level 3 portfolios and part of Levels 1 and 2 might not have in many cases a market price due to the fact that they are over-the-counter transactions, with specific risk. The over-the-counter derivatives account for a few trillion dollars in terms of nominal. Banking regulations as well as economic realities imposed a panel of metrics to assess banks exposure to over-the-counter derivatives. Two of them, the credit valuation adjustment and the debt valuation adjustment, are relevant cases as they have had repercussions on banks' balance sheets.

The credit value adjustment (CVA) refers to an adjustment made on the valuation of an over-the-counter derivative transaction in order to properly reflect the credit risk of the counterparty. The CVA allows the risky value of a derivative to be represented as the risk-free value less a specific term. For a given derivative instrument the CVA has the following form:

$$\mathbf{CVA}_T$$
$$= \widetilde{\text{LGD}} \cdot \int_0^T E_Q(\exp^{-r \cdot u} \cdot \max(V(u), 0)) \, dP(u) \tag{5}$$

where $Q$ is the risk neutral measure, $r$ is the interest rate, LGD is the loss given default, $V(u)$ is the derivative valuation at the moment $u$, $T$ is the maturity of the instrument, and $dP(u)$ is the infinitesimal variation of default probability for a specific counterparty.

One of the first banks to calculate CVA was Bank One Corp. in the late 1990s. Bank One Corp. simply adjusted the value of its over-the-counter derivatives portfolio for the perceived credit risk

of their counterparties. This led to an immediate result: Bank One Corp. promptly got sued by the Internal Revenue Service (IRS). The IRS claimed that this was only a clever scheme to understate profits and hence pay less tax. Bank One Corp. won the court case and the ruling indicated that if the company adjusted the value of a transaction for the counterparty credit risk then it also had to adjust it for its own credit risk. The court commissioned an expert report from Darrel Duffie, a Professor at Stanford University, which stated that the credit risk adjustment should reflect the credit quality of both parties to the transaction.

Thus, from its very inception CVA was meant to imply a bilateral measure. Therefore, in addition to the CVA a new metric was added to the counterparty risk metric panel called debt valuation adjustment (DVA). The DVA is typically defined as the difference between the value of the derivative, assuming the bank is default risk free and the value reflects default risk of the bank. For a given bank entering an over-the-counter derivative transaction, the DVA has the following form:

$$\mathbf{DVA}_T = \widetilde{\text{LGD}}_{\text{Bank}}$$
$$\cdot \int_0^T -E_Q(e^{-r \cdot u} \cdot \max(V(u), 0)) \, dP_{\text{Bank}}(u) \tag{6}$$

where $Q$ is the risk neutral measure, $r$ is the interest rate, LGD is the loss given default of the bank, $V(u)$ is the derivative valuation at the moment $u$, $T$ is the maturity of the instrument, and $dP_{\text{Bank}}(u)$ is the infinitesimal variation of default probability for the bank.

This principle found its way into international accounting systems (FASB 157 for the United States and the IFRS 13). The DVA metric has a very particular counterintuitive impact on the balance sheet of a bank:

- Whenever the credit quality of bank worsens (the rating is downgraded or the CDS spread increases) the banks will book a positive amount (asset), thereby creating a positive gain for that period.
- Whenever the credit quality of bank improves the bank will book a negative amount (liability) thereby creating a loss for that period.

In the period following the financial crisis many banks booked profit as a result of their degradation of the own creditworthiness. Some examples include:

- Citigroup on first quarter of 2009 reported a positive $2.5 billion mark-to-market due to its reduced credit quality.
- JPMorgan booked up to $1 billion worth of debit valuation adjustments as a result of its multi-billion dollar trading loss in 2012.
- In a similar move, Morgan Stanley stated that results for third quarter included positive revenue of $3.4 billion, or $1.12 per diluted share, representing a third of Morgan Stanley's net revenues due to changes in Morgan Stanley's DVA from the decline in the bank's credit worthiness.[6]

A detailed study published in 2011 showed the effect of[7] the DVA on a bank's profit related to the increase in their own CDS spread (Table 6). It is showed that a bank can generate up to $3 billion in gain over a few months just from the increase in its own credit spread.

---

[6]The truth behind CVAs, DVAs, and banking results, http://www.euromoney.com/Article/2930674/The-truth-behind-CVAs-DVAs-and-banking-results.html.
[7]CVA, DVA and Bank Earnings https://www.quantifisolutions.com/QDownloads.aspx?guid=ba61e664-bd28-4dd5-9bf1-9d3421248a64.

TABLE 6  Impact of Reduced Credit Worthiness on the DVA

| Bank | June CDS (bp) | Sept. CDS | Δ | DVA gain ($b) |
|---|---|---|---|---|
| Bank of America | 158 | 426 | 268 | 1.700 |
| Citigroup | 137 | 319 | 182 | 1.888 |
| Goldman-Sachs | 137 | 330 | 193 | 0.450 |
| JPMorgan | 79 | 163 | 84 | 1.900 |
| Morgan Stanley | 162 | 492 | 330 | 3.400 |

Source: *Quantifisolutions*.

# 5 OUTLOOK

Financial institutions and in particular investment firms must comply to complex accounting rules meant to provide investors and markets with a better idea of bank activity. The use of the mark-to-model for the valuation of derivatives portfolios has proven to be a source of misconduct. The mark-to-model gives to senior managers a real option for engineering the accounting figures depending on an unobservable input parameter. Therefore, valuations based on mark-to-model face risk because they can be manipulated based on circumstances.

New regulations imposing additional risk charges to banks have introduced additional variables in balance sheets depending on market fluctuations. With the variations in volatilities and credit spreads the prudential charges vary, thereby generating unrealized gains or losses for those institutions. Regulators give a lot of freedom to banks in regard with the choice of methods employed for computing the prudential risk metrics. Therefore, institutions can engage in capital arbitrages by using those methods that can adjust the variation of the risk metrics, like CVA and DVA in the desired direction.

# Fraud on the Market Theory

## 1 BACKGROUND

Basic Incorporated was a publicly traded company primarily engaged in the business of manufacturing chemical refractories for the steel industry, who was approached as early as 1965 or 1966, by Combustion Engineering, Inc., a company producing mainly alumina-based refractories.

Talks of a merger intensified in the years 1977 and 1978, resulting in a merger announce on December 20, 1978. Combustion's offer of $46 per share for Basic's common stock was accepted and Basic was taken off exchange the same day.

Upon news of the mergers the torment started for Basic due to the fact that before the merger, between 1977 and 1978, Basic made three announcements denying the merger rumors. Plaintiffs filed with class action lawsuit arguing that the falsity or misleading nature of the three public statements made them lose money as they sold the stock at a price lower than the offer price.

It is interesting to note that the sellers who sold Basic stock during the class period between October 1977 and December 1978 traded at a price between $20 and $30 per share and most made money through those sales. Nonetheless, the missing opportunity of selling at $46 triggered the litigation.

After a decade of legal battles, in 1988 the U.S. Supreme Court sided with the plaintiffs. This excerpt[1] from the Supreme Court's decision changed in a very radical way the framework of securities litigation in the United States

---

[1] The District Court certified respondents' class, but granted a summary judgment for petitioners on the merits. The Court of Appeals affirmed the class certification, agreeing that under the "fraud on the market" theory, respondents' reliance on petitioners' misrepresentations could be presumed, and thus that common issues predominated over questions pertaining to individual plaintiffs Basic Inc. v. Levinson, 485 U.S. 224 (1988) 485 U.S. 224 No. 86-279. Argued November 2, 1987, Decided March 7, 1988.

and worldwide. It is considered to be the most important legal reference after the Securities Act in 1934, establishing the fraud on the market theory.

The fraud on the market theory relies on the assumption than in a securities market, the price reflects fully the picture of all available information regarding the company, its finances, its business, and its prospects. This is nothing more than the efficient market hypothesis introduced by Fama in the early 1970s.

In addition, a misrepresentation, false news, or misleading statements can harm the investors directly or indirectly since price reflects the all available information and investors can be misguided even if they are not fully aware of the false information. Thus, the fraud on the market theory attaches the same degree of causality between rogue statements and investors' trades for cases when is or there is not direct reliance on the erroneous statements.

Under the fraud on the market theory a defendant can rebut the presumption of reliance by "any showing that severs the link between the alleged misrepresentation and either the price received (or paid) by the plaintiff, or his decision to trade at a fair market price."

## 2 BASIC'S BASICS

The fraud on the market theory is addressed[2] under Section 10(b) of the Securities Exchange Act of 1934 and the U.S. Securities and Exchange Commission (SEC)'s Rule 10b-5, which requires that in litigation a plaintiff must provide proof of:

- **Manipulation or deception**: Proof of misrepresentation and/or omission, false or deceitful information relevant to the case needs to be provided. Generally these are either financial misstatements, announcements regarding products in development, etc. (in the biotech industry, e.g., news about FDA approval).
- **Materiality**: The deception should be material, in other words be quantifiable and have an impact on the stock.
- **Scienter**: There should be an intent or knowledge of misrepresenting the reality that could impact the stock price.
- **Connection** with the purchase or sale of securities: The material misstatement should be related to the trades of the plaintiff. In general, both the misstatements and the trades should occur with a time frame.
- **Reliance**: The plaintiff reasonably relied upon the misstatement of the defender when investing.
- **Loss causation**: The losses flowed from the misrepresentations due to the plaintiff's reliance on that information.
- **Economic damage**: The plaintiff suffered an economic loss as a result of the fraud.

A class action suit is accepted if the elements related to the common reliance predominate over the individual one. The fraud on the market theory makes it easier for plaintiffs to file class action complaints, which was more difficult before the Basic case.

Courts assume that all plaintiffs indirectly relied on the alleged misrepresentation in making investment decisions with regard to the litigated stock through their reliance on market efficiency, which implies the stock's market price contains all the information. In other words, the plaintiff needs to show that the stock traded on an efficient market and they relied on price in making their buy/sell trades.

The Basic case and the resulting theory postulate that the aggregation of information flow is concomitant with the price discovery on the market. This might have been true a few decades ago when many investors traded based on information relative to a particular stock. In markets

---

[2]17 CFR 240.10b-5—Employment of manipulative and deceptive devices, https://www.law.cornell.edu/cfr/text/17/240.10b-5.

in which more than half of the volumes are driven by high-frequency trading the aggregation of information and prices in the market could follow different avenues, and prices cold reflect other things than the information relative to the stock.

# 3 FUND VS. HALIBURTON

A new development of the fraud on the market theory occurred with the *Halliburton vs. Fund* case, which started in 2002 and went through various phases until late 2014. Halliburton is a Texas-based provider of diverse services and products mainly in the oil and gas sector.

In the original case[3] Halliburton was charged with issuing a series of materially false and misleading statements that materially changed its revenue recognition policy to recognize revenue on claims and change orders relating to cost overruns, which its clients had not approved. The misrepresentations inflated Halliburton's reported revenues and earnings, thereby artificially inflating the price of Halliburton securities. On May 28, 2002, after the close of the market, Halliburton issued a press release announcing that the SEC was conducting an investigation into its accounting for cost overruns and its market price dropped by 3.3% in 1 day with very heavy trading volume.

Over almost a decade of litigation the case called for a debate around the very foundation of a securities class action: the presumption of reliance. The U.S. Supreme Court's decision was waited for with interest as it was an opportunity to tackle the fraud on the market theory, which has been contested by many theoreticians. On

June 23, 2014 the Court reinforced its support for the fraud on the market doctrine declining to overturn the *Basic vs. Levinson* decision. However, the U.S. Supreme Court granted to companies attacked in securities litigation the possibility to rebut the plaintiffs' presumption of reliance on an efficient market . Therefore in the early stages of the lawsuit the defendant needs to show that an alleged misrepresentation did not affect the stock price.

Two statistical tests were applied to Haliburton stock price in order to assess the reliance on market efficiency over the concerned period. Figure 1 shows the results of the density forecast test and "bubble" testing, which are explained in a dedicated chapter. The density forecast test, benchmarking the normal forecasting capacity test versus the normal inverse Gaussian, showed that during the class period the stock price returns were characterized by heavy tails. The same behavior was observed during the 2008 crisis. Sup-Augmented Dickey-Fuller (ADF) and generalized Sup-ADF tests showed that a price explosion might have occurred during the class period, but also in the post class period.

Figure 2 shows the results of the weak form efficiency tests for the Halliburton stock prices that were performed for a rolling window of 250 days with a holding period of 10 days. The Lo and MacKinlay, Chow-Denning, Wright, and the Portmanteau tests show violations in efficiency during the class period. These violations occurred also ulteriorly in other episodes.

In the *Halliburton vs. Fund* case the various efficient market hypothesis tests confirmed the fraud on the market theory. However, inefficiency in the Halliburton price did not occur only during the class period but also in other episodes. Fraud on the market could mean inefficiency but the reciprocal phase inefficiency means fraud on the market is not true. The current legal framework does not address clearly the fact that inefficiency does not always imply fraud, and this is probably a factor that leads to settlements in most securities fraud litigation.

---

[3]http://securities.stanford.edu/filings-case.html?id=102452.

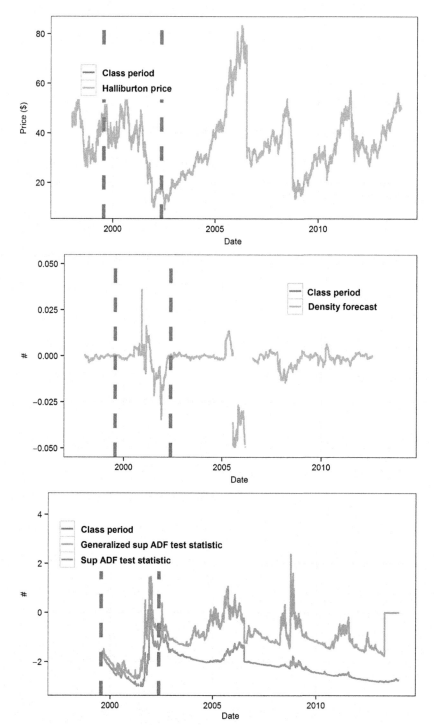

**FIGURE 1** Halliburton case: Up: Evolution of the Halliburton stock price. Middle: The density forecast test, benchmarking the normal forecasting capacity test vs. the normal inverse Gaussian. The test shows that during the class period the stock price returns were characterized by heavy tails. The same behavior was observed during the 2008 crisis. Bottom: Bubble, Sup-Augmented Dickey-Fuller, and Generalized Sup-ADF tests showed that a price explosion might have occurred during the class period, but also in the post class period.

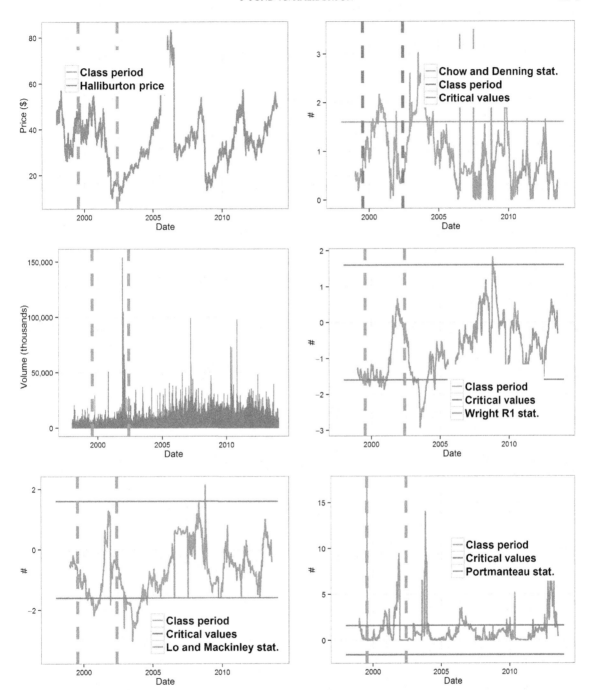

**FIGURE 2** Halliburton case: Weak form efficiency tests were performed for a rolling window of 250 days with a holding period of 10 days. The Lo and MacKinlay, Chow-Denning, Wright, and the Portmanteau tests show violations in efficiency during the class period. These violations occurred also ulteriorly in other episodes.

# 4 DRIVERS FOR FRAUD ON THE MARKET THEORY

When dealing with a securities fraud cases the fraud on the market theory should be proven or rejected from a quantitative point of view. As shown in the previous section, time series tests are not sufficient for distinguishing between efficient and inefficient firms.

Barber et al. [233] was among the firsts scholars to support that the application of the fraud on the market theory requires a detailed statistical analysis *at least at the preliminary stage of identifying the major efficiency drivers their inter-dependencies, and their relative contribution to efficiency.*

The drivers for efficiency that determine whether or not Fraud On the Market Theory (FOMT) can be applied are linked to factors that reflect the homogeneous spread of information about the security of all market participants, and include the depth of the market and the transaction costs. Markets do not become efficient automatically. It is the actions of investors and various traders, sensing arbitrage opportunities and putting into effect schemes to take profit from the market, that make markets efficient. A list of candidate efficiency drivers mentioned by the courts in various litigations was discussed by Barber et al. [233] and includes:

- **Volume of trade**. High volumes in a security mean more information incorporated in the price and thin volumes are associated with less efficiency. With the speculative funds and the allegations of market manipulation of high-frequency traders this assumption should be considered with caution.
- **Number of market makers**. Market makers inject liquidity in a given security's market and trade the security depending on the information in the market. If they make derivatives on those securities this could add a new layer of complexity and generally reinforce the efficiency.

- **Firm size**. Many researchers have shown that small firms (microcap) are more often involved in securities fraud cases as their stock is less efficiently priced. Enron and Worldcom are counterexamples of the size effect.
- **Bid-ask spread**. Reflects the liquidity of a given security. The higher the relative difference between the bid price and the ask price of a security the lower its liquidity is.
- **Volatility**. Securities with high volatility reflect the fact that the view of the market changes very quickly and new information alters the state of the security in a massive way. Electricity markets is one extreme example in this sense. Heterogeneous spread of information among the investors results also in high volatility, thereby being a sign of inefficiency.
- **Price level**. Low prices are associated with high volatility and implicitly to lower efficiency.
- **Number of analysts**. The larger the number of analysts following a security, the more efficient it tends to be. Analysts synthesize raw information and generate new analyses and recommend their views to investors in an independent manner, thereby contributing to the information aggregation and diffusion in the market.
- **Institutional investors**. Big funds and major investment firms are supposed to have better investment analysis tool than individual investors. Also, pension funds or other traditional long-term investors reallocate their portfolios less frequently than other more speculative investors. They tend to hold a more *buy and hold* view, thereby bringing support to the prices.

The above factors are not independent one from each other. In fact, a large firm trades on high volume, with few major banks as market makers, and a lot of analysts following its stock.

A smaller start-up company might be listed on Pink Sheets or in the best case on NASDAQ would have less liquidity, less analysts, and no dedicated market-maker.

To assess the contribution of each factor to the probability of classifying a stock as inefficient Barber et al. [233] employed a binary logit model as follows:

$$Y_i = \alpha + \beta_1 V_i + \beta_2 MM_i + \beta_3 SZ_i + \beta_4 BA_i$$
$$+ \beta_5 \sigma(r_{it}) + \beta_6 P_i + \beta_7 AN_i + \beta_8 NI_i + \epsilon_i \tag{1}$$

where $Y_i$ is a variable for the firm $i$ equal to 1 if the firm's stock is inefficient and otherwise, $\alpha$ and $\beta_1, \beta_2, \ldots$ are the regression coefficients for the factors $V_i$, volume, $MM_i$ market makers, $SZ_i$ size $BA_i$, bid ask spread, $\sigma(r_{it})$ volatility, $P_i$ price, $AN_i$ number of analysts, and $NI_i$ number of institutional investors. The study showed for a data set from the 1980s that volumes and number of analysts are the main drivers of efficiency.

## 5 SETTLEMENT: A QUEST FOR EFFICIENCY

The above analysis proposed by Barber et al. [233] offers a robust framework for distinguishing efficiency from inefficiency. However, in many litigation cases, this analysis is difficult to use as evidence due to its complexity and the fact that a stock should be benchmarked with other stocks. Out the 3898 securities litigation cases registered with the Stanford Securities Action Clearinghouse, 2019 have been settled for a total amount of $88 billion representing almost 1% of the total NASDAQ capitalization (2014 figures). Many of the defendants' lawyers noted that role of the fraud on market theory has facilitated the multi-billion dollars settlements for more than 25 years.[4]

In the aftermath of the Basic case in 1998 the theory was contested by many people at that time, and since then the morphology of the market has changed with few crises that impacted the markets, mainly the 2000 technology bubble and the 2008 financial crisis. Figure 3 shows the evolution of the number of litigations registered by the Stanford Clearinghouse, which shows a peak in the number of cases in 2000 when the Internet bubble exploded.

From a defendant perspective, FOMT enables securities class litigations to proceed without clear proof of actual reliance on alleged misrepresentation or omission. The defendant needs to bring proof that rebuts the presumption of reliance. Furthermore, addressing the fraud on the market theory is almost impossible. Market prices are very rarely (never) in line with the fundamental value and oscillate in the best cases around it. In addition to this point, all the market efficiency tests (for the weak form) would most likely reject the efficiency assumption on a period around the securities class period. But the efficiency is not a criteria that can separate fraud from normal securities. In the case of Halliburton discussed above, the tests for efficiency and density forecasting signaled inefficiency during the class period, and even in post class periods.

If we used an efficiency statistic like the Lo and MacKinlay [24] or Chow and Denning [25] statistics as an indicator for fraudulent securities the results would be surprising.

Figure 4 (left) shows the results of efficiency tests for a sample of 480 litigated NASDAQ stocks performed before and during the misrepresentation period. The difference between the Chow-Denning [25][5] statistics measured in a window during the "abnormal" period and in

[4]Supreme Court Leaves Fraud On Market Intact, Makes Life A Bit Harder For Securities Plaintiffs, http://www.

forbes.com/sites/danielfisher/2014/06/23/supreme-court-leaves-fraud-on-market-intact-but-makes-life-harder-for-securities-plaintiffs/#.
[5]NB. Here the test statistic is used from the Fischer perspective as an indicator to assess the level of efficiency rejection.

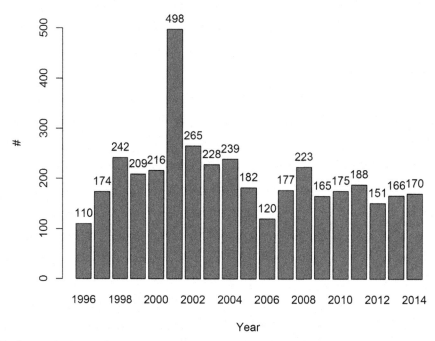

FIGURE 3    Evolution of securities litigation cases between 1996 and 2014. *Source: http://securities.stanford.edu/.*

a separate window before the class period was centered at zero. There was no relevant signal of inefficiency of the stock due to the class action.

In addition, the same statistic was measured for normal (nonlitigated) NASDAQ stocks during the same of time period. The higher the score the more inefficient the stock. The Gini coefficient of the statistics as an indicator for fraud is near zero as shown in Figure 4 (right).

An analogy with the oil market underlines this point. The extraction cost of physical oil varies from 1$ per barrel in Saudi Arabia and up to $30 in the northern hemisphere, but the Brent price was for many years way above $100. If oil futures were a stock they would surely not avoid class action suit.

## 6 OUTLOOK

Proving violation in market efficiency as a result of fraud is far from being an obvious task. The nature of financial markets is far from being fully understood and the main theories from 1970 by Black and Scholes [234] and Fama [45] still constitute the foundations of modern finance. These theories, built around the market efficiency hypothesis and the assumptions of nonarbitrage opportunities, are not agreed upon unanimously in the scientific community. Thus, assessing the fraud on the market only from external observations as market signals (i.e., price, volume, volatility) would fail to provide with relevant information.

The current legal framework is asymmetric in the sense that the fraud on the market theory incriminates fraud only when economic loss occurs from relying on misrepresentation. Goldberg and Zipursky [235] explained that there is no deceit when a misrepresentation negatively affects a losing transaction but the plaintiff never actually relied on its substance. This kind of plaintiff cannot complain of being manipulated in the requisite sense.

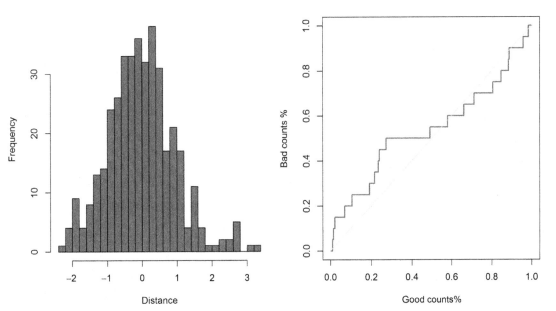

**FIGURE 4** Efficiency tests (left) for a sample of 480 litigated NASDAQ stocks performed before and during the misrepresentation period. The difference between the Chow-Denning statistics measured in a window during the "abnormal" period and in a separate window before the class period was centered at zero. There was no relevant signal of inefficiency of the stock due to the class action. Gini coefficient (right) for litigated vs. nonlitigated firm depending on the Chow-Denning statistic, used as classification score. The higher the score the more inefficient the stock [25]. *NB. Here the test statistic is used from Fischer perspective as an indicator to assess the level of efficiency rejection.*

There are many points that make the current FOMT framework debatable, but new developments in the financial markets might push the Court to reconsider the *Basic vs. Levinson* presumption.

Rule l0b-5 was also used in the recent ongoing case of *Providence vs. Bats Global Markets, Inc.*, related to high-frequency trading. In this case, the manipulation allegedly took place in infinitesimal intervals of time. Reliance of the price signal conditioned by the efficient hypothesis needs to be reassessed entirely. Rescaling the fraud on the market theory to millisecond intervals of time would imply that the reliance needs to be proved statistically based on the history of order and trades, thereby possibly leading to reopening the debate around the *Basic vs. Levinson* rule.

# Efficient Market Hypothesis Testing

## 1 BACKGROUND

Two hundred years ago in June 2015 Europe's and the world's destiny was decided on the hills of Waterloo, in Belgium when Napoleon's *Grande Armée* was defeated by the British army. At the very same time Nathan Meyer de Rothschild, one of the forefathers of the Rothschild banking empire, was making profits on the London securities exchanges using the fact that he knew about *Eagle's* defeat a few days before the rest of the public. This legendary episode in modern history showed that a heterogeneous spread of information among players in market can create asymmetry in terms of the price discovery process. In the early 1970s Fama [45] introduced the concept of an efficient market defined as follows:

A market in which prices always fully reflect available information is called efficient.

In an efficient market the price is an unbiased estimate of the true (fair) value of the security, and the evolution of the price oscillates around the true value going above and below the value,

the deviations behaving like a random variable. Fama [45] classified efficiency as in the following types:

- **Weak efficiency**: Based on the information set of the historic history of prices, the current price should reflect the information contained in all past prices, and all prediction methods using technical analyses should not be able to generate profits in the long term.
- **Semi-strong efficiency**: All publicly available information known to all investors including the past prices and reflected in the current price and approaches based on using new information (earnings, business news) should not be able to peak the mispriced stocks.
- **Strong efficiency**: Both public and nonpublic information known by investors are reflected in the current price.

The efficiency of a market relies broadly speaking on the fact that each investor adjusts their transactions rationally, the market does aggregate information in an efficient manner, and the equilibrium prices reflect all available information instantaneously.

## 2 STATISTICAL TESTS

The idea behind the statistical tests for assessing market efficiency (more precisely the weak form of efficiency) is that the more efficient a market of a security is, the more randomness there is in the time series of price variations. The perfect market in terms of efficiency is one in which price changes are random and also unpredictable, but not too random, as extreme variations in prices is not a sign of efficient price discovery. Further, in an ideal efficient market the current price is the best estimate of the price that can occur in the future, with the prices following martingales. There is an enormous amount of literature proposing various tests for market efficiency developed around the concept of random walk. A few of these tests are discussed here including the Lo and MacKinlay, Portmanteau, and Wright tests.

The variance-ratio test introduced by Lo and MacKinlay [24] assesses if stock prices follow random walks by using a simple specification test based on variance estimators.

If $P_t$ is the price of the assets at moment $t$ and $y_t = \log(P_t)$ is the price logarithm (with any dividends reinvested) then 1-day returns are $r_t = y_t - y_{t-1}$. Also, assuming the returns process is stationary, the variance of the return over $k$ day is $V(k) = \text{Var}(r_t + \cdots + r_{t+k-1})$. The Lo and MacKinlay test attempts to determine if the variance increases linearly with the time horizon with the null hypothesis $H_0$ assuming that:

$$\text{VR}(k) = \frac{\text{Var}(r_t + \cdots + r_{t+k-1})/k}{\text{Var}(r_t)} = 1 \quad (1)$$

The basic Lo and MacKinlay statistic is:

$$S_1(k) = \sqrt{(T)} \frac{(\widehat{\text{VR}}(k) - 1)}{\sqrt{2(2k-1)(k-1)/3k}} \to N(0,1) \quad (2)$$

with the following notations:

$$\widehat{\text{VR}}(k) = \frac{\hat{\sigma}(k)}{\sigma(1)}$$

$$\hat{\sigma}(k) = \frac{1}{k(T-k+1)(1-k/T)}$$
$$\times \sum_{t=k}^{T}(r_t + r_{t-1} + \cdots + r_{t-k+1} - k\mu)$$

$$\mu = \frac{1}{T}\sum_{t=1}^{T} r_t$$

When the series exhibit heteroscedasticity, the adjusted Lo and MacKinlay test becomes:

$$S_1(k) = \sqrt{T} \frac{(\widehat{\text{VR}}(k) - 1)}{\sqrt{\sum_{j=1}^{k-1} T \left(\frac{k-j}{0.5k}\right)^2 \frac{\sum_{t=j+1}^{T}(r_t-\mu)^2(r_{t-j}-\mu)^2}{\left(\sum_{t=1}^{T}(r_t-\mu)^2\right)^2}}}$$
$$\to N(0,1) \quad (3)$$

Both statistics tend asymptotically toward normal distribution.

Chow and Denning [25] test generalized the Lo and MacKinlay statistics for testing individual variance ratios. For a given value $k$ a more powerful approach is a comparison of all selected variance ratios with unity. Therefore, the revised null hypothesis is $H_0$: $\text{VR}(k_i) = 1 \; \forall \, i = 1, 2, \ldots, m$. and the corresbreak pondent statistics is:

$$S_1^*(m) = \underset{1 \leq i \leq m}{\max} |S_1(k_i)| \quad (4)$$

$$S_2^*(m) = \underset{1 \leq i \leq m}{\max} |S_2(k_i)| \quad (5)$$

Wright's [26] alternative nonparametric test using signs and ranks is complementary to Lo's test using signs and ranks of differences in place of the differences in the Lo and MacKinlay tests. Two pairs of statistics for signs ($R_1$ and $R_2$) and ranks ($S_1$ and $S_2$) are used for testing the hypothesis of random walk:

$$r_{1,t} = \frac{(K(r_t) - 0.5(T+1))}{\sqrt{(T^2-1)/12}}$$

$$r_{2,t} = \Phi^{-1}\left(\frac{K(r_t)}{T+1}\right)$$

where $K(r_t)$ is the rank of $r_t$ among $r_1, r_2, \ldots, r_T$ and $\Phi$ is the cumulative distribution function.

Wright's rank statistics $R_1$ and $R_2$ are defined as:

$$R_1(k) = \frac{T_k^{-1} \sum_{t=k}^{T} \sum_{j=1}^{k} r_{1,t-j+1}}{T^{-1} \sum_{t=k}^{T} r_{1,t}^2}$$
$$\cdot \sqrt{(2(2k-1)(k-1)/3kT} \qquad (6)$$

$$R_2(k) = \frac{T_k^{-1} \sum_{t=k}^{T} \sum_{j=1}^{k} r_{2,t-j+1}}{T^{-1} \sum_{t=k}^{T} r_{2,t}^2}$$
$$\cdot \sqrt{(2(2k-1)(k-1)/3kT} \qquad (7)$$

With the notation of the function $s_t = 2u(r_t, 0)$, $s_t(\mu) = 2u(r_t, \mu)$ with:

$$u(x,h) = \begin{cases} 0.5 & x > h \\ -0.5 & x \le h \end{cases} \qquad (8)$$

Wright's sign statistics $R_1$ and $R_2$ are defined as:

$$S_1(k) = \frac{T_k^{-1} \sum_{t=k}^{T} \sum_{j=1}^{k} s_{t-j+1}(r_t, 0)}{T^{-1} \sum_{t=k}^{T} s_t^2(r_t, 0)}$$
$$\cdot \sqrt{(2(2k-1)(k-1)/3kT} \qquad (9)$$

$$S_2(k) = \frac{T_k^{-1} \sum_{t=k}^{T} \sum_{j=1}^{k} s_{t-j+1}(r_t, \mu)}{T^{-1} \sum_{t=k}^{T} s_t^2(r_t, \mu)}$$
$$\cdot \sqrt{(2(2k-1)(k-1)/3kT} \qquad (10)$$

The Richardson and Smith [27] version of the Wald and Portmanteau tests from Escanciano and Lobato [28] for autocorrelation are complementary in the search for efficiency.

## ARENA PHARMACEUTICALS

### Background

Arena Pharmaceuticals[a] listed on the NASDAQ as "ARNA" is a clinical-stage biopharmaceutical company focused on oral drugs including the weight loss drug Lorcaserin. During the class period the company allegedly made false and misleading statements and failed to disclose the tests for Lorcaserin that indicated that the drug caused cancer in lab rats. When the results were made public, the Arena stock fell from a closing price of $6.85 on September 13, 2010 to $1.75 4 days later, when FDA's advisory committee rejected the drug.

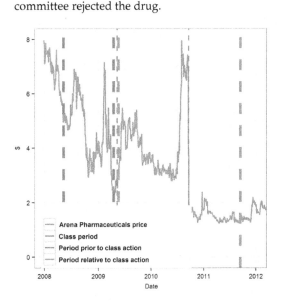

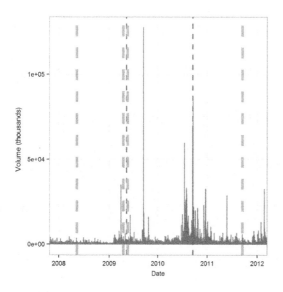

*Efficiency test*

Arena is a rare example of the statistical tests rejecting the efficiency during the period related to the class action suit and failing to reject it for the period prior to the class action. The Lo and MacKinlay ($S_1$), Chow and Denning ($S_1^*$), and Wald tests are able to differentiate between the efficiency of the two periods as reflected in the table below

| Statistic test | Period relative to class action | Period before the class action | Critical value |
|---|---|---|---|
| Chow and Denning ($S_1^*$) | 3.41 | 0.04 | 1.95 |
| Chow and Denning ($S_2^*$) | 1.61 | 0.04 | 1.95 |
| Lo and MacKinlay ($S_1$) | 3.41 | −0.04 | 1.95 |
| Lo and MacKinlay ($S_2$) | 1.61 | −0.04 | 1.95 |
| Wright $R_1$ | −0.95 | 0.80 | 1.99 |
| Wright $R_2$ | −0.95 | 0.80 | 1.99 |
| Portmanteau | 0.67 | 0.00 | 3.8 |
| Wald | 11.60 | 0.00 | 3.84 |

[a]Schueneman vs. Arena, http://securities.stanford.edu/filings-documents/1045/ARNA10_01/2010921_f01c_1001959.pdf.

As discussed further in the chapter dedicated to fraud on the market theory efficiency tests cannot assess independently if the efficiency necessarily points to fraud or other deceitful actions of the firm or other investors. The decision of the Supreme Court in relation to the *Halliburton vs. Fund case*, granting the defendants the right to show that their action did not inflict price variation could bring new meaning to efficiency tests.

## 3 TESTING BUBBLES

After the South Sea Company frenzy in the early eighteenth century, financial markets faced many bubbles and as many crashes, Black Tuesday in 1929 being one of the most dramatic examples.

Penny stock scams, microcap fraud, and pump-and-dump schemes have things in common with a "bubble" phenomenon, as in all these cases the price of a security is inflated far beyond its fundamental "fair value," and this inflation is accelerated by other investors that buy the security thereby boosting the exponential rise of price. The common points of manipulation and bubbles are also mentioned in the literature. Zhao [236] studied the unusual and puzzling stock price performance of USEC Inc., a company specializing in producing enriched uranium for nuclear plants. In July 2013 the stock price surged as much as 10 times during merely 16 trading days without apparent value-changing information being released.

Geng and Lu [237] studied bubble-creating stock attacks, an interesting form of market fraud, which is a mixture of manipulation and speculative bubbles in which speculators implicitly coordinate to pump up the stock price without any significant fundamental news and exploit behavioral-biased investors. The research provided empirical evidence in the Chinese stock market showing that stocks with low mutual fund ownership and stocks with high average purchase costs of existing shareholders are more likely to be attacked.

A few straightforward methods for testing a market for bubbles have been proposed by the recent works of Phillips et al. [31, 238]. These approaches include enhanced versions of the augmented Dickey-Fuller (ADF) test [239, 240]: Sup ADF test and generalized Sup-ADF test.

The testing procedure for the augmented Dickey-Fuller test for a unit root in time series is based on the model:

$$y_t = \alpha + \beta y_{t-1} + \gamma_1 \Delta y_{t-1} + \cdots + \gamma_p \Delta y_{t-p} + \varepsilon_t \quad (11)$$

where $p$ is the lag order and $\varepsilon_t \propto N(0, \sigma_t)$.

Phillips et al. [31] improved the basic version of the ADF test with a recursive approach that involved a rolling window ADF-style regression implementation. If the rolling window regression sample starts from the $r_1$th fraction of the total sample and ends at the $r_2$th fraction of the sample, where $r_2 = r_1 + r_w$ and $r_w$ is the fractional window size of the regression, the empirical regression model can then be written as:

$$y_t = \alpha_{r_1,r_2} + \beta_{r_1,r_2} y_{t-1}$$
$$+ \gamma_{r_1,r_2}^1 \Delta y_{t-1} + \cdots + \gamma_{r_1,r_2}^p \Delta y_{t-p} + \varepsilon_t \quad (12)$$

where $\alpha_{r_1,r_2}$ is the intercept, $\beta_{r_1,r_2}$ the coefficient on a time trend, and $p$ is the lag order of the autoregressive process computed on the window $r_1 T, r_2 T$. In these circumstances the unit root null hypothesis is $H_0: \beta = 1$ and the explosive root right-tailed alternative hypothesis is $H_a: \beta > 1$. The ADF statistic (based on this regression) is

denoted by $ADF_{r_1}^{r_2}$ from [238], where $ADF_0^1$ is the ADF statistics for the full sample. The right-sided unit root tests are informative about the explosive or submartingale behavior[1] in the time series and can be used for speculative bubble detection.

# AEGERION PHARMACEUTICAL

## Background

Aegerion Pharmaceuticals is a biopharmaceutical company founded in 2005 and listed on NASDAQ; it is engaged in the development and commercialization of novel therapeutics to treat debilitating and fatal rare diseases. Its main product is Juxtapid capsules, an adjunct to a low-fat diet and other lipid-lowering treatments.

## Class action

According to an ongoing class action suit Aegerion[a] allegedly made false and/or misleading statements, and failed to disclose material adverse facts about marketing its drugs in violation of the Food and Drug Administration (FDA). The increase of the stock started in early 2013 when the new drugs were announced. On November 8, 2013, news reports revealed that the company received an FDA warning letter about the fact that the new drug Juxtapid was misbranded and its distribution violated the law.

## Bubble testing

The two procedures Sup-ADF and GSADF that were applied to the Aegerion stock confirmed that a bubble occurred during the class action period between May and November 2013.

---

[1]It should be recalled that a discrete-time submartingale is a price time series $y_1, y_2, y_3, \ldots$ satisfying $E[y_{n+1}|\Phi_n] \geq y_n$, $\Phi_n$ being the filtration with all the information at the moment when the price is $y_n$.

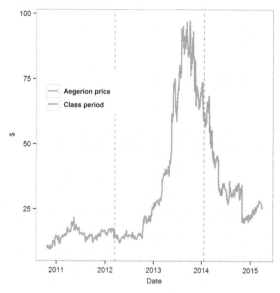

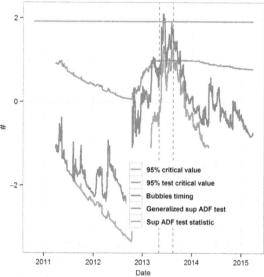

The Sup-ADF test introduced [238] for single-bubble detection searches for the maximum value of the test for all forward-looking windows on a given sample. The window size $r_w$ varies from the smallest sample window noted as $r_0$ to 1. In terms of the formalism in Equation 12 the starting point $r_1$ is 0 and the end point $r_2$ is chosen such that the statistic $\text{ADF}_0^{r_2}$ is maximized, which can be written as:

$$\text{SADF}(r_0) = \underbrace{\sup}_{r_2 \in [r_0, 1]} \text{ADF}_0^{r_2} \qquad (13)$$

A further improvement of the Sup-ADF test is the generalized Sup-ADF (GSADF), which leverages the idea of repeatedly running the ADF test regression on subsamples of the data in a recursive fashion. Thus, in addition to varying the end point of the regression $r_2$ from $r_0$ to 1, the GSADF test allows the starting point $r_1$ to change 0 to $r_2 - r_0$. The GSADF statistic searches for the biggest ADF statistic over all possible starting points and possible window length:

$$\text{GSADF}(r_0) = \underbrace{\sup}_{r_2 \in [r_0, 1], r_1 \in [0, r_2 - r_0]} \text{ADF}_{r_1}^{r_2} \qquad (14)$$

Figure 1 shows the application of the two tests for the case of an ongoing security litigation case involving Galena Biopharma, which allegedly misrepresented a few facts relating to its activity, thereby inflating the price of its stock.[2] Both tests confirmed the presence of a bubble during the alleged class period.

## 4 OUTLOOK

The most fundamental principle of all in gambling is simply equal conditions, e.g., of opponents, of bystanders, of money, of situation, of the dice box, and

On January 10, 2014, the company received a subpoena from the U.S. Department of Justice requesting documents regarding its marketing and sale of Juxtapid. Aegerion shares then dropped to $7.98 per share.

[a]Bodner vs. Aegerion Pharmaceuticals, http://securities.stanford.edu/filings-documents/1051/AEGR00_01/2014115_f01c_14CV10105.pdf.

[2]Michael E. Deering et al. vs. Galena Biopharma, Inc., et al., http://securities.stanford.edu/filings-case.html?id=105188.

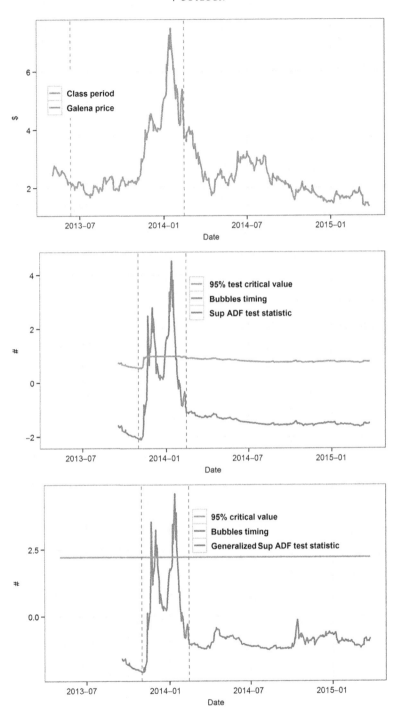

**FIGURE 1** Galena Biopharma bubble. The first graph shows the evolution of the stock price, the second the Sup-ADF test and the last graph GSADF test. Both tests confirm the presence of a bubble during the alleged class period.

of the die itself. To the extent to which you depart from that equality, if it is in your opponents favor, you are a fool, and if in your own, you are unjust. *Girolamo Cardano, Liber De Ludo Aleae (Book on Games of Chance) [241].*

Having fair conditions and homogeneous information for all players of a financial markets is only a prerequisite for achieving efficiency in price discovery in financial markets. Even in an ideal case when traders and investors have the same information about the *"dice box,"* there are many other factors that bring inequality and favor one or another player. First is access to liquidity, as a small number of investors are able to inject a significant amount of funds into a very short time in a market. Second is the structural role in a market of a player; many small investors tend to follow the actions of a bigger or more reputed investor. Also, a large number of small investors can synchronize their actions in order to distort the price signal and thereby create a mini-bubble; this action can appear as a natural evolution to other players.

The business culture also plays a role that is becoming increasingly crucial as markets become more globalized. The theory of efficient market hypothesis is often studied and probably was developed in the spirit of markets from developed countries, like the United States, which has one of the most transparent economies. However, in some emergent economies from the Far East, business is less transparent, with many listed companies in those countries disclosing less information than their European or North American peers.

Testing for market efficiency brings without doubt value in assessing the price discovery process, but its use on a standalone basis as evidence in securities fraud cases should be handled cautiously.

# Market Prices and Trading Activity

## 1 BACKGROUND

Financial models assume that prices follow stochastic processes and all trades, whether they are spot or derivatives, can be settled using that reference price and without changing the mechanics of the price dynamics. This hypothesis holds true in very efficient markets where the trading volume is homogeneously spread among a large number of traders. When markets dry in liquidity or large traders exist this assumption might be violated and the marginal contribution of a trader to a market's volume can be significant. Further, the diversity of liquidity-providing infrastructures as well as of the products traded raise new efficiency issues and justify market-impact models in which trading activity influences price.

Fraud on the financial market and more exactly market manipulation challenges this framework at another level and requires a change of paradigm. Market efficiency is perceived as a positive feature from a fraud on the market theory perspective, and a market integrating new information quickly would be seen as a safer than a *slower* market. If in many situations this holds true, in other ways of life a manipulator can use a very efficient market to give a signal through a set of trades to influence the price and then take advantage by reversing those trades.

Both situations with liquid and illiquid markets can present opportunities for manipulators based on the impact a trade can have on the global equilibrium of the market. In a seminal paper, Almgren and Chriss [242] proposed a widely used approach for modeling the costs arising from permanent and temporary market impacts following the execution of a portfolio of transactions.

The model aims to assess the impact of trading block of $X$ units of a security over a period of time $T$. The time horizon $T$ is divided into $N$ intervals of length $\tau = T/N$. The size of the portfolio held at moments $t_0, \ldots, t_N$ is $x_0 = X, \ldots, x_N$ and the number of units sold on the market is $n_1, \ldots, n_N$, where $n_k = x_k - x_{k-1}$, for $k \in \{1, \ldots, N\}$.

Assuming the initial price at moment $t_0$ price is $S_0$ and the initial value of the holdings is $X \cdot S_0$ the execution price evolves according to the interaction between the market and the trading blocks. Almgren and Chriss [242] introduced two kinds of market impacts:

- a *temporary impact* concerning the change in price caused the point in time asymmetry in supply and demand due to the execution of the portfolio activity.
- a *permanent impact* concerning a long-term effect of the trading activity over the price level.

The permanent impact on the price is described by the following equation:

$$S_k = S_{k-1} + \sigma \tau^{1/2} \xi_k - \tau g \left( \frac{n_k}{\tau} \right) \qquad (1)$$

where $\sigma$ represents the volatility of the asset and $\xi_k$ is a Brownian motion following a normal distribution $N(0, 1)$. The function $g(\bullet)$ reflects the permanent impact of the trading volumes on the price.

The temporary price impact is modeled though function $h(\bullet)$, reflecting the point in time change in price caused by a certain level of trading intensity: $n_k / \tau$. The temporary impact on the price is:

$$\bar{S}_k = S_{k-1} - h \left( \frac{n_k}{\tau} \right) \qquad (2)$$

The sum of the temporary and permanent impact on price can be found as follows:

$$\bar{S}_k = S_{k-1} + \sigma \tau^{1/2} \xi_k - \tau g \left( \frac{n_k}{\tau} \right) - h \left( \frac{n_k}{\tau} \right) \qquad (3)$$

With these notations the difference between the initial value of the holding and the value at which the full portfolio is executed constitutes the total cost of trading (CT):

$$CT = X \cdot S_0 - \sum_{k=1}^{N} n_k \cdot \bar{S}_k$$

$$= \sum_{k=1}^{N} \left( \underbrace{\tau g \left( \frac{n_k}{\tau} \right)}_{\text{Permanent impact}} - \underbrace{\sigma \sqrt{(\tau)} \xi_k}_{\text{Volatility impact}} \right) x_k$$

$$+ \underbrace{\sum_{k=1}^{N} n_k h \left( \frac{n_k}{\tau} \right)}_{\text{Temporary effect}} \qquad (4)$$

The expected value of the trading cost and the variance have the following forms:

$$\mathbb{E}(CT) = \sum_{k=1}^{N} \tau x_k g \left( \frac{n_k}{\tau} \right) + \sum_{k=1}^{N} n_k h \left( \frac{n_k}{\tau} \right) \qquad (5)$$

$$\mathbb{V}(CT) = \sigma^2 \sum_{k=1}^{N} \tau x_k^2 \qquad (6)$$

## 2 HIGH-FREQUENCY TRADING FOCUS

One avenue where the market impact model is applied is in high-frequency trading (HFT). In HFT the way execution impacts the price is fundamental to building a profit-taking strategy. The permanent impact can change the price pattern and if the algorithm is designed as such it can lead to risk-free profits, or in other words, to a negative expected cost.

Going back to the formulation of the market impact model the function for permanent and temporary impact $g(\bullet)$ and $h(\bullet)$, respectively, have a linear form:

$$g \left( \frac{n_k}{\tau} \right) = \gamma \cdot \frac{n_k}{\tau} \qquad (7)$$

$$h \left( \frac{n_k}{\tau} \right) = \epsilon \, sgn(n_k) + \eta \frac{n_k}{\tau} \qquad (8)$$

where the $\gamma$ and $\eta$ are the constants for the linear function impact and $\epsilon$ is related to the bid-ask spread and transactions fees.

Extending the linear assumption for the permanent price impact the relationship between the price at moment $t_k$ and moment $t_0$ is:

$$S_k = S_0 + \sigma \sum_{j=1}^{k} \sqrt{\tau} \xi_j - \gamma(X - x_k) \qquad (9)$$

Under this model specification, the impact size parameter $\gamma$ does not change with the interval length between transactions $\tau$. High-frequency trades would thus have the same impact on the micro-structure as slower trading. The parameter $\gamma$ is estimated based on the wheat prices intra-day quotes provided by Tickdata (http://tickdata.com/) during 2011 and 2012 using the following regression[1]:

$$|(S_k - S_{k-1})/\tau| = \text{const.} + \gamma(x_k - x_{k+1})/\tau + \xi^* \qquad (10)$$

where $\xi^*$ is the residual following $N(0, \sigma^*)$.

If the trades are aggregated on various intervals for $\tau$ and the $\gamma = \gamma(\tau)$ is estimated depending on the times between execution, the results show that $\gamma$ increases with the increase of the frequency of the trades. Figure 1 depicts the results of $\gamma$ estimation for a given day in the year. For smaller intervals between trades the $\gamma$ is higher; in other words, when trades are executed quicker in a shorter window of time, the permanent effect on price increases. The level of $\gamma$ is around $10^{-7}$, which is similar to the level given in the Almgren and Chriss [242] paper.

The same conclusion comes for the standard deviation of the residuals $\sigma^*$ shown in Figure 2. The higher the frequency of trade the higher the volatility effect on prices.

Figure 3 shows the interpolated $\gamma(\tau)$ curves on different days, indicating that the shape of the curve fluctuates over time. Of major importance are those cases when the curve peaks more than usual for low latency trades.

Figure 4 shows the estimations of $\sigma^*(\tau)$ for different days. The volatility impact fluctuates more for slower latency trades.

A variation of the basic market impact model enriches the framework with a drift $\mu$ aimed at capturing a trend in prices over the time horizon of a trade execution. Going back to the wheat futures intra-day quotes the permanent effect implied by the size of the orders blocks appears consistently, but the trend is not always relevant statistically:

$$S_k = S_{k-1} + \sigma \tau^{1/2} \xi_k - \tau g\left(\frac{n_k}{\tau}\right) - h\left(\frac{n_k}{\tau}\right) + \mu \tau \qquad (11)$$

The expected cost of trading and its variance under the assumption of a trend become:

$$\mathbb{E}(CT) = \sum_{k=1}^{N} \tau x_k g\left(\frac{n_k}{\tau}\right) + \sum_{k=1}^{N} n_k h\left(\frac{n_k}{\tau}\right) - \sum_{k=1}^{N} \tau \mu x_k \qquad (12)$$

$$\mathbb{V}(CT) = \sigma^2 \sum_{k=1}^{N} \tau x_k^2 \qquad (13)$$

Through a regression procedure the $\mu$ parameter is estimated. Figure 5 shows the estimates that are statistically significant at 95%. It can be observed that the drift for low latency is stronger compared to that for longer latency, the curve $\mu(\tau)$ being a decreasing function.

The data-mining analysis for assessing the market impact in the intra-day universe of the wheat Chicago Board of Trade (CBOT) prices notes two findings:

- The permanent effect of transactions on price increases for lower latency, underlining the potential effect of high-frequency trading on prices.
- When a trends in prices occurs, it tend to be stronger for higher frequency.

---

[1]The model assumption that the orders occur at equal length intervals is relaxed and the interval $\tau$, is estimated from the actual difference in the timestamps $\tau_1, \ldots, \tau_N$.

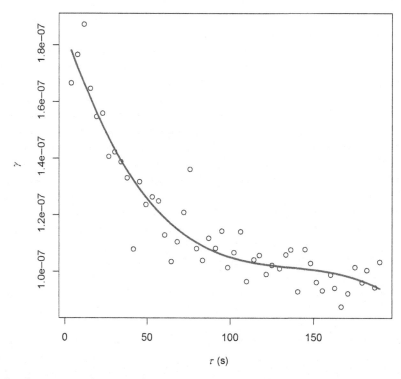

**FIGURE 1** Results of $\gamma$ estimation for a given day in the year. For a smaller interval between trades the $\gamma$ is higher; in other words, when trades are executed quicker in a shorter window of time, the permanent effect on price increases. The red curve (dark gray in print versions) represents the interpolation of the $\gamma$ estimates.

In regards to manipulation a wide panel of techniques, presented in a previous chapter, are employed in the HFT universe. Regulators and exchanges are in a continuously try effort to curtail the activity of trading firms to determine whether they are involved in illegal activity. The model impact framework can constitute a starting point in monitoring the activity of a market and provide a set of indicators of market normality or predatory behavior.

The cost of trading given in Equation 12 becomes strictly negative if a manipulation occurs. Therefore, a statistical test can be implemented with the following specifications:

- $H_0$ No manipulation occurs $\mathbb{E}(CT) \geq 0$
- $H_a$ Manipulation occurs $\mathbb{E}(CT) < 0$

Under the null $\mathbb{E}(CT)/\sqrt{(\mathbb{V}(CT))} \rightarrow N(0,1)$, and the null is rejected if the statistics $\mathbb{E}(CT)/\sqrt{(\mathbb{V}(CT))}$ fall below the value that corresponds to a confidence interval level.

## 3 DARK POOLS

Today traders have many avenues to execute orders including providers of dark liquidity: the dark pools. Dark pools are designed for big institutional investors willing to protect themselves when executing big trades. The risk of passing a large order over a public exchange is when other traders try to benefit from the information that such a big order is executed [243].

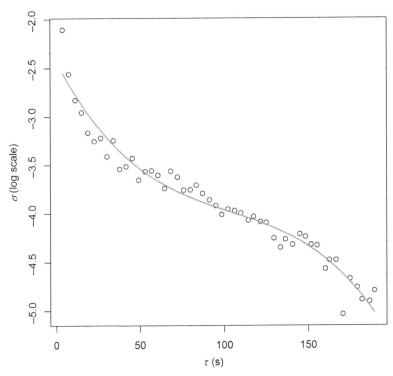

**FIGURE 2** Standard deviation of the residuals $\sigma^*$. The higher the frequency of trade the higher the volatility effect is on prices. The green curve (dark gray in print versions) represents the interpolation of the $\sigma^*$ estimates.

Market manipulation in dark pools was described as early as 2008 by Mittal [243] under the name of *"fishing"* which is a specific action whereby a manipulator sends a series of small orders to a dark pool to detect whether a large order is waiting for execution. Dark pools activity is generated mainly institutional liquidity with large orders. When the bait represented by those small orders is executed, this does reflect in theory that at the other end there is a big positions waiting for execution. Assuming the manipulator is looking for big buyers for a stock, the bait in the dark pool would be small sell orders. If the bait sends a positive signal to the manipulator he does the following [243]:

- He will buy the stock rapidly in the screen-based market in order to pump up the stock price.

- Dark pool transactions are usually executed at the midpoint of the displayed markets. If the manipulator succeeded in pumping up the price he will send a large sells order to the dark pool and sells at a higher price.
- The manipulator cuts his position on the exchange and prices fall to their fundamental level.

The market impact model in the presence of a parallel dark pool transaction is enriched with the block volume relative to the dark pool transaction $Z_{DP}$, which generates a gain $Z_{DP} * (S_N - S_0)$ when $S_N > S_0$ [244]. The scheme is illegal if this gain comes from the pumping of the market through a set of exchanged-based orders $n_1, \ldots, n_N$. The total expected cost of trading of both exchanged-based and dark pool transactions is:

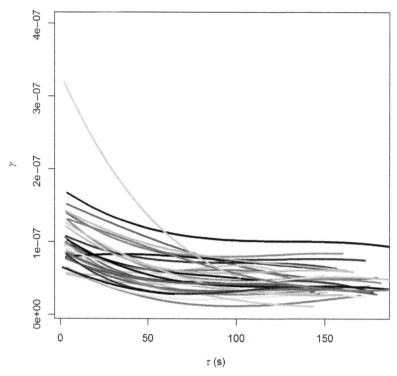

**FIGURE 3**   Estimation of $\gamma$ curves for different intervals $\tau$ on different days, indicating that the shape of the curve $\gamma(\tau)$ fluctuates over time. Of major importance are those cases when the curve peaks more than usual for low latency trades.

$\mathbb{E}(\text{CTDP})$

$$= \underbrace{\sum_{k=1}^{N} \tau x_k g\left(\frac{n_k}{\tau}\right) + \sum_{k=1}^{N} n_k h\left(\frac{n_k}{\tau}\right) - \sum_{k=1}^{N} \tau \mu x_k}_{\text{Manipulation cost}}$$

$$- \underbrace{(Z_{\text{DP}} * (S_N - S_0))}_{\text{Dark pool gain}} \qquad (14)$$

When $\mathbb{E}(\text{CTDP}) < 0$ the manipulation results in profit and the manipulator should compute *a priori* how much he should buy and at what price in order to move the market high enough to make a big profit from the large trade. The higher the $\gamma$ of the permanent impact the easier for the manipulator to pump the prices. He should also be sure that $\mu$ is non-negative to avoid fishing against the stream.

It is easy to see that the *fishing* is a key step for fruitful manipulation. Indeed, if the size of the trade cleared through the dark pool is not big enough the manipulator might end up with a loss, as the cost of moving the exchange price might be lower than the gain on the dark pool. The crucial point is to determine if the "fish" is big enough.

The dark pool example raises many questions around the role of efficiency. The fact that the dark pool and the exchange are individually efficient allows the manipulator to deploy the strategy. The information flow was efficient on the dark pool in the initial phase of the fishing. This allowed to the manipulator to have an advantage when trading at a loss on the exchange. The fact that the price signal reacts on the exchange following an increase in demand based on *dark info*

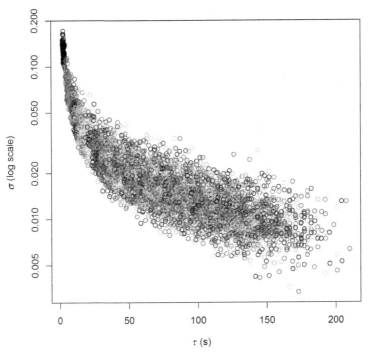

**FIGURE 4** Estimations of $\sigma^*(\tau)$ for different days. The volatility impact fluctuates more for slower latency trades.

is also an efficiency feature that facilitates a scam. In conclusion, if two trading infrastructures are efficient markets it's possible their sum might not be efficient.

# 4 MANIPULATION OPPORTUNITIES IN OVER-THE-COUNTER MARKETS

The literature explains in detail how a derivative market with a cash settlement can be manipulated or used as a manipulation tool for pumping the price of a stock [245]. There are also relevant studies about the manipulation of a derivative when the underlying stock is illiquid [246].

Another case of derivatives manipulation concerns over-the-counter (OTC) transactions, where there is no market for a derivative, which is generally an exotic derivative. In the absence of a new market the price is established through the controversial "mark-to model," the parameters being obtained from another derivative market that in most cases trades on thin liquidity.

Let's assume $V_t$ is the observed market price of a derivative of payoff $\Theta_T(S_t)$ at moment $t$, where $S_t$ is the price of the stock. The classic valuation is:

$$V_t = \mathbb{E}_Q(e^{-r(T-t)}\Theta_T(S_t)) = \mathbf{F}(S_t, \theta_t) \qquad (15)$$

where $\theta$ is a set of parameters as the volatilities or correlations used for the valuation of the contingency.

Let's assume also an OTC product with a payoff $\Xi_T(S_t^i, \theta_t)$ requiring the values of the parameters $\theta$ for its valuation.

Being traded on a thin liquidity market the risk neutral measure $\mathbf{Q}$ is not unique and also difficult to assess. Thus, the market value $V_t$ is based on the propensity of a trader to buy or sell in a certain range of prices, which leads most likely to class $\mathbf{B}$ of measures. This generates

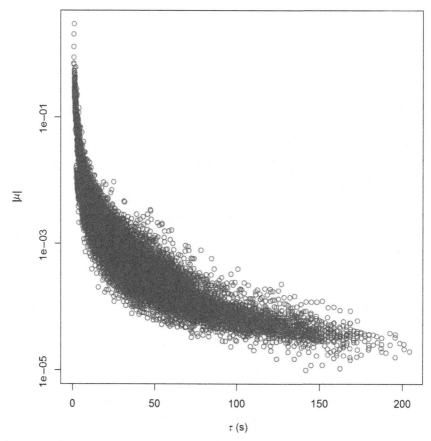

**FIGURE 5** $\mu$ estimates are statistically significant at 95%. It can be observed that the drift for low latency is stronger compared to that for longer latency, the curve $\mu(\tau)$ being a decreasing function.

a high and low value of the derivative, the observed price being in this range. Furthermore, the market implied value of parameters $\theta_t$ is in the range $\theta_t^l, \theta_t^u$:

$$V_t = \mathbb{E}_B(e^{-r(T-t)}\Theta_T(S_t))$$

$$= \mathbf{F}(S_t, \theta_t)) \in \left[\mathbf{F}(S_t, \theta_t^l), \mathbf{F}(S_t, \theta_t^h)\right] \quad (16)$$

Based on the market prices of derivatives the trader derives the market implied parameter $\theta_t^m$, which would correspond to the observed price $V_t^*$ computed as:

$$\theta_t^m = \mathbf{F}^{-1}(V_t^*) \quad (17)$$

With this parameter $\theta_t^m$ the OTC product with a payoff $\Xi_T(S_t^i, \theta_t))$ is valuated.

The market impact model applied to the price of the traded derivative $V_t$ can be written as:

$$V_k = V_{k-1} + \zeta \tau^{1/2}\xi_k - \tau g\left(\frac{n_k}{\tau}\right) \quad (18)$$

where $\zeta$ is the volatility of the derivative price, $\xi_k$ follows $N(0,1)$, $n_k$ are the blocks of derivative traded at interval $\tau$, and $g(\bullet)$ is the function describing the permanent market impact.

Extending this model to the value of the parameters $\theta$ its market impact dynamic can be expressed as:

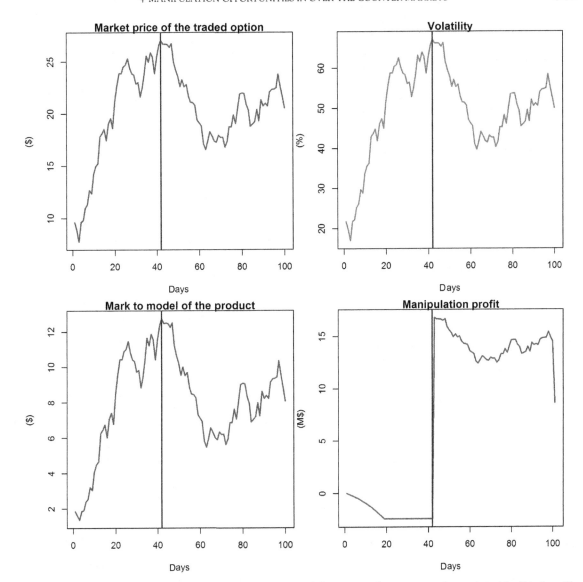

FIGURE 6   Manipulation of Mark to Model. The underwriter of the structured note pumps the market of the listed vanilla option until the moment the OTC derivative touches the trigger value for which the structured note becomes acceptable for the client. The underwriter keeps buying option and pumps the implied volatility until the mark to model of the barrier call reaches a peak value. At that point the structured note is sold and the commissions are paid by the client. Without support in the vanilla price the volatility goes back to its fundamental value.

$$\theta_k = \theta_{k-1} + \mathbf{F}^{-1}\left(\zeta\tau^{1/2}\xi_k - \tau g\left(\frac{n_k}{\tau}\right)\right) \qquad (19)$$

Thus, the parameters $\theta$ used to price the OTC product would depend on the permanent impact of the volume of derivatives traded. This impact is higher as the market is less liquid. Hence, when a bank wants to sell an OTC product,[2] it can pump up the price on the derivatives that generate the parameter $\theta$ in order to inflate the mark-to model of the OTC product.

For example, the underwriter of a structured note containing interest rate exotic options aiming to arbitrate the forward curve rate would have an incentive to trade intensively in the long tenors swaption market to drive the implied volatilities up, thereby making the structured note more valuable at underwriting.

The economy of a cost of trading assuming derivatives manipulation is expressed as:

$$\mathbb{E}(\text{CTM}) = \underbrace{\sum_{k=1}^{N}\tau x_k g(\frac{n_k}{\tau})}_{\text{Trade cost manipulation}}$$

$$- \underbrace{(\Theta_T^i(S_t^i, \theta_k) - \Theta_T^i(S_t^i, \theta_0))}_{\text{OTC manipulation gain}} \qquad (20)$$

A manipulation becomes possible ($\mathbb{E}(\text{CTM}) < 0$) when the gain from the OTC product in higher than the cost of pumping up the price of the listed derivative. To illustrate this type of manipulation let's assume a case for which the listed derivative is a plain vanilla market and the OTC product is a structured note with a barrier call up with an option embedded. The barrier option is not traded and the note is underwritten over the counter. For pricing it the implied volatility from the vanilla option is used.

- Vanilla ATM call: Spot = 100, Strike = 100, Interest rate = 0.02
- Market impact model: $g(x) = \gamma x$ with $\gamma = 0.00005$, $n_k = 100{,}000$, $\tau = 1$ day
- OTC barrier: Spot = 100, Strike = 120, Barrier = 105
- Structured note face value: $10 million and the underwriting commission is 5%

Figure 6 shows the outcome of a simulation where the underwriter of the structured note pumps the market of the listed vanilla option until the moment the OTC derivative touches the trigger value for which the structured note becomes acceptable for the client. The underwriter keeps buying options and pumps the implied volatility until the mark-to model of the barrier call reaches a peak value. At that point the structured note is sold and the commissions are paid by the client. Without support in the vanilla price the volatility goes back to its fundamental value.

## 5 OUTLOOK

Market impact models provide not only an advantage to understanding the dynamics of price depending on traded volumes but can be a useful tool for assessing the various misconduct that occurs. The new technologies used in trading as well as the diversification of infrastructures can increase the frequency and typology of manipulations and misconducts. The morphology of manipulation changes with the speed of technology, leaving regulators and market supervisors one step behind. Using market impact models can help determine if the dynamics of temporary or permanent impacts change over certain days or hours. These changes in impact functions can provide with warning signals when something abnormal occurs. Similar impact analysis tools are used by watchdogs in the sport betting market when monitoring intra-game betting patterns and can indicate if a game is rigged.

---

[2] Assume here that both the OTC product and the market derivative have positive sensibilities to parameters $\frac{d\Xi(\theta)}{d\theta} > 0$ and $\frac{d\tilde{V}(\theta)}{d\theta} > 0$.

# Order Book Analysis

## 1 BACKGROUND

As presented in the previous chapter the literature provides a rich spectrum of methods assessing the market impact at order level. However, at intra-day level, sometimes more than 95% [247] of orders are canceled before execution so an event study based on order book information would provide a full-fledged assessment especially when dealing with markets where high-frequency trading represents the biggest part volumes such as with the stock market.

Often slow intra-day traders try to guess the tendency of the market by looking at the upcoming order book on the market. Thus, they would know if the market is overbought or oversold by analyzing the relationship between bid and ask price as well as the block size of the foreseeable orders.

When algorithmic trading started to gain momentum people understood the role played by the order book and used this leading indicator for sending or extracting information from the market. Orders are sometimes placed and canceled in a structured way to influence the direction of the market, whereby slower traders have the advantaged. With the development of low-latency trading the price discovery process in many markets has become the results of war between algorithms and fast hardwares.

Specific manipulation strategies in the high-frequency trading universe like electronic front running, spoofing, or smoking use the order book for altering the supply-demand perception and to impose the desired market momentum. Therefore, studying the order book can provide investigators of such cases with useful information, but at it is probably not an effective tool to use to monitor misconduct.

## 2 MODEL THE ORDER BOOK DYNAMICS

The order book model introduced by Cont et al. [247] takes into account the limit orders sitting at the best bid and ask, assuming the bid price is $P^B$, the ask price is $P^A$, the bid size is $q^B$, and the ask size is $q^B$. The set of data is compared in the queuing between the events[1] $n$ and $n-1$, and depending on their relationships the following interpretations are given:

- $P_n^B > P_{n-1}^B$ or $q_n^B > q_{n-1}^B$ indicates an increase in demand
- $P_n^B < P_{n-1}^B$ or $q_n^B < q_{n-1}^B$ indicates a decrease in demand
- $P_n^A < P_{n-1}^A$ or $q_n^A > q_{n-1}^A$ indicates an increase in supply
- $P_n^A > P_{n-1}^A$ or $q_n^A < q_{n-1}^A$ indicates a decrease in supply

The contribution of each event $e_n$ to the supply/demand asymmetry is defined as:

$$e_n = \mathbf{1}_{P_n^B \geq P_{n-1}^B} q_n^B - \mathbf{1}_{P_n^B \leq P_{n-1}^B} q_{n-1}^B - \mathbf{1}_{P_n^A \leq P_{n-1}^A} q_n^A + \mathbf{1}_{P_n^A \geq P_{n-1}^A} q_n^A \tag{1}$$

The passage from the events queue $\ldots n-1, n$ to the chronological flow is straightforward as all events with the same timestamps $t_k$ are aggregated in a contribution $e_n^{t_k}$.[2] The order flow imbalance $\text{OFI}_k$ between $t_{k-1}$ and $t_k$ is a sum of individual event contributions $e_n$ over these intervals:

$$\text{OFI}_k = \sum_{t_{k-w}}^{t_k} e_n^{t_k} \tag{2}$$

---

[1] In the model implementation the data timestamp is measured with millisecond precision and a few sets can sit in the same timestamp. Therefore, the concept of event does not automatically imply a temporal sequence. This is also realistic as the orders that arrive on the book depend on the infrastructure used. Orders coming from fiber-optic servers near the exchange will arrive faster than orders placed by a sole trader from a cabin on the country side.
[2] This is a small variation from the original Cont et al. [247] proposal.

where $w$ is the window over which the flow imbalance is measured.

The order flow imbalance is a metric of supply/demand imbalance, which includes the full spectrum of the order book: trades, limit orders, and cancelations. In addition to the order imbalance the total volume of the event $e_{\text{fn}}$ is defined as:

$$e_{\text{fn}} = q_n^B + q_n^A \tag{3}$$

and the total cumulated size of events between $t_{k-1}$ and $t_k$.

$$\text{TI}_k = \sum_{t_{k-w}}^{t_k} e_{\text{fn}}^{t_k} \tag{4}$$

To complete the model framework $\Delta P_{t_k}$ is considered as the mid-price change at the moment $t_k$:

$$\Delta P_{t_k} = (P_{t_k} - P_{t_{k-1}})/\delta \tag{5}$$

the mid-price being the bid ask average $P_{t_k} = 0.5 \cdot (P_{t_k}^B + P_{t_k}^A)$.

The model proposed by Cont et al. [247] assumes the mid-price variation depends linearly on the order imbalance:

$$\Delta P_{t_k} = \beta + \text{OFI}_k + \epsilon_k \tag{6}$$

Another avenue to explore is to assess whether a relationship exists between the absolute mid-price variations and the total size of the event. Some research note that the total size of both bid and ask may have an influence on prices. This phenomena is assessed by the following:

$$|\Delta P_{t_k}| = \alpha_T + \beta_T \cdot \text{TI}_k + \epsilon_k \tag{7}$$

which searches for a relationship between the total market orders and the absolute price variations.

**TABLE 1** Regression Results for ($w = 25$)

| Day | 2013-01-09 | 2013-02-09 | 2013-03-09 | 2013-04-09 | 2013-05-09 | 2013-06-09 |
|-----|-----------|-----------|-----------|-----------|-----------|-----------|
| $R^2$ | 43% | 33.9% | 37.7% | 36.2% | 34.3% | 31.6% |
| $\beta$ | 4.261e−05 | 1.784e−05 | 2.172e−06 | 1.625e−06 | 1.991e−06 | 2.919e−06 |

*The $\beta$ values are statistically significant at 95% confidence interval.*

# 3 APPLICATION TO A NASDAQ STOCK ORDER BOOK

The framework described above is implemented for a NASDAQ stock price order book obtained from tickdata.com, and the order flow imbalance effect on price is measured on six different days in 2013. Table 1 shows the results for a window of 25 timestamps ($w = 25$). The $\beta$ values are statistically significant at 95% confidence interval. In addition, the casualty Granger test confirms their relationship of casualty from the order flow imbalance (OFI) index to the price variation when the number of lags considered is inferior to 10.

The regression results are show in Figure 1 for the 6-day considered. The variability of the OFI index explains 30-45% of the variability of price variation results, which is in line with the findings from previous researchers.

To assess the robustness of the results, the regression is performed for various values of $w$ with values between 1 and 50. For each value of $w$ the average timestamp difference is computed. Figure 2 shows the regression performances $R^2$ and $\beta$ for various average timestamp differences corresponding to different $w$ values. $\beta$ decreases with an increase of $w$, but the explanatory power $R^2$ increases and remains stable for average timestamp lags higher than seconds. The sensibilities of price variations to market imbalance is higher in the low-latency domain but the relationship is more robust when the latencies increase.

With these results a measure of the market depth is introduced by averaging the bid/ask queue sizes over intervals $t_{k_1}, t_k$:

$$(AD_k) = \frac{1}{2N_{t_{k-W}, t_k}} \sum^{n \in t_{k-W}, t_k} (q_n^B + q_n^A) \qquad (8)$$

where $N_{t_k, t_{k-w}}$ is the number of events between the moments $t_{k-W}$ and $t_k$. Assuming the price impact coefficient $\beta$ is constant over a given period of time, the following relationship is tested:

$$\log \beta_i = \alpha - \lambda \cdot \log(AD_i) + \epsilon \qquad (9)$$

which is aiming at assessing the relationship between the price impact coefficient and measure of market depth. This relation indicates how the variation in prices is linked to market depth. On an intra-day basis the market depth pattern typically follows the peak trading hour. Thus, if $\lambda$ is significant it might have an influence on intra-day price patterns Figure 3 shows the results of the regression, where the $R^2$ is around 45% and $\lambda = -0.4$ is statistically significant, confirming the influence of the market depth on the factor $\beta$.

Another interesting effect is the impact of the total bid/ask size on the price variations as expressed in Equation 7. The regression results are computed on a rolling window and show in Figure 4 for three trading days. Generally, the $R^2$ values are low but there are peak moments during the day when $R^2$ can go above 40%. The aim of this model is to assess whether the various techniques of *market jam* can influence price.

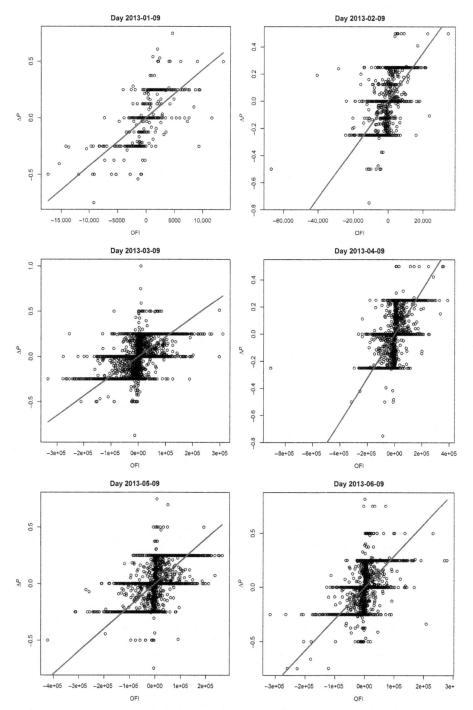

**FIGURE 1** Regression results. The variability of OFI index explains 35-40% of the variability of price variation for the 6 days considered.

III. INVESTIGATION CRIME ON FINANCIAL MARKETS (EMPIRICAL STUDIES WITH APPLICATIONS IN R)

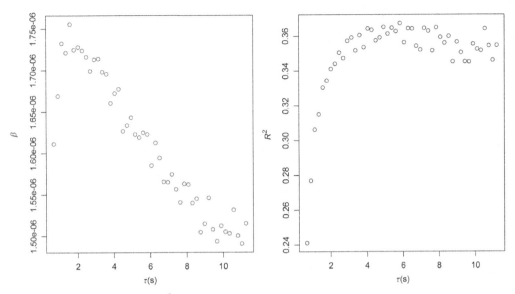

**FIGURE 2** Regression performances $R^2$ and $\beta$ for various average timestamp differences corresponding to different $w$ values. $\beta$ decreases with the increase of $w$, but the explanatory power $R^2$ increases and remains stable for average timestamp lags higher than seconds.

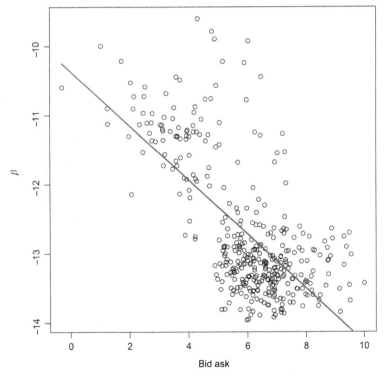

**FIGURE 3** Result of the regression between $\beta$ and market depth. $R^2$ is around 45% and $\lambda = -0.4$ is statistically significant, which the influence of the market depth on the factor $\beta$.

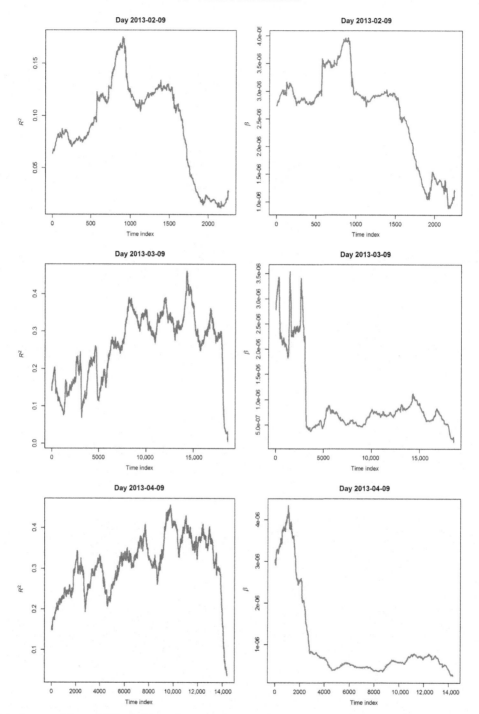

**FIGURE 4** Impact of the total bid ask size on the price variation. The regression results are computed on a rolling window of around 30 minutes for three trading days. Generally the $R^2$ values are low but there are peak moments during the day when the $R^2$ can go above 40%.

In some high-frequency trading manipulation techniques like smoking or spoofing, manipulators send many orders that are later canceled to either create intensity on the market and track other trader or for over-charging the market and blocking other traders. A high $R^2$ and a high sensibility can be the result of such manipulation techniques. Hence, to track this type of behavior the current analysis needs to be extended for a high number of trading days in order to assess the behavioral pattern for each stock and to be able to see warning signs if the above model has fluctuations in parameters.

## 4 OUTLOOK

Errare humanum est, perseverare autem diabolicum, et tertiaaltum frequentia negotiatione est. To err is human; to persist is of the devil, and the third possibility is high-frequency trading, *paraphrase of a Latin proverb*

The impact study of the order book on market prices become relevant in the context of high-frequency trading and is a good complement to the traditional impact model, which focuses only transactions [242]. Being able to draw a line between legal and illegal behaviors in the low-latency universe is a very difficult task and the gray zone is widening.

Monitoring dynamically the relationship between the supply and demand imbalance and the price dynamic, or the impact of the total market depth on price variation, can be useful for establishing micro-structure patterns for each stock, etc. If the $\beta$, $\beta_T$, or $\lambda$ moves away from their paths or exhibit unusual values this can be signal that an event occurred in the market at the micro-structure level, like the arrival of a new trader, a change in the trading algorithm of one of the investors, or a manipulation attempt.

## 1 BACKGROUND

The aim of an event study is to assess the extent to which security price returns around the time of an event became abnormal. An event study consists of building a model for a stock's expected returns and in measuring how much the observed returns, after the occurrence of an event, are different from those given by the model determined on the equilibrium of expected returns prior to the event. Event studies have a wide range of application for measuring the impact of mergers and acquisitions, financing decisions, corporate expenditure decisions, regulatory changes, and earnings announcements on the market price of a firm. In addition event studies are useful for understanding the capital market efficiency and nature of competition in the marketplace [248].

One of the first papers in the area of event study was published by Dolley [249] who studied the nominal price changes for stock splits, from 1921 to 1931. MacKinlay [250]

introduced more formalism in event studies noting that in a rational marketplace prices do respond to new information such as merger and acquisition news.

The application in securities fraud is mainly focused on the assessment of insider trading and market manipulation cases. Minenna [251] reviewed the implementation of event studies from the perspective of a regulatory body and in relation to the way it can be applied to monitor markets, especially for events such as insider trading or market manipulation. Wong [252] examined the efficiency of the Hong Kong stock market by investigating the abnormal price and volume performance surrounding corporate news announcements, finding strong evidence that points toward suspicious insider-trading activities among stocks of the China-affiliated firms listed in Hong Kong. Jeng et al. [253] found that insider purchases earn abnormal returns of more than 6% per year, and insider sales do not earn significant abnormal returns. Bouraoui et al. [254] investigated using event study methodology the market reaction to stock spams finding on a sample of penny stocks positive and significant abnormal liquidities for stocks targeted by manipulators for the period February 2006 through October 2008. Siering [255] investigated suspicious stock recommendations published via e-mail or on the Web finding that pump-and-dump campaigns have a positive stock market impact and that they are followed by a decline in stock prices within the subsequent days.

## 2 METHODOLOGY

Event studies methodologies include a large and variable panels of techniques from simple stock return-based analysis to more sophisticated multi-factorial models including traded volumes and sentiment indexes from unstructured data. Broadly speaking event study methods include the following the steps [248]:

1. Identify the event date(s) of interest
2. Define the event window
3. Establish the model for the security price returns
4. Estimate model parameters
5. Compute the abnormal returns
6. Conduct relevant statistical tests

The process identifying the event date(s) of interest and of the event window is shown in Figure 1 [250]. The main moments are the beginning and end of the event period $T_1$ and $T_2$, respectively. The event period is a window of a few days around the time information arrives. $T_0$ indicates the debut of the pre-event period serving as the estimation of the model, corresponding to the normal returns. The post-event period after the moment $T_2$ can be used to assess the impact of the event in the longer term.

### 2.1 Event Study Models

Several models for assessing abnormal returns have appeared over the past decades to evaluate the excess returns:

$$AR_{i,t} = R_{i,t} - R^*_{i,t}, t \in [T_1, T_2] \qquad (1)$$

where $AR_{i,t}$ is the abnormal return of firm $i$ and event date $t$ with $t \in [T_1, T_2]$, $R_{i,t}$ as the observed return of firm $i$ and event date $t$, and $R^*_{i,t}$ the *normal return* of firm $i$ conditioned by the information previous to the debut of event ($T_1$). A few models are used for determining $R^*_{i,t}$:

- The **mean-adjusted return model** discussed by Brown and Warner [256] assumes the returns of the firm oscillate around a mean value $\mu_i$:

$$R_{i,t} = \mu_i + \epsilon_{i,t}; \ E[\epsilon_{i,t}]$$
$$= 0 \ and \ \epsilon_{i,t} \propto N(0, \sigma_i) \qquad (2)$$

where $\epsilon_{i,t}$ are the innovations normally distributed. Despite being plainly specified, the model was reported as robust under several conditions and it could outperform more advanced methods.

- The **market-adjusted return model** considers that the returns of the stock are equal to the returns of the market index:

$$R_{i,t} = R_{m,t} + \epsilon_{i,t}; \ E[\epsilon_{i,t}]$$
$$= 0 \ and \ \epsilon_{i,t} \propto N(0, \sigma_i) \qquad (3)$$

where $R_{m,t}$ is the return on the market index during period $t$.

- The **market model** is the most commonly used model in the literature of event studies:

$$R_{i,t} = \alpha_i + \beta_i \cdot R_{m,t} + \epsilon_{i,t} \qquad (4)$$

where $\alpha_i$ and $\beta_i$ are estimated through linear regression. For time series with auto-correlation and heteroskedasticity, the appropriate method should be employed in the estimation process, respectively.

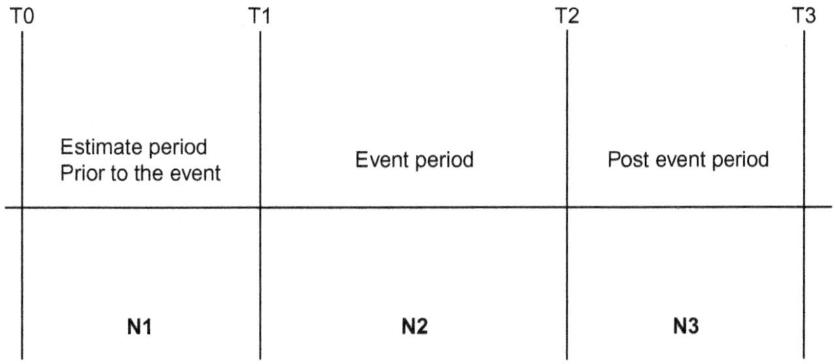

**FIGURE 1** Event study timeline. The main moments are the beginning and end of the event period $T_1$ and $T_2$, respectively. The event period is a window of a few days around the time information arrives. $T_0$ indicates the debut of the pre-event period serving as the estimation of the model, corresponding to the normal returns. The post-event period after the moment $T_2$ can be used to assess the impact of the event in the longer term [250].

- The capital asset pricing model (CAPM) model leverages the typical capital asset pricing model by time-series regression based on realized returns:

$$(R_{i,t} - r_{f,t}) = \alpha_i + \beta_i(R_{m,t} - r_{f,t}) + \epsilon_{i,t} \quad (5)$$

where $r_{f,t}$ is the risk-free rate at moment $t$.

- The **multi-risk factors model** proposes a multi-variate regression-based model on modeling the returns. The model introduced by Fama and French [257] improved the univariate CAPM model:

$$(R_{i,t} - r_{f,t}) = \alpha_i + \beta_{i,m} \cdot (R_{M,t} - r_{f,t})$$
$$+ \beta_{i,\text{SMB}} \cdot \text{SMB}_t$$
$$+ \beta_{i,\text{HML}} \cdot \text{HML}_t + \epsilon_{i,t} \quad (6)$$

where $\beta_{i,m}$, $\beta_{i,\text{SMB}}$, and $\beta_{i,\text{HML}}$ are the model parameters, $\text{SMB}_t$ is the excess return of small over big stocks measured by a market cap, and $\text{HML}_t$ is the excess return of stock with a high market-to-book ratio over stocks with a low market-to-book ratio at moment $t$.

- The **volume-driven models** as researched by Wong [252] also propose the study of trading volume surrounding announcements as in many cases high trading volumes are associated with the release and reception of information:

$$\ln(1 + V_{i,t}) = \ln(1 + V_{m,t}) + \ln(1 + V_{i,t-1})$$
$$+ \ln(1 + V_{i,t-2}) + \gamma_i \text{Day}_{i,t} \quad (7)$$

where $V_{i,t}$ is the traded volume of firm $i$ at moment $t$, $V_{m,t}$ is the market turnover volume at time $t$, and $\text{Day}_{i,t}$ are the weekday dummy variables that equal one for firm $i$ if the trading took place on that day and zero otherwise.

- The **news sentiment-driven models** enhance the market model [255, 258] with factors based on the sentiment analysis of web-based news concerning a firm:

$$R_{i,t} = \alpha_i + \beta_i \cdot R_{m,t} + \gamma_i \text{Sentiment}_{i,t} + \epsilon_{i,t} + \quad (8)$$

where $\text{Sentiment}_{i,t}$ is a sentiment index on news related to firm $i$ at moment $t$.

## 2.2 Statistical Tests

The model allows measuring the abnormal returns during the event period (test period) as the difference between the observed returns and those implied by the model. With a times series of abnormal returns $\text{AR}_{i,t}$ a few metrics can be built that serve as input for building relevant statistics. The aim of such a test is to assess whether the panel of abnormal returns is significantly differ-ent than zero. In other words, if an agent know-ing about the event *a priori* would be able to make a profit from placing the appropriate trades.

### 2.2.1 Abnormality Metrics

For the seminal market model the abnormal returns at moment $t$ are expressed by:

$$AR_{i,\tau} = R_{i,\tau} - (\hat{\alpha}_i + \hat{\beta}_i \cdot R_{m,t}) \quad t \in [T_0, T_2] \quad (9)$$

where $\hat{\alpha}_i, \hat{\beta}_i$ are the estimates of the parameters of the market model.

The average abnormal return during day $t$ for the full sample of stock returns in a portfolio with $N$ firms is:

$$AAR_t = \frac{1}{N} \sum_{i=1}^{N} AR_{i,t} \qquad (10)$$

The cumulative abnormal returns (CAR) are computed as the sum of abnormal returns across the time at firm level or cross-sectional:

$$CAR_{i,(T_1,T_2)} = \sum_{t=T_1}^{T_2} AR_{i,t} \qquad (11)$$

$$CAAR_{(T_1,T_2)} = \frac{1}{N} \sum_{i=1}^{N} CAR_{i(T_1,T_2)} \qquad (12)$$

To determine the abnormal returns across a time window or a portfolio comparable the standardized abnormal return is computed at a moment $t$ as:

$$SAR_{i,t} = \frac{AR_{i,t}}{S_{AR_{i,t}}} \qquad (13)$$

where the adjusted standard error is computed as:

$$S_{AR_{i,t}}$$
$$= \hat{\sigma}_{AR_i} \sqrt{1 + \frac{1}{T_1 - T_0} + \frac{(R_{m,t} - \bar{R}_m)^2}{\sum_{s=T_0}^{T_1}(R_{m,s} - \bar{R}_m)^2}}$$

$$\text{where } \hat{\sigma}^2{}_{AR_i} = \frac{1}{T_1 - T_0 - 2} \sum_{s=T_0}^{T_1} (AR_{i,s})^2$$

and $\bar{R}_m = \frac{1}{T_1-T_0} \sum_{s=T_0}^{T_1} R_{m,s}$ is the mean rate of return of the market index over the estima-tion period. It can be seen that $\sigma^2{}_{AR_i}$ is the standard deviation estimated from the abnormal returns from the estimation window and $S_{AR_{i,t}}$ is the standard deviation filtered over the event window.

The standardized abnormal returns for the firm $i$ over the time horizon of the event window $T_1, T_2$ is:

$$CSAR_{i,(T_1,T_2)} = \sum_{t=T_1}^{T_2} \frac{AR_{i,t}}{S_{AR_{i,t}}} \qquad (14)$$

and the standard deviation of CSAR is:

$$S_{CSAR_i} = \sqrt{(T_2 - T_1 + 1)\frac{T_1 - T_0 - 2}{T_1 - T_0 - 4}} \qquad (15)$$

### 2.2.2 Hypothesis Tests

One of the most common tests is Patell's [259], a standardized residual test applied for a one-day period or for a multi-day period. The null hypothesis of the cross-sectional test is defined as:

- $H_0$: $SAR_{(i,t)} = 0$ states the standardize abnormal return is equal to zero.
- $H_a$: $SAR_{(i,t)} \neq 0$.

The test follows the $t$-statistics:

$$SAR_{(i,t)} = \frac{AR_{(i,t)}}{S_{AR_{i,t}}} \to t(T_1 - T_0 - 2)$$

$$(N(0,1) \text{ for a big estimation window}) \qquad (16)$$

For the full cross-sectional test for a portfolio with $N$ firms the null hypothesis:

- $H_0$: $\mathbf{E}(\text{SCAR}) = \frac{1}{\sqrt{N}} \sum_{i=1}^{N} \frac{\text{CSAR}_{i,(T_1,T_2)}}{S_{\text{CSAR}_i}} = 0$
  states the cumulated standardize abnormal return is equal to zero.
- $H_a$: $\mathbf{E}(\text{SCAR}) \neq 0$.

with respect to the $t$-statistics:

$$T = \frac{1}{\sqrt{N}} \sum_{i=1}^{N} \frac{\text{CSAR}_{i,(T_1,T_2)}}{S_{\text{CSAR}_i}} \rightarrow N(0,1) \qquad (17)$$

A cross-sectional test aims to assess the impact of an event on a portfolio of stocks over the test period. The null hypothesis of the cross-sectional test is defined as:

- $H_0$: $\text{CAAR}_{(T_1,T_2)} = 0$ states the cumulative average abnormal return is equal to zero.
- $H_a$: $\text{CAAR}_{(T_1,T_2)} \neq 0$ implies there is a significant total average return following the event.

The statistics of the test have the expression and tends toward the normal law:

$$T = \frac{\text{CAAR}_{(T_1,T_2)}}{\hat{\sigma}_{\text{CAAR}_{(\tau_1,\tau_2)}}} \rightarrow N(0,1) \qquad (18)$$

where the variance estimator of the test is:

$$\hat{\sigma}_{\text{CAAR}_{i,(T_1,T_2)}}$$

$$= \frac{1}{\sqrt{N}} \sqrt{\sum_{i=1}^{N} (\text{CAR}_{i,(T_1,T_2)} - \text{CAAR}_{(T_1,T_2)})^2} \qquad (19)$$

## SEC METHODOLOGY

### Background

In the 1980s the SEC, the U.S. Securities and Exchange Commission, developed a quantitative procedure based on event-study methodology using an adapted version of the standardized abnormal returns test. The only particularity is that the SEC version is applied to the stock level and not the aggregated level [251].

### Test description

The estimation window is 120 days and the test window is 20 days. The model is a plain market model:

$$R_{i,t} = \alpha_i + \beta_i \cdot R_{m,t} + \epsilon_{i,t} \qquad (20)$$

and the abnormal returns are expressed as:

$$\text{AR}_{i,\tau} = R_{i,\tau} - (\hat{\alpha}_i + \hat{\beta}_i \cdot R_{m,t}) \quad t \in \overline{T_0, T_2}$$

where $\hat{\alpha}_i$, $\hat{\beta}_i$ are the estimates of the parameters of the market model.

The test uses the statistics of the standardized abnormal returns:

$$\text{SAR}_{i,t} = \frac{\text{AR}_{i,t}}{S_{\text{AR}_{i,t}}}$$

The null hypothesis of the cross-sectional test is defined as:

- $H_0$: $\mathbf{E}(\text{SAR}_{(i,t)}) = 0$ the information used by an insider or manipulator cannot generate abnormal returns.
- $H_a$: $\mathbf{E}(\text{SAR}_{(i,t)}) \neq 0$ the information used by an insider or manipulator does generate abnormal returns.

### 2.2.3 Long-Term Impact

Barber and Lyon [260] advocated the assessment of a post-event risk-adjusted performance measurement for long-horizon tests. There are two main methods for assessing and calibrating post-event risk-adjusted performance: the characteristic-based matching approach and the calendar-time portfolio approach.

The buy-and-hold abnormal return (BHAR) is nothing more than the difference between the realized buy-and-hold return and the normal buy-and-hold return:

$$\mathrm{BHAR}_{i,(T_1,T_2)} = \prod_{t=T_1}^{T_2}(1+R_{i,t}) - \prod_{t=T_1}^{T_2}(1+E[R_{i\tau}|\Omega_{i\tau}]) \tag{21}$$

The BHAR metric is in line with how an investor buys a unit of the stock and compares the total value in the long-term with or without the occurrence of the event. The cross-sectional mean buy-and-hold abnormal return for $N$ stocks is expressed as:

$$\overline{\mathrm{BHAR}}_{(T_1,T2)} = \frac{1}{N}\sum_{i=1}^{N}\mathrm{BHAR}_{i,(T_1,T2)} \tag{22}$$

The test proposed by Barber and Lyon [260] is:

$$T = \frac{\overline{\mathrm{BHAR}}_{(T_1,T_2)}}{\sqrt{\mathrm{var}(\mathrm{BHAR}_{i,(T_1,T_2)})\cdot N}} \tag{23}$$

## 2.3 Co-Integration Tests

The relationship between stock prices is usually assessed through the correlation metric, which can be applied only to stationary variables, keeping constant features over time. Market price signals are generally non-stationary and integrated of order one ($I(1)$). The price time-series are made stationary through differencing the logs ($\log(y_t) - \log(y_{t-1})$). When the integration order is different in time series, the correlation metric and even the basic regression outputs are spurious [261]. In addition, two non-stationary stock prices can share the same stochastic trend and are called co-integrated.

Two non-stationary time series of stock prices $x_t$ and $y_t$ are co-integrated if they tend to move together through time if there is a linear form $\alpha_0 \cdot x_t + \beta_0 \cdot y_t \rightarrow I(0)$, which is a stationary process. For instance, the levels of the Fed fund rate and the 3-year bond rate are non-stationary, while their differences are stationary, the same

being true for many spot and futures commodities prices.

The aim of co-integration is to detect a common stochastic trend in time series. A straightforward approach for co-integration testing is the two-step Engle-Granger test [262]. If a vector of time series is co-integrated, the long-run parameters can be estimated directly without specifying the dynamics because, in statistical terms, the long-run parameter estimates converge to their true values more quickly than those operating on stationary variables.

• In the first step parameters $\alpha$ and $\beta$ yield the best fit to the following model:

$$y_t = \alpha + \beta \cdot x_t + \zeta_t \tag{24}$$

The residual sequence $\zeta_t = y_t - \hat{\alpha} - \hat{\beta} \cdot x_t$ is then determined.

• The second step is to test for unit root in the residuals $\zeta_t$. An augmented Dickey-Fuller test procedure is used:

$$\Delta\zeta_t = \gamma_0 + \gamma_1 \cdot \zeta_{t-1} + \sum_{i=1}^{k}\delta_t\Delta\zeta_{t-i} + \epsilon_t \tag{25}$$

Under the null of no co-integration, the estimated residual is integrated in the first-order ($I(1)$) and all parameters are zero in the long run. Rejecting the null hypothesis implies co-integration and the alternative hypothesis is that the integrated variable $y_t$ co-integrates with $x_t$.

A more sophisticated test for co-integration of several times series integrated of order $1(I(1))$ is proposed by Johansen [263]. Stock prices of a similar firm can show co-integration, which is widely used in optimal portfolios and in hedging strategies today. In other words, stocks can share the same path. If an event occurs on one stock its path might deviate apart without bound and change the co-integration with other stocks. Other events like a crisis can drive stock on the same long-term path, thereby making them co-integrated. Therefore, co-integration can be used as a complementary tool in event analysis.

# 3 CASE STUDIES

A few applications of the metrics and tests for events studies discussed above are illustrated in order to show their utilization for various situations. The examples were chosen from the Stanford Class Action Clearinghouse[1] involving insider trading and misrepresentation of business and financial statements.

The effects of an insider trading event can be determined through the analysis of the abnormal returns to evaluate the gain generated by the insider [251]. There are few ways to justify the criminalization of illegal insider trading including misappropriation theory, such as information homogeneity, and market integrity. According to misappropriation theory material non-public information is the property of the firm and if an individual misappropriates material information, then he has "an absolute duty" to disclose that information to the other party [264]. The information homogeneity argument states that market efficiency is based on the fact that all investors have access to the same information and are able to impact the changes in information in the price in real time. If a party has privileged information it would create asymmetry and might create heterogeneous gain opportunities. Of course, the argument of market efficiency in the string form where all information including preferential should be captured in price is also used by those advocating for the non-incrimination of insider trading.

The market integrity argument [251] states that insider trader damages the market by implying that the underlying will need up-trading to a value that is different from its real intrinsic value.

For insider trading cases when a supervisor inflicts penalties or a class action is filed, the negative externality generated by an insider or his insider gain is computed deterministically based on the difference between the price after the disclosure of the information and the weighted average price of the insider open position, multiplied by the traded volumes.

The event analysis method provides a more econometric approach, based on the relationship between the returns of the stock and the returns of an index, before and after the event. For all cases the event is considered the announcement made around the end of the class period, which generally restates the activity or the performance of the firm.

In the chosen examples stocks are traded on NASDAQ and the benchmark market reference is the NASDAQ index.

- The Pharmos case involves both misrepresentation and insider trading,[2] the insiders shorting their stock after propagating allegedly false information. The case was settled.
- The Sonus case also involves financial misstatements and insider trading allegation.[3] The case was settled.

---

[1]Stanford Class Action Clearinghouse, http://securities.stanford.edu/.

[2]*Cohen vs. Pharmos*, http://securities.stanford.edu/filings-documents/1033/PARS05_01/2005124_f01c_Cohen.pdf.
[3]*Chin vs. Sonus Network*, http://securities.stanford.edu/filings-documents/1029/SONS04-01/20040212_f01c_Chin.pdf.

- The Dot Hill case involves an erroneous accounting practice of expense.[4] The case was dismissed.

In these cases its considered that times T1 and T2 are the beginning and end of the class periods as described in the class filings. For Pharmos and Sonus, which had clear insider trading allegations, it is crucial to assess the effect after the class period when the privileged information was released to the market. Therefore, the various metrics like the cumulative abnormal returns are assessed over a period of 40 days after the end of the class period.

Another important issue is to evaluate whether the abnormal returns were the consequence of the insider trades or a more systemic effect (structural breaks in the benchmark index). Hence, the abnormal returns are assessed for a set of stocks trading in the same market NASDAQ. Ideally, a cross-sectional test should not indicate any significant non-null abnormal return, and should confirm the same thing for the studied stock.

## PHARMOS CORPORATION

### Background

Pharmos is a bio-pharmaceutical company, listed on NASDAQ, that develops drugs to treat a range of neuro-inflammatory disorders. Pharmos's main product, Dexanabinol, was a synthetic non-psychotropic for the treatment of traumatic brain injury.[2]

### Class action

Pharmos and its directors announced that the product had good results in drug trails, which inflated the stock price. Moreover, between November 15, 2004 and December 1, 2004,

---

[4]*Buckner vs. Dot Hill*, http://securities.stanford.edu/filings-documents/1035/HILL_01/200626_o01c_Buckner.pdf.

allegedly knowing that the outcome of the trial was negative, Pharmo's directors sold more than 400,000 shares of Pharmos for proceeds of more than $1.6 million. When the true negative outcome of the Dexanabinol trials were announced on December 20, 2004, shares of Pharmos fell from $3.50 to $1.18 (a 66% decline).

### Event study

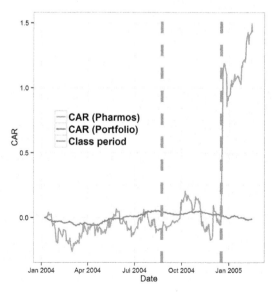

The figure shows the evolution of the stock price and the CAR for a portfolio of 527 NASDAQ stocks.

- The standardized residual test [259] rejects at a 95% confidence interval ($S = 1.76$) the null hypothesis with a statistic of zero average abnormal returns, thereby proving the alleged profit taken by Pharmos management.
- The CAR [250] test applied to the portfolio of NASDAQ stocks ($S = 0.46$) failed to reject the null hypotheses of the null abnormal returns.

## SONUS NETWORKS, INC.

### Background

Sonus asserts that it is a leading provider of packet voice infrastructure solutions for wireline and wireless service providers. The company claims to offer a new generation of carrier-class switching equipment and software that enable telecommunications service providers to deliver voice services over packet-based networks.

### Class action

The company had improperly and untimely recognized revenue, hence the net income and earnings per share published during the class period were allegedly materially false and misleading. On February 11, 2004, after the close of regular trading, Sonus announced that the company had identified issues related to both the timing of revenue recognized from 2003. Prior to that, Sonus insiders sold approximately $2 million in stock. As a result stock fell as low as $5.02 per share, a decline of $1.67 per share, or 24.9%, on extremely high trading volume.

**Event study**

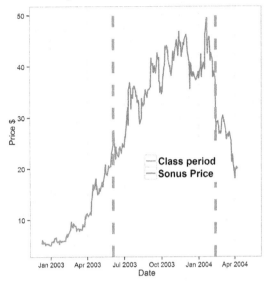

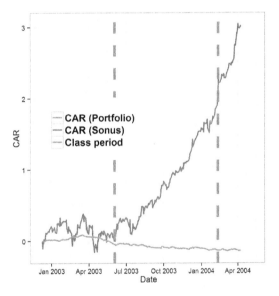

The figure shows the evolution of the stock price and the CAR for a portfolio of 527 NASDAQ stocks.

- The standardized residual test rejects at a 95% confidence interval ($S = 2.09$) the null hypothesis with a statistic of zero average abnormal returns, thereby underlining the alleged profit taken by the Sonus insiders.

- The CAR test applied to the portfolio of NASDAQ stocks ($S = 0.17$) failed to reject the null hypotheses of the null abnormal returns.

## DOT HILL SYSTEMS

### Background

Dot Hill is a U.S.-based company listed on NASDAQ that provides storage systems for organizations that require networked storage and data management solutions in an open-systems architecture.

### Class action

A class action suit was filed against Dot Hill for alleged inadequate internal accounting processes and controls that enabled Dot Hill management to manipulate the costs of goods sold and routinely and inappropriately misclassified expenses. Around February 3, 2005, Dot Hill announced it would be restating its 2004 unaudited financial results.

### Event study

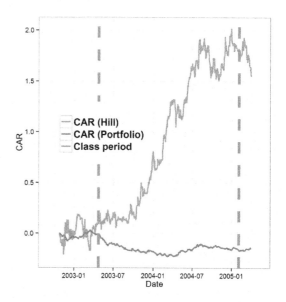

The figure shows the evolution of the stock price and the CAR for a portfolio of 527 NASDAQ stocks.

- The standardized residual test fails to reject at a 95% confidence interval ($S = 2.09$) the null hypothesis with a statistic of zero average abnormal returns. This finding is in line with the outcome of the case which was dismissed.
- The CAR test applied to the portfolio of NASDAQ stocks ($S = 0.17$) failed to reject the null hypotheses of the null abnormal returns.

## LONG-TERM IMPACTS

Long-term impacts can be assessed using the buy and hold abnormal returns (BHAR) test. For a sample of 649 stocks listed on NASDAQ the CAR and BHAR tests were assessed around the event represented by the default of Lehman Brothers in 2008. The holding period of buy and hold is considered to be 6 months. Both statistics are significant and reject the null hypothesis of zero abnormal returns. Interestingly, even in the long term it can be observed that there is no mean reversion effect in the abnormal return series.

### Co-integration

Co-integration between each stock price and the NASDAQ index is tested with the Engle and Granger tests in the period before and after the event. If before the event less than 5% of the stocks were co-integrated with the index, after the event no less that 19% of the stocks are co-integrated with the index. This could suggest that the stock was transmitted across the markets and some stocks would follow the same pattern.

These metrics indicating significant abnormal returns may not be linked to fraud or misconduct and may be the result of systemic factors. However, during crisis episodes like those that took place in 2000 and 2008 the number of securities litigation increases, which means the idiosyncratic factor may have led to economic losses for investors.

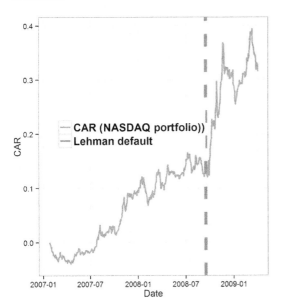

## 4 OUTLOOK

Regulatory bodies face the challenge of monitoring the markets for any suspect behavior or in relationship with allegations concerning a security. Event analysis methods are useful tools used by many securities watchdogs.

Currently markets have new issues related to high-frequency trading or micro-cap scams. However, traditional offenses like insider trading will still exist across markets, thereby raising the necessity of even more effective monitoring methods. Factorial models are leveraged for event analysis and a panel of tests are proposed for assessing the short-term or the long-term impact on a standalone at stock level or cross-section for a portfolio of securities. Co-integration is a necessary add-on to event study, especially for those offenses that involve trades in pair stock, something that often occurs in stock manipulation.

# CASE STUDIES
# (APPLICATIONS IN R)

# 4A

# LIBOR Manipulation

## 1 BACKGROUND

The LIBOR scandal erupted in June 2012 after the British bank Barclays was investigated by the Financial Conduct Authority.[1] Following the investigation Barclays settled for almost $480 million when it was charged by various prosecutors with attempt to manipulate LIBOR rates. Other institutions such as JPMorgan Chase and Citibank were also cited in the event, which quickly grew in amplitude.

Thus, it appeared that Barclays and other banks acted inappropriately between January 2005 and July 2008 by making U.S. dollar LIBOR and EURIBOR submissions that took into

account requests made by its derivative traders and were motivated by profit. Rate submissions that took into account the requests of its own business needs or tried to influence the submissions of other banks implied the published LIBOR rates were trying to be manipulated. The submitting panel could have benefited from this misconduct to the detriment of other market participants. When banks worked together, the risk of manipulation increased massively. Banks also acted inappropriately between September 2007 and May 2009 by making LIBOR submissions lower than the real market conditions that took into account concerns over the negative media perception of the bank's LIBOR submissions.

Liquidity issues were a particular focus for financial institutions during the financial crisis and banks' LIBOR submissions were seen by market analysts as a measure of their ability to

---

[1]Final notice for Barclays June 27, 2012, http://www.fsa.gov.uk/static/pubs/final/barclays-jun12.pdf.

raise funds to finance their assets with a highly uncertain value at that time. Senior management's concerns in turn resulted in instructions to reduce LIBOR submissions in order to avoid negative media attention.

Concerns about the nature of the LIBOR rates and banks' submissions were a part of the 2012 investigation. In 2008 a *Wall Street Journal* article[2] stated that major banks were contributing to the erratic behavior of a crucial global lending benchmark. The article noted that Citigroup Inc., WestLB, HSBC, JPMorgan Chase & Co., and UBS AG were among the banks that were reporting significantly lower borrowing costs for the London interbank offered rate, or LIBOR, than what another market measures suggest they should be. Faced with suspicions by some bankers that their rivals had been lowballing their borrowing rates to avoid looking desperate for cash, the *Wall Street Journal* article published the result of the benchmarking between the default-insurance market and the LIBOR rates. Thus, from late January 2008, as fears grew about possible bank failures, the two measures began to diverge, with reported LIBOR rates failing and default-insurance costs rising. The gap between the two measures was bigger for Citigroup, WestLB, HBOS, JPMorgan Chase & Co., and UBS than for the other 11 banks.

Following this article, academic research from Abrantes-Metz et al. [265] presented statistical evidence of patterns that appeared to be inconsistent with those normally expected to occur under conditions of market.

## 2  WHY MANIPULATE LIBOR?

From a technical point of view LIBOR is computed as the average of submitted rates by various banks. The LIBOR definition published by the British Bankers' Association (BBA) is: *the rate*

---

[2]Study Casts Doubt on Key Rate, http://www.wsj.com/articles/SB121200703762027135.

*at which an individual contributor panel bank could borrow funds, were it to do so by asking for and then accepting interbank offers in reasonable market size just prior to 11:00 London time.* Thus, every day at 11:00 a.m. (CET), Thompson Reuters receives the submission from the panel and computes an arithmetic average, eliminating the four highest and four lowest submissions.

Based on the prosecutor notes the LIBOR manipulation had two main goals that during two different periods:

- First, the banks from the submitting panel intentionally changed their LIBOR submission in order to influence the settlements of various derivatives products for which the banks were counterparties. Similar to the Forex manipulation the traders from the accused banks liaised with the submitters, disclosing their positions and their desired level of LIBOR that would guarantee a maximum utility for those positions.
- Second, during the financial crisis that peaked with Lehman's collapse, senior management from banks pushed for lower submissions to avoid the propagation of the fear concerning the liquidity crisis in the market.

### 2.1  Manipulating the Derivatives Mark-to Market

The British prosecutor's report underlined the collusion between the derivatives traders and the submitters in the banks with the aim to maximize their gains. Certain banks had defended themselves, saying that the bank itself could not profit directly from changes in interest rates as they had both assets and liabilities, which had a positive and a negative sensitivity with respect to the LIBOR.

LIBOR manipulation is a typical example of an act related to moral hazard. We consider a moral hazard as a real option given for free to a trader in order to enhance the likelihood of generating profits for a department within the organization by undertaking risk for the entire organization. This real option is reflected in the case of the LIBOR as a change in behavior and conduct by acting in an organized and continuous manner.

A relevant example is provided by the transcripts of the discussions between traders and submitters at Barclays published after the 2012 investigation:

- *We have an unbelievably large set on Monday (the IMM). We need a really low 3m fix, it could potentially cost a fortune. Would really appreciate any help.*
- *I really need a very very low 3m fixing on Monday—preferably we get kicked out. We have about 80 yards [billion] fixing for the desk and each 0.1 lower in the fix is a huge help for us. So 4.90 or lower would be fantastic.*

Assuming the bank sold an interest cap option to a client for $80 billion nominal he will receive payments at the end of each period in which the interest rate exceeds the agreed strike price (allegedly 4.90% as shown in Figure 1). One basis

point on 80 billion nominal would represent a $2 million difference, the client would not receive. Thus, if the LIBOR value is below 4.9% no payment from the bank to the buyer is made. The aim of the LIBOR manipulation in this case was to manipulate the payoff of the interest rate cap at the fixing date. Thus, a *mark-to market* of a derivative became the *mark-to manipulation*.

## 2.2 Manipulation During the Liquidity Crisis

From April 2007 the exposure of the major banks to the subprime crisis was a real concern since liquidity conditions had worsened dramatically. Liquidity issues became acute with the collapse of Northern Rock in September 2007 and the fall of Bear Stearns, which was bailed by JPMorgan in March 2008. By the third quarter of 2008 the fear concerned the solvency of financial institutions, following Lehman Brothers going to chapter 11 in September 2008 and the failures of Royal Bank of Scotland and HBOS in October 2008. The fear of negative perception of markets pushed the senior management with various banks to instruct the submitter to lower their LIBOR submissions during the period of market torment in late 2007 and early 2009.

## 3 METHODOLOGICAL FORENSIC CONSIDERATIONS

This section analyzes from a statistical perspective the case of LIBOR manipulation and tries to assess the severity of the allegation concerning the major banks with ties to the LIBOR scandal. As noted previously the attempt at manipulating the rate is a consequence of moral hazard. Thus, the bank had a free option to submit a rate that could drive the final rate closer to an advantageous value for its business.

In order to assess the possibility that one or few banks might alter the representation of LIBOR rates a few econometric tests are

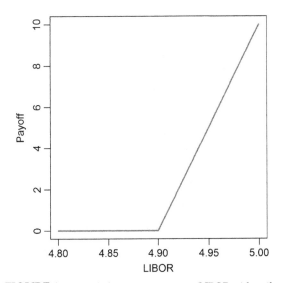

FIGURE 1    Payoff of an interest rate cap LIBOR with strike 4.90%.

conducted. These tests are a part of a forensic approach that could find incoherence from an independent external point of view. Forensic statistics as a topic is fit for the purpose of detecting anomalies in market behaviors without having non-public information. The methodology is focused on answering three questions:

1. Is the process of rate computation robust?
2. What is the impact of individual bank submission on the total rate and how did the contributions change over time?
3. What is the impact of a manipulation attempt from one bank or from a concert action of banks?

In order to answer to these questions a data set of USD LIBOR submissions constituted between 2005 and 2008 published by an independent analyst.[3] According to the data set, 16 banks were submitting daily rates for the LIBOR for each maturity. If the four highest submissions and the four lowest submissions are excluded the LIBOR is computed with a sample of 8 submissions, which here will be called $\mathbf{S}_8$. Let's define the following metrics:

1. LIB Observed$_M$ is the observed LIBOR for the maturity $M$.
2. LIB$_M$ is the LIBOR computed for the maturity $M$:

$$\text{LIB}_M = \frac{1}{8} \sum_{i=1}^{N} R_{i,M} \mathbf{1}_{R_{i,M} \in \mathbf{S}_8} \qquad (1)$$

3. LIBFS$_M$ is the full sample LIBOR for the maturity $M$ and is defined as the average of the submitted rates $R_{i,M}$ by each bank $i$ from the full panel of $N$ banks:

$$\text{LIB}_F SM = \frac{1}{N} \sum_{i=1}^{\dot{N}} R_{i,M} \qquad (2)$$

4. LIBRnd$_M$ is the LIBOR for maturity $M$ considering the submission of eight banks chosen randomly among the panel:

$$\text{LIBRnd}_M = \frac{1}{8} \sum_{N}^{j=1} R_{j,M} \cdot \mathbf{1}_{j \in \text{Rnd}(8,N)} \qquad (3)$$

5. LIBBank$_{M,B}$ is the LIBOR for maturity $M$ computed by the current rules considering the submission in the panel from which we exclude the bank $B$:

$$\text{LIBBank}_{M,B} = \frac{1}{8} \sum_{j \in 1:\dot{N} \text{ excluding } B} R_{j,M} \cdot \qquad (4)$$

6. LIBFSBank$_{M,B}$ is the full sample LIBOR for the maturity $M$ and is defined as the average of the submitted rates $R_{i,M}$ by each bank $i$ from the full panel of $N$ banks excluding the Bank $B$:

$$\text{LIBFSBank}_{M,B}$$
$$= \frac{1}{N-1} \sum_{j \in 1:\dot{N}-1 \text{ excluding } B} R_{j,M} \cdot \mathbf{1}_{R_{i,M} \in \mathbf{S}_8} \qquad (5)$$

Given these notations let's define the following spreads:

- FullSample Spread$_M$ = LIB$_M$ − LIBFS$_M$ is the difference between the official LIBOR, the maturity $M$, and the full sample LIBOR, computed on the entire panel.
- Random Spread$_M$ = LIB$_M$ − LIBRnd$_M$ is the difference between the official LIBOR the maturity $M$, and the random LIBOR computed on 8 random submissions from the full panel.

---

[3]We used the data set published by the English journal: "The Guardian," http://www.guardian.co.uk/news/datablog/2012/jul/03/libor-rates-set-banks.

- Panel Distance$_{M,B}$ = $R_{M,B}$ − LIBFSBank$_{M,B}$ is the difference between the submitted rate for the maturity $M$ by the bank $B$ and the full sample LIBOR computed excluding that bank.
- LIBOR Spread$_{M,B}$ = LIB$_M$ − LIBBank$_{M,B}$ is the difference between the official LIBOR, the maturity $M$, and the LIBOR computed from a panel excluding the submissions of bank $B$.

First, let's assess the robustness of the LIBOR computation method by analyzing the basic statistics of the FullSample Spread$_M$ and Random Spread$_M$. If the process is robust we would expect an average close to zero with a small standard deviation.

The structural breaks test of Bai and Perron [207] is applied for the Panel Distance$_{M,B}$ metric in order to assess if the submissions of an individual bank changed in pattern when compared to other institutions. We would expect to find a structural change around the crisis period in 2008, before Lehman defaults, when the financing conditions of banks were very difficult.

The structural breaks test shows that two important moments occurred in the submission of the major part of the panel: the summer of 2007 and the spring of 2008, which correspond to the beginning of the sub-prime crisis and to the beginning of the contagion, respectively (Table 1). At that time banks saw changes in their funding conditions, and yet each bank reacted differently. For instance, some banks submitted rates constantly higher than the panel (e.g., Barclays, Figure 2), some lower than the panel (e.g., HSBC and Citigroup), and others oscillated nervously around the panel's average (e.g., Bank of America, UBS).

Second let's assess the manipulation attempts and analyze for each bank the difference between its submissions and those of other banks in the panel. After the Barclays' investigation the Financial Services Authority (FSA) underlined that some banks showed better financing con-

**TABLE 1**  Breaks Points in the Panel Distance

| Banks | Dates for structural breaks |
| --- | --- |
| Barclays | 2007-08-27; 2008-05-28 |
| Citigroup | 2007-08-14; 2008-05-28 |
| JP Morgan | 2008-05-28 |
| UBS | 2007-08-03; 2008-04-15 |
| RBS | 2008-05-28 |
| Bank of America | 2008-05-28 |
| HSBC | 2007-09-12; 2008-05-28 |
| Norinchuckin | 2007-08-31; 2008-05-28 |
| BTMU | 2008-05-28 |
| Lloyds | 2008-05-28 |
| Rabobank | 2008-05-28 |
| WestLB | 2008-05-28 |
| Credit Suisse | 2008-05-28 |
| Deutsche Bank | 2007-10-19; 2008-05-28 |

ditions than were actually true, thereby communicating a lower LIBOR to the panel. While the LIBOR computation methodology is robust the impact of one bank communicating a lower LIBOR should not affect the outcome as it would be either diluted in the average or taken out by the filtering of higher submissions. Moreover, we assume a bank submitted a LIBOR rate 20 basis points lower than the real condition of financing at that time, which was during the crisis period. The "fixed spread" is modeled as a stochastic process. With these assumptions a simulated LIBOR with the "true" rates is constructed and the difference between the observed and simulated rates is considered. When replicating the simulation considering a concerted action of 2, 3, and 4 banks the results are astonishing.

The third question is far more complex and the answer is heavily dependent on the underlying assumptions. Figure 3 shows the relationship

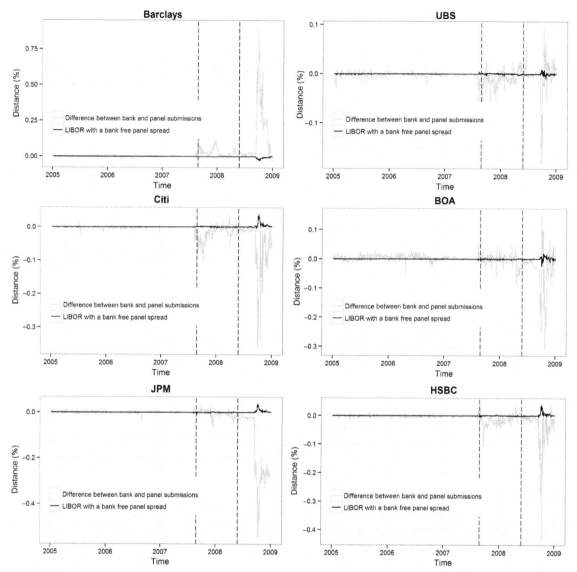

**FIGURE 2** Panel distance and impact of the bank submission for few banks from the panel (3 months USD LIBOR).

between the 3M USD LIBOR and the 3M Treasury rates of the U.S. Treasury notes.

The Bai and Perron test underlines two structural breaks that occurred in the nature of the relationship between the U.S. Treasury rates and the corresponding LIBOR on August 2007 and June 2008. Interestingly the breaks appeared at

the very same moment the banks from the LIBOR panel encountered changes in their submitting behavior, which is emphasized by the results on the Panel Distance$_{M,B}$ (Table 1). This moment likely corresponds to the beginning of the credit crunch in the summer of 2007 and to the first signs of the crisis in May 2008 that culminated

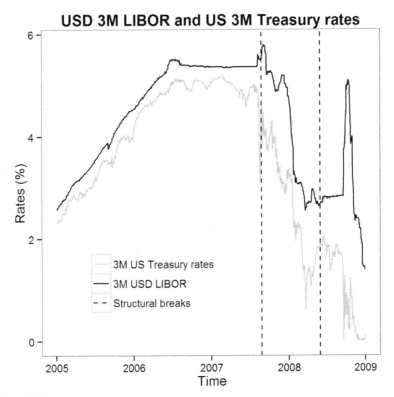

**FIGURE 3** LIBOR vs. UST.

with Lehman's default. The conditions on the capital markets at that time diminished the ability of banks to find liquidity, as the fear of contagion was enormous. The difference between the LIBOR and the official U.S. Treasury rates increased as shown in Figure 3. Obviously this structural change in market conditions affected the apprehension of the riskiness of banks on the credit markets. A high rate of funding (LIBOR) would imply a worse credit rating reflected in an inflated credit default swap spread.

A data set is constituted from CME Markit the quotations of credit default swaps (CDS) time series for each bank presented in the USD LIBOR panel. For each bank the corresponding CDS for all maturities corresponding to LIBOR rates (1 week to 12 months) is computed. The time series of the average CDS spread corresponding

to the banks included in the panel and the difference between the LIBOR and the U.S. Treasury for a 3 month horizon are shown in Figure 4. A visual inspection reveals that the two times series exhibit dependency, with a Pearson correlation of 62.5% and a Spearman correlation of 71.6%, which confirms the main assumptions that LIBOR submission and CDS are dependent.

## 4 STATISTIC RESULTS

The first phase assesses if the LIBOR computation process is robust. The behavior of the full sample LIBOR and of the random LIBOR compared to the observed LIBOR is studied. Basic statistics for the difference between the full sample LIBOR and the observed LIBOR and

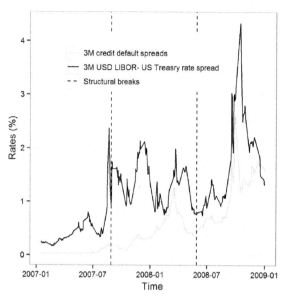

**FIGURE 4** Average 3M credit default swaps for the LIBOR panel banks and 3M Treasury rates vs. LIBOR spread.

spread becomes significant with higher standard deviation and with kurtosis effects. Thus, the impact of an one or few banks in the process could have been significant in altering the value of the LIBOR.

Excluding the submissions of each bank we can see that before 2008 the impact of individual submission was almost zero. The impact started to gain momentum in the spring of 2008 but with limited amplitude (<1 basis points). For more accuracy we perform elaborate tests in order to prove the robustness of the LIBOR computation. We show that the various spreads are limited in average and variance, with a stationary innovation.

**Proposition 1.** *An assessment of the full sample spread as the difference between the full sample LIBOR and the observed LIBOR given by the expression:*

$$|\text{LIBFS}_M(t) - \text{LIB}_M(t)| = \alpha + \epsilon_M(t)$$

*is made and the null hypothesis cannot be rejected within a 95% confidence interest:*

$H_0 : \alpha_M < 0.15\,\text{bp},$
   $\epsilon_M(t) < 1.5\,\text{bp}$ and $\epsilon_M(t)$ is stationary
$H_a : \alpha_M \geq 0.15\,\text{bp},$
   $\epsilon_M(t) \geq 1.5\,\text{bp}$ and $\epsilon_M(t)$ is not stationary

*Proof.* In Table 5 the results of Phillips-Perron test for innovation's stationarity and one sample *t*-test to show the upper limit of $\alpha$ are given. For variance of the innovation we used the one sample $\chi^2$ test for a population variance.    □

**Proposition 2.** *Considering the absolute difference between the random LIBOR and the observed LIBOR:*

$$|\text{LIBRnd}_M(t) - \text{LIB}_M(t)| = \alpha + \epsilon_M(t)$$

*the null hypothesis cannot be rejected:*

$H_0 : \alpha_M < 0.8\,\text{bp},$
   $\epsilon_M(t) < 1.5\,\text{bp}$ and $\epsilon_M(t)$ is stationary

the random LIBOR and the observed LIBOR per maturity, respectively, are given in Table 2. At first glance it can be observed that the differences are not significant for the entire considered history.

Table 2 shows the statistics of the full sample and random spreads for the data set of LIBOR time series between 2005 and 2008. Both spreads are not significantly different than zero. The standard deviation of the random computation is around 1-2 basis points, which shows that the process is overall stable.

Tables 3 and 4 show the same statics for the LIBOR time series but for a particular time period. Table 3 focuses on the early period of the subprime between September 2007 and May 2008, while Table 4 focuses on the period around Lehman's defaults between June and December 2008. During the early crisis the LIBOR computation method remained stable, but during the late phase of the crisis they started to show signs of higher sensitivity to underlying factors. We observe in Table 4 that the random

TABLE 2  Statistics of the Full Sample and Random Spreads Between 2005 and 2008

| LIBOR maturity/(%) | Full sample spread mean (%) | Full sample spread standard error (%) | Random spread mean (%) | Random spread standard error (%) |
|---|---|---|---|---|
| 1M | −0.001 | 0.013 | −0.001 | 0.019 |
| 2M | 0.000 | 0.011 | 0.000 | 0.017 |
| 3M | 0.000 | 0.009 | 0.000 | 0.017 |
| 4M | −0.001 | 0.008 | 0.000 | 0.012 |
| 5M | 0.000 | 0.007 | 0.000 | 0.013 |
| 6M | 0.001 | 0.007 | 0.001 | 0.014 |
| 7M | 0.001 | 0.006 | 0.001 | 0.012 |
| 8M | 0.000 | 0.006 | 0.001 | 0.013 |
| 9M | 0.000 | 0.006 | 0.000 | 0.013 |
| 10M | −0.001 | 0.006 | 0.000 | 0.012 |
| 11M | −0.001 | 0.007 | −0.001 | 0.014 |
| 12M | −0.002 | 0.008 | −0.002 | 0.015 |

TABLE 3  Statistics of the Random Spreads Between September 2007 and May 2008

| LIBOR maturity/(%) | Full sample spread mean | Full sample spread standard error | Full sample spread skewness | Full sample spread kurtosis | Random spread mean | Random spread standard error | Random spread skewness | Random spread kurtosis |
|---|---|---|---|---|---|---|---|---|
| 1M | 0.000 | 0.003 | 0.623 | 5.446 | 0.001 | 0.006 | 0.361 | 4.960 |
| 2M | 0.000 | 0.003 | −0.100 | 4.144 | 0.000 | 0.005 | 0.266 | 5.136 |
| 3M | 0.001 | 0.003 | 0.155 | 5.210 | 0.001 | 0.006 | 0.184 | 5.046 |
| 4M | 0.001 | 0.003 | 0.465 | 4.546 | 0.001 | 0.005 | 0.959 | 7.026 |
| 5M | 0.001 | 0.003 | 0.695 | 5.647 | 0.001 | 0.005 | 0.787 | 5.309 |
| 6M | 0.001 | 0.003 | 0.343 | 3.094 | 0.002 | 0.006 | 0.138 | 5.780 |
| 7M | 0.001 | 0.003 | −0.106 | 4.719 | 0.001 | 0.006 | 0.470 | 4.660 |
| 8M | 0.000 | 0.004 | −0.283 | 3.457 | 0.000 | 0.007 | −0.042 | 4.093 |
| 9M | −0.001 | 0.005 | −0.409 | 2.903 | 0.000 | 0.007 | −0.136 | 4.016 |
| 10M | −0.002 | 0.006 | −0.809 | 2.816 | −0.002 | 0.010 | −0.841 | 4.443 |
| 11M | −0.003 | 0.008 | −1.009 | 3.015 | −0.004 | 0.011 | −1.286 | 4.843 |
| 12M | −0.005 | 0.010 | −1.063 | 3.098 | −0.004 | 0.013 | −1.482 | 5.461 |

**TABLE 4** Statistics of the Theoretic and Random Spreads Between June and December 2008

| LIBOR maturity/(%) | Theoretic spread mean | Theoretic spread standard error | Theoretic spread skewness | Theoretic spread kurtosis | Random spread mean | Random spread standard error | Random spread skewness | Random spread kurtosis |
|---|---|---|---|---|---|---|---|---|
| 1M | −0.011 | 0.047 | −1.543 | 4.551 | −0.014 | 0.063 | −1.343 | 7.160 |
| 2M | −0.003 | 0.040 | −1.613 | 4.698 | 0.001 | 0.061 | −1.075 | 4.886 |
| 3M | −0.003 | 0.032 | −1.390 | 4.766 | −0.006 | 0.048 | −0.555 | 4.118 |
| 4M | −0.001 | 0.027 | −1.440 | 4.466 | 0.009 | 0.050 | −0.434 | 3.320 |
| 5M | 0.004 | 0.023 | −1.036 | 3.608 | −0.002 | 0.046 | −0.718 | 4.106 |
| 6M | 0.007 | 0.023 | −0.644 | 3.886 | 0.005 | 0.045 | −0.361 | 4.434 |
| 7M | 0.006 | 0.020 | −0.570 | 3.909 | 0.007 | 0.039 | −0.408 | 3.305 |
| 8M | 0.004 | 0.018 | −0.585 | 4.439 | −0.002 | 0.039 | −0.101 | 2.966 |
| 9M | 0.002 | 0.016 | −0.163 | 4.677 | 0.002 | 0.040 | 0.030 | 3.178 |
| 10M | 0.000 | 0.016 | 0.131 | 4.767 | 0.007 | 0.035 | 0.012 | 3.672 |
| 11M | −0.003 | 0.015 | 0.660 | 5.039 | −0.005 | 0.040 | 0.836 | 5.422 |
| 12M | −0.007 | 0.016 | 0.954 | 4.980 | −0.002 | 0.038 | −0.176 | 2.864 |

**TABLE 5** Statistics of the Full Sample Spreads Between 2005 and 2008

| (%) Maturity | Mean Chi-square test | | | Variance Chi-square test | | | Phillips-Perron test | |
|---|---|---|---|---|---|---|---|---|
| | $\alpha$ | $\alpha$ s.e. | $p$-Value | $\sigma(\epsilon)$ | $\chi^2$ value | $p$-Value | PP value | $p$-Value |
| 1M | 0.0038 | 0.0004 | 0.00 | 0.0129 | 761.94 | 0.00 | −111.73 | 0.01 |
| 2M | 0.0034 | 0.0003 | 0.00 | 0.0106 | 513.75 | 0.00 | −123.73 | 0.01 |
| 3M | 0.0029 | 0.0003 | 0.00 | 0.0086 | 341.15 | 0.00 | −137.07 | 0.01 |
| 4M | 0.0030 | 0.0002 | 0.00 | 0.0070 | 225.14 | 0.00 | −170.64 | 0.01 |
| 5M | 0.0030 | 0.0002 | 0.00 | 0.0063 | 185.53 | 0.00 | −368.58 | 0.01 |
| 6M | 0.0030 | 0.0002 | 0.00 | 0.0066 | 202.81 | 0.00 | −442.56 | 0.01 |
| 7M | 0.0028 | 0.0002 | 0.00 | 0.0058 | 153.84 | 0.00 | −513.79 | 0.01 |
| 8M | 0.0027 | 0.0002 | 0.00 | 0.0053 | 127.90 | 0.00 | −585.73 | 0.01 |
| 9M | 0.0028 | 0.0002 | 0.00 | 0.0050 | 116.63 | 0.00 | −698.13 | 0.01 |
| 10M | 0.0031 | 0.0002 | 0.00 | 0.0054 | 132.75 | 0.00 | −653.91 | 0.01 |
| 11M | 0.0035 | 0.0002 | 0.00 | 0.0060 | 167.55 | 0.00 | −457.33 | 0.01 |
| 12M | 0.0042 | 0.0002 | 0.00 | 0.0070 | 228.61 | 0.00 | −377.05 | 0.01 |

**TABLE 6** Statistics of Random Spreads Between 2005 and 2008

| (%) | Mean Chi-square test | | | Variance Chi-square test | | | Phillips-Perron test | |
|---|---|---|---|---|---|---|---|---|
| Maturity | $\alpha$ | $\alpha$ s.e. | $p$-Value | $\sigma(\epsilon)$ | $\chi^2$ value | $p$-Value | PP value | $p$-Value |
| 1M | 0.0062 | 0.0007 | 0.00 | 0.0218 | 659.09 | 0.00 | −606.4 | 0.01 |
| 2M | 0.0050 | 0.0005 | 0.00 | 0.0158 | 617.55 | 0.00 | −657.6 | 0.01 |
| 3M | 0.0052 | 0.0005 | 0.00 | 0.0150 | 671.14 | 0.00 | −1005.1 | 0.01 |
| 4M | 0.0047 | 0.0004 | 0.00 | 0.0124 | 461.98 | 0.00 | −1010.7 | 0.01 |
| 5M | 0.0046 | 0.0004 | 0.00 | 0.0119 | 573.98 | 0.00 | −749.7 | 0.01 |
| 6M | 0.0047 | 0.0004 | 0.00 | 0.0127 | 563.03 | 0.00 | −1043.9 | 0.01 |
| 7M | 0.0048 | 0.0003 | 0.00 | 0.0107 | 551.73 | 0.00 | −910.7 | 0.01 |
| 8M | 0.0049 | 0.0004 | 0.00 | 0.0118 | 639.04 | 0.00 | −756.8 | 0.01 |
| 9M | 0.0053 | 0.0004 | 0.00 | 0.0122 | 561.05 | 0.00 | −766.3 | 0.01 |
| 10M | 0.0057 | 0.0004 | 0.00 | 0.0117 | 582.03 | 0.00 | −904.7 | 0.01 |
| 11M | 0.0065 | 0.0004 | 0.00 | 0.0129 | 699.10 | 0.00 | −694.3 | 0.01 |
| 12M | 0.0070 | 0.0004 | 0.01 | 0.0135 | 645.81 | 0.00 | −878.9 | 0.01 |

$$H_a : \alpha_M \geq 0.8\,\text{bp},$$
$$\epsilon_M(t) \geq 1.5\,\text{bp and } \epsilon_M(t) \text{ is not stationary}$$

*Proof.* In Table 6 the results of the Phillips-Perron test for innovation's stationarity and one sample $t$-test to show the upper limit of $\alpha$ are given. For the variance of the innovation we used the one sample $\chi^2$ test for a population variance. □

**Proposition 3.** *In absolute value, the LIBOR spread* LIBOR Spread$_{M,B}$ *for each bank and each maturity is capped and stationary in the period before and after the crisis.*

*If the absolute value of the LIBOR spread is written and* $|\text{LIBFS}_M(t) - \text{LIB}_M(t)| = \alpha + \epsilon(t)$, *it cannot reject in the period before the credit crisis (before July 2007) the null hypothesis:*

$$H_0 : \alpha_M < 0.05\,\text{bp and } \epsilon_M(t) \text{ is stationary}$$
$$H_a : \alpha_M \geq 0.05\,\text{bp and } \epsilon_M(t) \text{ is not stationary}$$

*and it cannot reject in the period after the beginning of the credit crisis (after July 2007) the null hypothesis:*

$$H_0 : \alpha_M < 0.2\,\text{bp and } \epsilon_M(t) \text{ is stationary}$$
$$H_a : \alpha_M \geq 0.2\,\text{bp and } \epsilon_M(t) \text{ is not stationary}$$

*Proof.* In Table 7 for each bank in the period before the crisis and for the 3 months LIBOR the results of Phillips-Perron test for innovation's stationarity and one sample $t$-test to show the upper limit of $\alpha$ are given.

In Table 8 for each bank in the period during the crisis and for the 3 months LIBOR the results of Phillips-Perron test for innovation's stationarity and one sample $t$-test to show the upper limit of $\alpha$ are given (Figures 5 and 6). □

In order to assess the impact of a managed manipulation attempt a simulated LIBOR (3 months) is created assuming that one or more banks submitted lower rates than in reality (Figures 7 and 8). If the difference is modeled as a stochastic process with an average of 20 basis points and a variance equal to the observed variance of bank's submissions. The complete algorithm is:

**TABLE 7**   Statistics of the 3 Months LIBOR Spread for Each Bank of the Panel During the Pre-Crisis Period

| Bank | $\alpha$ | $\alpha$ s.e. | max($\alpha$) | $\chi^2$ value | $p$-Value | PP test | $p$-Value |
|---|---|---|---|---|---|---|---|
| Barclays | 0.0002 | 0.0004 | 0.0025 | −21.0897 | 0.0000 | −590.0508 | 0.0100 |
| Citigroup | 0.0001 | 0.0003 | 0.0025 | −34.1197 | 0.0000 | −545.7193 | 0.0100 |
| JP Morgan | 0.0002 | 0.0003 | 0.0025 | −22.2895 | 0.0000 | −585.1536 | 0.0100 |
| UBS | 0.0001 | 0.0003 | 0.0025 | −30.5261 | 0.0000 | −621.2913 | 0.0100 |
| RBS | 0.0002 | 0.0003 | 0.0014 | −30.1817 | 0.0000 | −659.1661 | 0.0100 |
| Bank of America | 0.0002 | 0.0003 | 0.0025 | −22.7831 | 0.0000 | −652.6114 | 0.0100 |
| HSBC | 0.0002 | 0.0003 | 0.0019 | −27.7683 | 0.0000 | −640.5213 | 0.0100 |
| Norinchuckin | 0.0002 | 0.0003 | 0.0025 | −23.4521 | 0.0000 | −637.3586 | 0.0100 |
| BTMU | 0.0002 | 0.0003 | 0.0023 | −22.5111 | 0.0000 | −637.8502 | 0.0100 |
| Lloyds | 0.0002 | 0.0003 | 0.0025 | −27.8567 | 0.0000 | −580.3935 | 0.0100 |
| Rabobank | 0.0002 | 0.0003 | 0.0022 | −28.2372 | 0.0000 | −691.0459 | 0.0100 |
| WestLB | 0.0001 | 0.0003 | 0.0018 | −33.0350 | 0.0000 | −643.2694 | 0.0100 |
| CreditSuisse | 0.0001 | 0.0003 | 0.0025 | −33.7590 | 0.0000 | −614.3785 | 0.0100 |
| Deutsche bank | 0.0002 | 0.0003 | 0.0025 | −28.1113 | 0.0000 | −556.7864 | 0.0100 |

**TABLE 8**   Statistics of the 3 month LIBOR Spread for Each Bank of the Panel During the Crisis Period

| Bank | $\alpha$ | $\alpha$ s.e. | max($\alpha$) | $\chi^2$ value | $p$-Value | PP test | $p$-Value |
|---|---|---|---|---|---|---|---|
| Barclays | 0.0009 | 0.0008 | 0.0045 | −20.7456 | 0.0000 | −172.4063 | 0.0100 |
| Citigroup | 0.0009 | 0.0007 | 0.0029 | −24.2823 | 0.0000 | −139.9996 | 0.0100 |
| JP Morgan | 0.0008 | 0.0008 | 0.0052 | −21.4354 | 0.0000 | −143.4283 | 0.0100 |
| UBS | 0.0009 | 0.0008 | 0.0050 | −21.2635 | 0.0000 | −178.7840 | 0.0100 |
| RBS | 0.0010 | 0.0009 | 0.0052 | −17.8869 | 0.0000 | −179.9779 | 0.0100 |
| Bank of America | 0.0008 | 0.0008 | 0.0036 | −23.6429 | 0.0000 | −184.5887 | 0.0100 |
| HSBC | 0.0010 | 0.0008 | 0.0052 | −18.9898 | 0.0000 | −148.3261 | 0.0100 |
| Norinchuckin | 0.0008 | 0.0007 | 0.0050 | −25.4175 | 0.0000 | −196.8340 | 0.0100 |
| BTMU | 0.0007 | 0.0007 | 0.0045 | −26.8654 | 0.0000 | −167.5826 | 0.0100 |
| Lloyds | 0.0008 | 0.0008 | 0.0052 | −21.5009 | 0.0000 | −159.4905 | 0.0100 |
| Rabobank | 0.0009 | 0.0009 | 0.0052 | −18.8297 | 0.0000 | −153.7776 | 0.0100 |
| WestLB | 0.0007 | 0.0007 | 0.0036 | −30.1669 | 0.0000 | −187.6266 | 0.0100 |
| CreditSuisse | 0.0007 | 0.0007 | 0.0041 | −26.9931 | 0.0000 | −203.6258 | 0.0100 |
| Deutsche Bank | 0.0009 | 0.0008 | 0.0041 | −22.3898 | 0.0000 | −154.6726 | 0.0100 |

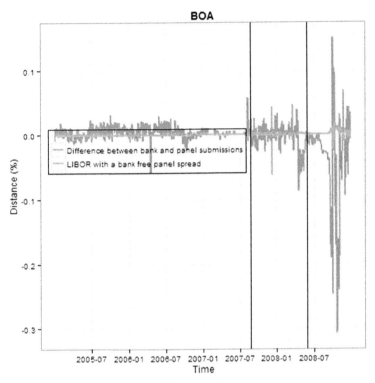

**FIGURE 5**  Panel distance and impact of the bank submission for Bank of America (3 month USD LIBOR).

$$\text{LIB Sim}_M = \frac{1}{8} \sum_{i=1}^{N} \underbrace{(R_{i,M} + \mu + \sigma \cdot \mathbf{B})}_{R_{i,M}^{\text{sim}}} \mathbf{1}_{R_{i,M}^{\text{sim}} \in \mathbf{S}_8}$$

(6)

The simulation results of manipulation attempts on the 3 month LIBOR are shown in Figure 9. The worst-case impacts for the case of one bank or worst-case combination are presented. It appears the impact of a single bank is limited with a maximum amplitude of 5 basis points. If the manipulation is considered as a result of concert action then the amplitude is considerably higher, reaching 10-15 basis points for the 3 month LIBOR. During the pre-crisis period we observe a very low impact of a simulated LIBOR fixing. Some impact occurs

after the beginning of the crisis in late 2007 and becomes significant if the fixing involves four institutions. Thus, it appears clearly that a single bank would not be able to change the LIBOR in a relevant way, as is reported by regulators and the media. Four or more banks in an organized *"cartel-like"* approach would be able to change the LIBOR. This event is apparently less likely to occur in the context of the financial industry as the impact of a LIBOR fix is not genuine and could be negative even for the group of banks originating the manipulation. But the crisis in 2008 brought a lack of confidence in markets and this issue generated probably a fear of gangrene in the interbank market, which led to an alleged attempt to present the brighter side of the picture. It should be recalled that during that period banks were not able to refinance

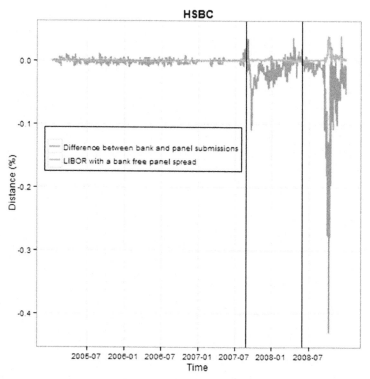

**FIGURE 6**  Panel distance and impact of the bank submission for HSBC (3 month USD LIBOR).

themselves totally on the inter-bank market (which generates the LIBOR).

## 5 SIMULATION: WHAT WAS THE TRUE LIBOR?

The real difficulty in assessing the amount of negative externality resulting from the LIBOR manipulation is the size of the drift from the true value. An article in the *Economist* noted that almost all the banks in the LIBOR panel were submitting rates that may have been 30-40 basis points too low on average.[4] Monticini and Thornton [266] investigated this issue by testing for structural breaks in the spread between

term-equivalent LIBOR and CD rates using daily data for the period January 2, 2004 through December 31, 2010. The research found evidence consistent with the hypothesis that the underreporting of the LIBOR rates by some banks reduced the reported LIBOR rates and that the average of 1- and 3-month LIBOR-CD spreads declined by nearly 5.5 basis points by mid-2007. The LIBOR-CD spreads eventually returned to their pre-underreporting levels.

The allegation of LIBOR fixing brought a lot of momentum around the topic, with authors claiming the need to change the way the rate is computed [267]. In an attempt to reconstitute the effect of an alleged manipulation, we focus first on the fundamental factors that drive the LIBOR. In the previous section we identified the U.S. Treasury rates and the credit spreads of the banks in the panel as potential factors. A bank

[4]The LIBOR scandal: The rotten heart of finance, http://www.economist.com/node/21558281.

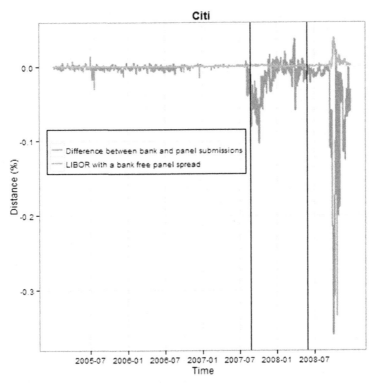

**FIGURE 7** Panel distance and impact of the bank submission for Citigroup (3 month USD LIBOR).

$B$ finances itself on the market for the horizon $M$ at a rate $R_{M,B}$, depending on the risk-free rate $r_M$, approximated by the Treasury rates, its credit quality $CS_{M,B}$, the available liquidity $LS_{M,B}$, and its specific risk $IS_{M,B}$, as shown by:

$$R_{M,B} = r_M + CS_{M,B} + LS_{M,B} + IS_{M,B} \qquad (7)$$

We consider here a simplified model that explains the difference between the rate of bank $B$ and the Treasury rates for a certain maturity $M$ depending on the credit spread the respective bank and maturity:

$$R_{M,B} - R_{\text{US Treasury},M} = \alpha + \beta \cdot CDS_{M,B} + \epsilon \qquad (8)$$

Moving further than Equation 8 the relationship with the credit spread is not stationary as we showed through the structural breaks test in the previous section. Following Hamilton [268] we assume a two-regime switching model explains the rate of one bank with its CDS. The idea is to affirm that there are several states in the LIBOR rate that switch following a transition matrix that is determined by a hidden factor [269]. This "hidden" factor could be determined by regulatory announcements, legislations, or interventions of new dealers on the market. Let's consider here that the "hidden" factor is in fact a fixing factor related to the tendency of the bank to submit the rates differently. A first regime is identified which is "normal" as it was in the period before the crisis and a second regime during the crisis when the manipulation allegedly had a significant impact. Nonetheless, as the purpose of this section is mainly focused on LIBOR modeling, we do not study the relevance of exogenous

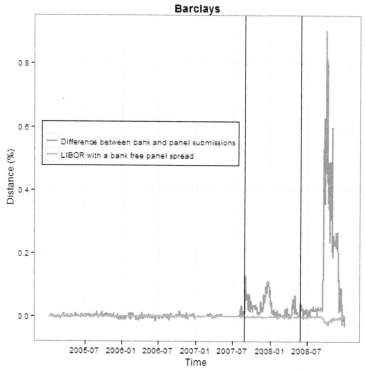

**FIGURE 8**    Panel distance and impact of the bank submission for Barclays (3 month USD LIBOR).

regulatory-like factors on the switching regimes, and we consider the existence of a Markov chain to explain these switches. The idea is developed in the following equation:

$$R_{M,B} - R_{\text{US Treasury},M} = \alpha_i + \beta_i \cdot \text{CDS}_{M,B} + \epsilon_i \ i \in 1,2 \tag{9}$$

Using the same model as introduced in Equation 8, we assume now that the parameter $\beta_i$ associated with each factor $f_i$, $i = 1, \ldots, 4$ has the following dynamics: $\beta_i = \beta_i^1(S_t) + \beta_i^2(1 - S_t)$, where $S_t$ follows a two-state Markov chain as shown in Figure 10, and $S_t = 1$ if $S_t$ is in State 1 and $S_t = 0$ if $S_t$ is in State 2.

The switch occurs with a probability $P$.

Table 9 gives the calibration of a Hidden Markov switching model that has two states and that allows the flip-flops of the factors: $\alpha$ the intercept, $\beta$ the sensitivity to the fundamental

factor, $\sigma$ the standard deviation of the innovations, and $p$ the probability of switch.

Following a factorial approach we attempt to rebuild a theoretic "true" LIBOR based on the relationship with the fundamentals [270]. From the Markov switching model calibration we rebuild a theoretic rate for each bank during the abnormal regime using the parameters of the normal regime. After reconstituting the theoretic submission for each bank we recompute the "true" theoretic LIBOR. The results for the 3M LIBOR are shown in Figure 11. It appears that the impact was significant in the period after July 2007 until the last quarter of 2008. The difference could be as high as 1% during certain periods. The theoretic and observed LIBOR should be considered as two boundaries of the real financing conditions in the markets at that time. The observed LIBOR tended to go near the

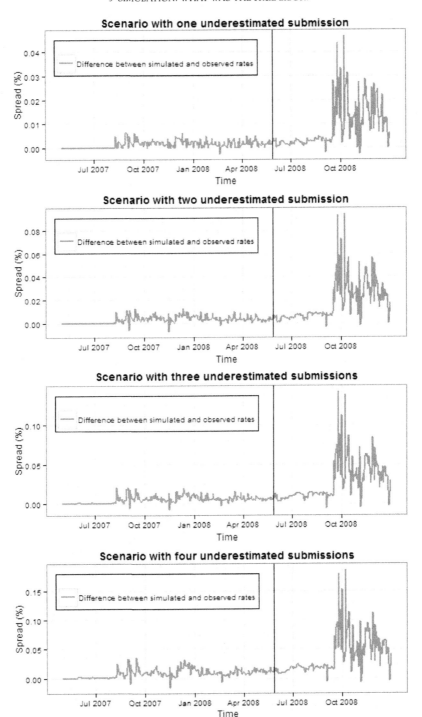

FIGURE 9   Simulation of manipulation attempts on the 3 month LIBOR.

**TABLE 9**  Switching Regime Regression Estimates for Each Bank Constituting the Panel

| | | Regime 1 | | | | Regime 2 | | | |
|---|---|---|---|---|---|---|---|---|---|
| **Bank** | **Param.** | **Estimate** | **Std. Err.** | **$z$-Value** | **$p$-Value** | **Estimate** | **Std. Err.** | **$z$-Value** | **$p$-Value** |
| Barclays | $\alpha_k$ | 0.0047 | 0.0002 | 17.070 | 0.000 | 0.0114 | 0.0010 | 10.9540 | 0.000 |
| | $\beta_k$ | 0.8620 | 0.0415 | 20.749 | 0.000 | 1.4097 | 0.1608 | 8.7619 | 0.000 |
| | $\sigma$ | 0.0022 | - | - | - | 0.0067 | - | - | - |
| | P | 0.5260 | - | - | - | 0.4740 | - | - | - |
| HSBC | $\alpha_k$ | 0.0042 | 0.0002 | 14.897 | 0.000 | 0.0095 | 0.0012 | 7.8084 | 0.000 |
| | $\beta_k$ | 1.4311 | 0.0609 | 23.490 | 0.000 | 2.6267 | 0.4024 | 6.5275 | 0.000 |
| | $\sigma$ | 0.0022 | - | - | - | 0.0059 | - | - | - |
| | P | 0.576 | - | - | - | 0.424 | - | - | - |
| UBS | $\alpha_k$ | 0.0038 | 0.0002 | 13.099 | 0.000 | 0.0148 | 0.0007 | 18.8654 | 0.000 |
| | $\beta_k$ | 1.6956 | 0.0476 | 35.568 | 0.000 | 0.1226 | 0.05695 | 2.1535 | 0.031 |
| | $\sigma$ | 0.0028 | - | - | - | 0.0051 | - | - | - |
| | P | 0.489 | - | - | - | 0.511 | - | - | - |
| JPMorgan | $\alpha_k$ | 0.0031 | 0.0002 | 12.927 | 0.000 | 0.0108 | 0.0009 | 11.1609 | 0.000 |
| | $\beta_k$ | 1.2699 | 0.2056 | 6.1739 | 0.000 | 1.9895 | 0.0561 | 35.421 | 0.000 |
| | $\sigma$ | 0.0014 | - | - | - | 0.0055 | - | - | - |
| | P | 0.532 | - | - | - | 0.468 | - | - | - |
| Bank of America | $\alpha_k$ | 0.0029 | 0.0002 | 13.577 | 0.000 | 0.0107 | 0.0008 | 12.1863 | 0.000 |
| | $\beta_k$ | 1.4937 | 0.0583 | 25.604 | 0.000 | 1.5001 | 0.1816 | 8.2576 | 0.000 |
| | $\sigma$ | 0.0012 | - | - | - | 0.0058 | - | - | - |
| | P | 0.493 | - | - | - | 0.507 | - | - | - |
| Citigroup | $\alpha_k$ | 0.0115 | 0.0008 | 13.134 | 0.000 | 0.0042 | 0.0002 | 19.85 | 0.000 |
| | $\beta_k$ | 0.7031 | 0.0683 | 10.281 | 0.000 | 0.5297 | 0.0178 | 29.67 | 0.000 |
| | $\sigma$ | 0.0050 | | | | 0.0018 | | | |
| | P | 0.438 | | | | 0.562 | | | |
| Credit Suisse | $\alpha_k$ | 0.0100 | 0.0015 | 6.5078 | 0.000 | 0.0057 | 0.0005 | 10.040 | 0.000 |
| | $\beta_k$ | 2.7401 | 0.4046 | 6.7712 | 0.000 | 1.1715 | 0.0604 | 19.378 | 0.000 |
| | $\sigma$ | 0.0056 | | | | 0.0037 | | | |
| | P | 0.252 | | | | 0.748 | | | |

**TABLE 9** Switching Regime Regression Estimates for Each Bank Constituting the Panel–cont'd

| Bank | Param. | Regime 1 | | | | Regime 2 | | | |
|---|---|---|---|---|---|---|---|---|---|
| | | Estimate | Std. Err. | z-value | p-value | Estimate | Std. Err. | z-value | p-value |
| Deutsche Bank | $\alpha_k$ | 0.0040 | 0.0002 | 14.070 | 0.000 | 0.0098 | 0.0010 | 9.6565 | 0.000 |
| | $\beta_k$ | 1.049 | 0.0516 | 20.334 | 0.000 | 1.5173 | 0.1819 | 8.3389 | 0.000 |
| | $\sigma$ | 0.0018 | | | | 0.0062 | | | |
| | P | 0.444 | | | | 0.556 | | | |
| Lloyds | $\alpha_k$ | 0.0028 | 0.0001 | 15.537 | 0.000 | 0.0118 | 0.0008 | 13.5901 | 0.000 |
| | $\beta_k$ | 1.8532 | 0.0415 | 44.621 | 0.000 | 0.8893 | 0.1458 | 6.0987 | 0.000 |
| | $\sigma$ | 0.0010 | | | | 0.0063 | | | |
| | P | 0.418 | | | | 0.582 | | | |
| Norin | $\alpha_k$ | 0.0039 | 0.0002 | 17.046 | 0.000 | 0.0117 | 0.0009 | 12.6852 | 0.000 |
| | $\beta_k$ | 1.3191 | 0.0773 | 17.051 | 0.000 | 1.5936 | 0.1960 | 8.1266 | 0.000 |
| | $\sigma$ | 0.0018 | | | | 0.0056 | | | |
| | P | 0.535 | | | | 0.465 | | | |
| RBS | $\alpha_k$ | 0.0040 | 0.0002 | 17.171 | 0.000 | 0.0098 | 0.0009 | 10.0266 | 0.000 |
| | $\beta_k$ | 0.8500 | 0.0266 | 31.913 | 0.000 | 1.4329 | 0.1545 | 9.2687 | 0.000 |
| | $\sigma$ | 0.0017 | | | | 0.0058 | | | |
| | P | 0.509 | | | | 0.491 | | | |
| Rabobank | $\alpha_k$ | 0.0115 | 0.0013 | 8.4300 | 0.000 | 0.0036 | 0.0006 | 5.7174 | 0.000 |
| | $\beta_k$ | 0.3086 | 0.1550 | 1.9903 | 0.000 | 3.0974 | 0.1682 | 18.4104 | 0.000 |
| | $\sigma$ | 0.0045 | | | | 0.0039 | | | |
| | P | 0.459 | | | | 0.541 | | | |
| WLB | $\alpha_k$ | 0.0033 | 0.0002 | 13.008 | 0.000 | 0.0077 | 0.0008 | 9.1651 | 0.000 |
| | $\beta_k$ | 1.0243 | 0.0345 | 29.670 | 0.000 | 1.9129 | 0.1804 | 10.5990 | 0.000 |
| | $\sigma$ | 0.0012 | | | | 0.0057 | | | |
| | P | 0.397 | | | | 0.603 | | | |
| BTMU | $\alpha_k$ | 0.0102 | 0.0009 | 11.4078 | 0.000 | 0.0040 | 0.0002 | 14.843 | 0.000 |
| | $\beta_k$ | 2.7440 | 0.3040 | 9.0265 | 0.000 | 1.8065 | 0.0685 | 26.346 | 0.000 |
| | $\sigma$ | 0.0058 | | | | 0.0019 | | | |
| | P | 0.493 | | | | 0.507 | | | |

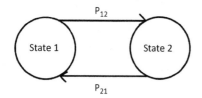

**FIGURE 10**  Switch Markov chain.

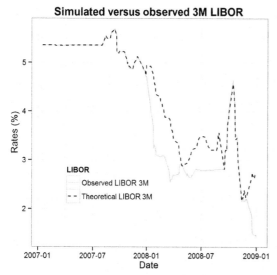

**FIGURE 11**  True Theoretic vs. Observed 3M LIBOR: The observed LIBOR tended to go near the true LIBOR in April 2008 shortly after the *Wall Street Journal* article. The difference increased afterward until the end of 2008.

true LIBOR in April 2008 shortly after the *Wall Street Journal* article. The difference increased afterward until the end of 2008.

# 6 IMPACT OF THE LIBOR MANIPULATION

In an attempt to assess the impact of the LIBOR manipulation Snider and Youle [271] explains that the best picture of aggregate exposure is given by aggregate revenue that banks earn from their derivative portfolios. Research shows that few major U.S. banks experienced

large net revenue increases in 2009 when the LIBOR fell dramatically. For instance, in the first quarter of 2009 Citigroup reported it would make $936 million in net interest revenue if interest rates fell by 25 basis points a quarter over the next year and $1935 million if they were to fell 1% instantaneously.

The impact of the LIBOR manipulation can be divided into three categories:

1. Impact on the over-the-counter interest rate derivatives indexed on LIBOR
2. Collateral damage on the municipalities' debts in the United States
3. Systemic impact on monetary policy

## 6.1 Impact on OTC Derivatives

A report published by the Bank of International Settlements in relation to over-the-counter (OTC) derivatives market activity in the first half of 2011[5] showed that the notional amount outstanding for OTC interest rate derivatives contracts all currency included was approximately $554 trillion. The break down of the U.S. dollar interest rate derivatives in the first quarter of 2009 is shown in Table 10.

Assuming that 1% of these contracts were affected by the manipulation of the LIBOR for

**TABLE 10**  Global over-the-counter Derivatives in Q1 2009 Exposed to USD LIBOR

| Product | Nominal (B$) | Gross market value (B$) |
|---------|--------------|--------------------------|
| FRA | 13,800 | 50 |
| Swaps | 126,573 | 4886 |
| Options | 13,000 | 411 |
| Total USD | 153,373 | 5347 |

---

[5]OTC derivatives market activity in the first half of 2011, Bank for International Settlements (November 2011), www.bis.org/publ/otc_hy1111.pdf.

an average of 2 basis points per quarter the total gains account for $5 billion.

## 6.2 U.S. Government Agencies' Debt

The LIBOR scandal peaked in the United States[6] in July 2012 when the Oakland City Council negotiated a termination without fees or penalties of an interest rate swap between Oakland and Goldman Sachs. Ending this agreement could save Oakland $4 million a year. The city of Oakland issued $126 million in variable interest rate bonds in 2005, with an associated interest rate swap in which Oakland would pay Goldman Sachs a fixed rate of 5.6775% until 2021 and in exchange, Goldman Sachs would pay Oakland an offset based on 65% of the LIBOR. Obviously a lower LIBOR rate due to manipulation would artificially inflate the payment of the city to the investment bank.

In 2013 the city of Philadelphia[7] was one of the last in litigation with major banks for the consequences of the LIBOR manipulation. Between 2009 and 2011, the city paid nearly $110 million altogether in termination fees to various banks to unwind swap agreements built around interest rates.

Experts' estimates[8] note that more than $200 billion in government agency swap contracts were affected by the rate manipulation. Assuming the average rate distance between the observed LIBOR and the "true" LIBOR is around 50 basis points, the total opportunity loss for

TABLE 11   **Negative Externalities:** Lower Limit of the Losses

| Target | Exposure to LIBOR (B$ per quarter) | Total loss (B$) |
|---|---|---|
| Derivatives | 153,373 | 5 |
| U.S. governmental agencies | 200 | 1 |
| LIBOR Bubble | 17,000 | ? |

the local municipalities in the United States was around $1 billion.

## 6.3 LIBOR Bubble

A more speculative consequence is related to the impact of the LIBOR manipulation to the monetary policy of the U.S. and the quantitative easing that followed the LIBOR manipulation.[9] The hypothesis that the low LIBOR rate communicated by banks influenced the cutting rate strategy of the U.S. Treasury cannot be rejected. Six years after those events the U.S. economy has a growth level higher than before the crisis, so the LIBOR bubble did not yet have negative impact. But if the trend in both GDP growth and market bull is nothing than a bubble the consequence risk could be very disruptive.

Table 11 shows the lower limit of the losses generated by the LIBOR manipulation.

## 7 OUTLOOK

Moral hazard is a key connection point between white-collar crime and abuse on financial markets. Manipulation of financial markets is one of the major concerns of investigators and regulators. The recent allegations of LIBOR manipulation prove the sensitivity of the issue.

---

[6]Goldman Sachs got break, but not cities, http://www.sfgate.com/opinion/openforum/article/Goldman-Sachs-got-break-but-not-cities-3711524.php.
[7]Philadelphia latest U.S. city to sue banks in Libor scandal, http://www.reuters.com/article/2013/07/29/us-usa-libor-philadelphia-lawsuit-idUSBRE96S0UZ20130729.
[8]U.S. Cities Get Fleeced in Libor Scandal, http://www.thefiscaltimes.com/Articles/2012/07/23/US-Cities-Get-Fleeced-in-Libor-Scandal#sthash.JYXJNZhx.dpuf.

[9]This New Libor "Scandal" Will Cause A Terrifying Financial Crisis, http://www.forbes.com/sites/jessecolombo/2014/06/03/this-new-libor-scandal-will-cause-a-terrifying-financial-crisis/3/.

However, the LIBOR manipulation cannot be the result of an institution acting alone. Before May 2008, an institution acting alone would not be able to change in a significant way the LIBOR rates. An organized attempt of two or more banks also not have produced significant results. After 2008 under the hypothesis of a bank acting solely, the changes in LIBOR rates would have been limited. However, an organized approach of at least four financial institutions could result in significant manipulation of the LIBOR. Our attempt at rebuilding a theoretic LIBOR shows that the impact was significant in the period after July 2007 until the last quarter of 2008. The difference was as high as 1% during certain periods. The theoretic and observed LIBOR should be considered as two boundaries of the real financing conditions in the markets at that time. The lower bound of total losses inflicted to the real economy is $6 billion.

# EURIBOR Manipulation

## 1 BACKGROUND

Allegations of interest rate manipulation were noted in scientific literature in 2007 by Abrantes-Metz and Addanki [272]. LIBOR and EURIBOR were the main interest rate benchmarks targeted by manipulators. The Barclays penalty in June 2012 for LIBOR fixing was followed by a wave of investigations especially in Europe. The outcomes revealed that the main actors included the Barclays, Deutsche Bank, Socit Gnrale, RBS, UBS, JPMorgan, Citigroup, and the brokers ICAP and RP Martin were organized into two separate illegal cartels that conspired to manipulate EURIBOR and LIBOR to benefit their own positions in the derivatives markets.

Barclays, Deutsche, Socit Gnrale, and RBS were accused of operating in a cartel between September 2005 and May 2008 in the euro interest rate derivatives market.[1]

Another cartel concerned the Japanese yen interest rate derivatives. Those involved in this group were UBS, RBS, Deutsche, JPMorgan, Citigroup, and RP Martin.

The investigation of the European Commission also noted the collusion between banks who were supposed to be competing with each other and the traders from the banks involved also exchanged commercially sensitive information relating.

---

[1]Libor and Euribor Fix Scandals: EC Fines Eight Banks 1.71 billion euros for Cartels, http://www.ibtimes.co.uk/libor-euribor-fixing-fines-european-commission-cartels-527395.

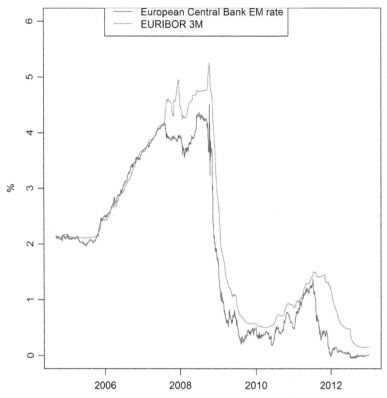

**FIGURE 1**    Evolution of EURIBOR 3 month and European Central Banks 3 month rate.

Figure 1 shows the evolution of the 3 month EURIBOR and of the European Central Bank's 3 month rate. The manipulation occurred the first time to influence the valuation of derivatives trade and the second time around 2008 for hiding the liquidity crisis banks faced and the increasing cost of the inter-banking lending. Thus, during that period they submitted lower levels than the real cost of funding.

## 2 ARCHITECTURE OF A CONTINUOUS CRIMINAL ENTERPRISE

EURIBOR is defined by the European Banking Federation (EBF) as *the rate at whicheuro interbank term deposits are being offered within the EMU zone by one prime bank to another at 11:00 am Brussels time.*

Between 2004 and 2009 almost 60 entities participated in the EURIBOR submission over various periods of time. Many entities entered or exited the panel due to absorption (e.g., Natexis) or mergers (e.g., Abn Amro, Banca Nationale di Lavoro). Compared to the 16 banks constituting the USD LIBOR panel the EURIBOR panel is bigger in size, more diversified internationally, and more heterogonous in terms of profile.

Figures 2 and 3 show the evolution of the rankof a bank in the submission panel. In theory a given bank should keep its rank stable over a period of time as its financing condition should not radically change, especially during of the credit cycle peak. But in practice it can be observed that many banks had a very volatile rank especially before 2009. Barclays, JPMorgan, or Rabobank had a lot of variability in their rank especially before 2008.

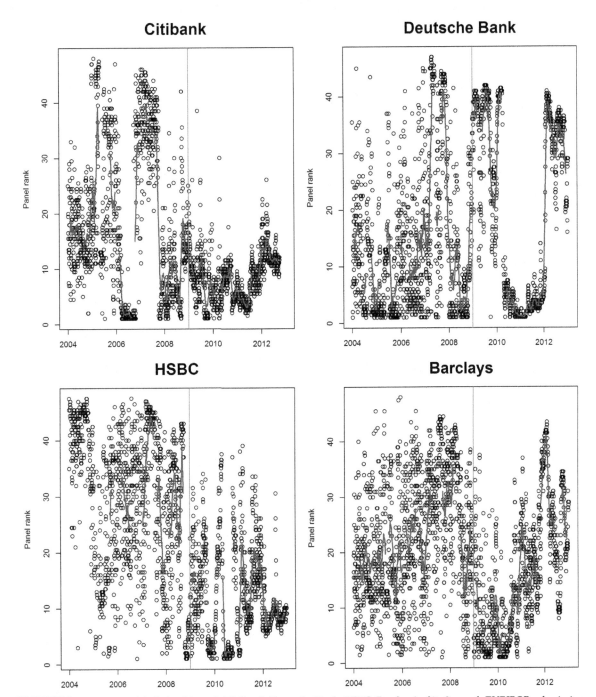

**FIGURE 2** Evolution of daily bank's rank (Citibank, Deutsche Bank, HSBC, Barclays) of its 3-month EURIBOR submission in the panel. The red line (dark gray in print versions) indicates the moving average of the ranks over a 40-day window.

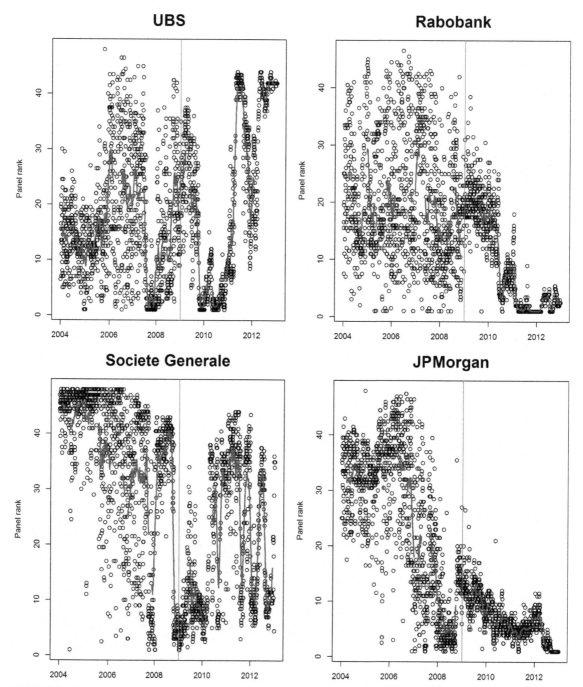

**FIGURE 3** Evolution of daily bank's rank (JPMorgan, SocGen, Rabobank, UBS) of its 3-month EUROBOR submission in the panel. The red line (dark gray in print versions) indicates the moving average of the ranks over a 40-day window.

All the examples depicted in Figures 2 and 3 are banks that had either a sure or alleged participation in the manipulation of EURIBOR and the fact that the rank of their submission was volatile might be partially explained by their involvement or alleged involvement in the EURIBOR rigging. After 2009 the ranks became more stable.

To manipulate the average of so many contributors with very volatile behavior it would be necessary that a large number of banks agree to submit a rate in a confined interval. As was shown for the case of LIBOR one bank cannot move the average, since it would require at least four banks to corroborate their actions. In the case of EURIBOR at least 10 banks would need to work together to move the benchmark. Coordinating the submission of four banks can be done by the banks themselves, while for 10 banks the communication becomes more complex. Therefore, such a large-scale manipulation would require buffers to collect the information from various banks and to send back suggested submissions to synchronize their actions. Figure 4 suggests an architecture for optimally deploying the EURIBOR rigging. As noted, this would involve "buffers" that would centralize and dispatch information to the manipulators.

The best candidate for this buffer role would be the broker and the clearinghouses. Among the firm investigated the broker RP Martin used its contacts with a number of JPY Libor panel banks that did not participate in the infringement, with the aim of influencing their JPY LIBOR submissions. Another big broker ICAP was also cited in the indictment.

Clearinghouses (e.g., LCH Clearnet, ICE, CME) are massive players in the rates markets and their initial margin calculation is also driven by the EURIBOR. The EURIBOR manipulation mostly involved other actors than the banks from the panel given the sophistication.

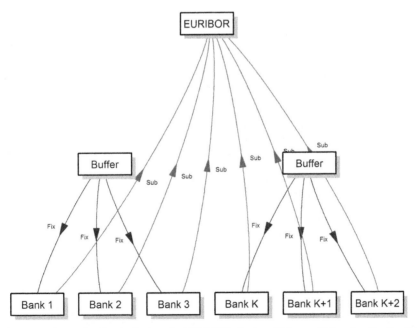

**FIGURE 4** Architecture for optimally deploying the EURIBOR rigging. This would involve "buffers" to centralize and dispatch information to the manipulators.

# 3 METHODOLOGICAL CONSIDERATIONS

Studying the dynamics of the rates submitted by banks during the concerned period can be useful for understanding if abnormalities appeared and also to understand the impact of the manipulation on the rates level. Therefore, in this section the following three questions will be addressed:

1. Wasthe submission process of each bank stable over time?
2. Wasthe relationship between the submissions of various EURIBOR maturity stable over time?
3. Whatwas the "true" value of the EURIBOR during 2008?

## 3.1 Concordance Agreement in the Panel Submissions

A first statistic aims to measure if the submission of the panel is consistent over time. Thus, for a given rate and for a few consecutive submissions of the panel we would expect the ranking of the submission in the panel to be constant and also concordant. This test is based on the idea that over a short period of time (1 week) the rank of the banks regarding the submitted EURIBOR is constant. One avenue for assessing the concordance of the submission of the panel for a few consecutive days is the Kendall's coefficient. Ideally for a perfectly concordant panel over time we would expect to find a value close to 100%.

Figure 5 shows the evolution of the Kendall W concordance for the 1-month EURIBOR

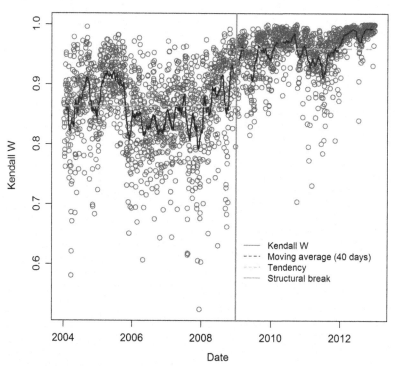

FIGURE 5   Evolution of the Kendall W concordance for the 1-month EURIBOR on 2 consecutive days.

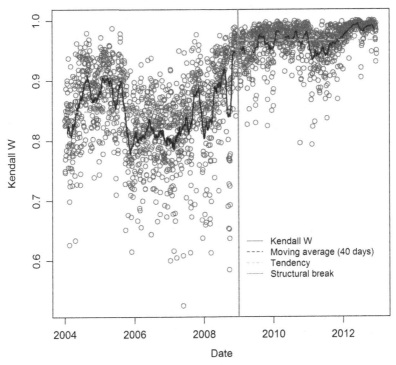

**FIGURE 6** Evolution of the Kendall W concordance for the 3-month EURIBOR on 2 consecutive days. The value decreases significantly in the period 2006-2007 and increases after 2009 in the post-manipulation period. The period when the concordance went below 80% corresponds to the manipulation of rates for altering the mark-to market of interest rate derivatives.

on 2 consecutive days. The value is globally above 80% and increase after 2009 in the post-manipulation period.

Figure 6 shows the evolution of the Kendall W concordance for the 3-month EURIBOR on two consecutive days. The value decreases significantly in the period 2006-2007 and increases after 2009 in the post-manipulation period. The period when the agreement went below 80% corresponds to the manipulation of rates for altering the mark-to market of interest rate derivatives.

Figure 7 shows the evolution of the Kendall W concordance agreement for the 6-month EURI-BOR on 2 consecutive days. The value decreases as low as 70% during the period 2006. The explanation of this finding is that the EURIBOR 6 month (and also the 3 month) is the most

commonly used benchmark for the settlement of derivatives. Therefore, manipulators had more incentive to rig the 6 months compared to the 1-month maturity. As a consequence the concordance for these submission is lower during the period of manipulation. The concordance increased after the manipulation period and was also influenced by the fall in interest rates.

## 3.2 Fixing the Forward-Rate Curve

Similar to the LIBOR case, the initial motivation for manipulating the EURIBOR was to distort the mark-to market of derivatives underwritten by banks. If a derivative was in the money at a given date the bank had an incentive to manipulate the benchmark for driving that derivative out of the money. As discussed in the

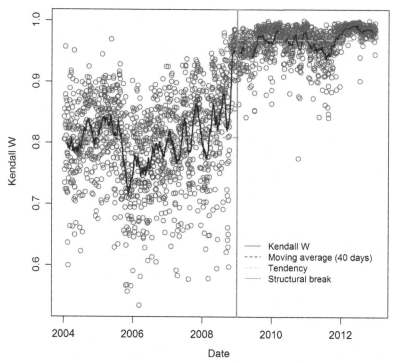

**FIGURE 7**  Evolution of the Kendall W concordance for the 6-month EURIBOR on 2 consecutive days. The value decreases as low as 70% during the period 2006. The explanation for this finding is that the EURIBOR 6 month (and also the 3 month) is the most commonly used benchmark for the settlement of derivatives.

previous chapter prior to 2008, exotic derivatives products depending on the steepness of the forward interest rate curve (steepener) were very popular on the markets. Here the value depended on the difference between a long-term rate and a short-term rate which was mainly the 3-month or 6-month EURIBORs. Long-term rates were more complicated to fix and the EURIBOR was more straightforward. The direction of the manipulation depended on the particular exposure of the banks involved and changed over time. Without knowing the price details of those derivative one way to assess this fact is to measure if the submissions of banks for various maturities were concordant. In other words, if a bank had a given rank in the panel from the 3-month EURIBOR it should have a close rank for the 6-month or 12-month submission.

If manipulation is involved in the key maturities than this rule should not be respected and the submission for different maturities should not be concordant. Figure 8 shows the evolution of the Kendall W concordance for the 3-month, 6-month, and 12-month submissions, cross-sectional for all banks. The concordance value is lower in the period prior to 2009 compared to after 2009. During 2006-2007 the agreement dropped to as low as 60%.

## 3.3 "True" EURIBOR

The last point concerns what would have been the "true" EURIBOR during the subprime crisis if the manipulation did not occur. The EURIBOR depends on the rate of the central bank (European Central Bank).

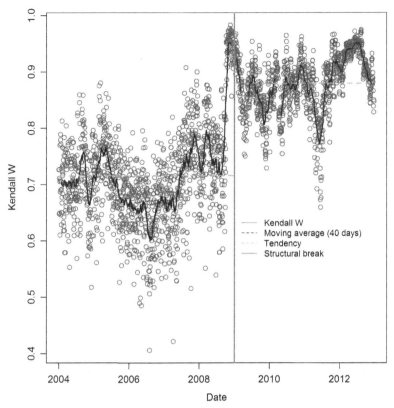

**FIGURE 8** Evolution of the Kendall W concordance for the 3-month, 6-month and 12-month submissions, cross-sectional for all banks. The concordance value is lower in the period prior to 2009 compared to after 2009. During 2006-2007 the concordance dropped to as low as 60%.

Figure 9 shows the structural breaks in the relationship between the variations of the EURIBOR 3M ($EUR_t$), the similar maturity rate of the Central bank ($\Delta DR_t$), and the average credit default swaps (CDS) spread for banks ($\Delta CDS_t$):

$$\Delta EUR_t \approx f(\Delta CDS_t, \Delta DR_t) \qquad (1)$$

The breakpoints are in November 2007 and in October 2008.

One way to estimate the relationship between the three variables is to regress the daily variations during the periods before, between, and after the breakpoints. However, this approach is restrictive if big variations occurs in the level of the rates. Therefore, an alternative is the vector autoregression (VAR) model, which has proven to be especially useful for describing the dynamic behavior of economic and financial time series and for forecasting [273]. Straightforward implementation in an R development environment was proposed by Zeileis [274] and Pfaff [275]. For the EURIBOR case a simple form is with one lag:

$$EUR_t = \beta_1 \cdot EUR_{t-1} + \beta_2 \cdot CDS_t + \beta_3 \cdot DR_t + \epsilon_t \quad (2)$$

Table 1 shows the results of estimations of the VAR model for the data set prior to November

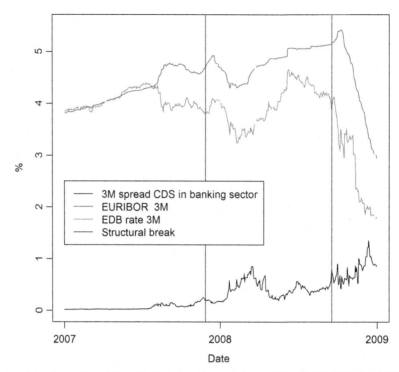

**FIGURE 9** Structural breaks in the relationship between the variations of the EURIOBOR 3M ($\mathbf{EUR}_t$), and the similar maturity rate of the Central bank ($\Delta DR_t$) and the average CDS spread for banks ($\Delta CDS_t$). The break points are in November 2007 and in October 2008.

**TABLE 1** Estimation of the VAR Model for the Data Set Prior to November 2007

| Parameter | Estimate | Std. Error | *t*-Statistic | *p*-Value |
|---|---|---|---|---|
| **EURIBOR lag(1)** | 0.983 | 0.0035 | 278.432 | 0.00 |
| **CDS** | 0.124 | 0.0222 | 5.605 | 0.00 |
| **DR** | 0.016 | 0.0034 | 4.746 | 0.00 |

**TABLE 2** Estimation of the VAR Model for the Data Set Between November 2007 and October 2008

| Parameter | Estimate | Std. Error | *t*-Statistic | *p*-Value |
|---|---|---|---|---|
| **EURIBOR lag(1)** | 0.997 | 0.006 | 147.908 | 0.0 |
| **CDS** | 0.028 | 0.009 | 3.092 | 0.00 |
| **DR** | 0.001 | 0.007 | 0.141 | 0.887 |

2007. Table 2 shows estimation of the VAR model for the data set between November 2007 and October 2008 and it shows that during this period the relationship between the EURIBOR, CDS, and euro rate is weaker than in the previous period.

For reconstituting the EURIBOR during the credit crunch period, the VAR dynamic estimate prior to November 2007 is applied to the factors observed in the crisis period. Figure 10 evolution of the observed 3-month EURIBOR and of the simulated theoretical EURIBOR. Between the end of 2007 and the last quarter of 2008 the 3M EURIBOR had a lower value than its theoretical level, the maximum difference reaching 100 basis points. This finding is in line

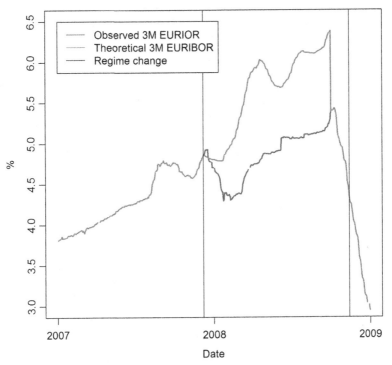

**FIGURE 10** Evolution of the observed 3-month EURIBOR and of the simulated theoretical EURIBOR. Between the end of 2007 and the last quarter of 2008 the 3M EURIBOR had a lower value than its theoretical level, the maximum difference reaching 100 basis points.

with the result concerning the USD LIBOR manipulation.

would represent 16 billion euros, the equivalent of the average yearly net profit of a major global bank.

# 4 COLLATERAL IMPACT OF THE EURIBOR MANIPULATION

## 4.1 Deposits

EURIBOR was the main reference used for establishing deposit remuneration and floating rates on loans in the Eurozone. The total deposits on the Eurozone toward the end of the EURIBOR manipulation period was around 16 trillion euros as shown in Table 3. A small variation of 10 basis points in the 6-month EURIBOR value

## 4.2 Toxic Credit Products

Prior to the crisis many city halls and municipalities across Europe took loans from banks with interest rate exotic derivatives embedded. The aim of such structured products was to diminish the cost of financial for local counties. During the financial crisis, due to unusual conditions and high volatility the exotic derivatives led to an exaggerated interest cost that reached as high as 15%. Thus, many counties became distressed and could not afford such

**TABLE 3**  Total Deposits on the Eurozone Toward the End of the EURIBOR Manipulation Period with a High of Around 16 Trillion Euros

| Country | 2003 | 2004 | 2005 | 2006 | 2007 | 2008 | 2009 |
|---|---|---|---|---|---|---|---|
| Germany | 3699.6 | 3807.4 | 3918.3 | 4103.9 | 4438.8 | 4686.9 | 4488.2 |
| France | 2249.5 | 2418.8 | 2513.4 | 2630.1 | 3045.8 | 3421.2 | 3437.3 |
| Spain | 999.5 | 1120.7 | 1392.2 | 1635.3 | 1956.2 | 2212.8 | 2247 |
| Italy | 1141.6 | 1215.1 | 1324.4 | 1503.9 | 1811.4 | 1986.7 | 2002.9 |
| Netherlands | 809.2 | 876.4 | 763.2 | 846.2 | 1012.1 | 1024.1 | 979.8 |
| Ireland | 282 | 336.9 | 411.7 | 496.7 | 535.9 | 694 | 663.6 |
| Belgium | 444.7 | 503.5 | 572.8 | 639.4 | 695.9 | 686.8 | 634.4 |
| Austria | 330 | 352.6 | 390.6 | 418.4 | 471.1 | 590.6 | 556.7 |
| Luxembourg | 370 | 398.7 | 443.5 | 468.7 | 527.3 | 559.2 | 480.7 |
| Total | 10,780 | 11,515.3 | 12,314.4 | 13,416.3 | 15,275.4 | 16,811.6 | 16,489.5 |

interest levels. In France, for instance, in 2010 from the estimated local public debt of about 160 billion euros, between 30 billion euros and 35 billion euros was in structured loans, and 20 billion euros of this number represented debts of municipalities in distressed situations due to the exotic derivatives.

The exotic derivatives embedded in the loans were very sensitive to the level of rates but also to the volatility, shape and steepness of the rate curve. In addition, many structured loans had embedded exotic derivatives depending on few currencies interest rates. The reference for all those derivatives was the EURIBOR and the LIBOR when dual or multiple currencies were involved. When during the crisis banks reported lower EURIBOR and LIBOR rates compared to the real cost, the differential between the long- and short-term rates changed as well as the interest rate differential between currencies, fact that activate the barriers in the exotic derivatives and led to the increase of the effective rate of the loan.

For example, if the activation of a barrier indexed on the difference between the 10-year swap and the 6-month EURIBOR created a snowball payoff this could generate an exponential increase in the loan's effective interest.

## 4.3 Eurozone Crisis

The EURIBOR manipulation came at the dawn of the Eurozone crisis as depicted in Figure 11. The rate rigging might have contributed to its amplification. The Eurozone distress was characterized by higher cost of debt of the Southern European countries compared to the Northern one requiring bailouts. This particularity consisted of the fact that the downfall in the credit cycle was juxtaposed over the increase in the sovereign debt in the Eurozone. The high EURIBOR rate was the signal that caused the European Central Bank to cut the rates. The banks with a lower rate during 2008 postponed the measure of the European Central

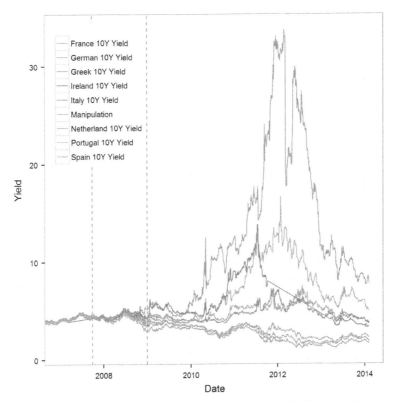

**FIGURE 11** EURIBOR manipulation came at the dawn of the Eurozone crisis. The Eurozone distress was characterized by a higher cost of debt of the Southern European countries compared to the Northern one requiring bailouts.

Bank and thus the worsening of the credit cycle at sovereign level came at the same time as the European Central Bank measure. The sum of these two effects amplified the crisis as explained by Frunza [276].

## 5 REVIEW OF PENALTIES APPLIED TO VARIOUS BANKS

Investigation of the EURIBOR and LIBOR manipulation is ongoing, but as of 2014 Deutsche Bank was fined 725 million euros, its biggest single penalty in history. Societe Generale was fined 446 million euros and RBS must pay 391 million euros. The combined fines for manipulating the yen London interbank offered rate and EURIBOR, the benchmark money-market rate for the euro, are the largest-ever EU cartel penalties. JPMorgan's infringement resulted in a 79.9 million euros fine. RP Martin got a 247,000 euros fine, while Citigroup's two remaining infringements cost them 70 million euros.

Zurich-based UBS and London-based Barclays Plc were not fined in the EURIBOR manipulation because they were the first to inform the EU of the cartels. UBS avoided a potential 2.5 billion euro fine and Barclays escaped a 690 million euro penalty. Citigroup also avoided an extra 55 million euro fine for blowing the whistle on one part of the cartel. Investigations were also opened against Crédit Agricole, HSBC, and JPMorgan. The cumulus of the penalties is reflected in Table 4.

TABLE 4   Penalties (Millions of Euro) Paid by Banks for the EURIBOR, LIBOR, and YBOR Manipulations

| Bank | Fine LIBOR | Fine EURIBOR | Fine YBOR |
|---|---|---|---|
| Barclays | 390 | | |
| Rabobank | | 774 | |
| Deutsche Bank | | 260 | 485 |
| Societe Generale | | 446 | |
| RBS | | 131 | 260 |
| Citigroup | | 70 | |
| RP Martin | | | 0.25 |
| ICAP | | 66 | |
| UBS | 1292 | | |
| JPMorgan | | | 80 |
| Lloyds | 280 | | |

# 6 OUTLOOK

The European Commission recognized the anti-trust and the cartel type behavior and started an ongoing investigation of the EURIBOR manipulation. However, a full-fledged picture of all the consequences has not yet been seen by any regulatory body, since in many cases of benchmark manipulation only the point in time impact of the trading book of the concerned banks are overseen by the regulators and investigators. The full effect on the real economy is often bigger and more important. In the case of the EURIBOR, the manipulation came at a time when the budgetary coordination of the Eurozone was weak and a small variation of the interest rate could have massive consequences in the way policies were designed and economic decision were made.

# The Madoff Case

## 1 BACKGROUND

At one time Bernard Madoff was perceived as an experienced professional with high authority in the Wall Street investment community. His broker-dealer firm Madoff Investment Securities founded in the 1960s was closely involved in developing the NASDAQ stock market, where Madoff served as chairman for many years. Bernard Madoff was also a founding member of the International Securities Clearing Corporation in London.

Despite his good reputation and credentials, in the torments that followed the Lehman collapse in 2008, the Madoff scam revealed itself from within after many doubts were raised by analysts and the investment community. Before dissecting the scam, it is important to depict in a few words the Madoff magic investment strategy that was able to provide double-digit returns for almost two decades.

Madoff employed a strategy referred to as a *split-strike conversion*, which is nothing more than a collar option structure on a basket of stocks. This involves purchasing a basket of 30-35 large-capitalization stocks with a high degree of correlation to the main market index. After the stocks were purchased, "out-of-the-money" call options on index were sold and "out-of-the-money" put options index were bought, thereby forming a collar structure aimed at reducing the variability of the investment.

A collar structure is shown in Figure 1 where the manager is long on the underlying, sells an out-of-the money call on that underlying, and buys a protective out-of-the money put. The strike of the call is obviously greater than the strike of the put. Thus, the investment evolves in a *tunnel* established by the strikes of the call and of the put.

The aim of a collar is that on a long stock position, selling a call increases the return and allows

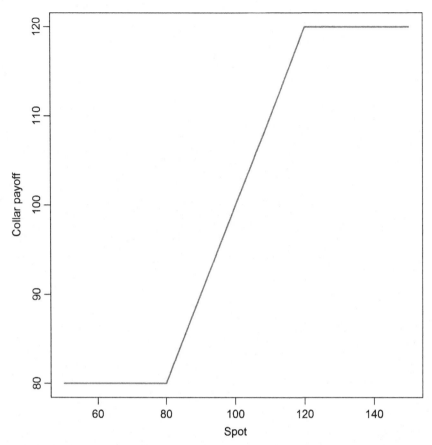

**FIGURE 1**   Collar payoff with a long position. The aim of a collar is that on a long stock position, selling a call increases the return and allows taking gains from bullish movements to the level of the short call strike price and the purchase of an out-of-the-money put funded with part or all of the call premium, which protects the position against a market downturn.

taking gains from bullish movements to the level of the short call strike price and the purchase of an out-of-the money put funded with part or all of the call premium and protects the position against a market downturn.

Figure 2 shows the investing process used by Madoff Investment Securities. Investors accessed Madoff's strategy through feeder funds such as Fairfield Sentry. The feeder funds generally did not mention Madoff's name or his firm name on their materials. Madoff established a firm in the United States in charge with the market mak-

ing and one in London more focused on family's finances. JPMorgan was the bank keeping the funds of Madoff's firm. Unusually Madoff's hedge fund was not a hedge fund either *de facto* or *de jure*. It was nothing more than a broker-dealer acting like a sophisticated prime broker for the feeders. Madoff Investment Securities was not able to make the market for all the options volume he needed. Therefore he traded the options over-the-counter for his strategy, so he had some counterparties, allegedly **UBS** and the defunct Merrill Lynch.

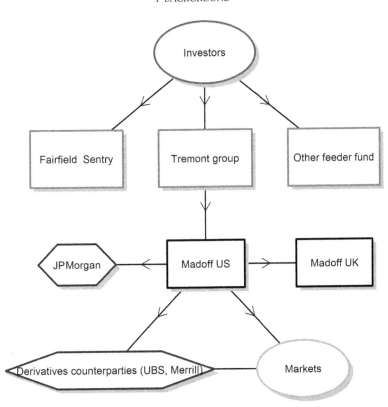

**FIGURE 2** Madoff's investment process. Investors accessed Madoff's strategy through feeder funds such as Fairfield Sentry. Feeder funds generally did not mention Madoff's name or his firm name on their materials. Madoff established a firm in the United States in charge with the market making and one in London more focused on family finances. **JPMorgan** was the bank keeping the funds of Madoff's firm. Unusually Madoff's hedge fund was not a hedge fund either *de facto* or *de jure*. It was nothing more than a broker-dealer acting like a sophisticated prime broker for the feeders. Madoff Investment Securities was not able to make the market for all the options he needed. Therefore he should trade the options OTC for his strategy, so he had some counterparties allegedly **UBS** and the defunct **Merrill Lynch**.

Strategically speaking, a broker-dealer and a hedge fund do have different business models; they finance themselves differently and remunerate themselves differently. Broker-dealers finance themselves on the short-term market and have various activities for clients and for their own accounts in an effort to transform volatility into profits. Hedge funds take funds from investors and invest in agreed-upon strategies. The access to markets is provided by the prime brokers. A traditional hedge fund has two streams of revenue: one being the management

fees, accounting for 1-2% of the total assets under management and the performance shares, accounting for 20% of the provided gains. A broker-dealer takes a commission on clients operations and also takes profit from the variations of the mark-to market of its derivatives portfolio.

Madoff's had a discretionary and not transparent remuneration based on the number of trades executed for deploying its strategy. As a broker-dealer Madoff financed itself at a very high cost, similar to a hedge fund. The cost of the funds was around 15% a year compared to 5%, which was the short-term financing cost for an average broker-dealer on Wall Street in 2008. It is questionable why this business model was chosen and what the benefits were.

Madoff's vehicle was not organized as a traditional hedge fund and many of its functionalities (depositaries, accounting, audit, brokerage, etc.) were either internalized or provided by a company managed by family and an inner circle friends as follows:

- Peter Madoff, Bernie's brother, was serving as Chief Compliance Officer for Madoff Securities International Ltd., for more than 40 years and ran the daily operations. He has served as vice chairman of the National Association of Securities Dealers (NASD), as member of its board of governors, and was as actively involved as his brother in the NASDAQ stock market as a member of its board of governors and its executive committee and as chairman of its trading committee.
- Shana Madoff, Peter's daughter, worked for Madoff Securities International Ltd. as a rules and compliance officer and attorney. She was married to Eric Swanson, who was part of the team conducting a SEC review of Madoff's firm in 2003.
- Mark and Andrew Madoff, both deceased, served as directors in the company in charge with trading floor and with sales activities.
- Ruth Madoff, Madoff's wife, was employed in the firm and helped Bernie in the various illegal actions.

His close friends for more than 25 years that were involved included

- Paul Konigsberg, the accountant in charge of the Madoff Family Foundation tax returns.
- Davif Friehling, the external auditor of the hedge funds.
- Frank di Pascali, the director of option trading who started working with Madoff in the early 1980s.

- Jeffry Picower, a businessman and investor in the fund who apparently knew about the scam and managed to pull out his funds with very good performance.
- Stanley Chais, another investor with preferential treatment.

This list provides an idea of how the scam was organized. The way the firm functioned, its business model, and the huge reliance on family members and friends in the daily operations is an unusual model for a respected financial institution.

Madoff's scheme generated the biggest loss in the history of the financial industry and was revealed to the investment community at the very moment the banking crisis unleashed its disastrous consequences on the economy. The web of funds managed by Bernie Maddoff was at that point the biggest hedge fund in the world in terms of assets under management. After the unwinding of the Madoff affair and with all the research showing how wrong the scheme was, several questions remain unaddressed:

1. Investors and mainly financial institutions do run extensive due diligences before placing funds in an alternative vehicle such as a hedge fund. Reputed institutions, mainly from Europe, which accounted for more than half of the Madoff contributions, such as AGF asset management Oddo and Cie, Dexia Asset Management, Santander, and Union Bancaire Privee, do regularly have in-depth review procedures of an investment vehicles by a team specialized in conducting such diligences. Why did those procedures fail to signal irregularities?

2. Madoff's scheme was too large and had many ramifications in various Wall Street institutions to remain unnoticed to a trained eye. Harry Markopulos, the whistleblower that alerted the SEC, could not have been the only one that saw the big picture. Hence, the obvious question then is what was the real

number of people aware of the scam that took part directly or indirectly for a profit?

3. To have such a huge amount of assets, most likely Madoff relied on some core investors that knew all along the timeline of the scam and about the true nature of the business. They were probably paid preferentially by the funds; in every Ponzi scam there are winners. Were all those special clients identified?

4. Madoff Securities were too large at least theoretically speaking to not be noticed by peers in the derivatives markets. It is certain that some traders from those institutions knew that something did not look right based on the volumes and type of trades Madoff was engaged in. Why would those Wall Street institutions prefer the *Omerta* instead of denouncing a practice that would most likely be very harmful and disruptive to its business?

5. To run such a large-scale operation any fund requires a license from regulators and authorities that are supposed to conduct in-depth reviews of their activity. Indeed, Madoff Securities was incorporated in the 1960s when it received its license, but regulators tend to do activity reviews periodically especially for systemic organizations. Why did those reviews not raise any flags and why they did not have the required level of detail?

6. The Madoff operation can be characterized as a full-fledged "mom and pop" investment boutique involving mainly members of his extended family. However, all big institutions interacting with other require third-party documents, audits, and reviews. Madoff managed to create an end-to-end operation where no external party was able to have a detailed view of his operations. Using a small audit firm, Friehling & Horowitz, with an uncertain status relative to U.S. accounting authorities Madoff managed to manipulate its performance without catching the

attention of any of its peers. Why did the regulators and counterparties accept those facts?

# 2 MARKOPULOS'S WARNINGS

> [...] I'm turning this case in because it's the right thing to do. Far better that the SEC is proactive in shutting down a Ponzi Scheme of this size rather than reactive. *Harry Markopulos's letter to SEC from November 2005*

Harry Markopulos, the man who figured out Madoff's scheme[1] sent no less than five letters to the Securities Exchange Commission between 2000 and 2008 warning about the misrepresentations and incoherence's in Madoff's enterprise. The best known letter, sent in 2005, was self-titled, The World's Largest Hedge Fund is a Fraud, contained detailed insight on the organization of the scam as well as no more than 29 red flags that should alarm every investor. A few of Markopulos[2] red flags included:

- Madoff Investment Securities was too secretive and did not allow proper external auditors. The firm also had an unusual remuneration scheme, in which he received a transaction fee from the feeder that also received management fees and performance bonuses from clients. Madoff Investment Securities was in fact a broker-dealer that used the contributions from the feeder to finance the market-making activity at a rate that was three times higher than its peers.
- Madoff had mostly non-American investors (with a few exceptions that apparently got their gains fully) and collected funds mostly

---

[1]The man who figured out Madoff's scheme, http://www.cbsnews.com/news/the-man-who-figured-out-madoffs-scheme-27-02-2009/.
[2]Madoff Securities is the world's largest Ponzi Scheme, https://www.sec.gov/news/studies/2009/oig-509/exhibit-0293.pdf.

from Europe, a fact that most likely bought him time in the eyes of U.S. regulators. Curiously many European fund managers considered themselves lucky if they could get *special access* to Madoff's scam.

- Madoff Investment Securities was a family business, which made it unique in the sector. Furthermore, only family members were given access to the secrets of the investment strategy.

- If Madoff was really implementing his strategy he might have been involved as a broker in illegal front-running. Since the 1980s Madoff had paid brokers to clear his customers orders through his broker-dealer firm. Those so-called a "legal kickback," gave Madoff the reputation of being the largest dealer in trading about 15% of the NYSE stock volume.[3] Madoff allegedly used the orders that other brokers placed through his firm to predict the market's move and with this strategy to provide superior returns. As a hedge fund it would not represent an issue but as a broker-dealer, what Madoff Investment Securities was in reality, this would be an illegal practice, taking advantage of information before sharing it with clients. His clients were the feeders (Figure 2, which had proper hedge fund status). This practice is in theory an offense called front-running.

- The split-strike conversion (collar) strategy cannot achieve a 12% average annual return for many years with much less negative returns. His low volatility in returns indicates he probably used a narrow collar with options close to moneyness, which are more expensive than out-of-the-money ones. Under this conditions, his returns would have even more difficult to justify.

- The volumes on the options market Madoff allegedly used were not sufficient for implement his option-based strategy. In addition, he was not a counterparty with the major option dealers from Wall Street like Goldman Sachs or Morgan Stanley.

- The Sharpe ratio of 2.55 for Fairfield Sentry Ltd. was much higher than the Sharpe ratios experienced by the rest of the hedge fund industry. As shown in Figure 3 the Fairfield's Sharpe ratio was in the 99th quantile in the distribution of the 5823 hedge fund performance from the Barclays hedge database.

## 3 PERFORMANCE METRICS

Many of the numeric fraud indicators presented in previous chapters would be red flags if applied to the time series of returns generated by the Madoff strategy. Figure 4 shows the distribution of the monthly returns of the Fairfield Sentry returns, and the basic statistics are given in Table 1.

### 3.1 Bias Ratio

The Bias ratio is the most popular metric used for assessing whether returns have been manipulated. During the Maddoff events the Bias ratio had allegedly indicated abnormal values as presented by software providers of the hedge funds industry[4]

For a given set of returns $R_i$ with mean $\mu_R$ and standard deviation $\sigma_R$, under the discrete form the Bias ratio can be expressed as:

$$BR = \frac{\sum_{i=1}^{M} R_i \cdot \mathbf{1}(0 \le R_i \le \sigma_R)}{\text{const.} + \sum_{i=1}^{M} R_i \cdot \mathbf{1}(-\sigma_R \le R_i \le 0)} \quad (1)$$

---

[3]The Regulation of Publicly Traded Securities, http://www.sec.gov/rules/proposed/s71004/s71004-587.pdf.

[4]Hedge Funds Risk And Replication, https://www.riskdata.com/resources/hedge_funds_risk_and_replication.html https://www.riskdata.com/files/news/Madoff_Bias_Ratio.pdf.

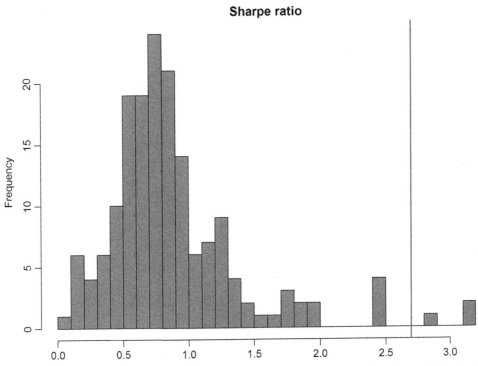

**FIGURE 3** Histogram of the Sharpe ratio. The Fairfield's Sharpe ratio (vertical line) is in the 99th quantile in the distribution of the 5823 hedge fund performance from the Barclays hedge database.

**TABLE 1** Basic Statistics for Fairfield's Returns

| Parameter | Value |
| --- | --- |
| Mean | 0.0089 |
| Median | 0.008 |
| Standard deviation | 0.0072 |
| Skewness | 0.807 |
| Kurtosis | 3.488 |
| Sharpe ratio | 2.67 |

The Bias ratio has the following properties:

1. $0 \leq BR \leq \infty$
2. if $R_i < 0, \forall i > 0$ then $BR = 0$
3. if $R_i > \sigma_R, \forall i > 0 \, R_i > 0$ then $BR = 0$
4. if $\mathbf{E}(R_i) = 0$ and $\mathbf{E}(R_i^3) = 0$ then $BR \to 1$

Highly illiquid securities have high serial correlation and hence the Bias ratio of such a fund will be higher than 1 and a high Bias ratio for funds to be invested in classic strategies should be an alarm signal.

In the Madoff case for the Fairfield fund the Bias ratio was **6.33**, a very high value that indicated that the returns might have not been genuine. Figure 5 shows the distribution of Bias ratios computed though a resampling approach from the initial target series of returns.

## 3.2 Discontinuity in Zero Test

Figure 4 gives a hint about the fact that returns distribution is positively skewed and is discontinuous in zero. Two tests are performed for assessing the smoothness of Fairfield's returns in zero as well as for the proportion of negative

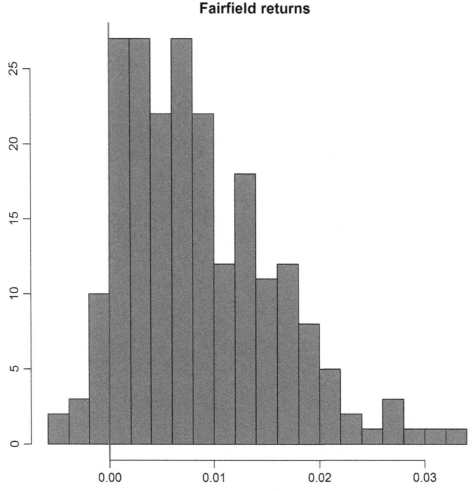

**FIGURE 4**  Distribution of the monthly returns of Fairfield's sentry returns. The red line (dark gray in print versions) indicates zero returns.

returns. Both tests revealed that the function was not smooth in zero with a discontinuity and that the number of negative returns was not appropriate to the shape of the distribution.

## 3.3 Ponzi Scam Test

A way to test if an investment has a Ponzi pattern is to assess whether its evolution total funds follow the trajectory described in the previous section. Statistically, for a given discrete time series of total assets from a fund $S^*_{t_i}$, where $t_i i = (1, 2, \ldots, N)$ are the reporting dates of the funds performance, which are generally monthly:

$$\mathbf{E}(S^*_{t_i}) = a \cdot e^{(b+r_m)\cdot t_i} + c \cdot e^{(d+r_m)\cdot t_i} + f \cdot e^{r_m \cdot t_i} \quad (2)$$

Assuming the expected value for the Ponzi funds can be represented as functional form $\Im(\theta)$ with $\theta = (a, b, c, d, f)$ for a given series of funds assets value the parameter $\theta$ can be estimated. The results of the estimations for the parameters

# Bias ratio

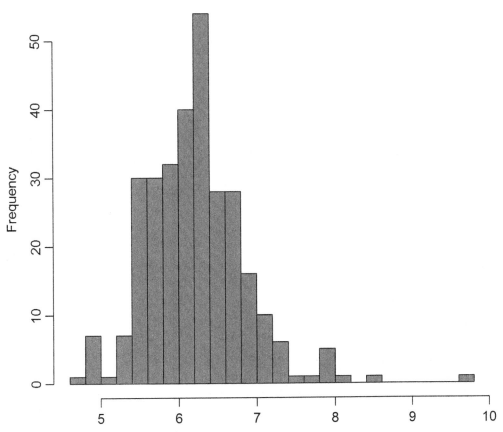

**FIGURE 5**   Bias ratio distribution for Fairfield's fund returns.

on the time series of the Fairfield Sentry case as well as the confidence intervals constructed via a resampling approach are presented in Figure 6. All parameters are statically significant at a 95% confidence interval denoting that the fund shows the typical behavior of a Ponzi scheme.

## 3.4 Relationship with Other Hedge Fund Markets

One of the points noted by many analysts is that Madoff's returns (Fairfield Sentry) did not look like any other hedge fund returns and were not correlated with any other financial market as shown in Figure 7. In addition, Madoff's strategy looked more like a fixed income investment not correlated to any other index. Based on Barclays hedge fund indexes database, two tests are performed:

- The correlation between Fairfield's returns and other hedge fuds indexes is computed and represented in a distribution. The correlation level is inferior to 30%, the highest being the Belgian Equity Index (BEL 20 Index).
- A Granger causality test searching the cause-effect relationship between

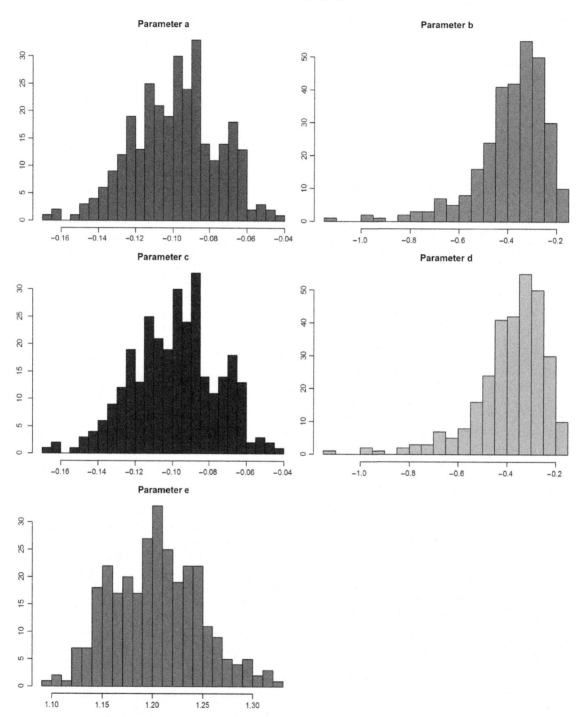

FIGURE 6   Ponzi scheme dynamic test. Estimations for the parameters on the time series of the Fairfield Sentry case as well as the confidence intervals constructed via a resampling approach.

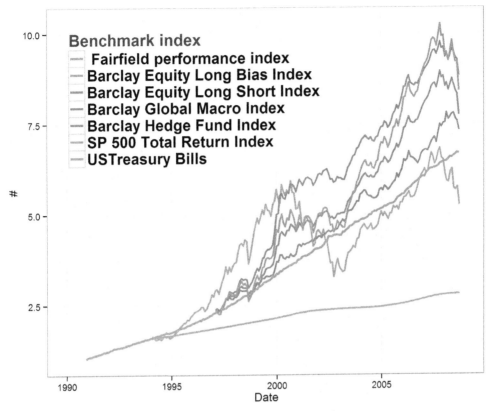

**FIGURE 7**   Maddoff scam. Fairfield performance index and various benchmarks.

the various indexes and Fairfield's returns rejects all causality with the exception of Barclays Merger Arbitrage Index and Barclays Multi-Strategy Index, which in practice are not indexes linked to Madoff's strategy. Both tests are depicted in Figure 8.

## 3.5 Benford's Law

The last statistical test assesses whether the returns reproved by Madoff were handled manually. Two tests are applied: the Benford test and the digits test. Figure 9 shows the first digit distribution for the returns of the Fairfield funds, which was Maddoff's main feeding fund.

The digits uniformity test described by Straumann [277], uniformity test that compares the percentage of observations ending in each digit 0 through 9 to its expected value of 10% under the null of a uniform distribution. The classic goodness-of-fit test U is asymptotically distributed.

$$U = \sum_{d=0}^{9} \frac{(D_d - M \cdot 0.1)^2}{M \cdot 0.1} \qquad (3)$$

where $D_d$ is the total number of observations ending in digit $d$ and $M$ is the total number of observations and the $U$ statistic is asymptotically distributed as a $\chi^2$ distribution with nine degrees of freedom.

Both tests reject the null hypothesis that the first digit follows the Benford's law and the last digit the uniform law, thereby indicating that

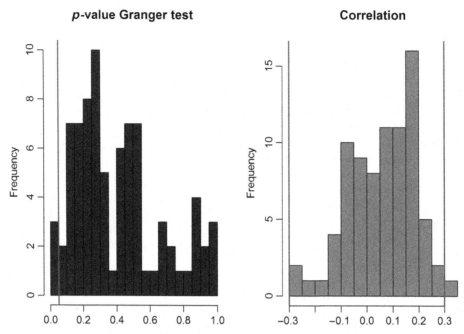

**FIGURE 8**   Fairfield returns relationship with hedge fund benchmarks.

the returns were subject to manual changes and thus they misrepresented the true performance of the fund.

## 4 SUCH A BIG CAKE FOR SO FEW PEOPLE

A fraud accounting for almost $50 billion that managed to keep going through two decades and overseen by a half dozen people from Madoff's family and entourage raises a few structural questions that go beyond financial and econometric aspects. Compared to the original Ponzi scheme, which used a relatively plain investment support, Madoff's was a complex investment scheme involving the market making of derivatives as explained above. When market making such an amount of derivatives corresponding to a high level of assets under investment, Madoff Securities became in fact one of the biggest actors in the derivatives market from Wall Street.

However, for those familiar with the sector the name Madoff was not associated until the 2008 investigation with derivatives activity.

It appears that many of the big names in the investment industry from Wall Street kept a low profile concerning Madoff's activities. What did they gain in exchange? It is known that an influential board member of both NASDAQ and NASD managed to obtain few favors from regulators. One of them concerned the naked short sale of stock, which is a very damaging practice on the capital markets. *Short sellers* were selling stock they did not own and were delivering after buying them when the prices dropped due to the bearish momentum created. Despite many irregularities in this area and regulators attempts to stop this practice Madoff obtained an exemption allowing market makers to sell short on a downtick. Both the SEC and Wall Street were grateful for his help and the rule for years was called the "Madoff Exemption."

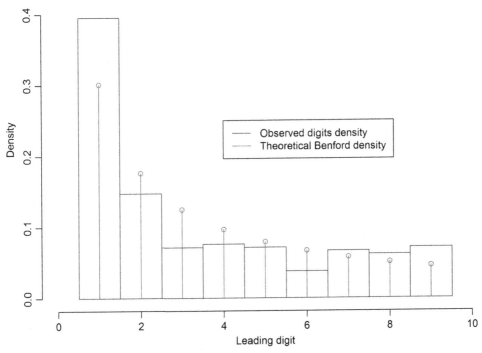

**FIGURE 9** First digit distribution for the returns of the Farifield fund which was Maddoff's main feeder fund.

Madoff is currently in the same detention facility[5] as the famous boss of the Colombo family, Carmine "the Snake" Persico, both serving life sentences. Both also inducted their sons in *the life* and, Carmine's son (Alphonse "Allie Boy") being the guest of the U.S. penitentiary system, and Madoff's both sons passing away after the scam was revealed.

During his detention Persico once presented to his inmates a hypothetical case study about a carpet-cleaning company and how he would not only control that company but would also have under his power the people who sold the carpet and the people who came and ripped it up before bringing it to the cleaners, explaining how all those combined businesses could garner over $1 million a year, for 20 or 30 years.[6] Telepathically or not Madoff replicated the scheme of his future inmate with the thinly veiled exception that the carpet cleaning was an investment firm and the 1 million figure was closer to 1 billion.

These facts are a coincidence, or maybe not. As recent unofficial investigation details note, Madoff was tied to many criminal groups including the American La Cosa Nostra. In 2009, the SEC charged several Madoff "feeders" with securities fraud related to their participation in the Madoff Ponzi. One of those charged was Robert Jaffe, who was also a partner with Madoff in a brokerage called Cohmad Securities. In

---

[5]Michael Milken, 60,000 Deaths, and the Story of Dendreon, https://www.sec.gov/comments/s7-08-09/s70809-4614.pdf.

[6]Mob Jail Hiss and Tell, http://nypost.com/2006/09/25/mob-jail-hiss-and-tell/.

his early years Jaffe was found to be running money for the Anguilo brothers (Donato and Francesco), bosses of the Boston-based Patriarca family allied with the New York Genovese family. Madoff knew through various relations people from the Michael Milkin era including Michael Steinhardt, the son of a reputed Genovese associate. Allegations were made recently that allege that Russian Mafia might have been a partner in Madoff's fund business in addition to Markopolis' statement in Congressional hearings that noted that Bernie had ties to the Russian Mafia and Latin American drug gangs.

# 5 OUTLOOK

*If you want to do something, you do it all.* **Carmine** *Persico, of the Colombo family*

Madoff's scam was not just a Ponzi scheme, it was a fraudulent enterprise where a small group of people managed to create a criminal process controlled from one end to another with no connection whatsoever with people outside the inner circle. This criminal governance structure, common to organized crime, depicts a behavioral model of which regulators and investigators should be aware of.

Further investigation will almost surely reveal even more information about this case. Nonetheless, one thing is clear: many of Madoff's peers including his banker did not alert authorities and seemed to accept his misbehavior. Indeed, Wall Street firms were not invested in his fund much. It was mostly private investors and European funds that had the privilege to share the $50 billion in losses.

CHAPTER

# 4D

# Enron-WorldCom

## 1 BACKGROUND

One month after the 9/11 tragedy, two enormous scandals hit the stock market: the defaults of Enron and WorldCom, the latter being the biggest bankruptcy in history until 2008 (Table 1). Despite being in different industries and having completely different levels of fraud both companies had one point in common: Arthur Andersen, a former audit and consulting firm and part of the Big-Five audit league. To misrepresent such enormous operations and conceal the true state of affairs, both companies needed the participation of the external auditors that certified their financial statements, which were the main inputs for investors and analysts in making their investing decisions.

Enron's case and to a lesser extent World-Com's is a cautious tale of the relationship between companies and auditors. In fact, during the recent financial crisis auditors certified accounts of many failed banks including Lehman, without having the real means, competence, or methods to valuate complex products. The Big-Five audit firms that certify the accounts of the big banks had a share in the propagation of the financial crisis and misconduct. The asymmetry between the banks' operators and auditors is significant, especially in regards to complex products or activities.

## 2 WORLDCOM

WorldCom was a U.S.-based provider of telecommunications services listed on NASDAQ under the name WCOM. WorldCom, Inc. began as a regional provider of telephone service and grew through acquisitions during the 1990s and expanding its operations in the Internet area. In a very competitive market with shrinking margins and a huge balance sheet to manage, World-Com's CEO Bernard Ebbers turned to rogue accounting practices in order to fuel the company's share price.

**TABLE 1**   Top 10 Bankruptcies by Asset Size

| Rank | Company | Date | Country | Sector | Assets (B$) |
|---|---|---|---|---|---|
| 1 | Lehman | 15-09-08 | US | Investment Bank | 691 |
| 2 | Washington Mutual, Inc. | 26-08-08 | US | Savings & Loan Holding Co. | 328 |
| 3 | **WorldCom, Inc.** | 21-07-02 | US | Telecommunications | 104 |
| 4 | General Motors | 6-01-09 | US | Manufactures & Sells Cars | 91 |
| 5 | Kaupthing Bank | 9-10-08 | Iceland | Banking | 87 |
| 6 | CIT Group, Inc. | 11-01-09 | US | Banking Holding Company | 80 |
| 7 | **Enron Corp.** | 12-01-01 | US | Energy Trading, Natural Gas | 66 |
| 8 | Conseco, Inc. | 17-12-02 | US | Financial Services Holding Co. | 61 |
| 9 | Chrysler, LLC | 30-04-09 | US | Manufactures & Sells Cars | 39 |
| 10 | Thornburg Mortgage, Inc. | 5-01-09 | US | Residential Mortgage | 37 |

*Enron and WorldCom are among the top 10 bankruptcies in history. Until 2008 WorldCom was the biggest company that ever failed.*

Thus, between 1998 and 2000 WorldCom reduced the provisions aimed to cover the liabilities of companies bought through an aggressive acquisition strategy. That reduction inflated the revenue massively by almost $3 billion. In addition, operating costs were not accounted as such but reclassified as long-term investments, thereby inflating the firm's assets by almost $4 billion and turning losses into profits.

The original complaint[1] filed in April 2002 stated that WorldCom:

- misrepresented its earnings as a result of recording inappropriately write-downs of goodwill and other intangible assets associated with WorldCom's acquisition of numerous telecommunication companies at premium prices.
- misstated the value of goodwill and other intangible assets associated with

WorldCom's acquisition of numerous telecommunications companies at premium prices.

After a big profit of $1.4 billion in 2001, WorldCom revealed in 2002 that it would have to take a big write-down of goodwill and intangible assets for $20 billion, an announcement that plummeted WorldCom's share price to close at $2.35 per share on April 29, 2002.

The auditor Arthur Andersen was also accused of violating federal securities laws by certifying WorldCom's financial statements. The WorldCom case is nothing more than a case of large-scale accounting fraud, consisting of diminishing liabilities and capitalizing costs. Such a fraud could have not been carried out without the participation of external auditors. Detecting such a fraud would have been almost impossible from the simple analysis of the price signal.

In the aftermath of the case, the firm filed for bankruptcy in July 2002. WorldCom re-emerged as MCI and was acquired by Verizon in 2005. The ex-CEO, Bernard Ebbers, was found guilty of fraud and sentenced to 25 years in prison.

---

[1]*Fadem vs. WorldCom*, http://securities.stanford.edu/filings-documents/1024/WCOM02-01/2002430_r01c_02CV3288.pdf.

# 3 ENRON

Compared to the WorldCom fraud case, Enron was much more complicated. While the World-Com scheme was based on simple capitalization of expenses, Enron employed a multitude of techniques and the panel of wrongdoing involved the creation of special-purpose entities as well as the use of energy derivatives as financial shenanigans.

Enron was created in 1985 from the merger of Houston Natural Gas and InterNorth, a Nebraska pipeline company. At the same time, the U.S. federal government deregulated the trade of natural gas. Enron, with the help of the consulting firm McKinsey, decided to develop a new activity in gas trading and in 1990 created a new subsidiary, Enron Finance Corp., run by Jeffrey Skilling, who was previously with McKinsey. The gas trading expanded and Enron became one of the main players in the American energy markets and at the same time led to company's fall.

## 3.1 A Silent Scam

The accounting background of Enron's fraud has been extensively discussed in the literature [278], but two aspects require a special attention: the impact of the misrepresentations on the price signal prior to the default and the role played by the energy derivatives in the fraud.

One of the main red flags concerning Enron was its $100 billion turnover figure. In only half a decade, Enron's sales increased 10 times in value from $9.2 billion in 1995 to over $100 billion in 2000. As shown in Table 2, the profit did not follow the trend of the turnover, and both the gross and net margin ratios contracted three and five times respectively during the same period.

Enron used on a large scale joint ventures and special-purpose entities as financial shenanigans [278]. Those entities were not consolidated, thereby hiding debt and losses. Starting in the mid-1990s, Enron began creating thousands of entities for various ventures or projects that would require massive infusions of capital. These entities were borrowing money based on Enron's credit grade, but they were not consolidated at the group level. In addition, Enron recuperated the cash from loans by selling energy or other services to those entities, thereby inflating its own cash flows.

As explained in the seminal book *Financial Shenanigans* [278], the effect of off-balance sheet entities went way beyond the simple debt disguise effect and in fact participated directly in inflating the Enron share price. As Cash was a scarce resource Enron used its own stock as assets to joint ventures. In addition, those special

**TABLE 2**  Enron's Sales, Gross and Net Profit

| ($ millions) | 2000 | 1999 | 1998 | 1997 | 1996 | 1995 |
|---|---|---|---|---|---|---|
| Sales | 100,789 | 40,112 | 31,260 | 20,273 | 13,289 | 9189 |
| Gross profit | 6272 | 5351 | 4879 | 2962 | 2811 | |
| *Gross profit to Sales Ratio (%)* | 6.2 | 13.3 | 15.6 | 14.6 | 21.2 | |
| Profit | 979 | 893 | 703 | 105 | 584 | 520 |
| *Profit to Sales Ratio (%)* | 0.97 | 2.23 | 2.25 | 0.52 | 4.39 | 5.66 |

*In only half a decade Enron's sales increased 10 times in value from $9.2 billion in 1995 to over $100 billion in 2000.*
*Source: Schilit [278] and Dharan and Bufkins [279].*

entities bought themselves Enron stock. As noted above these entities were not consolidated and in this way Enron managed indirectly to *long* its own stock and to support the price signal. This scheme worked as a butterfly effect. If the stock was increasing in value, Enron's own equity stake in the partnership increased and enable it to book additional revenue which further led to price inflation. In fact, $85 million of Enron's earnings were explained by this mechanism.

The financial engineering was certified and covered by auditors, thereby making it complicated to detect by an external analyst. In fact, even when the company started to get in trouble in the days prior to the bankruptcy filing when the stock was trading for $3, the three credit rating agencies (Moody's, Standard & Poor's, and Fitch) gave investment-grade ratings to Enron's debt. In October 2001, 16 out of 17 security analysts were recommending Enron as a *strong buy* or *buy*. Under these circumstances, the price signal did not exhibit unusual features. A structural break in the relationship between Enron and the Dow Jones Index returns occurred in July 2001, which coincides with the beginning of the class period in the first class action suit. Even the company's beta remained constant until it was too late. Figure 1 reflects the evolution of the Enron price and the tests for bubble detection based on the augmented Dickey-Fuller statistics. Enron's price reached its climax in 2000 at almost $100, but there is no evidence of a bubble.

Figure 2 shows some of the tests for assessing the weak efficiency hypothesis. With the exception of the Portmanteau test, which shows some serious serial correlation effects after 1999, the other tests do not show clear proof of inefficiency in the Enron returns. These findings are not surprising as the particularity of the Enron case was that all the information available in the market was distorted by Enron itself.

## 3.2 Enron the "Goldman Sachs" of Energy Trading

Mark-to-market accounting is noted in the post-Enron literature as one of the main tools responsible for the fraud. The company used mark-to-market accounting for its energy contracts, which it treated as financial contracts for this purpose. This allowed Enron to report expected benefits from future transactions into current period income. The mark-to-market itself was not the source of the fraud, but its application to a class of products have no observable market prices or parameters, which were later called Level III assets in the accounting standards.

Many works state that through the mark-to-market Enron was booking today the profits of forward sales, which were supposed to be delivered in the future. This idea is not entirely accurate as forward contracts in the energy markets and in particular in the gas market are different from other forward markets like FX. For example, one of the popular contracts in gas deals is the *swing contract*, which is also used in oil and electricity markets. A *swing contract* gives the holder the right to buy a predetermined quantity of gas at a predetermined price and allows some flexibility in the amount purchased and the price paid. Typically, a swing contract sheet stipulates the minimum and maximum gas per day and per month to be bought, the strike price, and how many times during the month the option holder can change the daily quantity of gas purchased.

Thus, for each day $t$ in the discrete time interval $t \in [0, t_N]$ the option holder can exercise a quantity $q_t$ satisfying:

$$0 \leq q_t \leq q_{max} \qquad (1)$$

where $q_{max}$ is the maximum quantity that can be delivered in a day.

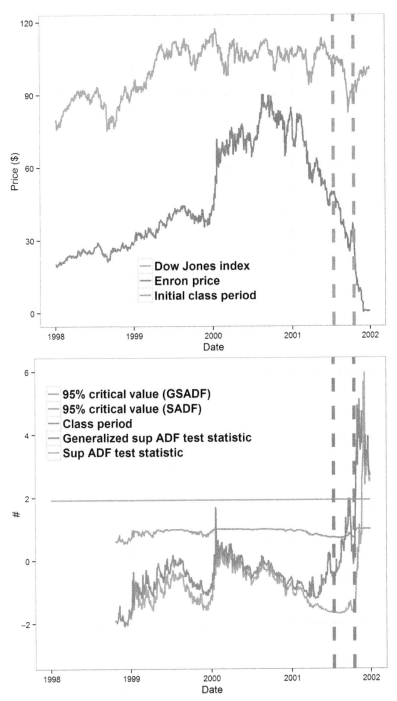

**FIGURE 1** Evolution of the Enron share price and the tests for bubble detection based on the augmented Dickey-Fuller statistics. The Enron price reached its climax in 2000 at almost $100, but there is no evidence of a bubble.

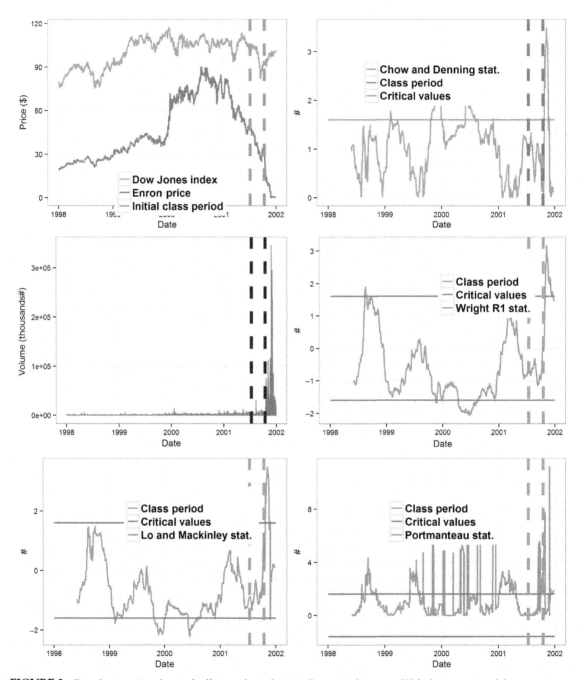

**FIGURE 2**　Tests for assessing the weak efficiency hypothesis in Enron stock returns. With the exception of the portmanteau test which shows some serious serial correlation effects after 1999, the other tests do not bring clear proofs of inefficiency in the Enron returns.

The global quantity consumed $Q_t$ is:

$$Q_{\min} \leq \sum_{i=0}^{N} q_{t_i} \leq Q_{\max} \quad i \in 1 \cdot N \qquad (2)$$

where $Q_{\min}$ and $Q_{\max}$ are minimum and the maximum quantities that can be delivered over the total period of $N$ days [280].

The pay-off of the swing contract is given at a day $t_i$ by:

$$(S_{t_i} - K_{t_i}) \cdot q_{t_i} \qquad (3)$$

where $S_{t_i}$ is the gas price and $K_{t_i}$ is the strike index constant on the agreed-upon interval of time. The valuation of such a contract is sophisticated and compared to basic financial forwards it has another degree of complexity linked to the variability of the gas to be delivered in the future. A very hot and dry summer in Northern California can deplete the hydro-power plants and increase the demand on gas for electricity production. Under this scenario the delivered quantities would reach the maximum, a fact that would also drive up the gas price in the secondary markets. The valuation of the swing contracts under this scenario as well the likelihood of such a scenario would be very complex. In fact, this flow of events actually happened between 2000 and 2001 during the so-called California Energy Crisis, when the state of California had a shortage of gas supply due to the market manipulation orchestrated by Enron.

In addition to the complexity of its valuation the gas delivery option has another particularity, which is its high dependency on the weather. No surprise again, Enron was one of the pioneers of weather derivatives and contributed to the development of the weather trades on the Chicago Mercantile Exchange. Enron had on its balance sheet over 5000 weather derivatives deals valued at over \$4.5 billion. These derivatives are very complex to value especially for multi-year contracts due to the fact that

weather forecasts are only reliable for 2-week timeframes. Like any other level III instrument, gas and weather derivatives could not be valued without professional advice. Thus, concerning the mark-to-market as the origin of fraud, in Enron's case it was more a *mark-to-management*. With no one being able to understand or price gas and weather derivatives, Enron's managers could adjust the balance sheet as they wanted.

Table 3 shows a break down of the Enron operating income between 1998 and 2000, emphasizing that the net operating income was driven by the derivatives activity. In fact, in 2000 the non-derivatives operation (classic distribution operation) were losing money.

With its increasing trading activity Enron started to compute and to communicate in its annual reports the value at risk measure with a 95% confidence interval for 1-day holding periods. As reflected in Table 4 the size of the 1-day Value at Risk (VaR) was \$89 million in 2000, representing a 162% increase compared to the previous year. The 1-day can be converted to a 10-day VaR by a plain time scaling. The corresponding capital necessary for backing the trading activity can be proxied as the 10-day VaR multiplied by a model correction factor ($K = 4$)

**TABLE 3** Enron Derivative Trading Income Compared to Other Sources of Income

|  | 2000 | 1999 | 1998 |
| --- | --- | --- | --- |
| Non-derivatives revenues | 93,557 | 34,774 | 27,215 |
| Non-derivatives expenses | 94,517 | 34,761 | 26,381 |
| Non-derivatives gross margin | (960) | 13 | 834 |
| **Other revenue (income from derivatives)** | 7232 | 5338 | 4045 |
| Other expenses | (4319) | (4549) | (3501) |
| **Operating income** | 1953 | 802 | 1378 |

*The net operating income was driven by the derivatives activity.*
*Source: Benston [281] and Partnoy [282].*

**TABLE 4** Profitability of Enron's Derivative Trading

|  | 2000 | 1999 |
|---|---|---|
| Derivative trading income (M$) | 7232 | 5338 |
| Value at risk 95% 1 day (M$) | 89 | 55 |
| Value at risk 95% 10 days (M$) | 281 | 174 |
| ROE of derivatives trading (%) | 642 | 768 |

*The resulting high level of ROE makes Enron more similar to a hedge fund than to an energy company.*

the return over equity (ROE) of the derivatives trading activity can be expressed as:

$$\text{ROE} = \frac{\text{Trading revenue}}{\text{VaR}_{10d} \cdot K} \quad (4)$$

The resulting ROE shown in Table 4 is in the 600-700% range, which is obviously a very high value, thereby making Enron more similar to a hedge fund than to an energy company.

### 3.3 Warning Signs

Starting in the fall of 2000 Jonathan Weil,[2] a New York journalist, warned about the volatility of Enron's business. Another analyst, Bethany McLean[3] noted the risk of cash depletion [283]. Besides the turnover inflation and the

California Energy Crisis events, there was a limited amount of public information. The publication of the Enron e-mail corpus[4] showed retrospectively that internally employees passed through a crisis period. Employee communication was more diverse with respect to people's formal positions and top executives had formed a tight clique with mutual support and highly brokered interactions with the rest of organization [284].

The Enron fraud was exposed by whistle-blower, Sherron Watkins, an Enron vice president. Enron's fall started in October 2001 when the auditing committee should have consolidated some of these partnerships and included their losses as a part of the company's financial results, which finally led to a $586 million reduction in previously reported net income.

### 3.4 Andersen

While WorldCom and Enron defaulted for financial reasons, Arthur Andersen was dismantled following the criminal charges in the Enron trial after being accused of evidence destruction. Enron was Andersen's second client in term of fees and provided both audit and consulting services. In addition, many of the chief financial executives and internal controllers were former Andersen auditors. In 2000 Enron's fees for Andersen were around $52 million, $25 million for audit, and $27 million for consulting services. In the torment of the events Arthur Andersen fired its lead audit partner for Enron, David Duncan, after learning that he had destroyed documents from the audit file, which did not avoid the criminal charges and caused the company to disband.

---

[2]*But at the heart of the situation is an accounting technique that allows companies to include as current earnings those profits they expect to realize from energy-related contracts and other derivative instruments in future periods, sometimes stretching over more than 20 years. Source: Energy traders cite gains, but some math is missing, The Wall Street Journal (Texas ed.) 9/20/2000, http://www.wsj.com/articles/ SB105545983187165000.*

[3]*In 1999, its cash flow from operations fell from $1.6 billion the previous year to $1.2 billion. In the first 9 months of 2000, the company generated just $100 million in cash. Source: Is Enron overpriced? Fortune, 3/5/2001, http://money.cnn. com/2006/01/13/news/companies/ enronoriginal_fortune/.*

[4]Enron Email Dataset, https://www.cs.cmu.edu/~./ enron/.

## ARTHUR ANDERSEN—AUDIT COWBOYS[a]

### Background

The Chicago-based audit firm was founded in 1913 by Arthur Andersen. For many years the firm supported the highest standards in accounting practice. In the 1980s Andersen developed a strong consultancy practice around technology. The consulting branch became independent in 2001 under the name of Accenture. In 2001 Arthur Andersen had 85,000 employees in 84 countries and generated $9 billion in fees.

### The Fall

During the 1990s Andersen expanded in terms of business and influence, with the turnover increasing almost five times in less than a decade. The culture was very aggressive from a technical and from a business point of view. The staff was pushed to go in-depth in their accounting reviews,[b] while partners were under pressure to generate new business fees. This is how the firm ended up providing both internal and external audit services to the same client as well as consulting services. Arthur Andersen had served as Enron's sole auditor for 16 years, also performing internal audits and providing consulting services. Enron, which was Andersen's client for almost 16 years, marked the end of the line and was representative of its edge-pushing culture.

### Aftermath

After the Enron episode, the U.S. Congress created the Sarbanes-Oxley Act imposing internal controls for the information flow to senior management in U.S.-listed firms. Auditors were also banned from providing consulting services to clients for which they provided audits. Being listed in the United States started to become expensive and at that time London started to gain momentum as a financial hub.

Arthur Andersen settled the various class action suit. In the WorldCom case the company agreed to pay $65 million.

[a] *Audit Cowboys* was the term used by few of the French AA alumni the author met in his early years at Ernst & Young.
[b] The auditor was in Andersen's view more a consultant rather than an accountant.

# 4 OUTLOOK

I view derivatives as time bombs, both for the parties that deal in them and the economic system. *Warren Buffet, 2002*

If moral hazard was noted as the main reason for the 2008 class of bankruptcies, in the case of the 2002 class the concentration of greed from the various actors implicated in the fraud seems to be the main factor. Auditors, analysts, investment banks, and rating agencies received substantial fees from Enron, and had no interest in digging further into Enron's business.

The special-purpose entities were also among the causes of the subprime crisis, with many of the credit portfolios being harbored in off-balance sheet structures. While the role of the auditors and of Enron's management were fundamental in the fraud, the vector of propagation was the complex montages such as the special-purpose entities and the gas/weather derivatives. Complexity automatically brings asymmetry between a firm's managers and its investors and implicitly creates a principal agent dilemma and auditors or consultants are not always in the best position to address the issue. Understanding the big picture is fundamental not only in financial crime assessment but in other areas as well. When a utility firm becomes a weather derivatives market maker or when a retail bank becomes an investment bank, for example, it should ring a bell to any investor.

# Rating Agencies and Crisis

## 1 BACKGROUND

Standard & Poors, Fitch, and Moody's are the main credit rating agencies, all based in the United States, that propose grades for debts underwritten by various organizations. The rating scale of each of the three agencies is given in Tables 1 and 2. The grades provided by these agencies are the main indicators used by analysts for making investment decisions in the area of debt or related vehicles. Ratings are also used by risk managers in overseeing the risk profile of portfolios or other assessments concerning collateral with a certain investment grade that should be held by an institution for regulatory reasons.

The scientific literature has shown that rating agencies are typically late with the lowering of ratings and often ignore numerous macroeconomic signals (e.g., Asian crisis or the credit crunch). Financial crisis noted weaknesses in the regulation of credit rating agencies as they were provided with both underwriting and rating services for structured credit products (e.g., Collateralized Debt Obligation (CDOs)); a conflict of interest is highlighted between serving clients for whom higher ratings of debt mean higher earnings and implicitly higher fees for the agencies paid by the sell side and accurately rating the debt for the benefit of the debt buyer/investor customers, who provide no revenue to the agencies. In 2011, concerns around the Eurozone crisis brought more attention about the role of credit rating agencies. It should be noted that most credit agencies are private companies that have many collateral activities (e.g., underwriting, consulting, IT systems).

As noted credit rating agencies have been incriminated over the past few years on two occasions:

- The subprime crisis (2007-2008). Credit agencies rated too optimistically the structured credit products that packaged the mortgages of American borrowers with low

**TABLE 1**   Rating Scale of Each of the Three Agencies

| Ranking | 1 | 2 | 3 | 4 | 5 | 6 | 7 | 8 | 9 | 10 | 11 |
|---------|---|---|---|---|---|---|---|---|---|----|----|
| S&P | AAA | AA+ | AA | AA− | A+ | A | A− | BBB+ | BBB | BBB− | BB+ |
| Moody's | Aaa | Aa1 | Aa2 | Aa3 | A1 | A2 | A3 | Baa1 | Baa2 | Baa3 | Ba1 |
| Fitch | AAA | AA+ | AA | AA− | A+ | A | A− | BBB+ | BBB | BBB− | BB+ |

**TABLE 2**   Rating Scale of Each of the Three Agencies

| Ranking | 12 | 13 | 14 | 15 | 16 | 17 | 18 | 19 | 20 | 21 | 22 |
|---------|----|----|----|----|----|------|------|------|----|----|----|
| S&P | BB | BB− | B+ | B | B− | CCC+ | CCC | CCC− | CC | C | D |
| Moody's | Ba2 | Ba3 | B1 | B2 | B3 | Caa1 | Caa2 | Caa3 | Ca | C | D |
| Fitch | BB | BB− | B+ | B | B− | CCC+ | CCC | CCC− | CC | C | D |

incomes. Hence, the risk was underestimated, which induced investors to make bad investment decisions.

- The Eurozone crisis (2011-2012), Credit agencies had added extra pressure on Eurozone sovereign bonds by an amplified downgrading of the obligors.

These two aspects will be discussed in the following section.

## 2 SECURITIZED SUBPRIME RESIDENTIAL MORTGAGES

Credit rating agencies were accused of misconduct and are used as an example of the effect of moral hazard on the relationship to the credit securitized investment products that flowed in the markets. White [285] exposed the fact that in the subprime residential mortgage debacle of 2007-2008, the three rating agencies played a crucial role. The conflict of interest between the sell-side and the buy-side was accentuated by the fact that the favorable ratings on the bonds that were securitized by subprime residential mortgages were the main factor in the successful underwriting and sale of these products to various categories of institutional investors from banks to hedge funds and from pension trusts to sovereign funds. The sale of those complex structured products inflated even more the

U.S. housing bubble and contributed in a full-fledged manner to its dismal end. When the U.S. real estate bubble started to lose momentum in mid-2006, many mortgage borrowers who were relying on a never-ending bubble in housing prices were not able repay their mortgages and defaulted. The initial hypothesis was that the three credit rating agencies were too optimistic and served the bond issuers who also were paying them fees for having the rating stamp. When prices of the structured mortgage bonds collapsed as a result of also being downgraded quickly by the same agencies that pushed them on the market, the consequences for the financial system were apocalyptic as many big institutions had invested in those products from the United States and overseas.

In the aftermath, the three agencies along with other connected institutions, were sued by private investors as well as by the U.S. government.

In the summer of 2007 two investment vehicles, the Cheyne and Rhinebridge structured vehicles, were in distress due to their exposure to the U.S. mortgages markets. Rhinebridge Plc[1]

---

[1]Rhinebridge Commercial Paper SIV May Not Repay Debt, http://www.bloomberg.com/apps/news?pid=newsarchive&sid=aEacPeg9pmLg.

was a structured investment vehicle[2] backed by the German bank IKB Deutsche Industriebank, which lost in only a few weeks about half of its value and was unable to pay its $1.2 billion debt consisting of commercial papers. Ironically, Rhinebridge was set up in June 2007[3] at the beginning of the euphony on the U.S. markets. Seventy-nine percent of Rhinebridge's holdings were in the U.S. and 80% were invested in mortgage-backed bonds, 83% of the assets having at that time the AAA rating. The German bank IKB was be bailed out by the end of 2007 by the German government.

After a few years of litigation in 2013 Moody's Investors Service and Standard & Poor settled the two long-running lawsuits that held them responsible for misleading investors about the risk of structured debt vehicles they had rated.[4]

The lawsuits concerning the Cheyne and Rhinebridge structured investment vehicles had accused Moody's, a unit of Moody's Corporation, and S&P, currently a unit of the McGraw-Hill Companies, of misrepresentation of the risks beared by the two entities. Morgan Stanley, which marketed both debt vehicles and helped structure the Rhinebridge one, also settled. All the accused organizations generated more than $700 million damages.

In 2013 the U.S. Department of Justice filed a lawsuit against Standard & Poor's Financial Services alleging that their ratings on structured credit products were inflated when they were relied upon by investors including many federally insured financial institutions. In the lawsuits S&P was accused of falsely representing that its ratings were objective, independent, and uninfluenced by S&P's relationships with investment banks. The government was seeking to obtain civil penalties for S&P's violations of three criminal fraud statutes: mail fraud, wire fraud, and financial institution fraud. Two years later in 2015 Standard & Poor's Financial Services agreed to pay $1.375 billion to settle with the U.S. Justice Department.[5]

# 3 EUROZONE CRISIS

While in the subprime crisis the rating agencies were accused of criminal frauds and settled in various courts, in the Eurozone crisis case things are more subtle. In fact, besides a few European politicians that accused the rating agencies of downgrading Eurozone bonds too much, the only relevant proof was brought by the scientific literature, which deserves review.

Gärtner et al. [286] used a benchmark macroeconomic model for ratings and showed that rating agencies do have some power to drive countries with a significant debt ratio into aggravation. The work shows that the PIIGS (Portugal, Ireland, Italy, Greece, and Spain) countries credit rating agencies appear to have played an aggravating role in the European sovereign debt crisis that unfolded in 2009.

Host et al. [287] indicated that the moment whencredit rating agencies decide to lower ratings, they act as an element of panic, instead of acting as an element of calming the market through the prediction of economic movements.

---

[2]A structured investment vehicle is an non-banking entity that borrows from the short-term commercial paper market to fund purchases of long-term asset-backed securities, thereby taking profit from the credit spread between its assets and liabilities.

[3]This finding is connected to another misconduct related to misselling as many of the Wall Street banks knew by that time the storm was close.

[4]Credit Rating Agencies Settle 2 Suits Brought by Investors, http://www.nytimes.com/2013/04/28/business/credit-rating-agencies-settle-lawsuits-over-debt-vehicles.html?_r=1&.

[5]Federal judge denies credit rating agency's motion to dismiss fraudlawsuit, http://jurist.org/paperchase/2013/07/us-district-court-denies-standard-and-poors-motion-to-dismiss-in-fraud-lawsuit.php.

The reputational crisis of credit rating agencies was assessed by Ryan [288] who raised the question of whether credit rating agencies they are credible in financial markets. The research notes that there may be a need to restrict the role of credit rating agencies in rating sovereign debt and stressed the need for increased regulation of the agencies.

Baum et al. [289] studied statistically the impact of credit rating agency announcements on the value of the Euro and the yields of French, Italian, German, and Spanish long-term sovereign bonds during the culmination of the Eurozone debt crisis in 2011-2012. Employing GARCH models the work showed that credit downgrade announcements affected negatively the value of the Euro currency and increased its volatility. Downgrading also increased the yields of French, Italian, and Spanish bonds but lowered the German bond's yields, although Germany's rating status was never assessed by the credit rating agencies. The credit rating agency announcements seemed to have significantly influenced crisis-time capital allocation in the Eurozone. Their downgrading caused investors to rebalance their portfolios across member countries, out of ailing states' debt into more stable borrowers' securities.

Alsakka and Ap Gwilym [290] examined the relationship between the foreign exchange market and the sovereign credit events prior to (2000-2006) and during the crisis (2006-2010) on a sample of countries in Europe and Central Asia. This research notes that rating agency signals do affect the same-country exchange rate and identifies strong spillover effects to other countries' exchange rates in the region, with the market reactions and spillovers being stronger during the financial crisis period than pre-crisis. Negative news from all three major agencies has an impact, while only Moody's positive news produces a reaction. Negative news from Fitch tends to have the strongest effect.

# 4 STATISTICAL TOOLS FOR ASSESSING THE CREDIT RATING

Analyzing the dynamics of ratings and the evolution of the relationship between the grades of various agencies requires specific tools, related to the particular nature of ratings. The methodology used by rating agencies is not fully disclosed and does rely on subjective qualitative factors. The credit rating agencies do not provide the debt issuer with *probabilities of default* of the obligator, but with a grade on an ordinal scale, each agency having its own scale. Nonetheless, rating users including risk managers and investment analyst do attach to the ordinal rating scale a continuous probability of default variables, computed through various methods. Ratings are theoretically ordinal data for a given agency just as a *AAA* means a better grade than *A*. However, depending on the investors' appetite for various grades they can be used as nominal data.

A straightforward way to assess the dynamics of credit rating agency behavior is to measure the evolution over time of the concordance of the three agencies for a given set of obligors. One would expect to observe a quasi-stable concordance as agencies do adjust their ratings based on the same information. A few strategies for assessing the concordance between various agencies need to be considered.

For dealing with ratings dynamics let's consider a sample of $N$ obligors denoted $X_i$ with $i \in 1, 2, \ldots, N$. Their rating measure $G_{X_i,j}(t)$ is defined on the set $N$ for the obligors $X_i$ from the agency $j$ at the time $t$.

Let's also consider a mapping function $F_j$: $N \to [0, 1]$ such as $Y_j(t) = F_j(G_{X_i,j}(t))$ is a continuous variable representing the default probability of that obligors. Under this assumption the concordance between two or more ratings agencies can be assessed for the defined population $X_i$ following concordance metrics with respect to the definition of Scarsini [291]. The efficient concordance metric for default probabilities should follow this property:

**Proposition 1.** *If $F(G(t))$ is uniquely defined then classic concordance measures $\kappa$ (i.e., Kendall $\tau$, Spearman $\rho$) can be applied to default probabilities from two rating agencies $Y_1(t)$, $Y_2(t)$ satisfying the following:*

1. *$\kappa$ is defined for every combination of $Y_1(t)$, $Y_2(t)$ of continuous variables*
2. *$\kappa$ is defined for every combination of $Y_1(t)$, $Y_1(t')$ if $t \neq t'$*
3. *$-1 \leq \kappa(Y_1(t), Y_2(t')) \leq 1, \kappa(Y_1(t), Y_2(t'))$*
4. *if $Y_1(t)$ and $Y_2(t)$ are independent then $\kappa(Y_1(t), Y_2(t')) = 0$*
5. *if $\kappa(Y_1(t), Y_1(t')) = 1$ then $Y_1(t) = Y_1(t')$*
6. *$\kappa(Y_1(t), Y_1(t')) = \kappa(Y_1(t'), Y_1(t))$ and $\kappa(Y_1(t), Y_2(t)) = \kappa(Y_2(t), Y_1(t))$*

*For many cases, the mapping functions $F(G(t))$ are not unique and in addition are not continuous. In fact, the mappings $F(G(t))$ are usually staircase functions and for each notch of the ratings the functions adjust to the next value of the probability of default. The extensions of properties from Proposition 1 for discontinuous variables or for discrete variables are not obvious as discussed by Nešlehová [292].*

Thus, assessing the behavior of the credit agencies through the bias of equivalent default probabilities might not give sound results and alternative ways of dealing with the ordinal data should be considered. A first option is to use nonparametric Kendall's coefficient $W$ concordance measures for assessing the original ratings.

Let's assume $C_j: N \rightarrow Q$, where $Q = (1, 2, \ldots, K)$ such as $z_{i,j}(t) = C_j(G_{i,j}(t))$ is a discrete variable representing the index order of the rating $G_i$ on the scale of the rating agency $j$.

For $k \in (2, 3)$ representing the number of agencies to be compared the following metric can be defined:

$$\bar{z}_{.j} = \frac{1}{n} \sum_{i=1}^{n} z_{ij} \tag{1}$$

$$\bar{z} = \frac{1}{nk} \sum_{i=1}^{n} \sum_{j=1}^{k} z_{ij} \tag{2}$$

$$SS_t = n \sum_{j=1}^{k} (\bar{z}_{.j} - \bar{z})^2 \tag{3}$$

$$SS_e = \frac{1}{n(k-1)} \sum_{i=1}^{n} \sum_{j=1}^{k} (z_{ij} - \bar{z})^2 \tag{4}$$

Kendall's coefficient $W$ is thus defined as $W = \frac{12SS_t}{m^2(n^3-n)}$.

Rating data do often present a number of ties, and the Kendall's coefficient $W$ is adjusted accordingly. Given the expected high number of ties the variance computation for $W$ presents convergence issues and a dedicated sampling method needs to be considered.

A second option is to explore the use of Cohen's kappa for assessing the degree of agreement between the credit ratings of various agencies.

The metric of Cohen's kappa is:

$$\kappa = \frac{\Pr(a) - \Pr(e)}{1 - \Pr(e)},$$

where $\Pr(a)$ is the relative observed agreement among raters and $\Pr(e)$ is the hypothetical probability of chance agreement using the observed data to calculate the probabilities of each observer randomly in each category. If the raters are in complete agreement, then $\kappa = 1$. If there is no agreement among the raters other than what would be expected by chance (as defined by $\Pr(e)$), $\kappa = 0$. Cohen's kappa can be extended for ordinal data if the amplitude of disagreement is weighted through various functions.

A third option is to explore an approach proposed by Jafry and Schuermann [293], which builds a metric of the migration speed for a rated population of obligors $X$ between moments $t$ and $t'$. Assuming the rating function $G_X$ gives a grade on a scale from 1 to $K$, the transition matrix $\mathbf{P}$

from the ratings $G_X(t)$ at moment $t$ and $G_X(t')$ at moment $t'$:

$$\mathbf{P}_{G_X(t),G_X(t')} = \begin{pmatrix} a_{1,1} & a_{1,2} & \cdots & a_{1,K} \\ a_{2,1} & a_{2,2} & \cdots & a_{2,K} \\ \vdots & \vdots & \ddots & \vdots \\ a_{K-1,1} & a_{K-1,2} & \cdots & a_{K-1,K} \\ 0 & 0 & 0 & 1 \end{pmatrix}$$

Let $I$ be the identity matrix that we note:

$$\tilde{P}_{G_X(t),G_X(t')} = P_{G_{X,1}(t),G_{X,1}(t')} - I \qquad (5)$$

The migration metrics is given by:

$$\mathrm{MM}(t,t') = (G_X(t),G_X(t')) = \frac{\sum_{i=1}^{K}\sqrt{\lambda_i \tilde{P}'\tilde{P}}}{K} \qquad (6)$$

where $\lambda_i$ are the eigenvalues of the matrix $\mathbf{P}$.

The migration metric satisfies the monotonicity condition that stipulates that for two transition matrices $\mathbf{P}$ and $\mathbf{P}^*$ $\mathrm{MM}(\mathbf{P}) > \mathrm{MM}(\mathbf{P}^*)$ if $a_{i,j} \geq a^*_{i,j}$ for all $i \neq j$ and $a_{i,j} > a^*_{i,j}$ for some $i \neq j$. Assuming that $\mathrm{MM}(\mathbf{I}) = 0$ then $\mathrm{MM}(\mathbf{P}) \geq 0$ unless $\mathbf{P} = \mathbf{I}$.

The migration metric also satisfies the distribution discriminatory features such that it can discriminate matrices having the same row-wise probabilities of change but different distributions across each row. Thus, if $a_{i,i} = a^*_{i,i}$ and $a_{i,j} \neq a^*_{i,j}$ for all $i \neq j$, then $\mathrm{MM}(\mathbf{P}) \neq \mathrm{MM}(\mathbf{P}^*)$.

The migration metric introduced above for evaluating the temporal migration can be generalized as a cross-sectional concordance measure for assessing the agreement of two rating systems:

$$\mathrm{MM}(G_{X,1}(t),G_{X,2}(t)) = \frac{\sum_{i=1}^{K}\sqrt{\lambda_i \tilde{P}'\tilde{P}}}{K}$$

**Proposition 2.** *If the classic concordance between two ratings systems is perfect $\kappa(G_{X,1},G_{X,2}) = 1$, then the migration between the two systems is $\mathrm{MM}(G_{X,1},G_{X,2}) = 0$*

*The disadvantage of the mobility metric is that it attaches the same weight in the mobility to upgrades as it does to downgrades. For assessing the speed of downgrade/upgrades, the migration rate metric introduced by Chakroun [294] can be used. From the matrix $\tilde{P}$ the metric is defined as:*

$$\mathrm{MR} = \sum_{i=1}^{K}\sum_{j=1}^{K}(i-j)\tilde{a}_{i,j} \qquad (7)$$

*The above metric can be modified for accounting only the downgrade speed as follows:*

$$\mathrm{MRD} = \sum_{i=1}^{K}\sum_{j=1}^{K}\mathbf{1}_{i-j<0}\tilde{a}_{i,j} \qquad (8)$$

*As for the case of the mobility measure (MM), the two metrics MR and MRD can be applied to assess the ratings' migration from one agency rating to another.*

In order to answer the question of *how large is large* for a concordance metric such as $\kappa$, $W$, MM, or MRD, we should assess its distributional properties. In the absence of any asymptotic theory, a straightforward and efficient way is through the resampling technique of bootstrapping. The method implemented for the concordance coefficient has the followings steps:

1 Independent bootstrap data sets $X_1^*, X_2^*, \ldots, X_{N_{Sim}}^*$ are drawn from the initial sample $X_i$. The number of resamples $N_{Sim}$ is large.

2 For each sample $X_j^*, j = i, 2, \ldots, N_{Sim}$ the concordance measure $\widehat{\kappa_{1j}^*} = (G_{X^*,1}, G_{X^*,2})$ is computed.

2 For each sample $Y_j^*, j = i, 2, \ldots, N_{Sim}$ the concordance measure $\widehat{\kappa_{2j}^*} = (G_{Y^*,1}, G_{Y^*,2})$ is computed.

3 The bootstrap cumulative distribution of the concordance measure values $\widehat{\kappa_1^*} - \widehat{\kappa_2^*}$ is constructed.

$$B(s) = (\#\,\widehat{\kappa_{1j}^*} - \widehat{\kappa_{2j}^*} < s) \quad -\infty < s < \infty \quad (9)$$

**4** The quantity $z_0 = \Phi^{-1}(B(\hat{\kappa}))$ is empirically computed.

**5** For a chosen critical value $\alpha$ (say $\alpha = 5\%$), we see if 0 falls within the $1 - \alpha$ range of $B(s)$.

To study the concordance of various agencies a data sample (around 20,000 obligors) of *long-term ratings* is built from the three main credit rating agencies (S&P, Fitch, and Moody's) gathered from financial databases (e.g., Bloomberg, Financial Times). The data is separated as sovereign, financial, and corporate obligors with reference to their origin country with good coverage since 2008, thereby making it a good candidate for testing the behavior during the Eurozone crisis. Figures 1 and 2 show the evolution of average equivalent default probabilities and distances to default ($DD = -N^1(PD)$), respectively, for the three rating agencies. The default probabilities have increased since 2008 on average for the considered portfolio.

Figure 3 shows the evolution of the mobility metric as a concordance measure between Standard & Poors and Moody's ratings for North American and European sovereign obligors. The

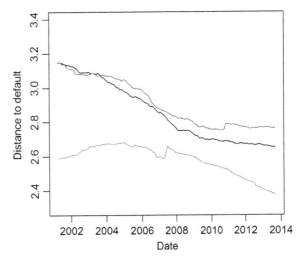

**FIGURE 2** Evolution of average equivalent distances to default ($DD = -N^1(PD)$) for the three rating agencies.

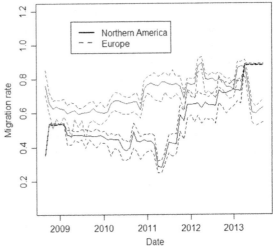

**FIGURE 3** Evolution of the mobility metric as a concordance measure of the Standard & Poors and Moody's for North American and European sovereign obligors. The dashed line indicates the 95% confidence interval.

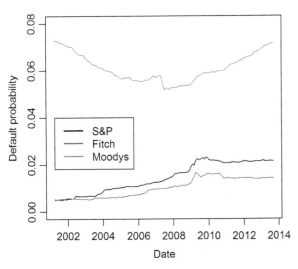

**FIGURE 1** Evolution of average equivalent default probabilities for the three rating agencies.

95% confidence intervals are also computed through bootstrapping. For European sovereign obligors, we can observe a lower agreement of the two agencies (Standard & Poors vs. Moodys)

as the mobility metric increases during the Euro crisis in 2009-2012. After 2013 the concordance for the North American has comparable levels with that for European ones. Figure 4 depicts the evolution of the Cohen's kappa as a concordance measure between the same agencies during the Euro crisis. It can be observed that Cohen's kappa for European obligors diminishes relatively to the North America ones during the crisis.

Figure 5 shows the evolution of Kendall's $W$ for European and American sovereigns measure for the agreement between Standard & Poor's vs. Fitch. It can be observed that for European sovereign obligors a lower agreement between agencies occur during the Euro crisis. The concordance between the two agencies is generally lower for European sovereign names than for North American obligors. Figure 6 shows the same analysis for Fitch vs. Moody's, which have similar levels of agreement concerning European and North American sovereign obligors during the Euro crisis.

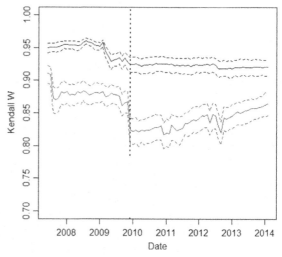

FIGURE 5  Evolution of Kendall's $W$ for European and American sovereigns: S&P vs. Fitch. The dashed line indicates the 95% confidence interval.

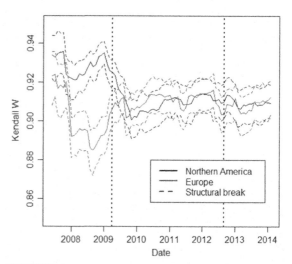

FIGURE 6  Evolution of Kendall's $W$ for European and American sovereigns for Moody's vs. Fitch.

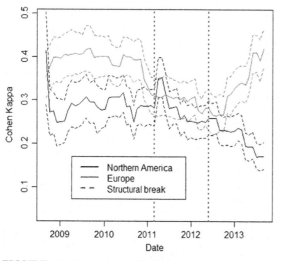

FIGURE 4  Evolution of the Cohen's kappa as a concordance measure of the Standard & Poor's and Moody's for North American and European sovereign obligors. The dashed line indicates the 95% confidence interval.

Figure 7 shows the evolution of the MM computes in the classic sense of Jafry and Schuermann [293] over a 1-year horizon for the S&P rating applied to European and American sovereign and financial obligors. After 2009 the

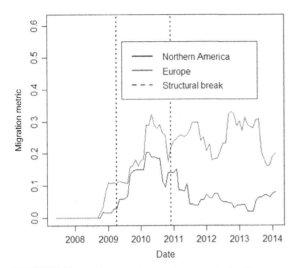

**FIGURE 7** Evolution of migration metric for European and American sovereignand financial obligors.

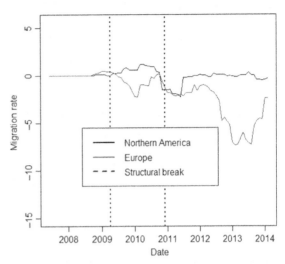

**FIGURE 8** Evolution of migration rate for European and American sovereign and financial obligors.

speed of migration of European sovereign rating is higher than the same measure for the North American counterparties. Long-term ratings are assumed by their nature to migrate very slowly even in periods of turmoil, which seems to be the case for North America but less so for the European obligors.

Figure 8 shows the evolution of the migration rate adapted to downgrades. The graph shows that the North American ratings are more stable in respect to downgrades compared to the European sovereign.

In conclusion, credit rating agencies had a lower degree of concordance during the Euro crisis compared to previous periods. The agreement between agencies for European sovereign obligors was lower compared to a similar measure of North American obligors. The migration speed of ratings during the Euro crisis for sovereign and financial obligors was higher for European names compared to the North American ones. The downgrading tendency of European Union sovereigns was stronger than the tendency of American sovereigns. The agencies (mainly S&P)

showed behavior that pushed toward more and faster downgrades in the European sovereign ratings, which most likely had a negative effect during the Eurozone crisis.

# 5 OUTLOOK

- Prime Minister Angela Merkel (2011): "Regarding the issue of rating agencies, I think it is important that we do not allow others to take away our own ability to make judgments."
- Finance Minister Wolfgang Schruble (2011): "I don't believe that Standard & Poor's has really understood what we in Europe have already set in motion,"
- European Minister Barroso (2011) even seriously suggested that, in order to break the dominance of the big three American agencies Moody's, Standard & Poors, and Fitch Brussels might have to develop a rival agency of its own.

Following the scandal related to the sub-primes and the reaction of the European politicians in regards to agencies' behavior during the Euro crisis, a series of regulations were implemented in both the United States and European Union.

The Dodd-Frank Wall Street Reform added a number of requirements for credit rating agencies concerning their internal controls, conflicts of interest with respect to sales and marketing practices, fines and penalties to agencies, disclosure of ratings performance statistics, third-party due diligence, disclosure of credit rating methodologies, disclosure of data and assumptions underlying credit ratings, and additional disclosure for ratings related to structured products.

The European Union also updated its regulations for credit rating agencies. These technical standards include:

- The disclosure requirements for issuers, originators, and sponsors on structured finance instruments.
- Reporting requirements for credit rating agencies on fees charged to their clients.
- Reporting requirements to credit rating agencies for the European Rating Platform. The European Rating Platform is a system to be set up by the European Securities and Markets Authority (ESAM), allowing investors to consult and easily compare all available credit ratings for all rated instruments.

Credit rating agencies have a big impact on the debt markets. Their regulation can bring more transparency in the process but will not address the issue of the oligopoly formed by the Big Three.

# 4F

# The FX Fixing Fix

## 1 BACKGROUND

Shortly after the case of LIBOR/EURIBOR another scandal erupted in relation to the Forex manipulation. The results of the investigation showed that even the biggest financial market has serious conduct breaches and the global integrity of financial markets is therefore seriously questioned. While the manipulation of niche markets like cocoa or rare metals affects a limited number of people the foreign exchange has a structural effect on the real economy, thereby underlining the increasing size of negative externalities generated by the investment industry.

Markets targeted by manipulation are in general niche markets traded on thin liquidity, heterogeneous information, or among a limited number of investors, thereby facilitating abuse. Nonetheless, since the recent crisis in addition to the classic price manipulation schemes a new type manipulations has arisen: manipulation of benchmarks. Verstein [295] showed that these benchmarks are written directly into industrial contracts, financial derivatives, statues, and regulations, and so their accuracy affects the economy every bit as much as the prices themselves. Benchmarks can be easier to manipulate than underlying prices if there is a joint effort by the counterparties establishing the benchmark. Such benchmarks are typically derived from only a snapshot of the market as in the case of Forex or even based on contributors as it was in the case of LIBOR. For example, benchmarks of exchange rates like the American to Canadian dollar (USD/CAD) reflect only trade prices during a two-minute period of trading (Figure 1). A manipulator of a "penny stock" would need to structurally alter the demand/supply equilibrium by injecting a

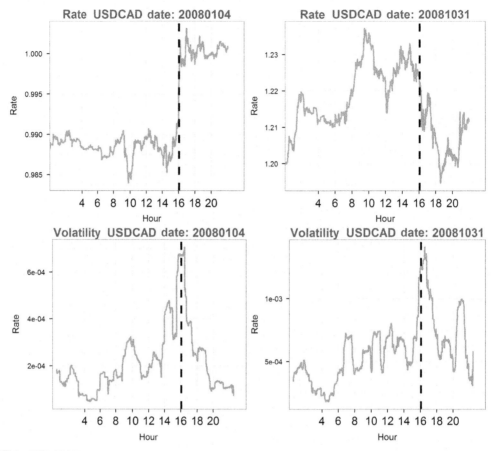

**FIGURE 1** USD/CAD.

significant amount of liquidity. In the case of a benchmark, a manipulator can strategically position trades, placing aggressive bids or asks in order to "move" the market at that point in time, thereby affecting the benchmark.

A pure price manipulation requires that one or few traders inject liquidity in a market or spread doubtful information and thereby alter the market efficiency. A benchmark manipulation requires that the majority of the benchmark contributors are organized in such way that they can influence the direction of the benchmark. In the case of the LIBOR they needed to agree on a value of the next-day benchmark in order to submit values that could jointly move the

benchmark in the desired direction. In the case of the Forex manipulation a group of banks making most of the volumes on that specific currency pair would agree to a target for a specific time. Various techniques can be used to move the price around a specific time when the client transactions are settled. The difference between LIBOR manipulation and FX manipulation is that LIBOR is communicated by banks, while the FX fixing is a real price observed by the market. Therefore, to manipulate LIBOR the submission needed to be rigged, whilst for the Forex case the rate at a certain moment was manipulated through various trades aimed at shifting the market. Table 1 shows the differences between the

**TABLE 1** Differences Between the Manipulation of Benchmarks and Manipulation of Price in Markets

| Manipulation | Requirements | Direct effect |
|---|---|---|
| Price | High liquidity or ability to spread misleading information | Affects market efficiency and changes the perception of investors |
| Benchmark | Cartel-type behaviors | Affects the market at a certain point in time and does not necessarily affect market efficiency |

**TABLE 2** 2013 Market FX Break Down by Type of Currency

| Currency | Instrument (B$) | | | | | |
|---|---|---|---|---|---|---|
| | Total | Spot | Forwards | FX swaps | Currency swaps | FX options |
| Total | 5345 | 2046 | 680 | 2228 | 54 | 337 |
| USD | 4652 | 1691 | 588 | 2030 | 50 | 293 |
| EUR | 1786 | 754 | 178 | 766 | 18 | 70 |
| JPY | 1231 | 612 | 123 | 332 | 11 | 153 |
| GBP | 631 | 227 | 69 | 301 | 5 | 29 |
| AUD | 462 | 196 | 50 | 183 | 6 | 27 |
| CHF | 275 | 84 | 27 | 149 | 1 | 14 |
| CAD | 244 | 93 | 36 | 101 | 2 | 12 |
| MXN | 135 | 57 | 14 | 58 | 1 | 6 |
| CNY | 120 | 34 | 28 | 40 | 1 | 17 |
| NZD | 105 | 39 | 11 | 50 | 2 | 3 |
| SEK | 94 | 27 | 12 | 53 | 1 | 2 |
| RUB | 85 | 37 | 9 | 37 | 0 | 3 |

Notes: *The total accounts for 200% as each currency is counted twice in the pair exchanges.*

manipulation of benchmarks and manipulation of price in markets.

The latest survey from the Bank for International settlements[1] shows that the average daily turnover in the global Forex market has reached $5.3 trillion, rising significantly from $4 trillion in 2010.

Table 2 shows the FX market nominal outstanding break down by type of currency in 2013.

The U.S. dollar, Euro, and British pound constitute most of the transactions. Spot transactions account for 38% of the total FX market.

Table 3 shows the evolution of the FX market per product type since 1998. Spot transactions have increased almost four times in volume during the past 15 years and have kept a stable share from the total amount of transactions.

The market break down per type of currency is given in Table 4. In 2001 the creation of the Euro replacing at that time more than a dozen currencies added a new player at the top. Euro

---

[1] FX market, http://www.bis.org/publ/rpfx13fx.pdf.

**TABLE 3** Evolution of the FX Market per Product Type Since 1998

| Instrument | Year (B$) | | | | | |
|---|---|---|---|---|---|---|
| | 1998 | 2001 | 2004 | 2007 | 2010 | 2013 |
| Spot transactions | 568 | 386 | 631 | 1005 | 1488 | 2046 |
| Outright forwards | 128 | 130 | 209 | 362 | 475 | 680 |
| Foreign exchange swaps | 734 | 656 | 954 | 1714 | 1759 | 2228 |
| Currency swaps | 10 | 7 | 21 | 31 | 43 | 54 |
| Options and other products | 87 | 60 | 119 | 212 | 207 | 337 |
| Exchange-traded derivatives | 11 | 12 | 26 | 80 | 155 | 160 |
| Total Forex instruments | 1527 | 1239 | 1934 | 3324 | 3971 | 5345 |

**TABLE 4** Evolution of Market Shares for Each Currency Since 1998

| Currency | Year (%) | | | | | |
|---|---|---|---|---|---|---|
| | 1998 | 2001 | 2004 | 2007 | 2010 | 2013 |
| USD | 86.8 | 89.9 | 88 | 85.6 | 84.9 | 87 |
| EUR | | 37.9 | 37.4 | 37 | 39.1 | 33.4 |
| JPY | 21.7 | 23.5 | 20.8 | 17.2 | 19 | 23 |
| GBP | 11 | 13 | 16.5 | 14.9 | 12.9 | 11.8 |
| AUD | 3 | 4.3 | 6 | 6.6 | 7.6 | 8.6 |
| CHF | 7.1 | 6 | 6 | 6.8 | 6.3 | 5.2 |
| CAD | 3.5 | 4.5 | 4.2 | 4.3 | 5.3 | 4.6 |
| MXN | 0.5 | 0.8 | 1.1 | 1.3 | 1.3 | 2.5 |

Notes: *The sum for all currencies is 200% accounting for all currency pair combinations.*

Forex transactions represent the second market after the U.S. dollar and before the Japanese Yen. Table 5 offers more clarification about what currency pairs have the highest volume of transactions, showing that the USD-EUR, USD-YEN, and USG-GBP have the biggest shares.

Table 6 shows the break down of the Forex spot transactions by counterparty type since 2008. Financial institutions account for the biggest shares.

## 2 ARCHITECTURE OF THE FIXING

Manipulating such a huge market can have both direct and collateral effects that can be immediate or latent. According to a report by the British regulator the Financial Conduct Authority (FCA) between January 2008 and October 2013 ineffective controls at five banks allowed Forex traders to put their banks' interests ahead of those of their clients. The banks failed to manage obvious risks around confidentiality, conflicts of interest, and trading conduct. From an operational point of view a currency "fix" known as a World Markets Reuters (WM/Reuters) fix and is agreed upon based on the price that currency trades at over a 60-second period is established on a daily basis. Many Forex transactions involving banks' clients are concluded at the reference "fix" rate. Having the information that a client was going to buy large amounts of the same currency the trader can "spill" the information by buying up the same currency just before the fix time in order to push up the rate higher. When the client concludes his deal at the fixed rate, the traders could sell at a profit. In a thin liquid market it would be enough to have one trader to conduct such an operation. In the Forex market, the biggest and most liquid

**TABLE 5** Currency Pairs Transactions

| | Year | | | | | | | | | |
|---|---|---|---|---|---|---|---|---|---|---|
| | 2001 | | 2004 | | 2007 | | 2010 | | 2013 | |
| FX | B $ | % | B $ | % | B $ | % | B $ | % | B $ | % |
| USDEUR | 372 | 30 | 541 | 28 | 892 | 26.8 | 1098 | 27.7 | 1289 | 24.1 |
| USDJPY | 250 | 20.2 | 328 | 17 | 438 | 13.2 | 567 | 14.3 | 978 | 18.3 |
| USDGBP | 129 | 10.4 | 259 | 13.4 | 384 | 11.6 | 360 | 9.1 | 472 | 8.8 |
| USDAUD | 51 | 4.1 | 107 | 5.5 | 185 | 5.6 | 248 | 6.3 | 364 | 6.8 |
| USDCAD | 54 | 4.3 | 77 | 4 | 126 | 3.8 | 182 | 4.6 | 200 | 3.7 |
| USDCHF | 59 | 4.8 | 83 | 4.3 | 151 | 4.5 | 166 | 4.2 | 184 | 3.4 |
| EURJPY | 36 | 2.9 | 61 | 3.2 | 86 | 2.6 | 111 | 2.8 | 147 | 2.8 |
| EURGBP | 27 | 2.1 | 47 | 2.4 | 69 | 2.1 | 109 | 2.7 | 102 | 1.9 |
| EURCHF | 13 | 1.1 | 30 | 1.6 | 62 | 1.9 | 71 | 1.8 | 71 | 1.3 |

Notes: *Break down volumes and timeline.*

**TABLE 6** Break Down of the Forex Spot Transactions by Counterparty Type

| | Year | | | | | | | | | | | |
|---|---|---|---|---|---|---|---|---|---|---|---|---|
| | 1998 | | 2001 | | 2004 | | 2007 | | 2010 | | 2013 | |
| Type | (B$) | % | (B$) | % | (B$) | % | (B$) | % | (B$) | % | (B$) | % |
| Dealers | 347 | 61.2 | 216 | 56.0 | 310 | 49.2 | 426 | 42.4 | 517 | 34.7 | 675 | 33.0 |
| Other financial institutions | 121 | 21.3 | 111 | 28.9 | 212 | 33.7 | 394 | 39.2 | 754 | 50.7 | 1183 | 57.8 |
| Non-financial customers | 99 | 17.5 | 58 | 15.0 | 108 | 17.0 | 184 | 18.3 | 217 | 14.6 | 188 | 9.2 |
| Total spot transactions | 568 | 100 | 386 | 100 | 631 | 100 | 1005 | 100 | 1488 | 100 | 2046 | 100 |

Notes: *Financial institutions account for the biggest shares.*

financial market, it is required to involve the biggest players of that market in order to be able to move it in the desired way. On top of that the various players should not have contrasting orders on the same day from different clients. For instance, if a big client wants to buy USD/CAN but another client of another bank wants to sell USD/CAN the interests of the two banks would conflict in terms of fixing.

Thus, benchmarking fixes at such a high level require very good organization and genuine governance. Therefore, banks and traders formed a cartel in a similar manner as was formed for the LIBOR/EURIBOR fix. Traders colluded to fix the currency's rate through conversations in chat rooms, usually via their Bloomberg or Reuters terminals. These groups, in which information was shared about clients' activity, used code names to identify clients without naming them. The cartel-type associations had nicknames such as, *the players*, *the 3 musketeers*, *1 team*, *1 dream*, *a co-operative*, and *the A-team*, or even more suggestive such as *the Cartel*, *the bandits' club*, and *the mafia* to swap confidential orders and set prices through manipulative tactics such as:

- **Front running**, a disruptive technique whereby the trader uses the information

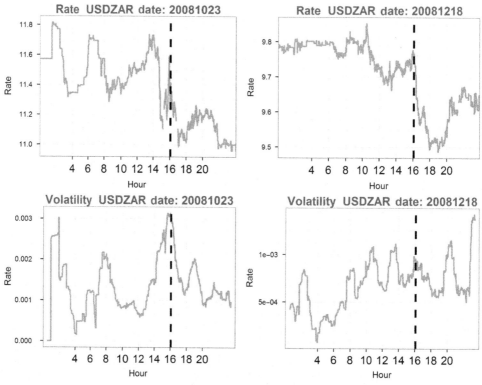

FIGURE 2    Example of the rate manipulation for the case of USDZAR.

about the operation of its client to make profit on its own account trades. For instance, a broker receives a market order from a customer based in South Africa to sell a large sum of Rand and to buy U.S. dollars but before placing the order for the customer, the broker buys on the future market the USD/ZAR, then places the customer's order for the big Rand sale, driving the rate of USD higher and allowing the broker to immediately sell his own future position, thereby generating a significant profit in a short time. As shown in Figure 2 when the order arrives at the fixing time the broker can make a significant profit from this scheme.

- **Banging the close**, a manipulative trading practice whereby a trader buys or sells a large number of futures contracts during the closing period of a futures contract (i.e., the

period during which the futures settlement price is determined) in order to benefit an even larger position in an option, swap, or other derivative that is cash settled based on the futures settlement price on that day.

- **Painting the tape**, a form of market manipulation whereby market players attempt to influence the price of a security by buying and/or selling it among themselves in order to create the appearance of substantial trading activity in the security. Painting the tape is an illegal activity that is prohibited in developed countries due to the fact that it creates an artificial price for a security. The term originated when stock prices were largely transmitted on ticker tape. The U.S. dollar to South African Rand shown in Figure 2 is a good example. It can be observed that the rate peaks intra-day around 16.00 and then comes back to its previous trajectory.

These manipulative techniques can be isolated or can occur frequently over a longer time horizon. In the latter case, the banks involved need good organization in order to coordinate their trades and to share extensively the options of their clients for determining what technique needs to be employed in a specific situation. Besides rigging, sharing clients' positions represents a big breach in the fiduciary duty of banks to its customers.

Among the banks investigated in the FX rigging are Bank of America Corp, Barclays, BNP Paribas, Citigroup, Credit Suisse, Deutsche Bank, Goldman Sachs Group, HSBC, Morgan Stanley, Royal Bank of Scotland Group Plc, and UBS AG. The 12 banks held an 84% global market share in currency trading, and were counterparties in 98% of U.S. dollar spot transactions.

The focus of investigators was to determine if what happened amounted to illegal actions like "front-running," "banging the close," or "painting the screen" or was just usual risk management techniques for clients. Not only in Forex markets but also in other markets banks often manage the risk of a jump in the price generated by a large order by spreading out the order among a few other counterparties before the "fix." Firms can legitimately manage the risk associated with big client orders by trading in the market and may make a profit or loss as a result. There is a very thin line between this risk adjustment and the market rigging. If the trades emanating around the fix are premeditated though a series of communication between the traders of various banks, then it is clear that illegal intent existed. Otherwise, if the trades are only based on a bank's intent to reduce the price risk, the action could not be consider as illegal.

As explained above banks used chat rooms and discussion groups in order to synchronize their strategies. Several of the investment banks involved have since banned the use of such chat rooms, which were also used during the LIBOR rigging.

# 3 STATISTICAL ASSESSMENT

To assess from an econometric point of view the behavior of intra-day rates[2] several aspects need to be considered. First, when traders decide to move the market around the "fix" an increased volatility at that moment might be observed. A second aspect is related to the rate level itself, which should have a peak or valley around the fix time. Lastly is the market efficiency assumption on the intra-day trades. If an agent can generate profit from trades around the fixing time knowing that a peak or a valley will appear means a breach in efficiency occurred. Therefore, the following statistic assessment would need to be studied:

- Intra-day volatility: The physical volatility is computed on the timestamps-based rate.
- Peak and valley detection: A tailored algorithm is implemented for peak detection. The frequency of peaks at the fixing time should be tests to determine whether they occur more frequently than in a random hour (the blind time) and also if the occurrences are independent.
- Market efficiency: A simple momentum strategy whereby an agent puts a buy or sell trade minutes before the fixing time, depending on the way the market went until that moment.

## 3.1 Intra-Day Volatility

Figure 3 depicts the evolution of the intra-day volatility computed on a rolling centered window of 60 min and averaged per year between 2001 and 2014. The volatility increases after 2008 depending on the systemic conditions related to

---

[2]Historical data base of the intra-day FX rate, www.forexite.com.

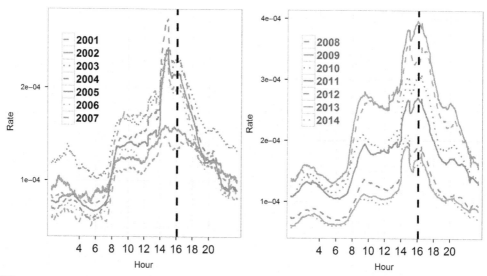

**FIGURE 3**  Evolution of the intra-day volatility for the USDCAD rate.

the financial crisis. It can also be observed that the relative difference between the fixing time (16 h) volatility and the average also increases after 2008 until 2014. These effects are noticed for many other currency pairs as will be emphasized in the following sections.

## 3.2  Peak Detection

The peak detection in a time series might seem trivial due to the simple property that the local value of the slope becomes zero wherever there are extremities. However, when the time series have a stochastic component this task encounter a few challenges. Schwartzman et al. [296] proposed a genuine and straightforward solution to the problem of detecting non-overlapping peaks in the presence of a stationary noise, where the number, location, and heights of the peaks are unknown. The solution developed by Schwartzman et al. [296] for the continuous case is applied in the discrete form for assessing the peaks in the intra-day Forex rates. This strategy is applied for both rates and volatility peaks detection. The valleys are detected with the peaks approach by

inverting the rate times series. The formalism is described below.

Let's assume that $y^*(t)$ is a time series of Forex rates and the $\mu(t)$ is the peak that needs to be detected and $y(t)$ is the normal component of the set. This can be expressed as:

$$y^*(t) = \mu(t) + y(t) \tag{1}$$

$$\Delta y(t) = y(t)\sqrt{h^*(t)}\epsilon(t) \tag{2}$$

where $h^*(t)$ is the variance of the rate and $\epsilon(t)$ are residuals.

The same logic can be followed for the variance, which has a peak as noted above around the fixing time (16 h):

$$h^*(t) = \gamma(t) + \zeta(t) \tag{3}$$

$$\Delta\zeta(t) = \zeta\sqrt{\xi(t)}\Delta\mathbf{B}(t) \tag{4}$$

where $\xi(t)$ is the variance of the stochastic variance $\zeta(t)$ and $\gamma(t)$ is the peak component.

Smoothing is required to avoid the small peak generated by the stochastic effect. However, in the market manipulation in many of the cases above the peaks occur only for few minutes, with the market coming back to normal afterward.

A smoothing process on the rate times series $y^*(t)$ could erase this effect and alter the quality of the statistical assessment of the manipulation. Therefore, for rate peak detection no smoothing filtration is used and for notation consistency it can be written that the $y_s^*(t) = y^*(t)$. The volatility is computed as a standard deviation of the returns per minute on a rolling window of 60 min, thereby also implying smoothing:

$$h_s^*(t) = \frac{1}{w} \sum_{t-w/2}^{t+w/2} (\Delta y(t)/y(t))^2 \quad (5)$$

The peaks around a specific timestamp $t_0[t_0 - L_d, t_0 + L_u]$ are localized by imposing a local maximum condition on the rate and on the local volatility of the following conditions:

$$T(t_0)$$
$$= \left\{ t \in [t_0 - L_d, t_0 + L_u] \frac{y_s^*(t + \Delta t) - y_s^*(t)}{\Delta t} = 0; \right.$$
$$\left. \frac{y_s^*(t + \Delta t) - y_s^*(t - \Delta t) + 2y_s^*(t)}{\Delta t^2} < 0 \right\}$$

$$T(t_0)$$
$$= \left\{ t \in [t_0 - L_d, t_0 + L_u] \frac{h_s^*(t + \Delta t) - h_s^*(t)}{\Delta t} = 0; \right.$$
$$\left. \frac{h_s^*(t + \Delta t) - h_s^*(t - \Delta t) + 2h_s^*(t)}{\Delta t^2} < 0 \right\}$$

The challenge of detecting the occurrence of the *16h fix* is to avoid the bogus peaks that can occur randomly for various reasons. Therefore, only the peaks that occur in a 2 min window around the 16h are considered.

The test employed here considers that an alleged manipulation occurs around the 16h window, noted $T(t_0)$, if a peak in volatility and rate is detected:

- $H_0$ $t \in T(t_0)$ $\mu(t) = 0$ $\gamma(t) = 0$
- $H_a$ $t \in T(t_0)$ $\mu(t) > 0$ $\gamma(t) > 0$

To clearly underline the manipulation effect the above test is conditioned by a threshold in the amplitudes of $\mu(t)$ and $\gamma(t)$ for a given $t_0$. Thus, the occurrence of a peak at $t_0$ is confirmed only if

in the window of length $L_d$ preceding $t_0$ there is a minimum such that the relative variations at the peak moment for both the rate and volatility are $l_u$ and $l_h$, respectively. The same conditions for the window of length $L_u$ following the moment $t_0$ are applied with the threshold $l_d$ for the return and $l_h$ for the volatility:

$$\exists t_u \in [t_0 - L_d, t_0] \text{ and } \exists t_d \in [t_0, t_0 + L_u]$$
$$: \frac{y_s^*(t_0) - y_s^*(t_u)}{y_s^*(t_u)} > l_u \left| \frac{y_s^*(t_d) - y_s^*(t_0)}{y_s^*(t_0)} \right| > l_d$$

$$\exists t_l \in [t_0 - L_d, t_0] \text{ and } \exists t_h \in [t_0, t_0 + L_u]$$
$$: \frac{h_s^*(t_0) - h_s^*(t_l)}{h_s^*(t_l)} > l_h \left| \frac{h_s^*(t_h) - h_s^*(t_0)}{h_s^*(t_0)} \right| > l_h$$

Table 7 shows the percentage of peaks at 16h and average size of the peak for the USD/EUR rate. The frequency of the peaks increase in 2008 and fall in 2014.

To test whether the peaks at the fix time occur randomly or are part of a pattern of peaks it is useful to compare the frequency of peaks detected at 16h and at a random time that we will call here the *blind hour*. This test compares the number of peaks in 16h intervals against another random **B** hour that is considered for all currencies 12h43 (Table 8). Let's consider $\pi_{16}$ the

**TABLE 7** USD EUR Rate

| Year | Percentage of 16 h peaks | Average size of peak |
|------|--------------------------|----------------------|
| 2007 | 6% | 0.00272 |
| 2008 | 20% | 0.00400 |
| 2009 | 21% | 0.00353 |
| 2010 | 22% | 0.00309 |
| 2011 | 18% | 0.00344 |
| 2012 | 11% | 0.00308 |
| 2013 | 15% | 0.00258 |
| 2014 | 7% | 0.00256 |

*Percentage of peaks at 16h and average size of the peak.*

**TABLE 8** Proportions of Peaks that Occur on the Same Day or on a Different Day

| Peaks at 16 h/Peaks at B | No | Yes |
|---|---|---|
| No | A | B |
| Yes | C | D |

probability of having a peak at 16 h and $\pi_B$ and the probability of having a peak at the **B** hour. The following statistic is considered:

$$z = \frac{\pi_{16} - \pi_B}{\sqrt{2\overline{\pi} \cdot (1 - \overline{\pi})/N}} \qquad (6)$$

where $\overline{\pi} = \frac{0.5 \cdot (NP_{16} - NP_B)}{N}$, $N$ is the total number of days, $NP_{16}$ is the number of peaks at 16 h and $NP_B$ is the number of peaks detected at B hour. The statistics of $z$ tend toward normal distribution:

$$z \to N(0, 1) \qquad (7)$$

The test applied for the current case is:

- $H_0 \; \pi_{16} = \pi_B$
- $H_a \; \pi_{16} > \pi_B$

The $Z$-test for proportion equality is synthesized in Table 11 for the main currencies and in Table 12 for the secondary currencies. With the few exceptions highlighted in the tables, the test shows that the frequency of the peaks at 16 h is superior to the blind hour. A few pairs of currencies such as EUR/CHF and GBP/CHF have this property for the years 2010 and 2011.

A version of the test for assessing whether proportions (probabilities of peaks) in several groups are the same was proposed by Wilson [297] and follows a $\chi^2$ statistic.

The Wilson test result is synthesized in Table 9 for the main currencies and Table 10 for the secondary currencies. They confirm the results from the previous $Z$-test. The highlighted values with high $p$-values indicate that for the respective currency pair and for that year the manipulation of the 16 h is not confirmed (Tables 11 and 12).

To be sure this increased proportions in peaks are not systemic a test is done to see if the peaks appear independently. McNemar's test [298] is a non-parametric (distribution-free) test that assesses whether a statistically significant change in proportion has occurred on a dichotomous trait at two time points in the same population. This test is widely applied in medical and psychological research. In the case of the FX manipulation for every currency pair the number of peaks at the fix hour and the blind hour, which occur simultaneously as reflected in Table 8, should be counted.

The null hypothesis of marginal homogeneity states that the two marginal probabilities for peaks appearing at the fixing hours and at the blind test hours are the same, i.e., $P_a + P_b = P_a + P_c$ and $P_c + P_d = P_b + P_d$. The null and alternative hypotheses are expressed as follows:

$$\mathbf{H_0} : \; p_b = p_c \qquad (8)$$
$$\mathbf{H_1} : \; p_b \neq p_c \qquad (9)$$

Here, $p_i$ denotes the theoretical probability of occurrences in cells with the corresponding label. The McNemar test statistic is:

$$\frac{(b - c)^2}{b + c} \to \chi_1^2 \qquad (10)$$

which follows the $\chi^2$ distribution with one degree of freedom.

The McNemar test result is synthesized in Table 13 for the main currencies and Table 14 for the secondary currencies. The test confirms that the peaks are independent for most of the currencies but fails to reject the dependence hypothesis.

## 3.3 Intra-Day Trading Based on Timing

The last assessment for the occurrence of a manipulation at the fixing hour is to test the efficient market hypothesis on an intra-day basis. If a trader had information that at 15 h the rate peaks he could determine a strategy that would profit from this information. Of course, if traders do arbitrate this information the market will

**TABLE 9** Wilson Test Result for the Main Currency Pairs Between 2001 and 2014

| Statistic/p-value | 2001 | 2002 | 2003 | 2004 | 2005 | 2006 | 2007 | 2008 | 2009 | 2010 | 2011 | 2012 | 2013 | 2014 |
|---|---|---|---|---|---|---|---|---|---|---|---|---|---|---|
| EURUSD | 5.700 | 5.900 | 7.600 | 5.100 | 4.900 | 5.700 | 3.000 | 4.100 | 4.200 | 5.700 | 4.600 | 2.800 | 6.100 | 3.300 |
| p-value | 0.000 | 0.000 | 0.000 | 0.000 | 0.000 | 0.000 | 0.001 | 0.000 | 0.000 | 0.000 | 0.000 | 0.003 | 0.000 | 0.000 |
| GBPUSD | 2.400 | 3.400 | 4.400 | 3.300 | 3.900 | 5.500 | 2.100 | 1.500 | 2.900 | 2.300 | 4.400 | 2.700 | 3.600 | 2.000 |
| p-value | 0.007 | 0.000 | 0.000 | 0.000 | 0.000 | 0.000 | 0.018 | 0.061 | 0.002 | 0.012 | 0.000 | 0.003 | 0.000 | 0.025 |
| USDCHF | 5.000 | 6.400 | 7.700 | 4.700 | 5.200 | 6.400 | 4.100 | 4.400 | 2.200 | 3.300 | 4.000 | 3.600 | 5.000 | 4.100 |
| p-value | 0.000 | 0.000 | 0.000 | 0.000 | 0.000 | 0.000 | 0.000 | 0.000 | 0.013 | 0.001 | 0.000 | 0.000 | 0.000 | 0.000 |
| USDJPY | 1.900 | 4.700 | 2.400 | 4.800 | 1.700 | 4.700 | 3.500 | 5.100 | 4.300 | 6.900 | 5.500 | 3.800 | 6.600 | 4.800 |
| p-value | 0.027 | 0.000 | 0.009 | 0.000 | 0.043 | 0.000 | 0.000 | 0.000 | 0.000 | 0.000 | 0.000 | 0.000 | 0.000 | 0.000 |
| EURGBP | 3.000 | 3.300 | 4.100 | 0.200 | 1.000 | 2.000 | 0.400 | 1.600 | −0.90 | 1.300 | 1.800 | 2.300 | 2.600 | 0.000 |
| p-value | 0.001 | 0.000 | 0.000 | 0.412 | 0.158 | 0.022 | 0.352 | 0.050 | 0.819 | 0.099 | 0.038 | 0.009 | 0.005 | 0.500 |
| EURCHF | 2.400 | 2.000 | 0.600 | −0.60 | 1.000 |  | 0.000 | 3.000 | 0.000 | 4.500 | 4.600 | 0.000 | 1.500 | 0.000 |
| p-value | 0.009 | 0.022 | 0.281 | 0.719 | 0.158 |  | 0.500 | 0.002 | 0.500 | 0.000 | 0.000 | 0.500 | 0.064 | 0.500 |
| EURJPY | 4.100 | 3.900 | 3.900 | 3.700 | −1.00 | 1.000 | 2.800 | 4.100 | 5.800 | 6.500 | 5.800 | 6.200 | 3.900 | 2.700 |
| p-value | 0.000 | 0.000 | 0.000 | 0.000 | 0.845 | 0.155 | 0.003 | 0.000 | 0.000 | 0.000 | 0.000 | 0.000 | 0.000 | 0.003 |
| GBPCHF | 0.300 | 3.500 | 3.900 | 0.500 | 0.900 | 2.600 | 1.100 | 2.300 | −0.40 | 2.900 | 3.600 | 1.400 | 2.000 | 1.100 |
| p-value | 0.379 | 0.000 | 0.000 | 0.304 | 0.180 | 0.005 | 0.143 | 0.010 | 0.666 | 0.002 | 0.000 | 0.075 | 0.024 | 0.139 |
| GBPJPY | 0.300 | 2.300 | 2.500 | 2.300 | 0.600 | 1.700 | 2.900 | 3.800 | 4.200 | 6.300 | 5.200 | 4.700 | 3.300 | 1.700 |
| p-value | 0.393 | 0.011 | 0.007 | 0.012 | 0.261 | 0.047 | 0.002 | 0.000 | 0.000 | 0.000 | 0.000 | 0.000 | 0.000 | 0.041 |
| CHFJPY | 3.900 | 3.700 | 3.800 | 4.000 | 1.500 | 4.300 | 2.000 | 2.200 | 6.600 | 5.600 | 3.600 | 4.600 | 2.900 | 1.000 |
| p-value | 0.000 | 0.000 | 0.000 | 0.000 | 0.066 | 0.000 | 0.021 | 0.015 | 0.000 | 0.000 | 0.000 | 0.000 | 0.002 | 0.155 |
| USDCAD | 3.100 | 1.700 | 4.700 | 3.200 | 4.400 | 3.600 | 0.700 | −0.30 | 4.900 | 4.800 | 6.200 | 5.300 | 5.100 | 4.100 |
| p-value | 0.001 | 0.042 | 0.000 | 0.001 | 0.000 | 0.000 | 0.241 | 0.634 | 0.000 | 0.000 | 0.000 | 0.000 | 0.000 | 0.000 |

*Continued*

**TABLE 9**   Wilson Test Result for the Main Currency Pairs Between 2001 and 2014—cont'd

| Statistic/ p-value | 2001 | 2002 | 2003 | 2004 | 2005 | 2006 | 2007 | 2008 | 2009 | 2010 | 2011 | 2012 | 2013 | 2014 |
|---|---|---|---|---|---|---|---|---|---|---|---|---|---|---|
| EURCAD | 4.300 | 6.200 | 4.300 | 1.600 | 4.000 | 4.100 | 1.300 | −0.40 | 1.000 | 3.600 | 4.300 | 2.600 | 5.800 | 2.500 |
| p-value | 0.000 | 0.000 | 0.000 | 0.059 | 0.000 | 0.000 | 0.103 | 0.637 | 0.170 | 0.000 | 0.000 | 0.004 | 0.000 | 0.006 |
| AUDUSD | 0.400 | 0.500 | 1.900 | 3.300 | 3.300 | 4.500 | 2.400 | 2.300 | 7.700 | 6.500 | 5.700 | 5.000 | 3.500 | 4.200 |
| p-value | 0.352 | 0.295 | 0.032 | 0.000 | 0.000 | 0.000 | 0.008 | 0.011 | 0.000 | 0.000 | 0.000 | 0.000 | 0.000 | 0.000 |
| AUDJPY | −0.50 | 3.300 | 0.700 | 2.800 | 0.400 | 2.900 | 1.900 | 3.400 | 7.900 | 8.700 | 7.300 | 7.100 | 3.300 | 2.500 |
| p-value | 0.685 | 0.000 | 0.251 | 0.003 | 0.361 | 0.002 | 0.026 | 0.000 | 0.000 | 0.000 | 0.000 | 0.000 | 0.001 | 0.006 |
| NZDUSD | | | 1.800 | 3.400 | 3.300 | 3.600 | 4.500 | 0.800 | 7.300 | 6.500 | 6.200 | 5.200 | 3.200 | 3.500 |
| p-value | | | 0.034 | 0.000 | 0.000 | 0.000 | 0.000 | 0.223 | 0.000 | 0.000 | 0.000 | 0.000 | 0.001 | 0.000 |

Notes: The highlighted values indicate that the features required for manipulation are not confirmed by the test.

**TABLE 10** Wilson Test Result for the Secondary Currency Pairs Between 2001 and 2014

| Statistic/p-value | 2001 | 2002 | 2003 | 2004 | 2005 | 2006 | 2007 | 2008 | 2009 | 2010 | 2011 | 2012 | 2013 | 2014 |
|---|---|---|---|---|---|---|---|---|---|---|---|---|---|---|
| NZDJPY | | | 2.500 | 1.700 | 1.600 | 2.600 | 4.200 | 3.400 | 8.000 | 8.000 | 6.800 | 7.600 | 4.400 | 3.500 |
| p-value | | | 0.006 | 0.044 | 0.055 | 0.005 | 0.000 | 0.000 | 0.000 | 0.000 | 0.000 | 0.000 | 0.000 | 0.000 |
| USDCZK | | | | | 1.800 | 4.100 | 1.200 | 2.000 | −0.10 | −0.70 | −1.50 | 1.600 | −0.70 | 0.500 |
| p-value | | | | | 0.040 | 0.000 | 0.121 | 0.023 | 0.549 | 0.772 | 0.932 | 0.057 | 0.744 | 0.295 |
| USDDKK | | | | | 4.200 | 5.900 | 2.900 | 3.800 | 3.100 | 4.800 | 4.100 | 3.200 | 5.300 | 3.500 |
| p-value | | | | | 0.000 | 0.000 | 0.002 | 0.000 | 0.001 | 0.000 | 0.000 | 0.001 | 0.000 | 0.000 |
| EURRUB | | | | | 4.000 | 6.000 | 3.400 | 5.200 | 2.700 | 3.600 | 3.700 | 3.300 | 2.500 | 2.100 |
| p-value | | | | | 0.000 | 0.000 | 0.000 | 0.000 | 0.003 | 0.000 | 0.000 | 0.001 | 0.006 | 0.016 |
| USDHUF | | | | | 0.900 | 4.200 | 2.100 | 1.400 | 0.200 | −0.60 | −0.20 | 1.200 | 2.100 | 2.000 |
| p-value | | | | | 0.172 | 0.000 | 0.019 | 0.087 | 0.413 | 0.738 | 0.592 | 0.109 | 0.017 | 0.022 |
| USDNOK | | | | | 4.400 | 6.200 | 3.200 | 2.700 | 6.300 | 4.700 | 3.900 | 4.400 | 4.900 | 1.100 |
| p-value | | | | | 0.000 | 0.000 | 0.001 | 0.004 | 0.000 | 0.000 | 0.000 | 0.000 | 0.000 | 0.143 |
| USDPLN | | | | | 3.900 | 5.400 | 1.200 | 1.800 | 1.800 | 3.700 | 3.600 | 3.300 | 4.600 | 3.400 |
| p-value | | | | | 0.000 | 0.000 | 0.114 | 0.038 | 0.038 | 0.000 | 0.000 | 0.000 | 0.000 | 0.000 |
| USDRUB | | | | | | | | −2.00 | −4.40 | −1.20 | 3.000 | 0.200 | 1.300 | 0.500 |
| p-value | | | | | | | | 0.978 | 1.000 | 0.879 | 0.001 | 0.424 | 0.095 | 0.300 |
| USDSEK | | | | | 3.400 | 5.700 | 2.900 | 4.200 | 4.100 | 6.600 | 5.800 | 3.500 | 4.700 | 3.500 |
| p-value | | | | | 0.000 | 0.000 | 0.002 | 0.000 | 0.000 | 0.000 | 0.000 | 0.000 | 0.000 | 0.000 |
| USDSGD | | | | | 1.700 | 0.800 | 1.000 | 2.500 | 1.900 | −0.40 | 3.000 | 1.400 | 1.400 | 1.400 |
| p-value | | | | | 0.041 | 0.206 | 0.158 | 0.006 | 0.029 | 0.648 | 0.001 | 0.080 | 0.078 | 0.078 |
| USDZAR | | | | | 2.200 | 4.000 | 2.700 | 2.200 | 3.700 | 5.700 | 3.300 | 2.800 | 0.900 | 2.400 |
| p-value | | | | | 0.014 | 0.000 | 0.003 | 0.014 | 0.000 | 0.000 | 0.001 | 0.002 | 0.195 | 0.009 |

Notes: The highlighted values indicate that the features required for manipulation are not confirmed by the test.

**TABLE 11** Z-Test Result for Minor Currencies Pairs

| Statistic/p-value | 2001 | 2002 | 2003 | 2004 | 2005 | 2006 | 2007 | 2008 | 2009 | 2010 | 2011 | 2012 | 2013 | 2014 |
|---|---|---|---|---|---|---|---|---|---|---|---|---|---|---|
| EURUSD | 30.600 | 33.700 | 55.300 | 24.800 | 23.000 | 30.700 | 7.900 | 15.900 | 16.800 | 30.600 | 19.600 | 6.800 | 35.500 | 9.700 |
| p-value | 0.000 | 0.000 | 0.000 | 0.000 | 0.000 | 0.000 | 0.003 | 0.000 | 0.000 | 0.000 | 0.000 | 0.005 | 0.000 | 0.001 |
| GBPUSD | 5.200 | 10.500 | 18.400 | 10.000 | 13.600 | 28.300 | 3.500 | 2.000 | 7.800 | 4.400 | 17.700 | 6.300 | 11.400 | 2.800 |
| p-value | 0.011 | 0.001 | 0.000 | 0.001 | 0.000 | 0.000 | 0.030 | 0.080 | 0.003 | 0.018 | 0.000 | 0.006 | 0.000 | 0.046 |
| USDCHF | 23.600 | 38.900 | 57.700 | 20.800 | 25.000 | 39.500 | 15.800 | 18.300 | 4.400 | 9.900 | 14.700 | 12.200 | 23.800 | 15.700 |
| p-value | 0.000 | 0.000 | 0.000 | 0.000 | 0.000 | 0.000 | 0.000 | 0.000 | 0.018 | 0.001 | 0.000 | 0.000 | 0.000 | 0.000 |
| USDJPY | 3.100 | 20.800 | 4.800 | 21.600 | 2.300 | 20.900 | 11.300 | 25.400 | 17.600 | 45.300 | 28.300 | 13.000 | 41.700 | 21.100 |
| p-value | 0.038 | 0.000 | 0.014 | 0.000 | 0.063 | 0.000 | 0.000 | 0.000 | 0.000 | 0.000 | 0.000 | 0.000 | 0.000 | 0.000 |
| EURGBP | 8.200 | 9.800 | 15.300 | 0.000 | 0.300 | 2.300 | 0.000 | 2.200 | 0.600 | 1.300 | 2.500 | 4.600 | 5.600 | 0.000 |
| p-value | 0.002 | 0.001 | 0.000 | 0.500 | 0.308 | 0.066 | 0.500 | 0.069 | 0.776 | 0.130 | 0.057 | 0.016 | 0.009 | 0.500 |
| EURCHF | 4.100 | 2.300 | 0.000 | 0.000 | 0.000 |  | 0.000 | 7.800 | 0.000 | 18.600 | 20.300 | 0.000 | 1.600 | 0.000 |
| p-value | 0.022 | 0.066 | 0.500 | 0.500 | 0.500 |  | 0.500 | 0.003 | 0.500 | 0.000 | 0.000 | 0.500 | 0.102 | 0.500 |
| EURJPY | 15.500 | 14.000 | 14.200 | 12.600 | 0.600 | 0.600 | 6.800 | 15.700 | 32.000 | 40.600 | 32.700 | 36.800 | 13.800 | 5.900 |
| p-value | 0.000 | 0.000 | 0.000 | 0.000 | 0.777 | 0.223 | 0.005 | 0.000 | 0.000 | 0.000 | 0.000 | 0.000 | 0.000 | 0.007 |
| GBPCHF | 0.000 | 10.800 | 13.900 | 0.100 | 0.400 | 5.000 | 0.700 | 4.900 | 0.100 | 7.900 | 12.300 | 1.400 | 3.200 | 0.700 |
| p-value | 0.439 | 0.001 | 0.000 | 0.366 | 0.271 | 0.013 | 0.197 | 0.013 | 0.612 | 0.003 | 0.000 | 0.115 | 0.036 | 0.208 |
| GBPJPY | 0.000 | 4.700 | 5.400 | 4.400 | 0.200 | 2.100 | 7.700 | 13.500 | 16.600 | 38.800 | 26.200 | 20.800 | 10.300 | 2.300 |
| p-value | 0.446 | 0.015 | 0.010 | 0.018 | 0.335 | 0.072 | 0.003 | 0.000 | 0.000 | 0.000 | 0.000 | 0.000 | 0.001 | 0.064 |

| | | | | | | | | | | | | | | |
|---|---|---|---|---|---|---|---|---|---|---|---|---|---|
| CHFJPY | 13.800 | 13.000 | 13.800 | 14.600 | 1.700 | 16.600 | 3.500 | 4.200 | 42.700 | 30.400 | 12.200 | 20.000 | 7.700 | 0.600 |
| p-value | 0.000 | 0.000 | 0.000 | 0.000 | 0.094 | 0.000 | 0.031 | 0.020 | 0.000 | 0.000 | 0.000 | 0.000 | 0.003 | 0.223 |
| USDCAD | 7.900 | 2.200 | 21.200 | 9.200 | 18.100 | 11.700 | 0.300 | 0.100 | 22.600 | 22.100 | 36.600 | 26.100 | 24.300 | 14.800 |
| p-value | 0.002 | 0.069 | 0.000 | 0.001 | 0.000 | 0.000 | 0.287 | 0.590 | 0.000 | 0.000 | 0.000 | 0.000 | 0.000 | 0.000 |
| EURCAD | 17.600 | 37.100 | 17.800 | 2.100 | 14.600 | 15.300 | 1.300 | 0.100 | 0.700 | 12.100 | 17.400 | 5.700 | 31.800 | 5.300 |
| p-value | 0.000 | 0.000 | 0.000 | 0.076 | 0.000 | 0.000 | 0.130 | 0.592 | 0.206 | 0.000 | 0.000 | 0.008 | 0.000 | 0.011 |
| AUDUSD | 0.100 | 0.100 | 2.900 | 10.200 | 9.900 | 18.700 | 5.200 | 4.800 | 57.600 | 40.600 | 31.000 | 23.300 | 11.100 | 15.800 |
| p-value | 0.400 | 0.359 | 0.043 | 0.001 | 0.001 | 0.000 | 0.011 | 0.014 | 0.000 | 0.000 | 0.000 | 0.000 | 0.000 | 0.000 |
| AUDJPY | 0.100 | 10.300 | 0.300 | 7.000 | 0.000 | 7.500 | 3.300 | 11.100 | 61.000 | 74.100 | 51.400 | 48.500 | 9.900 | 5.300 |
| p-value | 0.641 | 0.001 | 0.295 | 0.004 | 0.430 | 0.003 | 0.035 | 0.000 | 0.000 | 0.000 | 0.000 | 0.000 | 0.001 | 0.011 |

Notes: The highlighted values indicate that the features required for manipulation are not confirmed by the test.

**TABLE 12**  Z-Test Result for Minor Currencies Pairs

| Statistic/p-value | 2001 | 2002 | 2003 | 2004 | 2005 | 2006 | 2007 | 2008 | 2009 | 2010 | 2011 | 2012 | 2013 | 2014 |
|---|---|---|---|---|---|---|---|---|---|---|---|---|---|---|
| NZDUSD | | | 2.800 | 10.900 | 10.100 | 12.200 | 19.100 | 0.400 | 51.700 | 40.900 | 36.700 | 25.600 | 9.600 | 11.100 |
| p-value | | | 0.046 | 0.000 | 0.001 | 0.000 | 0.000 | 0.257 | 0.000 | 0.000 | 0.000 | 0.000 | 0.001 | 0.000 |
| NZDJPY | | | 5.700 | 2.500 | 2.100 | 6.100 | 16.500 | 11.000 | 61.900 | 63.100 | 45.400 | 56.000 | 18.500 | 11.100 |
| p-value | | | 0.008 | 0.056 | 0.073 | 0.007 | 0.000 | 0.000 | 0.000 | 0.000 | 0.000 | 0.000 | 0.000 | 0.000 |
| USDCZK | | | | | 2.600 | 15.800 | 0.900 | 3.500 | 0.000 | 0.400 | 1.900 | 2.100 | 0.300 | 0.100 |
| p-value | | | | | 0.054 | 0.000 | 0.175 | 0.032 | 0.500 | 0.739 | 0.914 | 0.073 | 0.700 | 0.359 |
| USDDKK | | | | | 16.200 | 32.700 | 7.000 | 13.400 | 8.800 | 21.500 | 15.400 | 9.400 | 26.200 | 10.700 |
| p-value | | | | | 0.000 | 0.000 | 0.004 | 0.000 | 0.001 | 0.000 | 0.000 | 0.001 | 0.000 | 0.001 |
| EURRUB | | | | | 14.600 | 34.100 | 9.700 | 25.000 | 6.800 | 11.700 | 12.300 | 9.400 | 5.300 | 4.000 |
| p-value | | | | | 0.000 | 0.000 | 0.001 | 0.000 | 0.005 | 0.000 | 0.000 | 0.001 | 0.011 | 0.023 |
| USDHUF | | | | | 0.600 | 16.800 | 3.600 | 1.500 | 0.000 | 0.300 | 0.000 | 1.300 | 4.000 | 3.500 |
| p-value | | | | | 0.215 | 0.000 | 0.029 | 0.108 | 0.456 | 0.702 | 0.546 | 0.131 | 0.023 | 0.031 |
| USDNOK | | | | | 18.300 | 37.100 | 9.000 | 6.500 | 37.800 | 21.200 | 13.900 | 18.100 | 23.100 | 0.700 |
| p-value | | | | | 0.000 | 0.000 | 0.001 | 0.005 | 0.000 | 0.000 | 0.000 | 0.000 | 0.000 | 0.197 |
| USDPLN | | | | | 14.200 | 27.500 | 1.000 | 2.700 | 2.800 | 13.000 | 12.500 | 10.400 | 20.400 | 10.200 |
| p-value | | | | | 0.000 | 0.000 | 0.157 | 0.049 | 0.047 | 0.000 | 0.000 | 0.001 | 0.000 | 0.001 |
| USDRUB | | | | | | | | 2.300 | 17.700 | 0.800 | 7.900 | 0.000 | 1.100 | 0.100 |
| p-value | | | | | | | | 0.934 | 1.000 | 0.810 | 0.003 | 0.500 | 0.147 | 0.363 |
| USDSEK | | | | | 10.600 | 30.500 | 7.500 | 16.400 | 16.300 | 42.400 | 32.400 | 11.000 | 20.300 | 10.900 |
| p-value | | | | | 0.001 | 0.000 | 0.003 | 0.000 | 0.000 | 0.000 | 0.000 | 0.000 | 0.000 | 0.000 |
| USDSGD | | | | | 1.300 | 0.200 | 0.000 | 5.200 | 2.300 | 0.000 | 7.900 | 1.300 | 0.500 | 0.500 |
| p-value | | | | | 0.123 | 0.341 | 0.500 | 0.011 | 0.064 | 0.500 | 0.003 | 0.131 | 0.239 | 0.239 |
| USDZAR | | | | | 4.300 | 15.500 | 6.700 | 4.400 | 13.100 | 31.200 | 10.100 | 7.300 | 0.600 | 4.900 |
| p-value | | | | | 0.019 | 0.000 | 0.005 | 0.018 | 0.000 | 0.000 | 0.001 | 0.003 | 0.226 | 0.013 |

Notes: *The highlighted values indicate that the features required for manipulation are not confirmed by the test.*

TABLE 13 McNemar Test Statistic for Major Currencies

| Statistic/p-value | 2001 | 2002 | 2003 | 2004 | 2005 | 2006 | 2007 | 2008 | 2009 | 2010 | 2011 | 2012 | 2013 | 2014 |
|---|---|---|---|---|---|---|---|---|---|---|---|---|---|---|
| EURUSD | 0.200 | 0.100 | 0.100 | 0.200 | 0.200 | 0.100 | 0.100 | 0.300 | 0.300 | 0.200 | 0.200 | 0.300 | 0.000 | 0.200 |
| p-value | 0.000 | 0.000 | 0.000 | 0.000 | 0.000 | 0.000 | 0.002 | 0.000 | 0.000 | 0.000 | 0.000 | 0.005 | 0.000 | 0.001 |
| GBPUSD | 0.500 | 0.300 | 0.200 | 0.400 | 0.200 | 0.100 | 0.300 | 0.600 | 0.500 | 0.500 | 0.100 | 0.200 | 0.200 | 0.200 |
| p-value | 0.028 | 0.001 | 0.000 | 0.003 | 0.000 | 0.000 | 0.041 | 0.161 | 0.006 | 0.036 | 0.000 | 0.008 | 0.000 | 0.065 |
| USDCHF | 0.200 | 0.100 | 0.100 | 0.300 | 0.100 | 0.100 | 0.100 | 0.300 | 0.500 | 0.400 | 0.400 | 0.300 | 0.200 | 0.100 |
| p-value | 0.000 | 0.000 | 0.000 | 0.000 | 0.000 | 0.000 | 0.000 | 0.000 | 0.033 | 0.001 | 0.000 | 0.000 | 0.000 | 0.000 |
| USDJPY | 0.500 | 0.300 | 0.400 | 0.200 | 0.500 | 0.100 | 0.300 | 0.300 | 0.300 | 0.100 | 0.100 | 0.200 | 0.100 | 0.000 |
| p-value | 0.073 | 0.000 | 0.029 | 0.000 | 0.136 | 0.000 | 0.000 | 0.000 | 0.000 | 0.000 | 0.000 | 0.000 | 0.000 | 0.000 |
| EURGBP | 0.300 | 0.200 | 0.200 | 0.900 | 0.300 | | 0.800 | 0.600 | 1.300 | 0.700 | 0.500 | 0.300 | 0.300 | 1.000 |
| p-value | 0.003 | 0.002 | 0.000 | 1.000 | 0.625 | | 1.000 | 0.132 | 0.451 | 0.268 | 0.122 | 0.027 | 0.011 | 1.000 |
| EURCHF | 0.100 | | 0.500 | 2.000 | | | 1.000 | 0.400 | 1.000 | 0.200 | 0.300 | 1.000 | 0.300 | 1.000 |
| p-value | 0.039 | | 1.000 | 1.000 | | | 1.000 | 0.005 | 1.000 | 0.000 | 0.000 | 1.000 | 0.146 | 1.000 |
| EURJPY | 0.300 | 0.300 | 0.300 | 0.300 | 1.700 | 0.600 | 0.400 | 0.400 | 0.300 | 0.200 | 0.200 | 0.200 | 0.300 | 0.200 |
| p-value | 0.000 | 0.000 | 0.000 | 0.000 | 0.454 | 0.424 | 0.005 | 0.000 | 0.000 | 0.000 | 0.000 | 0.000 | 0.000 | 0.013 |
| GBPCHF | 0.900 | 0.300 | 0.300 | 0.800 | 0.600 | 0.100 | 0.600 | 0.500 | 1.100 | 0.400 | 0.400 | 0.500 | 0.400 | 0.600 |
| p-value | 0.880 | 0.001 | 0.000 | 0.736 | 0.549 | 0.021 | 0.359 | 0.020 | 0.780 | 0.005 | 0.001 | 0.210 | 0.061 | 0.424 |
| GBPJPY | 0.900 | 0.500 | 0.500 | 0.500 | 0.800 | 0.400 | 0.400 | 0.400 | 0.400 | 0.200 | 0.200 | 0.300 | 0.400 | 0.300 |
| p-value | 0.896 | 0.029 | 0.019 | 0.040 | 0.664 | 0.115 | 0.003 | 0.000 | 0.000 | 0.000 | 0.000 | 0.000 | 0.001 | 0.077 |
| CHFJPY | 0.300 | 0.400 | 0.300 | 0.200 | 0.600 | 0.100 | 0.400 | 0.600 | 0.200 | 0.300 | 0.400 | 0.300 | 0.400 | 0.600 |
| p-value | 0.000 | 0.000 | 0.000 | 0.000 | 0.185 | 0.000 | 0.035 | 0.040 | 0.000 | 0.000 | 0.001 | 0.000 | 0.007 | 0.454 |
| USDCAD | 0.100 | 0.400 | 0.200 | 0.400 | 0.200 | 0.300 | 0.800 | 1.100 | 0.300 | 0.300 | 0.100 | 0.100 | 0.000 | 0.200 |
| p-value | 0.002 | 0.143 | 0.000 | 0.002 | 0.000 | 0.000 | 0.568 | 0.820 | 0.000 | 0.000 | 0.000 | 0.000 | 0.000 | 0.000 |

*Continued*

TABLE 13 McNemar Test Statistic for Major Currencies—cont'd

| Statistic/p-value | 2001 | 2002 | 2003 | 2004 | 2005 | 2006 | 2007 | 2008 | 2009 | 2010 | 2011 | 2012 | 2013 | 2014 |
|---|---|---|---|---|---|---|---|---|---|---|---|---|---|---|
| EURCAD | 0.300 | 0.200 | 0.300 | 0.600 | 0.200 | 0.200 | 0.700 | 1.100 | 0.800 | 0.400 | 0.200 | 0.200 | 0.100 | 0.300 |
| p-value | 0.000 | 0.000 | 0.000 | 0.161 | 0.000 | 0.000 | 0.233 | 0.818 | 0.419 | 0.001 | 0.000 | 0.012 | 0.000 | 0.017 |
| AUDUSD | 0.900 | 0.800 | 0.600 | 0.400 | 0.300 | 0.100 | 0.500 | 0.600 | 0.200 | 0.200 | 0.200 | 0.200 | 0.200 | 0.100 |
| p-value | 0.801 | 0.720 | 0.098 | 0.002 | 0.001 | 0.000 | 0.024 | 0.033 | 0.000 | 0.000 | 0.000 | 0.000 | 0.000 | 0.000 |
| AUDJPY | 1.100 | 0.400 | 0.800 | 0.500 | 0.900 | 0.300 | 0.600 | 0.500 | 0.100 | 0.100 | 0.100 | 0.100 | 0.300 | 0.300 |
| p-value | 0.724 | 0.001 | 0.590 | 0.009 | 0.856 | 0.005 | 0.063 | 0.001 | 0.000 | 0.000 | 0.000 | 0.000 | 0.001 | 0.015 |

Notes: The highlighted values indicate that the features required for manipulation are not confirmed by the test.

**TABLE 14** McNemar Test Statistic for Minor Currencies

| Statistic/p-value | 2001 | 2002 | 2003 | 2004 | 2005 | 2006 | 2007 | 2008 | 2009 | 2010 | 2011 | 2012 | 2013 | 2014 |
|---|---|---|---|---|---|---|---|---|---|---|---|---|---|---|
| NZDUSD | 0.600 | 0.400 | 0.300 | 0.300 | 0.300 | 0.500 | 0.500 | 0.200 | 0.200 | 0.200 | 0.300 | 0.200 | | |
| p-value | 0.119 | 0.001 | 0.001 | 0.000 | 0.000 | 0.012 | 0.000 | 0.000 | 0.000 | 0.000 | 0.000 | 0.000 | | |
| NZDJPY | 0.600 | 0.700 | 0.600 | 0.500 | 0.300 | 0.300 | 0.300 | 0.200 | 0.200 | 0.200 | 0.200 | 0.200 | | |
| p-value | 0.027 | 0.146 | 0.111 | 0.016 | 0.000 | 0.000 | 0.000 | 0.000 | 0.000 | 0.000 | 0.000 | 0.000 | | |
| USDCZK | 0.600 | 0.200 | 0.400 | 0.400 | 0.800 | 1.300 | 1.500 | 1.100 | 0.900 | 1.000 | 0.100 | | | |
| p-value | 0.096 | 0.000 | 0.118 | 0.020 | 0.435 | 0.410 | 0.079 | 0.795 | 0.724 | 1.000 | 0.021 | | | |
| USDDKK | 0.200 | 0.100 | 0.100 | 0.200 | 0.500 | 0.300 | 0.200 | 0.300 | 0.100 | 0.200 | | | | |
| p-value | 0.000 | 0.000 | 0.003 | 0.000 | 0.011 | 0.002 | 0.000 | 0.000 | 0.000 | 0.000 | | | | |
| EURRUB | 0.100 | 0.100 | 0.100 | 0.100 | 0.300 | 0.500 | 0.200 | 0.300 | 0.300 | 0.500 | 0.500 | | | |
| p-value | 0.000 | 0.000 | 0.006 | 0.000 | 0.001 | 0.028 | 0.000 | 0.001 | 0.001 | 0.054 | 0.302 | | | |
| USDHUF | 0.800 | 0.200 | 0.400 | 0.600 | 0.700 | 1.200 | 1.500 | 0.800 | 0.800 | 0.400 | 0.400 | | | |
| p-value | 0.542 | 0.000 | 0.029 | 0.265 | 0.219 | 0.620 | 0.115 | 0.434 | 0.380 | 0.001 | 0.267 | | | |
| USDNOK | 0.200 | 0.100 | 0.300 | 0.400 | 0.600 | 0.100 | 0.300 | 0.300 | 0.200 | 0.400 | 0.300 | | | |
| p-value | 0.000 | 0.000 | 0.002 | 0.004 | 0.024 | 0.000 | 0.000 | 0.000 | 0.000 | 0.003 | 0.180 | | | |
| USDPLN | 0.300 | 0.200 | 0.500 | 0.500 | 0.800 | 0.500 | 0.300 | 0.400 | 0.500 | 0.300 | 0.100 | | | |
| p-value | 0.000 | 0.000 | 0.332 | 0.136 | 0.466 | 0.009 | 0.000 | 0.000 | 0.003 | 0.000 | 0.012 | | | |
| USDRUB | | | | | | | 2.000 | 0.400 | 0.900 | 0.800 | 0.400 | | | |
| p-value | | | | | | | 0.508 | 0.043 | 1.000 | 0.572 | 0.180 | | | |
| USDSEK | 0.300 | 0.100 | 0.300 | 0.300 | 0.500 | 0.200 | 0.200 | 0.200 | 0.300 | 0.300 | 0.100 | | | |
| p-value | 0.001 | 0.000 | 0.011 | 0.001 | 0.003 | 0.000 | 0.000 | 0.000 | 0.000 | 0.001 | 0.039 | | | |
| USDSGD | | 0.500 | | 2.000 | 0.100 | | 0.500 | 0.300 | 0.000 | | | | | |
| p-value | | 0.688 | | 1.000 | 0.000 | | 0.508 | 0.041 | 0.062 | | | | | |
| USDZAR | 0.600 | 0.400 | 0.500 | 0.500 | 0.900 | 0.300 | 0.300 | 0.500 | 0.600 | 0.700 | 0.400 | | | |
| p-value | 0.047 | 0.000 | 0.008 | 0.004 | 0.586 | 0.000 | 0.000 | 0.002 | 0.028 | 0.129 | 0.344 | | | |

Notes: *The highlighted values indicate that the features required for manipulation are not confirmed by the test.*

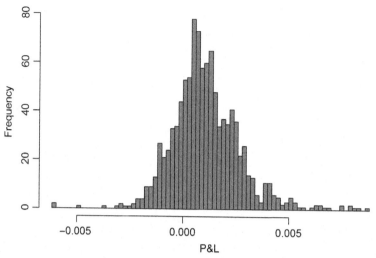

**FIGURE 4**  Histogram of the average daily profit for a trader arbitrating the 16 h peak.

get back its efficiency. The only problem is that the market is manipulated by the biggest player trading most of the volumes. The other speculators would not be able to pull up the required volume to reduce through arbitrage the effect of the manipulation. Therefore, the peak effect around the fixing hour would remain persistent in the market.

Figure 4 shows the empirical distribution of the average daily profit and losses generated by a trader which speculates the 16 h peak. The agent buys at the peak and afterwards when the rate comes back to the normal states he reverses the position.

The average of the daily returns from this strategy are tested for positivity at a 99.99% confidence interval. The results for the USD/EUR and GDP/EUR rates are given in Table 15 on a yearly basis since 2001. The average is significant for all years besides 2007 and 2006, and the level of the average return increases after 2008.

# 4 IMPACT ON THE REAL ECONOMY

## 4.1 Customer Opportunity Costs

The main visible negative externality generated by the Forex manipulation is the increased cost of spot trades for clients as a result of the banks pushing the rate in the direction that maximized their profits. Clients were essentially buying currency at inflated prices or selling at lower prices and the traders were making a profit on their behalf. These profits would not exist without the manipulation.

Let's assume a Swiss importer needed to purchase a large amount of U.S. dollars in order to pay an American supplier. In the example presented in Figure 5 assuming the Swiss importer buys dollars on that day based on the fixing rate he will pay more Swiss francs due to the rigging. Figure 6 shows the hourly distribution of the intra-day volatility emphasizing the fixing hour effect. The Swiss regulator FINMA investigated the two largest banks, UBS and Credit Suisse, related to the rigging of the CHF rate manipulation, but only UBS was fined.

## 4.2 Asian Currencies

While the transatlantic currencies pairs (e.g., USD/EUR, USD/GBP, USD/CHF, etc.) were shown to be clear targets of the 16 h "fix," the issues concerning the Asian currencies is more complex. The Hong Kong Monetary Authority investigated in 2014 the city's currency market

**TABLE 15** The Average of the Daily Returns from This Strategy are Tested for Positivity at a 99.99% Confidence Interval for EUR/USD and USG/GBP Through the $t$-Test

| Year | USDEUR | | | GBPUSD | | |
|------|---------|-------------------|---------|----------|-------------------|---------|
| | Mean P&L | Inferior conf. int | $p$-Value | Mean P&L | Inferior conf. int | $p$-Value |
| 2001 | 0.0007 | 0.0003 | 0.0009 | 0.0004 | 0.00 | |
| 2002 | 0.0011 | 0.0005 | 0.00 | | | |
| 2003 | 0.0010 | 0.0005 | 0.00 | 0.0009 | 0.0003 | 0.00 |
| 2004 | 0.0013 | 0.0008 | 0.00 | 0.0014 | 0.0008 | 0.00 |
| 2005 | 0.0008 | 0.0003 | 0.00 | 0.0010 | 0.0003 | 0.00 |
| 2006 | 0.0006 | 0.00 | 0.00 | 0.0004 | −0.0002 | 0.06 |
| 2008 | 0.0016 | 0.0010 | 0.00 | 0.0024 | 0.0017 | 0.00 |
| 2009 | 0.0013 | 0.0008 | 0.00 | 0.0014 | 0.0011 | 0.00 |
| 2010 | 0.0009 | 0.0005 | 0.00 | 0.0011 | 0.0007 | 0.00 |
| 2011 | 0.0015 | 0.0010 | 0.00 | 0.0010 | 0.0007 | 0.00 |
| 2012 | 0.0006 | 0.0001 | 0.00 | 0.0008 | 0.00 | 0.01 |
| 2013 | 0.0008 | 0.0002 | 0.00 | 0.0013 | 0.0008 | 0.00 |

and uncovered attempts to manipulate exchange rates, although there was no collusion between banks.[3] A Hong Kong-based trader working for Standard Chartered was suspected of Asian currency benchmark fixing by making requests to an overseas colleague between March 2009 and November 2010. However, there was insufficient evidence to suggest trades were actually made to achieve this. There was also a failed attempt by Deutsche Bank traders to influence the Hong Kong dollar spot rate in March 2009.

While no proof of manipulation was found of the Hong Kong dollar, Asia's biggest currency in terms of volumes on the FX market, the Japanese Yen, appears to have been heavily rigged as shown by the statistical analysis used in the previous section. A few examples of the New Zealand dollar-Yen rate are shown in Figure 7 and the intra-day volatility is given in Figure 8.

Figure 9 shows the evolution of the intra-day volatility, emphasizing the peak at the fixing hour. A few examples are depicted in Figure 10.

### 4.3 Algo Trading

Probably the most disruptive effect, which was not really covered by regulators, was in relationship to algorithmic (high-frequency) trading. Even the most basic algorithm would be able to capture on a historic basis that the market has a price bias around 16 h. The amount of profit that could be generated here is difficult to estimate and to assess as traders might be able to arbitrate between exchanges very easily.

In addition to the case of misconduct of the American hedge fund Renaissance Technologies that used computing power harbored by the banks infrastructure (e.g., Barclays) the question of a possible collusion between the hedge fund industry and the FX rigging appears naturally.

[3]Hong Kong clears banks of wrongdoing in foreign exchange probe, http://www.bloomberg.com/news/2014-12-19/hong-kong-clears-banks-of-wrongdoing-in-foreign-exchange-probe.html.

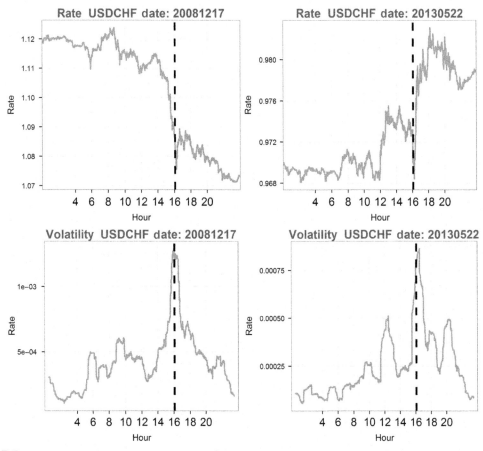

**FIGURE 5**  Manipulation of the USDCHF rate.

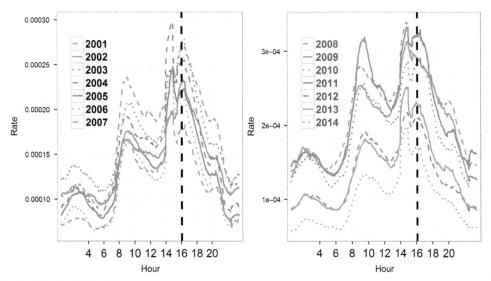

**FIGURE 6**  Volatility USD CHF.

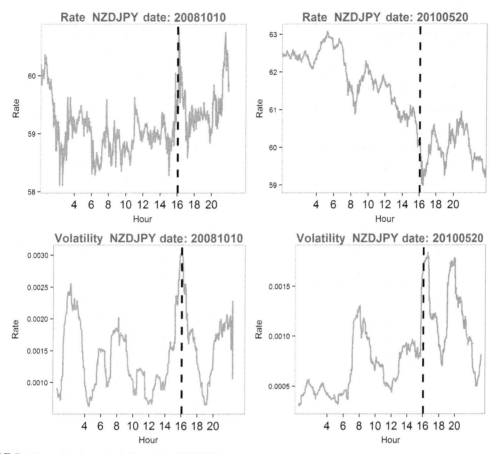

FIGURE 7    Example of manipulation of the NZDJPY rate.

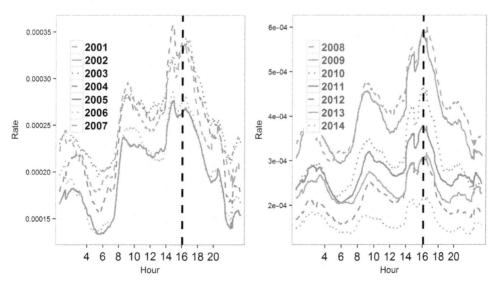

FIGURE 8    Intra-day volatility of the NZD/JPY.

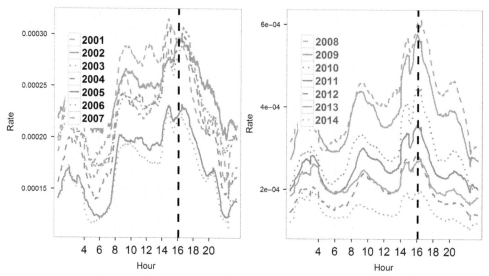

**FIGURE 9**  Intra-day volatility of the AUD/JPY.

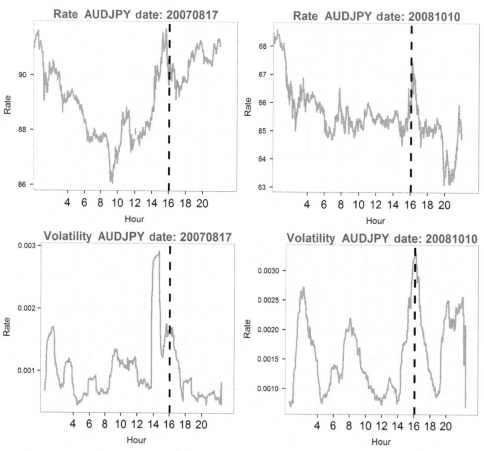

**FIGURE 10**  Example of manipulation of the AUD/JPY.

Banks also had information about the trigger client "stop loss" orders designed to limit the losses a client could face if exposed to adverse currency rate movement. Some of the manipulation could be related to targeting the stop loss level, which would cause a reaction of positions cutting from client, which would amplify the movements of the market. An algo trader could easily generate a profit by placing the appropriate orders around the level of stop loss of a big client.

Lastly, information did not circulate only between traders involved in rigging. Information appears to have been passed on to traders at other companies about big upcoming trades. All of this could have artificially raised or diminished the value of one currency against another.

## 4.4 Derivatives Transactions

If the rates were rigged, it could have affected the hedges multinational companies usually put in place to minimize their exposure to currency fluctuations. It could also have affected the value of options and funds tied to currency values. These can all affect investments made by ordinary shareholders and even the prices paid by consumers.

The derivatives could also be affected mainly in over-the-counter cases that had the 16 h close rate as reference rate. Most likely, the impact is minor but as a crime typology is important to indicate that benchmark manipulation can affect the derivatives market. If the fixing rate was a specified underlying rate in a derivatives contract this could have implications on clients' payoffs. Derivatives have nonlinear payoffs so the impact for the client is hard to evaluate. But if an option expires in a specific day and has the underlying reference linked to the rate fixing, a manipulation could reduce the payoff or to knock out the option if the product has barrier features.

TABLE 16 Break Down of the FX Rigging Fines Issued for Each the Banks and by Individual Financial Regulator

| (in $ million) | FCA | CFTC | FINMA | OCC | Total |
|---|---|---|---|---|---|
| UBS | 371 | 290 | 140 | | 801 |
| Citigroup | 358 | 310 | – | 350 | 1008 |
| JPMorgan | 352 | 310 | – | 350 | 1002 |
| RBS | 344 | 290 | – | – | 634 |
| HSBC | 343 | 275 | – | – | 618 |
| Bank of America | – | – | – | 250 | 250 |
| Total | 1768 | 1475 | 140 | 950 | 4333 |

## 5 AFTERMATH

In the aftermath total fines of $4.3 billion were issued to five banks and at least one arrest of a RBS trader was reported by British enforcement.[4] Table 16 shows the break down of the fines for each bank and by individual financial regulator.[5]

The highest penalties were given by the British Financial Conduct Authority for almost $1.7 billion. The two U.S.-based authorities, the Commodity Futures Trading Commission and the Office of the Comptroller of the Currency, fined both European and American banks for a total of $2.4 billion. The Swiss regulator Financial Market Supervisory Authority (FINMA) inflicted a fine only to its domestic bank UBS, which paid a little more than $800 million to settle its Forex-related suits. The Swiss bank is

---

[4]Five Banks Settle Forex Manipulation Charges For $3.4 billion, http://www.forbes.com/sites/greatspeculations/2014/11/12/five-banks-settle-forex-manipulation-charges-for-3-4-billion/.
[5]OCC Fines Three U.S. Banks Almost $1 billion in FX-Rigging Probe, http://www.bloomberg.com/news/articles/2014-11-12/occ-fines-three-u-s-banks-almost-1-billion-in-fx-rigging-probe.

currently under increased scrutiny and has had to keep bonuses down for all its employees working globally in foreign exchange and commodities trading.

To estimate the profit generated by various traders from the FX fixing in regards to sport transactions it would be sufficient to multiply the difference in rate that occurred as a result of the manipulation with the volume traded in a specific day. The sum over the full period of these gains would represent the illicit profit taken by a bank on a currency pair.

Mathematically the illicit profit can be expressed as the amplitude of the peak on the day a manipulation occurs multiplied by the volume of transactions on that day. A lower limit approximation can be obtained by multiplying the average peak by the number of extrapeaks compared to the blind hour and average volume:

$$\text{Profit} = \sum_{1}^{T} (R_t^{obs} - R_t^*) \mathbf{1}_{\text{Peak}} \cdot V_t$$
$$\geq \mathbf{E}((R_t^{obs} - R_t^*) \mathbf{1}_{\text{Peak}}) \cdot (N_{16} - N_b) \cdot \overline{V_t}$$
$$(11)$$

where $T$ is the total number of days, $R_t^{obs}$ is observed rigged rate, $R_t^*$ is theoretic real rate, $N_{16}$ is number of days with a 16 effect, $N_b$ is number of days that tested positive at the blind hour and $\bar{V}_t$ is the average daily volume.

This approach allows obtaining an estimator for the potential profit taken by banks from spot trades during the manipulation of rates for the main currencies. In the impact study it was assumed that the 1% of the daily trades were affected by fixing and that the daily volumes exposed to the manipulation were constant. Obviously this is a simplification but these approaches aim to provide a floor estimate of the impact. Table 17 shows the evolution of the lower limit of the rogue profits between 2008 and 2013 for the 10 most traded currencies pairs. The cumulated amount is at least $16.52 billion, accounting for almost five times the amount of the total penalties inflicted by various regu-

lators. The U.S. dollar/Euro (USD/EUR) market alone accounted for almost one-third of the total figure representing $5.5 billion. The other rates that generated profit through manipulation are the U.S. dollar/Japanese Yen (USD/JPY), U.S. to Australian dollars (USD/AUD) and U.S./Canadian dollar (USD/CAD).

The years when banks generated most of the rogue profits are 2011 and 2010 with $3.31 billion and $3.14 billion, respectively. As shown in the previous section there is evidence that the benchmark fix started probably way before 2008. The *16 h effect* could have been started in the early 2000s but the estimates from Table 17 present the negative externalities generated since 2008, in order to provide a figure that can be benchmarked with the actual penalties.

The amount of total externalities would be without doubt much higher if other collateral damages were included. The effect on the derivatives market as well as the algorithmic trading effect were not included in this estimation.

## 6 OUTLOOK

When he worked as a trader for an investment bank, Nero had to face the typical employee-evaluation form. The form was supposed to keep track of "performance," supposedly as a check against employees slacking off. Nero found the evaluation absurd because it did not so much judge the quality of a trader's performance as encourage him to game the system by working for short-term profits at the expense of possible blowups. *Black Swans [299]*

After the Forex manipulation the financial world raised the legitimate question of how trustworthy the markets actually are and how confident an investor can be in the signals received from them. On the one hand, if low volatility markets like interest rates or Forex can be manipulated the question about whether more volatile markets like oil, gas, and electricity are subject to manipulation comes naturally. On the other hand, if high liquidity markets are subject to manipulation what are the odds that niche markets like salmon or barley could be rigged?

TABLE 17  Estimated Gain per Year and per Currency

| Year | USDEUR | USDJPY | USDGBP | USDAUD | USDCAD | USDCHF | EURJPY | EURGBP | EURCHF | JPYAUD | All |
|------|--------|--------|--------|--------|--------|--------|--------|--------|--------|--------|-----|
| | | | | | | FX | | | | | |
| **2008** | 0.95 | 0.75 | 0.11 | 0.27 | 0.11 | 0.23 | 0.15 | 0.05 | 0.03 | 0.03 | 2.67 |
| 2009 | 0.94 | 0.44 | 0.23 | 0.75 | 0.30 | 0.08 | 0.19 | 0.01 | 0.00 | 0.09 | 3.03 |
| 2010 | 1.12 | 0.64 | 0.11 | 0.55 | 0.25 | 0.15 | 0.18 | 0.02 | 0.05 | 0.07 | 3.14 |
| 2011 | 1.05 | 0.52 | 0.20 | 0.60 | 0.31 | 0.29 | 0.15 | 0.02 | 0.08 | 0.07 | 3.31 |
| 2012 | 0.53 | 0.24 | 0.09 | 0.33 | 0.15 | 0.13 | 0.14 | 0.03 | 0.00 | 0.05 | 1.67 |
| 2013 | 0.95 | 0.82 | 0.18 | 0.25 | 0.15 | 0.22 | 0.07 | 0.03 | 0.00 | 0.02 | 2.70 |
| **Total** | **5.54** | **3.41** | **0.91** | **2.76** | **1.27** | **1.09** | **0.88** | **0.17** | **0.16** | **0.33** | **16.52** |

Hence, after the FX scandal the Platts oil benchmark faced scrutiny from European Union authorities for possible rigging and the U.S. Commodity Futures Trading Commission started investigating the ISDAFIX swaps benchmark. These suspicions will extend to other markets and other products mainly in commodities.

The Forex rigging case dealt with intra-day manipulation, hence the effect on the market price was not structural and did not affect the long-term levels of prices. The question naturally occurs is whether this type of manipulation involving a cartel can structurally affect the market. If rigging can occur over longer periods of time such as days or weeks, depending on clients positions or other structural factors, the manipulation can be systemic and impacts could be much more dangerous than what was discussed in this chapter.

# The Case of Greenhouse Gas Emission Allowances Market

## 1 BACKGROUND

The last case study discussed fraud on the carbon emission market, which is probably the most disruptive type of crime on a financial market in terms of losses and propagation speed.

The European Union agreed under the Kyoto Protocol to reduce its greenhouse gas emissions in the period 2008-2012 by 8% with respect to the 1990 levels. The adopted strategy for meeting this target was the establishment of a Europe-wide emission allowance market. The Emission Trading Scheme (EU ETS) was initiated in January 2005 and is still considered to be the largest single market for emission allowance trading, representing in 2007 approximately 45 billion euro. By 2009, the market amount to 3.8 billion tons of carbon, equivalent to 40% of the region's emissions. The so-called scheme was a "cap and trade" system whose objective was to cut greenhouse gas emissions by allocating emission allowances (allocated for free or auctioned), which could then be transferred between operators.

The main idea behind "cap and trade" is to reduce pollution not by taxing it but through a market mechanism, controlled by a cap level. Thus, with decreasing profile of the cap industries will see raising the price of pollution rights and will choose to drift their production toward greener technologies. The bottom line is that the price should be high enough for a certain cap level in order to stimulate the use of less-polluting technologies. Under a cap-and-trade emission trading scheme, a public authority (e.g., European Commission in the case of EU ETS) defines an annual upper limit (cap) on total pollutant emissions (e.g., greenhouse gas SOx). The cap is established on both a consolidated and local levels (per industry, region, or company). The authority issues a number of emission allowances (called EUAs for the case of European Union allowances) equal to the cap. Each permit gives the right to its owner to emit 1 ton of carbon dioxide equivalent. Generally the cap, the free allocation, and the auctioned volumes are the result of negotiations between the authority and the various polluters or industrial associations. The permits can be sold on an organized market through an auction, or allocated across industries. The authorities also define a compliance period, similar to a fiscal year, when the profit taxes are collected. At the end of each compliance period, polluting industries must own and consecutively surrender to the authority a number of permits equal to their actual pollution in that year. Obviously entities with fewer emissions than their allocated level could sell the surplus on the market and those entities with more pollution than allocated should buy the permits. This mechanism is nothing more than an exchange of marginal cost de-pollution curves.

Besides the European Union other countries or regions including Australia, New Zealand, South Korea, California, and Quebec have already passed cap-and-trade systems representing roughly less than 20% of the world's emission.

The issue with the emission allowances (EUA) was that under the European Union directive they were considered as supplies (i.e., goods, services) and therefore subject to value-added tax (VAT). The VAT is a type of consumption tax placed on a product whenever value is added at a stage of production and at final sale. The term VAT is most often used in the European Union. The amount of VAT that the user pays is the cost of the product, less the costs of materials used in the product that have already been taxed.

The VAT is paid by a company based on the difference between the collected VAT and the paid VAT. Thus, the carbon emission allowance (EUA) was at that time an instrument traded on a financial market, but each trader submitted a VAT payment to its domestic government.

VAT or missing trader fraud (MTF) frauds [300] based on pocketing governmental taxes is probably one of the most disruptive crimes for the economic system. In MTF's simplest form, a trader collects tax on sales and then fails to remit it to the government, e.g., by engineering bankruptcy. In MTF's more virulent form, the first and fourth factors are abused to trade repeatedly the same consignment of goods between companies set up for this specific purpose. It is this repeated cycling of goods that gives this version of fraud the common name "carousel fraud." Once the shell companies have been created, MTF is a relatively simple crime to commit, with the cycling of goods continuing to profit from one initial outlay.

## 2 VAT FRAUD ON CARBON MARKETS

### 2.1 Mechanism

The so-called VAT fraud carousel or MTF involving carbon emissions allowances, or carbon credits, is summarized in Figure 1.

The trading companies implicated in the scheme allegedly imported large volumes of carbon credits VAT-free from other countries and then sold the credits on French carbon market BlueNext having already marked up the price with the VAT. The market players purchasing the permits would then have been able to claim the VAT back from the French Government. However, the suspects allegedly never reported that VAT revenue, pocketing it instead.

The exchange handled a record 19.8 million metric tons of EU carbon permits on June 2, 2009. The previous record was 15.1 million tons on May 28, 2009. The exchanged volumes fell nearly to zero following the announcement of a reverse charge of VAT in the beginning of June

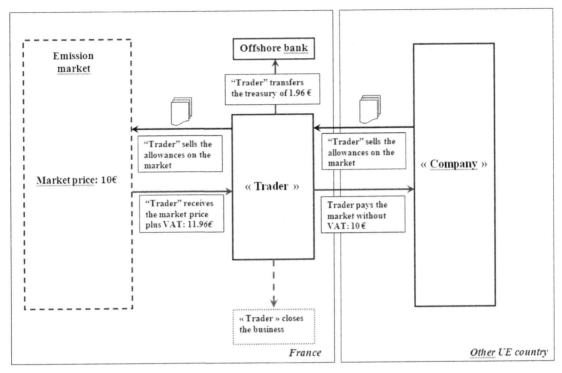

FIGURE 1    VAT carousel scheme.

2009. During the summer of 2009, a number of suspected cases of fraud were detected in several EU Member States, which led to different EU governments taking action by including the greenhouse gas emission allowances in the list of supplies to which a (domestic) reverse charge system could be applied. As a consequence in June 2009 the governments of France and The Netherlands removed the VAT from carbon permits (Figure 2).

## 2.2 Econometric Features

After drawing an accurate picture of the MTF mechanism on the carbon market this section focuses on the consequences of VAT fraud on the econometric features of the market. Thus, a forensic framework is designed to bring rationale proofs and to quantify the impact of the fraud. Our forensic methodology is based on

the validation of five hypotheses described as follows. First, given the rapid return and the low market surveillance the VAT carousel would emphasize a bullish tendency of volumes traded on the market. Second, in a market with a strong selling trend the prices would be pushed to bearish behavior, thereby showing an excess of negative skewness. Third, a market strongly influenced by one strategy (mainly sell-side) would show a breach in the efficient market hypothesis (EMH) assumptions mainly by auto-correlation effects. Fourth, the carbon prices would cease to respond to fundamental driving factors. Fifth, the carbon prices would show extra noise due to abnormal trading.

We divide the emission price time series into three periods: ante fraud, fraud, and post-fraud. The period limits are established based on prior test results and on public information about the MTF. For each period tests are performed for

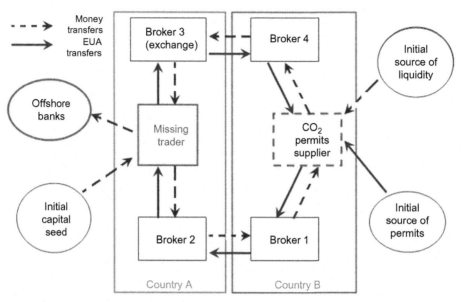

**FIGURE 2** VAT carousel on the carbon emission market. The blue dashed represent the payments and the plain ones represent the transfer of the carbon emissions. This scheme implies few brokers acting as intermediaries between the missing trader based in Country A and the supplier of permits placed in Country B. The supplier feeds its stocks from an initial source that could be an exchange or an industrial installation. Both the supplier and the missing trader are initially provided with capital in order to finance the working capital.

volumes, skewness, autocorrelation, fundamental factors, and extra noise and the results are compared for the three periods for the specific tests.

Our analysis shows that the VAT carousel represented a large part of the exchanged allowances and this massive scheme significantly influenced market prices. One consequence of the fraud is the unusually high volumes of permits exchanged in the market. In fact, in the pick weeks of the carousel the number of transactions was around 10 times higher than normal. After the ban of VAT on carbon trades the volumes dropped and stabilized to a basal regime in the last part of 2009.

As explained in Figure 1 the French carbon exchange was exposed to high quantities of selling that drove the market to significant contraction and to asymmetric behavior. The investigation continues on the fundamental level of

permit' prices during this period and also the dynamic of the skewness. In a market with a strong selling trend the prices would be pushed to bearish behavior, thereby showing an excess of negative skewness.

A statistical study that identified the "actual" main fundamentals for $CO_2$ prices through an arbitrage price theory (APT)-like model. Showed that oil, dark spread, spark spread, and CAC40 explain more than 75% of the $CO_2$ prices behavior and the dynamic feature of the dependencies [300]. These findings are used to demonstrate that during the VAT carousel the carbon prices ceased to respond to fundamental driving factors but recovered promptly after the VAT ban rule.

Figure 3 shows the exchanged volumes of permits on the BlueNext market. As expected it picked up on June 2 and dropped the day after the VAT ban announcement. This finding shows

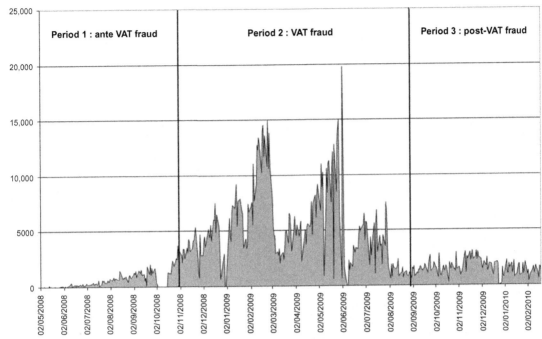

**FIGURE 3** CO$_2$ volumes exchanged on BlueNext from June 2, 2008 to February 2, 2010.

that on the one hand a big stake of volumes were linked to the VAT crime and on the other hand once the carousel was suspended the market lacked fundamental value, forcing the "clean" traders end the activity. Moreover, in February 2009 prices reached a historical low of 7 euros per ton, which is significantly less than the minimal estimated economic price of depolution, which is around 10 euros per ton, as can be seen in Figure 4.

Figure 5 shows the evolution of the carbon yield skewness measured on a moving window of 90 trading days. A phenomenon of skew reverse appears at the end of 2008 when the VAT carousel allegedly started. As the market became artificially long with large offerings the daily yields became predominantly negative. It should be noted that the VAT fraud was an absolute 19.6% return investment. The return was not linked by any means to market price, thereby pushing the permits to an unusual fundamental

level. The skewness reversed to non-negative levels shortly after the end of the VAT fraud.

Our next argument revolves around the fact that in a market strongly influenced by one strategy we would expect a significant autocorrelation effect. The investigation continues on the autocorrelation of carbon price returns on the three periods defined in the previous section. The Box-Ljung test rejects at 95% confidence level the null hypothesis on the ante and post-period and accepts it for the VAT period (Figure 6). The presence of autocorrelation and non-normality in EUA daily returns series is a strong indication of efficient market hypothesis breach. This finding is justified by the heterogeneous information spread in the carbon market due to the presence of some behavioral pattern across traders' strategies.

As discussed elsewhere the fraud on the market theory is closely linked to behavioral finance through the efficient market hypothesis (EMH).

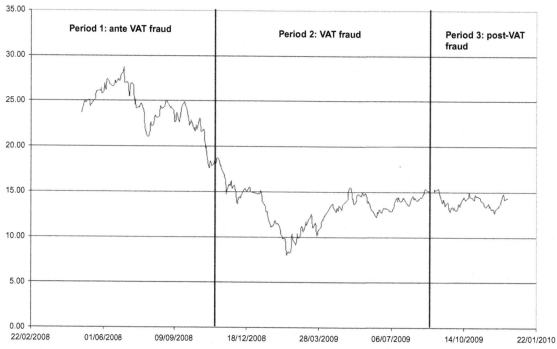

**FIGURE 4**  $CO_2$ emission prices from February 22, 2008 to January 22, 2010, and limits of the three periods: ante VAT fraud, VAT fraud, and post-VAT fraud.

The carbon allowances market is mainly driven by power producers that neutralize the carbon emission of their production on a regular basis. Hence, the carbon market is structurally linked to the power and fossils markets. On the one hand, the assumption that the carbon prices are driven by a quasi-stationary offer/demand equilibrium on energy exchanges might find an EMH framework. On the other hand, the regulated status of the market and the heterogeneous information spread are serious reasons for EMH violations and for the occurrence of correlated patterns of behavior. It is well known that in the absence of market drivers prices are driven more by behavioral biases and by psychological trading effects. An analysis (Figure 7) of the autocorrelation function over a 90-day moving window of daily returns shows that for periods allegedly linked to market uncertainty phenomena of persistence and time series trends occur. These facts

are emphasized by rejection of the Box-Ljung test for different periods. In fact, the EMH breach and the behavioral effect were determined by the opportunity of high returns via the VAT fraud.

In this section an arbitrage pricing theory model developed by Ross [301] is used to show the impact of the factors previously identified on the $CO_2$ price evolution to show calibration results with several noises. This calibration is done using EUA prices for the period 2006-2009. Using the historical time series let's consider some models based on residuals that go from the classical Brownian diffusion to more sophisticated generalized hyperbolic distributions.

The model supposes that a risky asset return follows a factor structure and has the following representation:

$$\tilde{r} = \bar{r} + \beta_1 f_1 + \beta_2 f_2 + \cdots + \beta_k f_k + \epsilon \qquad (1)$$

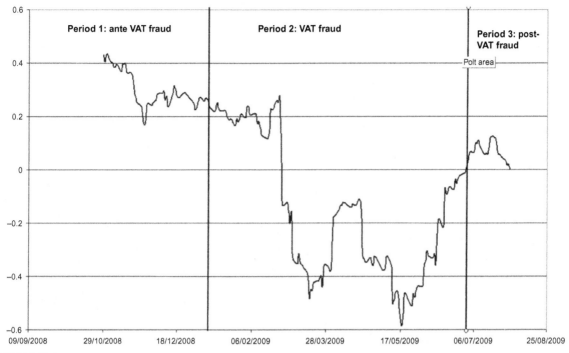

**FIGURE 5**  Skewness evolution of carbon yields computed using 90-day moving window.

where

- $\bar{r}$: The expected return of carbon allowance prices
- $\beta_i$: The factor loading of factor $i$
- $\epsilon$: The idosyncratic component
- $\mathbb{E}(f_i) = 0 \quad \forall i$
- $\mathbb{E}(\epsilon) = 0$

As described by Ross [301] and based on the underlying hypothesis that the markets are efficient the arbitrage price theory (APT) model assumes a Gaussian distribution of the residuals. Given the atypical nature of $CO_2$, the assumptions of the APT model are in some cases broken. Hence, the residuals do not follow a normal distribution and the dependencies are not stationary over time. In order to bypass this issue different distributions are used to replace the classic Gaussian modeling for residuals. We chose the functions $t$-student, GED, and normal

inverse Gaussian (NIG) because of their capacity to account for heavy tails.

Table 1 shows the results of our static calibration over the considered data set using a daily timestep for different residual distributions. The discriminator element is the log likelihood: the higher it is, the better the modeling. It appears that the level of dependencies of $CO_2$ price are generally close in the different models. However, the degree of fitness depends highly on the chosen model. Hence, the $t$-student distribution for residuals captures well the behavior of the residuals and offers a good explanatory ratio for fundamental factors.

The Ljung-Box test of residuals autocorrelation shows no presence of persistence at 99% significance for all the distributions.

We applied the $t$-student-based APT model to carbon prices for the period when the VAT carousel took place. The explained dependency

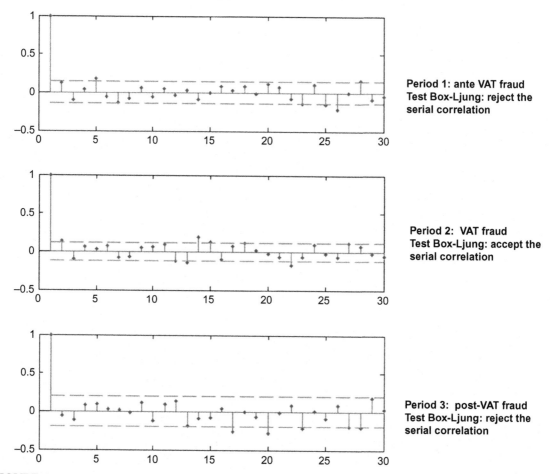

**FIGURE 6**  Autocorrelation tests for the three periods: ante VAT fraud, VAT fraud, and post-VAT fraud.

($R^2$) is represented and the model fitting (likelihood) on a moving window of 90 trading days. The results are presented in Figures 8 and 9.

Figure 8 shows the evolution of the explained dependencies during the period when the fraud allegedly occurred. The results indicate that the $R^2$ decreases significantly the end of 2008 and returns to normal after the summer of 2009. In fact, our APT model quantifies to a certain extent the link between the carbon yields and the fundamental factors. If at a certain moment the carbon price is linked to some new factors the accuracy of our model will diminish. This situation

occurred during the VAT carousel when prices were established mainly by the scheme traders, thereby responding less to fundamentals.

We could justify this downfall in model quality by the global bearish tendency on commodities markets and high volatility that occurred between the end of 2008 and the beginning of 2009. But to investigate this scenario we focused on the evolution of model likelihood. The likelihood estimates the accuracy of the distribution fit on residuals. Figure 5 indicates that the likelihood diminished significantly at the end of 2008 with a minimum in June 2009 and increased

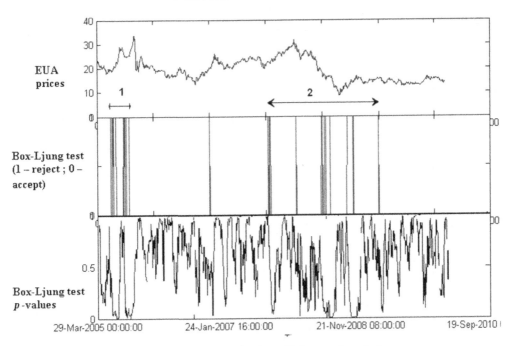

FIGURE 7  Autocorrelation tests for $CO_2$ emission prices using a 90-day moving window.

TABLE 1  Modeling Results

| | Residuals | | | |
|---|---|---|---|---|
| Factors | Gaussian | GED | t-Student | NIG |
| Oil | 0.131 | 0.103 | 0.122 | 0.116 |
| | [0.055 0.205] | [−0.149 0.352] | [0.070 0.174] | [0.063 0.169] |
| Dark spread | 0.262 | 0.2115 | 0.261 | 0.260 |
| | [0.231 0.349] | [0.014 0.468] | [0.221 0.304] | [0.221 0.302] |
| Spark spread | 0.002 | 0.0020 | 0.002 | 0.002 |
| | [−0.001 0.003] | [−0.009 0.033] | [0.000 0.004] | [0.001 0.004] |
| Equity | 0.12 | 0.157 | 0.160 | 0.168 |
| | [0.017 0.242] | [−0.213 0.543] | [0.088 0.247] | [0.097 0.250] |
| $R^2$ | 0.24 | 0.24 | 0.23 | 0.24 |
| Log likelihood | 2054 | 2087 | 2092 | 2094 |

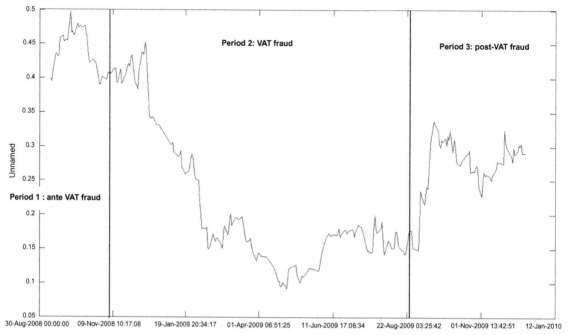

**FIGURE 8** $R^2$ evolution of APT model.

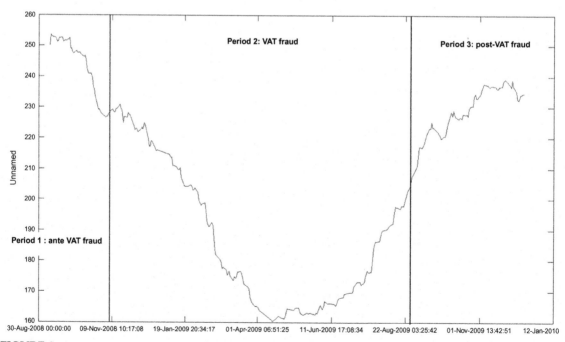

**FIGURE 9** Likely evolution of an APT model implemented for carbon price, with $t$-Student innovations.

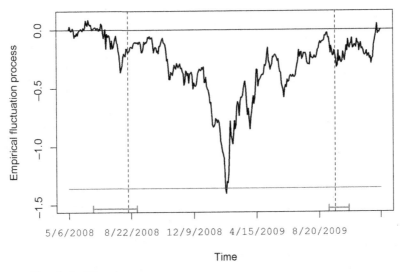

**FIGURE 10**  Structural breaks in $CO_2$ prices.

afterward. This finding shows that the residual noise of the model became stronger in the same period the VAT carousel was turning as a result of the trades that violated fundamental trends.

The previous results show that a trading "epiphenomena" occurred between August 2008 and June 2009. This "hidden trading" significantly changed the behavior of the carbon market, its price level as well as its relationship to other commodities such as oil and energy. The epiphenomena was pushed by high trading volumes ceasing after the VAT ban on carbon allowances. The link between the hidden trading pattern and the VAT carousel fraud is obvious, and the estimated loss for the French Government is at least 1.3 billion euros, given our estimations.

The structural break test of Bai and Perron [207] shows that in the relationship between the carbon prices and the loading factor presented above two structural breaks occurred in August 2008 and in September 2009 as shown in Figure 10. The graph reflects the evolution of the fluctuation process of the multivariate regression as described by Zeileis et al. [209]. These dates correspond to the period when the carbon fraud was acute on the market.

Statistics as a forensic instrument for tax fraud is a relatively new field but its actual applications are vast and future research in this area is justified. The VAT fraud on the carbon permits market that occurred between 2008 and 2009 represented a breach in the regulatory system. Beyond the fund-pocketing effect the scheme had a strong market manipulation effect, by drifting carbon prices behavior from its fundamental state. This situation was reversed immediately after the French Government banned the VAT trades. This type of analysis could be extended to other types of markets and trading systems to track or search for abnormalities or trading rules violations.

While the influence of the VAT fraud on the market's volume is an undisputed finding, the impact on market prices is still argued by regulators and exchanges. Obviously when massive volumes are traded through an exchange as a result of a fraud the market price tends to be very different from the fundamental level. Thus, the exchange does not quote anymore an underlying resenting the marginal depolution cost, but most likely the price of fraud instrument. The carbon market case is a clear-cut example of a market away from its fundamentals. It should be recalled that in cases where hedge funds "raid" a stock or another underlying they can move the price by trading less than 10% of the market volumes. The example of the rogue trades by Jerome Kerviel in 2008 when he allegedly accumulated very significant positions in the European stock indexes speak for itself. Thus, when Societe Generale cut the rogue positions markets across the globe felt the shock, which resulted in large intra-day variations.

In the case of the carbon permits the rogue volumes represented more than 80% of the BlueNext spot market. Moreover, the spot volumes were comparable to the futures market volumes. Figure 11 shows the evolution of the spot and futures volumes. To assess whether the spot volumes both the BlueNext spot trades

and the Intercontinental Exchange (ICE) intra-day futures are considered in order to provide an appropriate figure. Between October 2008 and October 2009 the spot trades accounted for more than 30% of the futures volumes. Usually the spot volumes represent only a small share of the futures trades, due to the use of leverage for the latter instrument. The ratio peaked in February-March 2009 when spot trades represented 70% of the futures volumes. This finding underlines not only a disequilibrium between the spot and the derivatives market, but also emphasizes a massive influx of liquidity on the spot market, given the fact that spot trades cannot use leverage as derivatives and require the use of liquidity. The preference for the use of liquidities for financial market trades is

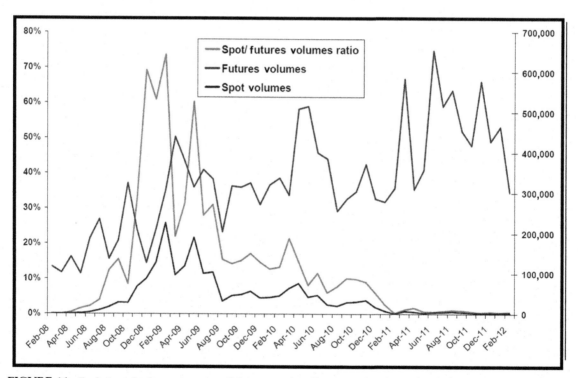

**FIGURE 11** Evolution of volumes on spot and futures market. The spot volumes are the sum of the BlueNext and ECX-ICE intra-day futures transactions. The futures volumes are the sum of all maturities transacted on ECX-ICE. The ratio of the spot/futures volumes peaked during the period of the VAT fraud January to July 2009. The ratio diminished progressively after the ban of the VAT on BlueNext, due to the fact that futures volumes increased over the last 2 years while the spot volumes fell.

uncommon in modern markets, since both institutions and corporations prefer derivatives (futures or forwards) as they are less cash intensive. The overwhelming preference for cash trades is even more illogical in the conditions where the credit market was blocked in 2009 after the default of Lehman Brothers and the subsequent financial crisis. Two questions then arise:

- Why did the market traders prefer "cash" trades?
- What was the source of the liquidities injected in the spot market?

For the first question the answer was given in the previous sections. Obviously the momentum of the spot trades was generated by the VAT traders and by the fact that futures had much heavier regulation and did not apply VAT. For the latter question, the answer is not trivial as clearly the liquidity sources could not be legitimate. The various investigations found a clear link between the VAT missing traders and the organized crime. A few networks were identified: the Israeli organization heavily implicated in the French market fraud, the Middle East—Pakistani implicated in the over-the-counter deals that appeared in the United Kingdom and the Eastern European organizations also played a significant role. The use of criminal funds as seed for the VAT fraud implied not only the capacity of replicating the strategy in various countries but also the capacity of laundering the seeding funds through the carbon market and the financial institution trading on this market.

Based on previous research by Guegan et al. [269] that assessed the link between the carbon prices and its drivers (power, oil, gas, and equity) the influence of the VAT fraud upon the carbon price is assessed. Assuming the EUA price would follow the energy-equity complex, the theoretical price from the end of October 2008 until 2009 is simulated (Figure 12). It can be observed that the theoretic price is significantly higher than the market price and the spread widens with the increase in fraud volume. The difference between the modeled and observed prices remains around a level of 2-3 euros even after June 2009 when the volumes decreased and BlueNext banned the VAT.

The fact that the market price fell below the fundamental level is explained by the change in the intrinsic nature of the stock exchanged on the market from an emissions reduction instrument to a systematic fraud vehicle. Obviously the amount of VAT pocketed by the rogue traders is independent of the EUA price and is only a function of the number of tours in the carousel as shown previously. Thus the VAT pocketed is similar to an "invisible dividend" provided by the EUA to its owner. Similar to the case of equity markets where each time a stock liberates a dividend its value diminishes, in the case of the carbon the EUA loses in price as the VAT is extorted through the organized exchange or through the over-the-counter mechanism. It is important to note that this contraction in price on markets reached by the VAT carousel was previously observed for other goods such as clothes, IT hardware, or mobile phones.

The VAT fraud might move the market into a low price clustered region away from the fundamental level as given by the APT model calibrated previously, with 2-3 euros of spread. This finding could be regarded suspiciously as the market price represents the equilibrium of offering and demand, thereby implying a comeback of the carbon prices at the equilibrium level before the fraud period. Thus, the spread implied by the model should fall toward zero after the VAT was banned from the organized exchanges. This fact is explained with two arguments derived from the structure of the carbon spot markets:

- First, the prices of the EUA since 2009 were highly uncertain and dependent on the future after 2012. The EU ETS was designed to create an increasing shortage in EUA compared to the free allocations for each

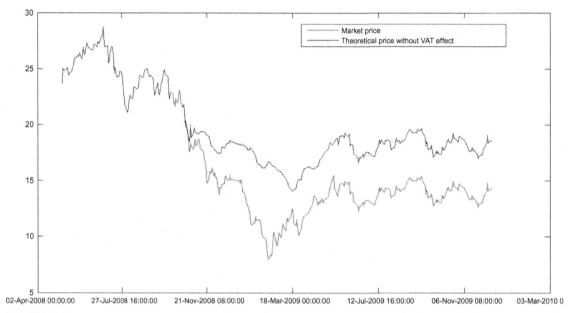

**FIGURE 12** Observed prices on the spot market and theoretical prices. Due to excessive VAT-related transactions the price of the EUA no longer reflected the offering/demand equilibrium for an emission permit. Instead, the market quoted an instrument generating a 19.6% return. Thus, the prices were significantly driven away from their fundamental value.

phase, thereby driving the prices to around 30 euros per ton. With the last double-dip economic recession and the industrial slowdown emissions diminished by more than 10% in 2009 and thus the EUTS became oversupplied with EUAs, putting pressure on the EUA price. Due to the portability of the EUA beyond 2012, the market began to price the expected deficit post-2012, thereby making the very nature of the market incomplete. Without developing these particularities, it appears that an incomplete market can have theoretically few levels of equilibrium, the market establishing more likely on an acceptance price. Under these conditions a shock in the offering/demand equilibrium could alter irreversibly the market price by pushing it to a different level. Therefore, the spread between the theoretic and the observed price would remain consistent even after the end of the VAT fraud on the spot exchange.

• Second, the carbon spot exchange was not only a vehicle for the VAT fraud but also part of a money-laundering platform as is shown in the next section.

## 2.3 Break Down of the VAT Fraud-Extorted Funds

The morphology of the VAT fraud has a degree of complexity that varies from basic scams implying one limited company acting as a missing trader to more sophisticated montages with dozen of entities spread in different countries.

Recently, the French Supreme Court condemned the owner of the French-based limited company ironically named "Crepuscule," allegedly implied in the carbon VAT fraud. This case represents the simplified form of the fraud, the limited company being a direct member of the emissions exchange BlueNext and also the missing trader, thereby making it easier to track. Other cases are much more complex with a lot of "buffer" brokers in the VAT carousel that act like legitimate layers in order to hide the company that commits the fraud. It would be naive to assume that the only alleged guilt pertains to the missing trader and to ignore the role of other elements in the carousel. Thus, the brokerage fees for those companies acting like buffers were higher than those for classic intermediation. For a market price of the EUA of 10-15 euros the gross amount of the extorted VAT was around 2-3 euros. The intermediation fees for the companies trading EUAs were around 8-15 cents. The brokers strategically linked to the VAT fraud had margins accounting for 15-30 cents per EUA, representing around 10% of the gross fraud value per EUA. The BlueNext transaction fees were around 2 cents per EUA when the fraud took place. This data allows us to reconstruct the chain value of the illegal profit-taking scam and to build the profile of those implicated in the crime. From the chain value it is possible to understand other criminal strategies juxtaposed on the operational framework of the VAT fraud.

Furthermore, respectable institutions were affected by the temptation of increasing their turnover. The prosecution of nine carbon traders from the reputed German Deutsche Bank in 2010 indicates the role of moral hazard in the financial system and also the popularity of the fraud among market professionals, as will be shown in the next section (Figure 13).

When analyzing the origin of the pocketed VAT two types fraud can be distinguished: the market cleared and the over-the-counter (OTC) versions. The first took place on the BlueNext exchange, the biggest spot market at the time in Europe. The exchange paid the VAT to allowances' sellers, thereby attracting directly or via various "buffer" brokers many flows that were a part of various scams. The advantage for a missing trader in terms of treasury and working capital is obvious, as the VAT amount was wired within few hours after the transaction

took place. As a comparison, on the OTC version the carousel needed to wait at least 1 month in order to obtain the VAT compensation from the local tax authority. The estimation of the market-cleared fraud was around 1.6 and 1.9 billion euros, while the amount of the OTC scam was estimated to be around 5 billion euros under some conservative assumptions. The amount given by the Europol for the OTC fraud represents the inferior bound estimate. Thus, if one assumes that 20% of the transactions are visible through the exchange and the rest are cleared OTC, the damage could be as high as 8-10 billion euros.

Strategic analysis shows that an initial investment of 100 million euros is "multiplied" through the VAT carousel in 600 million euros. It should be noted that a tour of a carbon credit in the carousel could be realized practically in few hours. Thus, a small initial investment could generate very quickly a significant amount of funds that could be reintroduced in the carbon market, thereby increasing considerably the market depth.

This finding is important not only for understanding the morphology of the VAT fraud but also the mechanisms that increased exponentially the spot-market volumes in a relatively short period between the end of 2008 and June 2009 (Figure 14).

The recent investigations by Frunza [1] led to the conclusion that there is a vertical integration effect between the missing trader entities and brokerages. Thus, the missing traders owned through various trustees small brokerage houses with a clean record meant to facilitate access to the market. These companies had an effect of co-minglement of permits from the carousel with normal transactions from industrial companies, which is part of the reason the fraud was more difficult to track. The co-minglement of permits implied obviously the co-minglement of funds, a practice very common in money laundering through capital markets.

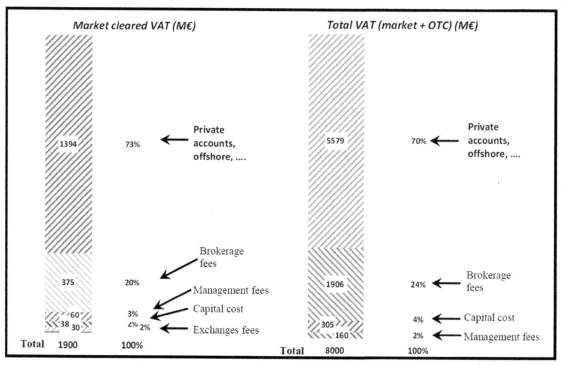

**FIGURE 13** Break down of the extorted funds in the carbon VAT fraud. The figure on the left shows the breakdown of the 1.9 billion euros pocketed via the BlueNext exchange. The extorted VAT funds net of brokerage cost, transaction fees, and other costs rose to 1.4 billion euros representing more than 73% of the total amount. The brokers' gross turnover was around 375 million euros accounting for 20% of the extorted funds. BlueNext's VAT-related gross revenue is estimated to be around 30 million euros, representing 2% of the total sum. The right-side figure shows the aggregated break down of both BlueNext cleared and over-the-counter VAT fraud. The value of the deturned VAT was around 5.6 billion euros representing 70% of the consolidated proceeds, while the brokers share was around 24% accounting for 1.9 billion euros.

While money laundering is one of the main charges in the majority of the indicted groups, its role as an independent crime is still not acknowledged by regulators and law enforcement. The interest and massive flows of funds on carbon markets through the VAT fraud it was also due to the fact that the funds obtained through the fraud were not only substantial but they were clean since they came from reputable financial institutions. The institution was either BlueNext depository's bank or another reputed bank for the OTC deals.

## 3 MONEY LAUNDERING

The illegal funds laundered through the capital markets are generated by illegal activities both from outside and from within the sector [302]. For illegal funds generated outside the sector, capital markets transactions are used as the mechanism for hiding the source of these funds. In the case of illegal activities carried out within the capital market itself (e.g., VAT pocketing, pump-and-dump schemes, insider trading,

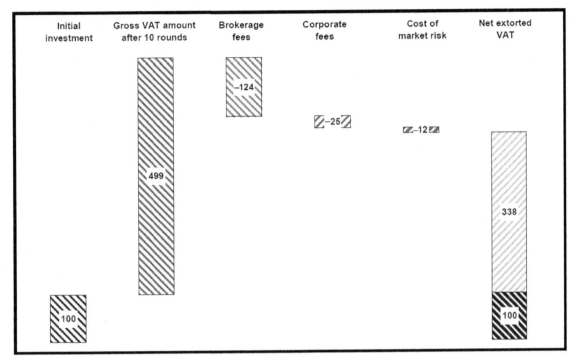

FIGURE 14  Chain value for a VAT missing trader. The carousel effect inflates the treasury account exponentially with each tour. Thus, after 10 rounds in the carousel an initial investment of 100 million euros increases to 499 million euros. The intermediation cost, corporate fees, and market volatility reduce the amount of the extorted VAT.

market manipulation) the market transactions or manipulations generate illegal funds that must then be laundered. In both cases, the organized capital markets appear to offer the launderer the potential for a double advantage in allowing him to launder illegal funds and to a certain extent to benefit from additional profit from the related frauds on financial markets. It is crucial to note that the "investing philosophy" of a money launderer is completely different from that of a classic investor, mostly due to a totally different interpretation of the risk/return. Thus, a money launder would accept introducing liquidity in very volatile markets (e.g., commodities) and undertake the significant losses as a cost of laundering the illegal funds. Obviously these risk-taking strategies can result in substantial gains that add to the benefit of having clean funds.

The emissions markets sector on a European scale was characterized until 2011 by its heterogeneity, the speed with which trading can take place (through electronic trading, for example), and the ability to execute transactions with little regard for national borders. On top of this the carbon physical trading was not specifically regulated across the 27 countries and access to the market was much easier than for other underlyings such as stocks or bonds. Thus, one could establish a carbon-trading entity through a simple limited company and have direct access to a national register of emissions permits and to a liquid market. These characteristics made carbon markets attractive to investors looking for a high speed, high liquid transitional and accessible market. These same characteristics, along with the sheer volume of transactions in EUA markets, made the sector a perfect tool not only for VAT fraud but also for the laundering of funds from criminal sources.

The estimation of laundered money, and more precisely laundered money through organized financial markets, is not an easy task, due to the lack of accurate and homogenous data. Nevertheless, a number of estimates have been published of the potential demand for money laundering using various methodologies. The consensus range estimation for laundered funds is between 2% and 5% of the global GDP [303]. Laundering fees, i.e., what money launderers charge their rogue clients, are estimated at 5-15% of the laundered amount according to Lal [304] and Reuter and Truman [305]. The estimations were determined by using a macro-economic approach that assumes that any revenue on which no tax is paid will need to be laundered in some way. A considerable body of literature, initiated by Tanzi [306], uses a method called the currency-demand approach, which measures the size of a cash-based underground economy depending on a particular level of taxes and extent of tax evasion.

## 3.1 Mechanism

As noted previously, VAT fraud indictments also contained allegations of money laundering for almost all cases in France, the United Kingdom, and Germany. If the crime was analyzed through the angle of the extorted VAT, the money-laundered phenomena received less attention from both investigators and professionals. The VAT carousel described in Figure 2 can be easily used as a money-laundering mechanism as described in Figure 15. The laundering mechanism can include all three phases: placement, layering, and integration. For example, a company X is financed from dirty funds in a Country C (that could be outside EU: e.g., Russian Federation, Georgia, or Montenegro).

Company X opens a subsidiary (Company Y) in a EU Country B that has a close economic relationship with Country C (e.g., Baltic Countries, Romania, Bulgaria), thereby transferring funds into the bank system inside the European Union and accomplishing the placement phase. Company Y joins an energy brokerage business and opens an account with a carbon national registry. With the originally dirty money Company Y buys with these funds EUAs from a Broker. A Company Z linked to the Company Y sells EUAs through its account with a Broker on an organized carbon Exchange (i.e., BlueNext). The selling order of Company Z is executed through a series of buffer brokers, aimed at cutting the direct link between the Exchange and the Company Y, thereby transferring the EUAs of Company Y from Country C to Country A where the exchange is based. Hence, the layering phase. The proceeds of the sale on the Exchange are delivered from a reputed bank based in Country A, thereby legalizing the funds and accomplishing the integration phase.

## 3.2 Estimate of Laundered Funds

In order to test the validity of the mechanism presented in the previous paragraph, we assess from an econometric angle what was considered to be an estimation of laundered funds on the emissions markets. Our method is top-down and based on a macro-economic estimation of theoretic volumes cleared by the spot exchanges. This approach is similar to the currency method, as we search to determine the share of transactions that fit an economic purpose and to explain the difference between the observed and predicted volumes. As discussed in the previous section, by their nature spot exchanges are supposed to be used by small- and medium-size carbon emitting companies in order to buy or sell their deficit or surplus of EUAs. The presence of speculators on spot markets is theoretically reduced, due to the classic appetite of speculators for leveraged markets (futures). The yearly allocation of EU ETS accounts for 2.1 billion tons of EUA between 2008 and 2012. The carbon-emitting

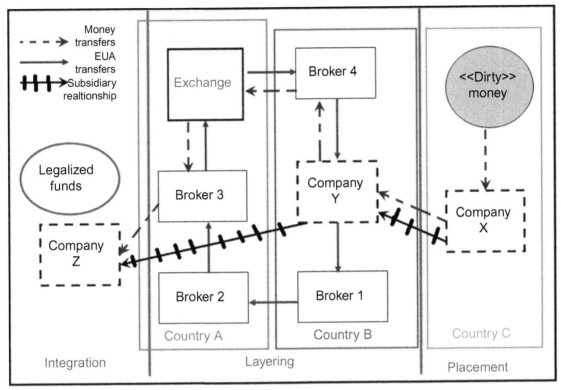

**FIGURE 15** VAT carousel as a money-laundering tool. A Company X is financed from dirty funds in a Country C (that could be outside EU). The Company X opens a subsidiary (Company Y) in a EU Country B, thereby transferring funds into the bank system. The Company Y buys with these funds EUAs from a Broker. A Company Z linked to Company Y sells EUAs through its account with a Broker on the carbon Exchange and transfers the EUAs of Company Y after passing them through a few buffer brokers. The proceeds of the sale on the Exchange are delivered through a reputed bank from Country A, thereby legalizing the funds.

industries can trade a maximum amount given by the difference between the allocated permits and the realized emissions. This represent on average 10% of the total allocations. The EUA/CER swaps represent another source of physical trades, which could account for around 20% of the total allocation. Thus, the potential for transactions is given by a grand total of 30% of the total annual allocations. This potential transition volume is divided among spot and futures markets, the latter having much more liquidity and being generally preferred by industries. Let's assume that 15% of the potential trans-

actions occurred on the spot exchange and the rest were executed through futures. It should be noted that in the carbon-emitting industries 75% of emissions are generated by electricity companies (RWE, Drax, EDF, or Vatenfall) that have a special division for market trading, similar to investments banks. These entities bring the quasi-totality of nonspeculative trades primarily through futures markets, thereby making our assumption conservative. Let's define the trading ratio as the product of the share of the total allocation potentially traded through organized markets and the proportion of spot trades. The

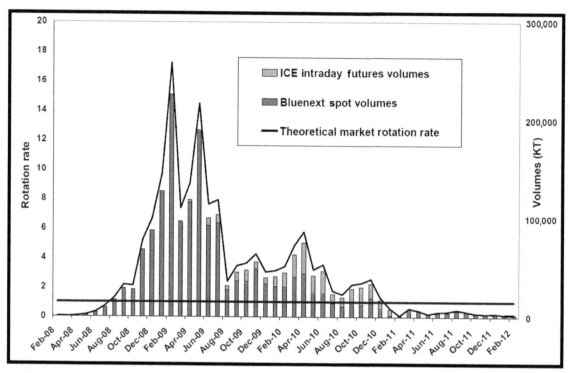

**FIGURE 16** Spot transaction and permit rotation rate. The rotation rate shows the ratio between the market spot volumes and the theoretical volumes that were supposed to be observed given the allocations of the various industries. The rate peaks during the period of the VAT fraud but remains relatively high until the beginning of 2011.

trading ratio multiplied by the annual allocation represents the theoretical volume that should be observed on the spot carbon markets.

We define the turnover ratio as the spot market volumes divided by the proportion of the trading ratio from the total allocation. In other words, it represents the fraction between the observed market volumes and the theoretic volumes:

$$\text{Turnover ration} = \frac{\text{Market volume}}{\text{Trading ration} \cdot \text{Allocation}} \quad (2)$$

Normally the turnover ratio is close to 1 as industries trade their deficit or surplus only once per year. A higher than 1 ratio would imply that

an EUA rotates in the market more than once, which is very similar to a carousel. It is expected that this ratio would peak in the first semester of 2009 in the most active time of the VAT fraud. This approach was used in a report by the French **Court of Audit**[1] that showed in February 2009 an EUA permit was traded no less than 16 times on average (Figure 16).

This estimate is consistent with the findings from previous sections that showed that for a rotation rate of 10 the carousel provided exponential progression of pocketed VAT. Nonetheless, the turnover ratio diminishes

---

[1]La fraude à la TVA sur les quotas de carbone, http://www.ccomptes.fr/content/download/1820/18256/version/1/file/Fraude_TVA_sur_quotas_carbone.pdf.

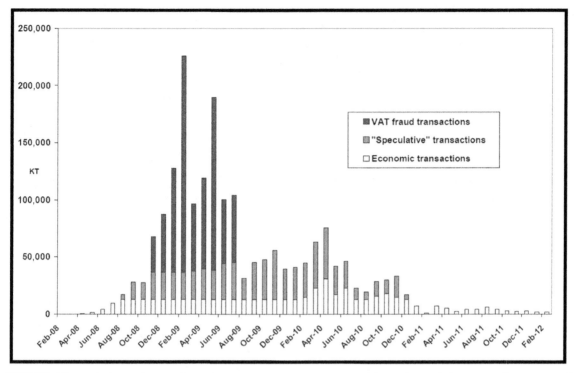

**FIGURE 17** Break down of spot volumes by origin. From August 2008 until December 2010 the spot markets transacted 1.9 billion tons. Around 0.8 billion tons were strictly linked to the VAT fraud on the BlueNext exchange and 0.5 Mt were the theoretical volumes generated by economic needs of industries. The difference of 0.7 Mt would have been of "speculative" origin, observed until January 2011.

when the fraud ended (September 2009) but remain unusually high (3x) and became normal toward the end of 2010. Figure 17 shows the breakdown of the market transactions in three categories: economic transaction, justified by the industries compliance trades, the VAT-fraud-related transactions, and the "speculative" transactions. The latter class has no financial explanation and likely represents trades that used the EUA as a support for transferring funds across the EU countries in transnational money-laundering schemes. Thus, the same scheme used for the VAT carousel was used was probably used for money laundering at the same time. This piece of evidence is perfectly coherent with the previous finding related to the VAT fraud: the crime-related origin of the

seed funds for the VAT carousel and the easiness to transfer both funds and permits through the EUA market. From August 2008 until December 2010 the spot markets transacted 1.9 billion tons. Around 0.8 billion tons were strictly linked to the VAT fraud on the BlueNext exchange and 0.5 Mt were the theoretical volumes generated by the economic needs of industries. A difference of 0.7 Mt would have been of "speculative" origin, observed until January 2011 and linked to the money-laundering effect, thereby implying a full amount of laundered fund of 9-10 billion euros. By the end of 2010 concerns of various fraud types and thefts that appeared on the carbon market brought massive attention from regulators, investigators. At the beginning of 2011 the spot markets closed temporarily

(BlueNext) or definitively (ICE intra-day) and with the massive indictments across Europe the carbon market became less attractive for criminals. As a consequence, the volumes on the spot market have fallen significantly since 2011 and carbon prices plunged much below 10 euros after June 2011.

# 4 OUTLOOK

This case presents only an aspect of fraud on the carbon markets, but other examples were given in previous chapters. This example shows that statistics can be used to measure and even detect fraud on markets where the drivers are genuinely defined. This approach could be used further as a monitoring framework for missing trader fraud on other markets like gas or power.

The main challenge of statistics as a forensic tool is to be able to provide signals in real time. However, launching an investigation takes at least 6 months to 1 year, thereby leaving a window where the model results can be consolidated and clear conclusions can be made.

# PART V

# PREVENTING CRIME AND PRESERVING MARKETS' INTEGRITY

# CHAPTER

# 5A

# Pros and Cons of Stronger Financial Regulation?

## 1 BACKGROUND

Crime and misconduct in financial markets are in most cases linked to financial regulations. Many of the reputed financial institutions as discussed in the previous chapters have been directly or indirectly involved in most types of white-collar crimes. In addition, many of the market infrastructures that aim to ensure the integrity of financial markets were targets or commingled in securities frauds. The question that comes naturally is whether regulatory frameworks of financial institutions can reduce financial crime. Furthermore, will the regulation be a deterrent for the propagation of fraud in securities?

Before analyzing these aspects it is necessary to define from a conceptual point of view the terms regulation and integrity.

A high-level framework, known as the regulatory dialectic, was introduced by Kane [307].

He notes that for any policymaker, a crisis may be described as a time of upheaval that *generates strong pressure for decisive changes in policy strategy. A regulation-induced banking crisis is an evolutionary process that is driven in Hegelian fashion by dialectical collisions of irreconcilable market and regulatory adjustments. For any regulated institution, change—not rest—represents the path of profit-making equilibrium. The Hegelian model of regulation assumes that the conflict between regulated parties and their regulators can never be completely eliminated. The contradictory forces at work in each round of adjustments are labeled the "thesis" and the "antithesis." Every sequence of adjustment and response produces a temporary "synthesis" that serves in turn as the "thesis" for a new round of action and response.*

Continuing the same conceptual framework the term *integrity* applied in the economic and financial regulatory spaces was defined by Erhard et al. [308] in the case of a system (or object) *as nothing more than but nothing less than that the design, the implementation of the design, and the use of the system (or object) are whole, complete, unbroken, sound, in perfect condition.* He showed that integrity handled this way is an important factor of production.

## 2 CAN BANKING REGULATION REDUCE THE RISK OF MISCONDUCT?

Studying cases of regulatory failures bring additional evidence on the prudential improvement axes concerning the occurrence of crime and misconduct. Historically, regulation was able to deal with issues retrospectively but failed to anticipate new issues in different circumstances, circumstances that in some cases led to white-collar crime (e.g., LIBOR manipulation, miselling). The recent financial crisis emphasized the fact that banking regulations have not reached their original goal of protecting investors. Regulations have imposed until now prudent rules for managing risk. However, they offered to financial institutions unique opportunities for regulatory arbitrages and incentives to push the their actions to the limits of the rules liaised to the less supervised activities.

In the 1970s and 1980s the bankruptcies of few financial institutions (e.g., Herstatt Bank[1]),

led to one of the most important set of recommendations, known as "Basel I." The prudential framework established by the first Basel Accord was simplistic, too general, and sometimes inadequate, thereby automatically leading to regulatory arbitrage. For example, the weighting of risk generated biases in the allocation of credit to reduce capital constraints, pushing the financial system from its optimal conditions. Credit institutions could make riskier loans and be more profitable without being penalizing in terms of prudential capital. These early subprimes formed the starting point for an initial reform of the Basel agreement, enacted in June 2004, that remained as Basel II. The second version of the agreement proposed a much finer grid of risk classes and had additional requirements with regard to the relationship between regulatory capital and economic capital. The Basel II prudential framework was already in place at the time the American subprime created a financial crisis followed by an economic crisis that spread worldwide. Different tools of the Basel framework did not give warning signals about risk exposure or help organizations manage the impact of the crisis. Indeed, the requirement of strengthening banks' capital due to Basel II led to regulatory niches for products with high yield and low capital charge. Banks used regulatory arbitrages focused on special purpose vehicles with very risky credit assets, allowing the consolidation of revenue for accounting purposes, but not of the underlying risks.

The various waves of regulation (Basel I, Basel II, Basel III; Figure 1) imposed over time an increase in the prudential capital of banks, which

---

[1]On June 26, 1974 German authorities declared the bankruptcy of Herstatt Bank, an institution active on the Forex market. Several counterparties who had sent payments in marks, but had not received the equivalent in dollars, lost the value of their transactions. The failure of Herstatt triggered a chain reaction that undermined the payment systems and settlements, showing the existence of systemic risk in the Forex market. Shortly after this event, at the initiative of Peter Cooke, the Director of the Bank of England, a committee was set up under the supervision of the Bank for International Settlements, bringing together central banks, regulators, and supervisory banking from G10 countries. They met in Basel four times a year, with the aim of promoting

international harmonization in terms of prudential banking control. The committee, however, had no authority and its deliberations were not legally binding. In 1988, the first Basel regulations established a single ratio, the Cooke ratio, which sets a minimum of 8% capital for all loans granted by banks.

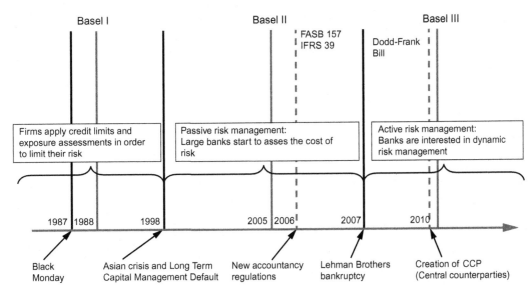

FIGURE 1   Various waves of regulation (Basel I, Basel II, Basel III).

resulted in a potential decrease in profitability. However, investors demanded a rate of return of about 15% from financial institutions, which has not changed with different waves of regulation. Obviously two mechanisms can adjust the profitability: either by reducing the capital burden or by increasing revenues on a constant risk. It is important to note that each wave of regulation aimed at in particular a typology of risks and offered the opportunity for banks to arbitrate for the calculation of capital charges between standard models and internal models. Obviously the cost of developing an internal model should provide a gain on consumption in capital. In a context where the banking industry is hyper-competitive, banks have an incentive to reverse engineer their modeling framework in order to optimize the capital charge.

In addition to those higher capital burdens as a result of regulation, banks need to push their actions closer to the legal edges to be able to provide the required returns. Therefore, it should not be a surprise that a structural market such as interest rated and Forex are subject to misconduct (manipulation) in these circumstances.

Classical principles of a free trade economy ensure that markets have the ability to self-regulate and that intervention of different regulatory actors is not helpful in the longer term. The "invisible hand" of Adam Smith would adjust dynamically the market mechanism to avoid inefficiencies. However, the banking sector, which by its nature is the symbol of the market economy, has been subjected over the past two decades to heavy regulatory constraints. The main reason for the introduction of a prudential framework in the banking system to protect investors. Nonetheless, the number of factors that affect investors' safety can hardly be covered by any policy or regulation. Regulations and state control cannot reach all fields of finance. Many financial processes and mechanisms are the result of old customs based on gentlemen agreements. When those rules are broken the results can be catastrophic.

This finding shows that the loop controls-arbitrage/misconduct-regulation can tend to become a "perpetuum-mobile." Given the structure of the banking system, financial regulations merely shift prudential boundaries to more amorphous zones that tend to be the most profitable but consume less capital. Under these conditions, institutions have to optimally exploit the opacity of the regulatory framework to expand and reiterate "off balance sheet" techniques in order to maintain the required profitability. Furthermore, obscure practices and involvement in extreme practices like money laundering, tax evasion, market manipulation, and misselling are also a result of this tendency to move the activity toward the amorphous zone of regulation. Concerning the misconduct and regulatory arbitrage, the invisible hand of Adam Smith pushed a part of the activity toward the less or not regulated financial twilight zone.

Before the "subprime" crises for example, poor quality loans were sold through dedicated semi-regulated entities. Thereafter, risky assets were shuffled into slices and then re-sold to banks that did not have a clear vision on primary debtors. In addition, the models used to calculate the risk tranches were designed to make them very attractive to investors. Furthermore, the juxtaposition of regulatory arbitrage strategies and the use of aggressive models generated a credit bubble and the crisis of 2007-2009.

This loop control-arbitrage/misconduct-regulation increases the variability of the balance sheets of financial institutions and causes a structural increase in risk basis. This mechanism is a factor that increases the risk of contagion and exposure to systemic risk. And in the case of a crisis, governmental entities are often called to the rescue. If a sovereign system imposes a regulatory framework that fails to limit the systemic crisis effect, is this enough to justify the bailouts?

There is not enough conceptual evidence to argue that stricter regulation will diminish crime and misconduct on the financial markets. Of course, regulation could clear up some of the current gray areas, but in the absence of proactive behavior regulators will always be one step behind the "wise guys". Two features of stronger regulation appear to limit the prevention of white-collar crime:

- First, regulation focuses on very specific areas leaving other potential zones of misconduct uncovered.
- Second, stronger regulation means more capital burden for banks that need to take more risk and sometimes misconduct risk to generate the same returns.

## 3 TAX ON FINANCIAL TRANSACTIONS

When issues around market integrity started to become more acute, the old idea of Tobin for financial transaction taxation started to have many supporters. The postcrisis debate on the introduction of a tax on financial transactions suffers from not fitting into a clear theoretical framework, consequently exposing the proposed measures to the most diverse critics. What is the precise calculation basis of this tax?[2] If the aim of this tax is to "punish" the banks, it must still be able to identify the operations that resulted in collective costs so that they constitute the base for future tax.

To what extent can a tax on securities transactions (purchase or sale of shares, for example) be a legitimate response to the production of negative externalities in the financial system? This counter-productive, and does not distinguish itself according to the motivation of operations [231]. Theoretically, the approach by assessment of the externalities is very rich and constitutes an indisputable base to the establishment of a fee. Before the beginning of the crisis, in June 2007 (with the closing of two credit funds

---

[2]The draft legislative resolution of the European Parliament, published in May 2012, states in its first article that "the starting point of this debate is to make the financial sector contribute part of the costs of the crisis," mentioning at the end of the same paragraph that it is to "create additional revenue to finance both the general budget... that specific policies, especially those related to development aid and the fight against climate change."

managed by Bear Stearns), U.S. banks practised large-scale prudential and accounting arbitrage,[3] consisting of closing of a loan portfolio carried at its nominal value and buying the same portfolio back in the form of structured credit products (e.g., CDO, Goldman's Abacus) valued at "fair value." The allocation of regulatory capital was less demanding on the secure loan portfolio than on the portfolio of underlying credits, resulting in capital relief. Above all, the market was not liquid, structured credit products were valued as mark-to-model either as level 2 (pricing model established on the basis of observable data) or as level 3, comprising of transactions valued on the basis of the pricing model, whose parameters are unobservable. The inability of any external scientific control of valuations had prompted many institutions to produce positive trading results on this portfolio segment or even to choose a business model focusing on structured transactions valued as "mark-to-model." The sharp downward revision of valuations has led to collective losses, and the cost has been paid by operators or institutions responsible for these operations.

To deal with negative externalities, the British economist Pigou (1877-1959) proposed a difference between the social cost and the private cost of activity to support economic agents. The internalization of externalities could be the theoretical basis of the future tax, of which the principle would be indisputable.

The current implementation of the tax on financial transactions in Europe might be the optimal response to tackling externalities, under the assumption that the base is only concerned with a very small fraction of the total transactions and where the purchase of shares can hardly be considered to be the product of moral risk behavior. The value of this tax disappears as it is not built on the principle of the internalization of the social cost associated with financial transactions initiated by banks. On the other hand, it is based on an imaginary distinction between speculative and hedging transactions, a distinction that exists only in a simplified world. As an illustration, derivatives are financial assets enabling both speculation on a favorable market movement and providing hedging in the event of an adverse scenario. The options have broken the boundary between coverage and speculation, and any tax based on this distinction could be challenged.

An alternative could be to substitute a Tobin with the Pigou tax applied to the derivatives portfolio, for which the valuation differences may be the cause of noninternalized collective losses. Within the financial instruments portfolio, the most suitable base is that of derivatives valued at the level 3 pricing model, known among professionals as "mark-to-myth." Analysis by externalities can be applied to other financial transactions, including securitization products. It can be considered that the transfer of risk, from the issuing institution to investors, in an information asymmetry context can trigger collective losses higher than those that would have been recorded if issuers were forced to keep their products.

The role of the current version of taxation of financial transactions is not a guarantee for bringing more integrity to markets. In fact, taxation could introduce additional frictions in the market, which could be an additional factor for the propagation of securities fraud. Markets need to be as transparent as they can be, and if an additional variable such as tax is not computed genuinely and efficiently this could obstruct efficiency.

---

[3]In light of the effect that those arbitrages had on the real economy they could be easily considered as misconduct. In fact, a prudential arbitrage can be harmless if employed on a small scale, say for a small bank or a limited size transaction, but could be very harmful to the economic system when implemented on a large scale.

# 4 OUTLOOK

Backward-looking regulations are not the best option for tackling both exposure to non-comprehensive financial risk and misconduct risk within organizations. Regulation should be proactive and allow more self-regulation. White-collar crime often appears due to the ignorance of individuals within an organization that limits their control of the prudential perimeter. Outside the prudential perimeter there is less concern. As the LIBOR manipulation showed, in the absence of an appropriate control for the submitted rates, misconduct can occur easily and go on for years without anyone noticing. The concept of regulation and its dialectics from Kane's perspective can evolve in defining prudential principles with less case-specific rules, thereby leaving more initiative for organizations.

# Efficient Frameworks for Financial Crime Surveillance

## 1 BACKGROUND

The increasing frequency and diversity of crime in financial markets with its massive impact on organizations has imposed the creation of dedicated functions within banks. The challenges involved in implementing a financial crime intelligence unit are multiple and concern not only the technical aspects but also its roles and responsibilities within an institution.

The major banks that have been issued penalties for types of misconduct have already started the process of creating such intelligence units. Of course, the pressure from regulatory bodies is one of the driving forces, but the optimality of such an financial intelligence unit is crucial for and organization's good functioning. The Basel II reform imposed the creation of risk management units integrated in the governance and decision-making process. Being regulation-driven, the risk management departments were not optimally fit for the purpose and failed massively during the recent economic crisis.

Financial intelligence units can face the same fate if their implementation is to satisfy regulations and not to address an organization's business-specific realties.

## 2 *BIG DATA* DILEMMA

One of the challenges faced by organizations in tackling financial crime through dedicated units is related to data. Identifying relevant data sources, creating new repositories, and being able to link all data sources are just a few of the aspects an organization needs to deal with. In recent years the term Big data has became more common in the financial industry. Big data is a set of systems and methods that make the exploitation of very large data sets within reasonable timeframes along with the storage required to support the volume of data (volumes of zettabytes $1000^7$ bytes) possible.

Technology providers and consultancies are pushing financial institutions for big data implementation, thereby implying the need for a

http://dx.doi.org/10.1016/B978-0-12-804494-0.00034-6

consistent multi-year budget for deploying such infrastructures. Mapping various repositories and maintaining the database are a few of the challenges of such a big data project. While big data can represent an interesting tool in terms of financial crime its efficiency is debatable.

First, compared to other areas of financial data like market risk management for instance, the scope of a financial crime is not clearly defined (i.e., the illegal vs. legal action might not be clearly defined *a priori*). For example, the FX manipulation case was considered by traders as a legal action in order to provide clients with a better price in a joint effort among banks. The investigators ruled that it was in fact misconduct and issued penalties. The financial crime unit might not look for very precise facts or metrics in the way a market risk manager would look for the number of days losses exceed the Value at Risk level. In many walks of life, a financial action could be classified as a crime only after it occurred and not before.

A person forcing on a door of a house during the night and carrying a revolver can be classified as a criminal before he enters a house and carries out the violent act. A trader executing trades on the futures market, sending a few confirmations to some over-the-counter counterparties, and canceling some trades cannot be classified in any way until a pattern is established.

This knowledge discovery process relies in many ways on unsupervised learning and implicitly on unlabeled data. Moreover, the scope of required data might be variable as with each offense new types of information need to be analyzed. For example, until Kerviel and Adobolis episodes, banks did not check the holidays periods of employees, the number of remote connections, and the physical access to various silos of the banks. Looking for this type of information became a necessity after 2011. Thus, creating a big data repository would not necessarily represent an advantage to the organization. Exploring the available data *in situ* and being able to

establish connections between the different types of information would represent a bigger gain.

Seconds a big data infrastructure would be optimal if the crime analysis relied mainly on data-mining techniques since other techniques relative to unstructured data exploration or basic statistics or capital stress testing are complementary to data-mining techniques. Furthermore, big data warehouses are not the most straightforward way to put all of the information together. *In situ* exploratory data analysis and data mining followed by cross-cluster inferences and final statistical analysis can be a more flexible and cost-effective approach.

The *big data* avenue brings with it as many opportunities as challenges. Nonetheless, dealing with financial crime within an organization should be done in a flexible way and also allow an appropriate time window to deal with suspicions that come up. As noted in the various case studies, time is an important factor in tackling financial crime and an event signaled too late or after too much mining even if is correctly signaled might be impossible to deal with and the losses unrecoverable. On the other hand, if an intelligence unit sends too many warning signals based on let's say fuzzy classification, then the cost of assessing all warnings in real time would be too high. Thus, an efficient system needs a balance between detection accuracy and speed of assessment.

## 3 EFFICIENT FRAMEWORK

When organizations do put in place a financial crime unit they should look for the most efficient approach in terms of system, power, and governance. Governance is a very sensible topic in relation to financial crime, but ideally this function should stay as far as possible in terms of hierarchy from the business units and also from the regulation-driven departments such as risk management. However, the crime intelligence unit should leverage the experience and systems of both business and risk units as well as other siloes of the bank without governance.

If many walks of life communities organize their own security forces in order to create a first defense against crime and a faster reaction taskforce for any possible issues. If a small town has local police and some neighborhoods have local security enforcements, why then would a bank not have an internal taskforce that would act like a police for financial crime with special powers and responsibilities? In some organizations, this role is assumed in part by auditors, risk managers, or other proxyholders.

In terms of systems the financial crime intelligence unit should be able to access data repositories from various siloes of the banks including the risk management, human resources, local financial crime analytics, clients data, and transactions stats, etc. For a multinational bank the framework implies an additional dimension: a country-specific vs. global function. For big global organizations, having local intelligence units can be an advantage in creating a first line of defense, but the financial crime intelligence unit as a global independent function is necessary due to the cross-country and cross-business dimension of financial crime.

Figure 1 shows the information flows in an efficient framework for a financial crime intelligence unit. The unit should be able to gather the data from various siloes of the banks as well from local intelligence units. Internal data can be completed by external data that is both structured and unstructured. Business experts can also define scenarios that are used further in the analysis process. The financial crime unit should be able to extract and link the various information sources from the various siloes and should have its own mining and statistical techniques in order to analyze the data. For instance, clusterings is an important step as a basic unsupervised learning technique. Each observation moving significantly away from other clusters needs to be looked at in more detail. Other analysis tools can include the statistics of risk data and human resources, traders' social network profiles, etc. As output the units can provide recommendations to regional financial crime units or to business units. They can also provide warning signals and recommendations for in-depth audits and investigations.

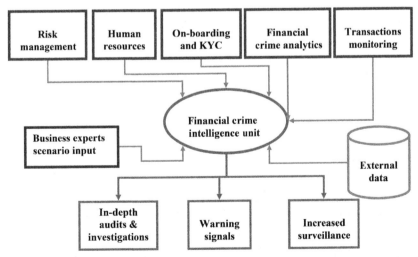

**FIGURE 1** Efficient framework for a financial crime intelligence unit. The unit should be able to gather data from various siloes of the bank as well from local intelligence units. Internal data can be completed by external data, both structured and unstructured. Business experts can also define scenarios that are used further in the analysis process.

# 5C

# Joint Structures for Tackling Financial Offenses: Criminal Investigators and Market Regulators

Crime on financial markets is not only a vast topic, but has many ramifications and requires a large spectrum of information during the investigation period. The main actors of financial markets and the markets themselves are overseen by various regulatory and monitoring bodies, both public and private. The sources of information and the targets of each agency are different and yet complementary for tackling financial crime. Banking regulators follow the implementations of prudential frameworks within organizations and securities market agencies oversee markets.

When financial offenses and misconducts do occur within organizations or market infrastructures in most cases there are warning signals that either regulators or investigators can use for investigation purposes (Figure 1). However, the agency that has the right information is not always the one conducting the investigation. For example, the figures for market risk and counterparty risk exposures for each bank are communicated to banking regulators. Generally agencies monitoring securities markets and crime investigators do not have or use this information on a regular basis. Cross-breeding in terms of information and methods would have been able

to tackle certain crimes and misconducts in a more efficient manner. Rogue trading positions like those held by Societe Generale trader Jerome Kerviel could have been better handled if risk and exposure metrics were crossed with exchange volumes and open interest data.

On the same topic, with the implementation in the European Union of EMIR (European Market Infrastructure Regulation, the Dodd-Frank European counterpart) and the building of specific data repositories of over-the-counter and cleared transactions, the French market regulator has been able to use the data to uncover market manipulation.[1] The European Supervisory Authority in charge with the EMIR implementation is the ESMA (European Securities and Markets Authority (ESMA)), while the AMF (Autorité des Marchés Financiers—Financial market Authority) regulates participants and products in France's financial markets

---

[1]French regulator finds market manipulation using Emir data, http://www.risk.net/risk-magazine/news/2375587/french-regulator-finds-market-manipulation-using-emir-data.

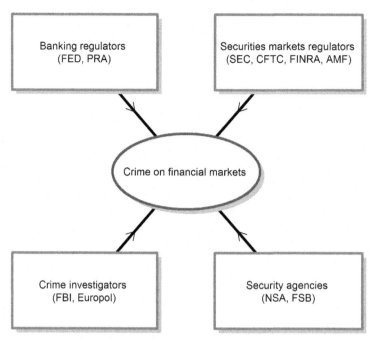

FIGURE 1  Regulatory bodies and investigators. Financial crimes generate warning signals that can be used by regulators or investigators.

as well as conducts investigations and issues sanctions. When both regulatory bodies share their data and methods the efficiency of tackling market abuse increases.

The trend of "joint ventures" among regulatory agencies is also happening in the Unites States. During the negotiations over the Dodd-Frank Act the idea to merge Commodity Futures Trading Commission (CFTC) and the Securities and Exchange Commission (SEC) surfaced and in 2012 a bill proposal was presented to the U.S. Congress.[2] It should be recalled that the SEC was created as a result of the 1929 crisis in order to re-establish order in the securities market. On a different and yet complementary agenda the CFTC was created to ensure the integrity of the derivatives market for those using it for hedging purposes. Both agencies target the securities market

from different angles, and with the merger proposal, the agency would be able to tackle complex manipulation schemes involving both spot and derivatives.

In the current economic and financial environment organizations tend to push their action toward the limits or the gray areas of regulation. Regulatory and monitoring agencies tend to assess whether those actions near the limits of regulations affect the integrity of a market or generate major systemic risks. This *defensive* attitude makes crime investigations more complicated and obviously more time consuming. Regulation and law violations are acknowledged as such whenever there is enough evidence to reject the null hypothesis that the underlying monitored actions are legal.

A change of paradigm in monitoring financial institutions and infrastructures is necessary. Thus, an activity can be considered as legal when there is enough evidence to reject the null evidence that the underlying actions are the

---

[2]Is an SEC and CFTC merger a perfect fit, http://www.fow.com/3321790/Is-an-SEC-and-CFTC-merger-a-perfect-fit.html.

result of misconduct or fraud. This way of distinguishing between legality and crime would extend the field of *a priori* suspicious actions. An in-depth monitoring or analysis could therefore be carried for find larger patterns. This paradigm would be applicable only in the investigation phase and not to issue sanctions. Unlawful behavior generating misconduct and fraud would be seen when the limits or gray area of legality are challenged. Therefore, it would be not inconceivable to consider a lawful behavior as something that "challenges" the limits and gray zone of illegality.

To this end all means of analysis including data mining and forensic statistics, economic analysis, and accounting should be used while illustrating the real need for the various public and private regulatory bodies to pool their resources. Sharing information and data is only one side of a full-fledged monitoring framework (the other side is the cross-breeding in terms of methods). Even regulatory bodies that survey the implementation of prudential liabilities like Basel III or Dodd-Frank should be aware of the crime investigation methods of organizations such as the Federal Bureau of Investigation, Europol, National Crime Agency, United Kingdom), or National Police Agency (Japan). As shown in the previous chapters many of the examples of misconduct from within regulated financial institutions involved professional individual that seemingly developed behaviors similar to those from organized crime. The manipulation of benchmarks such as LIBOR or the Forex rates speaks for itself. Thus, being able to understand the behavioral and conceptual aspects behind a traditional organized crime governance could be a real asset in combating crime even when it is generated by noncriminal elements.

Creating joint operative taskforces between crime investigators and regulators would present a few advantages compared to the current standalone situation:

- This type of structure would benefit from pooled resources, information flows, and infrastructures, which would allow better exploration of the available data, thereby giving a more accurate and holistic view of the activity of organizations and securities markets.
- The mosaic theory of intelligence gathering implies analyzing pieces of information or evidence that are not directly related to an offense or a crime but put all together result in a bigger picture that can provide useful indicators.
- Crime investigation methods in the prudential world imply among many other things a relaxing assumption of the regulatory framework assessment. Therefore, regulators need to assess a financial institution outside the perimeters of regulation and try to challenge that organization beyond the prudential aspect with a more economic sound effect. Using techniques specific to other agencies can present many advantages mainly in diversifying the methods of analysis. In this context, the role of data mining and of numerical techniques could play a crucial role in analyzing information from police or crime agencies. Reciprocally criminal investigation techniques could be leveraged for assessing the implementation of regulatory norms when looking for any flaws or possible gaps.

This trend exists currently within agencies that try to hire individuals with complementary skills. Intelligence crime units from banks and financial regulators have started to hire ex-law enforcement or intelligence services personnel. Additionally, crime investigators do hire ex-investment bankers or funds managers. Beyond this leverage in skill, the creation of task forces would enhance the efforts to tackle crime on financial markets in the foreseeable future.

# Epilogue

The origin of criminal behavior and the development of criminal enterprises within the financial industry involves a large panel of psychological and structural aspects of the sector. If the individuals using services provided by the industry are affected by ubiquitous crimes such as credit card fraud or insurance scams, the impact of this type of crime on financial markets on the real economy has a more serious and complex effect.

First, offenses tackling the markets affect investors and their confidence in the robustness of financial systems. Market manipulation or insider trading often lead to litigation prosecution by regulatory bodies. Hence, in many cases criminal behavior within a market can result in a general loss of confidence, withdrawal of liquidity, and a bearish tendency in the market. For example, the $CO_2$ emissions fraud led to the near dismissal of that market.

A second type of effect is the structural damage of the institution or group of institutions affected or employing the offenders. The default of Barings is the best known example, but this effect can cause an entire sector to lose confidence. The effect of misconduct in the credit derivatives market had a strong effect on the investment banking sector and reshaped the entire financial arena after the financial crisis. The systemic effects of financial crime on the real economy are still underestimated and insufficiently studied. It is realistic to question how the LIBOR/EURIBOR manipulation impacted the financial crisis and if the EURIBOR rigging amplified the Eurozone crisis.

The third consequence is linked to the concept of *fair value*, or even more precisely *unfair value*. Without getting into the foundations of the concept, market prices are used directly or as proxies for financial instrument valuation. Prices in markets affected by fraud can be misleading valuation of the assets or of a group of assets in a portfolio. For instance, the most recent allegations of Forex market rigging could have effects way beyond the perimeters of the buyers and seller involves in the manipulation. Significant manipulation of the Forex market could have a massive impact on many firms or investments using the Forex reference for business or accounting purposes.

The forth dimension is the political one. While we will not speculate here on particular investments or events (as we do in main text), a good example of the political dimension is the speculation that led to the rise in volatility of the agricultural markets. The *Arab spring* is believed to be generated among many things by the increase of price of grains and scarce supply to the North African countries. It's easy to see that altering the price of these commodities can have huge socio-political impact. The role of energy markets in the recent conflict in Donbass (i.e., Ukraine) or the strategies of hedge funds on distressed sovereign debt (i.e., Argentina) are other good examples of this point. The recent (July 2015) exacerbation of the Greek crisis re-emphasized the fact that investment banks (i.e., Goldman Sachs) played a major role in news of the Greek public debt in the years prior to country's entry in the Eurozone.

The financial literature is mainly focused on the assessment of markets' features and the construction of sound investment strategies, with reasonably mitigated risk. With a few exceptions, current research does not integrate the occurrence of offenses in financial markets both quantitatively and qualitatively. Of course, in the last 20 years, many researchers have noted that markets often show counterintuitive behavior with abnormal features very different from theoretical assumptions. Furthermore, some researchers have proposed also solutions for addressing the valuation of financial instrument under those abnormal condition. The abundance of pricing methods for derivatives in markets with abrupt variations and volatility clustering speaks for itself. However, analyzing markets in the light of the likelihood of criminal behavior is a recent phenomen.

The variety of crimes in the investment world requires a multi-disciplinary approach to analysis. The ethical mutations in society, the continual innovations in technology, and markets amplified by an increasing speed of information flow are the main challenges of this process.

On the one hand, despite the heavy involvement of technology and automatized processes in investment firms the human presence is still crucial in most operational decisions, thereby making it more vulnerable to error, misconduct, or fraud. On the other hand, technology is a useful asset in mitigating risk but in many situations it can used to disrupt financial systems. The example of Panther Energy Trading is relevant in this sense, as technology was used for high-frequency trading and to alter the market price market's price.

The recent financial crisis has made it clear that risk mitigation strategies are one step behind. Moreover, regulatory bodies put in place to address misconduct in the markets are far from having a prevention network in place. Financial crime investigation should be a discipline or a set of techniques used to look beyond risk mitigation and regulation strategies.

The outcomes of processes and systems based upon statistical and data mining techniques in financial crime analysis can highlight areas of risk or potential scenarios that could occur. To achieve this, information across all areas of business should be leveraged and explored on a continuous forward-looking basis.

# Bibliography

[1] M.-C. Frunza, Fraud and Carbon Markets: The Carbon Connection, vol. 5, Routledge, Abingdon, 2013.

[2] M. Lewis, Flash Boys: A Wall Street Revolt, WW Norton & Company, New York, NY, 2014.

[3] B. Biais, P. Woolley, High frequency trading, Manuscript, Toulouse University, IDEI, 2011.

[4] G. Scopino, The (questionable) legality of high-speed 'pinging' and 'front running' in the futures markets, Conn. Law Rev. 47 (2015).

[5] D. Cumming, F. Zhan, M. Aitken, High frequency trading and end-of-day manipulation, 2012. Available at SSRN 2145565.

[6] J.J. Angel, L.E. Harris, C.S. Spatt, Equity trading in the 21st century, Q. J. Financ. 1 (1) (2011) 1-53.

[7] E.S. Schwartz, The stochastic behavior of commodity prices: implications for valuation and hedging, J. Financ. 52 (3) (1997) 923-973.

[8] H. Geman, Energy commodity prices: is mean-reversion dead? J. Altern. Invest. 8 (2) (2005) 31-45.

[9] C.L. Gilbert, Commodit speculation and commodit investment, in: Market Review, 2010, p. 26.

[10] C. Pirrong, The Economics of Commodity Trading Firms, Trafigura, 2014.

[11] M.-C. Frunza, Aftermath of the VAT fraud on carbon emissions markets, J. Financ. Crime 20 (2) (2013) 222-236.

[12] J. Bollen, H. Mao, X. Zeng, Twitter mood predicts the stock market, J. Comput. Sci. 2 (1) (2011) 1-8.

[13] S. Chung, S. Liu, Predicting Stock Market Fluctuations from Twitter, 2011.

[14] R. Chen, M. Lazer, Sentiment Analysis of Twitter Feeds for the Prediction of Stock Market Movement.

[15] I. Zheludev, R. Smith, T. Aste, When can social media lead financial markets? Sci. Rep. 4 (2014).

[16] X. Zhang, H. Fuehres, P.A. Gloor, Predicting stock market indicators through twitter, Procedia Soc. Behav. Sci. 26 (2011) 55-62.

[17] M. Hu, B. Liu, Mining and summarizing customer reviews, in: Proceedings of the Tenth ACM SIGKDD International Conference on Knowledge Discovery and Data Mining, ACM, New York, 2004, pp. 168-177.

[18] M. Mantere, Stock market manipulation using cyberattacks together with misinformation disseminated through social media, in: 2013 International Conference on Social Computing (SocialCom), 2013, pp. 950-954.

[19] E. Ferrara, O. Varol, C. Davis, F. Menczer, A. Flammini, The Rise of Social Bots, 2014. arXiv preprint arXiv:1407.5225.

[20] D. Lee, Handbook of Digital Currency: Bitcoin, Innovation, Financial Instruments, and Big Data, Academic Press, Amsterdam, 2015.

[21] D. Chaum, A. Fiat, M. Naor, Untraceable electronic cash, in: Proceedings on Advances in Cryptology, Springer-Verlag, New York, 1990, pp. 319-327.

[22] R. Grinberg, Bitcoin: An Innovative Alternative Digital Currency, HeinOnline, 2012.

[23] G. Selgin, Synthetic Commodity Money, University of Georgia, Department of Economics, Athens, GA, 2013.

[24] A.W. Lo, A.C. MacKinlay, Stock market prices do not follow random walks: evidence from a simple specification test, Rev. Financ. Stud. 1 (1) (1988) 41-66.

[25] K.V. Chow, K.C. Denning, A simple multiple variance ratio test, J. Econ. 58 (3) (1993) 385-401.

[26] J.H. Wright, Alternative variance-ratio tests using ranks and signs, J. Bus. Econ. Stat. 18 (1) (2000) 1-9.

[27] M. Richardson, T. Smith, Tests of financial models in the presence of overlapping observations, Rev. Financ. Stud. 4 (2) (1991) 227-254.

[28] J.C. Escanciano, I.N. Lobato, An automatic Portmanteau test for serial correlation, J. Econ. 151 (2) (2009) 140-149.

[29] A. Malhotra, M. Maloo, Bitcoin—Is it a Bubble? Evidence from Unit Root Tests (March 1, 2014), 2014.

[30] J.B. Smith, An Analysis of Bitcoin Exchange Rates, 2014. Available at SSRN 2493797.

[31] P.C. Phillips, S.-P. Shi, J. Yu, Testing for multiple bubbles: historical episodes of exuberance and collapse in the S&P 500, 2013.

[32] A. Ramage, P.T. Craddock, M.R. Cowell, King Croesus' Gold: Excavations at Sardis and the History of Gold Refining, vol. 11, British Museum Press, London, 2000.

[33] D. Bryans, Bitcoin and money laundering: mining for an effective solution, Indiana Law J. 89 (2014) 441.

[34] T. Moore, N. Christin, Beware the middleman: empirical analysis of Bitcoin-exchange risk, in: Financial Cryptography and Data Security, Springer, Berlin, 2013, pp. 25-33.

[35] J. Abbott, D. Sheehan, The INTERPOL approach to tackling match fixing in football, in: Match-Fixing in International Sports, Springer, Berlin, 2013, pp. 263-287.

[36] R. Caruso, The basic economics of match fixing in sport tournaments, Econ. Anal. Policy 39 (3) (2009) 355.

[37] Sportradar, World Match-Fixing: The Problem and the Solution, Sportradar, 2014.

[38] KEA European Affairs, Match-Fixing in Sport: A Mapping of Criminal Law Provisions in EU 27, KEA European Affairs, 2012.

[39] Pantheon-Sorbonne and the International Center for Sport Security (ICSS), Protecting the Integrity of Sport Competition. The Last Bet for Modern Sport, University Paris 1 Pantheon-Sorbonne and the International Centre for Sport Security (ICSS), 2014.

[40] J. Anderson, Match Fixing and EU Policy in 2014: An Introduction, 2014. Available at SSRN 2449305.

[41] F.A.T. Force, Money Laundering Through the Football Sector, FATF/OECD, 2009.

[42] I. Fiedler, Online Gambling as a Game Chager to Money Laundering, 2012.

[43] S.D. Levitt, Why are gambling markets organised so differently from financial markets? Econ. J. 114 (495) (2004) 223-246.

[44] E. Franck, E. Verbeek, S. Nüesch, Inter-Market Arbitrage in Sports Betting, National Centre for Econometric Research, 2009.

[45] E.F. Fama, Efficient capital markets: a review of theory and empirical work, J. Financ. 25 (2) (1970) 383-417.

[46] W. Margrabe, The value of an option to exchange one asset for another, J. Financ. 33 (1) (1978) 177-186.

[47] M. Li, S.-J. Deng, J. Zhoc, Closed-form approximations for spread option prices and greeks, J. Deriv. 15 (3) (2008) 58-80.

[48] H.S. Shin, Measuring the incidence of insider trading in a market for state-contingent claims, Econ. J. (1993) 1141-1153.

[49] A. Bruce, D. Marginson, Power, not fear: a collusion-based account of betting market inefficiency, Int. J. Econ. Bus. 21 (1) (2014) 77-97.

[50] A.C. Constantinou, N.E. Fenton, et al., Profiting from arbitrage and odds biases of the European football gambling market, J. Gambl. Bus. Econ. 7 (2) (2013) 41-70.

[51] M. Duggan, S.D. Levitt, Winning isn't everything: corruption in sumo wrestling, National Bureau of Economic Research, 2000.

[52] Federbet, Annual fixed matches report '14, 2014.

[53] M.J. Dixon, S.G. Coles, Modelling association football scores and inefficiencies in the football betting market, J. R. Stat. Soc. Ser. C Appl. Stat. 46 (2) (1997) 265-280.

[54] M. Dixon, M. Robinson, A birth process model for association football matches, J. R. Stat. Soc. Ser. D Stat. 47 (3) (1998) 523-538.

[55] J. Goddard, I. Asimakopoulos, Modelling football match results and the efficiency of fixed-odds betting, Working Paper, Department of Economics, Swansea University, 2003.

[56] K.J. Kain, T.D. Logan, Are sports betting markets prediction markets? Evidence from a new test, J. Sports Econ. 15 (1) (2014) 45-63.

[57] W.C. Thompson, E.L. Schumann, Interpretation of statistical evidence in criminal trials: the prosecutor's fallacy and the defense attorney's fallacy, Law Hum. Behav. 11 (3) (1987) 167.

[58] D. Dwyer, The duties of expert witnesses of fact and opinion: R v Clark (Sally), Int. J. Evid. Proof 7 (4) (2003) 264-269.

[59] N. Fenton, M. Neil, The jury observation fallacy and the use of Bayesian networks to present probabilistic legal arguments, Math. Today (Southend on Sea) 36 (6) (2000) 180-187.

[60] D.L. Rubinfeld, Econometrics in the courtroom, Columbia Law Rev. (1985) 1048-1097.

[61] D.J. Leinweber, Stupid data miner tricks: overfitting the S&P 500, J. Invest. 16 (1) (2007) 15-22.

[62] A. Rajaraman, J.D. Ullman, Mining of Massive Datasets, Cambridge University Press, Cambridge, 2011.

[63] C.E. Bonferroni, Il calcolo delle assicurazioni su gruppi di teste, Tipografia del Senato, 1935.

[64] J.P. Shaffer, Multiple hypothesis testing, Annu. Rev. Psychol. 46 (1) (1995) 561-584.

[65] P. Good, Applying Statistics in the Courtroom: A New Approach for Attorneys and Expert Witnesses, CRC Press, Boca Raton, FL, 2001.

[66] C.R. Mann, Statistics in the courtroom, Law Prob. Risk 4 (2005) 1-3.

[67] B.B. Mandelbrot, The Variation of Certain Speculative Prices, Springer, Berlin, 1997.

[68] G.W. Schwert, Stock returns and real activity: a century of evidence, J. Financ. 45 (4) (1990) 1237-1257.

[69] J.J. Siegel, Stocks for the Long Run: The Definitive Guide to Financial Market Returns and Long-Term Investment Strategies, 2002.

[70] J.Y. Campbell, A.W.-C. Lo, A.C. MacKinlay, et al., The Econometrics of Financial Markets, vol. 2, Princeton University Press, Princeton, NJ, 1997.

[71] C.R. Knittel, M.R. Roberts, An empirical examination of restructured electricity prices, Energy Econ. 27 (5) (2005) 791-817.

[72] M.-C. Frunza, D. Guégan, Risk assessment for a structured product specific to the $CO_2$ emission permits market, J. Altern. Invest. 15 (3) (2013) 72-91.

[73] J.D. Hamilton, Analysis of time series subject to changes in regime, J. Econ. 45 (1) (1990) 39-70.

[74] E. Eberlein, K. Prause, The generalized hyperbolic model: financial derivatives and risk measures, in: Mathematical Finance Bachelier Congress 2000, Springer, Berlin, 2002, pp. 245-267.

[75] O. Barndorff-Nielsen, Exponentially decreasing distributions for the logarithm of particle size, Proc. R. Soc. Lond. A Math. Phys. Sci. 353 (1674) (1977) 401-419.

[76] T. Bollerslev, A conditionally heteroskedastic time series model for speculative prices and rates of return, Rev. Econ. Stat. (1987) 542-547.

[77] R.F. Engle, T. Bollerslev, Modelling the persistence of conditional variances, Econ. Rev. 5 (1) (1986) 1-50.

[78] R.T. Baillie, T. Bollerslev, H.O. Mikkelsen, Fractionally integrated generalized autoregressive conditional heteroskedasticity, J. Econ. 74 (1) (1996) 3-30.

[79] L.R. Glosten, R. Jagannathan, D.E. Runkle, On the relation between the expected value and the volatility of the nominal excess return on stocks, J. Financ. 48 (5) (1993) 1779-1801.

[80] D.B. Nelson, Conditional heteroskedasticity in asset returns: a new approach, Econ. J. Econ. Soc. (1991) 347-370.

[81] Z. Ding, C.W. Granger, R.F. Engle, A long memory property of stock market returns and a new model, J. Empir. Finance 1 (1) (1993) 83-106.

[82] R. Reider, Volatility Forecasting I: GARCH Models, New York University, New York, 2009.

[83] A. Ghalanos, Introduction to the Rugarch Package, 2012.

[84] H. Hong, B. Preston, Nonnested model selection criteria, 2005. Unpublished manuscript, Department of Economics, Columbia University, New York. Retrieved September 1, 2006.

[85] W. Breymann, D. Lüthi, ghyp: a package on generalized hyperbolic distributions, 2013, URL http://cran.r-project.org/web/packages/ghyp/vignettes/Generalized_Hyperbolic_Distribution.pdf.

[86] F.X. Diebold, R.S. Mariano, Comparing predictive accuracy, J. Bus. Econ. Stat. 20 (1) (2002).

[87] Q. Vuong, Likelihood ratio tests for model selection and non-nested hypotheses, Econ. J. Econ. Soc. (1989) 307-333.

[88] G. Amisano, R. Giacomini, Comparing density forecasts via weighted likelihood ratio tests, J. Bus. Econ. Stat. 25 (2) (2007) 177-190.

[89] F.X. Diebold, Comparing predictive accuracy, twenty years later: a personal perspective on the use and abuse of Diebold-Mariano tests, National Bureau of Economic Research, 2012.

[90] C. Diks, V. Panchenko, D. Van Dijk, Likelihood-based scoring rules for comparing density forecasts in tails, J. Econ. 163 (2) (2011) 215-230.

[91] T. Gneiting, R. Ranjan, Comparing density forecasts using threshold-and quantile-weighted scoring rules, J. Bus. Econ. Stat. 29 (3) (2011).

[92] J.E. Matheson, R.L. Winkler, Scoring rules for continuous probability distributions, Manag. Sci. 22 (10) (1976) 1087-1096.

[93] T. Gneiting, A.E. Raftery, Strictly proper scoring rules, prediction, and estimation, J. Am. Stat. Assoc. 102 (477) (2007) 359-378.

[94] C. Darwin, On the Origins of Species by Means of Natural Selection, Murray, London, 1859.

[95] J.H. Holland, Adaptation in Natural and Artificial Systems: An Introductory Analysis with Applications to Biology, Control, and Artificial Intelligence, MIT Press, Cambridge, MA, USA, 1975.

[96] J.H. Holland, Genetic algorithms, Sci. Am. 267 (1) (1992) 66-72.

[97] M.A. Kaboudan, Genetic programming prediction of stock prices, Comput. Econ. 16 (3) (2000) 207-236.

[98] J. Mańdziuk, M. Jaruszewicz, Neuro-genetic system for stock index prediction, J. Intell. Fuzzy Syst. 22 (2) (2011) 93-123.

[99] F. Allen, R. Karjalainen, Using genetic algorithms to find technical trading rules, J. Financ. Econ. 51 (2) (1999) 245-271.

[100] C. Neely, P. Weller, R. Dittmar, Is technical analysis in the foreign exchange market profitable? A genetic programming approach, J. Financ. Quant. Anal. 32 (4) (1997) 405-426.

[101] C. Dunis, A. Harris, S. Leong, P. Nacaskul, Optimising intraday trading models with genetic algorithms, Neural Netw. World 9 (1999) 193-224.

[102] T. Aftalion, Genetic algorithms for portfolio optimization, in: Graduate Artificial Intelligence. Proceedings of the Third International Conference on Genetic Algorithms, 2012, pp. 70-79.

[103] R. Rojas, Neural Networks. A Systematic Approach, Springer-Verlag, Berlin, 1996.

[104] V.S. Desai, D.G. Conway, J.N. Crook, G.A. Overstreet, Credit-scoring models in the credit-union environment using neural networks and genetic algorithms, IMA J. Manag. Math. 8 (4) (1997) 323-346.

[105] Y. Zhang, S. Bhattacharyya, Genetic programming in classifying large-scale data: an ensemble method, Inform. Sci. 163 (1) (2004) 85-101.

[106] C.-S. Ong, J.-J. Huang, G.-H. Tzeng, Building credit scoring models using genetic programming, Expert Syst. Appl. 29 (1) (2005) 41-47.

[107] C.G. Borroni, M. Zenga, A test of concordance based on Gini's mean difference, Stat. Methods Appl. 16 (3) (2007) 289-308.

[108] L. Scrucca, GA: a package for genetic algorithms in R, J. Stat. Softw. 53 (4) (2012).

[109] A. Konak, D.W. Coit, A.E. Smith, Multi-objective optimization using genetic algorithms: a tutorial, Reliab. Eng. Syst. Saf. 91 (9) (2006) 992-1007.

[110] K. Deb, A. Pratap, S. Agarwal, T. Meyarivan, A fast and elitist multiobjective genetic algorithm: NSGA-II, IEEE Trans. Evol. Comput. 6 (2) (2002) 182-197.

[111] D.F. Klein, Beyond significance testing: reforming data analysis methods in behavioral research, Am. J. Psychiatry 162 (3) (2005) 643.

[112] R.A. Fisher, The Design of Experiments, Oliver & Boyd, Edinburgh, 1935.

[113] T.A. Schonhoff, A.A. Giordano, Detection and Estimation Theory and its Applications, Pearson/Prentice Hall, Englewood Cliffs, NJ, 2006.

[114] S.T. Ziliak, D.N. McCloskey, The Cult of Statistical Significance, University of Michigan Press, Ann Arbor, 2008, p. 27.

[115] B.E. Hansen, Lecture Notes on Nonparametrics, University of Wisconsin, Madison, WI, 2009.

[116] A. Pagan, A. Ullah, Nonparametric Econometrics, Cambridge University Press, Cambridge, 1999.

[117] J.-N. Hwang, S.-R. Lay, A. Lippman, Nonparametric multivariate density estimation: a comparative study, IEEE Trans. Signal Process. 42 (10) (1994) 2795-2810.

[118] E.A. Nadaraya, On estimating regression, Theory Probab. Appl. 9 (1) (1964) 141-142.

[119] G.S. Watson, Smooth regression analysis, Sankhya Indian J. Stat. Ser. A (1964) 359-372.

[120] J. Racine, Q. Li, Nonparametric estimation of regression functions with both categorical and continuous data, J. Econ. 119 (1) (2004) 99-130.

[121] T. Hayfield, J.S. Racine, Nonparametric econometrics: the np package, J. Stat. Softw. 27 (5) (2008) 1-32.

[122] M. Schienle, Nonparametric Nonstationary Regression, University of Mannheim, Mannheim, 2008.

[123] J.N. Morgan, J.A. Sonquist, Problems in the analysis of survey data, and a proposal, J. Am. Stat. Assoc. 58 (302) (1963) 415-434.

[124] L. Breiman, J.H. Friedman, R.A. Olshen, C.J. Stone, Classification and Regression Trees, Wadsworth and Brooks/Cole, Pacific Grove, CA, 1984, 63 pp.

[125] M. Kenney, D. Patton, Firm Database of Emerging Growth Initial Public Offerings (IPOs), 1990-2010 (2013).

[126] T.M. Therneau, B. Atkinson, B. Ripley, et al., rpart: Recursive Partitioning, R package version, 3.1-46, 2010.

[127] E. Fix, J.L. Hodges Jr, Discriminatory analysis-nonparametric discrimination: consistency properties, DTIC Document, 1951.

[128] T. Hastie, R. Tibshirani, J. Friedman, J. Franklin, The elements of statistical learning: data mining, inference and prediction, Math. Intell. 27 (2) (2005) 83-85.

[129] K. Halvorsen, ElemStatLearn: Data Sets, Functions and Examples from the Book: 'The Elements of Statistical Learning, Data Mining, Inference, and Prediction' (2012.04-0 edn), 2012, URL http://cran.r-project.org/web/packages/ElemStatLearn.

[130] D.M. Hawkins, Identification of Outliers, vol. 11, Springer, Berlin, 1980.

[131] M.M. Breunig, H.-P. Kriegel, R.T. Ng, J. Sander, LOF: identifying density-based local outliers, in: ACM Sigmod Record, vol. 29, ACM, New York, NY, USA, 2000, pp. 93-104.

[132] E.M. Knorr, R.T. Ng, V. Tucakov, Distance-based outliers: algorithms and applications, Int. J. Very Large Data Bases 8 (3-4) (2000) 237-253.

[133] L. Torgo, M.L. Torgo, Package DMwR, 2013.

[134] M. Cremonini, D. Nizovtsev, Risks and benefits of signaling information system characteristics to strategic attackers, J. Manag. Inf. Syst. 26 (3) (2009) 241-274.

[135] L.A. Zadeh, Fuzzy sets, Inform. Control 8 (3) (1965) 338-353.

[136] K. Stoffel, P. Cotofrei, D. Han, Fuzzy methods for forensic data analysis, in: SoCPaR, 2010, pp. 23-28.

[137] K. Shang, Z. Hossen, Applying Fuzzy Logic to Risk Assessment and Decision-Making, Canadian Institute of Actuaries, Ottawa, ON, 2013.

[138] P. Cotofrei, K. Stoffel, Fuzzy extended BPMN for modelling crime analysis processes, in: Data-Driven Process Discovery and Analysis SIMPDA 2011, 2011, p. 13.

[139] E.H. Mamdani, Application of fuzzy algorithms for control of simple dynamic plant, Proc. Inst. Elect. Eng. 121 (12) (1974) 1585-1588.

[140] Z. Othman, K. Subari, N. Morad, Application of fuzzy inference systems and genetic algorithms in integrated process planning and scheduling, Int. J. Comput. Internet Manag. 10 (2) (2002) 81-96.

[141] J.C. Dunn, A fuzzy relative of the ISODATA process and its use in detecting compact well-separated clusters, J. Cybern. 3 (3) (1973) 32-57.

[142] J.C. Bezdek, Pattern Recognition with Fuzzy Objective Function Algorithms, Kluwer Academic Publishers, Dordrecht, 1981.

[143] Z. Ghahramani, Unsupervised learning, in: Advanced Lectures on Machine Learning, Springer, Berlin, 2004, pp. 72-112.

[144] A. Fahad, N. Alshatri, Z. Tari, A. ALAmri, A.Y. Zomaya, I. Khalil, S. Foufou, A. Bouras, A survey of clustering algorithms for big data: taxonomy & empirical analysis, IEEE Trans. Emerg. Top. Comput. 2 (3) (2014) 267-279.

[145] A.P. Dempster, N.M. Laird, D.B. Rubin, Maximum likelihood from incomplete data via the EM algorithm, J. R. Stat. Soc. Ser. B Methodol. 39 (1) (1977) 1-38.

[146] J.A. Bilmes, et al., A gentle tutorial of the EM algorithm and its application to parameter estimation for Gaussian mixture and hidden Markov models, 1998. Technical Report TR-97-021.

[147] C. Biernacki, G. Celeux, G. Govaert, F. Langrognet, Model-based cluster and discriminant analysis with the MIXMOD software, Comput. Stat. Data Anal. 51 (2) (2006) 587-600.

[148] C. Fraley, A. Raftery, L. Scrucca, Normal mixture modeling for model-based clustering, classification, and density estimation, 2012, URL http://cran.r-project.org/web/packages/mclust/index.html.

[149] C. Fraley, A.E. Raftery, Model-based clustering, discriminant analysis, and density estimation, J. Am. Stat. Assoc. 97 (458) (2002) 611-631.

[150] T. Zhang, R. Ramakrishnan, M. Livny, BIRCH: an efficient data clustering method for very large databases, ACM SIGMOD Rec. 25 (2) (1996) 103-114.

[151] R. Pamula, J.K. Deka, S. Nandi, An outlier detection method based on clustering, in: 2011 Second International Conference on Emerging Applications of Information Technology (EAIT), IEEE, New York, 2011, pp. 253-256.

[152] K. Zhang, M. Hutter, H. Jin, A new local distance-based outlier detection approach for scattered real-world data, in: Advances in Knowledge Discovery and Data Mining, Springer, Berlin, 2009, pp. 813-822.

[153] P. Dhaliwal, M. Bhatia, P. Bansal, A cluster-based approach for outlier detection in dynamic data streams (KORM: k-median outlier miner), 2010. arXiv preprint arXiv:1002.4003.

[154] A. Loureiro, L. Torgo, C. Soares, Outlier detection using clustering methods: a data cleaning application, in: Proceedings of KDNet Symposium on Knowledge-Based Systems for the Public Sector, 2004.

[155] A.S. Larik, S. Haider, Clustering based anomalous transaction reporting, Procedia Comput. Sci. 3 (2011) 606-610.

[156] K. Golmohammadi, O.R. Zaiane, Data mining applications for fraud detection in securities market, in: 2012 European Intelligence and Security Informatics Conference (EISIC), 2012 pp. 107-114.

[157] Q. Bsoul, J. Salim, L.Q. Zakaria, An intelligent document clustering approach to detect crime patterns, Procedia Technol. 11 (2013) 1181-1187.

[158] C.J. Burges, A tutorial on support vector machines for pattern recognition, Data Min. Knowl. Disc. 2 (2) (1998) 121-167.

[159] V.N. Vapnik, Vosstanovlenie zavisimostej po èmpiričeskom dannym, Nauka, Moscow, 1979.

[160] V. Vapnik, A. Chervonenkis, On a perceptron class, Autom. Remote Control 25 (1964) 112-120.

[161] V.N. Vapnik, The nature of statistical learning theory, Statistics for engineering and information science, URL http://books.google.lt/books?id=sna9BaxVbj8C, Springer, 2000.

[162] V. Vapnik, Statistical Learning Theory, Wiley, New York, 1998.

[163] S. Knerr, L. Personnaz, G. Dreyfus, Single-layer learning revisited: a stepwise procedure for building and training a neural network, in: Neurocomputing, Springer, Berlin, 1990, pp. 41-50.

[164] J. Weston, C. Watkins, Multi-class support vector machines, Citeseer, 1998.

[165] T. Hastie, R. Tibshirani, J. Friedman, T. Hastie, J. Friedman, R. Tibshirani, The Elements of Statistical Learning, vol. 2, Springer, Berlin, 2009.

[166] B. Efron, Better bootstrap confidence intervals, J. Am. Stat. Assoc. (1987) 171-185.

[167] L. Medema, R.H. Koning, R. Lensink, A practical approach to validating a PD model, J. Bank. Financ. 33 (4) (2009) 701-708.

[168] B. Efron, R. Tibshirani, Bootstrap methods for standard errors, confidence intervals, and other measures of statistical accuracy, Stat. Sci. (1986) 54-75.

[169] B. Pang, L. Lee, S. Vaithyanathan, Thumbs up?: sentiment classification using machine learning techniques, in: Proceedings of the ACL-02 Conference on Empirical Methods in Natural Language Processing, vol. 10, Association for Computational Linguistics, 2002, pp. 79-86.

[170] L. Auria, R.A. Moro, Support vector machines (SVM) as a technique for solvency analysis, 2008. DIW Berlin Discussion Paper.

[171] Z. Huang, H. Chen, C.-J. Hsu, W.-H. Chen, S. Wu, Credit rating analysis with support vector machines and neural networks: a market comparative study, Decis. Support Syst. 37 (4) (2004) 543-558.

[172] S.Y. Huang, Fraud detection model by using support vector machine techniques, Int. J. Digit. Content Technol. Appl. 7 (2) (2013) 32-42.

[173] D. DeBarr, H. Wechsler, Fraud detection using reputation features, SVMs, and random forests, in: Proceedings of the 9th International Conference on Data Mining, 2013.

[174] A. Sharma, P.K. Panigrahi, A review of financial accounting fraud detection based on data mining techniques, 2013. arXiv preprint arXiv:1309.3944.

[175] C. Gini, Variabilità e mutabilità, in: E. Pizetti, T. Salvemini (Eds.), Reprinted in Memorie di metodologica statistica, vol. 1, Libreria Eredi Virgilio Veschi, Rome, 1912.

[176] R.I. Lerman, S. Yitzhaki, A note on the calculation and interpretation of the Gini index, Econ. Lett. 15 (3-4) (1984) 363-368.

[177] T. Ogwang, A convenient method of computing the Gini index and its standard error, Oxf. Bull. Econ. Stat. 62 (1) (2000) 123-129.

[178] S. Yitzhaki, Calculating jackknife variance estimators for parameters of the Gini method, J. Bus. Econ. Stat. (1991) 235-239.

[179] E. Karagiannis, M. Kovacevic, A method to calculate the Jackknife variance estimator for the Gini coefficient, Oxf. Bull. Econ. Stat. 62 (1) (2000) 119-122.

[180] D.E.A. Giles, Calculating a standard error for the Gini coefficient: some further results, Oxf. Bull. Econ. Stat. 66 (3) (2004) 425-433.

[181] D. Tasche, Validation of internal rating systems and PD estimates, in: The Analytics of Risk Model Validation, Academic Press, New York, 2007, pp. 169-196.

[182] M.-C. Frunza, Computing a standard error for the Gini coefficient: an application to credit risk model validation, J. Risk Model Validat. 7 (1) (2013) 61-82.

[183] S. Newcomb, Note on the frequency of use of the different digits in natural numbers, Am. J. Math. 4 (1) (1881) 39-40.

[184] H. Poincaré, Répartition des décimales dans une table numérique, Calcul des probabilités, Gauthier-Villars, Paris, 1912, pp. 313-320

[185] F. Benford, The law of anomalous numbers, Proc. Am. Philos. Soc. (1938) 551-572.

[186] D.W. Joenssen, Two digit testing for Benford's law, in: Proceedings of the ISI World Statistics, 2013.

[187] T.P. Hill, A statistical derivation of the significant-digit law, Stat. Sci. (1995) 354-363.

[188] M.J. Nigrini, The detection of income tax evasion through an analysis of digital frequencies, Doctorat en sciences de gestion, Université de Cincinnati, Cincinnati, 1992.

[189] S.D. Graham, J. Hasseldine, D. Paton, Statistical fraud detection in a commercial lobster fishery, N. Z. J. Mar. Freshw. Res. 43 (1) (2009) 457-463.

[190] W.R. Mebane Jr, Note on the Presidential Election in Iran, University of Michigan, mis en ligne le 29, 2009.

[191] R.M. Abrantes-Metz, S.B. Villas-Boas, G. Judge, Tracking the Libor rate, Appl. Econ. Lett. 18 (10) (2011) 893-899.

[192] A. Karavardar, Benford's law and an analysis in Istanbul Stock Exchange (BIST), Int. J. Bus. Manag. 9 (4) (2014) p160.

[193] Z. Shengmin, W. Wenchao, Does Chinese stock indices agree with Benford's law? in: 2010 International Conference on Management and Service Science, 2010, pp. 1-3.

[194] P. Brown, A. Chua, J. Mitchell, The influence of cultural factors on price clustering: evidence from Asia-Pacific stock markets, Pac. Basin Financ. J. 10 (3) (2002) 307-332.

[195] R. Bharati, S.J. Crain, V. Kaminski, Clustering in crude oil prices and the target pricing zone hypothesis, Energy Econ. 34 (4) (2012) 1115-1123.

[196] M. Corazza, A. Ellero, A. Zorzi, Checking financial markets via Benford's law: the S&P 500 case, in: Mathematical and Statistical Methods for Actuarial Sciences and Finance, Springer, Berlin, 2010, pp. 93-102.

[197] D.W. Joenssen, T. Muellerleile, Package 'BenfordTests', 2013.

[198] K. Pearson, X. On the criterion that a given system of deviations from the probable in the case of a correlated system of variables is such that it can be reasonably supposed to have arisen from random sampling, Lond. Edinb. Dublin Philos. Mag. J. Sci. 50 (302) (1900) 157-175.

[199] W.K. Tam Cho, B.J. Gaines, Breaking the (Benford) law: statistical fraud detection in campaign finance, Am. Stat. 61 (3) (2007) 218-223.

[200] A.N. Kolmogorov, Sulla determinazione empirica di una legge di distribuzione, 1933.

[201] J. Morrow, Benford's law, families of distributions, and a test basis, 2007. Unpublished Manuscript.

[202] G. Judge, L. Schechter, Detecting problems in survey data using Benford's law, J. Hum. Resour. 44 (1) (2009) 1-24.

[203] L. Freedman, Watson's UN2 statistic for a discrete distribution, Biometrika 68 (3) (1981) 708-711.

[204] G.S. Watson, Goodness-of-fit tests on a circle, Biometrika (1961) 109-114.

[205] G.C. Chow, Tests of equality between sets of coefficients in two linear regressions, Econ. J. Econ. Soc. (1960) 591-605.

[206] J. Bai, P. Perron, Computation and analysis of multiple structural change models, J. Appl. Econ. 18 (1) (2003) 1-22.

[207] J. Bai, P. Perron, Critical values for multiple structural change tests, Econ. J. 6 (1) (2003) 72-78.

[208] R.L. Brown, J. Durbin, J.M. Evans, Techniques for testing the constancy of regression relationships over time, J. R. Stat. Soc. Ser. B Methodol. 37 (2) (1975) 149-192.

[209] A. Zeileis, F. Leisch, K. Hornik, C. Kleiber, Strucchange. An R Package for Testing for Structural Change in Linear Regression Models, SFB Adaptive Information Systems and Modelling in Economics and Management Science, WU Vienna University of Economics and Business, 2001.

[210] R. Feldman, J. Sanger, The Text Mining Handbook: Advanced Approaches in Analyzing Unstructured Data, Cambridge University Press, Cambridge, 2007.

[211] C.J. Fillmore, Frame semantics and the nature of language, Ann. N. Y. Acad. Sci. 280 (1) (1976) 20-32.

[212] M.P. Marcus, M.A. Marcinkiewicz, B. Santorini, Building a large annotated corpus of English: the Penn Treebank, Comput. Linguist. 19 (2) (1993) 313-330.

[213] P.M. Nadkarni, L. Ohno-Machado, W.W. Chapman, Natural language processing: an introduction, J. Am. Med. Inform. Assoc. 18 (5) (2011) 544-551.

[214] A. Voutilainen, NPtool, a detector of English noun phrases, 1995. arXiv preprint cmp-lg/9502010.

[215] E. Brill, A simple rule-based part of speech tagger, in: Proceedings of the Workshop on Speech and Natural Language, Association for Computational Linguistics, 1992, pp. 112-116.

[216] L. Rabiner, A tutorial on hidden Markov models and selected applications in speech recognition, Proc. IEEE 77 (2) (1989) 257-286.

[217] J. Lafferty, A. McCallum, F.C. Pereira, Conditional random fields: probabilistic models for segmenting and labeling sequence data, in: ICML '01 Proceedings of the Eighteenth International Conference on Machine Learning, 2001.

[218] A. Culotta, D. Kulp, A. McCallum, Gene prediction with conditional random fields, 2005.

[219] C. Sutton, A. McCallum, An introduction to conditional random fields for relational learning, in: Introduction to Statistical Relational Learning, MIT press, Cambridge, MA, USA, 2006, pp. 93-128.

[220] D. Gildea, D. Jurafsky, Automatic labeling of semantic roles, Comput. Linguist. 28 (3) (2002) 245-288.

[221] L. Màrquez, X. Carreras, K.C. Litkowski, S. Stevenson, Semantic role labeling: an introduction to the special issue, Comput. Linguist. 34 (2) (2008) 145-159.

[222] P.D. Turney, Thumbs up or thumbs down? Semantic orientation applied to unsupervised classification of reviews, in: Proceedings of the 40th Annual Meeting on Association for Computational Linguistics, Association for Computational Linguistics, 2002, pp. 417-424.

[223] K.W. Church, P. Hanks, Word association norms, mutual information, and lexicography, Comput. Linguist. 16 (1) (1990) 22-29.

[224] D.D. Lewis, Naive (Bayes) at forty: the independence assumption in information retrieval, in: Machine Learning: ECML-98, Springer, Berlin, 1998, pp. 4-15.

[225] P. Domingos, M. Pazzani, On the optimality of the simple Bayesian classifier under zero-one loss, Mach. Learn. 29 (2-3) (1997) 103-130.

[226] H. Zhang, The optimality of naive Bayes, in: FLAIRS 2004 Conference, 2004.

[227] T. Joachims, Text Categorization with Support Vector Machines: Learning with Many Relevant Features, Springer, Berlin, 1998.

[228] J. Haggerty, A. Karran, D. Lamb, M. Taylor, A framework for the forensic investigation of unstructured email relationship data, Int. J. Digital Crime Forensics 3 (3) (2011) 1-18.

[229] B.P. Green, A. Reinstein, Banking industry financial statement fraud and the effects of regulation enforcement and increased public scrutiny, Res. Account. Regul. 17 (2004) 87-106.

[230] L. Clerc, D. Marteau, Juste valeur et prix de modele: une comparaison internationale de la structure des portefeuilles de trading et du ratio rentabilite, Revue Econ. Financ. 115 (3) (2014) 305-322.

[231] M. Frunza, D. Marteau, Tax on Financial Transactions: Why a Pigouvian Tax is More Efficient than a Tobin Tax, 2012.

[232] K.S. Kolev, Do investors perceive marking-to-model as marking-to-myth? Early evidence from FAS 157 disclosure, 2008.

[233] B.M. Barber, P.A. Griffin, B. Lev, The fraud-on-the-market theory and the indicators of common stocks' efficiency, J. Corp. L. 19 (1993) 285.

[234] F. Black, M. Scholes, The pricing of options and corporate liabilities, J. Polit. Econ. (1973) 637-654.

[235] J.C. Goldberg, B.C. Zipursky, The fraud-on-the-market tort, Vanderbilt Law Rev. 66 (2013).

[236] X. Zhao, Trade-based manipulation or speculative bubble: a case study, Int. Bus. Econ. Res. J. 13 (4) (2014) 841-852.

[237] Z. Geng, X. Lu, Implicitly-Coordinated Stock Price Attack and Exploitation of Retail Investors' Behavioral Biases: Widespread Evidence in the Chinese Stock Market, 2014.

[238] P.C. Phillips, Y. Wu, J. Yu, Explosive behavior in the 1990s NASDAQ: when did exuberance escalate asset values? Int. Econ. Rev. 52 (1) (2011) 201-226.

[239] D.A. Dickey, W.A. Fuller, Distribution of the estimators for autoregressive time series with a unit root, J. Am. Stat. Assoc. 74 (366a) (1979) 427-431.

[240] S.E. Said, D.A. Dickey, Testing for unit roots in autoregressive-moving average models of unknown order, Biometrika 71 (3) (1984) 599-607.

[241] G. Cardano, Liber de ludo aleae, vol. 22, Franco Angeli, Milan, 2006.

[242] R. Almgren, N. Chriss, Optimal execution of portfolio transactions, J. Risk 3 (2001) 5-40.

[243] H. Mittal, Are you playing in a toxic dark pool? A guide to preventing information leakage, J. Trading 3 (3) (2008) 20-33.

[244] F. Klöck, A. Schied, Y.S. Sun, Price manipulation in a market impact model with dark pool, 2011. Available at SSRN 1785409.

[245] C. Pirrong, Manipulation of cash-settled futures contracts, J. Bus. 74 (2) (2001) 221-244.

[246] U. Horst, F. Naujokat, On derivatives with illiquid underlying and market manipulation, Quant. Finan. 11 (7) (2011) 1051-1066.

[247] R. Cont, A. Kukanov, S. Stoikov, The price impact of order book events, J. Financ. Econ. 12 (1) (2014) 47-88.

[248] G.H. Skrepnek, K.A. Lawson, Measuring changes in capital market security prices: the event study methodology, J. Res. Pharm. Econ. 11 (1) (2001) 1-18.

[249] J.C. Dolley, Characteristics and procedure of common stock split-ups, Harv. Bus. Rev. 11 (3) (1933) 316-326.

[250] A.C. MacKinlay, Event studies in economics and finance, J. Econ. Lit. (1997) 13-39.

[251] M. Minenna, A Supervisory Perspective on Insider Trading: Estimating the Value of the Information, 2000. CONSOB, Quaderni di Finanza, no. 2000-45.

[252] E. Wong, Investigation of market efficiency: an event study of insider trading in the stock exchange of Hong Kong. Unpublished thesis, Stanford University, Stanford, 2002.

[253] L.A. Jeng, A. Metrick, R. Zeckhauser, Estimating the returns to insider trading: a performance-evaluation perspective, Rev. Econ. Stat. 85 (2) (2003) 453-471.

[254] T. Bouraoui, M. Mehanaoui, B. Bahli, Stock spams: another kind of stock prices manipulation, J. Appl. Bus. Res. 29 (1) (2012) 79-90.

[255] M. Siering, All pump, no dump? The impact of Internet deception on stock markets, in: Proceedings of the European Conference on Information Systems (ECIS), 2013, p. 115.

[256] S.J. Brown, J.B. Warner, Measuring security price performance, J. Financ. Econ. 8 (3) (1980) 205-258.

[257] E.F. Fama, K.R. French, Common risk factors in the returns on stocks and bonds, J. Financ. Econ. 33 (1) (1993) 3-56.

[258] J.-Y. Delort, B. Arunasalam, M. Milosavljevic, H. Leung, The impact of manipulation in internet stock message boards, Int. J. Bank. Finance 8 (2009) 1-18.

[259] J.M. Patell, Corporate forecasts of earnings per share and stock price behavior: empirical test, J. Account. Res. (1976) 246-276.

[260] B.M. Barber, J.D. Lyon, Detecting long-run abnormal stock returns: the empirical power and specification of test statistics, J. Financ. Econ. 43 (3) (1997) 341-372.

[261] C. Alexander, A. Dimitriu, The cointegration alpha: enhanced index tracking and long-short equity market neutral strategies, 2002. ISMA Finance Discussion Paper.

[262] R.F. Engle, C.W. Granger, Co-integration and error correction: representation, estimation, and testing, Econ. J. Econ. Soc. (1987) 251-276.

[263] S. Johansen, Statistical analysis of cointegration vectors, J. Econ. Dyn. Control 12 (2) (1988) 231-254.

[264] K.A. Simon, The misappropriation theory: a valid application of section 10 (B) to protect property rights in information, J. Crim. Law Criminol. (1998) 1049-1086.

[265] R.M. Abrantes-Metz, M. Kraten, A.D. Metz, G.S. Seow, Libor manipulation? J. Bank. Financ. 36 (1) (2012) 136-150.

[266] A. Monticini, D.L. Thornton, The effect of underreporting on LIBOR rates, J. Macroecon. 37 (2013) 345-348.

[267] J.A. Garcia, Fixing the Benchmark-Wheatley Considers LIBOR Overhaul, 2012. Financial Regulation International (September, 2012).

[268] J.D. Hamilton, A new approach to the economic analysis of nonstationary time series and the business cycle, Econ. J. Econ. Soc. (1989) 357-384.

[269] D. Guegan, M.-C. Frunza, A. Lassoudière, Forecasting strategies for carbon allowances prices: from classic arbitrage pricing theory to switching regimes, Int. Rev. Appl. Financ. Issues Econ. 2 (3) (2010) 576-596.

[270] M. Frunza, Aftermath of the VAT Fraud on Carbon Emissions Markets, 2012. Available at SSRN 2070927.

[271] C.A. Snider, T. Youle, Does the LIBOR Reflect Banks' Borrowing Costs? 2010. Available at SSRN 1569603.

[272] R. Abrantes-Metz, S. Addanki, Is the Market Being Fooled? An Error-Based Screen for Manipulation, 2007.

[273] E. Zivot, J. Wang, Vector autoregressive models for multivariate time series, in: Modeling Financial Time Series with S-PLUS®, Springer, Berlin, 2006, pp. 385-429.

[274] A. Zeileis, dynlm: Dynamic Linear Regression, R package version 0.2-3, 2009. URL http://CRAN.R-project.org/package=dynlm.

[275] B. Pfaff, VAR, SVAR and SVEC models: implementation within R package vars, J. Stat. Softw. 27 (4) (2008) 1-32.

[276] M. Frunza, The Cost of Non-Europe of an Incomplete Economic and Monetary Union to Prevent Future Crises, 2014. Available at SSRN.

[277] D. Straumann, Measuring the quality of hedge fund data, J. Altern. Invest. 12 (2) (2009) 26-40.

[278] H. Schilit, Financial Shenanigans, Tata McGraw-Hill Education, New Delhi, 2010.

[279] B.G. Dharan, W.R. Bufkins, Red Flags in Enron's Reporting of Revenues & Key Financial Measures, 2008. Available at SSRN 1172222.

[280] X. Warin, Hedging Swing contract on gas markets, 2012. arXiv preprint arXiv:1208.5303.

[281] G.J. Benston, Fair-value accounting: a cautionary tale from Enron, J. Account. Public Policy 25 (4) (2006) 465-484.

[282] F. Partnoy, Enron and the Derivatives World, in: Corporate Fiascos and Their Implications, Foundation Press, New York, 2004 .

[283] B. McLean, Is Enron Overpriced? Fortune 143 (5) (2001) 122-126.

[284] J. Diesner, K.M. Carley, Exploration of communication networks from the Enron email corpus, in: SIAM International Conference on Data Mining: Workshop on Link Analysis, Counterterrorism and Security, Newport Beach, CA, Citeseer, 2005.

[285] L.J. White, Credit-rating agencies and the financial crisis: less regulation of CRAs is a better response, J. Int. Bank. Law 25 (4) (2010) 170.

[286] M. Gärtner, B. Griesbach, F. Jung, PIGS or lambs? The European sovereign debt crisis and the role of rating agencies, Int. Adv. Econ. Res. 17 (3) (2011) 288-299.

[287] A. Host, I. Cvečić, V. Zaninović, Credit rating agencies and their impact on spreading the financial crisis on the eurozone, Ekonomska misao i praksa (2) (2012) 639-662.

[288] J. Ryan, Credit rating agencies: are they credible? Int. J. Public Policy 9 (1) (2013) 4-22.

[289] C.F. Baum, M. Karpava, D. Schäfer, A. Stephan, Credit rating agency announcements and the Eurozone sovereign debt crisis, 2013. DIW Berlin Discussion Paper.

[290] R. Alsakka, O. Ap Gwilym, Rating agencies' signals during the European sovereign debt crisis: market impact and spillovers, J. Econ. Behav. Organ. 85 (2013) 144-162.

[291] M. Scarsini, On measures of concordance, Stochastica 8 (3) (1984) 201-218.

[292] J. Nešlehová, On rank correlation measures for noncontinuous random variables, J. Multivar. Anal. 98 (3) (2007) 544-567.

[293] Y. Jafry, T. Schuermann, Measurement, estimation and comparison of credit migration matrices, J. Bank. Financ. 28 (11) (2004) 2603-2639.

[294] O. Chakroun, Migration Dependence Among the US Business Sectors, DP HEC Montreal, 2008.

[295] A. Verstein, Benchmark manipulation, Boston Coll. Law Rev. 56 (2015).

[296] A. Schwartzman, Y. Gavrilov, R.J. Adler, Peak detection as multiple testing, 2010. arXiv preprint arXiv:1008.1924.

[297] E.B. Wilson, Probable inference, the law of succession, and statistical inference, J. Am. Stat. Assoc. 22 (158) (1927) 209-212.

[298] Q. McNemar, Note on the sampling error of the difference between correlated proportions or percentages, Psychometrika 12 (2) (1947) 153-157.

[299] N.N. Taleb, The Black Swan: The Impact of the Highly Improbable Fragility, Random House, New York, 2010.

[300] M.-C. Frunza, D. Guegan, A. Lassoudiere, Missing trader fraud on the emissions market, J. Financ. Crime 18 (2) (2011) 183-194.

[301] S.A. Ross, The Arbitrage Theory of Capital Asset Pricing, Rodney L. White Center for Financial Research, University of Pennsylvania, The Wharton School, 1973.

[302] Financial Action Task Force, FATF report: money laundering and terrorist financing in the securities sector, FATF/OECD, 2009.

[303] M. Camdessus, Money laundering: the importance of international countermeasures, 1998. Address delivered at the Plenary Meeting of the Financial Action Task Force on Money Laundering.

[304] B. Lal, Money Laundering: An Insight into the Dark World of Financial Frauds, Siddharth Publications, Delhi, India, 2003.

[305] P. Reuter, E.M. Truman, Chasing Dirty Money, Institute for International Economics, Washington, DC, 2004.

[306] V. Tanzi, The Underground Economy in the United States: Annual Estimates, 1930-80 (L'économie clandestine aux Etats-Unis: estimations annuelles, 1930-80) (La "economía subterránea" de Estados Unidos: Estimaciones anuales, 1930-80), International Monetary Fund, Washington, DC, 1983, pp. 283-305.

[307] E.J. Kane, Good intentions and unintended evil: the case against selective credit allocation, J. Money Credit Bank. (1977) 55-69.

[308] W. Erhard, M.C. Jensen, S. Zaffron, Integrity: A Positive Model that Incorporates the Normative Phenomena of Morality, Ethics, and Legality-Abridged (English Language Version), 2013. Harvard Business School NOM Unit Working Paper No. 10-061. Barbados Group Working Paper No. 10-01.

[309] N.P. Bollen, V.K. Pool, Conditional return smoothing in the hedge fund industry, J. Financ. Quant. Anal. 43 (02) (2008) 267-298.

[310] J. Brogaard, T. Hendershott, R. Riordan, High-frequency trading and price discovery, Rev. Financ. Stud. 27 (8) (2014) 2267-2306.

[311] D.M. Chance, Essays in Derivatives, Frank J. Fabozzi Associates, New Hope, PA, 1998.

[312] F.L. Chung, T. Lee, Fuzzy competitive learning, Neural Netw. 7 (3) (1994) 539-551.

[313] G. Crime, First page preview, Global Crime 6 (2) (2004).

[314] J.R. Crotty, Rethinking Marxian investment theory: Keynes-Minsky instability, competitive regime shifts and coerced investment, Rev. Radical Polit. Econ. 25 (1) (1993) 1-26.

[315] J. Danielsson, K. James, M. Valenzuela, I. Zer, Model risk and the implications for risk management, macroprudential policy, and financial regulations, 2014.

[316] G. Dorfleitner, C. Klein, Psychological barriers in European stock markets: where are they? Global Financ. J. 19 (3) (2009) 268-285.

[317] B. Engelmann, E. Hayden, D. Tasche, Testing rating accuracy, Risk 16 (1) (2003) 82-86.

[318] Q.C. Fisher, J.D. Giulio, J. Schutze, et al., Economic crime and the global financial crisis, Law Financ. Mark. Rev. 5 (4) (2011) 276-289.

[319] M. Frunza, Market Manipulation and Moral Hazard: Can the LIBOR be Fixed? 2013. Available at SSRN 2207703.

[320] M. Frunza, Could the LIBOR be Manipulated by a Single Bank? I2FC, Cambridge Science Publishing, Cambridge, 2013.

[321] W. Goetzmann, J. Ingersoll, M.I. Spiegel, I. Welch, Sharpening sharpe ratios, National Bureau of Economic Research, 2002.

[322] M. Hickman, A. Piquero, J. Greene, Police integrity: exploring the utility of a risk factor model, in: Police Integrity and Ethics, 2004, pp. 67-83.

[323] M. Khadka, B. Popp, K.M. George, N. Park, A new approach for time series forecasting based on genetic algorithm, in: CAINE, 2010, pp. 226-231.

[324] C.D. Manning, P. Raghavan, H. Schütze, Introduction to Information Retrieval, vol. 1, Cambridge University Press, Cambridge, 2008.

[325] D. Masciandaro, Global Financial Crime: Terrorism, Money Laundering, and Off Shore Centres, Ashgate Pub Limited, England, 2004.

[326] B. Pang, L. Lee, Opinion mining and sentiment analysis, Found. Trends Inf. Retr. 2 (1-2) (2008) 1-135.

[327] C. Perez, M. Lemercier, B. Birregah, A. Corpel, Spot 1.0: scoring suspicious profiles on twitter, in: 2011 International Conference on Advances in Social Networks Analysis and Mining (ASONAM), IEEE, New York, 2011, pp. 377-381.

[328] L. Petram, The World's First Stock Exchange, Columbia University Press, New York, 2014.

[329] O. Saito, Factor markets and their institutions in traditional Japan: Labour, paper for Conference The Rise, Organization, and Institutional Framework of Factor Markets, Utrecht, 2005.

[330] O. Saito, T. Settsu, Money, Credit and Smithian Growth in Tokugawa Japan, Hitotsubashi University, Tokyo, 2006.

[331] A. Schied, Order book resilience, price manipulations, and the positive portfolio problem, 2010.

[332] B. SchiilkopP, C. Burgest, V. Vapnik, Extracting support data for a given task, in: KDD-95 Proceedings, 1995.

[333] L. Snider, The technological advantages of stock market traders, in: How They Got Away With It: White Collar Criminals and the Financial Meltdown, Columbia University Press, New York, 2012, pp. 151.

[334] C. Kalb, Integrity in Sport: Understanding and Preventing Match-Fixing, SportAccord, 2013.

[335] D. Talay, Z. Zheng, Worst case model risk management, Finance Stochast. 6 (4) (2002) 517-537.

[336] G. Weiss, Born to Steal: When the Mafia Hit Wall Street, Warner Books, New York, 2003.

[337] US Senate, Minority Staff Report for Permanent Sub Committee on Investigations on Correspondent Banking: A Gateway for Money Laundering, Senate Committee on Government Affairs, 2001.

# Index

Printed in the United States
By Bookmasters